Criminal Law

The International Library of Essays in Law and Legal Theory

Second Series

Series Editor: Tom D. Campbell

Titles in the Series:

Freedom of Speech, Volumes I and II
Larry Alexander

Privacy
Eric M. Barendt

Comparative Legal Cultures
John Bell

Contract Law, Volumes I and II
Brian Bix

Corporate Law
William W. Bratton

Legal Positivism
Tom D. Campbell

International Trade Law
Ronald A. Cass and Michael S. Knoll

Sociological Perspectives on Law, Volumes I and II
Roger Cotterrell

Intellectual Property
Peter Drahos

Family, State and Law, Volumes I and II
Michael D. Freeman

Natural Law
Robert P. George

Commercial Law
Clayton P. Gillette

Competition Law
Rosa Greaves

Chinese Law and Legal Theory
Perry Keller

International Law, Volumes I and II
Martti Koskenniemi and David Kennedy

Constitutional Law
Ian D. Loveland

Interpretation of Law
D. Neil MacCormick and Fernando Atria

Human Rights
Robert McCorquodale

Anti-Discrimination Law
Christopher McCrudden

Medical Law and Ethics
Sheila McLean

Mediation
Carrie Menkel-Meadow

Environmental Law
Peter Menell

Criminal Law
Thomas Morawetz

Law and Language
Thomas Morawetz

Law and Anthropology
Martha Mundy

Gender and Justice
Ngaire Naffine

Law and Economics
Eric A. Posner

Japanese Law
J. Mark Ramseyer

Justice
Wojciech Sadurski

The Rule of Law
Frederick Schauer

Restitution
Lionel D. Smith

Company Law
David Sugarman

Freedom of Information
Robert G. Vaughn

Tort Law
Ernest J. Weinrib

Rights
Robin West

Welfare Law
Lucy A. Williams

Criminal Law

Edited by

Thomas Morawetz

University of Connecticut, USA

Routledge
Taylor & Francis Group
LONDON AND NEW YORK

First published 2000 by Dartmouth Publishing Company and Ashgate Publishing

Reissued 2018 by Routledge
2 Park Square, Milton Park, Abingdon, Oxon OX14 4RN
711 Third Avenue, New York, NY 10017, USA

Routledge is an imprint of the Taylor & Francis Group, an informa business

Publisher's Note
The publisher has gone to great lengths to ensure the quality of this reprint but points out that some imperfections in the original copies may be apparent.

A Library of Congress record exists under LC control number: 99039721

ISBN 13: 978-1-138-73043-4 (hbk)
ISBN 13: 978-1-315-18943-7 (ebk)

Contents

Acknowledgements

The editor and publishers wish to thank the following for permission to use copyright material.

Harvard University Press for the essay: Richard Wollheim (1993), 'Crime, Punishment, and "Pale Criminality"', in Richard Wollheim, *The Mind and Its Depths*, Cambridge, MA: Harvard University Press, pp. 112–31. Reprinted by permission of the publisher from *The Mind and its Depths* by Richard Wollheim, Cambridge, MA: Harvard University Press. Copyright © 1993 the President and Fellows of Harvard College.

Michigan Law Review Association for the essay: Dan M. Kahan (1997), 'Ignorance of Law *is* an Excuse – But Only for the Virtuous', *Michigan Law Review*, **96**, pp. 127–54.

Oxford University Press for the essay: Alan Brudner (1987), 'A Theory of Necessity', *Oxford Journal of Legal Studies*, **7**, pp. 339–68.

Southern California Law Review for the essay: Joshua Dressler (1989), 'Exegesis of the Law of Duress: Justifying the Excuse and Searching for its Proper Limits', *Southern California Law Review*, **62**, pp. 1331–86. Reprinted with the permission of the Southern California Law Review.

University of Chicago Law Review for the essay: John H. Langbein (1978), 'Torture and Plea Bargaining', *University of Chicago Law Review*, **46**, pp. 3–22.

University of Pennsylvania Law Review for the essays: Stephen J. Schulhofer (1995), 'The Feminist Challenge in Criminal Law', *University of Pennsylvania Law Review*, **143**, pp. 2151–207; Steven Shavell (1993), 'An Economic Analysis of Threats and their Illegality: Blackmail, Extortion, and Robbery', *University of Pennsylvania Law Review*, **141**, pp. 1877–903.

University of Virginia for the essay: Dan M. Kahan (1997), 'Social Influence, Social Meaning, and Deterrence', *Virginia Law Review*, **83**, pp. 349–95.

Lloyd L. Weinreb (1986), 'Desert, Punishment, and Criminal Responsibility', *Law and Contemporary Problems*, **49**, No. 3, pp. 47–80. Copyright © 1986 Lloyd L. Weinreb.

Wisconsin Law Review for the essay: Douglas N. Husak and Craig A. Callender (1994), 'Wilful Ignorance, Knowledge, and the "Equal Culpability" Thesis: A Study of the Deeper Significance of the Principle of Legality', *Wisconsin Law Review*, **1994**, pp. 29–69. Copyright © 1994 The Board of Regents of the University of Wisconsin System. Reprinted by permission of the Wisconsin Law Review.

Preface to the Second Series

The first series of the International Library of Essays in Law and Legal Theory has established itself as a major research resource with fifty-eight volumes of the most significant theoretical essays in contemporary legal studies. Each volume contains essays of central theoretical importance in its subject area and the series as a whole makes available an extensive range of valuable material of considerable interest to those involved in research, teaching and the study of law.

The rapid growth of theoretically interesting scholarly work in law has created a demand for a second series which includes more recent publications of note and earlier essays to which renewed attention is being given. It also affords the opportunity to extend the areas of law covered in the first series.

The new series follows the successful pattern of reproducing entire essays with the original page numbers as an aid to comprehensive research and accurate referencing. Editors have selected not only the most influential essays but also those which they consider to be of greatest continuing importance. The objective of the second series is to enlarge the scope of the library, include significant recent work and reflect a variety of editorial perspectives.

Each volume is edited by an expert in the specific area who makes the selection on the basis of the quality, influence and significance of the essays, taking care to include essays which are not readily available. Each volume contains a substantial introduction explaining the context and significance of the essays selected.

I am most grateful for the care which volume editors have taken in carrying out the complex task of selecting and presenting essays which meet the exacting criteria set for the series.

TOM CAMPBELL
Series Editor
The Faculty of Law
The Australian National University

Introduction

Many of the most familiar aspects of social coexistence defy easy understanding. Crime is a constant presence. Much of what counts as 'news' is news about crime. Much of our culture – novels, movies, television, theatre – is given over to stories about crime. Our imaginings and fears commonly betray a preoccupation with crime. And yet, this preoccupation is paradoxical. For most of us, crime is a much more ubitiquous presence in imagination than in fact. Comparatively rarely are most of us the perpetrators, victims or witnesses of crime.

Crime fascinates and mystifies us because it characteristically involves the disruption of order. Criminal acts produce arbitrary and cataclysmic harm. Often they defy rational explanation. Regardless of our individual propensities for risk-taking, we share a desire for security and safety. Among the most common threats to well-being – illness, natural disasters, war and crime – only the last two involve human agency and human choice.

Scholarship about crime, like legal scholarship in general, is now more interdisciplinary than it has ever been. Philosophers, psychologists, literary scholars, anthropologists, historians, economists, sociologists and political theorists have all migrated from their various disciplines to law schools in significant numbers. Many of those who have not strayed from their own departments also study crime. Accordingly, more points of view are focused on criminal law now than ever before. This collective effort to describe and understand what crime is and how we deal with it has no clear shape or trajectory. Within each discipline, and certainly among them, there remain profound disagreements about relevant methods, facts and goals. Perhaps this situation is inevitable. It is hardly to be regretted.

As a result, we produce more questions than answers. Significant essays may show us that we never really knew what we thought we knew, that received and familiar ways of conceptualizing crime are hardly to be taken for granted. In particular, the essays in Part I of this volume represent a series of critiques of received wisdom. Drawing on sociology, psychology, philosophy, critical feminist theory and economics, these scholars try to deconstruct and reassemble the ingredients of criminal law theory.

A particularly fertile area for reconsideration has been the intersection of criminal law, psychology and morality. While the topics of free will and responsibility have given employment to philosophers for over 2000 years, these thinkers have hardly left us definitive and wholly satisfactory accounts. Each generation of criminal law theorists needs to attend to questions about freedom and responsibility because the practice of criminal law requires a clear distinction between those who are to be held accountable for their actions and those who are to be excused. The essays in Part II are all about identifying and explaining the frontiers of responsibility.

If the topic of responsibility locates one hive of philosophical activity, the topic of punishment identifies another. Why we punish, how we punish, and what we achieve by punishing are among the concerns raised in Part III. Here, as elsewhere, new ways of thinking about desert, deterrence and condemnation march in step with sceptical misgivings about what we thought we knew: 'two steps forward, one step back'.

Jurisprudential Issues

In his magisterial 1978 treatise, *Rethinking Criminal Law*, George Fletcher commends the study of foreign legal systems to clarify the hidden structures of our own. In the first essay in Part I, Paul Robinson carries out a similar exercise in examining the covert structure of the Model Penal Code. He concludes that a penal code serves three functions: rule articulation, liability assessment and grading the seriousness of crime. He argues the Model Penal Code, and familiar domestic codifications of criminal law in general, fail to take account of the distinctiveness of each function. This has the effect of concealing from officials the underlying theory governing each function, and therefore has the practical result of compromising the law's performance of these functions.

Lloyd Weinreb (Chapter 2) commends a reconsideration of a different nest of issues: the psychology, morality and justification of punishment. He reminds us that both desert-based and utilitarian theories of punishment capture undeniable truths and, in their incompatibility, leave us with a conundrum. On one hand, desert is an indispensable and sufficient condition of punishment in a system that is based on freedom, responsibility and blameworthiness. On the other hand, as utilitarians never cease to remind us, our criteria for desert are endlessly controversial. Judgements about desert are characteristically vulnerable to the charge that they are arbitrary and psychologically untenable. (A different approach to reconciling utilitarian and desert-based intuitions about the justification of punishment is offered by Paul Robinson and John Darley in their essay in Part III.)

Drawing on Freudian psychology, Richard Wollheim, in Chapter 3, deepens our sense of Weinreb's conundrum about judgements of desert. He uses Freud's term 'pale criminality' for situations in which a sense of guilt does not follow from criminal activity, but precedes and precipitates it. Guilt in this sense is a motivational factor. Wollheim observes that recognition of 'pale criminality' forces us to confront the inadequacy, the thinness and the arbitrariness of our legal criteria for voluntariness. He concludes that 'law is an institution that misrepresents us to ourselves. It abets self-deception or self-disavowal' (this volume, p. 112).

Critical theorists also offer the criticism that criminal law embodies a kind of intellectual dishonesty and bad faith. They suggest not, as Wollheim does, that it rests on an untenable theory of human nature, but that it contains systemic bias. Stephen Schulhofer (Chapter 4) defends the feminist charge that criminal law is preoccupied with male concerns and male perspectives. Arguing that this criticism is 'accurate and uncontroversial', he concedes the difficulty of addressing it. Solutions do not seem to lie in the direction of equal treatment without regard to gender, since the *difference* between genders appears to play a crucial role in domestic violence, rape and issues of sentencing and imprisonment.

It is sometimes said that feminism offers a tool that illuminates some parts of criminal law, but not the perspective of criminal law in its generality. Economic analysis, when applied to criminal law, is said to have analogous limitations. Certainly, the behavioural model of economic rationality and the goal of efficient preference satisfaction have explanatory and normative applications within criminal law. The principles of law and economics help us understand why it makes sense to criminalize certain kinds of behaviour, why the criminal process sometimes fails in its goals, and how those goals may be achieved more sensibly. Nonetheless, the reasons why people commit crime, and the social and moral goals inherent in criminalization and punishment, often escape or transcend the categories of economic analysis. Steven Shavell (Chapter 5) is sensitive to these limitations. At the same time, his analysis of the criminalization of threats in blackmail and extortion shows the power of economic analysis in rationalizing important areas of law.

Doctrinal Issues: The Limits of Responsibility

The intersection of law and morality is a common preoccupation of the essays in Part II. All are concerned with legal doctrines that define the scope and limits of personal responsibility in the context of crime. And all suggest that, however much we try to observe the positivist mantra that the law is one thing and morality is another, our legal understanding of the boundaries of responsibility is permeated by normative assumptions and choices. These norms often play a subterranean role.

In Chapter 6 Douglas Husak and Craig Callender examine the principle of legality, the notion that there can be no liability or punishment without law. Moral wrongs alone do not count. Using the example of the law's treatment of cases of wilful ignorance, the authors question whether criminal law is as positivistic as the principle of legality implies. They point out instances in which the letter of the law is bent to accommodate a sense of fairness, and they suggest that the rule of law is governed less by the principle of legality than it is by deeper, often unacknowledged, ideas of justice.

Like the principle of legality, the principle that ignorance of the law is generally not an excuse seems to play a formal role in criminal jurisprudence. Dan Kahan (Chapter 7) challenges the standard account of why ignorance of the law does not excuse, namely that, once the laws are in force, citizens must be given an incentive to know them. Looking at the practice that elaborates the principle – at what counts as an application of the principle and as an exception – Kahan concludes that individuals are judged not just on the basis of law-conforming acts but on the moral quality of their values and motivations. When the actor's character justifies the result, ignorance is indeed an excuse. He observes that 'stealthy moralizing is in fact endemic to criminal law' (this volume, p. 27). Furthermore, he sees this as wholly defensible, if not inevitable, and objects only to disclaimers of it, to 'the duplicity that surrounds it' (ibid., p. 272).

Examining the law of duress, Joshua Dressler (Chapter 8) identifies another principle and practice that, as he argues, is covertly normative. He highlights the problematic quality of duress: on one hand, it does not fit our notion of a justification; on the other hand, it is an odd sort of excuse since it involves a knowing violation of a legal prohibition. For Dressler, the key to understanding duress as an excuse is not simply the descriptive conclusion that the actor made the sort of choice that most people would make, but the normative determination that she did not have a fair opportunity to act in conformity with the law. It is a question not of ordinary expectations but of legitimate ones in the light of fair understanding of moral strength.

The defence of necessity is as problematic as duress. Unlike other principles, necessity wears its normative character on its sleeve. A puzzle about necessity is not whether moral analysis is relevant in understanding and applying it, but what kind of moral theory is most helpful. In Chapter 9 Alan Brudner examines the competing claims of utilitarianism and rights theory to explain necessity. He argues that a utilitarian account of necessity cannot be reconciled with other aspects of criminal law, that it throws a wild card into determinations of liability by making them rest on a balance of harms. Instead, he contends the notion that those who are justified by necessity are acting out of a right and that this right has its defensible place in a hierarchy of value.

The essays in Part II reflect the influence of moral philosophy, the philosophy of action, and philosophical psychology on criminal law theory. The common denominator of each essay is the notion that we cannot evade controversial questions about what counts as a morally fair and psychologically appropriate expectation about behaviour. The effort to devise legal tests that escape the brambles of moral theory and psychology is an effort that, in each case, collapses in failure.

Punishment

Just as writers on criminal responsibility are rediscovering how difficult their topic is – both conceptually and morally – writers on punishment are also jettisoning familiar approaches in the light of their apparent inadequacy. Recent scholarly work is intellectually rich with respect to both topics. But, as the expression of more questions than answers, it has had, in the short run, little effect on practice.

The philosophy of mind – specifically reconsideration of the primitive disjunction between emotion and reason – inspires the rethinking of theories of punishment. A touchstone of this approach is Samuel Pillsbury's essay 'Emotional Justice: Moralizing the Passions of Criminal Punishment' (1991). Pillsbury reminds us of the survival of the Platonic assumption that reason and emotion are separate components of the soul. These two parts of the soul, or two aspects of our experience, are at war. Reason is to be trusted, and emotion tends to subvert reason. Thus, we must be prepared to resist the lures of emotion and avoid the mistakes to which it leads.

Arguably, we abandoned this primitive psychology during the Enlightenment and have recognized a more complex relationship between reason and emotion ever since. In fact, however, this distinction has stubbornly resisted extinction, and has appeared in familiar disguises throughout the nineteenth and twentieth centuries. Freud's bifurcation of the soul into the id and the ego resurrected its main elements for the twentieth century.

Pillsbury notes correctly that mistrust of emotion as the enemy of reason has survived with particular resilience in law. We are far more willing to acknowledge the necessary coexistence and interdependence of reason and emotion in private relationships than in public roles. Judges and juries, we think, should be dispassionate. Justice requires a kind of impartiality, and emotions are inherently partial. Accordingly, the subversion of reason by emotion is a constant threat to justice.

Proponents of this view habitually talk about emotion without specifying particular emotions, as if all emotions had the same characteristics. Pillsbury reminds us that this is nonsense. Drawing equally on empirical psychology and common sense, he argues that emotions have their own rationality and involve cognitive assessments. It is self-evident, I think, that such emotions as gratitude and resentment are appropriate only in certain factual settings and presuppose certain kinds of conditions and understandings. Indeed, legal categories and doctrines, such as those involving gifts, contracts and breach, or torts, anticipate that gratitude, resentment and other emotions will occur in certain circumstances and will make certain legal results appropriate.

Pillsbury emphasizes the role of such emotions as moral outrage and empathy as part of the dynamic of criminal punishment. The decision procedure for punishment would be incomprehensible if these emotions did not exist, and relevant evidence of circumstances that evoke these emotions should be presented. This does not mean that every emotion is *prima facie* relevant to a decision on punishment. But it does mean that the process involves the interplay of reason and emotion.

In the end, the very terms 'emotion' and 'reason' may be misleading insofar as it may be a fallacy that the two aspects of experience are separable. Every experience of emotion may in fact involve some process of reasoning and inference. And every instance of reasoning may be coloured by some emotion or other.

Only in the *exceptional* case does a determination about punishment follow from a full-fledged trial. John Langbein's essay (Chapter 10) discusses the controversial role of plea bargaining as the safety valve that allows most cases to be resolved without trial and ensures whatever efficiency the process has. In comparing the process of plea bargaining with medieval decision by torture, Langbein's piece is both descriptive and critical. He describes both processes as responses to legal contexts in which a standard of proof for criminal conviction was set too high for efficient crime control and determination of guilt. The medieval system, in which one could be punished following either confession or the convincing testimony of two eyewitnesses, made conviction of many criminals impossible. The unreliable method of torture as a test of guilt was devised to fill the gap. Similarly, Langbein argues, the inefficiencies of our current safeguards of constitutional justice make necessary the equally unreliable tool of plea bargaining.

Pillsbury and Langbein are concerned with how the process of deciding to punish works. Paul Robinson, John Darley and Dan Kahan, on the other hand, are concerned with the justifications of punishment. In Chapter 11 Robinson and Darley offer a clear and convincing method of reconciling two familiar and irreconcilable ways of justifying punishment: utilitarian theories and desert theories. Their suggestions are reminiscent of the influential writings of H.L.A. Hart (1968) and Joel Feinberg (1970) of a generation ago. They commend a two-level or rule-utilitarian theory whereby punishing on grounds of desert is by itself a system that leads to a law-abiding society and can thus be justified on a utilitarian basis. By the same token, deviations from decision-making in accord with desert are said to have unjustifiable costs with regard to crime control. Public confidence and support are crucial for efficient survival of the system, and they will be forthcoming as long as those who are punished are understood to deserve it. Thus judgements about desert and utilitarian considerations are melded in a system in which they are assigned first-order and second-order roles respectively.

Dan Kahan (Chapter 12) also sees the need to flesh out justificatory notions that have been treated simplistically. Just as Robinson and Darley show that utilitarian and retributive justifications are independent, Kahan shows that the economic model of deterrence is critically defective. This model explains law-breaking as a utilitarian decision that the benefits of law-breaking outweigh the expected disutility of punishment. Kahan argues that social meaning influences such choices, that one factor in choosing crime is the perception that others are breaking the law and that law-breaking is generally expected. He concludes that relevant perceptions reinforce and change reality, that society is more likely to be law-abiding when its members perceive that it is.

Conclusion

Most of the essays in this volume show the intimate connection between legal doctrine and moral assumptions and arguments. Agreement in legal theory and practice presupposes, more often than we realize, agreement in underlying moral convictions. Criminal law, more than other areas of law, depends on shared moral practices. The convictions that constitute such practices are often covert and unarticulated. Laying bare our agreements, disagreements and practices of debate is the ongoing task of scholarship.

References

Feinberg, Joel (1970), *Doing and Deserving*, Princeton: Princeton University Press.
Fletcher, George (1978), *Rethinking Criminal Law*, Boston: Little Brown and Company.
Hart, H.L.A. (1968), *Punishment and Responsibility*, New York and Oxford: Oxford University Press.
Pillsbury, Samuel (1991), 'Emotional Justice: Moralizing the Passions of Criminal Punishment', in Thomas Morawetz (ed.), *Criminal Law*, The International Library of Essays in Law and Legal Theory, First Series, Aldershot: Dartmouth.

Part I
Jurisprudential Issues

[1]

Copyright 1994 by Northwestern University, School of Law
Northwestern University Law Review

Printed in U.S.A.
Vol. 88, No. 3

ARTICLES

A FUNCTIONAL ANALYSIS OF CRIMINAL LAW

*Paul H. Robinson**

The criminal law has three primary functions. First, it must define and announce the conduct that is prohibited (or required) by the criminal law. Such "rules of conduct," as they have been called, provide ex ante direction to members of the community as to the conduct that must be avoided (or that must be performed) upon pain of criminal sanction. This may be termed the *rule articulation* function of the doctrine. When a violation of the rules of conduct occurs, the criminal law takes on a different role. It must decide whether the violation merits criminal liability. This second function, setting the minimum conditions for *liability*, marks the shift from prohibition to adjudication.[1] It typically assesses ex post whether the violation is sufficiently blameworthy "to warrant the condemnation of conviction."[2] Finally, where liability is to be imposed, criminal law doctrine must assess the relative seriousness of the offense, usually a function of the relative blameworthiness of the offender. This sets, in a general sense, the amount of punishment that is to be imposed. While the first step in the adjudication process, the liability function, requires a simple yes or no decision as to whether the minimum conditions for liability are satisfied, this second step, the *grading* function, requires judgments of degree. It must consider such factors as the relative harmfulness of the violation and the level of culpability of the actor.

This Article argues that these three primary functions of criminal law—rule articulation, liability assignment, and grading—are a useful way in which to analyze and organize criminal law doctrine. Modern criminal codes commonly acknowledge that criminal law serves each of these three functions. However, these same codes fail to see that a given code provision may serve one function but not another; the entire undifferentiated code is seen as serving these functions together. The Model

---

* Professor of Law, Northwestern University. Earlier drafts of this Article benefitted from criticisms by Ronald Allen, Andrew Ashworth, John Donohue, Antony Duff, Dennis Patterson, and participants of law school faculty workshops at Northwestern University and New York University.

1 For a general discussion of the distinction between rules of conduct and principles of adjudication, see Paul H. Robinson, *Rules of Conduct and Principles of Adjudication*, 57 U. CHI. L. REV. 729 (1990).

2 This is a Model Penal Code phrase. *See, e.g.*, MODEL PENAL CODE § 2.12(2) (1985).

Penal Code, for example, describes "[t]he general purposes of the provisions governing the definition of offenses" as:

> [1] to forbid and prevent conduct that unjustifiably and inexcusably inflicts or threatens substantial harm to individual or public interests;
>
> [2] to give fair warning of the nature of the conduct declared to constitute an offense;
>
> [3] to safeguard conduct that is without fault from condemnation as criminal;
>
> [4] to subject to public control persons whose conduct indicates that they are disposed to commit crimes;
>
> [5] to differentiate on reasonable grounds between serious and minor offenses.[3]

The first two purposes appear to embody the rule articulation function, the second two the liability assignment function, and the last the grading function. Part II of this Article dissects current criminal law doctrine in terms of these three functions and demonstrates that one can identify specific doctrines as serving specific functions.

The functional differences among doctrines have not been obvious in part because the current organizing structure of criminal law uses distinctions that obscure the law's different functions. The central organizing distinctions in criminal law doctrine have traditionally been those between offenses and defenses and between "actus reus" and "mens rea" requirements. Yet, as Part I demonstrates, each of these categories, as well as the subcategories into which they commonly are divided, contains doctrines that perform each of the three functions of rule articulation, liability assignment, and grading.

The failure of current theory and doctrine to recognize the distinctness of these functions has hurt the law's performance of each. Parts III, IV, and V of this Article give examples of doctrinal shortcomings that may be traced to insensitivity to the distinctiveness of each function.

I. The Standard Conceptualization: Offenses and Defenses; Actus Reus and Mens Rea

The distinctions between offenses and defenses and between actus reus and mens rea are criminal law's basic organizing distinctions for most lawyers, judges, and code drafters. The offense-defense distinction is reflected in the structure of modern codes. The Model Penal Code, for example, groups offenses in part II of the Code, leaving defenses for part I. The Code recognizes three kinds of defenses. Those relating to an actor's irresponsibility, such as mental illness and infancy, are contained in article 4 of part I. Those relating to the justification of an actor's

[3] *Id.* § 1.02(1). The order of the subsections is altered from the original. Over two-thirds of the states have adopted a criminal code modeled to some extent upon the Model Penal Code. *See Status of Substantive Penal Law Revision: Annual Report*, 60 A.L.I. Proc. 560-63 (1983) (tabulating extent to which states have adopted Model Penal Code).

conduct, such as self-defense and law enforcement authority, are grouped in article 3 of part I. Other miscellaneous defenses, such as duress, statute of limitations, consent, and de minimis, are included in article 2 of part I.

Modern codes also distinguish among kinds of offense elements, although they are more likely to use the modern terms "objective" and "culpability" elements rather than the older Latin labels "actus reus" and "mens rea" requirements. As for mens rea, modern codes typically follow the Model Penal Code in defining four "levels of culpability," as the Code prefers to call them: purpose, knowledge, recklessness, and negligence.[4] The remaining offense requirements typically are termed the offense's "actus reus." Included here are what the Code identifies as three kinds of objective elements: conduct, circumstances, and results.[5] (Each of the four culpability levels is specifically defined with respect to each of the three different kinds of objective elements.)[6] Also included in actus reus are the requirements of a voluntary act or an omission to perform a duty of which one is capable,[7] and of a causal connection between the conduct or omission and any required result.[8]

To summarize, the conceptual structure of criminal law embodied in modern codes might look something like this:

---

[4] MODEL PENAL CODE § 2.02.

[5] *Id.* § 1.13(9).

[6] *See id.* § 2.02(2). There are two exceptions: recklessness and negligence are not defined with respect to conduct. *See id.* § 2.02(2)(c)-(d); *see also infra* note 13 and accompanying text.

[7] *See* MODEL PENAL CODE § 2.01.

[8] *See id.* § 2.03. The term actus reus sometimes refers only to the voluntary act or omission requirement, sometimes to the conduct, circumstance, and result elements of an offense, and sometimes to both. *See generally* Paul H. Robinson, *Should the Criminal Law Abandon the Actus Reus-Mens Rea Distinction?*, *in* ACTION AND VALUE IN CRIMINAL LAW (Stephen Shute et al. eds., 1993).

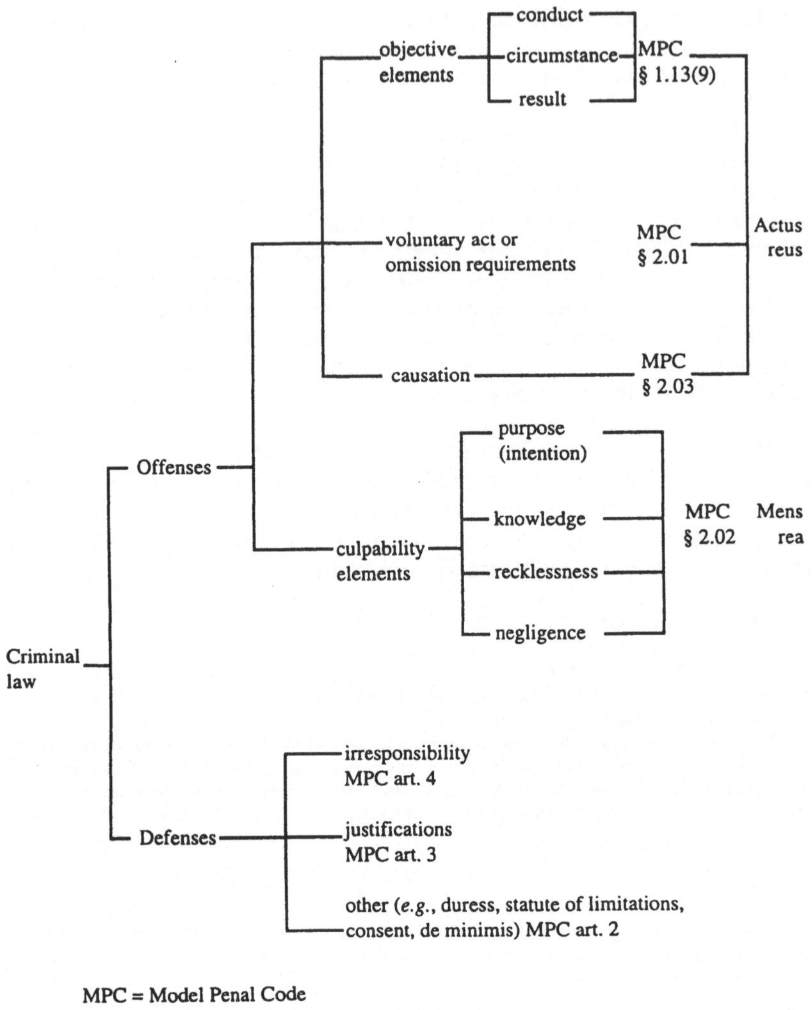

Figure 1

Presumably, current doctrine uses these organizing distinctions, rather than others, because they seem more useful than others in conceptualizing and analyzing criminal law. Let these distinctions, then, be the starting point for describing how different doctrines perform different functions.

One might initially estimate that the actus reus requirements define the prohibited conduct, the rule articulation function, and that the mens rea requirements, with the help of the general defenses, define the minimum requirements of liability for a violation, the liability function. A closer examination, however, suggests that the functional structure of current criminal law is somewhat different.

A. "Actus Reus" Requirements

The conduct and circumstance elements of offense definitions do contribute to the definition of the prohibited conduct, the rule articulation function, but result elements do not. Unlike conduct and circumstance elements, result elements are not necessary to define the prohibited conduct. The criminal law must prohibit an actor's conduct, not the conduct's result, because the law can influence only the actor's conduct. The law may claim to prohibit a particular result; however, the law actually means to claim that it prohibits actors from engaging in conduct that would bring about (or risk bringing about) that result. An actual resulting harm may make the violation more serious, some would argue, but the fortuity of whether the result actually occurs does not alter the nature of the conduct that constitutes the violation. The conduct remains objectionable notwithstanding the happenstance that the result does not occur.[9] Result elements, then, serve only to aggravate an actor's liability, the grading function.

Similarly, the causation requirement—defining the relation between an actor's conduct and a result that will give rise to an actor's accountability for the result—serves the grading function, not the rule articulation function. Like the requirement of a result, the causation rules determine when an actor's liability is to be aggravated because the actor is accountable for a harmful result. Because result elements and causation requirements are not necessary to define the conduct prohibited by the criminal law, it is not surprising that liability does not necessarily depend upon them. If a prohibited result does not occur or if a required causal connection is not established, the actor frequently is liable for a lesser offense, such as an attempt.[10]

Many of the omission and possession rules, which impose liability for an omission to perform a legal duty or for possession of contraband even in the absence of an affirmative act, contribute to the criminal law's definition of the conduct that is prohibited and required. Without the special duty requirements or the special prohibition for the possession of

---

[9] However, in some instances, as when less serious harms are only risked, the societal harm of the conduct may be too small to justify criminal condemnation. Conduct creating a low risk of a less serious harm may fall below the line of minimum seriousness required for adequate blameworthiness unless the harm actually occurs.

[10] This is always true for intentional offenses in jurisdictions that have general attempt statutes, as do nearly two-thirds of the states. See the general attempt statutes and their corresponding defense provisions cited at 1 PAUL H. ROBINSON, CRIMINAL LAW DEFENSES §§ 81(b) nn.16-17, 83(f) n.60 (1984 & Supp. 1992).

contraband, the law would not provide a complete description of what is acceptable and unacceptable conduct. Thus, aspects of the commission, omission, and possession rules serve the rule articulation function. However, other aspects of these actus reus rules do not serve the rule articulation function. The voluntariness aspect of the act requirement, the "physical capacity to perform" requirement of the omission doctrine, and the requirement in the possession liability rules that the actor know of his possession for a period sufficient to terminate the possession, do not define prohibited conduct. Rather, those requirements define minimum conditions for holding an actor condemnable for a violation by commission, omission, or possession, respectively. The rules of conduct continue to prohibit possession of certain drugs, even if the possessor of the drug is held nonliable because he did not know of the possession for a period sufficient to terminate it. Filing an income tax return remains a duty, although the nonfiling actor is not punished if it was physically impossible for her to file. In other words, the actus reus requirements of voluntariness, capacity, and knowledge of possession serve a liability function in the same way that many mens rea requirements do. For example, under the mens rea requirements, taking another person's property without permission remains a violation of the rules of conduct although the actor is held nonliable for such a taking where he was unaware of a risk that the property belonged to another person.

B. Mens Rea Requirements

We may tend to think of all mens rea or culpability requirements as serving analogous functions—the liability function of establishing the minimum culpability required for liability for a violation. Purpose, knowledge, recklessness, and negligence are defined as alternative levels of culpability. According to the Code, liability for an offense ordinarily may not be imposed unless one of these culpability levels is proven as to each objective element of the offense.[11] But as with actus reus requirements, by treating all mens rea requirements as a group, the doctrine obscures the different functions that the different requirements perform. Many culpability requirements do serve the liability function, but others do not. Let us examine more closely the nature of culpability requirements.

---

[11] "[A] person is not guilty of an offense unless he acted purposely, knowingly, recklessly, or negligently, as the law may require, with respect to each material element of the offense." MODEL PENAL CODE § 2.02(1). Thus, if the objective elements of an offense require that an actor take property of another without the owner's consent, the culpability elements of an offense might require, for example, that the actor purposely take what he knows is property while being reckless as to its belonging to another and reckless as to the owner's lack of consent. For a discussion of the sometimes complex and confusing process of determining the culpability requirements of an offense, see Paul H. Robinson & Jane A. Grall, *Element Analysis in Defining Criminal Liability: The Model Penal Code and Beyond*, 35 STAN. L. REV. 681, 699-702, 705-06, 710-19 (1983).

First, note that the four levels of culpability do not apply in a symmetrical way to the three kinds of objective elements. When we talk of culpability as to the existence of a *circumstance* element, we refer to the actor's culpability as to the then *present* circumstance. Any of the four culpability levels can apply. As to the circumstance that an actor's sexual partner is less than sixteen years old, for example, the actor may desire the partner to be under sixteen; he may be practically certain (know) that the partner is under sixteen; he may be aware of a substantial risk that the partner is under sixteen; or he may not be aware but should be aware of a substantial risk that the partner is under sixteen.[12] These culpability requirements are what might be called instances of *present circumstance culpability*, to remind us that they refer only to culpability as to then present facts.

When we talk of culpability as to a *result*, in contrast, we necessarily are talking of an actor's culpability as to a then *future* event. Culpability, required by the concurrence requirement to exist at the time of the conduct, as to an actor's conduct causing a result necessarily means culpability as to causing a result that does not at that moment exist. Again, any level of culpability can apply. With regard to an actor's culpability as to causing another's death, for example, the actor may desire to cause the death; he may be practically certain (know) that his conduct will cause the death; he may be aware of a substantial risk that his conduct will cause the death; or he may not be aware but should be aware of a substantial risk that his conduct will cause the death. These kinds of culpability are what might be called instances of *future result culpability*.

When we talk of culpability as to a *conduct* element, the full range of culpability levels does not apply. An actor can be purposeful only as to his or her *own* conduct. Absent a serious disability, an actor engages in conduct only if he desires to do so, if such is his "conscious object." An actor either wishes to engage in certain conduct or does not. Except for persons with control dysfunctions, it makes little sense to speak of an actor who knows or is aware of a risk that he is engaging in or will engage in certain conduct that he does not desire. The Code recognizes this in part when it fails to define "recklessly" and "negligently" with respect to a conduct element.[13] To remind us that only "purposely" is meaning-

---

[12] Apparently, the Model Penal Code drafters see no practical significance in the difference between desiring that a circumstance exists and knowing so. The Code defines "purposely" as to a circumstance as requiring only that the actor "*believes or* hopes" that the circumstance exists. MODEL PENAL CODE § 2.02(2)(a)(ii) (emphasis added).

[13] *See id.* § 2.02(2)(c)-(d). However, the Code does define "knowingly" as to conduct; an actor is "knowing" as to conduct when the actor "is aware that his conduct is of that nature." *Id.* § 2.02(2)(b)(i). What does the Code mean by being aware of the "nature" of one's conduct? Presumably, it means that the actor must be aware of the circumstances and results of the conduct. But, if this is what is intended, the drafters have created a troublesome overlap between culpability as to conduct and culpability as to a circumstance and a result, which the Code defines separately and differently. In any given circumstance or result element, how are we to know whether to apply the

ful with regard to one's performing conduct, we may wish to call this kind of culpability *conduct intention*.

Another important difference that characterizes culpability as to one's own conduct is that it can concern either *present* or *future* conduct. For all commission offenses, a *present conduct intention* is required, satisfied simply by showing that the actor did in fact intend to perform the bodily movements that he performed. For example, an actor does not satisfy this culpability requirement if he does not intend to push the victim but rather does so accidentally as he catches his balance from his own fall. A requirement of present conduct intention essentially duplicates the voluntariness requirement discussed above.

The requirement of a *future conduct intention*, on the other hand, has a critical independent role to play. It serves to show that the actor is planning to do more than what he has already done. Most prominently, attempt liability requires that the actor must intend, must have the "purpose," to engage in the conduct constituting the offense.[14] Such a future conduct intention also is present in substantive offenses that are or that contain codified inchoate offenses. Burglary, for example, requires that an actor enter a building "with purpose to commit a crime therein."[15] Note that the requirement of a *present* conduct intention applies to a corresponding objective element of offense definition, the conduct element, that the actor also must satisfy, just as the requirements of a present circumstance culpability and a future result culpability typically apply to a corresponding objective element. A requirement of a *future* conduct intention, in contrast, by definition has no corresponding objective element but rather exists on its own; the actor need not be shown to have performed the conduct.

In some instances the law requires that the actor have culpability as to *another person's* conduct. For example, the general inchoate offenses of conspiracy and solicitation, as well as complicity liability, require that the actor agree with or solicit or aid another with some level of culpability as to the other person engaging in conduct constituting an offense.[16] While one normally can be only "purposeful" as to one's own conduct, one can have any level of culpability as to causing or assisting another's

definition of culpability as to a circumstance or as to a result, or instead to subsume the circumstance or result into the "nature of the conduct" and thus apply the definition of culpability as to conduct. The Code provides no means of distinguishing conduct, circumstance, and result elements. If this broad interpretation of conduct is accepted—conduct includes the circumstances and results of conduct—one may wonder why the Code does not allow for culpability lower than knowing; one can be reckless or negligent as to the result or circumstances of one's conduct. The better view is to treat the circumstances or results of one's conduct as circumstance or result elements, each with a distinct culpability requirement (and to disregard the Code's definition of "knowingly" as to conduct). *See generally* Robinson & Grall, *supra* note 11, at 706-10.

14 MODEL PENAL CODE § 5.01(1)(c).

15 *Id.* § 221.1(1).

16 *See, e.g., id.* §§ 2.06(3)(a), 5.02(1), 5.03(1).

conduct. One may hope and desire that another will engage in certain offense conduct; one may not desire it but may know (may be "aware that it is practically certain")[17] that the other will engage in the conduct; one may be aware only of a substantial risk that the other will engage in the conduct; or one may not be aware but should be aware of a substantial risk that the person will engage in the conduct. Such culpability as to another's conduct can be either culpability as to another's present or future conduct. When it concerns another's present conduct, it is simply an example of a present circumstance. When it concerns another's future conduct, which is more often the case, as in solicitation, conspiracy, and complicity, it is a form of a future result. This form of culpability requires a showing that when the actor solicited, conspired with, or aided another, the actor had a given level of culpability as to causing or assisting the resulting conduct by the other person. Culpability as to another's conduct thus does not appear to present a culpability requirement different from present circumstance culpability and future result culpability.

Here, then, are four distinct kinds of culpability requirements—present circumstance culpability, future result culpability, present conduct intention, and future conduct intention—that are grouped together under current doctrine's standard purpose-knowledge-recklessness-negligence scheme. The reformulated distinctions described above are superior because they capture the different functions of mens rea requirements that current doctrine does not.

Only the requirements of a present circumstance culpability and a present conduct intention serve the liability function that we typically ascribe to culpability requirements. They set the minimum requirements for imposing criminal liability for a violation. We might call these "base culpability" requirements. Indeed, as noted above, even a present conduct intention has little practical effect in serving the liability function. It is rarely in dispute, and where disputed, duplicates the voluntariness requirement. Thus, of the four kinds of culpability requirements, present circumstance is generally the only one that establishes minimum liability conditions.

Just as result elements are never a minimum requirement for liability, their corresponding future result culpability requirements are never part of the minimum requirements of liability. (As we shall see, however, this may not be true where the future result culpability exists by itself in attempt liability, where no actual result is required.) Thus, future result culpability typically serves as part of the grading function. This is also the case for many future conduct intentions, such as the future conduct intention in burglary that turns the misdemeanor of trespass into the felony of burglary.

Both future result culpability and future conduct intentions also

[17] *Id.* § 2.02(2)(b).

serve a grading function when used to distinguish among different grades of violations with identical objective elements. The culpability requirements for homicide—murder (purposeful or knowing killing), manslaughter (reckless killing), and negligent homicide—are not designed "to safeguard conduct that is without fault from condemnation as criminal." Rather, they define the conditions for distinguishing between grades of unlawful homicide. Assault with intent to commit rape is another example.[18] The "intent to commit rape" element is used as a basis for increasing the grade of the offense over an assault without such intention. Burglary, as noted above, is a similar example. These culpability requirements serve "to differentiate on reasonable grounds between serious and minor offenses," to use the Model Penal Code phrase.[19] Future result culpability and future conduct intention, serving the grading function, might be termed instances of "aggravation culpability," to distinguish them from the base culpability requirements that serve the liability function.

Base and aggravation culpability may be the most common functions of culpability requirements, but in a few instances, chiefly in the definition of inchoate conduct, culpability requirements can serve the rule articulation function of defining the rules of conduct. That is, they are sometimes necessary to describe the conduct that the criminal law prohibits. In the general offense of attempt, for example, the conduct and circumstance elements of the substantive offense definition only begin to state the criminal law's prohibition. Defining the conduct prohibited by the attempt offense requires something more. A common requirement in modern codes, that the conduct constitute a "substantial step in a course of conduct planned to culminate in his commission of the crime,"[20] is inadequate in itself. As a purely objective matter, some conduct may constitute a "substantial step" toward commission of an offense but in fact be entirely innocent and acceptable conduct not meant to be prohibited. Such conduct becomes unacceptable and a societal harm only when accompanied by an intention to violate the substantive rules of conduct.

For example, lighting one's pipe is not a violation of the rules of conduct, unless it is a step in a plan to ignite a neighbor's haystack. Giving a young girl a ride is not a violation of the rules of conduct, unless it is done with the intention of sexually assaulting her. Thus, to describe the minimum requirements of prohibited conduct, the definition of a criminal attempt must include a state of mind requirement—the intention to engage in conduct that would constitute a rule violation.[21] (In

---

18 *See, e.g.*, CAL. PENAL CODE § 220 (West 1988).

19 MODEL PENAL CODE § 1.02(1)(e).

20 *Id.* § 5.01(1)(c).

21 The same analysis might be made for conspiracy and solicitation. Otherwise acceptable and innocent conduct may become a violation of the prohibition against conspiracy or solicitation if

contrast, the law can prohibit homicide without having to refer to the actor's mental state.) Here, the culpability requirements play a role similar to the conduct and circumstance elements of offense definitions.[22] Typically, such a rule articulation function for culpability requirements appears in "secondary prohibitions," such as those against complicity and inchoate offenses, and involves an intention to violate a "primary prohibition."[23]

Consider the kinds of culpability requirements that serve this rule articulation function. In the most typical attempt offense of incomplete conduct toward a substantive offense, a future conduct intention serves the rule articulation function. The examples above are of this sort: the

accompanied by an intention to conspire with or to solicit another to commit a substantive violation of the rules of conduct. However, conspiracy and solicitation might be distinguishable from attempt. One could argue that the rules of conduct ought to prohibit agreements with or solicitations of another to violate the rules of conduct, even if not done with the intention of causing a violation of the rules. Any agreement (even unilateral) to commit an offense and any solicitation of another to commit an offense might be seen as harmful conduct. The harmfulness of the conduct might not necessarily depend upon the actor's subjective state of mind. Therefore, the rules of conduct might appropriately prohibit all agreements and solicitations to commit an offense, whether intentional or inadvertent. That is, the rules might require one to avoid conduct that even accidentally gives the appearance of such an agreement or solicitation. Recall Henry II's rhetorical question, "Won't someone rid me of this troublesome priest?," which was mistaken as a directive to kill Thomas Beckett. One's lack of intent may suggest a lack of blameworthiness, but we nonetheless may wish to announce that even inadvertent agreements and solicitations are to be avoided. After all, one might argue, there is no analogously harmful "unintended attempt."

[22] An offense containing a criminalization mental element commonly contains culpability mental elements as well. In attempted assault, for example, the intention to engage in the conduct constituting the assault is a criminalization mental element; it is necessary for a description of the prohibited conduct. The same offense contains a culpability mental state requiring at least recklessness as to the victim being a person. Under MODEL PENAL CODE § 211.1(a), for example, the assault must be to another human being. MODEL PENAL CODE § 2.02(1) requires proof of culpability "with respect to each material element of the offense." That is, the definition of the prohibited conduct is complete even without this requirement; actors are warned not to attempt to assault persons even though this actor will not be punished for his assault because he was faultless or only negligent as to the victim being a person (*e.g.*, he attempted to abort what he believed to be an inviable fetus or he set a hunting trap for what he thought was a dog stealing his chickens).

[23] The conduct and circumstance elements of specific offense definitions define the primary prohibitions of the criminal law. But the criminal law prohibits not only conduct that violates primary prohibitions, but also conduct aiming toward that end. These secondary prohibitions proscribe assisting, attempting, soliciting, and conspiring to commit prohibited conduct. The secondary prohibitions thus enlarge the primary prohibitions: just as one may not violate a primary prohibition, neither may one assist or attempt or solicit or conspire to commit such a violation. Secondary prohibitions typically are of two sorts: (1) doctrines expanding the primary prohibition by imputing to the actor the conduct of another, as in complicity; and (2) doctrines expanding the primary prohibition by prohibiting conduct short of the substantive harm or evil, as in the inchoate offenses of attempt, conspiracy, solicitation, and possession. Secondary prohibitions sometimes are contained in general code provisions that incorporate by reference the offense definition containing the primary prohibition, as with general inchoate offenses and complicity provisions. Secondary prohibitions also sometimes are contained in specific offenses, such as special codified attempt provisions (*e.g.*, assault with intent to rape, burglary, and possession of burglar's tools). For further discussion, see *infra* part IV.A.

actor's intention to engage in future conduct, the conduct necessary to burn the haystack or to sexually assault the hitchhiker, makes his otherwise acceptable conduct unacceptable.

In other, perhaps more unusual, attempt cases, the actor has completed the conduct necessary for commission of the offense, but some other required objective element is missing. The actor pulls the trigger of a gun, which would kill another except that the gun is inoperative. The cases and literature call this a case of "factual impossibility." It was punished as an attempt at common law and is so punished in most American jurisdictions.[24] The actor's intention to engage in future conduct does not make his conduct criminal, but rather his future result culpability, his culpability as to causing another's death, does so.

In still other cases, an actor's otherwise acceptable conduct may be criminalized by his present circumstance culpability. The actor buys sugar believing it an illegal drug. His intention to perform some future conduct does not make his conduct unacceptable, nor does his culpability as to causing a prohibited future result. The conduct itself is entirely acceptable but is made criminal by the actor's belief that the powder is an illegal drug. Such a case of "legal impossibility," as the literature calls it, was not punished at common law. Today, it is punished under the Model Penal Code and the majority of American codes.[25]

To summarize, the incomplete conduct ("substantial step") addressed by subsection (1)(c) of the Model Penal Code's attempt provision[26] requires a future conduct intention. The completed conduct but missing result (factual impossibility) dealt with under subsection (1)(b) of the Code's provision requires a future result culpability. The completed conduct but missing circumstance (legal impossibility) dealt with under subsection (1)(a) requires a present circumstance culpability. Note that the functional distinctions identify and explain differences between the culpability requirements of the attempt categories used in modern codes. This is true even though the Code's provisions give no hint that the functional distinctions call for identifiably different culpability requirements. The functional distinctions also are useful in making the common law's notoriously difficult factual-legal impossibility distinction noticeably more workable. They also better focus the debate over whether liability should be imposed in cases of legal impossibility, as it is in cases of factual impossibility. In determining whether the two kinds of cases are meaningfully different, one can ask whether present circumstance culpa-

---

24 *See, e.g.*, MODEL PENAL CODE § 5.01(1)(a); Ira Robbins, *Attempting the Impossible: The Emerging Consensus*, 23 HARV. J. ON LEGIS. 377, 419-22 (1986); 1 ROBINSON, *supra* note 10, § 85(b). This form of attempt liability relies even more heavily than others upon an actor's subjective state of mind to justify liability, for the possibility of a successful violation exists only in the actor's mind.

25 Robbins, *supra* note 24, at 419-22.

26 MODEL PENAL CODE § 5.01.

bility is for some reason less appropriate as a ground for criminalization than future result culpability.

To conclude, while traditional analysis does not distinguish among culpability requirements other than among the levels of culpability—purpose, knowledge, recklessness, and negligence—a functional analysis suggests different relevant groupings of "mens rea" requirements—present conduct intention, present circumstance culpability, future result culpability, and future conduct intention. As later Parts of this Article will more fully illustrate, these functional distinctions can be useful in both applying and analyzing current doctrine.

The functions that different kinds of culpability requirements perform may be summarized as follows:

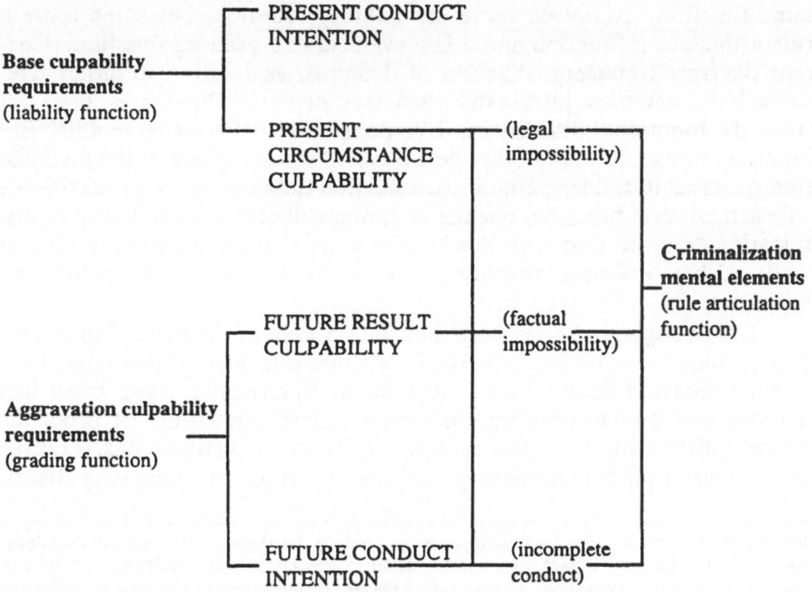

Figure 2

The presence of "base culpability" suggests that conduct that violates the rules of conduct is blameworthy. Present circumstance culpability requirements do most of this work. "Aggravation culpability" serves to aggravate an actor's liability over the minimum. Future result culpability and future conduct intention requirements perform most of this function.[27] Finally, on occasion, "criminalization mental elements" are

[27] Empirical evidence suggests that people perceive some sorts of culpability requirements as being more significant to grading than others. In a recent empirical study, subjects were given a

necessary to define the conduct prohibited by the criminal law. In incomplete conduct cases, future conduct intention performs this function. In completed conduct cases, the function is performed by future result culpability (factually impossible attempts) and, in some jurisdictions, by present circumstance culpability (legally impossible attempts).

C. Defenses

One might initially be tempted to see defenses as serving the liability function; the absence of any defense is a minimum condition for liability for a violation of the rules of conduct. That is, the presence of a defense bars liability for what otherwise would be a blameworthy violation. But, as with actus reus and mens rea requirements, not all defenses serve the same function. Many do serve the liability function, but some serve a rule articulation function and a few even serve a grading function. Current doctrine's conceptualization of defenses, as relating to either irresponsibility defenses, justification defenses, or "other" defenses, does not track the functional differences. Irresponsibility defenses serve a liability function, but so do many other defenses and some aspects of the justification defenses in modern codes. Justification defenses serve primarily the rule articulation function, but the common subjective formulation of justification defenses (more on this later)[28] gives them a liability function as well. Other defenses comprise a mix of defenses that include all functions.

I have suggested elsewhere that the concept of "defenses" draws together many very different sorts of doctrines and have raised what I see as the important distinctions among them. Specifically, I suggested that a more useful conceptualization would distinguish failure of proof defenses, offense modification defenses, (objective) justifications, excuses, and nonexculpatory defenses.[29] Let me structure the following discus-

---

number of scenarios describing similar instances of property destruction where the actor's culpable state of mind is different in each scenario. In one set of scenarios, his culpability as to causing the damage (a future result intention) is varied among the set. In another set of scenarios, his culpability as to the property being property of another (a present circumstance culpability) is varied among the set. (In each instance, his culpability level as to all other elements is held constant.) Subjects varied the degree of liability assigned to the actor according to his level of culpability as to causing the damage. His liability did not vary so much when his culpability as to ownership of the property varied. The subjects apparently perceived the actor's level of culpability as to causing the damage as much more important in determining the proper level of liability than the actor's level of culpability as to ownership. *See* PAUL H. ROBINSON & JOHN M. DARLEY, JUSTICE, LIABILITY AND BLAME (forthcoming 1994) (manuscript at 89-98, study 8, on file with author). This suggests that subjects in fact perceive the future result culpability as performing a grading function, while the present circumstance culpability does not. Without further research, it is unclear whether this pattern holds for other present circumstance culpability and future result culpability requirements.

28 *See infra* part III.C.

29 *See* Paul H. Robinson, *Criminal Law Defenses: A Systematic Analysis*, 82 COLUM. L. REV. 199 (1982); 1 & 2 ROBINSON, *supra* note 10.

sion around these distinctions, for they correspond somewhat better to the differences in defense functions.

Failure of proof defenses, which are simply instances of negating a required offense element, have been discussed above in the context of actus reus and mens rea. For example, mistake that negates a base culpability requirement (required culpability as to a present circumstance or required intention as to present conduct) serves a liability function. Mistake that negates an aggravation culpability requirement (required culpability as to a future result or required intention as to future conduct) serves a grading function.

Many offense modification defenses, which appear outside and independent of offense definitions, serve the rule articulation function. These doctrines, such as the consent defense, further modify or refine the conduct rules. While the rules prohibit conduct that risks causing bodily harm, an exception to the prohibition is admitted where the victim consents to a risk of minor injury or where the risk arises from participation in a lawful sporting event.[30] But other offense modification defenses perform a liability function. They serve to assure adequate blameworthiness for liability. The de minimis defense, for example, bars liability if the actor's conduct caused the harm or evil prohibited by the offense "only to an extent too trivial to warrant the condemnation of conviction."[31] Other defenses, such as renunciation, similarly refine the normal blameworthiness requirements for inchoate offenses.[32]

Justification defenses, objectively defined, perform exclusively a rule articulation function. The law recognizes that in some instances a greater harm may be avoided or a greater good achieved by allowing a person to do what the law normally prohibits. Burning another person's property, normally a violation, is tolerated (even encouraged) if the burning acts as a firebreak to save a town. Striking another person without that person's consent, normally a violation, is lawful if necessary to overcome resistance to a lawful arrest. A full account of what the law requires of persons must define the instances in which an actor is permitted, even encouraged, to do what the law otherwise deplores. In contrast, excuse defenses—such as insanity, immaturity, involuntary intoxication, and duress—serve exclusively a liability function. They define the instances in which an actor is held blameless for a violation of the rules of conduct. Nonexculpatory defenses serve none of the traditional functions of the criminal law, which is why they are disfavored and narrowly limited.[33]

30 *See, e.g.*, MODEL PENAL CODE § 2.11(2)(a)-(b).

31 *Id.* § 2.12(2).

32 Complete and voluntary renunciation, as defined in modern codes, *see, e.g.*, *id.* § 5.01(4), arguably undercuts an actor's blameworthiness by suggesting that the actor's earlier apparent intention to commit the offense was not in fact sufficiently resolute to warrant condemnation.

33 For a general discussion of nonexculpatory defenses, see Robinson, *supra* note 29, at 229-32.

II. Rule Articulation, Liability Assignment, and Grading

Having pulled apart current law to show how different doctrines serve different functions, let me reassemble it along the lines of the three basic functions. The doctrines that serve the rule articulation, liability, and grading functions may be summarized as follows:

Rule Articulation Function	**Liability Function**	**Grading Function**
Violation Doctrines	**Culpability Doctrines**	
Primary Violations: Conduct and circumstance elements of offense definitions	Base culpability requirements: primarily present circumstance culpability	Result elements of offense definitions Causation requirements
Legal duty requirements for omission liability; possession of contraband prohibition in possession offenses	Offense modification defenses relating to criminalization mental elements, such as renunciation defense, or to base culpability requirements	Aggravation culpability requirements: typically limited to future result culpability and future conduct intention Doctrines imputing aggravated culpability, such as felony murder
Offense modification defenses relating to conduct or circumstance offense elements, such as consent	Doctrines imputing culpability requirements, such as doctrines of voluntary intoxication and substituted mental elements	Miscellaneous offense mitigations and aggravations
Secondary Violations: Conduct toward a violation, such as attempt		
Assisting another in a violation	De minimis defense, setting minimum harm or evil requirements	
Criminalization mental elements	**Excuse Doctrines**	
Justification Doctrines	Voluntariness requirement, in commission offenses	
Justification defenses	Physical capacity requirement, in omission offenses	
	Requirement of knowledge of possession for a sufficient time to terminate the same, in possession offenses	
	Excuse defenses	

Figure 3

In determining which doctrines serve which function, the previous discussion has grouped them as if each doctrine serves exclusively one function or another. In fact, the interrelation of the doctrines is slightly more complex. A complete description of the minimum requirements for liability requires not only reference to the doctrines serving the liability function but also to those doctrines serving the rule articulation function. In other words, one prerequisite of liability is violation of the rules of conduct, as described by the doctrines serving the rule articulation function. Similarly, the criminal law's grading function cannot be performed by reference to the doctrines of grading alone. The doctrines of liability define the minimum grade in each instance. The doctrinal functions—ordered as rule articulation, liability, and grading—may best be thought of as having a cumulative relation: the doctrines serving a function include those serving previous functions. Their interrelation might be depicted as:

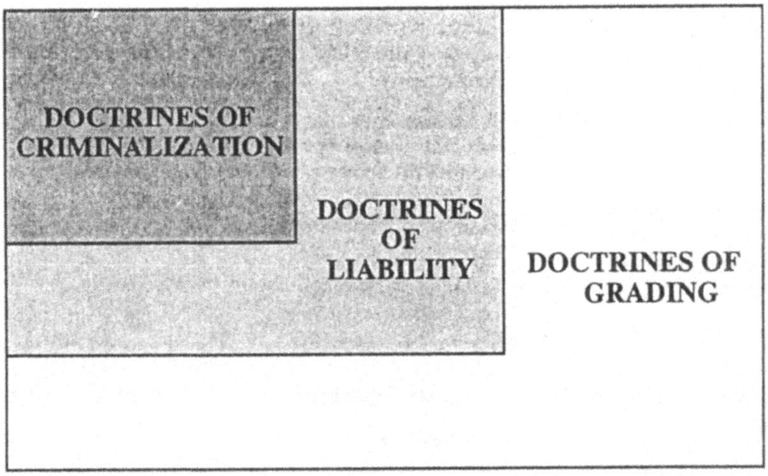

Figure 4

A comparison of this conceptualization to the Model Penal Code scheme diagramed in Part I might look roughly like the following:

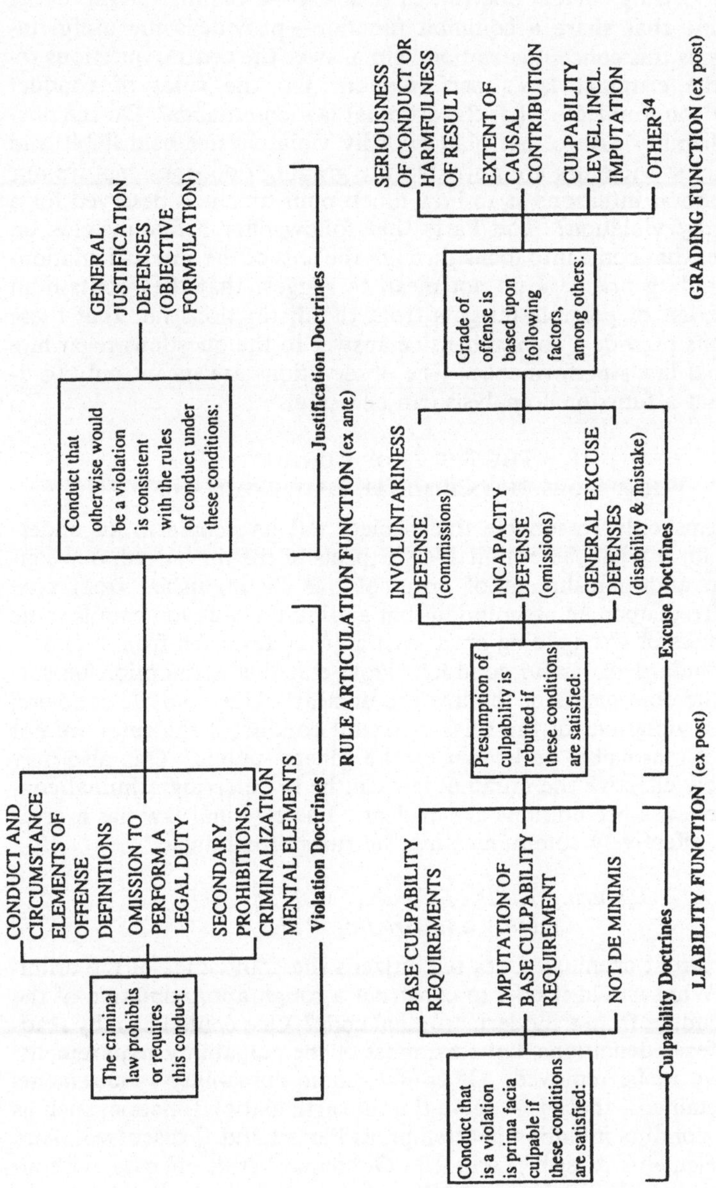

Figure 5

34 *See infra* part V.B-C.

Does viewing current doctrine in this way—grouping the aspects of the doctrine that share a common function—provide some useful insights? Does this conceptualization help answer the central questions regarding the criminal law's performance: Do the rules of conduct effectively communicate what the criminal law commands? Do the doctrines of liability assure that blameworthy violators are held liable and that blameless violators are not? Do the grading doctrines capture our common moral intuitions as to how much punishment is deserved for a blameworthy violation? The Parts that follow offer a few insights on these issues that come into focus through the lens of the rule articulation-liability-grading prism. I do not mean to suggest that they contain an exhaustive list of possible insights from the distinctions nor that these observations provide a comprehensive answer to the questions regarding the criminal law's performance. The observations are meant only to illustrate that a functional analysis can be useful.

III. The Rules of Conduct: What Does the Criminal Law Command?

It seems only reasonable that society tell its people in an understandable form what the criminal law expects of them. Indeed, our condemnation and punishment of criminals, as distinguished from civil violators, rests upon an assumption that a criminal violation entails some consciousness of wrongdoing or at least a gross deviation from a clearly defined standard of lawful conduct. How can this assumption be sustained if the commands of the law are unclear? How can we condemn and punish violations of the rules of lawful conduct if the rules are not and cannot reasonably be known by the general public? One also may wonder how effective the criminal law can be in deterring criminal conduct if the law's prohibitions are unclear. The criminal law has a great interest in effectively communicating the rules of conduct.

A. Obscuring Rules of Conduct with an Overlay of Liability and Grading Rules

Do current criminal codes tell citizens the commands of the criminal law? What would it take to construct a rough approximation of the rules of conduct from a modern criminal code? One could begin by reading the offense definitions, but then most of the culpability requirements would have to be removed. Of course, some culpability requirements must be retained—those that serve the rule articulation function, such as the future conduct intention in attempt, as Parts I and II discussed. And all result elements must be excluded. Of course, result offenses, without the results, are only risk-creation offenses, many of which already exist in the code. Manslaughter without death is reckless endangerment. In other words, some entire offenses, such as manslaughter, exist not to serve a rule articulation purpose but only to serve a grading purpose.

These "grading offenses" also must be excluded in an approximation of the rules of conduct. Also to be excluded are all the doctrines of aggravation, mitigation, and grading, noted in Part II. Some defenses also must be excluded, notably excuses and nonexculpatory defenses, while others are kept, such as justification defenses. (Although, as we shall see, only some provisions or parts of provisions relating to justification bear on the rules of conduct.) Another way of visualizing the difference between the rules of conduct and current criminal codes is to compare the chart of current conceptualization, at the beginning of Part I, to the first column of the functional analysis summary, at the beginning of Part II.

One may wonder whether it is possible for anyone other than a criminal law scholar to derive even a rough approximation of the criminal law's rules of conduct from a modern criminal code. The task is all the more difficult with the less systematic older codes that frequently codify arcane common law doctrine. Certainly, a statement of the rules of conduct will look substantially different than a code's collection of specific offense definitions. The undifferentiated commixture of rules of conduct, liability, and grading in a single code introduces significant complexity that obscures the rules of conduct. It seems unrealistic to expect the average person to read, understand, and govern their conduct by the rules of conduct embedded in any current criminal code.

In reality, the average person is left to ascertain the law's commands from his or her own moral intuitions about what ought to be prohibited, from word of mouth, or from press reports of criminal case dispositions. But each of these methods of communicating rules of conduct has serious shortcomings, many of which are created or exacerbated by present law's commixture of doctrines serving different functions.

Press reports of criminal case dispositions are necessarily ad hoc and frequently of questionable accuracy. Some criminal law professors and lawyers suggest that the press get the liability rules wrong more often than they get them right (sometimes for good reasons, as discussed below). Word of mouth can be worse; like the child's "telephone" game, every telling can introduce a slight variation in the story. And the original source of word of mouth information frequently is a press report. More on press accounts and word of mouth in the next section.

A community's shared intuitive notions will provide some guidance for the most serious offenses. Members of every culture probably understand that killing another person is wrong. But most cultures recognize exceptions, and the nature of these exceptions may not be quite so clear. (Can you kill a thief if that is the only way to stop his persistent theft of the garden vegetables you need to feed your family?) Especially in our multicultural society, which is predicted to grow even more diverse, it is dangerous to rely too heavily upon shared intuitive understandings as the source of society's conduct rules. While one might expect some shared notions of culpability and blame, necessarily matters of intuitive judgment, it is less clear that a citizen can reasonably be expected to intuit her tax obligation or the contours of criminally fraudulent conduct. Shared notions of desert may govern the liability and grading functions, but utilitarian concerns for protecting societal interests may heavily influence the definition of prohibitions and duties. Further, the existence of an intuitive understanding of conduct rules no doubt depends in some part on confirmation and reinforcement of such rules by existing moral authority, which in many societies is the criminal law as much or more than any other institution.

B. Confusing Conduct Rules and Liability Judgments: Ambiguous Acquittals

The difficulties inherent in an informal and ad hoc dissemination process are made all the more severe by the tendency of current doctrine to obscure the meaning of publicly reported dispositions. Reports of criminal case dispositions, in the press or by word of mouth or both, are doomed to confusion or inaccuracy because our public adjudication system frequently fails to provide information adequate to determine the disposition's meaning for the rules of conduct. For example, a verdict of "not guilty" may mean either (1) that the actor's conduct in the case *did not* violate the rules of conduct or (2) that the actor's conduct *did* violate the rules of conduct but that he does not have the minimum blameworthiness required to be held criminally liable for the violation. Thus, any acquittal might be understood either to approve or to disapprove the actor's conduct.

The state court acquittal of the officers who beat Rodney King illustrates the point. Many people found the acquittal outrageous because it seemed to condone the use of excessive and unnecessary force:

> [The verdict] sends out a message that whatever you saw on that tape was reasonable conduct.[35]
>
> [The verdict] tells me that police can do what they want. Everyone in the world saw that man get whipped and I don't know what the jury was seeing.[36]
>
> What does it take to prove they're guilty? They're saying, "So what if you videotape me, I still can beat you up."[37]

[35] Los Angeles Deputy District Attorney Terry White, *reported in* Seth Mydans, *The Police Verdict*, N.Y. TIMES, Apr. 30, 1992, at Al. Mr. White was the prosecutor in the case. *Id.*

[36] David Green, 32 year old northeast Washington construction worker, *reported in* Sue Anne Pressley, *Case Casts Long Shadow*, WASH. POST, May 1, 1992, at A1.

[37] Hilda Whittington, a Chicago nutritionist who is African-American, *reported in* Isabel Wilkerson, *Riots in Los Angeles*, N.Y. TIMES, May 1, 1992, at A23. In the same vein:

> It sends a very scary message to me. I can be driving my car and fitting a description. I try to respect cops as much as I can. I feel they should do the same. I'm very scared that something like this could happen to me.

Emilio Henry, an African-American senior at Texas Southern University, *reported in id.* Similarly:

> The verdict sends two messages. For those who wear the uniform of the law, the message is

> [I]t is an outrage that our system can't punish those—particularly police officers—who use the power and majesty of the state to beat some man senseless.[38]

But the issues at trial went beyond the propriety of the conduct; the trial also focused on the blameworthiness of the officers, including an examination of the danger that the officers felt, the confusion and uncertainty of the situation from the officers' perspective, the emotion generated by the preceding high-speed chase, and the training that the officers had for dealing with such a situation.

> In the words of defense attorney Michael Stone, their goal was to persuade jurors to view the incident "not through the eye of the camera but through the eyes of the police officers."
>
> . . . .
>
> . . . On the night in question, [the officers] confronted a 250-pound man who they believed—wrongly—to be intoxicated with the drug PCP, said to endow users with "superhuman strength."[39]

After hearing the evidence at trial, one juror explained the verdict this way:

> At one point, King lunged at and connected with Officer Powell. The cops were simply doing what they'd been instructed to do. They were afraid he was going to run or even attack them. He had not been searched, so they didn't know if he had a weapon. He kept going for his pants, so they thought he might be reaching for a gun . . . . I have no regrets about the verdict. I'll sleep well tonight.[40]

Another juror explained:

> [King] refused to get out of the car . . . so the police department had no alternative. He was obviously a dangerous person, massive size and threatening actions . . . . They're policemen. They're not angels. They're out there to do a lowdown dirty job. Would you want your husband doing it, or your son or your father?[41]

The conflict in perspectives arises in part because the simple verdict of "not guilty" fails to tell the whole story in a most important respect.

> that anything goes; for those whose only badge is their skin color, the message is to expect no justice from the criminal justice system.

Eddie Williams, president of the Joint Center for Political and Economic Studies, a D.C. think tank focusing on African-American affairs, *reported in* Paul Taylor, *A Case of Haunting Images and Perplexing Questions: Black Leaders Voice Deep Despair over a 'Great American Tragedy'*, WASH. POST, May 1, 1992, at A29.

[38] Jerry Brown, former Governor of California, *reported in* William Raspberry, *Where's the Outrage from White America?*, WASH. POST, May 1, 1992, at A27.

[39] Leef Smith, *Jury Was Asked to See Events As Police Did; Defense Depicted Officers in Urban Jungle*, WASH. POST, Apr. 30, 1992, at A25. Officer Powell explained to the jurors:

> He had very powerful arms. This was a big man . . . . I was completely in fear for my life, scared to death that if the guy got up again he was going to take my gun and there would be a shooting, and I did everything I could to keep him down on the ground.

Id.

[40] *The Jury's View*, WASH. POST, May 1, 1992, at A33.

[41] Smith, *supra* note 39, at A25.

The jurors voted "not guilty" presumably because they did not think the *officers* were sufficiently blameworthy to merit criminal conviction. Many persons hearing the verdict took it as approval of the officers' *conduct*. That is, the "not guilty" verdict was interpreted by some as condoning the conduct, whereas the jury may have reached the verdict upon finding inadequate blameworthiness, a subjective assessment, for what may well have been objectively excessive conduct.

What is needed is a verdict system that distinguishes "no violation" acquittals from "blameless violation" acquittals. If one were to follow the form of the "not guilty by reason of insanity" verdict, one might ask a jury to return a verdict of "no violation" (or just "not guilty") where the rules of conduct have not been violated, and a verdict of "not guilty by reason of mistake [or excuse]"[42] where the rules of conduct have been violated but where the violation is not blameworthy.

If the first Rodney King jury had returned the latter verdict, it might have better assured other citizens that the taped conduct was disapproved, not condoned. It might also have made it clearer to police officers that they are not authorized to engage in such conduct under similar circumstances in the future. But, as the next section illustrates, the success of such a verdict system depends upon the doctrine in fact distinguishing between the rule articulation issue and the liability issue. In the Rodney King case, that means that the doctrine must put distinct questions to the jury: (1) Was the conduct a violation? (2) If so, was the violation blameworthy? As we shall see, the doctrine governing the use of force in law enforcement mixes these questions, as indeed do all justification defenses.

Instead of clarifying and reinforcing the rules of acceptable conduct, the current verdict system can undercut and confuse an understanding of the rules. The tendency of current dispositions to confuse rather than educate may explain why we are not rushing to insist on wider dissemination of such dispositions or more careful reporting of them. The natural play in press and word of mouth accounts may well have a corrective effect, adding insights about what the disposition means for the rules of conduct, insights that the verdict itself fails to provide.

C. Mixing Rule Articulation and Liability Functions by Defining "Justified" Conduct Subjectively: The Failure to Define the Justified Conduct Rules

The rules of conduct are obscured not only by the overlay of liability and grading doctrines, as Part III.A discussed, but also by mixing func-

[42] The jury might be asked to give the particular grounds of excuse—"not guilty by reason of duress" or "not guilty by reason of mistake as to a justification"—but there seems little benefit from this requirement and it would require that the jurors come to agreement on the ground of exculpation.

tions in the formulation of a single doctrinal provision. An example with broad effect is the tendency of current codes, following the lead of the Model Penal Code, to obscure the rule articulation doctrines of justification by combining them inseparably with doctrines of liability. Was there justification for the use of force shown on the ghastly Rodney King videotape? The justification provision for use of force in law enforcement in most American jurisdictions is defined *subjectively*:

> [T]he use of force upon or toward the person of another *is justifiable when* the actor is making or assisting in making an arrest and *the actor believes* that such force is immediately necessary to effect a lawful arrest.[43]

This same form is used for most justification defenses. Self-defense commonly is defined to provide:

> [T]he use of force upon or toward another person *is justifiable when the actor believes* that such force is immediately necessary for the purpose of protecting himself against the use of unlawful force by such other person on the present occasion.[44]

Thus, according to the Code, King's beating was justifiable if the officers "believed" at that moment that the force was necessary for the arrest regardless of whether their belief was wrong.

It is the claim that the conduct was "justified" that caused outrage over the acquittal. For, as the previous section illustrates, many people reasonably interpret a finding of "justification" to mean that the conduct was proper and is condoned. In fact, the finding may reflect the opposite conclusion, that the conduct is disapproved. It is justified only in the sense that, when viewed from the actor's unique and possibly mistaken perspective, the actor believes the conduct to be justified. This crucial ambiguity assures that confusion over the meaning of an acquittal for the rules of conduct can occur in most justification cases.

The Model Penal Code drafters are not ignorant of the distinction between acceptable or unacceptable conduct. In a somewhat obscure provision, the definition of "unlawful force," the Code refers to "privileged" conduct, conduct which cannot lawfully be resisted (it is not "unlawful force" and therefore does not trigger a right to use defensive force).[45] Unprivileged conduct can lawfully be resisted. But the Code includes both privileged and unprivileged conduct within "justifiable" conduct. An actor's conduct is "justifiable" if it is within the rules of conduct (privileged) or if it violates the rules of conduct under the actual facts (unprivileged) but the actor mistakenly believes it is justified.[46] Because of this formulation of justification defenses, a jury is never asked to

---

43 MODEL PENAL CODE § 3.07(1) (emphasis added).

44 *Id.* § 3.04(1) (emphasis added).

45 *Id.* § 3.11(1) (defining "unlawful force" as used in justification defenses).

46 In the unprivileged justification case, the actor may receive a complete defense, despite his mistake, if his mistake is reasonable; if his mistake is honest but unreasonable, many jurisdictions provide a mitigation in liability. *See, e.g.*, *id.* § 3.09(2).

determine whether the conduct is objectively proper. The jury need only determine whether the actor's conduct was *either* (1) in fact proper, or (2) improper but the actor believed it proper. (Note that the members of the jury need not even agree among themselves as to which of these two alternatives is true. Thus, even the members of the jury may be unable to clarify an ambiguous acquittal.) The ultimate effect is that, even if a more refined verdict system were in place, the Code's subjective formulation of justification defenses leaves it unclear as to whether a jury should select a no violation or a blameless violation verdict.

To be clear, an excuse or mitigation for mistaken (unprivileged) justification is entirely appropriate, even necessary, as a means of imposing liability and punishment that match the actor's blameworthiness. The difficulty with subjectively defined justifications is not that they provide such a defense but that they fail to distinguish this excuse from liability from a defense arising from objectively justified (privileged) conduct. The failure can mislead people into thinking that conduct in violation of the rules of conduct is acceptable. Such subjective formulations of justification defenses might better be replaced with objective formulations, which accurately state the rule of conduct, and with separate provisions that give an excuse or mitigation for a mistake as to a justification.[47] A defense under the objective justification provision would give a no violation acquittal; a defense under the mistaken justification excuse would give a blameless violation acquittal.

D. *Mixing Conduct Rules of Risk-Creation with Liability Judgments of Risk-Taking: The Failure to Define Criminal Risks*

Another instance in which current doctrine combines and thereby confuses a rule articulation issue with a liability issue arises in defining what constitutes a criminal risk. Because danger may be created in an infinite number of ways and in an infinite number of situations, the prohibition must use risk as the defining concept; no specific set of acts and circumstances can adequately define the prohibited conduct.

Admittedly, describing the risks that the criminal law prohibits is a formidable task. It would be unwise to say simply: "No person shall engage in conduct that may cause injury to another person or damage to another's property." Some risks, even risks of personal injury to other persons, are tolerated by the criminal law. Part II noted at least three doctrines that tolerate risks. A victim's consent to a nonserious risk of injury is a defense. Creating a risk that avoids a greater risk typically gives rise to a justification defense. A prosecution for creating a trivial risk is subject to dismissal under the de minimis infraction defense. But

47 For a rare example of a code that segregates the issues of justification and mistake as to a justification by defining justifications objectively and providing a separate excuse provision, see N.D. CENT. CODE §§ 12.1-05-03, -04, -07, -08, -12 (1985).

consensual, justified, and trivial risks described by these doctrines represent only a minority of the tolerated risk situations. In nearly every instance of potential harm, the criminal law prohibits and punishes only the creation of risks of a certain probability and severity of harm under certain circumstances. If you decide to build a factory, drive to the theater, or open your umbrella, you necessarily create risks to others that did not previously exist. Part of the criminal law's rule articulation function is to tell persons beforehand which risks—what probability of how serious a harm under what circumstances—must be avoided. Yet, as we shall see, the doctrine fails to give even a clear general formula by which one can determine which risks are criminal.

The persons put at risk by your factory-building, driving, or umbrella-opening have not consented to such risks in the way that the consent defense of the criminal code requires.[48] Nor is the creation of such risks justified in the way that the justification defenses of the criminal code require.[49] The de minimis defense gives only a most general standard for determining whether a violation is de minimis: "too trivial to warrant the condemnation of conviction";[50] it provides little help in distinguishing criminal from noncriminal risks.[51] As we shall see, however, why the law tolerates some risks is similar in some respects to why the law recognizes the consent, justification, and de minimis defenses.

To determine whether creation of a risk is proper or improper, whether its creation is a violation of the rules of conduct, we need to know, among other things, the probability and the seriousness of the harm risked. Negligible risks of even serious harms are tolerated as the price we all pay to be part of a modern, industrialized society. We have all, in a sense, consented to such risks by choosing to remain in society knowing that such risks exist and are tolerated. Substantial risks of minor harms are similarly tolerated for similar reasons. Only significant risks of significant harms are criminalized, using a sliding scale between the two factors: the lower the probability, the more serious must be the potential injury to reach the point of criminalization.

In addition to the extent of the risk, the societal benefits of the risk also are relevant to whether it is tolerated. In an analysis analogous to

48 Consent is a defense if it "negatives an element of the offense or precludes the infliction of the harm or evil sought to be prevented by the law defining the offense." MODEL PENAL CODE § 2.11(1).

49 The lesser evils defense, the only justification that might be applicable, requires that the offense avoid a greater harm or evil. It does not authorize violations in order to create a *benefit*, such as financial profit from a factory or entertainment from attending the theater. Nor is the harm of getting wet likely to sufficiently justify conduct that is otherwise criminal. As the text discusses, however, the lesser evil defense's normative valuation of the actor's conduct has similarities to the assessment made in the definition of a criminal risk.

50 MODEL PENAL CODE § 2.12(2).

51 For example, it fails to give the most basic and most obvious guidance of directing attention to the extent of the harm risked and the probability of the harm occurring.

justification defenses, we tolerate a greater risk (probability *X* harm) if the effect of the risk is sufficiently desirable. The risks created by building a new factory might be justified by its productive potential but not justified if initiated to entertain the members of an explosives club. Whether any risk is justified by its purpose is a function of the relative values that society gives to the conflicting interests. Thus, each assessment of risk-creation requires an actor not only to make a complex judgment of probability and potential harm but also to balance competing community interests. An actor might find some guidance in whether such a risk in such circumstances has been tolerated in the past.[52]

Modern codes are not insensitive to the need to define the risks prohibited by the criminal law. The Model Penal Code, for example, includes in its definition of culpable risk-taking ("recklessness" and "negligence") the following:

> The risk must be of *such a nature and degree that, considering the nature and purpose of the actor's conduct* and the circumstances known to him, [its disregard/the actor's failure to perceive it] involves a gross deviation from *the standard of [conduct/care] that a [law-abiding/reasonable] person* would observe in the actor's situation.[53]

The nature and degree of the risk and the purpose for which it is undertaken are all taken into consideration. Further, these factors must be assessed in light of the community's standard of conduct.

But while the quoted provision accurately identifies the major factors that define criminal risk, it serves primarily to obscure the definition. To start, the quoted provision is not a definition of what will constitute *criminal risk-creation*. Rather, it is a definition of *culpable risk-taking*. The distinction is important. The definition does not define what risks are criminal; it does not define the real world risk-creation that is prohibited. Instead, it defines when an actor is culpable for taking a risk; it defines the mental risk-taking as to the existence of a circumstance or as to causing a result that makes the conduct blameworthy. The former issue—real world risk-creation—presents a rules of conduct issue: What is the kind and degree of risk of harm that an actor is prohibited from

---

52 But assumed knowledge of past "accepted" practice seems a weak reed on which to hang the notice called for by the legality principle (the notion that the state must place citizens on notice of a command before that command is legitimate). Further, to define an aspect of the rules of conduct by referring to "the standard of conduct [of] the [law-abiding/reasonable] person" is slightly circular. *See* Model Penal Code § 2.02(2)(c)-(d). No doubt the drafters assume that some shared understanding of "accepted" risks exists within the community. They may be right, but the law's reliance upon such an intuitive standard certainly ought to make us uncomfortable about whether this aspect of the rules of conduct adequately performs the notice function that the legality principle demands. On the other hand, no obvious alternative mechanism has as yet presented itself. The definition of criminal risk in a given instance is a complex matter that cannot (yet) be reduced to a more precise form. An actor's obligation under the rules of conduct is to try to discern "the standard of conduct [of] the [law-abiding/reasonable] person" and to avoid creating risks that, in light of this standard and the nature, degree, and purpose of the risk, are criminal.

53 *Id.* (emphasis added).

creating?[54] The latter issue—mental risk-taking—presents a liability issue: When is an actor to be held blameworthy for "taking a risk" that his conduct violates the rules of conduct? The distinction is between creating a risk of causing a harm and taking a risk of violating a rule.[55] The Code defines what risk-taking is culpable but does not define what constitutes a criminal risk.

As a doctrine of liability, the provision performs well. It is properly sensitive to the subtle difficulties in assessing whether the actor's risk-taking is culpable. The decisionmakers must take account of "the circumstances known to [the actor]" and to place the law-abiding/reasonable person "in the actor's situation." That latter requirement in particular permits courts great latitude to individualize the objective standard in judging the actor's culpability.[56] Finally, the provision permits liability only if the actor's conduct is a "gross deviation" from the standard of conduct of the law-abiding/reasonable person. The "gross deviation" standard is designed to give actors some, albeit vague, margin of error in adhering to the "standard of conduct of the [law-abiding/reasonable] person." Together, these requirements are meant to assure, as the doctrines of liability should, that an actor is held criminally liable for an offense only if he reasonably could be expected to have avoided the violation. But by formulating the definitions to perform the liability function, the Code fails in its rule articulation function.

By mixing the two functions, the Code invites a similar confusion in its readers. The following passage by a thoughtful and respected scholar is typical of descriptions found throughout the literature:

> Criminal liability is frequently predicated on negligence, which is *conduct that creates an unreasonable risk of harm* to an interest protected by the criminal law (negligence as to result), *or an unreasonable though sincere*

---

54 There is no comparable risk-creation for violations not involving a prohibited result. Where the prohibition is defined only in terms of conduct in certain circumstances, the circumstance either exists or does not. One does not *create* a risk of a circumstance; one can only *take* a risk that a circumstance exists. That is, one can act in disregard (or ignorance) of such a risk of the existence of the circumstance. As the text notes, determining whether an actor has engaged in such mental risk-taking is part of the liability function.

55 *See* Robinson, *supra* note 1, at 745-49.

56 The commentary makes clear that "in the actor's situation" may be interpreted as broadly as the court chooses. It may include not only the objective circumstances of the actor's "situation" but also characteristics of the actor.

> The standard for ultimate judgment invites consideration of the "care that a reasonable person would observe in the actor's situation." There is an inevitable ambiguity in "situation." If the actor were blind or if he had just suffered a blow or experienced a heart attack, these would certainly be facts to be considered in a judgment involving criminal liability, as they would be under traditional law. But the heredity, intelligence or temperament of the actor would not be held material in judging negligence, and could not be without depriving the criterion of all its objectivity. The Code is not intended to displace discriminations of this kind, but rather to leave the issue to the courts.

MODEL PENAL CODE & COMMENTARIES § 2.02 cmt. 4 (1985). In this respect, the drafters stray somewhat from the spirit of the legality principle.

> *belief* that one's conduct is not conduct which, under another description, is proscribed by the criminal law (negligence as to conduct). Negligent homicide is an example of a crime based on negligence as to result—i.e., *the creation of an unreasonable risk of death* that in fact eventuates in a death. Bigamy is an example of a crime that can be based on negligence as to conduct, as (for example) in those cases where one *unreasonably believes* in the validity of a prior divorce. The Model Penal Code's definition of criminal negligence is representative: [quotation of Model Penal Code section 2.02(2)(d)].[57]

Note the interchanging of risk-creation and risk-taking. Both are seen as a form of the single concept of "negligence," rather than as applications of the two very distinct functions of rule articulation and liability assessment. If negligence is meant to refer to the liability function of assessing whether a violation is sufficiently culpable, then analogous culpability requirements exist for both circumstance elements *and result elements*, bigamy *and negligent homicide*. Just as the prosecution must show that the bigamist's belief in the validity of the prior divorce was unreasonable, so too must it establish that the killer's failure to perceive the criminal risk of causing death was unreasonable. The difference between risk-creation and risk-taking is not related to the difference between result elements and circumstance elements, as the quoted passage suggests, but rather to the difference between the rule articulation function—defining the risks prohibited by the criminal law—and the liability function—defining the culpability that must accompany a violation before liability may be imposed.

Even if courts could dissect sections 2.02(2)(c) and (d) to extract the factors and analysis necessary to assess whether a risk is prohibited—the nature, degree, and purpose of the risk, and the community's balance of these as manifested in the standard of conduct of the law-abiding/reasonable person—the Code would fail in its function of defining the risks that are criminal. The quoted provision is contained in the definition of "recklessly" and "negligently." Thus, the dissection exercise is available only where the offenses criminalizing risk-creation use the terms "recklessly" or "negligently." This is sometimes the case, as in homicide.[58] But more frequently the Code defines risk-creation offenses as prohibiting a "substantial risk" or just a "risk" or a "danger" of a particular harm, using different phrases in different contexts.[59] The effect of this

[57] Larry Alexander, *Reconsidering the Relationship Among Voluntary Acts, Strict Liability, and Negligence in Criminal Law*, *in* CRIME, CULPABILITY, AND REMEDY 88-89 (Ellen F. Paul et al. eds., 1990) (emphasis added).

[58] A person is guilty of manslaughter "if he *recklessly . . . causes* the death of another human being." MODEL PENAL CODE §§ 210.1(1), 210.3(1)(a) (emphasis added). "A person is guilty of criminal mischief if he . . . *recklessly causes* another to suffer pecuniary loss. . . ." *Id.* § 220.3(1)(c).

[59] For example, the Code prohibits creation of a "substantial risk" of causing death (in § 211.1(2)(a), aggravated assault); creation of a "danger" of death or a "substantial risk" of death (in § 211.2, reckless endangerment); creation of a "substantial risk" of loss of entrusted property (in § 224.13); and creation of a "danger" of damage or destruction of a building (in § 220.1(2)(b), reck-

inconsistency is to exclude from the analysis of whether the actor has created a criminal risk the consideration of most factors deemed relevant by the Code drafters themselves: the nature, degree, and purpose of the risk, and the community's balance of these factors as manifested in the standard of conduct of the law-abiding/reasonable person. "Risk" might be taken to mean any risk; "substantial risk" might be taken to focus only on the degree of the risk (or possibly its nature). Nothing in the language suggests the need to assess the purpose of the risk-creation or the balance of competing interests.

The effect of the Code's failure to give guidance in defining criminal risks might seem minimized by the tendency of the Code to prohibit the most egregious risk-creation through offenses that require actual results, such as homicide. That is, if an actual result is required, we can avoid the problem of defining the mere risk of the harm that is criminal. But as most thoughtful readers have already discerned, requiring that the actual result have occurred does not avoid the need to determine whether the risk was criminal.[60] Defining reckless homicide (manslaughter) to require a death, for example, does not avoid the need to determine whether the actor's conduct in causing that death created a risk that was criminal. An actor might have caused the death through the creation of a risk that itself was noncriminal. To punish such an actor for manslaughter is to fail to distinguish him from the actor who caused a death by creating a risk that was itself criminal. This problem is the subject of Part V.A.

The need for clear guidelines in assessing the criminality of the risk is heightened by the human tendency to exaggerate the degree of a risk when it comes to fruition. The empirical literature reports this common phenomenon: persons significantly overestimate the extent of a risk if the risked result occurs.[61] This phenomenon may lead to liability for creating a criminal risk when in reality the created risk was not criminal. A death can occur even where the risk created is sufficiently low to be noncriminal. Yet, without a definition of criminal risk, how can this determination be made?[62]

---

less burning or exploding). The Code prohibits the "risk" of causing terror or serious public inconvenience (in § 211.3, terroristic threats). Also prohibited are a "risk" of causing a "substantial risk" of death through restraint (in § 212.2(a), felonious restraint) and a "risk" of causing a catastrophe (in § 220.2(2), risking catastrophe).

60 The use of result offenses to punish criminal risk-creation not only fails to avoid the need to define criminal risk but also creates several other special problems. For example, the resulting array of overlapping offenses may define the prohibited risk differently. In some instances of overlap between result and risk-creation offenses, the conduct creating a risk is prohibited and punished only if the harm comes about, but whether the harm will occur is a fact that the actor cannot know at the time he engages in the conduct. *See* Robinson, *supra* note 1, at 748-49.

61 Baruch Fischoff, *Hindsight Does Not Equal Foresight: The Effect of Outcome Knowledge on Judgment Under Uncertainty*, 1 J. EXPERIMENTAL PSYCHOL. 288, 298 (1975).

62 Nor is it enough, as discussed above, that the definition of culpable risk-taking tells us whether the actor's risk-taking was culpable. Liability for manslaughter is appropriate only if the actor was culpable *and* the risk created in fact is prohibited. At the very least, the doctrine should distinguish

A better approach would give independent definitions of criminal risk and culpable risk-taking. Risk-creation offenses, then, could properly be defined to prohibit creation of a "criminal risk" of the specific harm, incorporating by reference the general formula. This would replace the current practice, which defines these offenses by using either undefined terms such as "risk" or "substantial risk" or by using culpability terms that drop the requirement that the prohibited risk actually be created.

Using the language of the Model Penal Code, one could construct a definition of criminal risk something like the following:

> An actor creates a "criminal risk" of a result or "criminally risks" a result when he creates a substantial and unjustified risk that the result will occur. A risk is substantial and unjustified if, given its nature, degree, and circumstances, its creation is a gross deviation from the standard of conduct of a law-abiding person.

One could construct culpability definitions, again using Model Penal Code language, as follows (remember that the culpable risk-taking terms must be defined with respect to both result and circumstance elements):

> A person acts "recklessly" with respect to an element of an offense when he consciously disregards a risk that the circumstance exists or that his conduct will cause the result, as the case may be. (Same second sentence as in Code.)
>
> A person acts "negligently" with respect to an element of an offense when he should be aware of a risk that the circumstance exists or that his conduct will cause the result, as the case may be. (Same second sentence as in Code.)[63]

The only real change to the Code's current culpability definitions is the deletion of the phrase "substantial and unjustified" modifying the term "risk" in the first sentence of each definition. The substantiality and justifiability of the risk are matters of concern in defining criminal risk-creation, but they add nothing to the definition of culpable risk-taking that is not already covered by the culpability definitions' call, in the second sentence, to judge the blameworthiness of the actor's disregard or unawareness of the risk:

> The risk must be of such a nature and degree that, considering the nature and purpose of the actor's conduct and the circumstances known to him, [its disregard/the actor's failure to perceive it] involves a gross deviation from the standard of [conduct/care] that a [law-abiding/reasonable] person would observe in the actor's situation.[64]

Presumably, juries more easily will find "a gross deviation" where the risk is more "substantial" or more "unjustified."

---

reckless homicide convictions where the risk created is criminal from those where it is not. The current doctrine's failure to do so is examined more closely in Part V.A.

63 *See infra* text accompanying note 64.

64 MODEL PENAL CODE § 2.02(2)(c)-(d).

To illustrate the use of these terms, manslaughter might be defined as follows:

> An actor commits manslaughter if, with recklessness as to causing the death of another human being, he creates a criminal risk of such death and death results.

Of course, one might avoid such stilted definitions by having a general principle that liability for a substantive offense of risk-creation (as opposed to an inchoate offense) requires proof that the criminal risk in fact was created. With such a principle, which courts might supply even in the absence of a statutory provision, and a definition of a criminal risk, one could simply define manslaughter as "recklessly causing the death of another human being."

To conclude, my claim here is not that the Model Penal Code drafters are insensitive to factors important to the definition of criminal risk-creation or culpable risk-taking. That is, general formulae seem the best one can provide for guidance on these issues. My claim here is that by failing to see that the issues of risk-creation and risk-taking are distinct, the Code's general formula is less likely to effectively perform either task. (The discussion here focuses on the difficulties that such a mixture of function creates for the rule articulation function by failing to provide a definition of criminal risk. The difficulties that this mixture creates for the grading function by using culpability terms to define prohibited risks are examined in Part V.A.)

IV. The Doctrines of Liability: When Is a Violation of the Law's Commandments to Be Punished?

Recall that the liability function of criminal law doctrine arises from the special condemnatory nature of criminal law, which requires that criminal liability be based upon blameworthiness. If an actor's violation is blameless, he ought to be free from liability even though he may well have brought about the prohibited harm or evil. If an actor's violation is blameworthy, he ought to be liable. Does current doctrine impose liability on blameworthy violations and avoid liability for blameless violations? The legal literature contains a number of criticisms of the doctrine for a perceived failure in this regard. Two well-known examples are the lack of a general defense for a reasonable mistake as to the lawfulness of one's conduct and continued use of the felony murder rule. A functional analysis suggests some less obvious failures, both in setting culpability requirements and in formulating excuse defenses.

A. *Elevating Base and Aggravation Culpability Requirements as if They Were Criminalization Mental States: Improperly Limiting Attempt Liability*

An earlier discussion in Part I.B described four distinguishable kinds of culpability requirements: present conduct intention, future conduct intention, present circumstance culpability, and future result culpability.[65] Only the second is used as a criminalization mental state in cases of incomplete conduct toward an offense. The failure to see that the future conduct intention in attempt plays a different function than the other culpability requirements in an incomplete attempt has helped confuse many courts and code drafters into treating all attempt culpability requirements as if they perform the rule articulation function. It is true that this "purpose" or "intention" requirement is an appropriate additional requirement—beyond that required by the substantive offense—but it does not follow that this same elevated level of culpability should be applied to all other culpability requirements of attempts, which may serve other functions.

Consider a prosecution for attempted murder. Must it be the actor's conscious object (purpose) to cause the death, or is it sufficient, as it is for murder liability, that the actor know that his conduct is practically certain to cause the death? It is true that the actor's purpose *to complete the conduct* that would cause the death must be clear. Without this intention, the justification for criminalizing the otherwise innocent conduct disappears. But why should the minimum culpability requirements of the object offense—such as the culpability as to causing the death, a future result culpability—be elevated to purpose? Similarly, in a prosecution for attempted statutory rape,[66] must the actor have as his purpose that his partner is underage, or is it enough that he is aware that his partner might be underage (recklessness as to underage), as would be sufficient for liability for the completed offense? Clearly, his intention to go through with the intercourse, his future conduct intention, must be shown. In its absence there is no justification for criminalization. But why is recklessness as to age, a present circumstance culpability, no longer adequate in establishing the minimum culpability for liability?

The clumsiness of the common law's mental elements scheme may explain why the common law could not make the distinction between a criminalization mental state and a culpability mental state. Attempt was said to be a "specific intent offense."[67] It thus required more in the way of proof of culpable state of mind than a "general intent offense," where it was thought that the actor's intention could be inferred from his conduct. But the general intent/specific intent offense scheme, which did not distinguish between mental states as to different elements of the offense, made it impossible to require purpose as to completing the offense conduct while requiring mental states of less than purpose as to the elements of the substantive offense. Thus, once it was agreed that attempt

[65] The present conduct intention requirement is somewhat superfluous. *See supra* p. 864.

[66] *See, e.g.*, State v. Davis, 229 A.2d 842 (N.H. 1967) (affirming a conviction for attempted rape of a "woman child under the age of 16 years").

[67] *See, e.g.*, People v. Trinkle, 369 N.E.2d 888, 892 (Ill. 1977).

had a purpose requirement, which it surely had (the purpose to engage in the conduct constituting the substantive offense), it followed that this same purpose requirement applied to all offense elements.

The Model Penal Code replaces the common law "offense analysis" notion that each offense has a single culpability requirement with "element analysis."[68] Section 2.02(1) expressly requires a showing of culpability "with respect to *each material element of the offense*."[69] Yet it appears to hold to the common law rule that attempt liability requires the actor to be purposeful as to a result element even if the substantive offense attempted requires less. The commentary explains:

> The general principle is . . . that the actor must affirmatively desire to engage in the conduct or *to cause the result that will constitute the principal offense*.[70]

But why should this be the rule? Assume an actor places a bomb in a Selective Service office knowing it will kill the persons therein. He does not want to kill such persons—his object is only to destroy the building—but he knows that when he pushes the detonator the people are practically certain to be killed. If he is caught by police after the explosion causes deaths, he will be liable for murder. If he is caught just before he presses the detonator, he will not be liable for attempted murder. He will not be liable even though the prosecution can prove beyond a reasonable doubt that it was his purpose to engage in the conduct constituting the offense, pushing the detonator, and can prove that he has the culpability required for murder, knowledge that his conduct is practically certain to cause deaths. He may be liable for other offenses but will escape liability for attempted murder because it is not his *conscious object* to cause death.

The same principle would elevate culpability as to a circumstance element to the same "purpose" required as to future conduct, just as it elevates culpability as to a result element. Under this approach, an actor caught in bed on the verge of committing statutory rape will be free from

68 *See generally* Robinson & Grall, *supra* note 11.

69 Model Penal Code § 2.02(1) (emphasis added).

70 Model Penal Code & Commentaries § 5.01 cmt. 2 (emphasis added). Although modern codes have shifted to "element analysis," in which different culpability requirements may apply to different elements of the same offense, many modern courts and codes have followed the common law rule that attempt requires purpose as to the elements of the object offense. In *People v. Trinkle*, for example, after being refused further service, the resentful defendant fired a shot into a tavern, wounding a patron within. 369 N.E.2d at 889. The court affirmed a reversal of the defendant's conviction for attempted murder because, although murder required only "knowing" (or sometimes less) as to causing death, attempted murder required a specific intention, or purpose, to kill. The court reached this result despite the presence of an attempted murder statute that explicitly required only that the actor "*knows* [his] act creates a strong probability of death or great bodily harm." *Id.* at 890 (emphasis added). The court felt bound by the common law rule that "attempt is a specific intent offense" and attempt liability requires not only that the actor intend to engage in the conduct constituting the substantive offense but that the actor intend the prohibited result and the required circumstances of the substantive offense.

attempt liability even if he is aware that his partner may be underage and his purpose is clearly to engage in intercourse. To be liable for the attempt, it must be his "purpose" that his partner is underage.[71] Whether the law is wise to limit attempt liability in this way is questionable.[72] (While nothing on the face of the Model Penal Code's incomplete conduct provision would suggest a different rule regarding elevation of culpability as to a result from that as to a circumstance, the Code's commentary can be read to suggest that culpability as to a circumstance element need not be elevated.)[73]

The better approach is to see the criminalization mental state, such as the actor's future conduct intent to engage in the conduct constituting

---

71 Unlike the definitions as to conduct or results, "purpose" is defined with regard to a circumstance to require either a desire or an awareness of circumstances. *See* MODEL PENAL CODE § 2.02(2)(a)(ii) ("he *believes* or hopes") (emphasis added). Thus, "purpose" as to a circumstance requires no more than does "knowing" as to a circumstance.

72 There is some authority for a contrary view. In *State v. Galan*, for example, the defendant was charged with attempted trafficking in stolen property. The substantive offense required only recklessness as to the property being stolen but the defendant claimed that the indictment was defective because "an attempt . . . requires a specific intent which is incompatible with a reckless state of mind." 658 P.2d 243, 244 (Ariz. Ct. App. 1982). The attempt statute was similar to the Model Penal Code provision, except for the substitution of the term "intentional" for "purposeful," a common grammatical alteration. The court concluded:

> A common sense reading of the provision leads to the conclusion that the words "*intentionally* engages in conduct" refers, in this case, to the actions that make up trafficking like buying property . . . and that the words "*acting with the kind of culpability otherwise required for the commission of an offense*" requires only that the acts be accompanied by a reckless state of mind as to the circumstances attending the status of the property. A contrary conclusion would mean that the words "*acting with the kind of culpability otherwise required for the commission of an offense*" are superfluous.

Id. at 244-45 (alteration in original). (Deleted from the quoted passage is dicta suggesting that "intentionally engages in conduct" might also require proof that the actor intended to resell the property. This might well be required by the substantive offense of trafficking but it is hard to see such a requirement from the "engages in conduct" language.)

Some jurisdictions take a similar approach with respect to the culpability required as to a result. They require only that level of culpability as to causing a result required by the substantive offense; no elevation of culpability as a result is required for attempt. Indeed, some jurisdictions drop the Model Penal Code's "purpose" or belief language, leaving only the requirement that the actor be "acting with the kind of culpability otherwise required for commission" of the offense. MODEL PENAL CODE § 5.01(1). As the Utah Supreme Court concluded in *State v. Maestas*:

> [R]egardless of any requirements which the common law may impose concerning [specific intent in] "attempt" crimes; Utah law requires only "the kind of culpability otherwise required for the commission of the [completed] offense." Thus, there can be no difference between the intent required as an element of the crime of attempted first degree murder and that required for first degree murder itself.

652 P.2d 903, 904 (Utah 1982).

73 *See* MODEL PENAL CODE & COMMENTARIES § 5.01(1) cmt. 3 (Tent. Draft No. 10, 1960). (This unofficial revision in the commentary has not been noticed by many jurisdictions that use the Code's attempt provision.) But in support of elevation of culpability as to circumstance elements, see *supra* text accompanying note 69 (requiring a positive desire "*to engage in the conduct* or cause the result *that will constitute the principal offense*"). (And recall the Code's broad meaning of "conduct" to include the attendant circumstances of the conduct, *e.g.*, "having intercourse with a person under 16.").

the offense, as distinct from the culpability mental states required by the substantive offense, such as the future result culpability toward causing a resulting homicide or the present circumstance culpability as to the partner's age in statutory rape. The actor's future conduct intention is central to the definition of what constitutes a criminal attempt; the actor must have as his *purpose* to engage in the conduct that would constitute the offense. There is no apparent reason, however, why the culpability requirements of the substantive offense, which serve the liability function, must be elevated to purpose. The culpability requirements that adequately serve the liability and grading functions for the substantive offense ought to be adequate to serve those functions for attempt liability. If negligence as to a sexual partner's age is sufficient to establish culpability for statutory rape, why not for attempted statutory rape? If knowing as to causing a death is adequate for murder, why not for attempted murder?

One dramatic effect of the elevation-to-purpose approach is that it can bar liability altogether for conduct designed to create a prohibited risk of harm, specifically where the actor's attempt to create the risk is foiled. Consider a hypothetical: an actor is caught just as he is about to discharge toxic chemicals near a school soccer field, knowing the chemicals may cause the death of one or more of the school children. He cannot be liable for reckless homicide because no one is actually killed. He cannot be liable for endangerment because he had not yet created a risk of death or serious bodily injury (and did not believe that he had yet created such a risk).[74] One would think, however, that where we are lucky enough to catch him before he creates the risk, he ought to be liable for attempted endangerment. Similarly, where an actor is caught just before he buries toxic waste near the town reservoir and knows that, once completed, his conduct will create a risk of catastrophe, he ought to be liable for an attempt to commit the offense of risking catastrophe.[75] But under the elevation-to-purpose approach, neither actor can be held liable.[76] While the actor's awareness that the planned conduct creates the prohibited risk is sufficient for full offense liability if the risk is created, only purpose is adequate for liability where only attempt is charged. Because the actor's objective is to avoid costly disposal fees, rather than to endanger people, the actor is protected from attempt liability.

The drafters defend the Code's position by arguing that liability for attempts to create a prohibited risk would spread liability too far.[77] But

---

74 *See* MODEL PENAL CODE § 211.2.

75 *See id.* § 220.2(2).

76 Presumably, some regulatory offense governing the handling of toxic chemicals will impose some liability, but this hardly recognizes the seriousness of the violation.

77 The approach of the Model Code is not to treat such behavior as an attempt. Instead the Code creates a separate crime, a misdemeanor, for recklessly placing another person in danger of death or serious bodily injury. The Institute's judgement was that the scope of the criminal law would be unduly extended if one could be liable for an attempt whenever he recklessly or

why the actual creation of the risk ought to be determinative of liability is hard to understand. Successful and unsuccessful attempters have the same subjective culpability (and probably the same dangerousness). Indeed, the Code drafters use precisely this argument to support their view that the absence of resulting harm generally ought not reduce the grade of an offense; attempts generally are to be graded the same as completed offenses.[78] Yet, here, under their definition of attempt, the actor's failure to successfully create the intended risk does even more than reduce the grade of the violation—it exempts the actor from liability altogether.[79]

The discussion so far has focused on the most common case of incomplete conduct toward an offense. Is the analysis different for those cases where attempt liability is imposed when the actor's conduct is complete but the offense is factually or legally impossible? Where the actor's conduct is complete, no future conduct intention need be shown. We have the actor's conduct as evidence of his intention to engage in the conduct constituting the offense. Thus, even the analogy to the future conduct intention required in incomplete conduct cases does not explain a wish to elevate the required culpability above that required as to the circumstance and result elements of the substantive offense.

Reconsider the draft board terrorist who plans to bomb the draft board *knowing* that the bomb will kill the security guard but not *wanting* to kill the guard. If his bomb kills the guard, he will be liable for murder; knowing as to causing death is sufficient. As noted above, if he is caught just before he triggers the bomb, he will not be liable for attempted murder because his knowing culpability is insufficient; attempt liability here requires that he be purposeful as to the killing. Consider the case where he triggers the bomb but the explosive does not function due to moisture. His conduct toward the offense is complete—we know for certain that he was willing to carry the offense through to completion—but the result did not come about. Ought the actor escape liability for attempted murder because of the factual impossibility of completion?

All would agree that he ought not escape attempt liability. Even the Code agrees with this result. It creates an exception to the elevation-to-purpose requirement for cases in which the actor has completed his conduct but the result does not occur. Model Penal Code section 5.01(1)(b) provides that an actor is guilty of attempt if,

> when causing a particular *result* is an element of the crime, [he] does or

---

> negligently created a risk of any result whose actual occurrence would lead to criminal responsibility. While it was believed that the reckless creation of risk of death or serious bodily harm was grave enough for general coverage, even for this behavior misdemeanor penalties seemed more apt than the severer sanctions attached to felony attempts.

MODEL PENAL CODE & COMMENTARIES § 5.01 cmt. 2 (footnotes omitted).

78 MODEL PENAL CODE § 5.05(1).

79 Also note that such attempt liability is limited to those few instances in which the Code creates a substantive offense that punishes an actor for causing or risking a specified result. Result elements typically appear only in homicide, personal injury, and property damage offenses.

> omits to do anything with the purpose of causing or *with the belief* that it will cause such result without further conduct on his part.[80]

Such a reduction in the minimum culpability as to result from purpose to knowing is justified, in the drafters' view, because where the actor's conduct is complete,

> the manifestation of the actor's dangerousness is just as great—or very nearly as great—as in the case of purposive conduct. In both instances a deliberate choice is made to bring about the consequence forbidden by the criminal laws, and the actor has done all within his power to cause this result to occur.[81]

Some courts have reached the same conclusion and have argued that even the common law's specific intent requirement might be satisfied by such a belief that the result will occur.[82]

But the exception does not save the Code's provision from the criticisms voiced above. It does avoid elevation in the narrow case of substantive offenses, like murder, where knowledge as to causing a result is required and the conduct is complete. It does not, however, avoid the questionable results that occur where the actor's conduct is incomplete. The draft board bomber who is caught just before he detonates the bomb still escapes liability for attempted murder. The knowing culpability required for murder is still elevated to purpose for attempted murder.

Nor does the Code's exception avoid elevation and improper results where the substantive offense requires less than knowing as to causing a result. Consider the case of the toxic dumper who completes his conduct in dumping the chemicals but finds that suspicious investigators have substituted a similar looking nontoxic chemical. If the actor knows that his conduct would create a risk of death, then he might be liable for attempted endangerment under the Code's special rule (only knowing is required as to a result for completed conduct attempts). But assume that the actor is only reckless as to causing death. This is sufficient for the offense of reckless endangerment, but the Code will not permit liability for attempted reckless endangerment. This is so even though the actor has the culpability required for the substantive offense and has completed the conduct required for the offense. He cannot be held liable because the Code elevates the culpability requirement for attempt over that required by the substantive offense.

---

80 MODEL PENAL CODE § 5.01(1)(b) (emphasis added). The Code's commentary notes: "Thus when the charge is attempted murder or assault with intent to kill, it is error to permit conviction on a finding of reckless disregard for human life or intent to inflict grievous bodily harm." MODEL PENAL CODE & COMMENTARIES § 5.01 cmt. 2.

81 MODEL PENAL CODE & COMMENTARIES § 5.01 cmt. 2.

82 *See, e.g.*, People v. Krovarz, 697 P.2d 378, 383 (Colo. 1985). The *Krovarz* court upheld a conviction where a psychologically unstable defendant attempted robbery with a putty knife. The court, citing the Model Penal Code section 5.01(1)(b) commentary, concluded, "We agree with [the Model Penal Code] reasoning; a knowing attempt to attain a proscribed result is a sufficient culpable mental state to justify imposition by the legislature of attempt liability." *Id.* at 382.

It is true that there cannot be an "accidental attempt," in the sense that to "attempt" an offense one must intend to complete the conduct that would constitute that offense. One must have a future conduct intent. There is, however, such a thing as an attempt to cause an "accident," in the sense of an attempt to engage in conduct that would create the opportunity for an accident, that is, conduct that would create a risk. As long as the law is careful to require a conscious object to engage in *the conduct constituting the offense*, there seems little reason not to punish attempts to create risks and attempts that create risks.

The special intention requirement quite appropriately required in cases of incomplete conduct attempts is distinct from the other culpability requirements in such cases and has no application where the conduct is complete. No greater culpability than that required by the substantive offense ought to be required for attempt liability.[83]

B. Obscuring the Voluntariness Requirement's Shared Liability Function with Excuses: Distorting the Involuntary Act Defense

The voluntariness requirement typically is classed as part of the actus reus of each offense, as Part I.A noted.[84] Recall that most aspects of the actus reus serve a rule articulation or a grading function, describing the harm or evil of the offense and its seriousness. Functionally, the voluntary act requirement, or "involuntary act defense," is analogous to the criminal law's system of excuses, serving the liability function. Certainly,

[83] This position is not insensitive to the problems inherent in imposing liability where the actor has not gone far toward committing the offense. The less the actor has done, the harder to meet the culpability requirements. As a practical matter, a future conduct intention is harder to prove than a present conduct intention. Where the actor's offense conduct is incomplete, the prosecution has a significant burden in proving the actor's future conduct intention. Where the offense conduct is complete, the prosecution's task is easier. In completed conduct attempts, the required criminalization mental state is transformed from a burdensome future conduct intention to an almost pro forma present conduct intention. No special elevation of the object offense's culpability requirements is needed to reach this sliding scale between the extent of conduct and the importance of proving culpability.

[84] Voluntariness might be thought to be more akin to mens rea than to actus reus elements. Culpability elements at least concern the issue of accountability for harm caused; objective elements more clearly define the nature of the harm or evil. But this characterization is problematic as well. Under it, for example, an actor's involuntariness might be denied as a defense to a strict liability offense on the ground that proof of culpability is not required. *See, e.g.*, Roger Clark, *Accident—Or What Became of* Kilbride v. Lake*?*, *in* ESSAYS ON CRIMINAL LAW IN NEW ZEALAND 65 (Roger Clark ed., 1971) (discussing denial of involuntariness defense in strict liability case and arguing inappropriateness of such denial). But while public policy may support the imposition of strict liability for an offense, it does not follow that it supports the imposition of liability on involuntary actors, who are blameless under general principles of excuse. General excuses remain available to offenses of strict liability. And involuntariness, like the general excuses, ought similarly be available, without regard to the culpability requirements of the particular offense definition. The doctrine can make this point clear by characterizing involuntariness as a general excuse rather than an offense element.

the cases dealt with under the voluntary act requirement are at the extreme of the lack-of-volition spectrum. Such involuntariness represents the most nonvolitional form of conduct and is thus the most convincing ground for excuse, but it is not functionally different from other traditional conditional excusing conditions dealt with under the excuse defenses of insanity, immaturity, duress, and involuntary intoxication.

Like the general excuse defenses, the involuntariness defense is not unique to the particular offense at hand. Involuntariness does not mean the absence of the harm or evil of the offense, as does absence of other objective elements. When an actor assaults another during a seizure, our conclusion is not that the assault is not harmful and regrettable (indeed, civil liability may be permitted), but rather that the assault is undesirable but that condemnation is not appropriate in light of the involuntariness of the conduct. Nor is involuntariness consistent with a normal actor with normal capacities. It suggests either abnormal conduct or an abnormal actor, as do the conditions of excuse defenses. The other elements of an offense, in contrast, are consistent with an actor of normal capacities.[85]

The failure of current doctrine to recognize the functional similarity of the voluntary act requirement and the general excuse defenses has resulted in distortion in its formulation of the former. Because it is not conceptualized as an excuse, the voluntary act requirement has escaped significant limitations routinely placed on excuse defenses. The two most important are the requirement of a specific cause of the lack of control (a specific "disability") and the requirement that the disability cause a certain degree of control dysfunction.

As to the first—a specific disability requirement—the traditional excuses, such as insanity, duress, and involuntary intoxication, require proof that the actor's lack or impairment of control comes from a specific identifiable cause: mental illness, physical coercion, or intoxication, respectively. An involuntary act defense, in contrast, is permitted without regard to the cause of the involuntariness. Anything that causes an actor to perform a criminal act that "is not a product of [his or her] effort or determination" will qualify for the defense. The absence of a specific disability requirement might be justified on the ground that the lack of control in many involuntary act cases is so complete and dramatic that no other requirement is needed to assure blameworthiness. It is irrelevant whether the muscular movement comes from a grand mal seizure or

[85] One could maintain the conceptual similarity between involuntariness and other excuses by treating all excuses as negative elements of each offense. Indeed, the Model Penal Code seems to move toward this approach when it defines "elements of an offense" to include the absence of all general defenses, including excuses. MODEL PENAL CODE § 1.13(9)(c). However, such an approach hides the important conceptual distinctions between elements of an offense definition and general defenses. *See* Robinson, *supra* note 29, at 264-73.

from a reflex action. Such total lack of volition is an obvious and convincing ground for exculpation. No additional requirement is necessary.

But the absence of a disability requirement has the collateral effect of broadening the defense to cases beyond instances of complete lack of volition. That is, the freedom from a specific disability requirement gives the involuntariness defense a special role in the system of excuses as the catchall excuse, used where the actor's control is impaired by a disability other than one of those recognized in the traditional excuse defenses.[86] Hypnotism, for example, is not a recognized form of mental illness, defect, unlawful force, intoxication, or any of the other disabilities or sources of disability recognized by traditional excuse defenses. If an actor seeks an excuse for his conduct under hypnosis, he must invoke the involuntary act defense for which no specific disability is required.

This catchall use of the involuntariness defense is common where the actor's control is admittedly impaired but decidedly less impaired than the complete or nearly complete lack of control of a grand mal seizure or a reflex action. This use is problematic. Available evidence suggests that hypnotism, for example, can cause significant impairment of control under certain circumstances for certain persons, but not loss or even near loss of volition.[87] Similarly, somnambulism ("sleepwalking") has an effect in impairing an actor's control but does not render his conduct involuntary in the absolute or near absolute sense.[88] This extension of the involuntariness defense from cases of loss to cases of mere impairment of control is not limited to clever defense counsel or sympathetic courts. The Model Penal Code recognizes acts during both hypnotism and somnambulism as conclusively *involuntary* acts despite the lack of

[86] In Bradley v. State, 277 S.W. 147 (Tex. Crim. App. 1925), for example, the defendant was startled from sleep and in a somnambulistic state began randomly shooting into a dark room, killing his companion. The court held that the defendant lacked "conscious volition" and therefore could not be held liable. For other examples of this extended use of the involuntariness defense to cases of impairment, see Regina v. Charlson, [1955] 1 W.L.R. 317 (Chester Assizes) (acquitting on defense of automatism defendant who suffered from a cerebral tumor that gave rise to outbursts of impulsive violence); People v. Newton, 87 Cal. Rptr. 394, 402, 405 (Cal. Ct. App. 1970) (allowing complete defense to charge of criminal homicide based on physical injury causing action without awareness); Fulcher v. State, 633 P.2d 142, 145-47 (Wyo. 1981) (holding that blow to head producing "traumatic automatism," a condition affecting ability to control conduct and to perceive environment, is a defense).

[87] Conduct under hypnosis typically is not robotic, as is popularly thought, yet nonetheless can be odd and out of character. *See, e.g.*, ERNEST R. HILGARD, HYPNOTIC SUSCEPTIBILITY 6 (1965) (stating that the change in state under hypnosis is always relative, rather than absolute; thus the hypnotized subject has the ability to initiate action, such as delivering a speech); PAUL SCHILDER, THE NATURE OF HYPNOSIS 104 (Gerda Corvin trans., 1956) (asserting that the hypnotized subject is not a passive tool in the hypnotist's hands but retains his will and personal attitudes); GLANVILLE WILLIAMS, CRIMINAL LAW § 250 (2d ed. 1961) (citing evidence that the hypnotized actor may not be under complete control of the hypnotist and that the hypnotized actor's ego ideal exercises continuous control over relations). For a more detailed discussion of hypnosis as an excuse, see 2 ROBINSON, *supra* note 10, § 191.

[88] 2 ROBINSON, *supra* note 10, § 172(c).

evidence that such disabilities cause such loss of control.[89]

This expansion of the involuntariness defense from cases of loss to cases of mere impairment of control is not itself objectionable. The degree of impairment in such cases may not be severe but nonetheless may be sufficient to merit an excuse. And such impairment may result from disabling conditions that are as empirically confirmable as the traditional excuse disabilities of involuntary intoxication, insanity, and duress. Thus, this expansion of the defense may be useful because it generates a proper result in cases of blamelessness that otherwise would be denied a defense.[90]

However good the motivation, the characterization of volitionally impaired conduct as involuntary is problematic. Under traditional excuse principles, an excuse for impaired control short of involuntariness requires an inquiry into whether the degree of impairment is enough to render the actor blameless. This inquiry examines the actor's situation and compares the actor's conduct to that of the reasonable person in the same situation. The duress defense, for example, requires not only that "the actor engaged in the conduct charged to constitute an offense because he was coerced to do so," but also that "a person of reasonable firmness in [the actor's] situation would have been unable to resist [the coercion]."[91] The excuses of insanity and involuntary intoxication similarly require the jury to assess the *degree* of impairment of volition in the case at hand and to determine whether it is sufficient to support an excuse. The jury must find that the actor, at the time of his conduct, lacks "*substantial capacity* . . . to conform his conduct to the requirements of law." The standard of "substantial" capacity is intentionally "open-ended" in order to induce the jury to use its own intuitive sense of justice to determine whether the degree of impairment was enough to merit an excuse.[92]

To irrebuttably presume exculpating involuntariness in the absence of this inquiry into the extent of the impairment, as the Model Penal Code does, is to risk granting undeserved excuses. In cases of hypnotism and somnambulism, or wherever disabilities impairing control are treated as instances of lack of control, an actor may fail to meet the standard of impairment that a jury would require for excuse yet nonetheless gain an excuse if it is brought within the involuntary act defense. Indeed, whenever the voluntary act requirement is the claimed basis for a de-

---

[89] MODEL PENAL CODE § 2.01(2)(b)-(c).

[90] A hypnotic state can serve the purposes that a disability typically serves. The presence of a hypnotic state can be scientifically confirmed by a change in brain wave patterns. And, typically, the hypnosis is caused by another person, making the abnormality particularly effective in the blame-shifting function. Like the coercer in duress, the hypnotist presents an easy recipient for the blame.

[91] MODEL PENAL CODE § 2.09(1).

[92] MODEL PENAL CODE & COMMENTARIES § 4.01 cmt. 3.

fense, it creates the potential for improper exculpation if the actor's control is only impaired, not lost.

One could avoid these difficulties by recognizing that the voluntariness requirement serves the same liability function as the excuse defenses and imposes analogous requirements. If volition is not lost but impaired, the doctrine ought to demand the same inquiry into degree as do the excuse defenses. This can be done by adopting a new excuse of *impaired consciousness*,[93] for use in cases short of involuntariness, where the disability causing the impairment is other than one of the disabilities recognized by a traditional excuse.[94]

The central point here is that where an actor seeks excuse on a claim that he lacked adequate ability to control his conduct, the jury ought to inquire into the actual extent of the impairment to determine whether it is enough to render him blameless for his violation. The failure to include this basic requirement of excuse defenses in the formulation of the voluntary act requirement is consistent with a failure to see that these two aspects of criminal law doctrine in fact perform the same function and properly should have analogous requirements. This failure also creates procedural problems. Treatment of the voluntary act requirement as a universal actus reus element, rather than as an excuse defense, complicates the allocation of the burdens of proving the issue. Most jurisdictions allocate the burden of offense elements to the state but may have the defendant carry the burden for defenses. Thus, while voluntariness is functionally similar to the excuse defenses, the state is likely to be given the burden of proving voluntariness.[95] Indeed, Supreme Court case law

---

93 Such an excuse has been proposed by Glanville Williams for slightly different reasons. *See* WILLIAMS, *supra* note 87, § 157.

94 The defense provision might look something like the following:

Impaired Consciousness. An actor is excused for his conduct constituting an offense if,

(1) as a result of any physiologically confirmable disease or defect not specifically recognized or rejected as a basis for exculpation by another excuse,

(2) the actor

(a) does not perceive the physical nature or foresee the physical consequences of his conduct or does not know his conduct is wrong or criminal [lacks substantial capacity to appreciate the criminality/wrongfulness of his conduct], or

(b) is not sufficiently able to control his conduct so as to be justly held accountable for it [lacks substantial capacity to conform his conduct to the requirements of law].

95 The conditions supporting any of the general excuses are statistically rare; the actor has engaged in admittedly wrongful conduct, and the facts supporting the defense are uniquely within the knowledge of the defendant. Thus, a jurisdiction may wish to give the defendant the burdens of proof on general excuses. In contrast, offense elements are in issue in every case, and proof of the actus reus elements traditionally is required to establish that the actor has caused a societal harm, a burden traditionally and appropriately placed on the state. Allocation of the burdens of proof for excuses to the defendant is common. *See, e.g.*, 2 ROBINSON, *supra* note 10, §§ 173 nn. 6-7, 176 nn. 8-9, 177 nn. 4-5, 182 nn. 3-4. *See generally* Robinson, *supra* note 29, at 243-64. The failure to distinguish involuntariness from the offense elements makes inappropriate allocating the burden to prove involuntariness to the defendant. Regarding the burden of persuasion, compare People v. Furlong, 79 N.E. 978, 983 (N.Y. 1907) (placing burden of persuasion on defendant) and State v. Caddell, 215 S.E.2d 348, 363 (N.C. 1975) (determining that defense of unconsciousness (or automatism) is affirm-

may require this allocation if voluntariness is conceived of as an offense element.[96]

V. The Doctrines of Grading: How Much Punishment Is to Be Imposed for a Violation?

A functional analysis suggests some failures of current doctrine to properly grade violations. One kind of error is misformulation of grading because of a failure to see the function the formulation performs. The subjective definition of criminal risks, for example, gives liability treatment (focusing on an actor's belief that a risk is created) to a grading issue (whether the prohibited risk actually is created). A more common difficulty is the tendency of current doctrine to overlook the relevance to grading of factors that set the requirements for criminalization or liability. Sometimes the doctrine sees such factors as relevant to grading but does an unsystematic and incomplete job of varying grade with changes in the factors, as with the seriousness of the harm or evil or the actor's level of culpability. In other instances, as with causation, complicity, and excuses, the doctrine more generally fails to see the relevance of the factors to their grading function.

A. Mixing Liability and Grading by Using Culpability Terms to Define Prohibited Risks: Aggravation of Grade for Risk-Creation in the Absence of a Criminal Risk

Part III.D described the Model Penal Code's failure to define the risks that are criminal. Instead, the Code frequently defines risk-creation offenses by using the culpability terms "recklessness" and "negligence." Manslaughter is "recklessly causing a death"; negligent homicide is "negligently causing a death." Because culpability terms are necessarily subjective or individualized, the criminalization of these offenses is correspondingly subjective or individualized. This formulation is problematic because the Code punishment where a criminal risk actually is created is the same as where it is not created, where the actor only mistakenly believes it is created. Most jurisdictions take the view that the actual oc-

ative defense and therefore burden rests with defendant) with People v. Hardy, 198 P.2d 865, 872 (Cal. 1948) (placing burden of persuasion on prosecution).

96 The Supreme Court permits the burdens of production and persuasion to be shifted to the defendant for excuses but demands that they be allocated to the state for all offense elements. Patterson v. New York, 432 U.S. 197 (1977). To treat voluntariness as an offense element, then, is to foreclose the possibility of placing on the defendant either the burden of persuasion or the burden of production for involuntariness, no matter how strong a jurisdiction may judge the policy arguments in support of such allocation. This is particularly troubling given the use of the involuntariness defense as a catchall excuse, where the degree of impairment of control may be similar or even less than the degree of impairment of the traditional excuses, for which the burden of proof may be constitutionally shifted to the defendant. Conflicting expert opinions on matters of involuntariness, especially of the catchall type, common for many if not most general excuse defenses, make a beyond-a-reasonable-doubt standard difficult to meet.

currence of the offense harm or evil ought to increase the grade of liability. Thus, the actual creation of a criminal risk ought to be graded more seriously than where it is not actually created, all other things being equal.

Consider an actor who speeds at seventy-five miles per hour to avoid being late for an appointment and, in the process, kills a child who runs into the road. Assume that he unquestionably believes that he is taking a substantial and unjustified risk as to causing such a death, that given the circumstances known to him, his conduct is a gross deviation from the standard of care, as the definition of recklessness requires, and that his conduct causes the death. Under the Code, he is liable for manslaughter. Assume, however, that in fact his speedometer is broken and he is traveling only fifty-five miles per hour, the posted speed limit. His conduct admittedly creates a risk but no more of a risk than any other lawful driver creates on that road, a risk that is not, as an objective matter, a violation of the rules of conduct. Is liability for manslaughter still appropriate?

Criminalizing subjective risk-taking as to a result (the belief that one's conduct creates a prohibited risk) is not itself improper, for it is no different than punishing criminal attempts. Modern criminal law commonly bases liability upon an actor's externalization of her culpable state of mind. A difficulty arises here, however, because instances of criminalization of subjective risk-taking are not labeled or identified as instances of inchoate liability, but punished instead as full substantive offenses, as if the prohibited risk had actually been created. Under the Code, an actor is liable for manslaughter if he causes a death and, at the time of his conduct, has the required culpability as to the death (recklessness). The Code allows conviction for the full offense even if no criminal risk in fact is created.

If the actual harm or evil should aggravate liability—for example, by the actual creation of a prohibited risk—then liability for manslaughter is problematic. The actor's conduct is analogous to an impossible attempt. From his mistaken perspective, he satisfies the requirements of an offense by creating a criminal risk to pedestrians, but in fact he is wrong in his belief. If he is to be held criminally liable based upon his mistaken belief, by analogy to an impossible attempt, then only attempt liability is appropriate, not full liability for a substantive offense.

In defense of the Model Penal Code drafters, it is plausibly appropriate to punish an actor's subjective risk-taking the same as where the actor, with the same culpability, actually does create a prohibited risk. For example, while the Code is somewhat inconsistent in its implementation, it generally punishes attempts the same as the completed offense.[97] That is, the extent of the harm or evil attempted, but not its actual occur-

[97] *See* MODEL PENAL CODE § 5.05(1).

rence, affects the offense grade. The Code is not theoretically inconsistent, then, when it subjectivizes the definition of criminal risk.[98] Believing one is creating a prohibited risk and actually creating that risk are graded the same.

But if a jurisdiction disagrees with the Code's view that actual harm and actual risk are irrelevant, as a majority do, the code drafters in the jurisdiction must reverse the Code's provisions to reinstate the significance of the occurrence of the harm or evil. Thus, the Model Penal Code's provision grading attempt the same as the completed offense, for example, must clearly be dropped. And this typically is done.[99] But it is less obvious that the Code's treatment of criminal risk must be altered to eliminate its subjectivization of criminal risk. No jurisdiction that rejects the Code's disregard for resulting harm and evil also desubjectivizes, as it should, the Code's definition of criminal risk.

The problem is not unique to manslaughter. Whenever the Code uses an actor's culpability as the basis for liability, without requiring proof that the actor's conduct violates the rules of conduct, it potentially creates full substantive liability for an actor who simply believes, mistakenly, that his conduct is prohibited. The peculiarities go unnoticed because the rule articulation, liability, and grading doctrines are not distinguished. A purely subjective definition of criminal risk is obviously out of place in rules of conduct. It does not stand out in the current codes because the subjectivization is entirely appropriate in service of their liability function.

B. Incomplete and Unsystematic Use of Central Grading Factors

The most prominent distinction between the rule articulation and liability functions, on the one hand, and grading determinations, on the other, is between the yes-no nature of the former as compared to the gradient nature of the latter. Both rule articulation and liability determinations set minimum requirements. The grading determination must allot to each violator the appropriate amount on a spectrum of punishment. Yet, the doctrine frequently reverts to cutoff judgments for what in reality are issues of grading, resulting in part from the failure to distinguish grading from rule articulation and liability. Many of the issues of rule articulation and liability have an effect in assessing grade and, in that

---

98 Of course, the subjectivization of criminal risk is inconsistent with those aspects of the Code that do give significance to resulting harm, such as the grading difference between first degree felonies and attempted first degree felonies, *id.*, and between offenses that differ only in the resulting harm, such as that between manslaughter and reckless endangerment, *id.* §§ 210.3(1)(a), 211.2. *See generally* Paul H. Robinson, *The Role of Harm and Evil in Criminal Law: A Study in Legislative Deception?*, 5 J. CONTEMP. LEGAL ISSUES (forthcoming 1994) (discussing how the criminal law deals with the relationship between causing a prohibited harm and criminal liability).

99 *See* Robinson, *supra* note 98 (manuscript at 4-7).

capacity, require formulations that call for continuous rather than cutoff judgments.

It may seem that the doctrine fails to make degree judgments with regard to some of the most important determinants of grade, such as the seriousness of the offense harm or evil or the actor's level of culpability. That is, each offense typically requires proof of a given minimum culpability level and minimum harm or evil. But, when viewed as a whole, rather than one offense at a time, the doctrine does somewhat better. Many offenses exist only to establish a higher grade of liability over a "lesser included offense." For example, the doctrine takes account of the degree of seriousness of a threatened harm by creating different offenses to punish different harms. Thus, intentionally causing a death is murder, a first degree felony; intentionally causing serious bodily injury is aggravated assault, a second degree felony; intentionally causing bodily injury with a risk of death (use of a deadly weapon) is a third degree felony; intentionally creating a risk of death or serious bodily injury is endangerment, a misdemeanor.[100]

On the other hand, degrees of seriousness in some forms of harm are ignored by modern codes. Destroying a twenty story apartment building with an explosive and slightly scorching the side of an abandoned house trailer are the same grade offense.[101] The actor who causes permanent brain damage by repeatedly beating a robbery victim with a hammer is liable for the same grade offense as one who swings at the victim with the hammer but misses and then flees.[102] If the only role of result elements is grading, and the Code reflects this role by altering grade according to some harms (as in personal injury), one wonders why the Code does not more systematically alter grade according to the seriousness of the offense harm or evil.[103]

The doctrine also uses culpability levels to grade offenses, usually keying on future result culpability. This is done in homicide, for example, where an intentional killing is murder, a first degree felony; a reckless killing is manslaughter, a second degree felony; and a negligent killing is negligent homicide, a third degree felony.[104] Similarly, knowingly causing a catastrophe is a second degree felony, while recklessly doing so is a third degree felony.[105]

---

100 MODEL PENAL CODE §§ 210.2, 211.1(2), 211.2.

101 *Id.* § 220.1(1)(a), (4) (definitions of arson and "occupied structure").

102 *Id.* § 222.1(1).

103 The failure to recognize these differences in grading might arguably reflect a belief that actual resulting harm is irrelevant to the degree of liability; it is only the actor's subjective culpability that is relevant. But if that is the case, why does the Code include result elements at all? Why not define offenses in purely subjective terms? If subjective culpability is to be the central determinant of grade, the Code should generally take account of culpability level in grading. But, as the text notes, this is rarely done. *See generally* Robinson, *supra* note 98 (manuscript at 2).

104 MODEL PENAL CODE §§ 210.2, 210.3, 210.4.

105 *Id.* § 220.2.

But, again, varying the grade of a violation with the level of culpability as to the harm or evil is the exception rather than the rule. Few offenses other than homicide have their grade altered according to the actor's culpability level. This failure is particularly peculiar in the context of culpability as to a result since culpability as to result elements, like result elements themselves, serves *only* a grading function; thus one would expect the grading issue to be paramount in the drafters' minds. Yet, under most modern codes, an actor's culpability level as to causing a harmful result is frequently treated as irrelevant to the grade of his offense. The actor who starts a fire knowing that it will destroy another's building is liable for the same grade offense as one who is only reckless in doing so.[106] The actor who purposely creates a risk of catastrophe and the actor who recklessly does so are liable for the same grade offense.[107] The same is true for the actor who purposely creates a risk of death and the actor who recklessly does so.[108] If culpability level is relevant to grading, why should a code's grading scheme fail to systematically reflect it?

C. Dichotomous vs. Continuous Judgments: Using Rule-Articulation and Liability-Assignment Forms in Grading

While modern codes incompletely take account of the seriousness of the harm and the culpability level in grading a violation, they commonly fail to see the grading significance of some issues altogether. Causation, for example, is treated by modern codes as a simple yes-no issue. It is presented as a fixed point cutoff: either the actor is causally accountable for the result or she is not. The actor can be placed on one of only two points on the continuum of punishment, at the same point as where no result has occurred (the punishment point for an unsuccessful attempt, for example) or at the point of full causal accountability for the full result. This dichotomous rather than continuous formulation of causation does not stand out as unusual under current codes because such discrete forms are common, even typical, of the rule articulation and liability functions. But seeing causation as having a grading function suggests that it, like other grading issues, ought to be formulated to generate results along the continuum of punishment.

A recent empirical survey gave subjects a series of murder scenarios varying only in the actors' degree of causal connection with the death. The causal connection varied in both how necessary it was for the death to occur and in the remoteness of the result from the actors' conduct. The subjects assigned liability in a pattern that suggested that they were sensitive to the same factors recognized by current doctrine as relevant to

---

106 *Id.* § 220.1(2).
107 *Id.* § 220.2(2).
108 *Id.* § 211.2.

determining causation—the requirements of a necessary ("but for") cause and a result not "too remote or accidental"—but saw the issue of causation as one of degree rather than as dichotomous. The subjects did not require some minimum closeness in the causal connection to then impose full liability. Instead, the degree of liability assigned by the subjects ranged across a wide spectrum. Where the causal connection was weakest, by traditional necessary cause and remoteness criteria, the point of punishment was close to that for an unsuccessful attempt at murder. As the causal connection grew stronger, as death more directly and more immediately followed the actor's conduct, the subjects' imposition of liability increased.[109] This pattern is, of course, characteristic of grading factors.

Some writers have noted the analogy between causation and complicity.[110] An accomplice's aid to a perpetrator is a form of causal contribution to the offense. It should be no surprise, then, to find the same pattern of shared intuitions on causation, noted above, with regard to an actor's degree of assistance to a perpetrator. Current doctrine treats complicity as it does causation: as a dichotomous issue. In other words, it treats complicity in a fashion consistent with a rule articulation and minimum-liability function. But in an empirical survey similar in form to that discussed above, the subjects saw the nature and extent of complicity as an issue highly relevant to the grade of the violation. When given a series of scenarios similar in all respects except for the degree of the accomplice's causal contribution to the principal's offense—necessary versus sufficient, extent of contribution compared to the perpetrator and others—the subjects assigned different degrees of liability according to their perception of the degree of the accomplice's contribution.[111] This means, for example, that the subjects would never assign the same degree of liability to an accomplice helping to unload the drug shipment as to the organizer of the operation.

Note that the issue of grading according to degree of assistance to a perpetrator goes beyond the grading issue in causation in an important way. Causation is a grading issue from start to finish. Assisting a perpetrator, in contrast, is at base a rule articulation issue. Some minimum degree of complicity is required for liability. What this illustrates is that many factors relevant to rule articulation, or to the minimum requirements of liability, may well be relevant to grading as well. What is identified in this Article as the "doctrines of grading" are those doctrines that serve *only* a grading function. Recall the cumulative serial relation among the doctrines that serve the three functions, discussed in Part II.

---

109 ROBINSON & DARLEY, *supra* note 27.

110 *See, e.g.*, Sanford H. Kadish, *Complicity, Cause and Blame: A Study in the Interpretation of Doctrine*, 73 CAL. L. REV. 323 (1985); GEORGE P. FLETCHER, RETHINKING CRIMINAL LAW 369, 582 (1978).

111 ROBINSON & DARLEY, *supra* note 27.

To illustrate the point further, consider the current doctrine's treatment of excuse defenses as part of the liability function. They assure that criminal liability will not be imposed unless the actor could reasonably have been expected to avoid the violation. A failed duress defense, for example, means that, while some coercion may have been present, it was not sufficient to render the actor blameless for the violation. Does it follow, however, that the actor who fails to prove a duress defense is as blameworthy as one who commits the same offense with no coercion whatsoever? While the degree of mitigation may not be dramatic, most people would likely distinguish the two cases. When subjects in a research study were given a series of scenarios that differed in the amount of coercion exerted on the offender, they gave a complete defense in the extreme case but also varied the degree of liability in less severe cases according to the degree of perceived coercion.[112] If codes were to reflect this view, they would allow reductions in grade for excusing conditions short of a complete defense.

One might argue that while codes ought to take into account many more factors, they can only do so much. To try to account for even the most significant factors in grading would require a document even more complex than current codes. The complexity of the punishment judgment requires, the argument might continue, that the task be left primarily to the discretion of sentencing judges. Three kinds of arguments rebut this claim that codes must generally defer to judicial sentencing discretion: we need not defer, we ought not defer, and increasingly we do not defer.

Codes need not defer to judicial sentencing discretion. It is within our current ability to draft codes that take account of the most significant grading distinctions. This may well be difficult if the current multifunctional form of codes is maintained. As suggested here, current codes already try to do too much. If the functions are segregated, however, a separate document could provide a relatively sophisticated grading assessment in a workable form. I have discussed at length elsewhere the kinds of structures and drafting mechanisms that can be used.[113] There is great efficiency in using general principles, for example, to adjust an offense grade up or down according to culpability level, extent of the harm, causal contribution, degree of an actor's responsibility for his conduct, or some other relevant factor. Thus, a code can take account of a wide range of factors in setting the grade of a violation without requiring that the factors be redefined and restated in every offense definition.[114]

---

112 *Id.*

113 *See* Paul H. Robinson, *A Sentencing System for the 21st Century?*, 66 TEX. L. REV. 1, 14-58 (1987) [hereinafter Robinson, *21st Century*]; Paul H. Robinson, *Legality and Discretion in the Distribution of Criminal Sanctions*, 25 HARV. J. ON LEGIS. 393 (1988) [hereinafter Robinson, *Legality*].

114 *See generally* Robinson, *21st Century*, *supra* note 113, at 24-27 (discussing sentencing system that provides judges with a process, as well as relevant categories and factors).

So, for example, recklessness as to causing property damage might be a Class D misdemeanor, while purposely causing the same damage might be a Class C misdemeanor. (Such a system is likely to have many more offense grades than the seven or eight typical of current codes, however.)

I will not repeat here more of the discussion on drafting techniques for sophisticated yet workable grading provisions, but two additional general points are worth making. First, the grading task requires something less than the task of sentencing generally. Only the amount of punishment issue need be addressed in grading; the method of sanction issue (prison or house arrest or probation or fine, etc.) may be left to the discretion of sentencing judges without injuring the legality and related interests discussed below, as long as the sanctioning method or methods selected impose the amount of punishment called for.[115] Second, the need for simplicity in application is greatest where a document is intended for wide public dissemination and quick application, as with rules of conduct. If the grading rules are segregated from the functionally mixed provisions of current codes, they can become considerably more complex. We can expect trained and educated criminal adjudicators to apply more complex and more sophisticated provisions than would the untrained and uninstructed citizen. The adjudication process allows an opportunity for thoughtful and thorough application of grading rules that the real world application of conduct rules does not always permit.

A second set of arguments suggests that the code ought not defer to the discretion of sentencing judges—essentially the arguments supporting the legality principle. We ought to articulate the factors that affect the amount of punishment to be imposed because such articulated rules increase the uniformity of punishment among similar cases. Such articulated rules give notice of what conduct is deemed more serious and what less serious, in turn clarifying the deterrent threat for more serious offenses. Such rules also more systematically assure that each additional harm or evil will trigger additional punishment. Where a more-harm-more-punishment principle is adhered to, an articulated grading system better announces the principle and thereby better deters additional harms. Finally, an articulated grading system more effectively preserves for the legislature judgments about the relative seriousness of various societal harms, a judgment appropriately made by the legislative branch in a democratic system. No doubt there is a limit as to how precise a grading system can be. The thrust of these arguments simply suggests that we ought to adopt a system that embodies as much of the grading judgment as our current understandings allow us to articulate.

More comprehensive codification of grading factors also is called for by the tendency of some, including sentencing judges and commissioners,

115 *See generally* Paul H. Robinson, *Desert, Crime Control, Disparity, and Units of Punishment*, *in* PENAL THEORY AND PENAL PRACTICE (Antony Duff et al. eds., 1993).

to conclude that if the criminal code takes account of a factor it can no longer be relevant to grading. Consider the United States Sentencing Commission's treatment of excusing conditions short of a complete defense. As a Commissioner, I proposed that the federal sentencing guidelines contain a general principle of adjustment to account for excusing conditions that fall short of providing a complete defense.[116] Most of my colleagues strongly argued that the defendant had raised and lost on such issues at trial and ought not be able to raise them again. That is, they saw the present treatment of the issue, as one of dichotomous liability, as meaning that the factor could not properly be considered on the issue of grading. This is not an unreasonable conclusion to draw. It suggests, however, that where a code does not make clear that a factor is relevant to grading, judges and sentencing commissioners may mistakenly assume that it is not relevant, especially if the code recognizes and uses the factor in its liability function.[117]

A third set of arguments in support of an articulation of grading factors and principles is that this is in essence what many states and the federal system are doing as they develop more articulated "sentencing" systems. The movement has been characterized as one of *sentencing* reform, but in truth the vast majority of the reforms would accomplish precisely what the *grading* provisions of a criminal code do: set some general limits on the sentencing discretion of judges for a given kind of offense and offense circumstances. We have tended to keep this false grading-sentencing distinction because constitutional rulings on proof of *offense* elements limit the nature of possible reforms if those reforms appear to amend the criminal code, which sets out offense elements.[118] But it is not always easy to distinguish matters appropriate for legislative grading from matters appropriate for legislatively authorized limits on judicial sentencing, other than by the difference in their location in and out of the code. This is not an argument for petrifying sentencing systems, as constitutional rulings have done to much of criminal codes, but rather for allowing legislatures more freedom in structuring new ways to assess criminal punishment, perhaps by deconstitutionalizing some aspects of the proof requirements for criminal offenses.

---

116 *See* Robinson, *21st Century, supra* note 113, at 34-38.

117 I think it wrong to draw this implication from the code's failure to use a factor in grading. A better interpretation of the code's treatment would be that some factors are more important in grading than others and that some are more easily reduced to defensible categories than others. Note that the Commission was persuaded that degree of complicity should be adopted as a grading/sentencing factor even though it is a factor recognized by the code and used only in a minimum-requirements role. *See* U.S. SENTENCING COMM'N, FEDERAL SENTENCING GUIDELINES MANUAL §§ 3B1.1, 3B1.2 (West 1992).

118 *See* McMillan v. Pennsylvania, 477 U.S. 79 (1986) (noting that traditionally no prescribed burden of proof on sentencing factors, Court finds preponderance of evidence standard constitutionally acceptable for proof of sentencing guideline factors).

VI. Summary and Conclusion

This Article suggests that the criminal law has three primary functions: announcing ex ante the rules of conduct, its rule articulation function; determining ex post whether an actor's violation is blameworthy and deserves condemnation as criminal, its liability assignment function; and assessing the general amount of punishment due, its grading function. The current conceptual structure of criminal law, as reflected in the structure of modern codes, shows little sensitivity to these distinct functions. Indeed, the current structure frequently masks functional differences. This masking is unfortunate because, this Article suggests, a functional analysis can provide useful insights in assessing how well the doctrine is performing its functions and how its performance might be improved.

Does the criminal law tell persons what the law commands of them? For a society that complains of the breakdown of shared understandings of acceptable behavior, we do considerably less than we could to make the rules of acceptable conduct accessible to the average person. The rules of conduct can be made clearer by segregating them into a separate code designed to be read by the average person rather than by attorneys and judges. We can improve the educational effect of criminal adjudications by avoiding the ambiguity of acquittals and dismissals. This requires that two alternative, and contradictory, grounds for acquittal be distinguished: no liability because no violation of the rules of conduct; and no liability, despite a violation of the rules of conduct, because the violation is not blameworthy. Ambiguities of this sort inherent in criminal code doctrines also can and should be remedied, for example, by defining justification defenses objectively and providing a separate excuse defense or mitigation for a mistaken justification. It also means defining criminal risks objectively so that persons can better judge the risks that are prohibited. The blameless creation of a prohibited risk should be exempt from liability under separately defined culpability requirements. Is it not possible, and desirable, to have a simpler, clearer statement of the rules of conduct? Might it not be useful to produce a set of rules the basics of which fifth-graders could begin to discuss in their "citizenship classes" and that could form the basis for discussion of a citizen's obligations in classes continuing through high school or beyond?

Does the criminal law impose liability on blameworthy violators and only blameworthy violators, its liability function? Confusion over the function of different aspects of the doctrine results in formulations that fail to answer this question. Current doctrine fails to impose deserved liability on some attempt violations, for example, because it requires elevation of all culpability requirements of the object offense to purposeful. This elevation results from the mistaken view that the very demanding future conduct intention required for criminalization of incomplete attempts must be applied to all other culpability elements, including those that serve only liability or grading functions. Similarly, current doctrine's involuntariness defense fails to require a showing of sufficient impairment of control to exculpate because it fails to see that both the voluntariness requirement of the "actus reus" and the general excuse defenses perform analogous liability functions and ought to have analogous minimum requirements. The first error—the culpability requirements for attempt—occurs because the doctrine fails to see that different mental elements in attempt are functionally different. The second error—too broad an involuntariness defense—illustrates the reverse sort of error, where the doctrine fails to see that two defenses are functionally similar; the involuntariness defense serves the same function as the general excuse defenses.

Does the criminal law properly distinguish among different grades of violations? Again, confusion over function may account for an underutilization or a failure to consider factors that have a significant effect on grade, at least as significant as factors that the doctrine does take account of. In some cases, the failure is rather obscure because the functional confusion is hidden within a misconceived doctrinal formulation, for example, where culpability terms, designed for a liability function, are used to define prohibited risk, a rule articulation function. The resulting effect is to distort the grading function by aggravating a violation to actually creating a criminal risk when in fact the risk existed only in the actor's mind.

Underutilization of grading factors is somewhat more apparent where the doctrine fails to take account of such significant differences as the extent of resulting harm and differences in culpability level. Relevant grading factors are sometimes ignored altogether, such as differences in an actor's degree of causal accountability for a result, in causal contribution to a violation by another, and in the degree of dysfunction and impairment short of complete excuse. These weaknesses in current grading schemes result in part from a failure to make an independent assessment of the doctrine's performance of this function.

Whether criminal law doctrine ought to be reconceptualized around its three primary functions remains unclear. More experience in using these functional distinctions may give a better sense of whether such reconceptualization is warranted.[119] One can imagine a separate document specifically drafted to perform each function: a code of conduct

[119] Clearly, reconceptualization around the functional distinctions would be better than the present conceptualization summarized in Part I. It is unclear, however, whether another structure might be more useful. For an example of a structure somewhat closer to that of current law, see Robinson & Grall, *supra* note 11; Robinson, *supra* note 29, at 199-291; Paul H. Robinson, *Imputed Criminal Liability*, 93 YALE L.J. 609-76 (1984) (suggesting a three-part structure of offense definitions, general defenses that would provide a defense even if the elements of the offense definition are satisfied, and doctrines of imputation that would impose liability even if the elements of the offense definition are not satisfied).

written for the general public to announce the criminal law's rules of conduct; a code for the adjudication of violations to determine whether the blameworthiness conditions are sufficiently satisfied to justify criminal conviction and condemnation; and a grading/sentencing code that takes account of the range of factors that affect our assessment of the amount of punishment called for. This last code might be supplemented by a set of guidelines to help sentencing judges decide the method by which the amount of punishment previously determined ought to be inflicted, a decision that may be subject to factors unrelated to the offender's degree of blameworthiness and informed by empirical evidence on the sanctioning method that will best prevent future offenses by this or other potential offenders.[120]

The code of conduct for the public, the liability code, and the grading code might have different structures, reflecting their different functions. The first ought to be simple yet comprehensive, preferably using objective criteria and easily understood standards.[121] Here the legality principle ought to be applied so as to maximize notice of the conduct that is criminal. The second and third, which are directed to judges, lawyers, and, through instructions, to juries can be more complex and judgmental.

The liability code need only assess whether the minimum requirements of blameworthiness are satisfied; a discrete yes or no decision is sufficient. The procedural safeguards for this determination ought to be high, for it is at this stage that the criminal justice system's jurisdiction over the offender is established and the condemnation of conviction is dispensed. The legality principle ought to be applied here in a way that maximizes the uniformity in treatment of similar cases.

The grading code, in contrast, calls for judgments on matters of degree. The factors influencing amount of punishment typically will range across a continuum. The challenge here is to quantify the factors and find where on the continuum a particular offender falls and how the relevant factors interrelate in assessing the amount of punishment called for. The judgmental nature of such decisions, as well as the fact that the authority for criminal jurisdiction has previously been established, suggests that procedural rules and adherence to legality can be somewhat more flexible here than at the liability stage.[122]

---

120 For a discussion of such a system and its special virtues, see Robinson, *21st Century*, *supra* note 113, at 53-58; Paul H. Robinson, *Hybrid Principles for the Distribution of Criminal Sanctions*, 82 Nw. U. L. Rev. 19, 34-36 (1987); Robinson, *supra* note 115.

121 For example, New Jersey has pending a proposal to reformulate its justification defenses in an objective form on the theory that this will make it easier to train police on the rules for permissible use of force. *See* New Jersey Attorney General's Task Force on the Use of Force in Law Enforcement, Report 105-08, 115-16, 128-32 (1992).

122 For further discussion of the grading and sentencing as a single process, its difference with the liability assessment function, and the implications of these functional similarities and differences, see Robinson, *Legality*, *supra* note 113, at 396-400.

It is premature to propose seriously these kinds of ambitious reforms. An investigation of their feasibility and attractiveness is a study in itself. But it is not premature to suggest that analysis of criminal law doctrine in light of its functions gives insights into how to improve current doctrine's performance. Some insights and their corresponding reforms are described here.[123] No doubt others can use functional analysis to reveal other weaknesses and to formulate other reforms.

[123] Given the financial and political limitations on other methods for improving the performance of the criminal law, the kinds of reforms proposed here may be worth considering. Most are within our control and do not call for additional resources.

[2]

DESERT, PUNISHMENT, AND CRIMINAL RESPONSIBILITY

LLOYD L. WEINREB*

I
INTRODUCTION

The crucial element in any theory of punishment is its treatment of the matter of desert. For the retributivist, desert is the sole basis on which punishment properly is imposed; he is accordingly obliged to explain how desert attaches and, more particularly, how it is translated into a measurement of punishment. Those have proved to be difficult tasks. Objectors to the retributivist position not only question whether a person can be said to be guilty in the sense required by desert. They question also whether desert, if it is a meaningful concept, by itself justifies the deliberate infliction of pain; if pain itself is not a good and no good consequences are in view, they argue, the question can have only one answer. To fortify those questions, they challenge retributivists to make their position concrete and specify what punishment attaches by way of desert to specific crimes.[1]

Utilitarians, on the other hand, have the greatest difficulty not defending desert but getting rid of it. They are asked if they can even explain the concept of punishment, as distinguished from other kinds of public obligation, without reference to desert. If desert is not relevant, why would they not, to attain a desirable end, punish the innocent, that is, those who do not deserve to be punished? In response, utilitarians proffer elaborate arguments to show the instrumental value of punishing the guilty and only them; but tacitly or even explicitly, the real proof of the correctness of their arguments is that the results are consistent with considerations of desert, which is enough to undermine the conclusion the arguments are intended to support.[2]

---

* Professor of Law, Harvard Law School.

1. The justification of punishment has been discussed extensively in philosophical and legal writing. Two excellent survey articles, which together suggest the range of the literature are by Benn, *Punishment*, in 7 THE ENCYCLOPEDIA OF PHILOSOPHY 29 (1967), and Greenawalt, *Punishment*, in 4 ENCYCLOPEDIA OF CRIME AND JUSTICE 1336 (1983), *reprinted in* 74 J. CRIM. L. & CRIMINOLOGY 343 (1983). Both contain useful bibliographies.

Although the summary statements of the retributive and utilitarian positions that I have provided here scarcely do justice to the subtlety of the arguments on both sides, no purpose would be served by a more thorough exposition. The fine distinctions that are made are all efforts to account satisfactorily for desert.

2. *See* Rawls, *Two Concepts of Rules*, 64 PHIL. REV. 3 (1955); *cf.* H.L.A. HART, PUNISHMENT AND RESPONSIBILITY 18-22 (1968). In a highly regarded book, Herbert Packer argued forcefully that the only justification for criminal punishment is utilitarian: the prevention of crime. H. PACKER, THE

To end the impasse, a variety of composite theories have been proposed.[3] Those who favor the use of punishment to reform or rehabilitate the criminal may recognize that only those who so deserve may be punished but urge that utilitarian considerations ought to determine the extent of punishment. If desert is a condition of punishment, it is not credible that it operates like a sluice gate; for we all know that pain can be greater or less, and no explanation is given why it should be regarded as indivisible so long as it is deserved. The suggestion that the individual desert of the traffic offender and the murderer or, less dramatically, the petty shoplifter and the bank robber, has no comparative bearing on their punishment, provided it has been established that they deserve to be punished at all, makes no sense.[4]

LIMITS OF THE CRIMINAL SANCTION 35-70 (1968). ("The case for an essentially preventive view of the function of criminal law is unanswerable; anything else is the merest savagery." *Id.* at 66.) According to Packer, if we were certain that the costs of punishment, including the harm inflicted on those who are punished as well as more general societal and individual costs, were less than the benefits, considerations of culpability—blameworthiness for commission of an offense—might be disregarded. But the utilitarian calculus is not certain, and for that reason there are instrumental reasons to require culpability as a condition of punishment. *Id.* at 62-70.

> [A] purely preventive view, reinforced as that view is today by a scientific and deterministic attitude toward the possibilities for controlling human conduct, carries the danger that single-minded pursuit of the goal of crime prevention will slight and in the end defeat the ultimate goal of law in a free society, which is to liberate rather than to restrain. Human autonomy is an illusion if we make it conditional on human perfection.

Id. at 66. Packer straddles the question whether uncertainty about how to achieve utilitarian goals should be regarded simply as our current state of knowledge or as an *a priori* assumption.

> As we find ourselves gaining more nearly exact knowledge about the sources and control of deviant behavior, the pressure from the behavioral position upon this rationale will become very strong and may prove to be irresistible. The more confidently we can predict behavior and the more subtly we can control it, the more powerful will be the temptation to relax the constraints that inhibit us at present from aggressively intervening in the lives of individuals in the name of crime prevention. But the millennium will not announce itself with unmistakable clarity. And skeptics about its advent may then as now find some merit in a limiting rationale for the criminal sanction.

Id. The value of human autonomy, on which Packer's argument finally rests, requires recognition of desert, not simply as a fence against excessive utilitarian zeal, but because desert is part of the meaning of autonomy. *See infra* pp. 74-75.

3. Occasionally it is suggested that each of the two theories may provide a separate and independent, sufficient justification for punishment. *See* Flew, *The Justification of Punishment*, 29 PHIL. 291, 306-07 (1954); Mundle, *Punishment and Desert*, 4 PHIL. Q. 216, 228 (1954).

4. Packer's theory is not strictly subject to this objection because he relies on desert not to justify the imposition of punishment but to limit its imposition even though it may be justified. *See* H. PACKER, *supra* note 2. But if, as he says, "once a decision to punish has been made and justified on other grounds, the rehabilitative ideal should be fully used in deciding what kinds of punishment should be imposed," *id.* at 67, the protection afforded by his limiting principle is likely to be very weak indeed. That reinforces the conclusion that the basis for the principle is not entirely instrumental. Insofar as it is not instrumental, it is subject to the objection.

See also Morris & Miller, *Predictions of Dangerousness*, 6 CRIME AND JUSTICE 1 (1985). The authors argue that predictions of dangerousness are a proper basis of punishment provided the punishment does not exceed "what would be justified independent of that prediction. Thus, concepts of 'desert' define the upper limits of allowable punishment." *Id.* at 6. They say that we are ordinarily unable to state with precision what is a "just" [i.e., deserved] punishment; the most we can do is conclude that a punishment is "not unjust." Since there is usually a range of punishments that are not unjust, the utilitarian consideration of dangerousness has room within which to operate. *Id.* at 37. Although Morris and Miller assert, not without reason, that the practical effect of full implementation of their proposals would be to restrict the implicit or explicit reliance on predictions of dangerousness in the actual criminal process, *id.* at 38, their theoretical model makes one skeptical of how significant their

Another kind of composite theory, which probably comes closest to the reflective judgment of most people, is that utilitarian considerations ought to determine what conduct is criminal but that considerations of desert restrict the imposition and extent of punishment in a particular case.[5] Such a position appears to accommodate what is most persuasive about retributive and utilitarian theories. By separating justification of the law from justification of punishment under the law, it avoids the useless infliction of punishment and, at the same time, punishes according to desert. The proposed separation, however, is illusory. For it is the law's definition of guilt that determines who will be punished. When utility and individual desert do not coincide, one or the other of the theory's distinct principles must give way. If it were shown, for example, that utilitarian values would be served by the punishment of persons who engage in certain conduct involuntarily—say, while sleepwalking or drugged—under this theory, ought the law provide that such involuntary conduct is a crime? If so, does the theory allow a person who commits such a crime to be punished? Evidently it is intended that utilitarian considerations govern only the kinds of conduct that are criminal and not the exculpatory (or inculpatory) significance of the actor's individual circumstances, which depends on desert. That limitation gives away everything to the retributive view, no matter what the basis on which some kinds of conduct are made criminal and not others.[6]

The inconclusiveness of the theoretical debate has noticeably little effect on practical issues. Although the punishment (or absence of punishment) in particular cases and the extent and manner of punishments generally arouse controversy, it usually turns out that if a person deserves to be punished, there are good consequential reasons to punish him; and if there are good

---

limiting principle of desert really is. Their program could be put into effect only if we were able to predict accurately. Against the weight of well-supported empirical predictions developed for that purpose, how much force would the notion of an upper limit of not unjust punishment have?

5. Among those who have espoused some version of this position are: H.L.A. HART, *supra* note 2; Greenawalt, *supra* note 1; Rawls, *supra* note 2.

6. Oddly, the point is brought out most clearly in J.D. Mabbott's justly famous article, *Punishment*, 48 MIND 152 (1939), in which he rejects all utilitarian justifications of punishment. Mabbott argues that the connection between punishment and crime is all that need be considered. "The only justification for punishing any man is that he has broken a law." *Id.* at 158. While he is prepared to allow utilitarian considerations to enter into the formation of the law, that issue, he says, is altogether irrelevant to the question of punishment. As for desert, he regards it simply as a matter of whether the law has been broken. Mabbott described his theory as retributive, and it is generally so regarded. *But see* Flew, *supra* note 3, at 298-306. If anything, it is rejected as too exclusively retributive. In fact, however, it is on its own terms neither retributive nor utilitarian. It requires neither kind of justification. According to Mabbott's theory, if the law were the product of an altogether irrational process, the fact of violation would still "justify" punishment of the violator. Mabbott is correct, I believe, in denying that utilitarian considerations are essential to a justification of punishment. He is able to eliminate direct consideration of desert as well only because he tacitly assumes that for utilitarian or other reasons, the law will not inculpate someone who is not responsible for his conduct.

The requirement that conduct not be declared criminal except on utilitarian grounds excludes the possibility that crime will be defined according to a dogmatic notion of desert unrelated to the humanly good—equated with sin, as it were. But retributive theories rarely include such elements anymore and certainly need not.

consequential reasons to punish him, that is what he deserves.[7] So whatever one's theory, the outcome is about the same. The short explanation for this happy coincidence is that, for whatever reason, criminal law is concerned largely with intentional conduct. Since desert attaches most easily to such conduct, which also can be deterred by the threat of punishment, desert and utility coincide.

The slight practical importance of theories of punishment is illustrated in another way by a small number of persistent doctrinal problems in the criminal law, old chestnuts that keep first-year classes in a state of suspense and are discussed repeatedly in the literature without resolution. Their common element is that a person's liability to be punished or the extent of his punishment is affected by a circumstance beyond his control. Included among such cases are those in which the law provides that punishment be greater or less according to the seriousness of the harm, which may vary independently of the actor's conduct: felony murder, misdemeanor-manslaughter and negligent homicide generally, and fully executed, failed attempts. Included also are cases in which the occasion for conduct that makes a person liable is an extraordinary situation not of his own making and the situation itself fully explains his conduct: self-defense against an "innocent aggressor" or an act necessary to preserve oneself that unavoidably exposes another person to the same peril. Also, cases in which the actor's liability depends on the fault or absence of fault of the victim: homicide provoked by the victim or by someone other than the victim, or defense of a third person who is or is not the person originally at fault.[8] The difficulty of these cases is not that the applications of the retributive and utilitarian theories are in conflict. On the contrary, the theories point in the same direction; only this time neither of the theories justifies the outcomes that the doctrines dictate. The peculiar, troubling feature of the cases is that the doctrines persist, despite the absence of justification according to both theories.

In view of the intractability as well as the practical irrelevance of the abstract issue, it is perhaps not surprising that the theory of punishment is usually treated as a philosophical digression from the main concerns of the criminal law, as if we were clear about when it is correct to punish even if we

---

7. Greenawalt observes shrewdly:

> Theories of justification are often built with existing practices in mind and do not usually stray too far from the reflective moral views of ordinary citizens. The fact that sharply divergent philosophical theories can have closely similar implications across a broad range of actual practices is less a startling coincidence than a product of the existential basis on which those theories are constructed.

Greenawalt, *supra* note 1, at 1345, *reprinted in* 74 J. CRIM. L. & CRIMINOLOGY at 360-61.

8. There are other types of cases that fall more or less within the same description, although those that I have mentioned are the most obvious and important. For a thorough review of such cases, see Schulhofer, *Harm and Punishment: A Critique of Emphasis on the Results of Conduct in the Criminal Law*, 122 U. PA. L. REV. 1497 (1974).

cannot sort out exactly why it is correct.[9] The inability of the most widely held composite theory to maintain a separation between declaring when conduct is criminal and imposing punishment illustrates, however, that within the criminal law the theory by which punishment is justified must be determinative of the fundamental issue of criminal responsibility. Ordinarily, the issue is presented in the context of a specific defense, like insanity or duress; and it is discussed with relation to the specific facts in terms that are not limited to criminal law: causation, voluntariness, intent, and so forth. The general theoretical justification of punishment may not appear to be immediately relevant. But whatever relationship there may be between responsibility and punishment more generally, criminal responsibility renders one susceptible to punishment. A theory of criminal responsibility must literally be a theory of punishment. And if the problem of desert is central to the latter it must likewise be central to the former.

There is reason to believe, therefore, that closer attention to the matter of desert and its relation to punishment will shed light on general and specific doctrinal problems of the criminal law. Of particular interest in that connection is the apparent disregard of considerations of desert in the resolution of concrete issues despite its controlling significance abstractly. If an explanation can be found for those doctrines that persist despite a lack of justification on either retributive or utilitarian grounds, it may help to account also for criminal responsibility in the more usual case, where both doctrines appear to provide the justification independently but inconsistently.

The debate about punishment harbors an ambiguity related to the above that is generally overlooked, and which seems to me critical. It is seldom clear whether punishment is conceived as a strict implication of desert, so that "deserves to be punished" is a unitary, albeit complex, idea, or as a distinct and separable consequence of desert, so that one could properly regard a person as deserving of punishment without answering the question whether he ought to be punished. Proponents of the retributivist view sometimes seem to believe that what they have to defend is not the criminal's desert as such but punishment, more particularly the painful aspect of punishment. And opponents sometimes sound as though they do not object to the idea of the criminal's desert but only to the useless infliction of pain as a consequence; they might agree that abstractly a person deserves to be punished but disagree about carrying out the punishment if there are not utilitarian reasons for doing so.[10]

A similar ambiguity may often be found in statements of the relationship between responsibility and desert. Appearing to concede that the criminal is responsible for his conduct, or at least not arguing that he is not, the

9. That is not to say that the philosophers or the more philosophic-minded of the legal writers have not made the connection. *See, e.g.*, Kadish, *Complicity, Cause and Blame: A Study in the Interpretation of Doctrine*, 73 CALIF. L. REV. 323 (1985).

10. There are additional questions about the imposition of punishment, such as who has authority to punish. The utilitarian objection that I am considering here is independent of those questions.

utilitarian may assert that nothing follows about the criminal's desert; he may claim, indeed, that a reference to desert is either only a curious way of talking about responsibility or is meaningless altogether.[11] In response, the retributivist may find himself defending what looks like a move from responsibility to desert. Once again, it may not be clear whether the retributivist believes that desert follows unavoidably from responsibility or is something additional, which needs to be defended and can be rejected independently.[12]

The conception of punishment as separable from desert is, I believe, a mistake, as is the conception of desert as separable from responsibility. Doubts about punishment for crime that are expressed as doubts about the correctness of inflicting pain uselessly are doubts about desert itself. If it were clear that a person deserved to be punished, the fact that punishing him would require the infliction of pain would not itself be a reason not to punish him, even though the punishment would predictably do no good. Equally, if it were clear that a person was responsible for a wrong, his desert (and therefore the propriety of punishment) would follow without more. Doubts about a person's desert are, at bottom, doubts about his responsibility from a moral point of view.[13]

There is, therefore, a relationship between responsibility and punishment, mediated by the idea of desert, which requires no additional argument. Thus

11. The overlooked ambiguity spares the utilitarian the burden of explaining what responsibility without desert means. I do not believe that the idea of responsibility without desert can be sustained. *See infra* p. 74.

12. In each case, the appearance of separability is fortified by a question that we are unable to answer satisfactorily even though desert seems to have been established in principle. Sometimes, *pace* Kant, one may question whether those having authority to punish ought to carry out a deserved punishment, because of strong utilitarian considerations to the contrary. The difference between cosmic justice and human justice, which in this context Kant disregards, is that the latter requires a decision; justice is not the only human goal, and another goal can sometimes be preferred without overthrowing justice altogether (as a departure from it would overthrow justice as part of the determinate natural order). That makes it easier to believe that desert is not by itself a reason to punish when we do. The apparent separability of desert and responsibility is fortified by our inability to specify what precisely a person deserves, even though the facts establishing his responsibility are undisputed.

13. It follows that I disagree with the assertion that strict retributive justifications for punishment "can be shown to be either denials of the need to justify it, or mere reiterations of the principle to be justified, or disguised utilitarianism." Benn, *An Approach to the Problems of Punishment*, 33 PHIL. 325, 327 (1958). See also H. PACKER, *supra* note 2, at 38-39 where he states that the argument "that it is right for punishment to be inflicted on persons who commit crimes . . . has no useful place in a theory of justification for punishment, because what it expresses is nothing more than a dogma, unverifiable and on its face implausible." Benn observes: "Appeals to authority apart, we can provide ultimate justification for rules and institutions, only by showing that they yield advantages." Benn, *supra*, note 1, at 326 (footnote omitted). He says also: "[R]etributive justifications in general are unsatisfactory for the very reason that they refuse to look to the consequences of a rule, thereby denying a necessary part of the procedure for justifying it." *Id.* at 329. Unless he is only stipulating what he means by justification, which is unlikely, Benn seems here to assume the very point at issue. One needs to distinguish at least between justification on a basis other than consequences and a refusal to consider consequences, however serious, at all. The former does not require the latter. I argue in this article that punishment for desert is an implication of an aspect of the human condition, freedom and responsibility, that is not open to question (although, as I also argue, it is antinomic). The justification of retributive theories is simply our recognition of human responsibility.

far, the retributive position is correct. At the same time, the causally determinate background of human action undermines our conclusions about individual responsibility and, equally and inescapably, undermines desert as a basis for punishment. To the extent that they depend on rejection of retributivism, the utilitarian's consequential arguments are sustained. The two positions are contradictory, and the effort to join them in a unified theory of punishment must fail, even though each considered separately may point in the same direction as the other.

In order to overcome the contradiction, one would have to adopt the ontological premise of normative natural order—that is, that the causally determinate background of our actions is itself according to our desert. Such a premise, however, contradicts the opposition between freedom and cause or, as it may be put, the separation between normative and descriptive discourse—"ought" and "is." The substantive doctrines of the criminal law indicate that the separation, beyond challenge abstractly, is not always maintained in our experience.

It is the purpose of this article to elaborate and explain those very abstract and, in some respects, counter-intuitive propositions. Section two of the article contains some ruminations about the connection between responsibility and desert generally. In section three, I discuss criminal responsibility and the problematic doctrines of the law, in which the connection between responsibility and desert, as it is ordinarily understood, is weak. In section four, I describe how these problems of crime and punishment would be viewed from the normative ontological perspective.

It is not part of my purpose to convince anyone that that perspective is correct. No more than anyone else, can I make sense of the claim that "what is, because it is, ought to be," at least without the aid of some theological or other metaphysical hypothesis that puts the matter beyond debate. Rather, the normative ontological perspective accounts, on its own terms, for a fundamental aspect of the organization of our experience—human freedom, responsibility, and desert—which is not itself open to question. Furthermore, the manner in which we now account for that aspect of our experience, which preserves the separation between what is and what ought to be, is subject to the same objections, to the same extent, as the perspective that we reject. All that renders the latter acceptable to us, and the former not, is the conventional pattern of our thought. These conclusions do not validate the utilitarian resolution of the problem of punishment. For, as I have said, freedom and responsibility, and with them, desert, are given directly in our experience.

II

RESPONSIBILITY AND DESERT

It is usually the case when a judgment about a person's desert is questioned that the explanation offered to defend the judgment is descriptive. Asked to explain an assertion that Harry deserves to be punished, one is likely to respond with just a description, which may be simple or elaborate, of what Harry did. There is no logical trap waiting to be sprung in that small observation. It reflects, I think, only that we are likely to withhold a judgment about desert unless we are confident of the underlying normative principle, which we expect others also to perceive and accept. If someone questions the judgment, we assume that he lacks information about the facts, not that he is unaware of or doubtful about the principle. So, asked to explain why Harry deserves to be punished, one is likely to say, "He left her bruised and battered," or "He promised to do otherwise," rather than "It is wrong to beat up people," or "People shouldn't make promises unless they mean to keep them." Of course, after hearing a description of Harry's conduct, the questioner might reply, "So what if he did?" The speaker would then have to tender the normative principle; but more than likely, he would be considerably puzzled about the need to do so.

Facts that explain why a person deserves to be punished have to be described in a certain way; or, one may prefer to say, they have to include a certain kind of fact. They must refer to the person as an actor, not simply someone who was affected or someone the effect on whom contributed to other effects. Furthermore, as an actor, he must be presented as responsible for the conduct in question.[14] So far as desert is concerned, nothing else counts, because only insofar as he is responsible does a normative principle come into play at all. His responsibility need not eliminate from the description reference to other causes without which the event would not have occurred as it did (although it may eliminate some). Harry "started the fire"; just the same, there would have been no fire had there not been a pile of leaves (left, perhaps, by someone else) and a strong wind, not to mention all the other general conditions of combustion.

Although this attribution of responsibility is critical, typically it is not explicit but is built into the description of an event and, unless challenged, taken for granted. Nevertheless, one can challenge an assertion about desert by questioning the implicit attributive element, while agreeing with the normative principle being applied and accepting the factual description in every other respect. Such challenges comprise the whole range of what we call excuses. Sometimes, an excuse goes to the brink of denying that one's conduct caused the event. It suggests that we look elsewhere in the situation for the significant cause and regard the person's involvement as only an attendant condition, a kind of physical link between the cause and the effect. Someone on a bus who bumps into another person, for example, may offer as an excuse, "I was shoved," or, "The bus stopped short," and think that an apology is not strictly in order. Other excuses acknowledge the actor's intention to bring about the result, but deny that he is responsible in the required sense because of some fact about him, which may pertain only to the

14. I rely for the moment on the familiar notion of responsibility that we use all the time without difficulty. It is part of the program of this article to elucidate some aspects of this notion more precisely.

event in question or more generally: he was "only a child," or was delirious, or was an addict or insane. One may agree that conduct was intentional and that one is responsible for it in general, but deny his responsibility in a particular respect that made it violative of the normative principle. So, one may excuse himself, saying, "I was not thinking about that," or "I thought you wouldn't mind," or "I thought at the time it was the right thing to do." Such excuses may approach a denial that the conduct violated a normative principle at all.

The range of such responsibility-denying excuses is large and may be said to include any explanation that avoids desert except, at one extreme, the denial of any causal connection whatever—the event would have been the same whatever the actor had done—and, at the other, rejection of the underlying normative principle, so that one affirms his responsibility but claims that he deserves well or at least not ill.[15] For all their concrete variety, whether they focus attention away from the actor or toward some particular aspect of him or his conduct, excuses have a good deal in common. Although, like many descriptive concepts, they may incorporate a reference to an evaluative standard, they purport to describe what is the case; they are cast descriptively rather than prescriptively. Furthermore, although there are identifiable, more or less distinct types of excuse along the range from no causal connection to no moral fault, the types tend to collapse into one another. Responsibility must be for something; unless conduct is an event, a happening that perceptibly alters the state of things, there is nothing to which a normative principle can be applied, and no excuse is necessary or

---

15. Although the difference between an excuse and a denial of causal responsibility or rejection of a normative principle is one that we recognize and has significance generally, cases at either end of the range of excuses may not easily be labeled as an excuse or something else. One may, for example, respond to an accusation of thoughtlessness toward his sibling, "I am not my brother's keeper." That may be a statement of fact—the law or some other positive code does not make me responsible for my brother's well-being—or it may be a rejection of the implied obligation. Or it may be a bit of both. If the person who responded that way were pressed and he insisted that he had no obligation to look after his brother, the reply, "That's no excuse," would be out of place, because he was not offering an excuse at all; rather he was asserting that he needs no excuse, for his conduct was not at fault. On the other hand, if he were to insist only that he was not legally obligated to look after his brother, that would be an offer of an excuse (of a somewhat special kind) to which the reply might well be, "That's no excuse." At the other end of the range, the denial of causal responsibility, which makes an excuse otiose, may be mixed up with a sort of excuse. For example, a person who is accused of failing to prevent some harm may respond, "I had nothing to do with it," without denying that he was aware of the harm and was able to prevent it; any number of other persons could also have prevented the harm and he was no more implicated than they. His response is perhaps not a denial that someone ought to have acted; it may fit ambiguously between a denial of causal responsibility and a claim that, given the number of other persons on whom the obligation fell equally, he (as well as any other person in his situation) ought to be excused from individual responsibility. The important point for the present purpose is not precisely how a specific exculpatory statement is catalogued, but that there is a category of "excuses": statements that acknowledge both causal responsibility and the normative principle but deny an attribution of desert, on grounds peculiar to the actor's case. *See generally* Fletcher, *The Right and the Reasonable*, 98 HARV. L. REV. 949 (1985); Greenawalt, *The Perplexing Borders of Justification and Excuse*, 84 COLUM. L. REV. 1897 (1984) (both discussing the various doctrines known as "excuses" in the criminal law).

appropriate.[16] The larger a harm or loss, the more likely we are to look for a human agent and, having found him, the more likely we are to regard him as morally responsible. On the other hand, the greater the moral fault, the more likely we are to identify conduct as the effective cause of whatever harm results; whereas if the fault is small, we are more likely to look around for another cause among the circumstances.

The excuses that we offer and accept help to clarify what we mean by responsibility and desert. They presuppose that a person is responsible for his conduct and desert can attach only insofar as the conduct is self-determined, and that whether conduct is self-determined or not is a matter of fact.[17] An attribution of desert requires that a person have exercised a capacity to direct his actions for himself (even if by taking no action). Also, since an "action" does not consist entirely[18] of a determination of the will but occurs as an event in the world, it requires a sufficiently stable natural order, a setting of non-self-determining things that respond predictably to events.[19] Neither of those requirements is, in general, problematic. Without insisting that the capacity for self-determined action is either necessary or sufficient to constitute the category of "persons," it is true at least that the capacity is a central definitional element of the category.[20] And in fact the two requirements seem like structural conditions of our experience of a world of persons and things. Although we can look behind them in a particular case or perhaps be persuaded to shift an object or type of object from one category to the other, we cannot within our experience question them in principle.

Our practice of making excuses indicates that there is another requirement for an attribution of desert, which stands on very different footing. Unless the

16. That is not to say that one can only be responsible if there is a perceptible harm. One may be responsible for driving recklessly, even though, as it turns out, no one is injured. The idea that it is sinful to lust in one's heart, Matthew 5:28, is not an exception; it regards lust as the effect of an exercise of will.

17. To say that it is a matter of fact is not to say that it is easily ascertained or is observable in a simple way, but that it purports to say what is the case and not what ought to be the case. As I argue below, however, the notion of self-determination is not fully intelligible unless the distinction between fact and value is somehow overcome.

It is more usual to say that conduct must be "voluntary" in order for a person to be responsible, rather than that it must be "self-determined." The criminal law typically refers to voluntariness. *E.g.*, MODEL PENAL CODE § 2.01 (1985). The ambiguity of the concept of voluntariness in this context, which makes it so useful in ordinary discourse (and in the criminal law), makes it less useful here. It may be used to characterize the actor's attitude—willing or unwilling, eager or reluctant—towards conduct for which all would agree he is responsible as well as all the gradations of pressure up to and even including compulsion to act. While the idea of self-determination is not always easily applied, it is more precise and, for reasons explained in this essay, gets at the critical question.

18. Or perhaps at all—? I do not wish to take up the difficult problem involved in the idea of will or a will.

19. That is true even if the action is nothing but a bodily movement. Insofar as there are "mental events," they also are included.

20. A great deal more could be said on that subject. I am not especially troubled by the notion of a "person" who has few, or none, of the characteristics of a human being. Science fiction thrives on such possibilities. Nor am I troubled by the notion of a creature that has all of the other characteristics of a human being but is not a person. Some robots may come close. Still, I do not think that the category of persons could be made independent of such ordinary identifying characteristics altogether.

capacity to determine one's action is not merely individual but *personal* in a strong, constitutive sense, an attribution on the basis of how the capacity is exercised seems altogether arbitrary; for the attribution attaches to a particular person and not simply to a person or to any person. It is to avoid just such arbitrariness that we reject immediately vicarious liability for the acts of another, if there is nothing to connect the person in question and the actor.[21] So far as the law is concerned, of course, there is nothing vicarious about Smith's liability, say, for homicide if it is Smith who fired the fatal shot. The very person who pulled the trigger is the person who goes to prison. We are there regarding Smith, however, not simply as an autonomous self, a self-determining, individual entity, but as a person in the ordinary sense, with concrete attributes and an actual history: height, weight, hair color, intellect, habits, desires, upbringing, education, job experience, family relationships—the whole lot. As to all that, he is not autonomous at all; on the contrary, he simply is who he is, Smith and no one else. (If his present attributes are the effects of his actions in the past, those actions were taken by Smith as he was then.) And it is clear that those nonautonomously acquired attributes are implicated in the actual exercise of the capacity for self-determination that calls forth the attribution of desert. Yet, non-autonomous factors in a situation are just what we regularly allow as excuses.

So we begin a retreat. It is not personal characteristics like height or intellect as such nor one's history as history that accounts for desert. Nor is it any combination of characteristics and history. Rather it is the self-determined action. And no combination of one's characteristics and history *fully* determines what his action is. If one is a person—if that basic requirement of desert holds at all—then one has always the capacity to determine one's actions. If not, then desert is out of the question. But that has already been conceded.

Maybe so. But, indisputably, a person's characteristics and history powerfully affect how he acts; and if the investigation is pursued far enough, it may look as though the autonomous capacity that remains is squeezed into a corner. Why should all the rest be disregarded? Why do some things count as excuses and not others? Anyway, when we finally isolate the autonomous self from the factors that compose the person as he is, it looks like the autonomous self of anyone at all, an undifferentiated locus of decision without any personal characteristics that bind it to the person we have in view. Otherwise it would not be truly autonomous.

Coming at the matter from the other end, one might ask why self-determined conduct has the significance it has for desert? The consequences of the conduct may not affect the person himself at all. How does he, being unchanged, incur a susceptibility to some change as his due, presumably because something else (by his action) is changed? That unfamiliar form of the question almost breaks out when a person declares that he is sorry for

21. *See generally* Kadish, *supra* note 9.

what he has done and therefore that he does not deserve to be punished. Why should he be made to feel pain because his conduct sometime in the past was wrong, as he now recognizes? If we believe his declaration—as sometimes we must—and punish nonetheless, desert seems to attach to the conduct and not to the person, while the punishment attaches exclusively to the person, as gratuitous pain.[22]

Perhaps when we speak about self-determined conduct we really mean not a determination *by* the self but a determination *of* the self, of which the conduct is evidence: something like, "That being the person he has determined himself to be, then this, which is the due of such a person, is what he deserves." That has a neat aspect, a person's desert attaching uniquely to him because he has determined himself to be that person. But it seems rather remote and abstract, as if desert attached to a self that we never quite encounter and not to the flesh and blood person who is actually punished. One may amplify the argument by a reference to the person's character (of which the conduct is evidence) as the basis of punishment, rather than an abstract self.[23] But that seems to have the matter backwards from the point of view of desert. On that basis, if a bad character refers to anything other than regular bad conduct (even to a disposition to engage in bad conduct), surely the person is less deserving of punishment when he behaves badly, since he would have had to work harder to behave well than someone who has a good character. The suggestion that there is greater joy in heaven from one sinner saved than from all the angels seems a bit unfair to those who have no impulse to sin.

If the willingness to excuse conduct in certain circumstances but not others betokens an inconsistency in the abstract idea of desert, excuses also indicate a good deal about how attributions of desert are made concretely. We seem generally to start with a model of responsible action defined not by the nature of the act but by reference to the notion of a person, an abstraction loosely associated with an adult human being identified as such by physical characteristics alone. In the absence of special excusing circumstances, that model is presumed to be applicable, and the attribution is taken for granted. Although the nature of the act is not conclusive either way, conduct outside a range of normal behavior may prompt an inquiry to see whether there are circumstances of excuse or mitigation. The "range of normal behavior" refers not only to human behavior in general but also to the particular person, so that if someone behaves "out of character," we look for an explanation. There does not seem to be any general principle that determines definitively what factors count as a sufficient explanation to displace responsibility; often,

---

22. That attachment seems to be true even though personal identity is continuous over time. What is the connection between this person's conduct in the past and his punishment now, if the conduct left him unchanged? The short response is that the question misunderstands the notion of desert from the start and proceeds from a consequentialist point of view. But the question remains: What then is desert, which makes consequences beside the point?

23. *Cf.* D. HUME, ENQUIRIES CONCERNING THE HUMAN UNDERSTANDING AND CONCERNING THE PRINCIPLES OF MORALS 98-99 (L.A. Selby-Bigge 3d ed. 1975) (posthumous ed. 1777).

the degree of abnormality of the conduct, inconclusive by itself, seems relevant to the conclusion. In the end, the only way to demonstrate that an attribution of desert or a failure to attribute desert is mistaken is by a comparison with other agreed cases. If that leaves some cases in doubt, it is enough for most. Since we know, without benefit of explanation, that persons sometimes are responsible and sometimes not, the lack of a general explanatory theory does not invalidate our conclusions.[24] One may add that, despite the importance that we may attach privately to judgments about desert, they commonly have little "official" impact. If we disagree, each of us is able to give effect to his own judgment without disabling others from giving effect to theirs.

The fact that we do make concrete attributions of responsibility and desert in this way, as an ordinary aspect of our experience that seems to flow directly from our recognition of other persons, has led some philosophers to deny that there is any abstract problem. When we speak of a person's desert, they urge, we do not mean to imply anything about the ultimate desert of the person to be the person she is—whatever that might mean. We mean only that this person—as she is now—has done well or ill. We identify her as an actor and express our approval or disapproval of the act, nothing more. In Professor Nozick's apt phrase, desert does not have to go "*all the way down*."[25] If *all* that a person is had to be deserved in order for her to deserve at all, there could be no person as the subject of desert. The effort to apprehend an autonomous self in isolation from a person's characteristics and life history is misconceived from the start.

Professor Strawson has made a more elaborate argument to the same general effect. There is, he says, no contradiction between the perception of ourselves as autonomous and deserving (the "participant" standpoint) and the perception of ourselves as constituted by characteristics and history nonautonomously acquired (the "objective" standpoint):

> [T]he appearance of contradiction arises only if we assume the existence of some metaphysically absolute standpoint from which we can judge between the two standpoints I have been contrasting. But there is no such superior standpoint—or none that we know of; it is the idea of such a standpoint that is the illusion. Once that illusion is abandoned, the appearance of contradiction is dispelled. We can recognize, in our conception of the real, a reasonable relativity to standpoints that we do know and can occupy. Relative to the standpoint which we normally occupy as social beings, prone to moral and personal reactive attitudes, human actions, or some of them, are morally toned and propertied in the diverse ways signified in our rich vocabulary of moral appraisal. Relative to the detached naturalistic standpoint which we can sometimes occupy, they have no properties but those which can be described in the

24. Immediately above, I suggested that responsibility is associated with the idea of a person, whereas here I observe that persons are responsible "sometimes." It seems preferable to accept the ambiguity of ordinary speech, which will, I think, mislead no one here, rather than to wrestle with ways to avoid it.

25. R. NOZICK, ANARCHY, STATE, AND UTOPIA 225 (1974).

> vocabularies of naturalistic analysis and explanation (including, of course, psychological analysis and explanation).[26]

That is not an evasion of the problem, Strawson says, because the duality of the human condition in this respect is simply a matter of fact. Sometimes we see one image and sometimes another; but our vision is not defective, nor can we even say what it would be like to bring the two images into single focus at the same time. Our experience of ourselves as persons in the natural world starts from the dual points of view, which are not subject to correction.

Strawson's account may alleviate our perplexity because it appears to separate the abstract problem of desert from questions about individual desert in concrete circumstances. As for the former, as he says, we cannot even describe what we want. As for the latter, we ordinarily know unhesitatingly which of the alternative points of view to adopt. Even to say that we "adopt" a point of view is too much; rather, we simply perceive from one point of view or the other.

The separation between the abstract problem and concrete instances cannot always be maintained as Strawson proposes, however. When an attribution of desert is challenged on the kind of grounds that, if accepted, constitute an excuse, the abstract issue is made concrete by evidence that supports the "objective" standpoint. Not every such explanation will be accepted; the very core of Strawson's argument about dual standpoints is that not every such explanation can be accepted, although in principle one might be offered in every case. If we insist on the attribution, despite the actual or theoretical availability of an explanation from the other standpoint, we have to provide an answer to the protest, "I don't deserve this." Similarly, if we reject an attribution of desert, we have to be able to withstand the challenge, "Why not?" Even if we are not able to say exactly what sort of answer would be satisfactory, the question that troubles us is not one that we decide to ask, and I do not see how we can decide not to ask it.[27] Strawson seems to dismiss

26. P.F. STRAWSON, SKEPTICISM AND NATURALISM: SOME VARIETIES 38 (1985). *See* Strawson, *Freedom and Resentment,* 48 PROC. BRIT. ACAD. 187 (1962), *reprinted in* P.F. STRAWSON, FREEDOM AND RESENTMENT 1-25 (1974).

27. In a recent insightful study of the doctrines of excuse in the criminal law, Michael Moore has argued persuasively that the basis of excuse cannot be simply that a causal explanation has been found for the conduct in question. If that were the basis of excuse, all our conduct would in principle be excusable and individual responsibility would be eliminated altogether. Moore, *Causation and the Excuses,* 73 CALIF. L. REV. 1091 (1985). On the contrary, he argues, "it is perfectly compatible to think both that persons are autonomous and that everything they do is caused by some set of factors external to their will." *Id.* at 1132. Like Strawson, Moore points to the indubitable reality that human beings are responsible over much of their lives. He suggests that our imprecise, partial, or occasional moral attitudes that express sympathy and understanding for a wrongdoer who has had an "unfortunate" past are, in the context of our total moral experience, misconceived, except in the specific areas in which an excuse is recognized. Finally, he thinks it is possible to unify the discrete excuses in a theory about the exercise of "practical reasoning capacities." *Id.* at 1148. Excuses are recognized, he says, when practical reasoning capacities are impaired.

Moore and I are in considerable agreement. We agree entirely about the basic point that a causal explanation cannot ipso facto eliminate responsibility. We agree that our experience of ourselves and others conclusively contradicts any such simple dichotomy. We disagree, however, about what to do next. For it is not only our moral experience that has to be rendered plausible and coherent. Pervasively throughout other areas of our experience a causal explanation *does* count as sufficient.

that whole aspect of the matter with the observation that "human actions, *or some of them*" are fit for moral appraisal.

III

CRIMINAL RESPONSIBILITY

Criminal law is the most explicit and formal communal application of what Strawson calls the participant standpoint. When the community declares that someone is guilty of a crime, it affirms his responsibility and gives it consequences. For the most part, as one would expect, the law follows our general understanding. The ordinary assumption, expressed indirectly by the requirement of mens rea, is that a person is responsible for his acts. Although they are not entirely congruent, most of the grounds of excuse in everyday life also constitute defenses against an accusation of crime.[28]

The legal doctrines that define a specific defense of this kind resolve the general issue of responsibility by prescribing a line of separation between the participant and objective standpoints. So long as the doctrines themselves are accepted on their own terms, their application appears to be a matter of fact, which, however difficult or complex, is to be determined like other factual issues. If the doctrines are called in question, the general issue emerges. Unlike challenges to other principles of law, the doctrinal questions about responsibility seem themselves to be questions of fact, albeit of a different order from questions about their application. If we consider whether the defense of insanity or intoxication or duress ought to be modified in some way, the question that apparently needs to be answered is not whether a person in such circumstances *ought* to be (regarded as) responsible but whether he *is* responsible, whether we *can* properly regard him as responsible. Or if, speaking more carefully, we say that the question before us is whether the person ought to be held criminally responsible, the answer to the question seems to depend unequivocally on the question whether he is in fact responsible.[29]

The price of validating our moral experience in the manner that Moore chooses is, at least without further explanation, a deep rupture in the framework of our general experience of the world. (I am doubtful that he can unify our excuses by reference only to practical reasoning capacities. The apparent ground of unification, surely, is that some other, presumably causal, process has taken over and wiped out those capacities.)

Moore focuses principally on responsibility; I suspect that he would find it less easy summarily to dismiss the causal assault if he had discussed desert more explicitly. Yet responsibility and desert, as I believe he agrees, are indissolubly linked. In the end, Moore and I agree that what is at stake, stated most generally, is a fundamental difference between persons and things. The issue between us is how far to (try to) go to unpack that difference and how to go about it.

28. Not all of the grounds of exculpation that the criminal law denominates as "excuses" are excuses in the ordinary sense. *See supra* note 15. *See generally* Fletcher, *supra* note 15; Greenawalt, *supra* note 15.

29. Occasionally, the two questions appear to be separated not only formally but substantively. The verdict of "guilty but insane" suggests such a separation. *See generally* McGraw, Farthing-Capowich & Keilitz, *The "Guilty But Mentally Ill" Plea and Verdict: Current State of the Knowledge*, 30 VILL. L. REV. 117 (1985); Note, *The Guilty But Mentally Ill Verdict and Due Process*, 92 YALE L.J. 475 (1983). If the questions were truly regarded as separate, the appropriate verdict would be "guilty and insane." Similarly, in some discussions of duress and voluntary intoxication, those who would restrict the

In his famous *Durham* opinion, Judge Bazelon, writing about the insanity defense, said:

> The legal and moral traditions of the western world require that those who, of their own free will and with evil intent (sometimes called *mens rea*), commit acts which violate the law, shall be criminally responsible for those acts. Our traditions also require that where such acts stem from and are the product of a mental disease or defect as those terms are used herein, moral blame shall not attach, and hence there will not be criminal responsibility.[30]

The *Durham* test of insanity finally failed because the gradations of mental competence could not be reduced to two mutually exclusive descriptive categories along the lines that the test indicated. Subsequent cases showed that one might conclude that an act was the product of a mental disease or defect and nevertheless conclude that the person was not altogether without responsibility. But so far as the operation of the criminal law is concerned, Judge Bazelon was correct. There is no room for two standpoints. If it is established that the defendant's act is the product of causes beyond his control, criminal responsibility is removed.[31]

The difficulty of this "either-or" framing of the general issue was exposed dramatically in *Powell v. Texas*,[32] in which the defendant sought to challenge the claim that he was responsible directly, without reference to a specific legal doctrine of excuse. He was charged with being drunk in a public place and defended on the ground that he was a chronic alcoholic. In an opinion for four Justices of the Supreme Court, Justice Marshall upheld the trial court's ruling that chronic alcoholism was not a defense. Distinguishing the earlier *Robinson* case,[33] in which the Court had invalidated a conviction for being a narcotics addict, Justice Marshall said:

> [T]he entire thrust of *Robinson*'s interpretation of the Cruel and Unusual Punishment Clause is that criminal penalties may be inflicted only if the accused has committed some act, has engaged in some behavior, which society has an interest in preventing, or perhaps in historical common law terms, has committed some *actus reus*. It thus does not deal with the question of whether certain conduct cannot constitutionally be punished because it is, in some sense, "involuntary" or "occasioned by a compulsion."[34]

---

defense offer arguments that seem to suggest that doing so will have the effect of increasing obedience to the law without any exercise of responsibility by the person in question. A strictly behaviorist analysis of human action allows that approach.

30. Durham v. United States, 214 F.2d 862, 876 (D.C. Cir. 1954) (footnote omitted), *overruled*, United States v. Brawner, 471 F.2d 969 (D.C. Cir. 1972).

31. In practice, the criminal law hedges its answer to the factual question in much the way that we do in our ordinary, unofficial moral assessments. Not only the defense of "diminished responsibility," which is recognized in some jurisdictions, but also various doctrines of mitigation and gradation of offenses as well as the exercise of discretion in sentencing may allow a considerable measure of shading, which no doubt sometimes reflects uncertainty whether the defendant was responsible at all rather than a clear conclusion that he was "less" or "partially" responsible. Nevertheless, insofar as the defendant is found guilty, the question whether he was responsible for his conduct must have been answered in the affirmative.

32. 392 U.S. 514 (1968).

33. Robinson v. California, 370 U.S. 660 (1962).

34. 392 U.S. at 533.

In a dissenting opinion joined by three other Justices, Justice Fortas stated his disagreement bluntly: "Criminal penalties may not be inflicted upon a person for being in a condition he is powerless to change."[35] Justice White, who voted to uphold the conviction on other grounds, sided with the dissent on the main issue.[36] He said, even more plainly than Justice Fortas, that if one cannot be punished for a condition, neither can he be punished for conduct that follows inescapably from the condition; if Justice Marshall's reference to an "actus reus" meant otherwise, he was wrong.

According to the general principles of criminal law, if the result in *Powell* is acceptable at all, it is because the evidence does not entirely convince us that the defendant "couldn't help it." Justice Marshall alludes to such doubt, without attempting to explain or justify it, in the parenthetical phrase, "in some sense." In effect, he straddles the question whether Powell's defense is inadequate factually or legally.[37] But unless Justice Marshall would say that, constitutionally at least, responsibility is unnecessary for criminal responsibility, or guilt, if the defense is not inadequate factually, then it is incomprehensible how it can be inadequate legally. Justice Black wrote a separate opinion, in which he skirted the issue of responsibility in a different way. He defended Powell's conviction on utilitarian grounds, and added, not incidentally, that the jailing of alcoholics might be regarded as a form of therapy (!) and that in any case there seemed to be no practical alternative.[38]

The courts have reached results similar to those in *Powell* in a number of other cases in which the defendant asserted without benefit of an established defense that he was powerless to avoid committing the criminal act.[39] It is evident that the judges are aware of the abstract issue at stake and troubled by the prospect that the foundations of the criminal law might be undermined by the relentless advance of a method of inquiry—Strawson's objective standpoint—that dismisses the explanatory value of individual free will and responsibility from the start. The issue is present, albeit less vividly, in all the cases in which the defendant relies on a defense that constitutes an excuse from responsibility. In all of them, one may ask on what basis, consistently with other cases, the law adopts one standpoint or the other. If we care to stalk it, the issue lurks in every case whatsoever.[40] Its ubiquity emerges briefly and dramatically into the open when the law assesses criminal responsibility according to circumstances that are unmistakably beyond the actor's control.

35. *Id.* at 567 (Fortas, J., dissenting).

36. *Id.* at 548 (White, J., concurring).

37. Elsewhere in his opinion, Justice Marshall gives a general basis for doubting the conclusion that Powell's act was not voluntary, but he does not make clear whether the doubt is factual or legal. *Id.* at 521-26.

38. *Id.* at 537-40 (Black, J., concurring).

39. *E.g.*, United States v. Davis, 772 F.2d 1339 (7th Cir. 1985) (compulsive gambling); United States v. Gould, 741 F.2d 45 (4th Cir. 1984) (same); United States v. Torniero, 735 F.2d 725 (2d Cir. 1984) (same), *cert. denied*, 469 U.S. 1110 (1985); United States v. Lyons, 731 F.2d 243 (5th Cir.) (en banc) (narcotics addiction), *cert. denied*, 469 U.S. 930 (1984); United States v. Moore, 486 F.2d 1139 (D.C. Cir.) (same), *cert. denied*, 414 U.S. 980 (1973).

40. *See generally* Kelman, *Interpretive Construction in the Substantive Criminal Law*, 33 STAN. L. REV. 591 (1981).

1. *Felony Murder (and Negligent Homicide and Attempts).* The felony murder doctrine has a long history in English and American common law and is retained in most recent codifications.[41] It provides, with qualifications that need not be considered here, that if a person is killed or dies in consequence of the commission of a felony, the felon is criminally liable not only for the felony but also for the death, which is treated as murder.[42] According to the traditional doctrine, the death constitutes murder no less even though the felon took steps to avoid harm to anyone and was altogether unaware of (and incapable of avoiding) the danger.

The short way to explain this peculiar doctrine is similar to H.L.A. Hart's response to what he called the "definitional stop" in discussions about punishment.[43] If all that troubles us is that the death is called "murder," call it something else to distinguish it from an intentional killing; there is no reason to make so much of a mere lack of linguistic invention. But even if the doctrine were recast as a heightened penalty for the felony itself if someone is killed, the crucial problem of fortuity remains. Why ought we punish for an accident? The troublesome feature about felony murder is not just that the death increases the felon's punishment but that the death is attributed to him at all and qualifies his conduct differently from that of other felons committing the same act.

The question may be asked from any perspective.[44] From the point of view of retributivists, why ought the felon be punished for a consequence that he did not intend and was not reasonably foreseeable—for what, speaking plainly, he did not do.[45] Utilitarians point out that one can scarcely be dissuaded or deterred from doing what one has no intention or expectation of doing in the first place. Other utilitarian justifications have been suggested; but they fare no better. The argument that an occasional conviction of murder will deter commission of the underlying felony is met by the response that we could do as much, more efficiently, by convicting every tenth felon of

---

41. The doctrine was abolished in England in 1957, Homicide Act of 1957, 5 & 6 Eliz. 2, ch. 11, § 1, and has been abolished in a few states. The current state of American law is reviewed in People v. Aaron, 409 Mich. 672, 299 N.W.2d 304 (1980), in which the Supreme Court of Michigan abrogated the doctrine judicially. *See generally* Crump & Crump, *In Defense of the Felony Murder Doctrine*, 8 HARV. J. L. & PUB. POL'Y 359 (1985).

42. The case is more complicated but the principle is the same if more than one person engages in the commission of the felony. If the death is not attributable to one felon in particular (for example, the victim of the felony dies of a heart attack later), all the felons are liable alike. If the death is accidental but caused by the action of one felon, accessorial liability makes the act of one the act of all and, once again, all are liable. *See, e.g.*, People v. Stamp, 2 Cal. App. 3d 203, 82 Cal. Rptr. 598 (1969), *cert. denied*, 400 U.S. 819 (1970) (heart attack); State v. Best, 44 Wyo. 383, 388-89, 12 P.2d 1110, 1111 (1932) (accidental killing by one felon).

43. H.L.A. HART, *Prolegomenon to the Principles of Punishment*, in PUNISHMENT AND RESPONSIBILITY 1-5 (1968).

44. For an extensive discussion of supposed retributive and utilitarian justifications of result-based punishments generally, see Schulhofer, *supra* note 8.

45. In Enmund v. Florida, 458 U.S. 782 (1982) (5-4 decision), rejecting capital punishment for felony murder, the Supreme Court observed: "Putting Enmund to death to avenge two killings that he did not commit and had no intention of committing or causing does not measurably contribute to the retributive end of ensuring that the criminal gets his just deserts." *Id.* at 801.

murder (or sentencing him equivalently) whether or not anyone had died.[46] The argument that the felon is at least put out of the way for a time does not explain why this particular felon is put out of the way for a longer time than others who commit the same felony.

There are responses. Retributionists point to the commission of the felony, itself a serious intentional wrong. Utilitarians also point to the felony and its dangerousness, as evidenced by the actual result. But if it is the felony that attracts the punishment, for retributive or utilitarian reasons, why is it meted out some times and not others? The last stand of retributivists and utilitarians alike is an effort to eliminate the element of fortuity. Given the limitations of our capacity to observe and measure intention and dangerousness, it is reasonable for us to qualify the act itself by its consequences.[47] The death, then, is not the basis for greater punishment; rather it is good enough evidence for the true basis, which is the especially wrongful and dangerous conduct of the actor. That argument, however, is an attempt to swallow whole what is indigestible in small bites. Sometimes, it is true, the felon's claim that the death was an accident may be suspect or it may be traceable to the special dangerousness of his act.[48] But the felony murder doctrine is not cast in terms of those explanations, and it extends much further than they would allow.

The most interesting feature of the felony murder doctrine is its resilience. In two celebrated series of cases, the California courts and the Pennsylvania courts displayed how difficult it is to eliminate the doctrine even though its irrationality from the point of view of either retribution or utility is fully understood.[49] Most remarkable in this respect is the Model Penal Code's effort to have it both ways. The Code's provisions are the product of careful academic and professional discussion unpressured by the urgencies of an actual case. Having rejected the felony murder doctrine on the straightforward ground that "the criminal law does not predicate liability simply on conduct causing the death of another"[50] and "there is no basis in experience for thinking that homicides *which the evidence makes accidental* occur with disproportionate frequency in connection with specified felonies,"[51] the Code restores the doctrine as a presumption that a person who commits any

46. *See* O.W. HOLMES, THE COMMON LAW 48 (1963).

47. In some cases, in which the felon does not challenge his causal responsibility but only his intention, the felony murder doctrine may just lessen the prosecutor's burden of proof on a particularly difficult issue of fact. Even so, one may ask why the stringent requirements of proof are relaxed in this situation.

48. See Schulhofer, *supra* note 8, at 1588-99, for a careful discussion of the dangerousness argument.

49. The California cases are reviewed in Taylor v. Superior Court, 3 Cal. 3d 578, 477 P.2d 131, 91 Cal. Rptr. 275 (1970). For a more recent discussion of the California cases see People v. Dillon, 34 Cal. 3d 441, 668 P.2d 697, 194 Cal. Rptr. 390 (1983). For Pennsylvania, see Commonwealth *ex rel.* Smith v. Myers, 438 Pa. 218, 261 A.2d 550 (1970).

50. MODEL PENAL CODE § 210.2 commentary at 36 (1980).

51. *Id.* at 38.

of six designated felonies had the requisite state of mind for murder.[52] With disarming frankness, the commentary to this provision acknowledges that the results are likely to be about the same either way; what is important, it says, is that a conviction on the new basis "rests solidly on principle."[53] What principle?[54]

The puzzle of felony murder is duplicated at another level in cases of negligent homicide and what is called misdemeanor manslaughter. Once again, the actor is at fault and, but for his fault, the victim would not have died. The ordinary basis of responsibility, however, is missing; the death was neither intended nor so likely that it should be regarded as part of the act that was intended. Even so, the actor is held criminally liable not just for his negligence (or misdemeanor) but for the death, and sentenced accordingly. Another person, whose conduct is the same without resulting in a death, is punished much less or not at all.[55] The most common explanation for treating the two cases differently is that otherwise either the negligent conduct will go unpunished, because a jury will not convict if the penalty is severe, or the homicide will be punished too lightly. That, however, only deflects the puzzle from the law to the attitudes of the jurors or the public generally. Why, one wants to know, would jurors react that way? Why does the case that is characterized as homicide call for more severe punishment?[56]

The relevant fortuities are not only those of the surrounding circumstances; they include the unapparent and, from the point of view of the defendant, fortuitous condition of the victim himself. The well-known rule is that "you take the victim as you find him."[57] In one often cited case, a person who committed a minor assault was found guilty of manslaughter, because the person he struck was, unknown to the defendant, a hemophiliac and died from a small injury.[58] Almost certainly in such a case, one would say that the

52. MODEL PENAL CODE § 210.2(b) (1980). The six felonies are robbery, rape or deviate sexual intercourse by force or threat of force, arson, burglary, kidnapping, and felonious escape.

53. MODEL PENAL CODE § 210.2 commentary at 39 (1980).

54. The attraction of the felony murder doctrine for the Anglo-American (more recently the American) legal mind does not seem to be duplicated elsewhere. The commentary to the Model Penal Code states that "felony murder is unknown as such in continental Europe." MODEL PENAL CODE § 210.2 commentary at 40 (1980).

55. There is not a fixed rule that separates conduct from its consequences. If the consequences are substantial, they may contaminate a description of the conduct so that it does not appear to be the same as conduct that has different consequences. If Smith and Jones both drive through a red light and someone is killed as a consequence of Jones' act, we may say that Smith "drove carelessly" and that Jones "killed a pedestrian."

56. The argument about jury "nullification" is discussed at length and with great precision with respect to result-based crime generally in Schulhofer, *supra* note 8, at 1522-57. Schulhofer concludes that in only a small number of rather special cases the argument is "not demonstrably fallacious" but remains speculative even in them. *Id.* at 1557. *See* Crump & Crump, *supra* note 41, at 363-69. They argue that since the public perceives a crime from which death results accidentally as more serious than the same crime not attended by a death, various social purposes are served by treating the crime as qualitatively different.

57. *E.g.*, W. LAFAVE & A. SCOTT, CRIMINAL LAW 261 (1972). Perhaps accidentally, the rule makes the fortuity sound like something that the actor does.

58. State v. Frazier, 339 Mo. 966, 98 S.W.2d 707 (1936).

victim died of hemophilia, not that the actor had killed him; the law opts for the latter.[59]

Fortuity plays a role also in the law of criminal attempt. Some conduct punishable as an attempt falls short of the conduct that constitutes the completed crime. In such cases, an explanation for punishing the attempt less severely may perhaps be available from the retributive or the utilitarian perspective.[60] Explanation is ordinarily lacking if the conduct is complete and would constitute the crime but for a circumstance unknown to the actor.[61] The actor simply gets the benefit of the accident that makes his attempt not succeed.[62] As in the case of negligent homicide, one may deflect the puzzle from the law onto the jury; but the puzzle remains.

2. *Self-Defense against an "Innocent" Aggressor.* Straightforward cases of self-defense, in which a person kills someone who would otherwise have killed him, are explicable on retributive or utilitarian grounds. One who is unjustifiably threatened with death (or serious injury) does no wrong if he avoids the threat, even at the (unavoidable) cost of the life of whomever threatens him; the latter can avoid the harm to himself by ending his own wrongful conduct before it is too late.[63] Nor does any consideration of the general good dictate that the intended victim of an assault spare his assailant's life at the cost of his own.[64] The law satisfies also a general sense of appropriateness—what we like to call "poetic justice"—since the person at fault has borne the injury he had intended to inflict on someone else. We may acknowledge that aspect of the situation by describing his death as "really" self-inflicted, although, of course, it really is not.

---

59. In this, as in other similar situations, whether or not the act of the defendant is regarded as the cause of the death would ordinarily depend a good deal on one's assessment of the defendant's blameworthiness. *See supra* p. 56. The jury, of course, need not find the defendant guilty of homicide. It is instructed separately about each of the elements of the crime, including causation. Probably, separation of the issues in that way makes it easier to reach the ultimate conclusion of responsibility.

60. Among the possible explanations are (i) that the defendant might have desisted at the last minute, (ii) that the defendant's intention may not be certain until it is fully executed, and (iii) that the criminal law ought not be concerned with bad intention as such, which an uncompleted crime too much resembles. Usually such arguments are made to support postponement of liability for an attempt until the crime is all but complete and will be completed unless prevented. They may also serve, albeit rather weakly, to explain why punishment is less for the attempt than for the completed crime. The explanation will be more or less convincing according to how near to the completed crime the attempt comes.

61. The overworked problem of "impossibility" arises in some cases of this kind. For one effort to sort out the badly entangled strands of the problem, see L. WEINREB, CRIMINAL LAW 724-30 (4th ed. 1986).

62. The intended victim also gets the benefit of the accident, but there is no reason why the actor ought to be treated alike in that respect. He intended that the crime occur, and the victim, so to speak, intended that it not occur.

63. The doctrine of "withdrawal" allows a person who has effectively ended his own assault on another person to defend himself if the latter unnecessarily continues to assail him. *E.g.*, United States v. Grover, 485 F.2d 1039 (D.C. Cir. 1973).

64. That is true at least if we know nothing more about the parties and the event than who assaulted whom. The circumstances and the issues that may be raised are a great deal more complex than I indicate here. As uncomplicated statements, these generalizations are, I think, acceptable.

Most cases in which the need to act in self-defense is only apparent fit the same pattern without too much trimming. The appearance of a need to use deadly force typically arises from an actual assault; the difference between appearance and reality is not that what looked like an assault was not one in fact but that the assailant was not threatening as great a harm as it appeared. Even though there has been an unnecessary death, the retributive and utilitarian considerations that apply in a case of actual self-defense apply here as well. There is no retributive basis for punishment of a person who has acted, according to the apparent circumstances, as the law authorizes him to act; from a moral point of view, his conduct is not distinguishable from that of someone who acts in actual self-defense. The calculation of utility may be more complex. It is possible that on balance lives would be saved if persons were required to confirm absolutely the need to use deadly force before they used it. But we have no access to evidence that would support such a conjecture; and without more evidence, it seems unlikely.[65] As between the conduct of the victim that creates the appearance of a need to use deadly force and the conduct of the actor who uses it, there is not much to choose one way or the other as the cause of the homicide. If there is not so strong a sense of poetic justice, one may still regard the victim's death as, in some sense, self-inflicted.[66]

The cases of defensive homicide that most trouble the theories of criminal law are those in which the conduct of the person who is killed, insofar as it constitutes a threat, is not regarded as self-determined, because he is unaware and has no reason to be aware that his conduct endangers someone else or because he is acting to save his own life in circumstances for which he has no responsibility. Although actual cases are few, the situation may not be as unlikely as one supposes. It encompasses not only the law teacher's corny case of the birdwatcher threatened by a near-sighted hunter,[67] but any situation in which there is a means of escape for only one person from a deadly peril that threatens two: a supply of food that will sustain one but not two stranded hikers; a life raft that will support one but not two persons overboard, and so forth.[68]

65. The law requires that the appearance of necessity be enough to convince a reasonable person. Someone who unreasonably believes that he is threatened by another person and responds with deadly force is guilty of homicide.

66. With some imagination, one can posit a case in which the conduct that creates an apparent need for someone to act in self-defense is entirely innocent; the person has no reason to suppose that his conduct appears to someone else to threaten his life. Such a case of an "innocent apparent aggressor" would be assimilated to the case of an innocent actual aggressor, discussed below, especially the *faute de mieux* case in which there is no reason to label one party or the other the aggressor at all, except that the (innocent) conduct of one threatens the life of the other (who is also innocent). In such a case, there is no question of poetic justice. One may want to add that there is no question of justice of any kind.

67. *See* L. WEINREB, *supra* note 61, at 226.

68. The category might be extended to cases involving more than two persons, of whom fewer than all can be saved. The famous case of United States v. Holmes, 26 F. Cas. 360 (C.C.E.D.Pa. 1842) (No. 15,383) is an example. Such cases are usually thought to raise special questions of process—drawing lots and so forth—that, interestingly, are not much discussed even hypothetically if only two persons are involved and the issue is simply "him or me."

I am aware of no rule of law that resolves such cases clearly. The doctrine of self-defense applies to defensive acts against a person who unjustifiably threatens the actor. The doctrine of necessity refers to avoidance of a harm greater than that caused by one's conduct, which perhaps applies when more lives are saved than taken but certainly does not apply to a choice of one's own life over that of another person.[69] Neither the retributive nor the utilitarian argument dictates an outcome. The situation is described abstractly without reference to fault of either person; and, even if we admire an attitude of self-sacrifice, we suppose that we cannot and in any event ought not in general deter persons from competing for self-preservation.[70]

One might expect, therefore, that the criminal law is simply silent. Perhaps in actual practice it usually is silent; such cases when they arise are bound to be extraordinary and likely to call for resort to the informal processes of the law, like an exercise of prosecutorial discretion. The general doctrinal position of the law is, I think, more complicated. So far as one can discern any rules, the law is that a person can act to preserve himself, but only without aggression against another. That sounds correct; it is consistent with the doctrine of self-defense, which excuses the victim of aggression who responds with defensive force. What counts as aggression when two persons are threatened by the same peril and only one can escape is, however, far from clear.

The survival of each person being a barrier to the survival of the other, one might regard the legal principle allowing the use of deadly force in necessary self-defense as available to both. I am fairly confident that the law would resolve the problem by concluding that if either person acts in a way that would be criminal in ordinary circumstances, his act will constitute him the aggressor and determine the issue of self-defense and, ultimately, homicide. While both are in the water, each may swim as fast as he can; but if the slower swimmer tries to impede the other by any kind of physical assault he is an "aggressor," against whom the other person can use whatever force is necessary to defend himself. The raft supporting only one person, whoever reaches it first acts defensively against the "aggression" of another person who tries to board it. The result is clearer if one supposes that the person on the raft was on it from the moment the ship went down and that the other person swims up some hours later.[71] The same results in principle would, I

69. *E.g.*, MODEL PENAL CODE § 3.02 (1985), which provides in part: "(1) Conduct which the actor believes to be necessary to avoid a harm or evil to himself or to another is justifiable, provided that: (a) the harm or evil sought to be avoided by such conduct is greater than that sought to be prevented by the law defining the offense charged . . . ."

70. One might want to say that utilitarianism dictates an outcome in principle and that only a contingent factor, our inability or failure to gather enough information, leaves the outcome in doubt. Any such principle would most likely be so abstract and the facts required for its application so many and so inaccessible that it would not be applicable at all as a practical matter. For reasons suggested at the beginning of this article and discussed more fully below, I believe that the excuse "not enough facts" is an evasion of the deficiency of utilitarianism generally.

71. Or suppose that while the ship is going down one person discovers that his life vest is defective and grabs the vest of another person just as the latter is about to put it on. Even though the

think, be reached in other kinds of situation involving a joint peril. If two hikers had enough food for only one to survive, the person carrying the food would prevail, even though their division of responsibilities had been made without any view to their current situation.[72] In the birdwatcher/hunter situation, where one person's act unknown to him threatens the life of another person, the result would also turn, I think, on a small fault. If either of the two were a trespasser, for example, bizarre as it sounds, I believe that that would be decisive. If neither were at fault at all, the one whose act threatened to kill would, *faute de mieux*, be labeled the aggressor so that the other would be allowed to use deadly force in self-defense.

If my reading of the law in such cases is correct, the outcomes bear considerable resemblance to felony murder. In both kinds of situation, the act to which liability for homicide attaches seems unable to bear so much weight, because the death was unintended and unforeseen or because the intention to kill was incidental to the imposed necessity to save oneself. The felon chooses "freely" to commit the felony, whereas the person in the water is "forced" to choose. On that basis, most people would probably regard the latter as less culpable. So far as the death is concerned, however, the felon did not choose to kill anyone at all, whereas the person in the water, forced or not, did choose to save his life by taking the life of another innocent person. The comparative moral judgment is not so clear.

Various analyses of the cases involving a mutual peril have been suggested. The critical element, however, which they do not address, is that the fault that makes a person an aggressor is swamped by the necessity that causes him to act as he does. But for the necessity, he would not have committed the act. The necessity unquestionably excuses the act itself. Without such an act, the person would be allowed to save himself, even if a consequence of doing so were the death of another person. Yet when the act and the death are connected, the fault is reinstated not with respect to the act but with respect to the homicide. The short way through that labyrinth is usually simply that a person is allowed to save his own life but not by taking

---

distribution of the defective vest was entirely a matter of chance, the invasion of the latter person's brief possession would make the former person the aggressor.

72. A friend who works in the field of criminal law has expressed some doubt. Suppose that Smith and Jones are hiking. As they agreed when they planned the trip, Smith bought and is carrying the food. Jones paid for the camping permit and is carrying the tent. They become lost, have small hope of being discovered or finding their way out for a long time (an avalanche), and there is food in Smith's pack sufficient for the survival of only one. If Smith, using only the force necessary to defend himself while fending off Jones' attempt to take the food, kills Jones and eats the food, is he (rescued the next day in time for both to have been saved, the usual surprise) guilty of homicide? Surely not. If Jones overcomes Smith's resistance and takes the food, is he guilty of homicide if Smith dies and it is proved that he would have survived if he had had the food? I think so. The situations are, at any rate, perceptibly distinct. Perhaps it is Jones' aggressive act, rather than Smith's possession of the food that makes the difference. If so, what about Smith's calmly sitting down to (his) dinner, while Jones sits on his haunches and watches? If the person carrying the food is not the owner, or the sole owner, the situation is more complicated; so is the law of theft. To simplify the problem (by complicating the facts) suppose that Smith and Jones, who are strangers to one another, are sole survivors of an airplane crash on a mountain. Before the crash, Smith stuffed the food on his luncheon tray into his pockets.

the life of someone else. Stated that simply, however, the argument proves too much or too little; it is only the characterization of an act as "aggression" that allows us to distinguish self-defense from what is equally life-saving but not self-defense. That characterization turns on a "fault" that, in the circumstances, would not be a fault at all but for the death.

3. *Fault of the Victim.* The doctrine of provocation, by which an intentional killing that would otherwise be murder is "reduced" to voluntary manslaughter, is usually understood as a concession to human frailty: in extreme circumstances, a person may be so provoked that even homicide is, to some degree, comprehensible. Having been provoked, he is less at fault (according to the retributivist) or he was less subject to the deterrent effect of the law (according to the utilitarian). Although the doctrine is not always expressly so limited, it is clear that what is principally included are provocations by the victim of the homicide. Cases are extremely rare in which the source of the provocation is someone or something else.[73] The Model Penal Code broadens the circumstances of mitigation to include any "extreme mental or emotional disturbance for which there is reasonable explanation or excuse."[74] Even under that extended formulation, it is doubtful that provocation by a third person will often be accepted, at least if the victim and the third person are not related. Paradigmatically and almost always in practice, therefore, the doctrine of provocation gives some recognition to the victim's own fault as a factor mitigating the liability of the actor. One might just say that the victim "asked for it" and let it go at that. But that is again a reference to poetic justice and has nothing to do with the purposes of criminal law. From both the retributive and utilitarian perspectives, the source of the provocation by itself should make no difference.

The doctrine—now under attack—that one who goes to the aid of someone engaged in combat with another person acts "at his peril" invites a similar interpretation.[75] From the retributive point of view, a reasonable mistake about whom to aid ought not affect the qualification of one's act. Someone who mistakenly but reasonably identifies the wrong person as the victim of the combat and goes to his aid is not at fault; his mistake may be occasion for regret, but strictly morally, his conduct is as commendable as if he had made no mistake. Utilitarian arguments fare no better. The peril of being mistaken may make people less willing to meddle without adequate information; or it may simply make them less willing to intervene at all, even when there is no mistake and intervention would be desirable. It is impossible to say which; but a requirement that a mistake be reasonable rather than that there be no mistake seems likely to come nearer to our general objectives.

---

73. For an example, in which the court concluded, as I suggest here, that the doctrine of provocation does not apply unless the victim is the source of the provocation, see People v. Spurlin, 156 Cal. App. 3d 119, 202 Cal. Rptr. 663 (4th Dist. 1984).

74. MODEL PENAL CODE § 210.3(1)(b) (1985).

75. *See* W. LAFAVE & A. SCOTT, *supra* note 57, at 397-99.

The peril rule, however, satisfies in a peculiar way an aspect of responsibility or desert that the excuse of reasonable mistake does not. If the intervenor unavoidably uses deadly force against an aggressor to save the life of the latter's intended victim, the aggressor's death can without much strain be described as caused by his own self-determined conduct and attributed to his own fault, as in a case of self-defense. If the intervenor goes to the aid of the aggressor and kills the intended victim, an innocent person is dead, and the aggressor's fault and the death are clearly separate. Unless the aggressor invited the intervention, it is too much to hold him responsible for the intervenor's self-determined mistaken act, however reasonable it may have been. The doctrine that an intervenor acts at his peril avoids an outcome that would force us to treat the death as an accident, despite the entire innocence of the victim, the fault of the aggressor, and the error of the intervenor. By allowing us to fix responsibility on a human actor, it brings the situation closer in one important respect to cases of self-defense, even though apparent necessity is recognized in the latter and not the former.

The doctrines discussed on the preceding pages are not all of a piece. There are many differences among them; according to the usual distinctions of the criminal law, they do not readily compose a coherent category. Some, like felony murder and negligent homicide, attempts, and provocation, have familiar and recurrent applications in the mine run of criminal cases. Occasions for application of others, notably the innocent aggressor, are extremely rare. Nor are the doctrines separately or collectively an invariable or inextricable part of the criminal law. All are the subject of criticism and, to one degree or another, have been questioned, limited, or rejected in some jurisdictions. Nevertheless, they are illustrative of a tendency of the law sometimes to give the consequences of conduct significance for criminal responsibility that they would not be given by reflective normative judgment. As a result, the defendant's punishment, in comparison with that of other defendants, may be greater or less, without justification according to either retributive or utilitarian theories of punishment. For the most part, these types of cases are treated as idiosyncratic and unrelated departures from a largely consistent theoretical ideal. From a sufficient distance, however, they display a common pattern. The tendency that they illustrate appears most strongly when (1) there is a very substantial harm, (2) the harm would not have occurred but for the specific, identifiable fault of a specific person,[76] and (3) no other person is manifestly so much in control of the event that his conduct is regarded as the cause of the harm.[77] The doctrines are,

76. The third-party defense case seems to fit this description least well because the fault in question is not a moral failing in any respect but only a (reasonable) mistake; that case is also, however, the one in which the actor's causal responsibility for the death is most unequivocal.

77. See, for example, cases in which a policeman kills an innocent person while trying to prevent commission of a felony. His involvement is regarded as highly relevant to the felon's liability, even though it is a consequence of the felon's conduct. *Compare* Commonwealth *ex rel.* Smith v. Myers, 438 Pa. 218, 261 A.2d 550 (1970) (liability rejected) *with* People v. Hickman, 12 Ill. App. 3d 412, 297 N.E.2d 582 (1973), *aff'd*, 59 Ill.2d 89, 319 N.E.2d 511 (1974), *cert. denied*, 421 U.S. 913 (1975)

furthermore, sufficiently resistant to change to suggest that, despite their factual variety, they may have a common source.

IV

THE NORMATIVE ONTOLOGICAL PERSPECTIVE

The criminal law's occasional, discordant emphasis on normatively separable faults, which is described in section three, is generally regarded as a mistake. The attraction of responsibility for a harm to a fault to which the harm is related only by "but-for" causation is understood to be a response, "human" but theoretically misconceived, to our grief and anger at the harm itself—an irrational "striking out" at someone without whose wrongful conduct the harm would not have occurred. When we are confronted by the death of an innocent person in the course of a felony, it is not surprising that the accurate statement, "If you hadn't committed the felony, she would still be alive," should become "You killed her," and finally, "You murderer!" Whatever fortuities were also necessary to the result are swept from view by the aspect of the occurrence for which responsibility is clear. Similarly, the survivor of a joint peril whose deliberate act was the cause alike of his survival and the non-survival of someone else bears the burden of the death. We may understand his situation and mitigate the crime. Just the same, he had no greater right to life than the person he "killed." The nonsurvivor was in the same peril, and, as between the two. . .. The doctrines about provocation and defense of a third person likewise are presumed to reflect a strongly felt "intuitive" response to the situation, rather than a reflective judgment.

Although the doctrines that support such results contradict our usual, well-settled understanding of the conditions in which responsibility and susceptibility to punishment attach, they are not, or not simply, a mistake. They reflect the deep ontological assumption that human experience is contained within, or composes, a normative order. That assumption appears on the surface in the cases that trouble us, because it is extended beyond its conventional limits; but it is just as essential to our resolution of untroubling cases and, except as a matter of convention, no better validated in the latter than in the former. Far from challenging the assumption, its untoward extension can be perceived as a deep, inexplicit reinforcement of it. In none of the cases is it exact to say that the assumption is correct or not correct except, once again, conventionally. It is a structural element of human experience as we know it.

(liability approved). Cases in which a felon is held vicariously liable for the act of a co-felon do not contradict the relevance of this factor. The former's liability is based on principles of vicarious liability that are independent of the considerations involved here. *See generally* Kadish, *Complicity, Cause and Blame: A Study in the Interpretation of Doctrine*, 73 CALIF. L. REV. 323 (1985). The provocation cases are perhaps contradictory; it depends on how strongly one construes "manifestly . . . in control." (Provocation, of course, is taken to induce a loss of control by the actor. But that is self-control, a somewhat different, although not unrelated, matter.) If one so regards those cases, this factor has to be regarded as relevant often but not always.

The heart of the matter is the problem about desert. It is not simply that we sometimes have a difficult time deciding whether to hold a person responsible or not. Nor is it, fully stated, that we know persons are (sometimes) free and responsible and we cannot account for their freedom consistently with their place in a determinate natural order.[78] Rather the problem concerns the conditions of freedom itself. Freedom without desert is a descriptive concept without normative significance. It is like the freedom of a plant after the trellis collapses or of a dog that gets out the gate. Both are free in a way they had not been before; but desert does not attach because we do not regard them as responsible for how the freedom is played out.[79] That by itself is not a difficulty; we need only affirm, as we do, that the exercise of normatively significant freedom gives rise to desert. Desert, however, seems to require that a person's acts be *both* free *and* determinate. Unless they are free, the person cannot be said to be morally responsible, and desert is out of the question. By the same token, a person is not responsible for circumstances beyond his control—circumstances, that is, that are not the product of his freedom. But then, unless the conditions in which a person acts are fully determined according to his desert, they are arbitrary from a moral point of view; furthermore, unless such deserved conditions fully determine his action, an attribution of desert according to how he exercises his freedom also is morally arbitrary. If freedom requires desert, it seems to require that the exercise of freedom itself be determinate. But if desert requires freedom, that is a contradiction. Desert cannot depend on freedom and at the same time freedom depend on desert.

The contradiction is avoided if either dependence is rejected. The usual method of avoidance nowadays is to reject the dependence of freedom on desert. So, Nozick insists, desert does not have to go "all the way down." Strawson's resolution of the problem comes out in the same place for essentially the same reasons, as must any account that accepts the fundamental opposition between freedom and cause and the limitation of responsibility and desert to freedom. In the end, freedom is made independent of desert because desert is not—cannot be made—independent of freedom.

This account of freedom reflects how we ordinarily think about these matters. We do, as Nozick and Strawson say, affirm that a person deserves well or ill without insisting that he have deserved all the factors that might explain his conduct. We believe that a person may be free and responsible even though he does not deserve to be and to have all that he is and has. There is no basis for that account, however, except the very contradiction that

---

78. Strawson's statement of the problem as consisting of two incompatible standpoints frames it this way.

79. Compare the Epicurean doctrine that explained free will by a "swerve" or absolutely undetermined motion of atoms that are otherwise subject to strict causal laws. *See* A. LONG, HELLENISTIC PHILOSOPHY 56-61 (1974). Such a doctrine might contribute to a condition of *ataraxia*, or quietude, by eliminating indeterminacy. As an account of human freedom and responsibility, it is hopeless. The Greek word *tyche* referred to both chance and necessity.

it is offered to resolve: the fact that we do deserve even though many, and in principle all, of the constituents of our freedom are themselves ultimately determinate causally and (therefore) not according to desert. So far as the problem of desert itself is concerned, convention aside, it is just as convincing to affirm the opposite: since we do deserve and desert is not morally arbitrary, it does *not* depend on freedom. The determinate factors that compose our freedom, although beyond our control, are themselves deserved. Desert does go all the way down or, more comfortably perhaps, it is as if desert goes all the way down. Although the two solutions are precisely opposed, neither one has an advantage over the other; according to both, albeit from different perspectives, desert is morally arbitrary.

The current preference for the former solution reflects our concentration on desert (or justice) as a problem of ethics. The reality of freedom, arbitrary or not, is assumed; and desert is tied to it. Earlier, the problem was stated in ontological terms. The deservedness of our natural condition, determinate or not, was assumed; and freedom was tied to it. The idea of a normative order immanent in nature is built as deeply into the classical Greek conception of what there is as the idea of causation is built into ours.[80] More familiarly, normative natural order is the core of the Christian conception of divine Providence (or the Eternal Law, in the system of Thomas Aquinas) and, particularly, the conception of original sin.[81] One way or another, it is part of any philosophy that bases the meaning and significance of human existence on something other than what is imparted by human beings themselves. Considered abstractly, it seems to be not much more than a matter of philosophic currency and intellectual preference as well, of course, as deep convention whether one regards desert as arising out of conditions that are morally arbitrary or regards the natural order as morally significant. Both are indemonstrable, unanalyzable assumptions that rest finally on our recognition of human beings as morally responsible: persons rather than things.

The cases described in section three are troubling because criminal liability arises from a circumstance that ordinarily would be regarded as unrelated to the defendant's exercise of freedom. In cases of felony murder and fortuitous homicide generally, the felon's act is fully described—"used up"—without reference to the death, which was not forewarned in the circumstances at the time of the act. So far as his conduct is concerned, the death makes no difference. Therefore, it is argued, the death does not affect the felon's desert and ought not affect his punishment. As an event in the natural order, the death is not a fortuity. It is not a random occurrence that "just happened." On the contrary, the events leading to the death are determinate; and, in particular, the death would not have occurred but for the commission of the felony. That, however, gives no comfort so far as the

80. Among the concepts that gave expression to the idea are *moira*, *kosmos*, and *physis*, which we translate inadequately as, respectively, fate, cosmos or order, and nature.

81. The reference to Divine Providence explicitly removed the problem beyond the range of human understanding.

felon's liability is concerned. For, if the death is regarded in that way—Strawson's objective standpoint—freedom is excluded from consideration, and there is no question of responsibility or desert at all.

Even if, by a willing suspension of disbelief, we were to adopt the ontological approach to the problem of desert, we seem no nearer a solution. The idea of normative natural order does not mean that a person can be said to deserve anything at all; it does not mean that, willy-nilly, he deserves to be punished because someone has died in Casablanca.[82] In this case, the death is closer to home; the felony, which itself *is* an exercise in freedom, is discernibly causally related to the death. Even so, normative natural order refers to the dispensations of nature. It requires that individual desert be determinate and, therefore, not subject to determination by human dispensation. The judgment that the felon is guilty of murder and deserves to be punished as a murderer is pronounced not by nature but by us. Of course, we may *say* that the felon is a murderer: "You killed her. You murderer!" But can we believe it? Whatever speculative perspective one adopts, concretely the question is whether a person is morally accountable for an occurrence that he neither intended nor had any reason to anticipate. We do one way or another regard persons (with all their determinate attributes) as free and morally responsible. We do not regard them as responsible without limit. Why do we go beyond the ordinary limit here?

If desert is regarded ontologically, the cases that trouble us are distinctive not because their circumstances are especially compelling evidence of normative natural order but the opposite, because they call that assumption peculiarly into question. In a case of felony murder, the death of an innocent person would not have occurred but for commission of the felony. Although we are acquainted with natural fortune and misfortune of all kinds, here the intervention of what we think of as a humanly (that is, self-determined) wrongful act strains the assumption that the death is within a normative order at all; the explicit evidence of normative disorder is too great. By identifying the commission of the felony as the cause of the death and attributing the death to the felon, it is as if we exculpate nature (which is not without some responsibility).[83] But-for causation, which ordinarily is not enough for an attribution of responsibility, is enough in this case. Although from an ethical perspective, the result contradicts our understanding of desert and seems unjust, from the ontological perspective, punishment of the person who is responsible is restorative of normative order.[84]

---

82. At least not without some explanation. J.B. Priestley's play, *An Inspector Calls*, is along these lines. J.B. PRIESTLEY, SIX PLAYS 291 (1979).

83. Compare the observation of Joel Feinberg: "When something scandalous has occurred and it is clear that the wrongdoer must be one of a small number of suspects, then the state, by punishing one of these parties, thereby relieves the others of suspicion and informally absolves them of blame." J. FEINBERG, DOING AND DESERVING 105 (1970).

84. It may be helpful to consider the position of the doomed hero in Greek tragedy. Oedipus does everything in his power to avoid the oracle's prediction and fulfills it nevertheless. He and his children suffer beyond any possible personal desert, as we should regard it, because of the wrong of Laius, his father. The end of the tragedy is not a confirmation of the meaninglessness of human

A similar approach helps to explain the other puzzling doctrines. In cases of self-defense against an innocent aggressor, the critical circumstance that determines who is the survivor is a self-determined act of one of the two persons. Any outcome is affected both by the actions of the two persons and by "natural" circumstances: their resourcefulness, speed, strength, and so forth, as well as factors like the height of the waves, the temperature of the water, or whatever. The significance of describing a wrongful act as "aggression" is precisely that it identifies the act as an alteration of the outcome as it would have been determined by nature and defeats a reference to the normative order of nature itself (including the attributes of the persons) to account for the death. Nature being exculpated, holding the survivor liable follows. Similarly, to allow provocation from a source other than the victim to reduce an intentional killing from murder to voluntary manslaughter would appear to leave a portion of responsibility for the harm undistributed among the human actors; what is in question, however, is not a natural occurrence, but the self-determined, wrongful act of another human being. So also, if the victim of aggression is killed by the act of a third person, who mistakenly goes to the aid of the aggressor; unless the person who intervenes is liable, the occurrence of the harm as a consequence of his mistaken act is too strong evidence of normative *dis*order.

Although we think of desert as dependent on freedom, from the ontological perspective all that it requires is the causal connection itself; we need only say, as a descriptive matter, that the conduct in question caused, or was a cause of, the harm for which the person is held responsible. If liability follows without more, the result is not more fortuitous than the combination of personal factors that account for the conduct itself. (The victim of the felony had a bad heart; the felon had a bad upbringing.) Coming at the matter in this way, there is not a sharp break between the special, troubling cases and all the straightforward cases of criminal liability; if, as Nozick says, desert does not have to go all the way down, why should it have to go all the way out? The break that we perceive is one of convention, albeit deep convention, only. The criminal law departs from convention in order not to undermine the conventional basis of desert altogether, by calling into question whether a person can ever truly be said to have acted with freedom and responsibility despite the determinate conditions of his existence.

---

existence—that "chance is all in all," as Jocasta had said—but an affirmation that there is meaning and moral sufficiency. *See* SOPHOCLES, *Oedipus the King* (D. Grene trans.) in 2 THE COMPLETE GREEK TRAGEDIES: SOPHOCLES 9 (D. Grene and R. Lattimore, eds. 1959). For Jocasta's remark, see *id.* at 52, line 977.

Sometimes it is suggested that a requirement of culpability is justified on the utilitarian ground that it protects us against the fear and disturbance that would be aroused if we knew that we might be found guilty and punished for acts that we could not help but commit. *Cf.*, H.L.A. HART, *supra* note 2, at 46-47, 181-82; H. PACKER, *supra* note 2, at 64-65. That may be true, although I doubt that most people are concerned concretely about the kind of loss of control that is posited. The possibility of guilt without punishment might feed a more general fear of undeserved harm, no matter what the source. *See infra* note 85. From that larger perspective, the fixing of blame in these special cases is reassuring.

Assigning responsibility as it does in these cases, the criminal law remains close to our ordinary, unreflective judgments.[85] We do look upon the felon as "in some sense" responsible for his victim's death, whether or not it was an accident. We do tend to think of the person who provokes another person to a homicidal response as "in some sense" getting what he deserves or, as we say, his "just deserts." There is something that calls for requital if a person alters the "natural" odds in a struggle for survival with another person, even though no one deserves to have the natural odds in his favor, or if his mistaken intervention leaves the innocent victim of an act of aggression dead. The doctrines of the criminal law that give effect to these attitudes stand out not because their treatment of responsibility as such seems immediately and obviously defective but because it has consequences and calls for a justification we are unable to provide.

The disturbing feature of *Powell v. Texas* and other cases in which the defendant claims to be excused from criminal responsibility on the basis of an unrecognized etiological explanation for his conduct can be seen in a similar light. Probably it is easier to comprehend, if not agree with, the conclusion that Powell was responsible than the conclusion that a felon is responsible for a fortuitous death or that a person is culpable despite the necessity that obliges him to take away another person's means to safety. Powell's alcoholism is at least a condition of the person himself. We may be inclined to believe that he voluntarily became an alcoholic, which makes him deserving of something, even if not for the act of public drunkenness as such. We may, therefore, regard the conviction of Powell as problematic or a mistake, but comprehensible nonetheless; whereas the felon's conviction of murder looks like a mistake of another order and incomprehensible. From a nonarbitrary moral standpoint, however, Powell's alcoholism is not different from the circumstances surrounding the felony that produced the death. In both cases, it is simply something that happened.

The disagreement among the Justices had very little to do with how chronic alcoholics would actually be treated. As Justice Black's opinion indicated most clearly, as a practical matter there was little to distinguish Powell's conviction and punishment from a noncriminal disposition. The difference between the theoretical positions of the majority and the dissent is much greater. If Powell is deemed not responsible, we must either clearly identify the special excusing circumstances that take the case out of the realm of freedom or risk undermining desert in every case. For the general premise that conduct is subject to causal order applies universally; and if that is not a normative order in one case for reasons not specific to it, it need not be in any other. Powell's conviction avoids that general problem, but only by brushing aside strong evidence that he in particular really was not able to control his

85. There is abundant psychological evidence that people tend to see normative significance in natural occurrences. *See* M. LERNER, THE BELIEF IN A JUST WORLD (1980); Lerner & Miller, *Just World Research and the Attribution Process: Looking Back and Ahead*, 85 PSYCHOLOGICAL BULL. 1030 (1978). Both works contain extensive bibliographies.

behavior.[86] Approached in that way, Justice Marshall's statement that it is enough for criminal liability if a person has engaged in "some act . . . some behavior," even if it was "in some sense 'involuntary' " seems as much a recognition of the fundamental issue as an evasion of it.

V
CONCLUSION

From the foregoing, one may conclude that a satisfactory general theory of criminal responsibility is unattainable. Such a theory, unless it were just a summary description of specific doctrines without explaining them, would have to provide defensible general reasons for regarding some kinds of determinate conditions and circumstances as excluding freedom but not others. It would have to answer the question, "How far down is desert?" But there is in principle no answer. Even if we were able to develop statistical correlations between complex sets of personal characteristics and specific harmful conduct, the most we could achieve would be consistent application of predictions of relative dangerousness. If we were to base the availability of an excuse on such predictions, the lines that we drew would not demarcate a general theory of criminal responsibility; rather, they would indicate abandonment of the concept altogether.[87]

We are led back to the theories of punishment. As justifications for the practice of punishment, neither the retributive theories nor the utilitarian theories are satisfactory. Retribution fails from the utilitarian perspective because desert cannot be demonstrated and punishment for desert alone seems futile. Utilitarianism fails from the retributive perspective because desert cannot be dismissed and punishment for its utility alone seems unjust. The preceding discussion indicates that the source of the problem lies a step further back. Once it has been determined that punishment is deserved, no further justification for carrying out the punishment is necessary or appropriate. Punishment follows directly from desert because only if desert is fulfilled can we be regarded fully as persons—free, morally responsible, and deserving—at all. Our willingness to punish now as desert requires is not only a recognition of freedom; it is also a condition of desert, and therefore freedom, thereafter. Desert without punishment, or moral responsibility without desert, is incoherent as a general rule, even though other considerations may dictate in exceptional cases that punishment not be imposed. The utilitarian argument that desert is an insufficient or unnecessary basis for punishment is in fact a rejection of desert altogether. It

86. *See* Powell v. Texas, 392 U.S. 514, 555-63 (1968) (Fortas, J., dissenting).

87. We should have to face starkly the puzzle that the concept of criminal responsibility allows us usually to avoid: Ought a prediction of a higher degree of dangerousness make a person more subject to the operation of the criminal law or less? Compare the controversy whether the defense of insanity ought to be available to a "psychopath." *E.g.*, MODEL PENAL CODE § 4.01(2) commentary at 174-75 (1985); ROYAL COMMISSION ON CAPITAL PUNISHMENT, REPORT, CMD. 8932, at 135-40 (1953). *See generally* Morris & Miller, *Predictions of Dangerousness*, 6 CRIME AND JUSTICE 1 (1985).

is the argument, in ethical terms, that desert is morally arbitrary or, in ontological terms, that normative natural order is unintelligible. As I have indicated, I do not believe that the argument is incorrect; only our awareness of ourselves and others as persons, acting freely and morally responsible, concludes the issue to the contrary. The utilitarian avoids that response by driving a wedge between desert and punishment and focusing his attack on the latter. But there is no space between them. Punishment or a failure to punish for utilitarian reasons defeats the conditions of desert on which freedom itself depends. It regards persons as things, fit for whatever purposes are acceptable. The utilitarian does not really believe that. If he did, he could not object to the retributive position, as he does, on moral grounds.

[3]

VII Crime, Punishment, and "Pale Criminality"

Richard Wollheim

1. In his essay "Murder and the Principles of Punishment"[1] H. L. A. Hart refers at two different places, in two distinct contexts, to the mental or subjective factors that operate in the mind of the criminal. This essay was written in 1957, or during the great British debate on capital punishment, which terminated in 1965 in abolition, and the essay is touched by a subdued eloquence that the solemn occasion fired and chastened.

The first of these references occurs when, breaking off from a consideration of the statistics of murder, punishment, and deterrence, Hart asks what the principles are to which men appeal when they argue about the death penalty. Hart has already had something to say, in this and earlier essays, notably the "Prolegomenon to the Principles of Punishment," about how we should segment the issues involved in any such discussion, and let me first remind the reader of his proposals, for I do not believe that there is anyone who has tried seriously in the intervening years to resolve these problems and who does not owe Hart a massive debt for the framework he constructed.

Penology abounds in answers, but to recognize the differences between them gets us nowhere until, Hart points out, we recognize that penology also abounds in questions and that many different answers are often answers to different questions. So we may ask, (one) What is punishment? (two) What justifies a system of punishment?, (three) Whom may we punish?, and (four) How severely may we punish? There is the question of *definition,* there is the question of *general justifying aim,* there is the question of *liability,* and there is the question of *amount:* the two latter questions, those of liability and amount, the Who? and the How much? questions, being conflatable into one question, or that of *distribution.*

A further point that Hart makes suggests an elaboration of the framework. Any tolerable answer to the first question, or any adequate definition of punishment, must, he contends, include a clause to this effect:

that in standard cases punishment is for an offence against legal rules, or for a crime. Why the clause? And, for that matter, why the proviso it contains? The point of the proviso, or of inserting "in standard cases" into the clause, is to prevent the definitional stop being applied to such discussions as whether it is permissible to punish hostages or the relations of offenders. To say in such cases "But that wouldn't be *punishment*" blocks legitimate consideration of what is objectionable in such practices. However, the point of the clause itself is to bring out, to make clear, that in general a penal system, or a system that allots punishment to certain kinds of behaviour, presupposes a criminal system or a system that denounces certain kinds of behaviour as offences. Penal system and criminal system are two different kinds of system, and the elaboration I had in mind is that presumably we can ask of the criminal system some of the questions already asked of the penal system. So we can ask for the definition of a crime and, more significantly, we can ask for the general justifying aim of a criminal system.

I return to penology and the questions we can ask of a penal system. How are they to be answered? The definition of punishment—the point I have just been making, or the clause it must contain, apart—need not detain us, but a broad condition that Hart lays down upon how the remaining three questions—general justifying aim, liability, and amount—are to be answered is of real concern to us. It is this: that, if the general justifying aim of a penal system can be constructed out of purely utilitarian or consequentialist materials, the issues of liability and amount cannot be settled in this way. They cannot be settled consequentially without grave insult to our ethical intuitions. More precisely, the upper limits of distribution—that is, of liability and amount compounded—may be fixed by appeal to consequences: for punishment that is in excess of efficacy is clearly unwarranted: but any precise determination of punishment that falls below this ceiling requires us to invoke another social value. Hart calls this value Justice or Fairness. It is Justice or Fairness that requires us, in determining what precise penalty should be imposed upon an offender, to take account, either at the point of conviction or at the point of sentencing, of such questions as whether he was ignorant of what he was doing or of the circumstances that he was in, whether he was under duress, whether he was mentally abnormal, or whether he had peculiar difficulty in keeping the law. Justice requires us to take account of these factors and to temper punishment accordingly, even if from a utilitarian point of view the adjustments they lead us to make bring about a less desirable result. For a possibility we must face is that they will weaken the consequentialist or deterrent value of the law. The factors that Justice asks us to consider are in effect the mental or subjective factors operative within the criminal mind, and it is in this context, of the competing claims of Utilitarianism and Justice, that Hart makes the first of his two references to them.

The second reference occurs later, at the end of a substantive examination of the case for capital punishment as a deterrence. Hart divides the case into two parts. There is the statistical argument, whose findings prove singularly inconclusive, and there is the argument provided by common sense. Hart considers them in turn, very judiciously, and he then turns and directs our attention to this somber disquieting thought:

> Those who base their advocacy of the death penalty on this rough 'commonsense' psychology must seriously consider psychological theories that run in the other direction. For at present theories that the death penalty may operate as a stimulant to murder, consciously or unconsciously, have some evidence behind them. The use of the death penalty may lower, not sustain, the respect for life. Very large numbers of murderers are mentally unstable, and in them at least the bare thought of execution, the drama and notoriety of a trial, the gladiatorial element of the murderer fighting for his life, may operate as an attractive force, not as a repulsive one.[2]

2. In 1916 Sigmund Freud collected under the general title "Some Character-Types Met with in Psychoanalytic Theory" three essays wide-ranging in scope, of which the third is called "Criminals from a Sense of Guilt."[3] I do not know whether Hart had this essay in mind when he wrote the passage I have quoted, but in it Freud tells us how he was led on from accounts that patients regularly gave him of youthful misdeeds to ponder the criminal activities that some carried out while they were actually in treatment with him. Analysis revealed two things: first, that these forbidden actions were done largely because they were forbidden, and, secondly, that doing them, or being detected doing them, brought mental relief.

How could this be? And Freud sought to restore intelligibility to these actions by proposing that the agent already, independently, suffered, consciously or unconsciously, from a heavy burden of guilt, and it was in order to lighten this burden that he embarked on his course of criminal action. The action served the guilt in two distinct ways. In the first place, it gave the guilt, which up till then appeared to float free, something on which to suspend itself: it rationalized the guilt. Secondly, by bringing punishment in train, the action offered the guilt a way of dissipating itself: the guilt could not only be rationalized, it could be purged. What secured this explanation was the independent evidence for the preexistent guilt provided by (I quote Freud) "a whole set of other manifestations and effects." And as to the origin of that sense of guilt which is now the motivating force, Freud had no difficulty in tracing it back to the incestuous and murderous wishes omnipotently entertained at the height of the Oedipal phase. That these wishes were omnipotently entertained is significant for the explanation that Freud offered in that it means that for the adult agent there would be no subjective register, there would be at most bare knowledge, of the fact that the objects of his wishes were things that he had merely desired to do as opposed to things that he had actually done. And, given the enormity of these things—sexual intercourse with the mother, dismemberment and destruction of the father—it is barely surprising that the aspirant criminal could feel that any crime he contemplated was barely a match for the guilt that already tormented him.

For these criminals from a sense of guilt Freud appropriated a phrase of Nietzsche's, which serves as one of the chapter-headings of *Thus Spake Zarathustra:* it has come to be translated as 'pale criminal'. Criminals from a sense of guilt are pale criminals. With them guilt precedes and explains, rather than, as we like to think is usually the case, follows on and is explained by, the crime they commit.

Freud combined, as ever, boldness of speculation with modesty in the face of the facts. He ends his essay characteristically: "Let us leave it to future research to decide how many criminals are to be reckoned among these 'pale' ones."[4]

3. In pointing out how in "Murder and the Principles of Punishment" Hart makes a dual reference to the subjective factors in the criminal mind, once in so far as they function as excusing conditions, and once in so far as they contribute to what we can now think of as pale criminality, I was not suggesting that in Hart's eyes pale criminality is an excusing condition.

However, the question must raise itself: *Is* pale criminality an excusing condition? And one thing that Hart does is to make clear what kind of question this is, and how it is to be answered. It is a matter of whether pale criminality amounts to non-voluntariness, and whether it amounts to non-voluntariness in turn is a matter of what are the mental facts of the case. And it is, I believe, worth emphasizing that, in arguing that the issue whether, when certain conditions obtain, they make an action done under them non-voluntary, or excuse it, is a matter of mental fact, or a matter of the difference that these conditions make subjectively, Hart was in effect dissociating himself from two views of excusing conditions, both of which were philosophically influential at the time he was writing and may still be. These two views would settle the question whether a condition is or isn't exculpatory on a very different basis.

The first view makes the issue a linguistic issue. It is to be settled by reference to what the words in which the law formulates the offence mean. The issue is a matter of whether, when the condition obtains, the agent's act still falls within the extension of terms such as 'voluntary', or 'responsible', or 'free'. The second view makes the issue a legal issue. It is to be settled by reference to what pleas the law permits an accused person to enter. The issue is a matter of whether, when the condition obtains, the prima facie offender is legally entitled to cite the condition in order to get his action condoned or mitigated. It is not hard to see what Hart would have objected to in these two views. Both views invoke some agency outside the mind—language in one case, the law in the other—to arbitrate the issue of responsibility, and on neither view is it intelligible how we could come to criticize or to transcend (on one view) what ordinary language requires us to say or (on the other) what positive law recognizes as due process.

Hart then psychologizes—more precisely, he repsychologizes—*mens rea,* but, in returning to this tradition, Hart evidently thinks that it is no part of the philosophy of law to propose a general framework of the mind within which this fragment can be embedded. I wish to take a few steps beyond the point at which Hart thinks it wise to stop.

4. Any convincing account of what non-voluntary action is—more specifically, any account that is convincing and provides the materials for determining whether particular types of action are or are not voluntary—must cohere with general motivational theory. It must exhibit non-voluntary action as a mutant, as a motivational mutant, of voluntary

action. This is because the non-voluntariness of an action must be a characteristic of how it came to be performed, and it is implausible that the motivation of non-voluntary action should be not just different from but discontinuous with that of voluntary action. Accordingly we must ask: What is different about the motivation of an action when it is performed under conditions that in special circumstances the law will, or at any rate should, recognize as excusing?

In future I shall call such conditions excusing conditions, but a word on the circumlocution: "conditions that in special circumstances the law will, should, recognize as excusing conditions." The circumlocution makes the unabstruse point that the law calls certain conditions excusing only when they lead to an action that would otherwise be a crime—that is, when there is indeed something to excuse. But there is no reason to believe that those very same conditions cannot also lead to actions where there is nothing to excuse. Nor is it mere pedantry that makes me make this last point. There is a real danger that the motivation of non-voluntary action might elude our grasp because we take too narrow a view of the scope of the phenomenon we are trying to understand. Prejudice blinds us to its full range. For I believe it to be more than a merely theoretical possibility that there should be non-voluntary action where there is nothing to excuse. It strikes me that a great deal of action that is done, say, out of conscientiousness, or out of loyalty, is less than voluntary.

And now I have another explanatory point to make before I return to the principal argument. In discussing the conditions, the psychological conditions, that make actions done under them non-voluntary, I am using the term 'action' in a full-blooded sense: I mean, what might be called 'acts of commission'. I exclude 'acts of omission', though, of course, the law is also concerned with them and recognizes a way of deciding when they are or are not voluntary. Whether my account can be extended to cover them is therefore an important point, but is not one which I consider in this lecture.[5]

I return from this parenthesis to the question how non-voluntary action is to be accommodated within general motivational theory, and my first observation is that motivational theory allows itself to be formulated to different degrees of elaboration. At the top level it can be formulated schematically. Then it merely identifies the different motivational factors and specifies how they must interrelate to be jointly effective. An example of this schematic formulation is the desire-belief theory, which tells us that actions are caused by paired desires and beliefs so related that the agent believes of the action that it is a good means, perhaps the best means available, towards the satisfaction of the desire. It is relevant for me to say at this stage that I subscribe to the desire-belief theory. However, what the schematic formulation fails to tell us is how, or the mechanism by which, the motivational factors prove effective. The desire-belief theory, for instance, doesn't tell us how suitably interrelated desire and belief prod the agent into action. However just this is what we should expect motivational theory to tell us when it is elaborated at the bottom level: at any rate this is the degree of elaboration in which I shall be interested in this lecture. And it is my conviction, which I shall illustrate rather than argue for, that what this requires, or what is needed in order to achieve this degree of elaboration, is that the phenomenology should be filled in. Motivational theory, elaborated so as to provide the mechanism of motivation, has to tell us what it is like, subjectively, for the agent when the factors that have been identified for us by the theory schematically formulated lead to action.

Now once it is recognized that motivational theory admits of different degrees of elaboration, once it is recognized that there are at least these two degrees of elaboration, the question must arise: On what level should we formulate it if we want to exhibit what is distinctive about the motivation of non-voluntary action? Will the schematic formulation suffice to capture what is so special about excusing conditions, or do we have to introduce the phenomenology?

At this point the excusing conditions fall conveniently into two broad groups. If we want labels for them, we may call them the cognitive conditions and the conative conditions, without attaching great theoretical weight to the nomenclature. Typical of the cognitive conditions is whatever brings it about that the agent's action was a mistake. Typical of the conative conditions is whatever brings it about that the agent's action was done under duress or was something that he couldn't stop himself from doing. And this division of excusing conditions into these two groups is of present relevance in the following way: that to show why the cognitive conditions excuse can be managed within motivational theory at the top or schematic level, whereas to do the same thing for the conative conditions requires the further elaboration of motivational theory; we must call upon the phenomenology of motivation.

5. The claim, just made, that schematic motivational theory provides an adequate framework within which to show why the cognitive conditions excuse I shall substantiate within the specific context of desire-belief theory. We can see the competence of desire-belief theory to account for the exculpatory character of cognitive conditions once we bear in mind the three following facts: (one) that desire-belief theory yields for every particular action what we might call the agent's desire-belief schedule, which lists the motivating factors, (two) that each desire-belief schedule lists the relevant desires and beliefs in an opaque fashion or intensionally, and (three) that the voluntariness or non-voluntariness of an action is always relative to a certain description true of it. Now it is a consequence of these three facts that the desire-belief schedule for a given action is more informative than we might initially expect it to be. *Ex hypothesi* it will tell us what motivated the action: it will tell us which desires and which beliefs, opaquely characterized, were effective. But it will also circumscribe the descriptions under which the action is voluntary. For an action can be voluntary under a certain description only if two conditions are fulfilled: the description is true of the action *and* the description occurs on the desire-belief schedule in the characterization of one of the effective beliefs. It works like this: Imagine that a particular drug is administered to an old woman and it kills her outright. Now the administration of the drug cannot be viewed as a case of voluntarily killing the old woman if on the agent's desire-belief schedule there is no belief to the effect that the drug might have a lethal character—and the agent's beliefs have been formed with adequate conscientiousness. It is only if the agent had some inkling of what the drug could do that he is a candidate for murdering her.

Now the cognitive conditions are defined as those which result from a mismatch of the following sort: There is a description true of a certain action which an agent has done; in the standard case it is a description in which the law takes a punitive interest; but at the same time there is not to be found in the agent's mind any belief to the effect that the action, or the outcome of the action, falls under this description. This is common to the cognitive conditions, and they then differ amongst themselves in the actual causation they invoke for this mismatch. If this is right, then it is evident that desire-belief theory, or (to put it more generally) schematic motivational theory, can fully exhibit how the cognitive conditions excuse, for such a theory can readily show how the satisfaction of these conditions ensures the non-voluntariness of the action under the description at issue. To exculpate the agent we do not have to consult anything outside his desire-belief schedule.

6. But all this changes radically when we turn from the cognitive to the conative conditions. For, when the conative conditions hold, it is not, as we might at first think, simply a matter of our turning from the agent's beliefs to the agent's desires in order to understand why his action is non-voluntary. To grasp the non-voluntariness of the action, we need more information than turns up on the agent's desire-belief schedule. This articulates a familiar intuition that, when an agent does something which he couldn't help doing or which he had to do, what is at stake is not just the desires that he had, it is the hold that these desires had over him. It is not to the desires, it is to their imperiousness, that we should look, though it may well be the case that certain desires, or certain kinds of desire, desires with certain histories, have a tendency to acquire the required imperiousness.

To understand the conative conditions, to see how they exculpate, and to do this within general motivational theory, we must go on to motivational theory in its elaborated form. We must be able to exhibit the imperiousness with which certain desires demand satisfaction as a mutant of the way in which desires ordinarily achieve outlet, and this means that we need motivational theory not simply in the form of an inventory of motivational factors: it must tell us how they become efficacious. If I am right about this requirement, we need a filling of phenomenology. We must drop a level.

At this point, in proposing a shift of level for motivational theory, I also intend to introduce another shift: a shift that is terminological, but also more than terminological.

So far in talking about desire as a motivational factor, I have followed current philosophical practice and used the term in a very broad sense, which is required if desire and belief between them are to exhaust the motivational inventory. There is no harm in this usage provided it is taken for the artificiality that it is: in moral theory, where this provision seems ignored, the usage is, I suspect, harmful. However, in the rest of this lecture I shall use desire in a narrower sense, which approximates to the ordinary usage. In this narrower sense, desire contrasts itself, on the one hand, with merely wanting to do or be something, which falls short of desire proper, and, on the other hand, with an emotion or mood, which is likely to generate a number of desires proper. What makes this terminological shift opportune is that, if we are to say anything informative about how motivational force is achieved, we need to look at the motivational factors closer up, in finer detail, than the broad sense of desire permits. At the same time the shift can be effected without any loss of generality that we might come to regret. This is because, when the conative conditions hold, it is desires in the narrow sense, not desires in the broad sense, that are likely to be involved. They are the things that gain undue power.

So: How do they do so? In proposing an answer to this question I shall abridge some arguments that I have elsewhere elaborated.[6]

The first point to be noted, and it is a very general point, and fatal to behaviourism, is that most of the dispositions that persons have—and this includes desires—lead to action, when they do so, not directly but indirectly. Directly they lead to mental states. By mental states I mean transient events occurring in the mind, of a sort that are held to make up the life of the mind, or the stream of consciousness, and which are endowed with phenomenology. It is then in response to the phenomenology of his mental states that the person acts. More specifically, mental dispositions manifest themselves in appropriate mental states, and appropriateness here means that the mental states have a phenomenology such that when the person acts in response to it he furthers the role of the disposition. The role of the disposition I shall take as primitive. The normal course of motivational flow is then from dispositions through mental states to action.

Phenomenology, the distinctive attribute of mental states, is in fact a complex attribute, the two constituents of which are (in my terminology) intentionality and subjectivity. The intentionality of a mental state is its thought-content, and the subjectivity of a mental state is its experiential character, or 'feel' as philosophers used to say, or, as they now say, what it is like for the subject to be in that state, and the relevance of this distinction for the present discussion is that the motivational flow that passes from disposition to action has, as it passes through the mental state, two pathways open to it. It can pass solely through the thought-content of the mental state: it can activate just its intentionality, and ignore its subjectivity. But it is a distinctive feature of our psychology, doing as much as anything else to separate us from the lower animals (whoever they may be) and from intelligent machines (whatever they might be), that the flow from disposition to action can also pass through the subjectivity of the mental state: it can exploit the experiential feel of the state, getting that to move the person to action.

Let me illustrate the two pathways. I take as my example not a desire but an emotion: say, the fear of snakes. Now let us assume that the behaviour in which the fear of snakes issues, that which furthers its role, is flight. Now the two pathways along which fear of snakes will lead to flight, given the appearance of snakes, are these: On the one hand, fear will give rise to a mental state whose intentionality consists of recurrent thoughts amounting to the drumroll of, This is no place to be, This is terrible, I must get out of here, If I don't get out of here something worse will happen. And in response to these thoughts and to nothing else, the person starts running. On the other hand, fear might give rise to a mental state whose subjectivity warrants us in thinking of it as a state of terror. In addition to the drumroll of thoughts, the person experiences sudden weakness, a dryness of the throat, utter incertitude, quivering in the chest, visions of pain and destruction, and it is in response to these further aspects of the mental state as well as to the thoughts that it contains that the person starts running. When this second pathway is followed, I shall say that the mental state lures the person to action. To allay doubts, let me say that 'lure' is also a causal notion.

Of these two pathways, the second, besides the general significance that it has for psychology, possesses a very special efficacy, and it is no accident that many of our more exigent dispositions regularly have resort to it in initiating action. They exploit lure. And, amongst our most exigent dispositions are, of course, those of our desires which attain imperiousness and cause involuntary actions.

Is there anything to be said about the distinctive phenomenology, that is, intentionality plus subjectivity, of those mental states which desire induces when it motivates action along the second pathway? I believe there is, at any rate in rough general terms. Generally, roughly, we may say that, when desires motivate action along this second pathway, they lead us to imagine what we desire to do or be. It is the envisagement of these events or states of affairs that work upon us as lure, and the force that combined intentionality and subjectivity bring to bear upon us, as opposed to the force of intentionality uncombined, becomes more in evidence as we move into the realm of the imperious desires.

Just one amplification: When we imagine outcomes under the influence of desiring them, we do not imagine these outcomes neutrally. We conjure them up as desirable or as offering pleasure, and this colouring partly accounts for the way in which the imagination lures. It is indeed I believe here, in the motivational force of imagination, that we find such truth as there is to the ancient doctrine of psychological hedonism. It is not the case that everything we desire we desire for the pleasure it will bring, nor is it the case that when we act on our desires we necessarily believe that our actions will achieve pleasure for us. But what I believe to be the case is that, when we desire something and in consequence imagine it, desire also leads us to imagine it as pleasurable, and it is this that precipitates us into action.

We are now, I believe, on the brink of understanding what is distinctive about the motivation of non-voluntary action when the non-voluntariness can be ascribed to the fact that the conative conditions hold. For the conative conditions coincide with an intensification of the way in which we imagine the outcome of our desires. By intensification I mean an increase in the vivacity, or an increase in the persistence, with which these imaginings crowd in upon us. Lure escalates to seduction or to intimidation.

This suggestion is grounded in introspection, though it exceeds introspection. For I am not contending that every such case of intensified imagination is conscious or even preconscious. It will often be unconscious. Then it will be based on self-interpretation.

However, one decided merit of the suggestion is that it allows us to make sense of two distinctions which independently recommended themselves. This is a further argument in its favour.

The first distinction, which is one that moral philosophy habitually elides, is that between, on the one hand, how we evaluate something that we desire, or the importance of the desire, and, on the other, how forceful the desire is, or the irresistibility of the desire. Under the blanket term 'strength of desire' these two issues are often run together. But this must be wrong. The tragedy of much crime is that the criminal sacrifices satisfactions that are very dear to him, or upon which he sets a high value, for the sake of satisfactions that may very well mean nothing to him, but to which he cannot say No. In this lecture I have nothing to say about the importance of desire; I am concerned only with the force of desire; and mostly I want to make the point that the two are not the same.

The second distinction, a related distinction, which my suggestion makes it easier for us to recognize, is that between understanding why an agent desires something and understanding why an agent acts on his desires. For one way of coming to appreciate this second distinction is to see that, though there will certainly not be a single answer to the question why we desire something, for that depends on what we desire, there very well might be a single answer to the question why we act on our desires. For there very well might be a single mechanism that impels us into action, and just what my suggestion does is to offer such an answer.

The second distinction is one that we manipulate in thinking about criminality. We manipulate it in order to distance ourselves from criminality. And, by talking of manipulating it, I mean that we conflate the distinction, and yet we recognize it. For instance, we say of the criminal, "I don't see how anyone could do such a thing"—as though that were the unbridgeable gap between him and us. But, if I am right, it requires no great leap of the imagination to see this, given that he has the desires that he has. What we are very unlikely to be able to see is why he has those desires, why he desires what he desires. But then the criminal himself is likely to be in exactly the same position. When the serial murderer Dennis Nilsen recounts how, as he casually got up and went out to the kitchen to fetch some string or a tie out of which to make a noose for the young man with whom he had been drinking and listening to music, the thought entered his mind, "Oh Stephen here I go again,"[7] he is thereby revealing something which the psychology of the criminal law tries to disavow. His murderousness surprises him as much as us.

One plausible response to this last point is worth considering. Someone might grant me that the criminal could fail to understand why he had a certain desire and simultaneously be so haunted by images of its satisfaction that he was driven to acting on the desire: yet, the objector would go on, this co-existence must be short-lived. For surely the criminal's incomprehension of his desire must have the effect of diminishing the pleasure that attaches to the images of its satisfaction, with the result that intimidation or seduction will be attenuated to lure, and then lure to indifference.

But the response is narrow-minded. If there is any diminution of the pleasure with which the outcome of the criminal's desire is invested, it is this diminution that it is likeliest to be short-lived. And the reason is that, within our psychology, an incomprehensible desire glamourizes its object in a way that is not true of a comprehensible desire. By 'glamourize' I mean that the desire suffuses its object with an aura that is not subject to testing either in reality or in imagination. For a point I have not had time to mention is this: if it is ordinarily the case that a desire in motivating action first causes the person to imagine the desire fulfilled, and this image of fulfilment lures him to act, there is also a danger to this mechanism. It may misfire. Imagining what he desires may cause the person to reconsider his desire: the image of fulfilment can come to serve as a test of the desire, and the person may respond to what he has imagined in such a way that there is a change of desire. This, I repeat, is something that readily happens in ordinary circumstances, and for these purposes the line between the ordinary and the extraordinary is drawn by whether the desire is comprehensible or incomprehensible. Accordingly, so long as the desire remains incomprehensible, then, should for a moment the person be able to imagine the outcome of this desire as no more pleasurable than it is likely to prove in reality, the next moment this will alter, the effect of judgment will prove unstable, and pleasure will flow back in and reinvest the object. Glamour will be restored, and lure consolidated.

7. I pause at this point because I may have given the impression that the conative conditions and their claim to have exculpatory force can be understood entirely in terms of the intensification of lure. Incomprehensible desires are at work leading the person to imagine their outcome with such vivacity or such persistence that he is intimidated or seduced into acting upon them. I believe that this account is highly promising for many of the conative conditions, but, if pale criminality is to be reckoned amongst them, pale criminality is certainly a pathological phenomenon, and pathological motivation requires us to take account of a new factor.

To retrieve this factor I propose that we return to pale criminality.

Freud's 1916 discussion of pale criminality is manifestly inadequate for a rather obvious reason. It is broken-backed. The central insight of Freud's essay is that there is a certain type of criminal in whom conscience is not, as wiseacres assume, too weak. On the contrary, conscience is too strong, and criminality is inspired by its strength. I am sure that this is a brilliant insight, and it is appealing for the neat way in which it offends common sense. But it is from this point onwards that the inadequacy of Freud's account manifests itself. For the account now shifts character, and becomes purely energic. Guilt here, like sexuality in certain other places, is treated purely as a quantity pressing for discharge, and both the crime that the guilt motivates and the punishment that the crime secures are assigned no special significance. But it is a notorious fact that, unless such energic accounts are supplemented by some story couched in psychological, not in energic, terms, indicating what the crime and what the punishment mean to the pale criminal, they are useless. They encourage error in explanation. If, for instance, a masochist falls down in the street and sprains his ankle, we cannot explain this as a case of his satisfying his erotic desires: however pent up his sexuality, however painful the injury, there is no explanation unless and until we can establish that he effected a connection between the suffering he seeks and the suffering he receives. For his masochism to be satisfied he must, by some association, have eroticized the accident.

If we ask how the nexus can be formed in the case of the pale criminal, the likeliest story is that the criminal, in finding the punishment purgative, thinks of those from whom it comes as continuous with, or as persisting versions of, those against whom the original, the Oedipal, wishes were directed. He must, in other words, identify the authors or the agents of the penal authority with the internalized parental figures. Thus can the punishment seem to the criminal not a mere contingent misfortune: like the masochist's accident. However, once we have taken this first step in reconstructing the pale criminal's perception of things, it is natural to go on to believe that he will identify the crime he commits with the early wishful assaults upon the parents' bodies.[8]

But, it might now be objected, this reconstruction of the pale criminal's perspective has been achieved at too high a price. For the most original, indeed the most arresting, feature of Freud's 1916 proposal has now been abandoned. The crime is no longer motivated solely by the desire for punishment, it is now motivated also by whatever it was that found expression in the early Oedipal wishes. The neat reversal of common sense, so that guilt explains crime, has been ironed out.

But this objection is not just. For if, on the new integrated account, crime is not motivated solely by the desire for punishment, if the perceived nature of the crime also adds to its appeal, there is this to be noted: that one crucial reason why a breach of the law is identified with a renewed attack upon the parents is because the law and the parents are both, in the criminal's perspective, punishing forces. In attacking, in reattacking, the parents, the criminal *is* seeking punishment.

8. I have however taken the revised account of pale criminality thus far, not so much for its substance, as to indicate the structural alterations that it requires in motivational theory. The key to these alterations lies in the term 'phantasy', and they are alterations necessitated by any pathological condition if the motivation it supplies is to be theoretically understood.

The pale criminal has desires: we have seen that. He has beliefs: we have seen that. But, in so far as his mind lies under the influence of phantasy, these beliefs and desires do not co-exist in comparative autonomy: the desires seeking satisfaction and using beliefs only as a means to attaining it, the beliefs seeking confirmation. Rather in his mind desires and beliefs are interlocked, so that desires reinforce the very beliefs on which we might expect them to be conditional, and beliefs in turn are the products of desires whose fulfilment they anticipate. So, if we find it plausible to think that underlying the pale criminal's behaviour is a phantasy which unites (one) his continuing aggression against his parents, (two) a belief that they are consummately punitive, and (three) the desire for punishment, then the phantasy will entwine them in the following way: hostility to the parents reinforces the belief that they are punitive, and this belief in turn arises in response to the desire for punishment.

Phantasies offer their own gratifications, and this is one reason why they are formed, but they also press for outlet. When they do, and are efficacious, two things happen. First, if the subject has not already done so, he projects the phantasy on to the world: he sees the world through it, and the points of contact between the phantasy and the world are given by the subject's identifications. Secondly, the subject acts out the phantasy: he acts upon the world in such a way that would be rational only if the world conformed to it.

There are many interesting ways in which acting out a phantasy differs from acting on a desire. These differences correspond to ways in which motivational theory needs to be adjusted if, or when, it is to accommodate phantasy as a motivational factor. I want to consider just two differences between acting-out and acting on. I select them because of their relevance to the question which we are inexorably approaching but which I shall leave unanswered: that is, whether pale criminality is, and so should be recognized as, an excusing condition.

Of course, before we turn to the differences between acting and acting-out, there is this similarity: that a phantasy, like a desire, can obliterate voluntariness through the way in which mental states appropriate to it invasively occupy the mind. In the case of phantasy this invasion of the mind will invariably be unconscious.

And now for the differences. In the first place, phantasy has a tendency, unremarked of desire, to draw into its orbit emotions, feelings, desires that might ordinarily be expected to run counter to it. A criminal phantasy, for instance, will recruit solicitude: solicitude (it may be) for the victim, or for the victim's victims. But the upshot will be, not that the crime is arrested or impeded, but that it is more certain: solicitude, somehow or other, insists that the crime is perpetrated. Secondly, when the subject acts out his phantasy, the effect that what he does has upon him is that it appears to confirm or to cement what was antecedently the case. Nothing seems new. For this reason he is denied satisfaction or pleasure, and for this very same reason he has no sense that the desires or the beliefs that the phantasy imprisons have in any way been put to the test. All he can do is, when the occasion seems opportune, when the appropriate identifications have been established, to re-enact the phantasy. The pale criminal, if he cannot break the mould of the phantasy, must repeat his crime.[9]

This last point brings us back to Professor Hart. For, though Hart does not undertake to provide us with a list of excusing conditions, nor does he attempt an account, which is what I have been offering, of how conditions amount to non-voluntariness, what he does do is to offer a rationale why non-voluntariness should exculpate. He shows what is superior about a system of social control that moves only against voluntary actions. And one of the points that he makes is that only under such a system does the citizen trade off actions against satisfactions. It may very well be that Hart, in making this point, had particularly the cognitive conditions in mind. I don't know. But my claim is that it also works for the conative conditions. They excuse those actions in which the subject is deprived of a plus, which would be pleasure, to set beside the law's minus, which would be punishment.

9. I want to end on a speculative note. Speculation consorts with the thinker this lecture honours.

It is certainly true that, if pale criminality is indeed an excusing condition, this confronts penal systems with a severe challenge: How is it within the forensic capacity to detect such a condition? But this is an epistemic or practical challenge, and the challenge that I wish to pose in conclusion is, if it is to be taken seriously at all, a more profound challenge. It transcends practical difficulties, and it confronts any penal system: even one which has recognized the exculpatory force of pale criminality. It is a challenge to any system of the kind whose virtues Hart has laid out for us: any system which attaches penalties to voluntarily committed offences.

The challenge that I have in mind presupposes one assumption about human nature and one view about social institutions. Dismiss either, and the challenge needn't trouble us. But can we dismiss them? The assumption about human nature is to the broad effect that pale criminality enjoys, in some way to be made clear, a centrality in our psychology. It is not an assumption about the distribution of a certain form of behaviour, it is an assumption about motivation, and it holds that *in foro interno* we have a disposition, which is bound up with what is deepest in us, to do what is forbidden, and to do it for that reason. The view of social institutions is that, if not all, many of them imply a particular psychology, and, if the particular psychology that they imply is in point of fact false of human nature, then the institution is at fault because instead of facilitating, it impedes, self-knowledge.

Now, if it is true of any institution that it has inscribed into it a psychology, this is likeliest to be the law: particularly the criminal law. And, though the details of this psychology must be very complex, what it cannot, what it must not, include, surely, is the thesis that we are motivated to do what we are enjoined not to do. The law would be, I suggest, a very grim institution if it embraced the conclusion that it made it more difficult for us to do whatever its injunctions asked of us. Accordingly, if pale criminality is central, the law is an institution that misrepresents us to ourselves. It abets self-deception or self-disavowal.

One way of bringing the present challenge into focus, one way of appreciating its radicalism, is to ask what system of social control those who present it would prefer. The answer, of course, might be, None, for it might be that there was no conceivable system that did not have a false psychology, a psychology that denied pale criminality, built into it. But if there were, by the standards of the challenge, a preferable system, it seems that it would be one that did not wait for an offence to be committed and whose operation consisted in something like an educative process. We can envisage systems of this sort, ranging from the repressively preventitive to the benignly therapeutic, but any such system would have to abandon totally not just the term 'punishment' but the phenomenon. I barely have to point out the relevance of this last remark. For no one has argued more incisively than Hart against those hybrid systems of social control which first borrow from a penal system the crucial condition of an offence that has been committed, and then, rejecting the claims of Justice, distribute, according to the criteria of social hygiene, punishment, which they and the system of social control they are likely to sponsor, prefer to call 'treatment'. The challenge that I am considering does not lead towards, in fact it leads away from, the ideas of, say, Lady Wootton and now Professor Stern.

We do not however take this challenge seriously unless we are prepared to raise the further question, How much security from criminal behaviour are we entitled to expect? How much protection can we rightly claim from those with whom we share our psychology? If, not criminality, but the seeds of criminality, are, in some identifiable way which the science of mind can make clear, present in all of us, how far are we right to distance it from us?

We know how politicians would answer this question. They would say that we are entitled to as much protection as is consistent with the demands of justice, *and a bit more*. But politicians have constituencies, philosophers do not, and yet social philosophers have often written as if tomorrow they might wake up and find themselves in elected office. I think that such a heavy assumption of civic responsibility is inimical to free inquiry.

And let me make it clear that the question that I have in mind is this: How far, if the need arose, should we be prepared to sacrifice security for self-knowledge? It is not: How far should we be prepared to sacrifice security for the greater expression of aggression? After all, our society, our world, tolerates aggression on a massive scale. It not merely tolerates it, it idealizes it. And, to compound the matter, it tolerates it in ways that perpetuate self-ignorance, self-error, and self-disavowal. For the ways in which it tolerates aggression are labelled with distinctions, and, though they are not distinctions that correspond to no differences whatsoever, they are distinctions that grossly exaggerate the differences they register. The distinctions that I am thinking of are retaliation *versus* attack, deterrence *versus* intimidation, defence forces *versus* terrorists. In each case the arsenals of violence that the nation-state has at its disposal are approved of, and the ruses to which desperate men are driven are thought of as unspeakable. Such rhetoric does not advance self-knowledge, even if the powerful sleep better for it.

But to return to the profound challenge itself: Should we listen to it, even if the only outcome is to leave us dissatisfied with the only institutions we can conceive ourselves as having? Or is there nothing to it? I have no means of evaluating it: though I must confess that—to re-use a term I have appropriated as a term of art—I experience its lure.[10]

[4]

THE FEMINIST CHALLENGE IN CRIMINAL LAW

STEPHEN J. SCHULHOFER†

INTRODUCTION

Feminist criticism of criminal law and criminal justice administration has proliferated over the past decade and now touches scores of doctrinal, practical, and theoretical issues. These critiques and the associated proposals for reform are usually acknowledged to be controversial (and even "radical") by proponents and opponents alike. Yet, across a wide range of issues, the feminist position has its basis in a simple fact that cannot be considered debatable: criminal law is, from top to bottom, preoccupied with male concerns and male perspectives.

In this Article, I explain why this seemingly tendentious claim is not only accurate but uncontroversial. I then seek to show how the male orientation of existing criminal law creates both the necessity for reform and a major obstacle to doing it well.

The feminist challenge is to adapt male-oriented criminal laws and practices to the concerns of a group of victims and offenders who are normally left out of the picture. This turns out to be difficult, and not just because of a lack of empathy for the needs of women. Factoring female victims and female offenders into the criminal law equation is hard because of many conflicting concerns and commitments that most Americans share. Three conflicts in particular will be central to the discussion that follows.

First, although we want women to be treated the same as men, sometimes equality cannot be achieved by treating two groups of people the same way. We need to take differences into account.

---

† Julius Kreeger Professor of Law and Criminology and Director of the Center for Studies in Criminal Justice, University of Chicago. Portions of this Article were presented at McGeorge Law School in November 1994, at the Annual Meeting of the American Political Science Association in September 1994, and at the University of Chicago Law School in November 1993 as the Wilbur G. Katz Lecture. Research for this Article was supported by the Russell J. Parsons Faculty Research Fund and the Sonnenschein Fund at the University of Chicago Law School. I have also benefited from the research assistance of Kimberly Dunn and Katharine Moir, and from the comments of Kathryn Abrams, Albert Alschuler, Mary Coombs, Anne Coughlin, Deborah Denno, Joshua Dressler, Leslie Goldstein, Elena Kagan, Dan Kahan, Jane Larson, Larry Lessig, Dorothy Roberts, Cass Sunstein, Michael Vitiello, Joan Williams, and Laurie Wohl.

Yet drawing categorical distinctions between men and women undermines our ideals. This is the familiar debate concerning sameness versus difference. It pervades discussions of gender in other areas of the law and discussions of equal treatment for racial minorities, the handicapped, and other groups.[1] The debate plays out with some unexpected twists in criminal justice.

A second dilemma is that we want to be sensitive to the nuances of context when gender issues are at stake. But effective protection of women also requires that women have clear-cut rights protected by clear rules. This is the old debate concerning rules versus discretion. Again, it plays out with some unexpected twists in criminal justice.

A third dilemma concerns the limits of theory. We need theory to help pinpoint the problems confronting women and to help organize thinking about solutions. But theory is not up to the task. Indeed, I will argue that in criminal justice, theory can never be equal to the task.

Much of contemporary feminist discussion and scholarship center on developing new theories or on parsing the differences among theories and defending commitments to one of them or another. One theory emphasizes formally equal treatment.[2] A major competitor is a theory stressing the ways that culture and social practice subordinate women under laws that are formally neutral.[3] A third theory emphasizes context, caring, and connection in lieu of what it views as a "male" commitment to abstract rights defined without regard to context.[4] One scholar has iden-

---

[1] *See, e.g.*, MARTHA MINOW, MAKING ALL THE DIFFERENCE: INCLUSION, EXCLUSION, AND AMERICAN LAW 21 (1990) ("The dilemma of difference grows from the ways in which this society assigns individuals to categories and, on that basis, determines whom to include in and whom to exclude from political, social, and economic activities.").

[2] *See, e.g.*, Wendy W. Williams, *The Equality Crisis: Some Reflections on Culture, Courts, and Feminism*, 7 WOMEN'S RTS. L. REP. 175, 175 (1982) (stating that courts should "rule that the privileges the law explicitly bestows on men must also be made available to women"); Wendy W. Williams, *Notes from a First Generation*, 1989 U. CHI. LEGAL F. 99, 99 (identifying the "'formal' equality" approach as "an insistence that laws not embody explicit sex-based distinctions").

[3] *See, e.g.*, CATHARINE A. MACKINNON, FEMINISM UNMODIFIED: DISCOURSES ON LIFE AND LAW 40 (1987) (discussing the "dominance approach" to the equality question); Christine A. Littleton, *Reconstructing Sexual Equality*, 75 CAL. L. REV. 1279, 1282-84 (1987) (noting that courts routinely apply "phallocentric standards 'equally' to men and women's different reproductive biology or economic position to yield . . . unequal results for women").

[4] *See, e.g.*, CAROL GILLIGAN, IN A DIFFERENT VOICE: PSYCHOLOGICAL THEORY AND

tified seven distinct feminisms: liberal, radical, marxist, socialist, psychoanalytic, existentialist, and post-modern.[5] And that taxonomy still leaves out a few.[6] We can say, with only slight exaggeration, that feminist legal theory and feminist jurisprudence have become synonyms for feminist scholarship in law schools today.[7]

I do not attempt here to define and distinguish the many varieties of feminist theory because I wish to draw attention to a problem that is common to all of them. The difficulty, not a new one, is that broad propositions do not solve concrete cases; or they solve too many cases very poorly. The problems confronting women in criminal justice run so deep and have such complex links to the goals and structures of law that theory is inherently incapable of carrying us very far along the path toward effective solutions. The problems can be worked out only by paying close attention to particulars.

I begin this Article by describing how the criminal justice system is dominated (incontrovertibly so) by a preoccupation with men and male perspectives. I then focus on four problems that particularly concern women as potential victims or offenders—domestic violence, rape, sentencing policy, and prisons. Finally, drawing some common lessons from the four discussions, I suggest the need for a rather skeptical attitude toward high theory in the

---

WOMEN'S DEVELOPMENT 17 (1982) (discussing the importance of the ethic of care to women's self-definition).

[5] *See* ROSEMARIE TONG, FEMINIST THOUGHT: A COMPREHENSIVE INTRODUCTION 1-8 (1989).

[6] *See, e.g.*, Katharine T. Bartlett, *Feminist Legal Methods*, 103 HARV. L. REV. 829, 836-67 (1990) (discussing feminist practical reasoning, consciousness-raising, and related methods of epistemological inquiry).

[7] There are, to be sure, significant counterexamples: some recent legal scholarship considers potential reform with a close eye on the institutional or doctrinal specifics of legal change. *See, e.g.*, Mary E. Becker, *Politics, Differences and Economic Rights*, 1989 U. CHI. LEGAL F. 169, 171 (discussing the economic effects of formal equality); Herma H. Kay, *Equality and Difference: A Perspective on No-Fault Divorce and Its Aftermath*, 56 U. CIN. L. REV. 1, 3 (1987) (exploring the concrete effect of no-fault divorce reforms); Jane E. Larson, *"Women Understand So Little, They Call My Good Nature 'Deceit'": A Feminist Rethinking of Seduction*, 93 COLUM. L. REV. 374, 454-71 (1993) (examining specific elements of a legal cause of action for sexual fraud); Deborah L. Rhode, *Feminism and the State*, 107 HARV. L. REV. 1181, 1195, 1197-98 (1994) (focusing on institutional details necessary to promote feminist goals in the areas of physical security and equal employment opportunity). A related example, largely pragmatic in tone, although not as detailed in its reform prescriptions, is SUSAN ESTRICH, REAL RAPE 80-91 (1987) (discussing various reform statutes focusing on the problem of rape).

search for a feminism that can guide reform in criminal justice and, perhaps, other areas. Despite the undoubted importance of theoretical insight, the most effective tools of reform at the present juncture are likely to be eclectic and atheoretical, and the most effective feminist scholarship is likely to be one that attends to the complexities of specific institutions and procedures. What is needed, I suggest, is a feminism of particulars, a recognition that real solutions are likely to lie deeply embedded in the details.

I. WHY CRIMINAL LAW IS "MALE"

The criminal justice system fits almost perfectly Lincoln's conception of a government of the people, by the people, and for the people. It fits perfectly, if you are willing to equate "the people" with the male half of the population. Criminal law is—and has been for centuries—a system of rules conceived and enforced by men, for men, and against men.

There are counterexamples but not many. The law against prostitution, which might make sense as a way to protect young and poor women from sexual exploitation, is not enforced that way. It is enforced almost exclusively against women.[8] The law notices women but prosecutes those it should be protecting. In many instances law enforcement does benefit and protect women. But overwhelmingly, criminal law is designed and implemented with men in mind.

This observation should be considered completely uncontroversial. One way for the reader to confirm its accuracy is simply to pause for a moment and attempt to picture a typical offender. What does he look like? *He* is inevitably the subject of the inquiry. The criminal offender is disproportionately male, overwhelmingly so. In 1983, men and boys, 49% of the U.S.

[8] *See, e.g.*, RICHARD SYMANSKI, THE IMMORAL LANDSCAPE: FEMALE PROSTITUTION IN WESTERN SOCIETIES 88 (1981) (noting that although New York law was changed in 1964 to criminalize both male prostitution and the act of patronizing a prostitute, the effect of the change was minimal; in 1977, the number of males arrested was less than one-tenth the number of females arrested). Recent attention to the need for sanctioning prostitutes' customers has not substantially changed this picture. *See* Eleanor M. Miller et al., *The United States*, *in* PROSTITUTION: AN INTERNATIONAL HANDBOOK ON TRENDS, PROBLEMS, AND POLICIES 300, 313 (Nanette J. Davis ed., 1993) (noting the persistence of arrest patterns in which 70% of prostitution arrests are of females, while male customers account for only about 10% of arrests).

population, represented 78% of all property offenders and 89% of all violent offenders.[9]

What about victims? The Women's Movement has taught us to be far more aware of the victimization of women, and there is a widespread sense that women are disproportionately victimized by violence.[10] There is an important truth in that perception, but it is a complex truth. It is a truth that statistics seem to contradict.

The victims of reported crime are disproportionately male, again overwhelmingly so. Justice Department statistics indicate that compared to women, men are 123% more likely to be the victims of robbery and 161% more likely to be the victims of an aggravated assault.[11]

One's immediate reaction, given widespread perceptions of disproportionate victimization of women, is that statistics of this kind must be distorted, and in part this is true. The great majority of victims of domestic violence are female.[12] Outside of prisons and other custodial institutions, over 90% of rape victims are

---

[9] *See* BUREAU OF JUSTICE STATISTICS, U.S. DEP'T OF JUSTICE, REPORT TO THE NATION ON CRIME AND JUSTICE 41 (2d ed. 1988) [hereinafter REPORT TO THE NATION].

[10] *See* S. REP. NO. 197, 102d Cong., 1st Sess. 33 (1991) ("Women bear the disproportionate burden of some of the most pernicious crimes, like rape, and some of the most persistent crimes, like beatings in the home."); S. REP. NO. 545, 101st Cong., 2d Sess. 30-31 (1990) (noting "a spiralling 'gender gap' of violence . . . [in which] female victimization is increasing faster than male victimization (at least for some crimes)" (citations omitted)).

[11] *See* BUREAU OF JUSTICE STATISTICS, U.S. DEP'T OF JUSTICE, CRIMINAL VICTIMIZATION 1991, at 6 (1992) [hereinafter VICTIMIZATION IN 1991].

[12] In measuring domestic violence, a number of surveys suggest that male partners are victimized at about the same rate as female partners. *See* MURRAY A. STRAUS ET AL., BEHIND CLOSED DOORS: VIOLENCE IN THE AMERICAN FAMILY 266 (1980) (reporting a rate of 12.0 for husband-to-wife violence compared to a rate of 11.5 for wife-to-husband violence); Murray A. Straus & Richard J. Gelles, *Societal Change and Change in Family Violence from 1975 to 1985: As Revealed by Two National Surveys*, 48 J. MARRIAGE & FAM. 465, 470 (1986) (reporting that in 1985, the rate of husband-to-wife violence was 113 per 1000 couples, while the rate of wife-to-husband violence was 121 per 1000 couples). But the overall data on the rates of assault by victim gender present a misleading picture because the assaults experienced by male victims tend to be concentrated disproportionately in the milder forms of slapping or hitting; the female partners are much more likely to suffer the most serious assaults. *See* Irene H. Frieze & Angela Browne, *Violence in Marriage*, *in* FAMILY VIOLENCE 163, 181 (Michael Tonry & Norval Morris eds., 1989) (noting that "the average number of severely violent assaults by a husband against a nonviolent wife was three times greater than the average number of wives' assaults on nonviolent husbands").

female.[13] Yet rape and domestic violence are vastly underreported and underprosecuted.[14]

For other violent crimes, victimization rates are much higher for males than for females, and reporting problems cannot explain all of the difference. Household victimization surveys, a reasonably effective check on underreporting (except for domestic violence), show much higher victimization rates for men.[15] In homicide, an offense for which victimization data are extremely reliable, we find that men and boys, 49% of the population, represent 74% of homicide victims.[16] Over their lifetimes, men are about three times more likely than women to become the victims of homicide.[17] For an African-American man, the chance of becoming a homicide victim is four-and-a-half times higher than for an African-American woman, and sixteen times higher than for a white woman.[18]

Women's disproportionate victimization is nonetheless a reality, but it is a complex one, rooted not only in raw numbers but in judgments about the vulnerability of female victims and, perhaps,

---

[13] The Justice Department's household survey data indicate that only 8% of reported rape victims are male, but these data do not include the rapes (largely male) that occur in institutional settings, such as prisons. *See* BUREAU OF JUSTICE STATISTICS, U.S. DEP'T OF JUSTICE, HIGHLIGHTS FROM 20 YEARS OF SURVEYING CRIME VICTIMS 9 (1993). There are no reliable data on the incidence and prevalence of rape in prisons, but some studies, extrapolating from crude survey data, estimate that among inmates of prisons, jails, and juvenile "reform schools," there may be as many as 290,000 male rape victims per year. *See* Stephen Donaldson, *The Rape Crisis Behind Bars*, N.Y. TIMES, Dec. 29, 1993, at A11. That figure is more than double the Bureau of Justice Statistics' estimate for the number of female rape victims annually, although many believe that the number of female victims is much higher. *See id.* Inattention to sexual assault in prisons does not only harm the men who are its immediate victims; some observers believe that men and boys who are sexually victimized in custodial institutions are more likely to become rapists themselves when they are released. *See id.*

[14] *See, e.g.*, S. REP. NO. 197, at 38 (noting that "[r]ape and domestic violence are some of the most underreported crimes in America"); S. REP. NO. 545, at 33 (noting witness testimony to the effect that "rape is still underreported and underprosecuted"); MARGARET T. GORDON & STEPHANIE RIGER, THE FEMALE FEAR: THE SOCIAL COST OF RAPE 34-37 (1991) (discussing the underreporting of rape).

[15] *See* VICTIMIZATION IN 1991, *supra* note 11, at 6 (finding 40.3 violent crimes against men per 1000 persons, but only 22.9 violent crimes against women per 1000 persons); REPORT TO THE NATION, *supra* note 9, at 27 (reporting that while men suffer assault at a rate of 32 per 1000 persons, women suffer assault at a rate of only 17 per 1000 persons).

[16] *See* REPORT TO THE NATION, *supra* note 9, at 28.

[17] *See id.*

[18] *See id.*

an assumption of some contributory fault with regard to many of the victims on the male side: victims who provoked fights, assumed risks, or went looking for trouble. The victimization of women seems disproportionate not simply to women's share of the population but to their desert; the victimization of women seems particularly unfair. The proper complaint, therefore, is not that the victimization statistics lack "objectivity," because observations about women's disproportionate victimization involve an irreducible normative element. That perceptions about women's victimization rest in part on socially constructed value judgments does not, of course, render such perceptions invalid or unimportant.

What the data themselves suggest is that the criminal justice system's preoccupation with male offenders and male victims is not exclusively an artifact of cultural bias in reporting and charging behavior. In part, this preoccupation reflects the nature of the underlying phenomenon of crime in our society and probably most others. Nor would we expect (or want) progress for women to increase women's participation as offenders or as homicide, robbery, and assault victims.[19] So for the foreseeable future, the raw material of criminal justice is likely to remain, to an overwhelming extent, disproportionately male in character.

Under these circumstances women have, until very recently, remained at the margins of thought about criminal justice problems. The criminal justice system has been run by men, against men, and for the benefit of men. Not so much different from the rest of society, but more so.

The Sections that follow consider some of what needs to be done to correct that imbalance in four areas of special concern to women—domestic violence, rape, sentencing, and prisons.

---

[19] On the possibility that women's independence and increased workforce participation might increase women's rates of offending, see *infra* text accompanying notes 125-29. For a discussion of connections between women's independence and society's stereotypes of women as criminals, see Susan N. Herman, *Thelma and Louise and Bonnie and Jean: Images of Women as Criminals*, 2 S. CAL. REV. L. & WOMEN'S STUD. 53, 62 (1992); Elizabeth V. Spelman & Martha Minow, *Outlaw Women: An Essay on* Thelma and Louise, 26 NEW ENG. L. REV. 1281, 1281 (1992).

II. DOMESTIC VIOLENCE

Lack of attention to domestic violence has a venerable tradition in the criminal justice system. Failure to prosecute abusive husbands was not just the result of inattention, because for centuries, the criminal law gave the husband an affirmative privilege to beat his wife in order to provide her with what was seen as appropriate chastisement and instruction.[20] The husband's formal privilege of chastisement was abolished by the end of the nineteenth century,[21] but wife beating continued. The extent of it cannot be measured precisely, but even the cautious studies point to high levels of abuse: 28% of all women experiencing a violent assault at some point in their marriages; 16% of married women assaulted by a spouse in a single year.[22]

This culture of spousal abuse coexists with a police practice of not arresting wife beaters, especially in cases perceived as "ordinary" misdemeanor assaults.[23] Many episodes of domestic violence involve life-threatening attacks, assaults with guns, knives, and other weapons, or brutal battering that leaves serious physical injuries. Police are likely to take such cases more seriously than the much

---

[20] *See* Anne M. Coughlin, *Excusing Women*, 82 CAL. L. REV. 1, 40-41 (1994) (noting that the husband's right to chastise his wife stemmed from "the belief that married women suffered from a volitional disability"); Joyce E. McConnell, *Beyond Metaphor: Battered Women, Involuntary Servitude and the Thirteenth Amendment*, 4 YALE J.L. & FEMINISM 207, 232 (1992) (noting that "[t]he batterer's belief in a man's right to chastise his partner and to coerce sexual services remains entrenched in the law"). Blackstone attempted to rationalize the husband's privilege of chastisement by connecting it to the marital coercion doctrine, under which a husband could be liable for crimes the wife might commit in his presence (actual or constructive). It was only fitting, Blackstone argued, that the husband have a corresponding privilege of chastisement in order to deter his wife from actions that would expose him to criminal liability. *See* 1 WILLIAM BLACKSTONE, COMMENTARIES 432 ("For, as he is to answer for her misbehaviour, the law thought it reasonable to intrust him with this power of restraining her, by domestic chastisement, in the same moderation that a man is allowed to correct his servants or children . . . .").

[21] *See, e.g.*, Fulgham v. State, 46 Ala. 143, 143 (1871) (abolishing a husband's right to chastise his wife); The Queen v. Jackson, 1 Q.B. 671, 681-82 (1891) (abolishing the right of marital chastisement in England); *see also* Bernadette D. Sewell, Note, *History of Abuse: Societal, Judicial, and Legislative Responses to the Problem of Wife Beating*, 23 SUFFOLK U. L. REV. 983, 984 (1989) (noting that legal authorization of marital chastisement "continued to exist in many Western cultures until the late nineteenth century").

[22] *See* Frieze & Browne, *supra* note 12, at 179.

[23] *See* LAWRENCE W. SHERMAN, POLICING DOMESTIC VIOLENCE: EXPERIMENTS AND DILEMMAS 26-27 (1992) (describing patterns of underenforcement of domestic violence laws).

more numerous domestic disturbances classified as misdemeanors—those involving loud arguments, slapping, shoving, and kicking.[24] Arrest rates in spousal abuse cases range from a low of only 12% to a high of no more than 50%.[25] Up through the 1970s, police training materials instructed officers to avoid making an arrest whenever possible,[26] and in several states, the majority of police departments had explicit policies against making arrests in domestic assault cases.[27]

Advocates for battered women brought a number of lawsuits challenging these practices on sex discrimination grounds.[28] There is, however, a problem in trying to attack police practices in this way: arrest rates are very low in all kinds of assault cases, even those involving assailants who are strangers to the victim.[29] Yet the woman who is repeatedly abused by her partner probably needs police protection much more than a man who gets into a fight in a bar. So lawyers working for battered women shifted their focus from one of trying to eliminate sex discrimination to one of trying to eliminate discretion. Mandatory arrest is now the solution favored by many leading advocates for battered women.[30]

---

[24] *See id.* at 26 (noting that police widely ignore domestic violence that involves only slaps and kicks).

[25] *See* Delbert S. Elliott, *Criminal Justice Procedures in Family Violence Crimes*, *in* FAMILY VIOLENCE, *supra* note 12, at 427, 438.

[26] *See* ROGER LANGLEY & RICHARD C. LEVY, WIFE BEATING: THE SILENT CRISIS 164-65 (1977) (citing the Detroit Police Department's General Orders which imply that domestic violence is not a crime); Elliott, *supra* note 25, at 435 (noting that "[t]here is little question that the . . . 'hands off' view predominated prior to the early 1970s" and that "[p]olice training materials clearly specified that, when responding to domestic disputes, arrest was to be avoided whenever possible").

[27] *See* Lawrence W. Sherman & Richard A. Berk, *The Minneapolis Domestic Violence Experiment*, POLICE FOUND. REP., Apr. 1984, at 7, 8.

[28] *See, e.g.*, Thurman v. City of Torrington, 595 F. Supp. 1521, 1531 (D. Conn. 1984) (denying the defendant's motion to dismiss a Fourteenth Amendment claim that police provided less protection to women abused by spouses or boyfriends than to victims of nondomestic violence); Bruno v. Codd, 396 N.Y.S.2d 974, 979 (Sup. Ct. 1977) (denying a police department's motion for summary judgment on charges of inadequately protecting women from their abusive husbands), *rev'd*, 407 N.Y.S.2d 165 (App. Div. 1978) (mem.), *and aff'd*, 393 N.E.2d 976 (N.Y. 1979); *see also* Joan Zorza, *The Criminal Law of Misdemeanor Domestic Violence, 1970-1990*, 83 J. CRIM. L. & CRIMINOLOGY 46, 53-60 (1992) (documenting the history of sex discrimination in suits filed against violent husbands).

[29] *See* Elliott, *supra* note 25, at 438-41 (examining the similarity between arrest rates for assaults committed against family members and for similar violent crimes perpetuated against strangers).

[30] *See, e.g.*, Clifford Krauss, *Keeping in Touch with the Victims of Domestic Violence*, N.Y. TIMES, Nov. 21, 1994, at B3 (noting victims' advocates' praise for mandatory

A. *Mandatory Arrest Through the Lens of Feminist Jurisprudence*

Domestic violence, a central issue in the struggle to assure dignity and equality for women, is extensively discussed in feminist literature.[31] Yet there has been little effort to consider how battles over theoretical commitments or attempts to refine theoretical paradigms might inform efforts to begin solving this critical problem.

One obvious irony involves the manner in which the tactic favored by many feminist reformers (mandatory arrest) collides with the part of feminist theory that advocates open-textured standards and attention to the nuances of relationships. Feminists inspired by the work of Carol Gilligan[32] reject inflexible rights as a distinctively male conception.[33] Police officers who do not arrest battering husbands are not being very "male" in that sense. They are making ad hoc judgments, based on their intuitions about the whole situation.

This sort of police discretion is presumably not what Gilligan really meant by an ethic of care and connection. Nevertheless, the example highlights a more general point about the supposed clash between a male ethic of rights and a female ethic of context and relationship. There is nothing especially feminist about an ad hoc, discretionary approach to making decisions. It all depends on the values that inform the exercise of the discretion. Nor should we automatically count as "feminist" any ethic that emphasizes caring, connection, and the continuity of relationships. There are situations where that ethic is not only out of place, but dangerous to women.[34] Everything depends on the particular problem, the

---

arrest policies instituted in New York City).

[31] For references to the recent literature, see SANFORD H. KADISH & STEPHEN J. SCHULHOFER, CRIMINAL LAW AND ITS PROCESSES 829 & n.2 (6th ed. 1995).

[32] *See, e.g.*, GILLIGAN, *supra* note 4.

[33] *See, e.g.*, M. Kay Harris, *Moving into the New Millennium: Toward a Feminist Vision of Justice*, PRISON J., Fall-Winter 1987, at 27, 32 ("[In Gilligan's research] [m]en were more likely to employ a 'rights/justice' orientation [toward moral issues] and women were more likely to reflect a 'care/response' orientation . . . ."); Frances Heidensohn, *Models of Justice: Portia or Persephone? Some Thoughts on Equality, Fairness and Gender in the Field of Criminal Justice*, 14 INT'L J. SOC. L. 287, 295-96 (1986) (noting that men become "detached, autonomous and individualized" in their quest for justice, while women tend to focus on context and caring).

[34] An "ethic of care" poses related dangers in such criminal justice contexts as the juvenile court movement, civil commitment of the mentally ill, and rehabilitative models of sentencing. *See* Stephen J. Schulhofer, *The Gender Question in Criminal Law*, SOC. PHIL. & POL'Y, Spring 1990, at 105, 124. In particular,

values presupposed, and the kinds of people who will make the judgments. As Kathleen Daly observes:

> When court officials define crime and impose sanctions, they use relational reasoning and an ethic of care toward defendants .... This female voice may not contain the same relational concerns that women (or feminists) desire, but that is different from saying that men's form of legal reasoning does not contain relational, caretaking, or responsibility concerns. Thus, the problem in criminal-court practices is not that the female voice is absent, but that certain relations are presupposed, maintained, and reproduced.[35]

Scholars associated with what is often called "radical feminism" approach this problem from the opposite direction. They argue that women should have an absolute right to bodily integrity and protection from aggression.[36] Formal equality (a "liberal feminist" stance) is a poor benchmark here because men involved in fights and minor assaults do not have the same need for state protection from one another that women have for protection from assaultive men. Thus, even if the police are equally inattentive to acquaintance assaults when victims are men or women, the state's seemingly even-handed inaction is nonetheless an affirmative policy that contributes to the subordination of women.[37] For feminists committed to this view, society has an obligation to use arrest powers vigorously when a man violates a woman's right to physical safety.[38] This is a coherent perspective, and surely an appealing

---

> the model of caring and connection [is flawed] because . . . conflicting interests are inherent in any criminal justice system that serves society's interests in deterrence and social protection. A system of criminal law premised on caring and connection will simply mask conflict and invite the abuses that vague standards of intervention have produced over and over in ostensibly benign programs.

Id. (citation omitted).

[35] Kathleen Daly, *Criminal Justice Ideologies and Practices in Different Voices: Some Feminist Questions About Justice*, 17 INT'L J. SOC. L. 1, 2 (1989).

[36] *See, e.g.*, MACKINNON, *supra* note 3, at 41 (noting that in domestic relationships, battery of women tends to be ignored, whereas "[w]hen [men] are hit, a person has been assaulted").

[37] *See id.* at 76 (arguing that when government refuses to prosecute for marital rape, "the woman's obligation to deliver sexually is effectively enforced by the state").

[38] *See* Kathleen Waits, *The Criminal Justice System's Response to Battering: Understanding the Problem, Forging the Solutions*, *in* FEMINIST JURISPRUDENCE 188, 202 (Patricia Smith ed., 1993) (arguing that "[a]rrest of the batterer is the central element of an effective police response"); Zorza, *supra* note 28, at 66 (arguing that in order to deter batterers effectively, more severe sanctions should be imposed).

one, but it takes no account of the psychological, social, and institutional dynamics that determine whether, and under what conditions, a "get tough" approach will really help a particular victim or women in general.

B. *Evaluating Mandatory Arrest*

Good policy for domestic violence cases depends less on the theoretical appeal of either "absolute rights" or "relational reasoning" than on the actual effect of laws and policies that translate these conceptions into operational strategies. In Minneapolis, police conducted an experiment to determine the effect of arrest in misdemeanor assault cases.[39] The result was dramatic support for mandatory arrest: by every measure, arrest was reported to be more effective than other responses such as counseling the parties or sending the suspect away.[40] The results were widely reported and enthusiastically received; numerous police departments adopted rules requiring arrest in domestic assault cases, and more than a dozen states enacted statutes mandating that approach statewide.[41] By 1989, only five years after the study results were released, 84% of urban police agencies reported having mandatory or preferred arrest policies for domestic violence cases.[42]

Unfortunately, the rapid and uncritical acceptance of the Minneapolis findings was premature because flaws in the study made it hard to be sure that reported deterrent effects of arrest were not spurious.[43] To afford a more complete picture, experi-

[39] *See* Lawrence W. Sherman & Richard A. Berk, *The Specific Deterrent Effects of Arrest for Domestic Assault*, 49 AM. SOC. REV. 261, 262 (1984) (reporting the results of the Minneapolis study).

[40] *See* Sherman & Berk, *supra* note 27, at 7. For an example of early warnings about possible flaws in the Minneapolis study and the need for caution in interpreting its findings, see Elliott, *supra* note 25, at 453-54.

[41] *See* Lawrence W. Sherman & Ellen G. Cohn, *The Impact of Research on Legal Policy: The Minneapolis Domestic Violence Experiment*, 23 L. & SOC'Y REV. 117, 129 (1989) (noting that "[t]he publicity about the Minneapolis experiment did reach a large number of police departments and may have had a substantial . . . influence on policy"); Zorza, *supra* note 28, at 64-65 nn.182-86 (citing to the applicable state statutes).

[42] *See* Lawrence W. Sherman, *The Influence of Criminology on Criminal Law: Evaluating Arrests for Misdemeanor Domestic Violence*, 83 J. CRIM. L. & CRIMINOLOGY 1, 23-24 (1992).

[43] Some of the deterrence effects were inferred from official arrest records, but such records cannot reveal whether arrest is deterring subsequent violence or only subsequent reports. The Minneapolis study attempted to control for this problem through follow-up interviews with victims, but there was a large falloff in victim

ments testing the effects of mandatory arrest were repeated, among broader demographic groups and with better data-collection procedures, in five other cities.[44] In three of them, arrest had a greater deterrent effect than other responses only in the short run; the effect tended to diminish over time, and within a year after the initial intervention, suspects who had been arrested were *more* likely to engage in repeat violence than those who had merely been warned.[45] A reanalysis of the Minneapolis data revealed a similar pattern in that city.[46] Over time, in other words, arrest often seems to have an "escalation effect," aggravating the subsequent violence.

Advocates for battered women have attacked these more recent studies, especially the "do nothing" strategy they seem to support. As one attorney writes, "We do not consider eliminating arrest for . . . [robbery], [just] because it may not deter a particular . . . class of individuals."[47] Unfortunately, that is a dangerous answer. The objective here is to protect battered women. If arrest is not doing that, we need to consider using other solutions, either in conjunction with arrest or as an alternative to it. Moreover, the danger is not just that arrest may not deter, but that in some situations, arrest may make matters worse. Mandatory arrest may cause more violence to the very women we are trying to help.

Other unintended harms to women have emerged as well. In mandatory arrest jurisdictions, police are sometimes obliged to arrest the abused woman because her partner alleges that *she* had hit

---

participation in the follow-ups, and the follow-up study was limited to only six months, a period when temporary deterrence effects may dominate to the extent that court proceedings remain possible. *See* Elliott, *supra* note 25, at 453 (noting that only 49% of the victims in the Minneapolis study completed all 12 follow-up interviews).

[44] *See* SHERMAN, *supra* note 23, at 15-18 (reporting results from similar experiments conducted in Omaha, Charlotte, Milwaukee, Colorado Springs, and Miami).

[45] *See id.* at 17, 188-87 (describing an initial deterrent effect of arrest, followed by a subsequent escalation in the likelihood of repeat violence in Omaha, Charlotte, and Milwaukee).

[46] In Minneapolis, the deterrent effects of arrest (measured by victim interviews) decayed over time and disappeared after six months. *See id.* at 197. Although the Minneapolis study did not collect victim interview data after six months, the trend of the data suggests the possibility of an escalation effect after the six-month point. (When repeat violence was measured by official arrest records, arrest had a clear deterrent effect that continued for the entire 18-month period studied. *See id.* But official records may present a misleading picture of the actual level of battering, if arrest deters victims from reporting subsequent incidents to the police.)

[47] Zorza, *supra* note 28, at 66.

him.[48] And there is some indication that visible, highly popular mandatory arrest programs have permitted legislators to reduce their support for more costly solutions like shelters for battered women.[49]

Surprisingly, the tentative Minneapolis study and its recommendations for a more punitive approach received widespread attention and an immediately favorable reception, but public officials and the media have either attacked or ignored the more thorough studies that suggest the opposite conclusion.[50] Theoretical and ideological commitments to punitive strategies and to a rights-oriented response to aggression seem to dominate any concern for designing operational programs which actually help abused women. Yet the best available evidence suggests that an across-the-board policy of mandatory arrest should be anathema to feminists. As Lawrence Sherman writes, using mandatory arrest to fight domestic violence "may make as much sense as fighting fire with gasoline."[51]

C. *Selective Mandatory Arrest?*

An important qualification to this pessimistic assessment of mandatory arrest emerges when data from the follow-up studies are disaggregated. The escalation effect seems especially strong when the batterer is unemployed, but arrest does appear to have a net deterrent effect when the husband has a job or other marks of social stability.[52] That finding triggers a further series of dilemmas. Should we arrest only the employed? If not, should we arrest in all cases, knowing that this will harm some women? A third possibility is to leave the decision to each officer on the spot. That would probably give us the worst of both worlds: police would arrest blacks and the underclass while letting off middle-class white

---

[48] In Connecticut, mandatory arrest policies reportedly led to the arrest of both spouses in 14% of the cases. *See* Jan Hoffman, *When Men Hit Women*, N.Y. TIMES, Feb. 16, 1992, (Magazine), at 23, 26. Moreover, if children are present and no other caretaker for them is available, the children may have to be placed in state custody until one of the parents is released. *See id.*

[49] *See* SHERMAN, *supra* note 23, at 255.

[50] *See id.* at 135-36 (describing political attacks on empirical research and the unwillingness of the Wisconsin legislature to repeal its mandatory arrest statute after the Milwaukee study had indicated the harmful effects of that policy); *id.* at 266 (describing sparse press coverage of the Milwaukee findings); Sherman & Cohn, *supra* note 41, at 129 (stating that publicity about the Minneapolis study reached a large number of police departments and had a substantial influence on policy).

[51] SHERMAN, *supra* note 23, at 210.

[52] *See id.* at 155.

offenders with a warning.[53] In practice we would get warnings when arrest might really help and arrest when it is most likely to be counterproductive.

A final possibility is to leave the choice up to the victim.[54] This seems a promising option, but it too conceals dilemmas and risks. Victims know the offender better than the police do and may be able to predict whether his arrest will be an effective deterrent. Deference to the victim's wishes also may strengthen her self-esteem and empower her within the relationship. Yet there are important countervailing concerns. Few victims will be aware of the long-run escalation effects of arrest or of the complex roots of that phenomenon. Moreover, the victim will have to make her decision at a moment of great stress with little relevant information and little time for reflection.[55] Even if the police talk privately to the victim in a separate room, the offender may perceive that her preferences control the arrest decision, and if so, the escalation effects of arrest could be aggravated. Deference to the victim could backfire in another way if victims who fear retaliation are deterred from expressing their preference for arrest.

The effects of deferring to the victim's preferences are worth studying carefully, but there is little reason to hope that such a policy will offer a panacea for the dilemmas we have been considering. In any case, to underscore the obvious, theoretical conceptions of domination and related commitments to "empowering the victim"[56] provide little practical guidance to those who want to find a way to help women caught in abusive relationships. The value of deference to victim preferences turns on the specific methods used to make that policy operational and on the complex, multidirectional effects that those methods will have in practice.

---

[53] *See, e.g.*, Caroline Forell, *Stopping the Violence: Mandatory Arrest and Police Tort Liability for Failure to Assist Battered Women*, 6 BERKELEY WOMEN'S L.J. 215, 221 (1991) (summarizing results of a Duluth study in which minority males comprised 8.5% of those arrested under a policy of mandatory arrest, but comprised 33% of arrestees when the decision to arrest was left to police officers' discretion).

[54] *See, e.g.*, David A. Ford, *Prosecution as a Victim Power Resource: A Note on Empowering Women in Violent Conjugal Relationships*, 25 L. & SOC'Y REV. 313, 330 (1991) (evaluating deference to victim preferences in deciding whether to arrest and prosecute batterers).

[55] To make matters worse, a significant number of domestic violence victims (21% in one city studied) are intoxicated at the time police arrive on the scene. *See* SHERMAN, *supra* note 23, at 207.

[56] *See* Ford, *supra* note 54, at 317-20 (discussing empowerment theories).

D. *Getting Tougher: Giving Content to "Arrest"*

Instead of seeking to minimize arrest, especially for unemployed husbands, a more promising approach might be to consider *more* severe sanctions for all categories of offenders. Indeed, mandatory arrest may appear ineffective or dangerous in part because the response being advocated ("arrest") is mainly a slogan, not a fully specified policy. In many cities, suspects arrested on domestic violence charges are free within a few hours; among the six cities in which mandatory arrest experiments were conducted, average times in custody varied from twenty-four hours to only two.[57]

The constitutional right to bail[58] accounts for some of the rapid release times and may make that feature of the current landscape difficult to change. Nonetheless, rapid release times probably are not a major cause of the ineffectiveness of mandatory arrest, because most of the experiments show some deterrence over the short run, even when suspects spent very little time in jail.[59] The problem is that the deterrence effect of arrest tends to dissipate, and escalation effects begin to dominate, roughly six months after the arrest.[60] The decay of deterrence effects could be slowed by making the initial arrest a more unpleasant experience, but that approach obviously risks making the escalation effects more severe as well.

There is another reason why mandatory arrest is primarily a slogan, not a concrete policy. To advocate "arrest" says nothing about what should happen after the arrestee's inevitable release on recognizance or money bail. Husbands arrested for misdemeanor assault are almost never prosecuted.[61] An obvious option is to combine the increased use of arrest with a greater determination to get convictions and jail time. But the available data permit little confidence that prosecution provides the easy answer. In Milwaukee and Charlotte, two cities in which mandatory arrest appeared to produce an escalation effect, the percentage of suspects prosecuted

---

[57] *See* SHERMAN, *supra* note 23, at 140-42. Longer times in custody did not correlate cleanly with either the deterrence effects or the escalation effects, perhaps because times were poorly measured, and other factors that affect the severity of the arrest experience (jail conditions, for example) were not measured at all. *See id.*

[58] *See* U.S. CONST. amend. VIII.

[59] *See* SHERMAN, *supra* note 23, at 129, 141.

[60] *See id.* at 189.

[61] *See* Sherman, *supra* note 42, at 29 (reporting that in Minneapolis, only 4% of those arrested were ever convicted, and in Milwaukee, only 1% were ever convicted).

and convicted was only 1% and 28% respectively.[62] But substantial escalation effects also occurred in Omaha, a city where 64% of the arrestees were prosecuted and convicted.[63]

Normatively, as well, the increased-prosecution approach poses uncomfortable choices. Since employed offenders seem to be deterred by arrest alone,[64] do we reserve prosecution and jail time for the unemployed? That's not easy to live with. Or do we jail all the offenders? If so, the men who had jobs often will lose them, and middle-class wives who have sought help in the past may now be afraid to call the police. And no matter which way we resolve these issues, we still cannot be sure that a more punitive approach will have a net deterrent effect overall. For the chronic, seriously violent batterer, vigorous prosecution and substantial prison time are usually appropriate. But unless we are willing to treat every episode of domestic assault as a felony deserving a year or more in prison, the deterrent and incapacitative effects of punishment, in cases not involving a weapon or serious bodily injury, are inherently limited.

E. *Other Alternatives*

Because mandatory arrest and other punitive responses have such problematic effects, other options need to be explored. Yet the array of promising alternatives is meager.

One seemingly constructive approach is for the officer on the scene to refer the abuser to counseling services, possibly with the added inducement of a court order or a threat to arrest after any repeat episode. Unfortunately, evaluations of this option are just as pessimistic as those concerning the use of arrest. There is as yet no evidence that counseling reduces the offender's propensity for repeat violence.[65] What is worse, because women are more likely to remain with an abuser who is in counseling, the likelihood of further victimization actually increases when the counseling option is used.[66] Thus, counseling, like mandatory arrest, actually seems

---

62 *See* SHERMAN, *supra* note 23, at 141-42.

63 *See id.*; Franklyn W. Dunford et al., *The Role of Arrest in Domestic Assault: The Omaha Police Experiment*, 28 CRIMINOLOGY 183, 193 (1990).

64 *See supra* text accompanying note 52.

65 *See* SHERMAN, *supra* note 23, at 249 (noting that "no randomized experiment yet demonstrat[es] that court-ordered counseling can reduce the frequency or prevalence of repeat domestic violence"); Zorza, *supra* note 28, at 67 (noting that "completing batterer treatment made no difference in stopping future violence").

66 *See* Zorza, *supra* note 28, at 67 (suggesting that victims may be "deceived" into

associated with an escalation effect. Such findings obviously do not mean that counseling *cannot* be helpful. Outcomes may depend on the structure and quality of the counseling programs, the kinds of offenders who participate in them, the degree to which participation is coerced, and so on. Well-conceived programs certainly deserve to be funded, tried, and tested, but until that can be done, the counseling option needs to be viewed with caution.

Orders of protection can backfire in a similar way. As a popular component of domestic violence reform legislation, orders of protection have proved notoriously ineffective, largely because statutory mandates and newly created rights have not been accompanied by commensurate efforts to provide necessary resources or to educate police, court officials, and victims in the proper use of new procedures.[67] As a result, such orders may serve only to foster misplaced confidence that ultimately leaves victims at greater risk.[68] Except in the case of the most determined aggressors, orders of protection probably can contribute to the protection of abused women, provided they are backed by thorough training and better resources. In the absence of substantial and sustained institutional support, however, they risk causing more harm than good.

Another important approach is to expand the availability of shelters for battered women, so that victims can more easily leave abusive relationships. Police called to the scene of a domestic assault could be required to explain that option and to offer to transport the victim directly to a shelter if she wishes. Lawrence Sherman suggests this approach as a possible way for police to protect the victim against both the long-run escalation effects of arresting the abuser and the short-run dangers of leaving the scene without arresting him.[69]

Theoretical commitments and intuitions of fairness prompt resistance to this approach, however. Why should the victim be the

---

reconciling with abusers in counseling because the victims may think that counseling will produce an end to the violent behavior).

[67] A study by the National Institute of Justice found that police often fail to inform victims of available remedies, fail to serve the orders of protection on the abuser (thus nullifying their effect), and fail to arrest when orders of protection are violated. *See* Peter Finn, *Civil Protection Orders: A Flawed Opportunity for Intervention*, *in* WOMAN BATTERING: POLICY RESPONSES 155, 182 (Michael Steinman ed., 1991).

[68] *See* Janice Grau et al., *Restraining Orders for Battered Women: Issues of Access and Efficacy*, WOMEN & POL., Fall 1984, at 13, 27 (calling for improvement of the procedures for obtaining, and enforcing, restraining orders).

[69] *See* SHERMAN, *supra* note 23, at 208-10.

one who has to leave her home? Why not require the *abuser* to leave? Of course, the victim still can reject the offer; she could not be *required* to leave. But when a police officer refuses to arrest the abuser and encourages the victim to accept transportation to a shelter, we can hardly view state policy as simply facilitating the exercise of a wholly "voluntary" choice.

The Minneapolis experiment tested the option of requiring the abuser to leave the premises (ostensibly for eight hours) without arresting him.[70] In reality, however, the abuser was free to return as soon as the police left. Only arrest or an order of protection will keep the abuser out of the home, but these responses can be ineffective and dangerous, as we have seen. In any case, the Minneapolis experiment showed that requiring the abuser merely to leave produced high rates of repeat violence.[71] Against that background, the fact that the victim has a right to remain on the premises, while the abuser has none, can be dispositive only as a matter of pure theory. When a terrorist is spraying the street with bullets, those of us who have the right to remain on the sidewalk may prefer not to stand our ground. In an imperfect world, discretion may be the better part of valor. And the world of efforts to control domestic violence is hedged by imperfections at every turn.

F. *Developing Effective Responses*

The preceding considerations suggest that sharply etched, theoretically satisfying positions are unlikely to carry us very far toward effective solutions to the problem of domestic violence. Helpful responses are more likely to be complex, eclectic, costly, and elusive.

Several components of a constructive policy nonetheless can be identified. First, complex and contingent response strategies must not obscure the message that spousal abuse is a *crime* and that it will not be tolerated. Every police response must be structured to send the offender a clear warning that domestic violence is unacceptable and that future incidents will be met with increasingly punitive responses. Similarly, to combat any police tendency to take domestic violence cases cavalierly, officers need guidelines that require an energetic response. Mandatory arrest serves that function but only

---

[70] *See* Sherman & Berk, *supra* note 27, at 7, 9.
[71] *See id.* at 7, 12.

at some risk to the women we are trying to help. A more useful rule of thumb, therefore, would not insist on arrest per se, but mandatory action—action of some sort, from a list of strong, constructive alternatives,[72] and a mandatory report (normally in writing), both to ensure a thoughtful response and to inform officers who might be called to the same address in the future.

Specific response options will necessarily reflect the services and programs (including prosecution programs) available in the particular jurisdiction; over the longer run, effort should focus on strengthening and evaluating alternative approaches. For chronic offenders and cases involving serious injuries, a vigorous prosecution program should assure substantial jail or prison terms. In the most minor cases, a stern warning or a reference to counseling may be appropriate, especially if records are adequate to assure that there have been no prior episodes of violence involving the same couple. For cases falling in between these extremes, arrest or some other means of separating the parties should be considered, with choices depending on the woman's desire to preserve the relationship, the history of past abuse, and other relevant circumstances. Where resources and back-up procedures permit, it may be appropriate to require the husband to leave and stay away long enough for the wife to obtain an effective order of protection. But if that avenue seems unlikely to afford real safety for the woman, an offer to transport her to a shelter may be appropriate, if that is the course she prefers.

The spousal-abuse problem illustrates two general points that apply to criminal justice and to probably most other areas of the legal system. First, legal, social, and institutional details are critical. Second, quick-fix statutes and doctrinal change do very little, and may even backfire, unless they are backed by changes in attitudes, personnel, and resources.

III. RAPE

I have just suggested that rigid rules will not work well in domestic violence cases. There, we need to rely on flexible standards. For rape statutes, I reach the opposite conclusion.

---

[72] *See* SHERMAN, *supra* note 23, at 253-56 (listing options including transporting the victim to a shelter, taking the suspect or victim to a detoxification treatment center, and allowing the victim to decide if an immediate arrest should be made).

At one time, the law of rape openly denied equality to women, for example, in rules that required special corroboration for rape complaints.[73] Formal inequalities have largely disappeared, but the problems have not. Most of the problems stem from the highly contextual way that the formally equal doctrines of rape law are applied in practice. As in the case of arrests for domestic violence, the law is quite preoccupied with the nuances of the relationship between the alleged offender and the victim. What is missing is not a jurisprudence of context. What is missing is sufficient respect for what should be clear-cut rights.

Because the current feminist critiques are by now familiar, I will sketch the problems and the prevalent criticisms rather quickly. Then I will suggest a perspective that is a bit different from the ones most often discussed.

A. *The Prevailing Law of Rape*

The controversies are framed by a definition of rape that has been with us since the time of Blackstone—intercourse by force and without consent.[74] There have been two important waves of statutory reforms, the Model Penal Code revision in the 1950s and revisions inspired by feminist reformers in the 1970s.[75] New statutes relaxed the rules of evidence and tinkered with the definitions of force and consent. But all of the statutes accepted the basic framework, which still requires both force and nonconsent.[76]

---

[73] *See, e.g.*, United States v. Wiley, 492 F.2d 547, 550-51 (D.C. Cir. 1973) (establishing that a person may not be convicted of a "sex offense" unless the testimony of the victim is corroborated by, for example, medical evidence); *see also* Note, *The Rape Corroboration Requirement: Repeal Not Reform*, 81 YALE L.J. 1365, 1366-72 (1972) (recounting the history and status of the corroboration requirement). *Wiley* was overruled by United States v. Sheppard, 569 F.2d 114, 117 (D.C. Cir. 1977) (holding that corroboration of the victim's testimony is no longer a requirement for conviction in a sex offense case). Nearly all American jurisdictions have abandoned special corroboration rules applicable only to rape complaints. *See* KADISH & SCHULHOFER, *supra* note 31, at 371 (noting that no American state now requires corroboration in forcible rape cases).

[74] *See* 4 WILLIAM BLACKSTONE, COMMENTARIES 210 (defining rape as "carnal knowledge of a woman forcibly and against her will").

[75] For a discussion of the background and specific elements of the reforms of the 1950s and the 1970s, see Stephen J. Schulhofer, *Taking Sexual Autonomy Seriously: Rape Law and Beyond*, 11 L. & PHIL. 35, 36-40 (1992).

[76] *See id.* at 38-39.

The reforms of the 1970s made convictions somewhat easier, but important kinds of abuse still are not covered by statutory language. Two examples from recent cases will serve to illustrate my points.

1. The defendant meets the victim in a singles bar, and she gives him a ride home. When they get there, she turns down his invitation to come inside, but he is not about to take "no" for an answer. He takes her car keys from the ignition and pleads with her to come in for a few minutes. It is 1:00 a.m., in an unfamiliar neighborhood, and she is frightened, so she goes with him under protest. In his room, he presses her for sex. She keeps saying "no" and starts to cry, but she eventually submits so that he will let her leave.[77]

The appellate court said it would uphold the rape conviction in this case, but only because there was evidence that the defendant had threatened the victim with direct physical harm.[78] Why should that detail be critical to the result?

2. The defendant and the victim live together for several months. He often beats her to make her meet his sexual demands. Eventually, she moves out, but one day they meet again and go to a friend's house to talk. The defendant bluntly announces that he wants sex, but she refuses. He orders her to lie down on a bed. She freezes in fear, while he undresses her and penetrates her.[79]

Should that kind of behavior be sufficient to make out a case of rape? The North Carolina Supreme Court said the evidence of nonconsent was overwhelming. But it also said there was no proof that the defendant had used force. So it reversed the conviction.[80]

These are situations where the defendant's behavior is egregiously wrong, by any standard of common decency. But existing conceptions of force and nonconsent are not clear enough to make the conduct illegal.

B. *Strategies for Reform*

Most reformers responding to problems such as those described above make essentially two points: 1) "no" means no,[81] and 2) force should extend from explicit to implicit threats, from

---

[77] *See* State v. Rusk, 424 A.2d 720 (Md. 1981).

[78] *See id.* at 728.

[79] *See* State v. Alston, 312 S.E.2d 470 (N.C. 1984).

[80] *See id.* at 475-76.

[81] *See, e.g.*, ESTRICH, *supra* note 7, at 102 (maintaining that the law should define "consent" in such a way that "no" means no).

violence to implicit power.[82] These points are plausible, and they are certainly widely accepted. But on close inspection, these solutions turn out to be misdirected.

1. "No" Means No

It is hard to see why the claim that "no" means no should be considered a revolutionary idea, but many people are still hotly debating it. In a recent article, Professors Husak and Thomas marshalled social science surveys in which many women say that, for them, "no" *does not* mean no.[83] The authors conclude that contemporary American culture does not give a verbal "no" the meaning of unequivocal nonconsent that I and others have attributed to it. They write that "Schulhofer's proposal [to treat a verbal "no" as sufficient to establish nonconsent] is not without cost to women [because] it distorts rather than accurately represents [existing social] convention[s] . . . ."[84]

These objections to treating "no" as unequivocal evidence of nonconsent reflect conceptual, as well as political, disagreement. "No" means no is in part a cultural claim and an advocacy slogan; as such it invites skeptics to question what "no" really does mean. The usual feminist response to such skeptics has been to reassert forcefully that "no" does mean no and that any non-Neanderthal male should agree.[85] It is not surprising that feminists would be reluctant to concede that "no" might ever mean yes (apart from cases of abject false consciousness). Yet much of this debate results from misunderstanding the significance of empirical data for what is ultimately not an empirical issue. For law, the relevant question

---

[82] *See, e.g.*, Susan Estrich, *Rape*, 95 YALE L.J. 1087, 1115 (1986) (arguing that courts should "understand force as the power one need not use (at least physically)").

[83] *See* Douglas N. Husak & George C. Thomas III, *Date Rape, Social Convention, and Reasonable Mistakes*, 11 L. & PHIL. 95, 122 (1992). In a recent survey of Texas female undergraduates, 39.3% reported that they had said "no" when they meant yes, and 60.8% of the sexually experienced women in the survey said that they had done so. *See* Charlene L. Muehlenhard & Lisa C. Hollabaugh, *Do Women Sometimes Say No When They Mean Yes? The Prevalence and Correlates of Women's Token Resistance to Sex*, 54 J. PERSONALITY & SOC. PSYCHOL. 872, 874 (1988). The authors are quick to point out that this pattern of communication, although rational for some women, can teach men to disregard women's refusals and thereby increase the incidence of rape. *See id.* at 878.

[84] Husak & Thomas, *supra* note 83, at 113.

[85] *See, e.g.*, CATHARINE A. MACKINNON, TOWARD A FEMINIST THEORY OF THE STATE 175 (1989) ("If rape laws existed to enforce women's control over access to their sexuality, . . . no would mean no . . . .").

is the effect that *should be* attributed to a woman's use of the word "no."

Although not decisive, the empirical landscape is obviously relevant here, because in an inquiry about what people mean when they speak, no one would want to give a word a meaning for legal purposes that is utterly at odds with ordinary usage. But the matter becomes a legal issue precisely because the usage of the word is not uniform throughout the culture. It can hardly be fatal to the feminist position, therefore, to discover that women who say "no" do not always mean the same thing. Because they do not, mistakes are possible. And so long as neither law nor culture develops rules to permit uniform appraisal of such mistakes, some of them can plausibly be described (although this will pain many feminists) as reasonable. The proposition that, for legal purposes, "no" means no is, therefore, primarily a normative claim about how the word *should be* understood in the face of ambiguity about its actual meaning in any given context.

The objection that taking "no" to mean no will make it "harder for some women to get what they want"[86] therefore misses the point of such a proposal. As with any default rule, the legal proposition that "no" means no does not claim infallible accuracy; to the contrary, the absence of empirical consensus is its raison d'etre. It presupposes ambiguity and seeks to allocate the risk of the inevitable misunderstandings.

As a normative claim, the proposition that "no" should be taken to mean no is not subject to any plausible objection. True, as Husak and Thomas note, this "proposal designed to make it more difficult for men to get away with rape might have the . . . effect of making it harder for some women to get what they want."[87] But this cost, inevitable for any default rule, is in no way comparable to the costs that are incurred by the traditional approach that Husak and Thomas, among others, prefer. That approach makes it harder for *other* women to get what they want, in this case women who have sought to avoid male sexual impositions by expressing their desires in plain language. There can be little doubt about which set of frustrated expectations is more serious or more deserving of legal protection.

---

[86] Husak & Thomas, *supra* note 83, at 114.

[87] *Id.*

Although the "no"-means-no claim should not be controversial, the more serious difficulty is that this proposition offers surprisingly little help. In real cases, the "no" is often followed by some form of equivocal acquiescence, or even a "yes." How should the "no"-means-no rule apply in cases like that?

One approach suggested is to use something like the *Miranda* rule. In police interrogation, a consent to talk about a crime is considered involuntary if an initial "no" is followed by any questions or comments that persuade the person to talk.[88] The argument is that a similar approach should apply in rape cases: a woman's consent would be invalid if her "no" was followed by cajolery or psychological ploys that led her to acquiesce.[89]

That approach sounds plausible until you try to apply it to situations involving dates or acquaintances. Suppose a woman says "no" to her lover before dinner and then changes her mind after several hours of intimate conversation? Would the consent have to be considered invalid? That cannot be the right result. The only way to sort out these problems is to focus on the conduct that leads to a "yes"—in other words, whether the persuasions are improper. "No" means no just does not help sort out whether the things that happen after the "no" are legitimate or abusive. And even if the "no" is clear and persistent, the "no"-means-no rule is still insufficient because it only serves to establish nonconsent, and under existing law nonconsent is insufficient to establish rape: the prosecution must prove "force" in addition.[90]

2. The Meaning of "Force"

The other strand in current reform proposals is to tackle the problem by expanding the conception of force. Many rape reformers stress that force can take the form of strength that a man does not need to use.[91] Force can involve not only physical violence but also other kinds of power.[92] This approach reflects the theories of male dominance developed by Catharine MacKin-

---

[88] *See* Miranda v. Arizona, 384 U.S. 436, 473-74 (1966).

[89] *See* ESTRICH, *supra* note 7, at 40-41 (contrasting the rule that "no" is insufficient to establish nonconsent in rape to the rule in custodial questioning that "a suspect's 'no' must mean no, and questioning must cease").

[90] *See supra* text accompanying note 76.

[91] *See* Estrich, *supra* note 82, at 1115.

[92] *See id.* (noting that existing law "create[s] a gulf between power and force").

non[93] that are now supported by many moderate feminists[94] and by several courts.[95]

Some women worry that the dominance approach, which is intended to strengthen women, may wind up making them feel weak and more vulnerable.[96] The cultural effect of these debates is tricky, but it is not really decisive for the criminal law. The sexual pressure on women is real; the law cannot wish that away or wait until all men "get it."

The more important concern for law is that recognizing the power of male sexual pressure does not solve the legal problem because, as usual, a major part of the legal problem is a boundary ("line-drawing") problem. Despite the undoubted value of legal analysis or cultural criticism that points to commonalities between physical violence and social, economic, or psychological pressure,[97] the job of legal scholarship is not finished until a workable boundary between permitted and regulated conduct has been identified.[98] And in the case of rape, the boundary problem is acute. If

---

[93] *See* MACKINNON, *supra* note 3, at 40 (arguing that "[g]ender is . . . a question of power, specifically of male supremacy and female subordination").

[94] *See, e.g.*, ESTRICH, *supra* note 7, at 63 (arguing that one of the problems with "'force' as a standard is . . . that it is too narrowly defined").

[95] *See, e.g.*, State *ex rel.* M.T.S., 609 A.2d 1266, 1277 (N.J. 1992) (stating that the requirement of "physical force" is satisfied any time the defendant penetrates a woman against her will); State v. Etheridge, 352 S.E.2d 673, 680 (N.C. 1987) (holding that "force" may be "actual, physical force or . . . constructive force in the form of fear, fright, or coercion").

[96] *See, e.g.*, Vivian Berger, *Not So Simple Rape*, CRIM. JUST. ETHICS, Winter-Spring 1988, at 69, 75 (reviewing ESTRICH, *supra* note 7) (arguing that Estrich's approach may lead the law to "patronize" women). A related theme is sounded and expanded in a number of recent revisionist attacks on the feminist program. *See, e.g.*, KATIE ROIPHE, THE MORNING AFTER: SEX, FEAR, AND FEMINISM ON CAMPUS 163 (1993) (arguing that teaching women to "recognize" behavior as sexual harassment may train them to think like victims).

[97] *See, e.g.*, Commonwealth v. Mlinarich, 498 A.2d 395, 416 (Pa. Super. Ct. 1985) (Spaeth, J., dissenting) (arguing that "forcible compulsion" includes nonphysical compulsion); *see also* Lucy R. Harris, Comment, *Towards a Consent Standard in the Law of Rape*, 43 U. CHI. L. REV. 613, 643-45 (1976) (arguing for the criminalization of sexual coercion via threat of nonphysical harm).

[98] *Cf.* Robin L. West, *Legitimating the Illegitimate: A Comment on* Beyond Rape, 93 COLUM. L. REV. 1442 (1993). Professor West's article criticizes a male scholar's proposal to draw lines between permissible and impermissible sexual pressures, and suggests that the very effort to mark such a boundary and to condone conduct on one side of the line is in itself inappropriate. *See id.* at 1452-59. The article is filled with interesting and insightful cultural criticism, but its implication that such line-drawing efforts are inappropriate in principle seems unfair not only to the author of the proposal, but to the women who are seeking helpful responses to inadequacies in the law of rape.

disparities in economic and social power are sufficient to establish coercion, then force is pervasive in human affairs. If disparity of size, strength, and fighting ability are sufficient to establish force, rape is implicit in nearly every heterosexual relationship.

The move to expand the conception of force thus has much truth to it but no stopping point. In that sense, it is too radical. That is a common reaction to Professor MacKinnon's approach.[99] But the dominance approach is also too conservative because it remains linked to notions of force. In actual administration, it is almost certain to be held back by the cultural preconceptions that determine what force means to the many police, prosecutors, judges, and jurors who are not feminists. Efforts to expand accepted conceptions of force can offer interest and excitement to conversations within feminist circles, but as these approaches rest upon accordion-like notions of power or pressure, they inevitably lead the discussion into an area where boundaries will be unclear and social consensus will be elusive.

We all face pressures and constraints on our choices every day. The pressing problem for feminist jurisprudence and legal reform is to provide tools for determining *which* pressures are excessive or improper. A "dominance" analysis offers little guidance here, unless we want to treat conduct as rape whenever the pressures deployed are deemed "excessive," "unreasonable," or "unfair." A recent Pennsylvania decision takes essentially that view in equating the "forcible compulsion" required for rape with "using superior force—physical, moral, psychological or intellectual—to compel a person to do a thing against that person's volition."[100] But even if we by-pass the obvious vagueness problems entailed in deploying such a standard against economic inducements, emotional pressure, and the like, this approach will not necessarily work well for the women we want to protect, because there is no guarantee that prosecutors and juries will accept a feminist perspective on when such pressures are improper.

---

[99] *See, e.g.*, Berger, *supra* note 96, at 75 (arguing that "[t]o treat as victims in a legal sense all of the female victims of life is at some point to cheapen, not celebrate the rights to self-determination [and] sexual autonomy . . . of women").

[100] Commonwealth v. Rhodes, 510 A.2d 1217, 1225 (Pa. 1986); *see also Mlinarich*, 498 A.2d at 404 (Spaeth, J., dissenting) (defining "forcible compulsion" to mean to constrain or compel "by physical, moral, or intellectual means or by the exigencies of the circumstances"); *cf.* MODEL PENAL CODE § 213.1(2)(a) (1980) (punishing conduct as "gross sexual imposition" if it produces submission to intercourse by "any threat that would prevent resistance by a woman of ordinary resolution").

Three recent proposals attempt to draw more specific lines. Professor Donald Dripps argues that physical violence should not be the only factor sufficient to render sexual intercourse criminal, and he proposes a crime of "sexual expropriation" to punish certain nonviolent impositions as an offense distinct from rape.[101] His analysis rests on a "commodity theory" that sees "sexual cooperation as a service much like any other," in which "erotic assets" are exchanged for monetary or nonmonetary compensation.[102]

This concededly "unromantic notion of sex"[103] provides a poor basis for understanding the dynamics of personal relationships, and it tends to entrench and endorse much of the sexual pressure that women so often experience as problematic. Although Dripps seems to acknowledge that "some nonviolent pressures should be criminal,"[104] the only nonviolent impositions actually covered by his proposal are cases in which the woman is unconscious or mentally incompetent, or in which she has expressly refused consent.[105] The Dripps proposal would thus impose no criminal sanctions in cases of silence or ambivalence about consent, nor would it punish cases of express acquiescence produced by nonviolent pressure, however serious. In a recent Montana case, a high school principal allegedly got a student's consent to sex by threatening to prevent her from graduating.[106] The court held that its sexual assault statute required a threat of physical harm and that the principal's alleged conduct therefore was not criminal.[107] Professor Dripps evidently would agree with the result, not only as a matter of statutory interpretation but as a matter of policy. Indeed, he concludes by "argu[ing] for *limiting* the reach of criminal liability to cases in which the defendant either causes sex through violence or engages in sex over the victim's expressed refusal."[108]

Professor Susan Estrich suggests a different approach. She, like Dripps, would treat an expressed refusal (but not silence or ambivalence) as sufficient to establish nonconsent. She goes further

---

[101] *See* Donald A. Dripps, *Beyond Rape: An Essay on the Difference Between the Presence of Force and the Absence of Consent*, 92 COLUM. L. REV. 1780, 1799-1805 (1992).

[102] *Id.* at 1786.

[103] *Id.*

[104] *Id.* at 1800.

[105] *See id.* at 1807 (including these conditions in a model sex offense statute).

[106] *See* State v. Thompson, 792 P.2d 1103 (Mont. 1990).

[107] *See id.* at 1106-07.

[108] Donald A. Dripps, *More on Distinguishing Sex, Sexual Expropriation, and Sexual Assault: A Reply to Professor West*, 93 COLUM. L. REV. 1460, 1463 (1993) (emphasis added).

than Dripps in two respects. She argues that "[t]he 'force' or 'coercion' that negates consent ought to be defined to include extortionate threats and misrepresentations of material fact."[109] And she concludes that such conduct should be called "rape," not some other offense.[110] This seems a sensible way to begin thinking about factors that taint consent. But Estrich unfortunately does not spell out her notion of either extortion or misrepresentation. Because her concept of rape could extend even to a partner who insincerely professes true love for his or her date, many committed feminists are dubious about Estrich's analysis.[111] Without further detail, the approach seems either plausible but vague, or clear but far too broad.

The New Jersey Supreme Court's recent, much-discussed decision in *State ex rel. M.T.S.*[112] adopts a third solution. The case dealt with the interpretation of a statute punishing conduct as "sexual assault" when intercourse is committed by "physical force or coercion."[113] The court held that this requirement is met by the force inherent in the act of intercourse itself, whenever the act is nonconsensual.[114]

This approach succeeds in criminalizing nonviolent sexual misconduct but with several costs. The statute prohibiting "force or coercion," without any mention of nonconsent, is in effect rewritten to prohibit nonconsensual intercourse without regard to force (other than that intrinsic to intercourse). Under this view criminality turns on the validity of consent; the court specified that consent must be "freely-given"[115] but provided no standard for making this determination, beyond its rejection of physical violence as a touchstone. Thus, for cases where there is express acquiescence, induced by problematic means, the seemingly specific New

---

[109] ESTRICH, *supra* note 7, at 102-03.

[110] *See id.* at 103 ("The crime I have described may be a lesser offense . . . but it is a serious offense that should be called 'rape.'").

[111] *See, e.g.*, Berger, *supra* note 96, at 75 (arguing that Estrich's broad conception of force "may backfire and ultimately damage the cause of women"); Lynne N. Henderson, *What Makes Rape a Crime?*, 3 BERKELEY WOMEN'S L.J. 193, 228 (1988) (reviewing ESTRICH, *supra* note 7) (criticizing Estrich for "poorly . . . thought out" proposals that "suffer from the same flaws and difficulties as current laws"). For a discussion of whether deception should invalidate consent, see Schulhofer, *supra* note 75, at 88-93.

[112] 609 A.2d 1266 (N.J. 1992).

[113] N.J. STAT. ANN. § 2C:14-2c(1) (West 1982).

[114] *See M.T.S.*, 609 A.2d at 1276-77.

[115] *Id.* at 1277.

Jersey approach ultimately draws no line at all. And the court placed such misconduct in the same statutory grading category as physically violent rape, an offense that is punishable in New Jersey by a minimum of five years in prison.[116]

Dominance is not the way to get at this problem. The underlying concern here is to protect a woman's autonomy in matters of sexual choice. The autonomy concern needs to be addressed directly, not as a by-product of definitional debates about force.

3. Protecting Autonomy

Autonomy is not self-defining, of course. Stating the problem as an autonomy question amounts to a nonsolution if violations of autonomy are equated with coercion by excessive pressure.

An alternative approach is to define autonomy as the right to protection from those interferences that our culture and our legal system already consider impermissible.[117] This seemingly minimalist approach to the problem has unexpected power in serving to identify sexual behavior that is unambiguously improper.

It is important to stress that in advocating reliance on this very "thin" conception of autonomy, I do not imply moral approval for all conduct outside its reach. Many troubling forms of sexual pressure manage to avoid use of threats that are prohibited by existing principles within our culture. Economic pressure, for example, can have powerfully constraining effects on freedom of action, and decisions to accept sexual intimacy for economic reasons are appropriately regarded as "unfortunate, unattractive, or degrading."[118] That such pressures will not always violate the minimalist conception of autonomy I develop here is not a reason to insulate them from moral or psychological criticism or from the eventual adoption of more ambitious legal standards. The conception of autonomy I want to spotlight is not intended as the end of dialogue or legal development. Rather, it simply offers a baseline that is relatively uncontroversial in its moral and cultural presuppo-

---

[116] Because *M.T.S.* was a juvenile case, the trial court was able to grant the defendant a suspended sentence. *See id.* at 1269. In an adult prosecution, New Jersey law would not permit suspension of the minimum five-year term except under "'truly extraordinary and unanticipated circumstances.'" State v. Johnson, 570 A.2d 395, 398 (N.J. 1990) (citation omitted).

[117] *See* Schulhofer, *supra* note 75, at 69-71 (developing a theory of sexual autonomy based on existing conceptions of impermissible interference with bodily integrity and freedom of choice).

[118] *Id.* at 86.

sitions. Yet this minimalist starting point has significant power to extend the scope of available legal protections.

Several examples will illustrate the far-reaching implications of the conception of autonomy that is already broadly accepted within our culture. First, when is consent lacking? "No" means no, obviously. But an intrusion on the person requires more than just the absence of a clear "no." A physical intrusion on the person requires actual permission.

Would anyone think that a medical patient's ambivalence, or an ambiguous "maybe," was a consent to medical treatment or surgery? Obviously, anything less than clear affirmative permission would never count as consent. Imagine Atlas, an Olympic weightlifter, consulting a doctor about whether to have surgery on his elbow. The doctor really wants to perform the operation. He thinks Atlas will be very happy with the experience. But the weightlifter is uncertain. He thinks things may not work out the way the doctor has promised. And there is a risk of picking up a serious infection. So Atlas hesitates, says he just is not sure. Can the doctor just go ahead and start cutting? Would we ever treat the weightlifter's silence or indecision as equivalent to consent? No, obviously, but why not? No one compelled him to submit. If he really objected, all he had to do was say so! Yet we would never consider silence or ambivalence as equivalent to consent for surgery. To say that is not to patronize Atlas; it is simply to recognize an obvious violation of the physical autonomy of his person.

Why should the physical autonomy of a woman's body not be entitled to the same respect in a sexual encounter? Clear proof of an unequivocal "no" should not be required. Consent for an intimate physical intrusion into the body should mean in sexual interactions what it means in every other context—affirmative permission clearly signaled by words or conduct.[119] There are many ways to make permission clear without verbalizing the word "yes," and permission certainly need not be in writing. But permission must be an affirmative indication of actual willingness. Silence and ambivalence are not permission.[120]

---

[119] *See, e.g.*, WASH. REV. CODE ANN. § 9A.44.010(6) (West 1988) (defining consent to mean "that at the time of the act of sexual intercourse there are actual words or conduct indicating freely given agreement to have sexual intercourse"); *M.T.S.*, 609 A.2d at 1278 (defining consent as "affirmative and freely-given authorization for the specific act of sexual penetration").

[120] Contextual differences between surgery and sexual intimacy suggest somewhat different mechanisms for protecting autonomy in the two situations. The doctor's

Next, what if a woman does agree? What kinds of constraints violate her autonomy? Autonomy cannot mean freedom from all constraints upon choice, but it does entail freedom from those constraints that our culture identifies as illegitimate. The scope of that freedom is marked by the rights to bodily integrity and personal independence that existing legal principles already protect.[121] This modest conception of personal autonomy offers boundaries that are specific and, yet, far reaching.

One example is sexual harassment in the workplace. This looks like an area that is hardly ripe for criminal sanctions. But if a supervisor tries to get sexual favors by offering a promotion (or by threatening to veto one), he is confronting the employee with alternatives (no matter whether we call them offers or threats) that his position gives him no right to impose. If the supervisor used his position to get an economic payoff from the employee, he would be guilty of extortion.[122] If a professor threatened to withhold a good grade or a good recommendation until he got some cash from a student, again he would be guilty of extortion.[123]

The worker or student should have the same right to control her sexuality that she has to control her wages or her bank account. What makes the woman's consent invalid is not that the supervisor's act involves too much pressure. What makes the consent invalid is that rules already settled in our culture deny the supervisor the right to require an employee to choose between her promotion and her legally protected interests. One of those interests should be—and is—her sexual independence. For the same reason, the high school principal who allegedly obtained sex from a student by threatening to block her graduation[124] should certainly be guilty of a crime.

---

expertise can justify a special duty of disclosure, and the complexity of the risks may suggest the need for a conception of informed consent much more stringent than that which is appropriate in a sexual encounter.

[121] *See* Schulhofer, *supra* note 75, at 69-71 (discussing the scope and objectives of legal protection of autonomous choice in the area of sexual intimacy).

[122] *See* MODEL PENAL CODE § 223.4 commentary at 223 (1980) (offering as an example of extortion the case of a "foreman in a manufacturing plant who requires the workers to pay him a percentage of their wages on pain of dismissal or other employment discrimination").

[123] *See id.* (noting as an example of extortion the case of a "law professor who obtains property from a student by threatening to give him a failing grade or to influence a prospective employer to hire someone else").

[124] *See supra* text accompanying notes 106-07.

Two variations will make the implications clearer. Suppose that a highly paid fashion model wants to land a film role to enhance her career. The company's casting director says that unless she sleeps with him, she will not get the part. If you are looking for excessive pressure, this case will seem a lot harder than that of the student or employee. You may not feel sympathy for the model at all. But whether you feel sympathy or not, the violation of her autonomy is the same as in the previous cases. The man's action is extortionate, just as if he had insisted on a side-payment in cash. There is an improper constraint on the woman's freedom of choice under background rights that are already settled in our culture.

The converse of the model's situation, the "hard case" for this analysis, is that of a needy mother of four who finds a partner willing to support her. Suppose that the relationship deteriorates, and the man threatens to kick her out of the apartment unless she continues to meet his sexual demands. Obviously, the needy mother has far less freedom of choice than the successful fashion model does. But the relevant question has to be whether the man's threatened actions are illicit. In the model's situation, the pressure may be slight, but it is clearly impermissible. In the mother's case, the pressure, though severe, might not be illicit. A sexual quid pro quo is not a legitimate condition of ordinary employment, but sexual fulfillment *is*, for both men and women, an appropriate and valued goal of ongoing, intimate personal relationships. Thus, although the man's action in imposing a sexual condition on his willingness to continue his relationship with the needy mother could be criticized as insensitive in many contexts, it nonetheless involves an exercise of *his* autonomy that society ordinarily considers legitimate and worthy of social protection. It makes sense to ask whether the nature of the relationship is sufficient to give her a right to remain in the apartment or to receive financial support, and if she does have such a right, the man's threats should render any consent to sex invalid. But if existing norms do not protect her from this sort of economic pressure, then her decision to remain in the relationship, although highly constrained, is not improperly tainted, and her consent to sex would therefore be valid.

With these principles in mind, we can return to the cases mentioned earlier—the man who takes the woman's car keys and the man whose intimidated girlfriend no longer tries to fight back. In the first case, there is a kind of consent, ultimately the woman says "OK," but the consent is tainted by a clear violation of her right to leave. In the second case, there is never any affirmative permission at all. These cases make clear that one thing missing in the law of rape is some way to punish sexual misconduct that is not physically violent. It is as if we had a law against armed robbery but no law against theft. The way to fill that gap is not to try expanding what we mean by force but to have statutes punishing, as an offense distinct from forcible rape, any sexual imposition without valid consent. Thus, the men in these two cases should, at a minimum, be convicted of sexual misconduct.

We get these results without having to sort out degrees of force and without having to treat women as dominated or disempowered. The key is in the background structure of rights and privileges that determine what uses of personal power and institutional position are permissible, against either the weak or the strong, against either men or women in our society.

This approach identifies a baseline of existing rights, and it leaves room for evolution in the standards for valid consent. Respect for a woman's autonomy should mean that her interest in controlling her sexual choices receives just as much protection as any person's interest in controlling her property, her labor, or her freedom of action in other areas of life.

IV. SENTENCING

I turn now to a set of problems facing female offenders. Women constitute an ever-increasing proportion of all defendants, and they are facing increasingly serious charges, especially in the federal courts.[125] One explanation attributes these changes to women's increasing independence and growing participation in the workforce.[126] But this "liberation hypothesis" is now generally discredited as an explanation for women's apparently rising crime

---

[125] *See* BUREAU OF JUSTICE STATISTICS, U.S. DEP'T OF JUSTICE, WOMEN IN PRISON 3 (1994) [hereinafter WOMEN IN PRISON 1994] ("[T]he number of women sentenced for a violent offense rose from 8045 to 12,400 during the [1986-1991] period."); RITA J. SIMON & JEAN LANDIS, THE CRIMES WOMEN COMMIT, THE PUNISHMENTS THEY RECEIVE 78 (1991) (reporting that from 1980 to 1985, the female incarceration rate increased from 11 per 100,000 to 17 per 100,000).

[126] *See, e.g.*, FREDA ADLER, SISTERS IN CRIME: THE RISE OF THE NEW FEMALE CRIMINAL 13-15 (1975) (claiming that women's advances in "fields of legitimate endeavor" have been paralleled by advances in "the world of major crimes"); RITA J. SIMON, WOMEN AND CRIME 19 (1975) (noting that a major hypothesis regarding women's criminality is that women's participation in financial and white collar crimes should increase as their participation in the workplace increases, as such participation will expose them to greater opportunities for committing such crimes).

rate.[127] *Thelma and Louise* notwithstanding, economic and psychological liberation seem to play a small role in accounting for the growth in women's rates of offending.[128] Far more important factors appear to be the feminization of poverty and the "War on Drugs."[129]

Along with the increase in the number of women facing long sentences is a major shift in the way they are sentenced. Until the late 1970s, American sentencing judges had essentially unbridled discretion.[130] This approach seemed to help women, as they often received less severe punishment than men convicted of similar crimes.[131] The reason for this preferential treatment remains unclear. Some of the differences seem traceable to something like "chivalry"—male judges felt protective toward a female defendant, except when she violated gender norms by committing a violent crime.[132] Probably a more important factor was judges' desires to protect the children of convicted women.[133] In any event, discretion helped women, although maybe not for the right reasons.

But that was the 1950s and 1960s. In the 1990s, sentencing discretion has gone the way of the dinosaur, especially in the federal courts. The new order is dominated by mandatory minimums and inflexible guidelines.[134] Part of the egalitarian spirit of our age is

---

[127] *See* Joseph G. Weis, *Liberation and Crime: The Invention of the New Female Criminal*, CRIME & SOC. JUST., Fall-Winter 1976, at 17, 17 (challenging the assertion that a causal relationship exists between women's liberation and their criminal behavior).

[128] *See, e.g.*, Roland Chilton & Susan K. Datesman, *Gender, Race, and Crime: An Analysis of Urban Arrest Trends, 1960-1980*, 1 GENDER & SOC'Y 152, 167-68 (1987) (arguing that the most plausible explanation for rising women's crime rates, in particular black women's crime rates, is their declining economic situation).

[129] *See id.*

[130] *See* Stephen J. Schulhofer, *Due Process of Sentencing*, 128 U. PA. L. REV. 733, 735-37 (1980) (describing sentencing regimes that were common until the 1970s).

[131] *See* Ilene H. Nagel & John Hagan, *Gender and Crime: Offense Patterns and Criminal Court Sanctions*, *in* 4 CRIME AND JUSTICE: AN ANNUAL REVIEW OF RESEARCH 91, 129-34 (Michael Tonry & Norval Morris eds., 1983) (finding that women receive preferential treatment in the sentencing process); Darrell Steffensmeier & John H. Kramer, *Sex-Based Differences in the Sentencing of Adult Criminal Defendants: An Empirical Test and Theoretical Overview*, 66 SOC. & SOC. RES. 289, 297 (1982) (finding that "[p]referential treatment of female defendants appears to be consistent . . . across most offense categories").

[132] *See* Nagel & Hagan, *supra* note 131, at 112-15 (articulating the "chivalry/paternalism thesis").

[133] *See* Kathleen Daly, *Rethinking Judicial Paternalism: Gender, Work-Family Relations, and Sentencing*, 3 GENDER & SOC'Y 9, 19-22 (1989) (discussing the significant influence that the protection of children has on the sentencing of female defendants).

[134] *See* Stephen J. Schulhofer, *Assessing the Federal Sentencing Process: The Problem

the directive in the Sentencing Reform Act of 1984 that federal sentencing guidelines must be "entirely neutral" as to the race, socioeconomic status, and sex of the offender.[135]

In practice, that neutrality has been a mixed blessing. To illustrate the paradoxes of neutrality, I will outline the structure of sentencing under guidelines in the federal courts and then take up three issues that pose special problems for women: pregnancy, children, and recidivism.

A. *The Federal Sentencing Guidelines*

The guidelines promulgated by the United States Sentencing Commission establish a normal sentencing range for each offense and identify aggravating and mitigating factors that either alter the normal sentence range or provide an authorized basis for an upward or downward departure.[136] Circumstances not identified by the Commission are impermissible grounds for upward or downward departure unless they involve some factor "not adequately taken into consideration by the Sentencing Commission in formulating the guidelines."[137] Applying the egalitarian mandate of the Sentencing Reform Act of 1984, the Commission listed a number of factors that ordinarily cannot justify a departure from the guideline sentence.[138] Among the factors "not ordinarily relevant" are age, mental and emotional conditions, physical condition, and family responsibilities.[139] Gender is even more suspect. This factor, the Commission has said, is *never* relevant.[140]

Is Uniformity, Not Disparity, 29 AM. CRIM. L. REV. 833, 851 (1992) (stating that "[t]he federal sentencing process is pervaded by unwarranted *similarities* in the treatment of substantively distinguishable cases"); Stephen J. Schulhofer, *Rethinking Mandatory Minimums*, 28 WAKE FOREST L. REV. 199, 200-02 (1993) (describing mandatory minimums and their goals).

[135] Pub. L. No. 98-473, tit. II, ch. II, § 217(a), 98 Stat. 1987, 2019 (codified as amended at 28 U.S.C. § 994(d) (1988)).

[136] *See* 18 U.S.C.S. app. § 1A (Law. Co-op. 1994); *see also* Stephen Breyer, *The Federal Sentencing Guidelines and the Key Compromises upon Which They Rest*, 17 HOFSTRA L. REV. 1, 8-31 (1988) (explaining the background and operation of this system).

[137] 18 U.S.C. § 3553(b) (1988).

[138] *See* 18 U.S.C.S. app. § 5H (Law. Co-op. 1994) (listing offender characteristics not ordinarily relevant to the determination of whether a sentence should be outside the applicable guideline range).

[139] 18 U.S.C.S. app. § 5H1.1 (regarding age), § 5H1.3 (regarding mental and emotional conditions), § 5H1.4 (regarding physical conditions), § 5H1.6 (regarding family responsibilities).

[140] *See* 18 U.S.C.S. app. § 5H1.10.

Against the background of prior judicial sentencing practices, these changes will clearly produce more severe sentences for women. That in itself cannot tell us that the changes are wrong. A woman convicted of a crime should face the same penalty as a similarly situated man. But there are several special problems. The following section explores the problems for women that are presented by this seemingly sensible conception of neutrality.

B. *The Paradoxes of Neutrality*

1. Pregnancy

The first problem for a neutrality approach is that men do not get pregnant. Yet in *United States v. Pozzy*,[141] the First Circuit held that a defendant's pregnancy ordinarily cannot justify reducing a long prison sentence that the Guidelines would otherwise require.[142]

The intuition that *Pozzy* sets an unjustifiably harsh rule is understandable, and critics of the Guidelines sharply attacked it. Professor Albert Alschuler[143] and Professors Marc Miller and Daniel J. Freed[144] argue that the holding in *Pozzy* is unsound. Professor Myrna S. Raeder, in the most comprehensive study on the issue, concludes that "[u]nquestionably, pregnant women . . . should be eligible for downward departures in the current Guidelines regime."[145]

This issue, however, is a troubling one, not only for fair sentencing policy, but for women's interests in particular. No one likes sending a pregnant woman to prison. But convicted men enter prison with serious medical problems too. For too long, women's interests have been undermined by practices that singled out

---

[141] 902 F.2d 133 (1st Cir.), *cert. denied*, 498 U.S. 943 (1990).

[142] *See id.* at 138-39. On occasion, district judges in the Second Circuit have granted downward departures on the basis of pregnancy, without being challenged on appeal. *See* Myrna S. Raeder, *Gender and Sentencing: Single Moms, Battered Women, and Other Sex-Based Anomalies in the Gender-Free World of the Federal Sentencing Guidelines*, 20 PEPP. L. REV. 905, 948 (1993) (discussing Second Circuit cases that neglected to follow the standard set forth in *Pozzy*).

[143] *See* Albert W. Alschuler, *The Failure of Sentencing Guidelines: A Plea for Less Aggregation*, 58 U. CHI. L. REV. 901, 911 (1991) (criticizing *Pozzy*).

[144] *See* Marc Miller & Daniel J. Freed, *Offender Characteristics and Victim Vulnerability: The Differences Between Policy Statements and Guidelines*, FED. SENTENCING REP., June-July 1990, at 3, 3-4 (criticizing restrictions on the departure power in cases such as *Pozzy*).

[145] Raeder, *supra* note 142, at 949.

pregnancy for different treatment than that accorded health problems in general.[146] Our starting point on this question should therefore be the assumption that, all else equal, we will strive to treat pregnancy like other medical conditions. Pregnant women, therefore, should probably lose on their claim to special treatment, unless there is reason to treat pregnancy differently from the health problems that male inmates suffer.

One special feature of pregnancy is that poor medical care in prison may endanger not only the offender but an innocent party, the child. If the prison cannot provide safe birthing facilities and adequate neonatal care, there is surely a case for special treatment. But because pregnancy, unlike other medical problems, is a short-term condition, a sentence reduction is not necessary to deal with this concern; the judge can simply delay the date of entry into prison until after the child is born.[147] In any event, pregnant inmates are no longer unusual, and many state and federal prisons now provide modern facilities that can equal or exceed the quality of care these women would be likely to receive in the outside world.[148]

Other major differences between pregnancy and the medical concerns of male inmates tend to undermine claims for special treatment. Pregnancy usually is not life-threatening, and it often occurs by choice, unlike cancer, for example. As a result, any rule allowing sentence reductions for pregnancy would have unique potential for manipulation.[149] I am not enthusiastic about the results in the pregnancy cases, but on balance the courts are right to disregard pregnancy in most circumstances.[150]

---

[146] *See, e.g.*, Geduldig v. Aiello, 417 U.S. 484, 494 (1974) (holding that the exclusion of pregnancy from disabilities covered under a California statute did not deny women equal protection of the law).

[147] This approach will raise a new question, of course: how to deal with the offender who has responsibility for an infant child. Under some (but by no means all) circumstances, such family responsibilities could justify more lenient punishment of the convicted mother. For a discussion of this issue, see *infra* notes 151-60 and accompanying text.

[148] *See, e.g.*, Anita G. Huft et al., *Care of the Pregnant Offender*, 3 FED. PRISONS J. 49, 51 (1992) (discussing the health-care facility at Lexington, Kentucky for federal inmates who have high-risk pregnancies).

[149] *Cf.* United States v. Arize, 792 F. Supp. 920, 921 (E.D.N.Y. 1992) (granting downward departure where a female drug courier was unaware of her pregnancy at the time of the offense and where loss of child custody was possible).

[150] The issue needs to be approached case-by-case because pregnant offenders (many of whom have drug or alcohol problems) often face high-risk pregnancies. If a jurisdiction's prisons do not have appropriate obstetrical services available, there is

2. Family Ties

Although pregnancy ordinarily should not be treated differently from the medical problems that men suffer, a "neutral" approach to family ties is a different matter. In the old days, white-collar defendants were able to win leniency by using their family responsibilities to evoke sympathy.[151] Judges were reluctant to take the breadwinner away from his children, and the ignominy of accusation and conviction were often viewed as substantial sanctions for the white-collar defendant.[152] That instinct helped middle-class offenders, but the unemployed, especially underclass blacks, often received harsher sentences.[153] The Sentencing Commission responded to the race and class biases of the old system by specifying that community ties, employment, and family responsibilities ordinarily will not justify a departure from the guideline sentencing range.[154]

This is generally a sensible rule, but as usual, it was crafted with men in mind. The "family responsibility" rubric is the same, but the real problem is different when the defendant is a woman with three preschool age children. Compared to a male prisoner, a female pri-

---

a strong case for special consideration. But a similar point can be made with respect to other medical conditions that cannot be treated properly in prison. A male inmate's health problems ordinarily endanger only the offender himself, but improper treatment and consequent risks of permanent injury or death are not permissible punishments for whatever offense sent the offender to prison. *See* Estelle v. Gamble, 429 U.S. 97, 104 (1976) (holding that "deliberate indifference to serious medical needs of prisoners" violates the Eighth Amendment), *cert. denied*, 434 U.S. 974 (1977).

[151] *See* STANTON WHEELER ET AL., SITTING IN JUDGMENT: THE SENTENCING OF WHITE-COLLAR CRIMINALS 152-54 (1988) (reporting that prior to the recent sentencing guidelines, judges imposed either short sentences or no prison term on white-collar offenders "to avoid eliminating the [offender's] contribution to community and family").

[152] *See id.* at 144-45 (reporting that judges typically considered public indictment, conviction, and loss of community status to be significant forms of punishment for the white-collar offender and that "[m]ost judges . . . wonder whether the imposition of additional suffering is justifiable").

[153] Available statistical studies do not, however, show unambiguous racial disparities in sentencing. *See* 1 RESEARCH ON SENTENCING: THE SEARCH FOR REFORM 93 (Alfred Blumstein et al. eds., 1983) (noting that "[w]hile there is no evidence of a widespread systematic pattern of discrimination in sentencing, some pockets of discrimination are found for particular judges, particular crime types, and in particular settings").

[154] *See* 18 U.S.C.S. app. § 5H1.5-.6 (Law. Co-op. 1994) (stating that employment records, family ties and responsibilities, and community ties "are not ordinarily relevant in determining whether a sentence should be outside the applicable guideline range").

soner is twice as likely to have dependents who lived with her prior to her incarceration.[155] A welfare check can often replace the only kind of family support that many male offenders ever provide, but when the mother goes to prison, the children lose their primary caretaker. This may not be a disaster for the children if the parent is an abusive drug addict or if close relatives can offer a stable and supportive home. But children are much more likely to face problematic alternatives when the incarcerated parent is their mother. Among male prisoners who have minor children, 88.5% report that the children are living with their mother, while only 22.1% of the female prisoners with minor children report that those children are living with their father.[156] When long-term imprisonment of the mother will mean uncertain placements in foster care for all of a child's formative years, the social cost of "neutral" policy can be enormous. Yet 10.5% of female inmates (compared to only 1.7% of male inmates) have children who are assigned to a foster home or to an institutional placement after the parent's incarceration.[157]

The rule making family ties irrelevant thus creates a false equality between offenders in very different situations. It also makes fairness among offenders the sole question, when fairness to the children should be one of the court's major concerns. Equal treatment here—if it is equal treatment—can have a devastating effect on young lives. Yet in most of the federal circuits, courts have been "fairly hostile to child-based departures,"[158] even when the offender was the single mother of five young children.[159] As a result, the

---

[155] In 1986, 52.6% of all female prisoners, but only 27.5% of all male prisoners, had been living with minor children just before they entered prison. *See* BUREAU OF JUSTICE STATISTICS, U.S. DEP'T OF JUSTICE, WOMEN IN PRISON 6 (1991) [hereinafter WOMEN IN PRISON 1991] (noting that 67.5% of female prisoners, but only 54.4% of male prisoners, had minor children when they entered prison, and that among the prisoners who had minor children, 78% of the women, but only 50.5% of the men, had lived with those children before entering prison).

[156] *See id.*

[157] *See id.* (noting that percentages are based on those inmates who had children under age 18).

[158] Raeder, *supra* note 142, at 945; *see also* United States v. Bieri, 21 F.3d 811, 814, 817-18 (8th Cir.) (denying downward departure when both the mother and father of two children, ages four and seven, were convicted of drug violations), *cert. denied*, 115 S. Ct. 208 (1994).

[159] *See* United States v. Headley, 923 F.2d 1079, 1082-83 (3d Cir. 1991) (finding that although the district court had the power to depart downward when sentencing a mother of five, no court that had considered the issue had found parenthood to be an extraordinary circumstance justifying such a departure); *cf.* United States v. Chestna, 962 F.2d 103, 107-08 (1st Cir.) (affirming the district court's denial of downward departure based on the convict's position as the mother of three young

equal treatment concept has been a disaster, not just for women, but for sensible policy. What we now need is more discretion, and more recognition of family ties as a legitimate basis for a shorter sentence or a less restrictive type of incarceration.

Such an approach need not entail a formal privilege of special treatment for women as such, because departures presumably should be authorized for primary caretakers or single parents of either gender under appropriate circumstances. But the appearance of formal equality here should not by itself satisfy us that a special departure rule would be evenhanded and fair. The reality is that such a departure rule will not look, and will not be, fully neutral between the sexes. Nearly all of the offenders who will benefit from it will be women.[160] An overwhelmingly disproportionate impact of this sort should raise serious fairness concerns in most contexts. What makes such an impact tolerable in connection with sentencing is the manner in which the incarceration of single parents affects their children.

3. The Likelihood of Recidivism

Recidivism poses a third problem for the equal treatment approach. A key factor in determining guideline sentencing ranges is the need for incapacitation, based on the likelihood of recidivism and especially the likelihood of future violence. Sentencing tables reflect judges' perceptions about the potential violence of the typical offender,[161] and of course the typical offender is male.

---

children), *cert. denied*, 113 S. Ct. 334 (1992). In the Second and Ninth Circuits, the courts have been somewhat more willing to view a female offender's family responsibilities as a permissible basis for a downward departure under some circumstances. *See, e.g.*, United States v. Johnson, 964 F.2d 124, 129-31 (2d Cir. 1992) (affirming a downward departure based on extraordinary family circumstances consisting of the defendant having sole responsibility for raising four young children); Raeder, *supra* note 142, at 942-44 (discussing the Second and Ninth Circuits' willingness to grant a downward departure for single-parent mothers and noting one case in which the Tenth Circuit did so as well). On occasion, male defendants have benefitted from such departures as well. *See, e.g.*, United States v. Sclamo, 997 F.2d 970, 972-74 (1st Cir. 1993) (affirming downward departure for a man who played an important role in the development of an emotionally disturbed child with whom he lived).

[160] *See supra* notes 155-57 and accompanying text (discussing the fact that female offenders are much more likely than male offenders to have dependents living with them prior to incarceration, and noting that children are more likely to suffer when the incarcerated parent is their mother).

[161] For example, in the federal system, the U.S. Sentencing Commission generally attempted to follow typical past practice in setting guideline sentencing ranges for

The danger that a first or second offender will return to crime, especially to violent crime, is not the same for women as it is for men. This is not simply a false stereotype. Nor is it an area where we can make accurate judgments by excluding group generalizations and by relying entirely upon facts other than the individual's gender. Women really are different in this respect. Whether as a result of nature or nurture, and in this case the differences are probably due to both, women (including female offenders) are far less prone to violent aggression than are men.[162]

Modern equal protection doctrine seems strongly, perhaps unalterably, opposed to reliance upon statistical differences between the sexes as a basis for justifying categorical differences in treatment. In *Craig v. Boren*,[163] the Supreme Court held unconstitutional an Oklahoma law that prohibited the sale of 3.2% beer to males under the age of 21 but permitted sales to females over the age of 18.[164] The state got nowhere with statistics indicating that young males were more likely than females to drive while intoxicated.[165] The Court noted that the state's statistics were subject to "obvious methodological problems," and that properly analyzed, the "statistical disparities between the sexes [were] not substantial."[166] Nonetheless, the Court also stressed broader principles; it concluded that "proving broad sociological propositions by statistics is a dubious business, and one that inevitably is in tension with the normative philosophy that underlies the Equal Protection Clause."[167]

Although *Craig v. Boren* might be explained by the fragility of the statistical differences that the State invoked, the same is not true of *Reed v. Reed*,[168] *Frontiero v. Richardson*,[169] and *Weinberger v.*

both first offenders and repeat offenders. *See* Breyer, *supra* note 136, at 7 ("[I]n creating categories and determining sentence lengths, the Commission, by and large, followed typical past practice, determined by an analysis of 10,000 actual cases." (citations omitted)).

[162] *See supra* text accompanying note 9. For a discussion of repeat violence by women who have already committed a first offense, see *infra* notes 182-83 and accompanying text.

[163] 429 U.S. 190 (1976).

[164] *See id.* at 190-91.

[165] *See id.* at 200-04.

[166] *Id.* at 202, 203 n.16. In one random survey of Oklahoma City drivers, blood-alcohol levels indicating intoxication were found in 14.6% of the male drivers and 11.5% of the female drivers. *See id.* at 203 n.16.

[167] *Id.* at 204.

[168] 404 U.S. 71, 76-77 (1971) (holding that a statutory scheme that draws distinctions between sexes solely for administrative convenience violates the Constitution).

[169] 411 U.S. 677, 690-91 (1973) (finding that statutes that accord "differential

Wiesenfeld.[170] In these cases the Court struck down efforts to use sex as a decision-making factor, even though sex appeared to have substantial value in predicting an admittedly important fact. In *Reed*, the state's apparent premise, in preferring men to women as administrators for decedents' estates, was that men were more likely than women to have experience in formal business matters.[171] In *Frontiero* and *Wiesenfeld*, Congress had mandated hearings on dependency for men but not for women seeking certain statutory benefits, on the ground that husbands were less likely to be dependent on their wives than vice versa.[172] The Court held that such generalizations, even if empirically accurate, could not justify categorically different treatment of the sexes.[173] The hostility to empirical generalization in these cases nonetheless may be explained by two facts. First, the differences between the sexes were themselves the products of gender discrimination and cultural impediments to women's ability to lead independent lives. Second, the facts for which gender was used as a proxy (business experience and dependency) could be ascertained more directly and more accurately by a factual hearing.

Closer to the present problem—that is, sharp, statistically valid gender differences that are not simply the results of past discrimination—is *City of Los Angeles v. Manhart*.[174] In *Manhart*, the Supreme Court barred employers from using male-female differences in life expectancy as a basis for requiring women as a group to pay higher pension-annuity premiums.[175] Technically, *Manhart* held only that the salary differentials violated the nondiscrimination requirements of Title VII of the Civil Rights Act of 1964,[176] but the Court's

---

treatment to male and female members of the uniformed services for the sole purpose of achieving administrative convenience" violate the Due Process Clause of the Fifth Amendment).

[170] 420 U.S. 636, 637-39 (1975) (finding unconstitutional a gender-based differential in Social Security survivors benefits which discriminated against men whose wives were deceased); *see also* Califano v. Goldfarb, 430 U.S. 199, 201-02 (1977) (finding unconstitutional a gender-based differential in Social Security survivors benefits which required a widower to show dependence on his deceased wife).

[171] *See Craig*, 429 U.S. at 202 n.13.

[172] *See Wiesenfeld*, 420 U.S. at 644 (noting that "the framers of the Act legislated on the 'then generally accepted presumption that a man is responsible for the support of his wife and children'" (citation omitted)); *Frontiero*, 411 U.S. at 681 (surmising that Congress intended to make an economical law that took advantage of the fact that women tend to be the dependant spouse).

[173] *See, e.g.*, *Craig*, 429 U.S. at 202 n.13; *Frontiero*, 411 U.S. at 688-89.

[174] 435 U.S. 702 (1978).

[175] *See id.* at 707-11.

[176] Pub. L. No. 88-352, tit. VII, § 703(a), 78 Stat. 241, 255 (codified as amended

reasoning would seem to suggest that such differential treatment would, in the case of a public employer, violate the Equal Protection Clause as well.[177]

One obvious argument for gender distinctions in sentencing is that, in contrast to the pension-annuity situation, the purpose and the primary effect of differential treatment in sentencing would be to help women, not to impose additional burdens on an already disadvantaged group.[178] But the cases leave little if any room for the "benign purpose" path around the neutrality requirement of the Equal Protection Clause. Women were more favorably treated by the gender classifications held unconstitutional in *Craig*, *Frontiero*, and *Wiesenfeld*. Only when more favorable treatment for women can be seen as compensating for disadvantageous conditions suffered by women in the past does the Court seem prepared to uphold gender-based affirmative action remedies.[179] If this perspective is controlling, the sentencing of female offenders seems a poor case for affirmative action preferences. Yet does it really make sense, either

---

at 42 U.S.C. § 2000e-2(a)(1) (1988)) ("It shall be an unlawful employment practice for an employer . . . to . . . discriminate against any individual with respect to his compensation, terms, conditions, or privileges of employment . . . .").

[177] *See Manhart*, 435 U.S. at 711. Because *Manhart* was a Title VII case, there was no need to prove that differential treatment was adopted because of, and not simply in spite of, the gender of the disadvantaged group. *Cf.* Washington v. Davis, 426 U.S. 229, 239 (1976) (holding that a facially neutral classification violates the Equal Protection Clause only when there is proof of purposeful discrimination). But that requirement appears inapplicable in constitutional challenges to statutes that draw explicit distinctions along racial or gender lines. *See, e.g.*, *Craig*, 429 U.S. at 204, 210 (holding that an explicit gender-based differential in an Oklahoma statute violated the Equal Protection Clause, without requiring proof of discriminatory purpose, when the differential was not substantially related to a legitimate statutory objective). In any event, the statutory holding in *Manhart* could be read to imply that categorical gender differences in sentencing guideline ranges would violate requirements of gender neutrality in the Federal Sentencing Reform Act of 1984, Pub. L. No. 98-473, tit. II, ch. II, § 217(a), 98 Stat. 1987, 2019 (codified as amended at 28 U.S.C. §994(d) (1988)), even if such sentencing differentials were supported by statistics indicating substantial gender differences in the rate and seriousness of recidivism.

[178] Of course, seemingly favorable treatment has the potential to reinforce stereotypes and thus to backfire in the long run. *See* Orr v. Orr, 440 U.S. 268, 283 (1979) (noting that "[l]egislative classifications which distribute benefits and burdens on the basis of gender carry the inherent risk of reinforcing stereotypes about the 'proper place' of women and their need for special protection"), *cert. denied*, 444 U.S. 1060 (1980). All "benign" preferences are subject to this caveat.

[179] *See, e.g.*, Califano v. Webster, 430 U.S. 313, 317-18 (1977) (upholding a Social Security-related statute which provided higher old-age benefits for women); Schlesinger v. Ballard, 419 U.S. 498, 505-08 (1975) (upholding differential tenure periods for male and female naval officers); Kahn v. Shevin, 416 U.S. 351, 355-56 (1974) (upholding a statute granting a larger property tax exemption to women).

in terms of fairness to women or in terms of effective crime control policy, to sentence female offenders to the same long incapacitative sentences that are thought necessary in the case of potentially violent males?

The gender differences that we are considering are not small. In the *Manhart* case, the difference in annuity costs between men and women was found to be roughly 15%.[180] Sex-specific differences in the propensity for violence in the general population are roughly 800%—eight to nine times higher for men than for women.[181] When the focus is narrowed to individuals who have already committed one offense, gender differences diminish but remain substantial. Young men begin their criminal careers earlier than young women, they commit more offenses of greater seriousness, and their criminal careers begin to taper off much later than those of the women.[182] In one study, the propensity for violence

---

[180] *See Manhart*, 435 U.S. at 705.

[181] *See supra* text accompanying note 9; *see also* 1 CRIMINAL CAREERS AND "CAREER CRIMINALS" 25 (Alfred Blumstein et al. eds., 1986) [hereinafter CRIMINAL CAREERS] (noting that male arrest rates for violent crimes were 8.3 times greater than female rates for 1980); Darrell J. Steffensmeier, *Sex Differences in Patterns of Adult Crime, 1965-77: A Review and Assessment*, 58 SOC. FORCES 1080, 1090-92 (1980) (noting that male arrest rates for violent crimes were nine times greater than female rates for 1965 and eight times greater for 1977). Independent victimization data corroborate the arrest data and tend to negate any inference that differential arrest rates are due to differences in willingness to report or arrest female offenders. *See* Michael J. Hindelang, *Sex Differences in Criminal Activity*, SOC. PROBS., Dec. 1979, at 143, 153 (suggesting that "sex is a central correlate of *involvement* in the crimes examined and cannot be dismissed as simply an artifact of biases in the processes culminating in arrest").

[182] *See, e.g.*, Deborah W. Denno, *Gender, Crime, and the Criminal Law Defenses*, 85 J. CRIM. L. & CRIMINOLOGY 80, 82, 94, 104-06 (1994) (basing these conclusions on empirical data drawn from a longitudinal study of biological, psychological, and sociological predictors of crime). Similarly, female offenders released from prison are less likely to commit a subsequent offense and are much less likely to be returned to prison than are men. *See* BUREAU OF JUSTICE STATISTICS, U.S. DEP'T OF JUSTICE, RECIDIVISM OF PRISONERS RELEASED IN 1983, at 5 (1989) (finding that while 47.3% of men released from prison in 1983 were reconvicted within three years, only 38.7% of women were reconvicted); BUREAU OF JUSTICE STATISTICS, U.S. DEP'T OF JUSTICE, RETURNING TO PRISON 4-5 (1984) (finding that in all states except Massachusetts, "the proportion of recidivists among males was substantially higher than for female releasees"). There is some limited evidence to the contrary. In one study of active heroin users, self-reported crime rates were quite similar for males and females, except for burglary, an offense for which the average male offender committed five times more offenses than the average female offender. *See* CRIMINAL CAREERS, *supra* note 181, at 67-68. On the basis of this data, the authors speculated that large differences in male and female arrest rates arise primarily from differences in rates of participation in crime, and that once active, females commit crime at rates similar to those of the active males. *See id.* at 67. This conclusion may, however, be an

among young offenders who had already committed one offense was three times higher for the men than for the women, and among those who had committed three offenses, 48% of the men but *none* of the women went on to commit further crimes.[183]

When the base expectancy of violence is substantially different for the sexes, and when gender gives us predictive information we probably cannot get in any other way, neutrality again becomes, in effect, a form of unjustified discrimination against women. Particularly in the case of sentences that have a large incapacitative component, such as recent "three strikes and you're out" legislation,[184] there is reason for some discretion to alter the normal sentence on the basis of gender, and perhaps other factors (such as age) that are indicative of low recidivism risk. From this perspective some gender-based differentials in sentencing should have sufficient justification to pass constitutional muster even under intermediate-level or "strict" scrutiny. As in the case of family ties, there are good reasons to support sentencing rules that are not fully neutral between the sexes.

V. PRISONS

Women's prisons are another major growth sector of the criminal justice economy. In 1980, there were over 13,000 women in federal and state prisons[185] and roughly 9000 in county jails.[186] We now have over 50,000 women in federal and state

---

artifact of the focus on the population of active heroin users and appears to differ sharply from the results observed in birth cohort studies that draw upon a more representative sample of both offenders and the general population. *See, e.g.*, Neil A. Weiner, *Violent Criminal Careers and "Violent Career Criminals": An Overview of the Research Literature*, *in* VIOLENT CRIME, VIOLENT CRIMINALS 35, 105 (Neil A. Weiner & Marvin E. Wolfgang eds., 1989) (finding the male rate of recidivism to be approximately three times higher for men than for women in the 1958 cohort); Denno, *supra*, at 105 (reporting that males are far more likely than females to be chronic repeat offenders and that "female chronics committed fewer and less severe crimes than their male counterparts").

[183] *See* Weiner, *supra* note 182, at 105.

[184] *See, e.g.*, Violent Crime Control and Law Enforcement Act of 1994, Title VII, § 70001, Pub. L. No. 103-322, 55 Crim. L. Rep. (BNA) 2365-66 (to be codified at 18 U.S.C. § 3559(c)) (requiring mandatory life imprisonment for defendants previously convicted of either two or more serious violent felonies, or one or more serious violent felonies and one or more serious drug offenses); CAL. PENAL CODE § 1170.12(c)(2)(A) (West Supp. 1995) (requiring sentencing to an indeterminate term of life imprisonment in cases where the defendant has two or more prior felony convictions).

[185] *See* WOMEN IN PRISON 1991, *supra* note 155, at 7.

[186] *See* BUREAU OF JUSTICE STATISTICS, U.S. DEP'T OF JUSTICE, CORRECTIONAL

prisons[187] and another 40,000 in county jails.[188] Over one million women are incarcerated in local jails at some point each year.[189] Since the early 1980s, the male prison population has grown by 112%, while the female prison population has grown by 202%.[190]

The growing number of women in prison partly reflects the "equal treatment" stance that now governs sentencing. But equal treatment ends the minute the sentencing hearing is over. Once offenders enter the correctional system, men and women face entirely different regimes.

The differences do not always disadvantage women. Physical danger and insecurity are problems for some female prisoners, but these risks seldom compare to the pervasive threats of rape and physical assault that are commonplace for male prisoners.[191]

Female prisoners face other kinds of difficulties, however. Women are typically housed in facilities separate from men.[192] Moreover, because there are fewer women in prison, the facilities are usually smaller and draw from a much wider geographical area; most states have only one women's prison for the entire state.[193] In the federal system, the main prisons for women are in West Virginia, Kentucky, Texas, and California, so women from the Northeast and Midwest are often sent over one thousand miles from their homes.[194]

POPULATIONS IN THE UNITED STATES, 1991, at 13 (1993) [hereinafter CORRECTIONAL POPULATIONS] (basing estimates on 1978 data).

[187] *See* BUREAU OF JUSTICE STATISTICS, U.S. DEP'T OF JUSTICE, PRISONERS IN 1992, at 4 (1993) [hereinafter PRISONERS IN 1992].

[188] *See* CORRECTIONAL POPULATIONS, *supra* note 186, at 9.

[189] Because jail stays are typically short and because jail census data reflect only the number of inmates in jail at any one time, such one-day census data greatly understate the total number of inmates incarcerated over the course of the year. In 1991, a total of over 1,187,454 women were admitted to jail, and 1,154,110 were released. *See* BUREAU OF JUSTICE STATISTICS, U.S. DEP'T OF JUSTICE, JAIL INMATES 1991, at 2 (1992).

[190] *See* WOMEN IN PRISON 1991, *supra* note 155, at 1.

[191] On the problem of rape in men's prisons, see *supra* note 13 and accompanying text.

[192] *See* NICOLE H. RAFTER, PARTIAL JUSTICE: WOMEN, PRISONS, AND SOCIAL CONTROL 184 (2d ed. 1990) (reporting that of the 80 prisons that held women in 1988, 74% excluded males entirely, and several others were almost entirely segregated by sex).

[193] As of 1988, 44 of the states held all of their female inmates at one or two central locations. *See id.* at 181.

[194] *See* Sue Kline, *A Profile of Female Offenders in the Federal Bureau of Prisons*, FED. PRISONS J., Spring 1992, at 33, 36.

Differences in the programs available to male and female prisoners are striking. Men's prisons in Michigan offer vocational training in twenty areas, but until recently, the women's prison offered only five programs—most focused on such skills as short-order cooking and handicrafts.[195] In Idaho, the women's prison offers only two vocational programs, one of which teaches the women how to make decals.[196] In Louisiana, the only program for women is a sewing class.[197] In Montana, the women's prison has job slots available to only 18% of the inmates, and only two programs are offered—sewing and data entry.[198] The Nevada prison system offers male inmates vocational training in a wide variety of positions, but the women can choose only from domestic jobs.[199] In Nebraska, the men's penitentiary offers a program leading to a college degree in business administration, while the women's prison offers only a certificate—not a degree—in "secretarial technology."[200]

The problem here is not just that women are not offered the same programs provided for men. Consider the programs that are offered to the women: sewing, decals, handicrafts, and cooking. Visiting American prisons in the 1990s is like taking a time machine back to the high schools of the '50s, where the boys took Shop, and the girls learned cooking, baking, and sewing—glorified under the name of Home Economics.

The major problems for women in American prisons are thus numbers and "nature."[201] The number of female prisoners is no longer so small, but it is still small relative to the number of men in prison.[202] This means fewer programs and greater separation

---

[195] *See* Glover v. Johnson, 478 F. Supp. 1075, 1086-87 (E.D. Mich. 1979).

[196] *See* RAFTER, *supra* note 192, at 188.

[197] *See id.* at 187.

[198] *See* Memorandum of Professor Melissa Harrison Submitted to the Montana House Appropriations Committee (March 9, 1993) (on file with author).

[199] *See* McCoy v. Nevada Dep't of Prisons, 776 F. Supp. 521, 525 (D. Nev. 1991).

[200] The course in "secretarial technology" was instituted at the women's prison only when a lawsuit challenging unequal educational opportunities was set for trial. *See* Klinger v. Nebraska Dep't of Correctional Serv., 824 F. Supp. 1374, 1399-1402 (D. Neb. 1993), *rev'd sub nom.* Klinger v. Department of Corrections, 31 F.3d 727 (8th Cir. 1994), *and cert. denied*, 115 S. Ct. 1177 (1995). Prior to that time, the Nebraska Department of Corrections had offered no on-site post-secondary education for its female prisoners, although it offered many college courses and degree programs to men. *See Klinger*, 824 F. Supp. at 1399.

[201] *See* RAFTER, *supra* note 192, at 179 (noting that gender stereotypes motivate prison programming and affect staff attitudes toward female inmates).

[202] *See* PRISONERS IN 1992, *supra* note 187, at 4 (indicating that women constitute

from families. Assumptions about women's nature mean that the programs which are offered tend to deny women the skills they need for economic and psychological independence.

The third problem for female prisoners—the third "N"—is inertia. Because male prisoners outnumber women by about twenty to one,[203] and because male prisoners are much harder to control, men's problems and needs always dominate the agenda of prison administrators. What women get is the fourth "N"—neglect. Or the fifth "N"—nothing. Yet, what can be done?

A. *Constitutional Litigation*

Female inmates have brought many equal protection challenges, but they have won few real victories. The lack of progress seems due, in part, to the kinds of problems that pervade all institutional reform litigation. In 1979, a federal district court found equal protection violations at Huron Valley, Michigan's only women's prison, where vocational and rehabilitational opportunities were substantially inferior to those afforded at the state's prisons for men.[204] Yet when the court attempted to appoint an independent administrator for the facility, after almost ten years of persistent noncompliance with the court's decree, the Sixth Circuit set aside the order because "[t]he record . . . strongly suggests that the district court has not attempted to exhaust a number of methods to enforce its order that are less intrusive."[205] The appointment of an independent administrator was finally upheld in 1991, fourteen years after the inception of the litigation.[206]

Most class action suits on behalf of female prisoners have ended in settlements, with consent decrees promising improvement in facilities and vocational opportunities.[207] Yet gains have been modest because the consent decrees have proven difficult to enforce and because states can avoid equal protection problems by simply cutting back on facilities and programs made available to more favorably treated prisoners.[208]

---

less than 6% of the inmates in American prisons).

[203] *See id.*

[204] *See* Glover v. Johnson, 478 F. Supp. 1075, 1083-94 (E.D. Mich. 1979).

[205] Glover v. Johnson, 855 F.2d 277, 287 (6th Cir. 1988).

[206] *See* Glover v. Johnson, 934 F.2d 703, 713-15 (6th Cir. 1991).

[207] *See* RAFTER, *supra* note 192, at 201-02.

[208] *See* Molar v. Gates, 98 Cal. App. 3d 1, 20 (4th Dist. 1979) (finding that the state can comply with equal protection requirements by simply abolishing special privileges afforded male prisoners rather than granting them to women); *see also* RAFTER, *supra*

Beyond these familiar difficulties shared by all reform litigation are a series of problems that grow out of the unique complexities of gender. Does the Fourteenth Amendment require neutrality and equal treatment, or do differences between men and women permit different programs and facilities for the two groups? The contending "isms" of modern feminism do not help much here, and the theoretical debate over "sameness" versus "difference" has shed little light on the issues.

In *Canterino v. Wilson*,[209] a federal district court found substantial disparities between the programs available to Kentucky's male and female prisoners. Women had fewer opportunities to qualify for work-release and study-release programs; they were often denied minimum-security classification (and thus denied eligibility for release programs) simply because of an assumption that any social contact with men would lead to pregnancy.[210] The court held that the women had been denied equal protection,[211] but the Sixth Circuit vacated and remanded, holding in a brief opinion that there was no proof that the lesser programs had been afforded to the women because of their gender.[212]

The Eighth Circuit was more explicit in *Klinger v. Department of Corrections*.[213] The court there held that substantial differences between programs at Nebraska's men's and women's prisons, including vocational training for female inmates that was limited to traditional "women's" occupations and the denial of college-credit courses, did not violate equal protection because the male and female prisoners were "not similarly situated for purposes of prison programs and services."[214] The court supported that conclusion by noting that, compared to the women's prison, the men's prison housed six times as many inmates, had a higher security rating, and the average stay for its inmates was two to three times longer.[215] The court also noted that the female inmates were more likely to be

---

note 192, at 202 (noting that "[e]ven when a court decides in favor of inmates, the result is usually only another long struggle to achieve compliance"); Judith Resnik, *The Limits of Parity in Prison*, J. NAT'L PRISON PROJECT, Fall 1987, at 26, 28 (noting that "[e]quality can be achieved either by bringing one group up to the other or by reducing the benefits of the group that was 'better off'").

[209] 546 F. Supp. 174 (W.D. Ky. 1982).

[210] *See id.* at 204-06.

[211] *See id.* at 206-08.

[212] *See* Canterino v. Wilson, 869 F.2d 948, 954 (6th Cir. 1989).

[213] 31 F.3d 727 (8th Cir. 1994), *cert. denied*, 115 S. Ct. 1177 (1995).

[214] *Id.* at 731.

[215] *See id.*

single parents and victims of physical or sexual abuse, while the male inmates were more likely to be violent and predatory criminals.[216] Ironically, the fact that the female inmates were less violent offenders, incarcerated for shorter periods, for less serious crimes, became the basis for justifying *less* generous programs for the women.

The *Klinger* court's justification for disparate treatment of women in prison stands in sharp contrast to the approach of cases like *Reed v. Reed*[217] and *Craig v. Boren*.[218] Many of the differences between the male and female inmate groups are solely the result of the state's decision to segregate them in separate facilities. Differences between the men and the women that are not state created could be relevant for some purposes. I have argued, for example, that the less violent character of female offenders can sometimes justify shorter sentences for them as a group.[219] Such differences likewise might have a legitimate bearing on the kinds of programs best suited to the needs of particular offenders. But since gender in this context is a crude proxy for the rehabilitative needs of the individual inmate, statistical generalizations, even if valid, cannot justify conclusive gender-based categories that preclude an individual factual inquiry.[220] Nor, in any event, can any differences between the sexes justify denying women higher education and well-paid jobs that they need as much as men do. In the Nebraska prisons, the programs for women are not only different in content but simply less generous in every respect.

Although the *Klinger* court's use of dissimilar situations to obviate any equal protection inquiry is surely incorrect, it is more difficult to specify what the nondiscrimination principle affirmatively requires in terms of programs and facilities for female prisoners. The constitutional mandate is obscure, in part, because there is little agreement about what the right policy directions for reform should be. The history of prior reform efforts is not encouraging.

---

[216] *See id.* at 732.
[217] 404 U.S. 71 (1971).
[218] 429 U.S. 190 (1976).
[219] *See supra* notes 161-84 and accompanying text.
[220] *See supra* text accompanying notes 163-84.

2202 *UNIVERSITY OF PENNSYLVANIA LAW REVIEW* [Vol. 143: 2151

B. *The Policy Dilemmas and Their History*

Feminist concern for women in prison predates modern feminism by close to a century and mirrors many of the modern themes. Until the latter part of the nineteenth century, female prisoners were usually housed at the same locations as the men, although often in a separate wing or annex of the men's buildings.[221] Typically, large numbers of women were thrown together in a single large cell, long after the penitentiary system of one-person cells had been introduced for the men.[222] The women were also vulnerable to all kinds of exploitation by male prisoners and guards.[223] In all other respects, female prisoners were ignored.[224]

The enlightened response to nineteenth century prison conditions was what became known as the Reformatory Movement.[225] It stressed rehabilitation for both male and female prisoners, and its guiding principle for the women was separation—women were to be housed in separate facilities, supervised by a separate staff of female guards and administrators.[226] The Reformatory Movement was very modern in stressing how women's different needs created a strong case for separate treatment under the benevolent guidance of female supervisors.[227]

---

[221] *See* RUSSELL P. DOBASH ET AL., THE IMPRISONMENT OF WOMEN 61 (1986) (discussing the separation of women into exclusive female wings and the appointment of separate female wardens and matrons in British prisons in the mid-nineteenth century); RAFTER, *supra* note 192, at 7 (noting that the Women's Annex built in 1837, adjacent to the Ohio Penitentiary, was one of the first structures designed specifically for female prisoners); Lucia Zedner, *The Prison for Women*, *in* THE OXFORD HISTORY OF THE PRISON: THE PRACTICE OF PUNISHMENT IN WESTERN SOCIETY (Norval Morris & David J. Rothman eds., forthcoming 1995).

[222] *See* RAFTER, *supra* note 192, at 4.

[223] *See* DOBASH, *supra* note 221, at 61 (noting that in the mid-nineteenth century United States, "women were held in cramped, insanitary gaols and often subjected to sexual assaults by wardens").

[224] *See* RAFTER, *supra* note 192, at 5 (noting that as a general rule "female prisoners almost wholly lacked supervision").

[225] *See id.* at 23-82.

[226] *See id.* at 184.

[227] *See id.* at 41-51. Similar themes were evident in the development of the federal government's first prison for women at Alderson, West Virginia. *See* Claudine SchWeber, *"The Government's Unique Experiment in Salvaging Women Criminals": Cooperation and Conflict in the Administration of a Women's Prison—The Case of the Federal Industrial Institution for Women at Alderson*, *in* JUDGE, LAWYER, VICTIM, THIEF: WOMEN, GENDER ROLES, AND CRIMINAL JUSTICE 277, 284-85 (Nicole H. Rafter & Elizabeth A. Stanko eds., 1982) (noting that a mostly female staff ran Alderson).

The Reformatory Movement's approach to female prisoners had two serious flaws. First, it linked its conception of women's special needs and special capacities for rehabilitation to a program that stressed training in household tasks and domestic service outside the home.[228] Second, it focused primarily on the needs of white working-class offenders, many of them morals offenders who would not have been in prison at all if they were men who had engaged in similar conduct.[229] Underclass and minority women usually remained in strictly custodial institutions, often in wings of a male prison, and faced extremely harsh regimes of punishment.[230]

Nonetheless, for all its flaws, the Reformatory Movement was a significant step forward for its time. It survived and prospered from the 1870s until the 1930s. Then a new round of progressive reforms, which focused on corruption in and mismanagement of men's prisons, led to pressures for greater professionalism, more centralized management, and control over the fiefdoms of individual wardens in both male and female prisons.[231] This development had nothing to do with the women's prisons per se, but it doomed their creativity and independence.[232] After the 1930s, separate women's prisons remained, but they dealt in punishment; innovative programs were eliminated; women remained separate, and once again they were neglected.[233]

---

[228] *See* RAFTER, *supra* note 192, at 39 (noting that vocational programs focused on training female inmates in domestic skills).

[229] *See id.* at 35-36 (noting that women were committed to reformatories under long-term sentences on convictions of fornication, drunkenness, and other minor crimes for which men typically were not sent to prison at all).

[230] *See id.* at 87 (noting that in 1930 Tennessee, "[t]he situation was especially grim for black women" and that "the 'Negro Wing' was 'almost constantly overcrowded'" (citation omitted)).

[231] See SchWeber, *supra* note 227, at 287, for an account of these developments in the federal system. In the individual states, women's reformatories were also undermined by the financial stresses of the 1930s. Throughout the country, prison administrators who were pressured for space in their maximum security prisons transferred out the hard-core female felons who had been held there; these women then had to be housed at reformatories. *See* RAFTER, *supra* note 192, at 81-82. The population of less serious offenders who had made up the group in women's reformatories was either severely diluted by the serious felons or was pushed out entirely (and transferred to local jails) to make room for offenders who were not suited to the rehabilitative focus of the reformatory approach. *See id.*

[232] *See* SchWeber, *supra* note 227, at 298-99 (chronicling the effects of this change at Alderson, West Virginia).

[233] *See* RAFTER, *supra* note 192, at 81 (detailing the demise of the Reformatory Movement).

In the 1970s, reformers again drew attention to the neglect of female prisoners. The 1970s reformers attributed most of the problems to the prevailing policy of separating and centralizing the female inmates.[234] The preferred solution was called cocorrections, essentially coed prisons, where men and women housed in the same buildings share many programs and facilities.[235] The idea was to reduce geographical displacement and permit cost-effective delivery of services.[236] Building on the same insight, a 1985 law review note argued that sexually segregated prisons violate the Equal Protection Clause and that a gender-neutral system of inmate assignment for most offenders is constitutionally required.[237]

Coed prisons have been tried extensively since the 1970s, but generally they have been a disaster for women. When small numbers of women are dispersed to coed prisons, they are vastly outnumbered by the men at each site. Men's needs dominate, and once again the women get neglected, even more so than before.[238] There is also a concern about safety and security. You do not have to be a rocket scientist to foresee that there will be security problems when you mix men and women in coed prisons. It is the men who pose the problem, but it is much harder to restrict and supervise the movements of 500 men than to guard closely forty or fifty women. So the women bear the brunt of tight security measures in coed prisons.[239]

By the late 1980s, most women's advocates and prison administrators had lost their enthusiasm for coed prisons.[240] There remain several mixed-sex prisons, but they retain few features of the coed model: prisoners are tightly separated by sex, and there is little sharing of programs and facilities;[241] in a few instances the

---

[234] *See* Claudine SchWeber, *Beauty Marks and Blemishes: The Coed Prison as a Microcosm of Integrated Society*, PRISON J., Spring-Summer 1984, at 3, 4-5.

[235] *See id.*

[236] *See id.* at 3.

[237] *See* Rosemary Herbert, Note, *Women's Prisons: An Equal Protection Evaluation*, 94 YALE L.J. 1182, 1182 (1985).

[238] *See* RAFTER, *supra* note 192, at 204 (noting, for instance, that in coed prisons "men forced women out of programs by assuming a right to the best positions").

[239] *See* SchWeber, *supra* note 234, at 6-7 ("The burden of upholding this [no physical contact] policy falls heaviest on women inmates who must often be escorted or whose activities must be supervised.").

[240] *See* RAFTER, *supra* note 192, at 184 (describing the demise of the coed movement).

[241] New York's Albion Correctional Facility, for example, housed 332 men and 116 women, but the sexes were segregated from one another except in prison industries and food service jobs, college and health service classes, visiting, and certain special

only coed feature is the housing in a mainly female prison of a small number of much older, minimum security males.[242] For all practical purposes, the coed movement is now virtually dead.[243]

C. *Toward Effective Solutions for Female Prisoners*

The difficulties of cocorrections drive us back to separating the women, probably–for many states–in a single, centralized facility. That means that the best hope for female prisoners may be a doctrine of separate but equal. No one wants to invoke *Plessy v. Ferguson*[244] as a shining model, but what is abhorrent for the races in education may be a sensible solution for the sexes in prison.

A separate but equal approach will require us to have a concrete working conception of equality, a daunting task in this context. It makes little sense to afford weightlifting facilities for large numbers of inmates, as in men's prisons, if the women are not interested in using them. Nor does it make sense to deny women programs they do want (like courses in child rearing and prenatal care) just because such programs are not offered to or demanded by men. Inmate needs and preferences are one helpful measure of the kinds of services that should be offered, but this yardstick must be used cautiously, lest programs simply mirror and reinforce role stereotypes that the offenders bring with them to prison. Preparation for jobs and the enhancement of marketable skills should be priorities. Yet effective pursuit of these goals will sometimes require different programs for the women. And expenditure levels for men and women probably should not be held to strict per-capita equality, since program costs can be much higher for small groups of women than for large groups of men.

The search has to be for parity in the services delivered to women and to men. What is needed is what I would call "comparable worth" at the receiving end of the programs. Judged by this standard, the programs afforded to female inmates in the Nebraska prison system, although upheld by the court in *Klinger*,[245] should

---

programs. *See* SchWeber, *supra* note 234, at 5.

[242] An example is the 93% female prison at Clinton, New Jersey. *See id.*

[243] *See* RAFTER, *supra* note 192, at 184.

[244] 163 U.S. 537, 548 (1896) (holding that the separation of passengers of different races into separate railroad cars does not violate the Fourteenth Amendment). *Plessy* became the basis for the doctrine of separate but equal in education. *See* Brown v. Board of Educ., 347 U.S. 483 (1954) (overruling *Plessy*).

[245] *See supra* text accompanying notes 213-16.

clearly be regarded as constitutionally inadequate. Comparable worth may not be the best solution for wage discrimination in the labor market,[246] but it does make sense in assessing programs for women in prison.

No one concept or doctrine, of course, will magically solve all of the difficulties. As in the other areas of criminal justice I have surveyed, theoretical conceptions of neutrality, preferential treatment, empowerment, and the like are much less important than the particular strategies used to make feminist goals operational. Plausible ideas can easily backfire unless they are rooted in a close analysis of legal and institutional processes, and unless they are coupled with adequate funding and political support. That makes reform especially tricky in prisons, because when it comes to providing services for drug sellers and other offenders, funding and political support are not in overabundant supply.[247]

CONCLUSION

The four topics discussed in this Article make clear the overriding importance of particulars. Some may wonder whether the topics are representative—whether I have selected four unusually intractable problems. But if we wanted to pick issues for their intrinsic importance to female victims and female offenders, could we skip domestic violence, rape, sentencing, and prisons?

In stressing the particular and the concrete, I do not aim to deprecate the contributions of theory. As indicated at the outset, my concern about the limits of theory states a dilemma. We need theory, but theory cannot do all the work. The sweeping generalizations of high theory provide excitement in preaching to the choir, but too often they prove inapt, unhelpful, or positively counterpro-

---

[246] *See, e.g.*, Daniel R. Fischel & Edward P. Lazear, *Comparable Worth and Discrimination in Labor Markets*, 53 U. CHI. L. REV. 891, 918 (1986) (noting that comparable worth "has none of the appropriate incentive effects and fails to provide compensation for past wrongs to the appropriate parties"); Paul Weiler, *The Wages of Sex: The Uses and Limits of Comparable Worth*, 99 HARV. L. REV. 1728, 1756-79 (1986) (discussing the difficulties of adopting the comparable worth approach); *cf.* Mary E. Becker, *Barriers Facing Women in the Wage-Labor Market and the Need for Additional Remedies: A Reply to Fischel and Lazear*, 53 U. CHI. L. REV. 934, 940 (1986) (developing a case in favor of comparable worth).

[247] *See* Resnik, *supra* note 208, at 28 (noting that "[a]s overcrowding increases and interest in rehabilitation diminishes, many vocational and educational programs are reduced").

ductive when the time comes to address the problems of working institutions and the task of producing real improvement for women.

Many strands in contemporary feminism emphasize the importance of context and particulars as sources of insight into social and legal conditions that are oppressive to women.[248] A comparable insistence on doctrinal and institutional specifics is often lacking, however, in the discussion of proposals to redress these conditions. What has been missing from the dialogue, and is now most needed, is a feminism of process and particulars, a recognition that real solutions are likely to lie very deeply embedded in the details.

Because details are critical, and because change itself is guaranteed to bring problems, a natural reaction is that the status quo is not invidious after all. A common response to the feminist challenge is just the point with which I began—the recognition that bringing women into the equation is hard to do. For skeptics, this recognition translates into a do-nothing conclusion. The difficulty of social and legal change is where the discussion stops. My approach in this Article has been different. The difficulty of change was where I started. Change *is* difficult. But it is also long overdue.

---

[248] *See, e.g.*, Bartlett, *supra* note 6, at 849-63 (discussing feminists who emphasize reasoning from context); *see also* Margaret J. Radin, *The Pragmatist and the Feminist*, 63 S. CAL. L. REV. 1699, 1707 (1990) (noting that "[p]ragmatism and feminism largely share . . . the commitment to finding knowledge in the particulars of experience").

[5]

AN ECONOMIC ANALYSIS OF THREATS AND THEIR ILLEGALITY: BLACKMAIL, EXTORTION, AND ROBBERY

STEVEN SHAVELL†

The subject of this Article is the making of threats and the working of, and social need for, laws against them. I emphasize blackmail—by which I mean threats to expose information unless money (or something else of value) is surrendered—but I devote attention also to extortion (threats to cause injury to a person or to his property in the future) and to robbery (threats to do immediate physical harm to a person), as well as to certain commonly made threats that are not illegal (for example, threatening to withdraw business unless price is lowered).[1]

Section I of the Article is concerned with a purely descriptive, theoretical analysis of threats, assuming that parties act in a largely self-interested way and with due forethought.[2] The point I initially consider is that to the degree that threats will yield gains, potential threateners will invest effort in obtaining information for purposes of blackmail and, more generally, in placing themselves in positions allowing them to make threats. Likewise, to the extent potential victims fear threats, they will endeavor to avoid becoming vulnerable to threats. This preparatory behavior of threateners and of victims will be affected by legal rules that punish threats. By reducing the anticipated return from threats, the rules discourage threateners from devoting effort to the making of threats and lead victims to do less to protect themselves from threats.

---

† Professor of Law and Economics, Harvard Law School. I wish to thank Louis Kaplow and A. Mitchell Polinsky for comments, Paul Taylor for research assistance, and the National Science Foundation for research support.

[1] The term "blackmail" is sometimes interpreted more broadly than it is here, to encompass extortion. In fact, the early meaning of blackmail was limited to threats to do physical harm. For a recent discussion of blackmail and extortion, see James Lindgren, *Unraveling the Paradox of Blackmail*, 84 COLUM. L. REV. 670, 673-76 (1984); for an extensive description of blackmail and extortion in English law, see Glanville L. Williams, *Blackmail*, 1954 CRIM. L. REV. 79; and for an examination of the evolution of the crimes of robbery, blackmail, and extortion in English law, see W.H.D. Winder, *The Development of Blackmail*, 5 MOD. L. REV. 21 (1941).

[2] This feature of the analysis (along with its consequentialist normative aspect, to be described) is, of course, the hallmark of "economic" analysis of law and explains the use of the word in the title of the present Article.

After examining behavior preparatory to threats, I investigate the actual making of threats, focusing on the very real question of how a threat can succeed. A person making a threat faces a double problem. On one hand, his threat must be credible. The intended victim must believe there to be a significant chance that the threat will be carried out if and only if he does not accede to it; otherwise, he may have insufficient reason to bow to the will of the threatener. On the other hand, the victim must believe that if he *does* reward the threatener, he, the victim, will gain thereby and not merely set himself up for further threats. These difficulties may render success in threat-making somewhat problematic, and I discuss partial solutions to them for threateners (for instance, I suggest that although the second difficulty involving repeated demands is often inevitable, a threatener may still be able to induce his victim to pay if the amount repeatedly demanded is appropriately small). Difficulties in making threats combined with possibilities of miscalculation lead to the risk that demands will be rejected and threats actually executed.

In Section II of the Article, I inquire about the social undesirability of threats and the social advantages of laws punishing them. In so doing, I employ a consequentialist notion of social welfare and evaluate threats with reference to their three types of effect: (1) those concerning threateners' and victims' preparatory behavior; (2) the anxiety and worry suffered by victims (whether or not threats ultimately are carried out); and (3) results flowing from the carrying out of threats or the satisfaction of demands. In examining the utility of legal rules for discouraging undesirable threats, I consider, among other things, the virtues of punishing preparatory behavior versus punishing the making of threats versus punishing the execution of threats.

In both sections, I apply the analysis to the three major types of threats.[3] Regarding blackmail, I am naturally led to consider issues surrounding the social versus the private harm (or good) done by disclosure of information, and also issues involving the reporting of crime and law enforcement. The latter arise when the information a blackmailer threatens to reveal pertains to commission of a crime, for then blackmail itself might be thought to serve as a supplementary form of punishment.[4]

---

[3] *See supra* note 1 and accompanying text.

[4] I argue, however, that rewards for reporting crime are superior to blackmail as a device for enhancing law enforcement, so that blackmail should be illegal even when

In Section III of the Article, I offer concluding remarks. I should also say at the outset that I do not achieve any striking novelty here; I depend in many respects on the recent thoughtful analyses of blackmail by Landes and Posner, Ginsburg and Shechtman, and Lindgren.[5]

I. Descriptive Analysis of Threats

A. *Behavior Preparatory to the Making of Threats*

A person must often engage in certain preparatory activity to place himself in a position allowing him to make a threat. To carry out blackmail, a person must obtain information about the intended victim that the latter does not want revealed. To commit robbery, a person must find a potential victim in circumstances where he could not defend himself or secure help. Of course, it could be that a person fortuitously finds himself in a position allowing him to make a threat, as where a person chances upon information embarrassing to another. But individuals frequently undertake purposeful activity to gain advantages permitting them to make threats.

Similarly, potential victims of threats will want to reduce their vulnerability to threateners; they can do this in two ways. First, they can diminish the scale of the activities that expose them to risk. A person worried about the risk of blackmail from his infidelity can lower the number of unfaithful acts in which he engages; a person worried about the risk of blackmail from commission of a crime can reduce the number of crimes he commits; or a person worried

the blackmail information concerns criminality. *See infra* text accompanying notes 37-38.

[5] *See* Douglas H. Ginsburg & Paul Shechtman, *Blackmail: An Economic Analysis of the Law*, 141 U. PA. L. REV. 1849 *passim* (1993); William M. Landes & Richard A. Posner, *The Private Enforcement of Law*, 4 J. LEGAL STUD. 1, 42-44 (1975); Lindgren, *supra* note 1, *passim*. I am also informed by the following articles examining blackmail from an economic perspective: Ronald H. Coase, *The 1987 McCorkle Lecture: Blackmail*, 74 VA. L. REV. 655 (1988); Daniel Ellsberg, *The Theory and Practice of Blackmail*, *in* BARGAINING: FORMAL THEORIES OF NEGOTIATION 343 (Oran R. Young ed., 1959); Richard A. Epstein, *Blackmail, Inc.*, 50 U. CHI. L. REV. 553 (1983); Richard A. Posner, *Blackmail, Privacy, and Freedom of Contract*, 141 U. PA. L. REV. 1817 (1993). The present Article appears to add to the existing economically oriented literature chiefly in its descriptive analysis of threat-making. It also differs, though, in various ways in its normative analysis (see especially the discussion of whether blackmail is socially undesirable when the information that might be disclosed concerns a crime) and is more general in that it considers different types of threats.

about robbery can reduce the number of times he is out and about at night. Second, a person can take precautions to lower the likelihood of threats given the scale of his activity. For instance, a person who has arranged a meeting with a lover in a hotel room can exercise the precaution of checking for hidden cameras and can double-lock the door.

The general influence of legal rules on the preparatory behavior of threateners and of victims is apparent. Rules that penalize the making of threats or their execution lower the expected return from this activity,[6] and thus should lower the preparatory effort expended by potential threateners setting up threats. Threateners' preparatory efforts will also fall if such effort is itself punished (for instance, if drilling peepholes to be employed subsequently to obtain information for blackmail is penalized). A reduction in threateners' preparatory efforts will in turn lead potential victims not to fear threats as much, and will therefore increase the scale of the activities that expose them to risk and reduce their precautions.

B. *The Making of Threats: A Basic Model*

Let us now assume that a threatener is in a position to make a threat and discuss a simple model in which threats are made only once.[7] Here, the central issue will be the credibility of the threat, by which is meant the victim's belief that the threat will be carried out if and only if he does not satisfy the demand made of him. Consider Figure I on the following page.

As illustrated, threatener *T* makes a demand of victim *V*, which *V* either accepts or rejects, and then *T* either carries out his threat or does not. Assume as well that if *T* carries out his threat, he will bear a cost or enjoy a benefit and that *V* will suffer a harm.

What constitutes rational behavior for the parties in this situation? *V* should often reject *T*'s demand because his threat will not be credible. Specifically, suppose that it is costly for *T* to carry out his threat. Then *T* will do nothing whether or not *V* accepts his demand, so *V* should reject it. Similarly, suppose that it will give *T* pleasure to carry out his threat. Then *T* will carry out his threat whether or not *V* accepts his demand, so again *V* should reject it; he would gain nothing by accepting the demand.

---

[6] *See infra* part I.B.

[7] For discussion of repeated threats, see *infra* part I.C.

FIGURE I
MAKING THREATS: THE SINGLE DEMAND MODEL

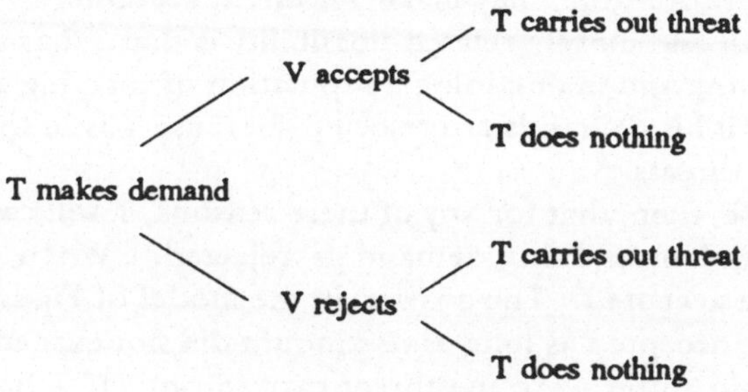

Plainly, for it to be rational for *V* to accept *T*'s demand, it must be that *T*'s threat will be carried out if, but only if, *V* rejects the demand; for then *V* will profit by meeting the demand. When will *T*'s threat be carried out if and only if his demand is rejected? Several answers suggest themselves.[8]

One possibility is that *T* will bear zero cost in carrying out his threat (as might nearly be true if the threat is to shoot a robbery victim or to reveal information about a blackmail victim). In this case, *T* will be happy to carry out his threat if his demand is rejected, and also happy not to carry it out if his demand is accepted. In other words, a statement that *T* would carry out his threat if and only if his demand is rejected is credible (even though barely so).

A second possibility is that *T* has the psychological makeup whereby he would become angry about rejection of his demand. If so, *T* would want to carry out his threat if his demand is rejected, but may not want to do so if it is accepted, perhaps because he

[8] *See generally* THOMAS C. SCHELLING, THE STRATEGY OF CONFLICT 21-52, 81-203 (1960) (discussing how parties may make their threats credible and specifically mentioning among other elements the third and fourth possibilities noted below); Ellsberg, *supra* note 5, at 343-63 (amplifying Schelling's points in the context of blackmail).

would then feel grateful or because there is a cost to carrying out the threat.[9]

A third possibility is of an entirely different nature: that *T* will make a contract to have the threat carried out by a third party if and only if his demand is rejected. Such a contract, if legally or otherwise enforceable, may make *T*'s threat credible.[10]

A fourth and closely related possibility is that *T* has an interest in establishing and maintaining a reputation of carrying out threats if and only if his demands are rejected—because *T* is in the business of making threats.[11]

Suppose, then, that for any of these reasons, *T* will carry out his threat if and only if his demand is rejected. When would his demand be accepted? The answer, in the model of Figure I, is that it would be accepted as long as its amount did not exceed the harm that *V* would suffer were the threat carried out. If *T* has accurate knowledge of the harm that *V* would suffer, he will demand exactly this amount, extracting the maximum from *V*.[12]

Imperfect information, however, can lead to rejection of demands and execution of threats. If *T* overestimates the harm to *V*, *T* may demand more than *V* would be willing to pay; *V* will thus rationally reject the demand, and *T* will then carry out his threat.[13] Another way that imperfect information may lead to inefficient

---

[9] A numerical example may be useful here. Suppose that if his demand were rejected, *T* would obtain a benefit of 10 from carrying out the threat, whereas if his demand is accepted he would bear a cost of 5 from carrying out the threat; in either case, if he does nothing, his gain is 0. If *T*'s demand is rejected, he will clearly carry out his threat, for a gain of 10 exceeds 0; but if his demand is accepted, he will not carry out his threat because he would rather gain 0 than lose 5.

[10] I say "may" because there are a variety of difficulties that may arise with such contracts (apart from ensuring their enforceability). Suppose, for example, that *T* would derive pleasure from revealing information about *V*. Even if he made a contract with a third party for that party to reveal information if and only if his demand were not met, if his demand were met, *T* himself would still have an interest in revealing the information. Hence, accepting *T*'s demand would do *V* no good.

[11] Equivalently, *T* may sell his ability to make a threat (as by selling embarrassing information) to such a business.

[12] Suppose that the harm *V* would suffer if the threat is carried out is 100 and that *T*'s threat is credible. If *T* knows that 100 is the harm *V* would suffer, *T* will know that any demand he makes up to 100 will be accepted by *V*, so *T* will ask for 100 (or just under 100), and *V* will be willing to pay that amount.

[13] If *T* thinks the harm that *V* would suffer is very likely to be 100 and very unlikely to be 50, *T* will rationally demand 100: for usually this amount will be accepted, and when it is not, all that happens—assuming the situation in note 9, *supra*—is that *T* gets angry and carries out his threat, gaining 10 instead of 100. The alternative of obtaining 50 for sure is not as good. Thus, when the harm *V* would suffer is indeed 50, *V* will reject *T*'s demand of 100, and *T* will carry out his threat.

decisionmaking is that *V* may mistakenly think that *T* will not carry out his threat and thus reject it, only to see the threat carried out.[14]

Finally, consider the question whether *T* will want to make a demand in the first place (assuming that he is in the position to do so). The answer depends on the return he can expect from a demand, and the cost of making it and of possibly carrying out a threat. In the simplest case, where he and *V* have perfect information and *T*'s demand is credible, *T* will obtain a gross return equal to the harm to *V*, so he will make a threat if the expected costs of so doing are less than this amount. If *T*'s information is imperfect, he will compare his expected return to his expected costs.

How do legal rules affect the behavior of parties, given that a threatener is in a position to make a threat? Rules that penalize the making of threats and their execution will generally increase the expected cost of making threats, and thus reduce the number of occasions in which a threatener will decide to make a threat. The threshold of gross return from a threat will have to be higher before a person who is in a position to make a threat will decide to do so. Furthermore, such rules may limit the circumstances in which threats are credible and reduce the probability that a threatener will make a threat.

To amplify this discussion, consider how the probability of detection and conviction for a threatener is determined. First, by making a threat, he suffers a risk of capture, as someone, especially the victim, may obtain proof of his behavior. Second, the victim's acceptance of a threatener's demand provides an additional opportunity for proof of his behavior to be obtained.[15] Third, the carrying out of a threat may affect the probability of detection. In some contexts, executing a threat will increase the chances of detection, for it may furnish an additional opportunity for proof of a threat to be obtained. Also, the carrying out of a threat may

---

[14] In the example given in note 9, *supra*, suppose that, contrary to fact, *V* thinks it very likely that *T* will bear a cost of 5 in carrying out his threat whether or not *V* rejects the demand. *V* will not believe that *T* will carry out the threat if he rejects the demand, so that *V* will reject *T*'s demand, and *T* will carry out his threat.

[15] A complication with regard to a discovery that *T* is accepting payments is that this in itself may well not be illegal. If it is not illegal, then *T*'s acceptance of payments must be combined with other evidence for it to help in convicting *T* of making threats. Similarly, *T*'s execution of a threat may not be illegal (suppose the threat is to expose information) and thus must be combined with other evidence to assist in convicting *T*. For further discussion on this point, see *infra* part II.B.

increase the incentive of the victim or someone else to report the threat, as where a blackmail victim, having been exposed, no longer has anything to fear from reporting, or where a robbery victim becomes angry and wants revenge. It is possible, however, that the carrying out of a threat will reduce the probability of detection (for instance, if the threat is to kill the victim, thereby eliminating a source of information about the threat). If, though, the carrying out of a threat would increase the exposure of the threatener to detection, then the likelihood that his threat would be credible would be reduced by the presence of the legal rules under consideration.

Of course, the magnitude of the effect of legal rules depends importantly on the probability of detection and conviction, and this in turn depends on the likelihood of observation by third parties or the report of threats by victims.

C. *The Making of Threats: Model with Repeated Demands*

Let us now examine an extension of the basic model allowing for the possibility of repeated demands and repeated threats. In this version of the model, the new issue that arises is that if the victim accepts an initial demand, that may well not result in his being free from further demands. Consider Figure II on the following page.

The assumption is that after *V* accepts or rejects, *T* has the option of making another demand in addition to the option of carrying out his threat or doing nothing. It is also assumed that the situation portrayed repeats itself, that after *V* accepts or rejects a possible second demand, there may be a third demand, and so on.[16]

---

[16] The diagram reflects the implicit assumption that *T* will not resume bargaining if he ever carries out his threat or does nothing. This assumption is made for simplicity but has justification in certain situations. For instance, in blackmail, if *T* carries out his threat and exposes information, he no longer can carry out a threat.

FIGURE II
MAKING THREATS: THE MULTIPLE DEMAND MODEL

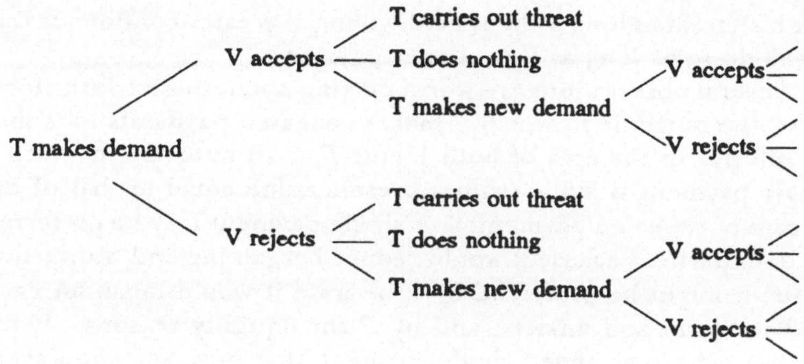

To understand the new issue, assume that *T*'s threat is credible—that he will carry out his threat at any stage if and only if his demand is rejected (for concreteness, one might assume that *T* would become angry if his demand were rejected). Now consider *T*'s decision if *V* accepts his initial demand. *T* will be best off making a new demand if there is any probability that it will be accepted.[17] Moreover, this logic applies at every stage. Hence, both *T* and *V* will realize that *T* will be making repeated demands. What does this imply? It implies that what *V* purchases when he makes a payment to *T* is freedom from the threat for one period, until *T* makes the next threat. Hence, for *V* to be willing to pay *T*, *T*'s demand each period must be "small," equal only to the value of freedom from the threat during the periods between demands. A succession of payments of this size is, however, quite rational for *V*

---

[17] If *T* makes a new threat, he will obtain a positive expected return. If he does nothing more, he obtains zero. If he carries out his threat, he gains nothing or bears a cost. Hence, *T* would make a new demand.

to make.[18] Further, notice that there is a self-reinforcing aspect of the situation under discussion: both *V* and *T* know that if *T* were ever to carry out his threat, he would as a consequence lose all future payments—he would be killing the goose that lays the golden eggs. This should make *T* want to continue to refrain from carrying out his threat as long as he is paid, giving *V* greater confidence that *T* will do so as long as *V* continues payments.

Several observations are worth making about these conclusions. First, the outcome in which *V* makes repeated payments to *T* may be inferior in the eyes of both *V* and *T* to an outcome in which a single payment is made (with a present value equal to that of the stream of repeated payments). A single payment may be preferred by both parties because it would reduce bargaining and transaction costs; it might be preferred by *V* because it would mean an early end to worry and anxiety, and by *T* for liquidity reasons. If the parties want to arrange a single payment, they must somehow avoid their joint problem that *T* will have an incentive to make repeated demands. One way in which a single payment could be arranged is, in principle, for *T* to give *V* the power to threaten him when the first payment is made. Notably, as I will discuss subsequently in the context of blackmail, *T* could give *V* information that *T* would not want revealed; thus, after the first payment, *V* and *T* would each be able to threaten each other. and hence, after a single payment, there might be no more demands. Another way in which the problem might be solved is that *T* may be in the business of making threats and thus, as discussed above, want to maintain a reputation that will inure to his long run benefit. If so, *T* would have a reason to drop the matter after *V* made a single payment.[19]

---

[18] A complete example may be helpful. Suppose that, as in note 9, *supra*, if *T*'s demand is ever rejected, he would become angry and obtain a benefit of 10 from carrying out his threat, but whenever his threat is accepted, he would sustain a cost of 5 were he to carry out his threat. Suppose as well that if *T* ever carries out his threat, *V* will suffer a loss of 20 for each and every period thereafter. In this situation, it is reasonable for *T* to demand 20 (or just under this amount) and to have the strategy of carrying out his threat if and only if any demand is rejected. Also, it is reasonable for *V* to pay 20 every period. In the terminology of game theory, this constitutes a perfect equilibrium. Specifically, if *T* has the stated strategy, it is obviously rational for *V* to accept *T*'s demand each period. *T*'s strategy is also rational for him to pursue at each stage, for if he ever carries out the threat or drops the matter, the game is over and he obtains less than 20, whereas if he makes another demand he will obtain 20. While this is only an example, I conjecture that it illustrates the nature of a solution to the repeated threat model under wide conditions. (This model, it seems, deserves to be studied formally.)

[19] Similarly, *T* could conceivably contract with a third party to make only a single

This is not to say, however, that *V* and *T* will necessarily want to arrange a single payment. *T* may prefer a stream of payments because only in this way can he extract a share of *V*'s future earnings. If *V* receives income over time from employment or a business (and cannot borrow against future earnings), then the only way *T* can obtain a significant share of *V*'s income is to take it in a series of payments. For this reason, if the harm that *T* could impose on *V* by carrying out his threat is sufficiently large, *T* may prefer to collect a stream of payments.

A second observation is that the possibility that imperfect information will lead to rejection of demands and the carrying out of threats appears to be greater in the repeated context. There are more opportunities for demands to go wrong, to exceed what *V* is willing to pay. Further, over time, the value *V* places on freedom from execution of the threat may change, as may his willingness to make payments. If *T* fails to gauge properly *V*'s situation, he may ask for too much and be rejected, and that may in turn prompt performance of the threat.

Third, the influence of legal rules is altered somewhat in the repeated context. The repetition of payments means that there are more chances for *T* to be caught, and thus suggests that the power of the legal rules to deter is greater than would otherwise have been appreciated.

D. *Application to Different Types of Threat*

1. Robbery

How do robbers make their threats credible? First, if a robber carries a weapon that he appears to know how to employ, not only does he have a threat that is large in magnitude, but also one which may be easy for him to execute (to pull a trigger is virtually effortless) and one which, if carried out, may not increase (and could reduce) his likelihood of being caught. Hence, we may sometimes envision the situation as one in which the cost of carrying out a threat is small, making credibility of the threat easier to establish. Second, the possibility that a robber may enjoy carrying out his threat if he is thwarted may also be relevant. The personality type given to this reaction is probably correlated with certain characteristics of robbers (lack of education, anomie), and

---

demand.

self-selection may also be at work—individuals with the personality type may choose to become robbers. In any case, we would expect to see attempts by robbers to convince victims that they would not mind, or would enjoy, carrying out threats if their demands are not met. Thus, robbers often display behavior patterns that lead victims to believe they are confronting sociopathic individuals who will carry out their threats. Robbers may commit minor acts (shove someone, push a knife to a person's throat) to help persuade victims that they are dealing with individuals who are willing to carry out threats. Despite the various efforts of robbers to make their threats credible, they obviously do not always succeed, and for this reason as well as others, robbers often commit violence.

It should be remarked that the issue of repeated threats is moot with regard to robbery. In a robbery situation, repeated threats are not possible, as once a person turns over his possessions to the robber, that is the end of the matter.

Legal rules against robbery undoubtedly reduce the amount of robbery substantially, despite the incidence of this crime. If there were no laws against robbery, the levels of precaution taken by potential victims and the curtailment of their activities arguably would be extraordinary, as would the efforts by robbers to commit robbery.

2. Extortion

An extortionist's problem of making his threat credible is in some respects more difficult than a robber's, because the extortionist's threat is not immediate and apparent and because his victim will have time to defend himself. While extortionists probably attempt to solve their credibility problems by the general techniques used by robbers, it also seems that they resort more often than do robbers to groups (neighborhood gangs, organized crime) with long-term stakes in maintaining a reputation for carrying out threats.

The threat of the extortionist often can be repeated, unlike that of the robber, for the nature of the extortionist's threat usually lends itself to repetition. If the threat is to burn down a store, for instance, this can ordinarily be repeated. We would therefore expect on the general grounds advanced above that extortion demands would be repeated. Moreover, an extortionist frequently would not want to arrange a single payment because the extortion victim often earns money over time and thus will yield more if the extortionist collects repeatedly. Thus, it is not surprising that extortion demands are in fact usually repeated (at least this is my impression).

There is little to add about the effect of legal rules to what has already been said.[20] To the extent that extortion threats are anticipated, it would seem that there is an enhanced opportunity to catch an extortionist, other things being equal. Moreover, since organizations often are involved in extortion and organizations are easier to detect than single parties, extortion may be easier to detect than what might otherwise be supposed. The implication is not, of course, that we would expect to see extortion stamped out, and we do not. Rather, it is that the legal rules against extortion are probably effective in deterring a tremendous amount of that activity; in the absence of the enforcement of legal rules against extortion, we would likely be overrun by extortionate enterprise.[21]

3. Blackmail

It appears that a blackmailer should often face less difficulty in making his threat credible than a robber or extortionist because the cost of executing a blackmail threat is likely to be small by comparison. The direct cost to a blackmailer of actually carrying out his threat is ordinarily trivial; it takes almost no effort to mail a photograph or a document to someone. The cost to a blackmailer of carrying out his threat probably inheres mainly in any resulting increase in the risk of his being caught and punished. But the blackmailer can usually reveal his information anonymously, using the mail or the telephone. And even if he is caught revealing information, this is not a crime (unlike the extortionist's or the robber's threats), so it might be difficult to successfully prosecute the blackmailer in the absence of independent evidence that he had made a threat. All this suggests that the blackmail threat is frequently not very hard to make credible. Accordingly, blackmailers should not usually need to rely on a group's reputation to

---

[20] *See supra* parts I.A-C.

[21] In areas where the legal system is ineffective or has broken down, such as in regions of Bolivia and Colombia today, extortion is well known to engender serious avoidance efforts on the part of potential victims, extending even to the creation of private protective armies to act against extortionists. At the same time, the efforts of extortionists to set up opportunities for their activities are extensive. This is a chief occupation of certain guerrilla and bandit groups. *See* James Brooke, *Kidnapping and "Taxes" Transform Guerrilla Inc.*, N.Y. TIMES, July 24, 1992, at D1.

enhance the credibility of their threats, and it appears that blackmail is usually an individual activity.[22]

The threat of blackmail is one which can be repeated. A blackmailer virtually always retains the ability to reveal information. Even if he wants to extinguish his ability to reveal information, there is usually no way to convince a blackmail victim that the blackmailer does not have copies of photographs or other proof of the information the victim does not want revealed.[23] This means that the victim should expect repeated demands and that a small stream of repeated payments will be made. This may also sometimes be seen as a problem by a blackmailer and his victim. Although I have no direct evidence that it is so regarded, one sees occasional reference to the issue in accounts of blackmail,[24] and one certainly sees reference to the point that demands are seldom made only once.[25]

With regard to the effect of legal rules on blackmail, it is frequently difficult to obtain evidence that a blackmailer made a threat. Blackmail threats are occasions in which information is communicated, perhaps only verbally, and can ordinarily be concealed or designed so that the blackmailer's identity cannot be established. Moreover, the blackmailer can sometimes phrase the threats in a nuanced way to avoid crossing the line of criminality, even though the meaning of the threats will be clear to victims. Further, the victim of a blackmail threat may well have an incentive to hide the threat from the authorities, for reporting it may result

---

[22] *See, e.g.*, MIKE HEPWORTH, BLACKMAIL: PUBLICITY AND SECRECY IN EVERYDAY LIFE 46-60 (1975) (describing traits and accounts of blackmail by master blackmailers).

[23] There are exceptions to this statement. Suppose that I am blackmailing murderer V with the threat that I will turn over to the authorities the murder weapon, a gun, that I have in my possession. If I instead surrender the gun to V, I will end my ability to make further demands. But such instances appear to be rare.

[24] Consider, for example, the following conversation about blackmail in a detective novel by Lawrence Block:

> "You pay it once and it's over."
>
> "Back on Square A. How do I know that?"
>
> "Because when you pay over the money, I give you a handle on me. I did something a few years ago. I could go to jail for it for a long time. I can write out a confession giving all the details. I'll give it to you when you pay the fifty thou . . . . That locks me in, keeps me from doing a thing."
>
> . . . .
>
> Finally she said, "It might work."

LAWRENCE BLOCK, TIME TO MURDER AND CREATE 45-46 (Jove Books 1983) (1977).

[25] *See* HEPWORTH, *supra* note 22, at 42 (discussing recurring demands for money as both a feature of blackmail and frequent cause of the blackmailer's undoing).

in disclosure of the information he wants to keep secret. Unlike the victim of an extortion or robbery threat, the blackmail victim may suffer more if the threatener is brought to justice than if he is not. It is true that there is scope for the state to protect the blackmail victim from exposure of the information, but this will often be impossible.[26] In addition, as explained above, the chances of convicting a blackmailer who carries out his threat are not high. Hence, one suspects that the ability of legal rules to prevent blackmail is often circumscribed.

At the same time, this limitation does not mean that the rules are of negligible effect. In their absence, it is probable that the scope of blackmail would be vastly increased due to growth of businesses specializing in this activity.[27] All manner of activity aimed at gathering information for purposes of blackmail would occur, as would efforts to entice people into embarrassing situations. Furthermore, potential victims would take protective measures that they do not take today because of the remoteness of the chance of blackmail.

An additional issue concerning the effect of rules against blackmail involves situations where a blackmailer's information pertains to the commission of a crime. In such cases, does blackmail increase deterrence of crime, that is, the probability and magnitude of punishment for crime?

The illegality of blackmail would seem to reduce the probability that crime is punished, where by "punished" I mean either that the criminal is punished by the state *or* by having to pay a blackmailer. Because people will generally have less incentive to obtain information about the commission of crimes when blackmail is illegal, criminals who would have been discovered and then blackmailed may not be if blackmail is illegal. For instance, a neighbor of *X* who has a suspicion that *X* committed a crime and would blackmail him were this legal may not bother to investigate (say by looking for stolen goods) due to the illegality of blackmail. It is true that the illegality of blackmail will tend to increase the reporting of crime to

---

[26] For instance, the time the victim spends in court may be hard to conceal from co-workers or from a spouse, and may lead to discovery of the information that he wants to hide. Additionally, if the information is that the person committed a crime, he will be reluctant to go to the authorities, unless they had granted him immunity from prosecution (even in this case, he might be reluctant to go forward).

[27] *See* Epstein, *supra* note 5, at 562 ("[T]here would then be an open and public market for a new set of social institutions to exploit the gains from [legalized blackmail].").

the authorities when people already have information about the commission of a crime;[28] if *X*'s neighbor already knows that *X* committed a crime, the neighbor might report this if blackmail is illegal but may have kept quiet and committed blackmail if the law permitted otherwise. Such an event, however, amounts to a shift in the medium of punishment, not in the probability of punishment.

It appears, though, that the illegality of blackmail will often tend to increase the magnitude of punishment. As just mentioned, the illegality of blackmail should result in people who have information reporting it to the state more frequently than otherwise, and under plausible assumptions the state's punishment will be more severe than a blackmailer's. In particular, suppose that the criminal sanction includes imprisonment and that the assets of the victim are not very large. Then the maximum amount of money a blackmailer could extract would create less disutility for the criminal than the criminal sanction. For example, an embezzler with $5000 in assets could pay a blackmailer at most $5000, but spending fifteen years in jail would be a considerably more serious punishment. Moreover, part of the criminal sanction is public humiliation, a situation which is avoided in a blackmail arrangement. Hence, the suspicion is that with regard to many serious crimes, there would be a systematic reduction in the magnitude of punishment were blackmail allowed. The importance of this dilution in sanctions is great when one takes into account two groups of individuals who frequently have information about criminals but also have easy access to the criminal justice system: law enforcement officers and the victims of crime. If each were free to blackmail criminals, there would be a pronounced alteration from punishment by the criminal justice system to punishment through blackmail, with a substantial decrease in the magnitude of punishment.

The conclusion from this analysis of the effect of the illegality of blackmail on deterrence of crime is then ambiguous in principle, since the likelihood of punishment should fall even though the magnitude should rise.[29]

---

[28] Of course, many people will neither report crime nor commit blackmail, but the illegality of blackmail can only increase reporting to the state by people who already possess information about crime.

[29] *See* Jennifer G. Brown, *Blackmail as Private Justice*, 141 U. PA. L. REV. 1929, 1936 (1993). The conclusion, however, treats all else as given. I will argue below that when the possibility of rewarding people for reporting crimes is taken into account, the conclusion will change. The legality of blackmail should not be looked upon as needed to increase the probability of punishment, since the offer of rewards can

4. Commonly Made Threats in Commercial Life and Other Legally Permissible Threats

There are a multiplicity of threats that are not illegal. I will make no attempt to characterize them, as they are so various, but will consider three for contrast with the types of illegal threats discussed above. The first is the typical threat made in commerce, to withdraw business unless price (or some other term) is favorably adjusted—for instance, a buyer's threat that he will not purchase an item unless the price is lowered from $100 to $75. Such threats are often made credible by the existence of alternative opportunities. If the buyer could indeed buy the item for $75 elsewhere and the seller knows this, the buyer's threat would be credible. The fact that such threats may be made and carried out leads to changes in preparatory behavior, that is, in a buyer's search for relevant markets and a seller's efforts to lower costs enabling him to meet demands.

A second legal threat of interest is the right of a person who suffers a civil wrong to bring suit against the injuring party unless he is paid an amount in settlement. This threat is made credible by the ability of the injured party to go to court and collect a judgment. A natural question to be asked about the legality of such threats is whether they allow substantially reduced punishment of liable parties. It seems that they do not, at least in a comparative sense: settlements in the civil context should not permit as much reduction in punishment as would "settlements" of criminal cases (legal blackmail arrangements between victims of crimes and criminals). Contrast, for instance, the likely settlement in a civil case in which the defendant would be liable for $50,000 with the criminal case in which the embezzler with only $5000 in assets would be imprisoned for fifteen years. In the civil case, the settlement would approximate $50,000, the social sanction, whereas in the criminal case, the settlement of $5000 would represent far less punishment than the social sanction of lengthy imprisonment. The source of the difference is that the civil sanction is monetary, while the criminal sanction includes imprisonment.

A third example concerns a threat to take some action with one's property unless one is given a payment or something else of value in exchange. For example, a person might threaten to erect a fence around his property that his neighbor would find objection-

---

accomplish that.

able unless the neighbor agrees to constrain his bothersome dog. Such threats may or may not be credible, depending notably on whether the threatened act appears to be in the self-interest of the threatening party (whether a person is really bothered by his neighbor's dog or whether a person would find his own fence objectionable).

II. Normative Analysis of Threats

A. *General Effects of Threats on Social Welfare*

The influence of threats on social welfare can be divided into three categories. The first is the welfare consequences of threats for preparatory behavior. As a general matter, efforts expended by threateners putting themselves in a position to carry out threats is a social waste; such effort is not producing anything of value for final consumption. Similarly, precautions taken by potential victims avoiding threats reduce social welfare. The scaling back of activities that expose victims to the risk of threats, however, may or may not be socially undesirable, depending on the social value placed on those activities. If an activity is socially disapproved, such as a criminal activity, then any reduction in its level due to threat-making is socially desirable.

The second category is the welfare consequences of the making of threats themselves. I mention this because the making of threats, independently of whether they eventually are executed, can create fear and anxiety in victims.[30] This disutility, especially if it extends over a long period, is potentially a significant detriment to social welfare. Thus, it would seem to be most relevant in a context of repeated threats, or at least where there is a long-lasting ability to carry out threats. It also needs to be noted that the fear of execution of threats is explicable in terms of our analysis. As previously mentioned, the possibility of miscalculation by the parties can lead to the blackmailer carrying out his threats. Accordingly, it

[30] Although it is customary in economic analysis to restrict attention to actual outcomes, such as whether a threat to expose an embarrassing fact is ultimately carried out, in the present context it seems important to take into account the effect of the risk of the actual outcome on the mental state of the threatened party. It seems that when the risk surpasses some threshold, the threatened party will worry, that is, play over in his mind what would happen if the threat were carried out, and that this type of mental activity creates substantial disutility. If so, worry is a factor that ought to weigh in the welfare calculus, along with any "actual outcome."

is rational for a victim in a context of repeated threats to harbor a fear that at some point, a threat may be carried out.

The third category is the welfare consequences flowing from payment of demands or the carrying out of threats. If a payment is made, we often think of this as having no welfare significance in itself, as being a mere transfer of purchasing power, and I will make this assumption unless otherwise noted. But what will be of consequence to welfare is the carrying out of threats, due to imperfect information and miscalculation. The nature of the welfare effects of the execution of threats depends on the type of threat. If the threat is to do harm to a person or to property, it will lower welfare, other things being equal. If the threat is to reveal information, it may or may not be undesirable.[31]

The overall effect on welfare of the making of threats, therefore, is determined by the net impact of the three sources of welfare change due to threats.

B. *Optimal Use of the Law Against Undesirable Threats*

If it is desirable to discourage the making of threats because they lead to undesirable consequences, the law can be applied at three different stages: to the preparatory behavior of potential threateners, to the making of the threats, and to the collection of payments or the execution of threats.

When is it socially desirable for the law to intervene? The answer is that if deterrence is weak, as I will suggest will often be the case, the law should intervene at all three stages; all available opportunities to deter the unwanted behavior should be taken.[32]

With regard to the preparatory behavior of threateners, we can imagine that if a person is setting up eavesdropping devices for the purpose of blackmail, there is an opportunity for legal intervention. This legal strategy, however, suffers from the difficulty in differentiating innocent behavior from that which is preparatory to the making of threats. If, for instance, a person is prowling the halls of

---

[31] *See infra* part II.C.

[32] This argument implicitly rests on the assumption that society cannot necessarily raise deterrence adequately by increasing the magnitude of punishment. Hence, society may need to increase the number of occasions in which it punishes in order to achieve a deterrence goal. *See* Steven Shavell, *Deterrence and the Punishment of Attempts*, 19 J. LEGAL STUD. 435, 436-37 (1990) (explaining why, to achieve deterrence, it may be desirable for society to punish not just acts that result in harm, but also acts that happen not to—namely, attempts).

a motel with a camera, it will be hard to demonstrate from this alone that he was planning to take photographs for blackmail; or if a person is walking the streets searching for a robbery victim, it will be hard to demonstrate that this was his intent.

When the law is applied to the making of threats, there are also problems with deterrence. With regard to all three types of threat, there is the basic problem that the threatener selects his time and method of threat-making so as to avoid detection. Blackmail, as discussed, also involves the perversity that if the victim reports the threat, this itself may result in the revelation of information that he seeks to avoid. Further, as also discussed, blackmail and extortion threats may be hard to substantiate. Altogether, then, one supposes that the use of penalties only for the making of threats would not be sufficient to generate adequate deterrence of threats.

When the law is applied at the third stage, where payments are made or where threats are carried out, there again may be problems with detection.[53] Consider first that it may not be easy to catch a person collecting a payment. He can arrange a surreptitious pickup of funds (using agents, drop-offs, and the like) or other devices (such as "buying" property at a reduced price). Further, what if he is caught taking money? Without any direct evidence about his having made a threat, it might be hard to obtain a conviction of a person who took payment, since this in itself is not illegal (a threatener might say that he merely found money in a bag). If, though, the person who took payment could be shown to have directed an effort to do so secretly, a conviction would be easier. Thus, catching a person taking payments would be likely to result in a conviction only in the latter case or where there already existed some, but not sufficient, evidence of threat-making (if proof of threat-making had been sufficient, a conviction would already have been obtained). Consider next the carrying out of threats. Again, this will be done by threateners in such a way as to avoid detection, and as was mentioned above, in the case of blackmail, is not a crime in itself.

This discussion suggests that the ability to deter threats is weak enough to warrant legal intervention at all three stages, not just at the stage of the making of threats.

---

[53] Here, I speak only about extortion and blackmail, as I assume that the second and third stages of threat-making are coincident in the case of robbery.

C. *Application to Different Types of Threat*

1. Robbery and Extortion

As indicated earlier, robbery and extortion generate a substantial amount of preparatory activity on the part of potential victims and potential threateners, all of which is a social waste. Moreover, the threats generate anxiety on the part of potential victims. With robbery, the anxiety may be short-lived, if intense, although the memory of the event can create disutility. With extortion, which is likely to be repeated, the anxiety is suffered over a long period.

Also, the threats involved in robbery and extortion are to do harm to person or property, and since threats are sometimes carried out, this is another element that makes robbery and extortion socially undesirable. If the threats are not carried out, there are transfers of funds. If we regard these transfers as a wash, then there is no more to say about them. But when extortion affects businesses, as it frequently does, product prices will often rise as a consequence. This in turn will lower social welfare in a familiar way: consumers will be led to purchase alternative goods that they do not really prefer and which are not really cheaper but only appear so because of the high extortion-related price of goods sold by extorted merchants.

In sum, the effects of robbery and extortion are unambiguously to reduce social welfare, which justifies the use of legal rules against these threats.

2. Blackmail

Consider first blackmail where the information that might be disclosed pertains to a *socially harmless activity or fact*. An example is engaging in conventional sexual intercourse with one's spouse, or even taking a shower, where in either case the blackmail threat is to reveal photographs of the activity. Note that it is perfectly rational for the blackmail victim not to want such photographs revealed even though the activity in question is socially harmless. Personal modesty would lead most people not to want such photographs revealed; a very definite positive value, perhaps high for some people, would be put on preventing their revelation.

In such cases, blackmail is almost, but not entirely, analogous to robbery or extortion and thus seems socially undesirable. Specifically, the efforts to undertake blackmail and the efforts to guard against it are social wastes, and the reduction in the scale of potential victims' activities is a social detriment since the activities are not harmful yet benefit those who engage in them. If people take showers less frequently (for example, when they are in hotel rooms), they experience a loss in utility for no socially good reason. The making of threats also creates anxiety, which has a similar negative effect on one's welfare.

But the influence on social welfare of the actual revelation of information, should it occur, is ambiguous. By assumption, revelation of information always harms the victim. However, the effect on others of revelation of information is unclear. Consider the case of photographs of a person taking a shower being sent to the person's co-workers. It could be that those who see the photographs would not enjoy viewing them in any sense; rather, they would feel awkward, especially when in the presence of the blackmail victim. Another possibility, though, is that people might enjoy seeing photographs of a person taking a shower. For example, the blackmail victim may be an extremely attractive young woman and her male co-workers may take a prurient interest in the photographs. Thus, in theory, it is not apparent how revelation of information would affect social welfare.

Because the exposure of information when blackmail threats fail may produce a net social benefit, it is theoretically possible that blackmail is not socially undesirable even though the acts in question are socially innocuous. This case, however, seems a rather unlikely one (and it must always be kept in mind that the whole issue of exposure of information is limited in importance because it applies only when blackmail does not succeed and the blackmailer nevertheless carries out his threat). Thus, it appears that one may safely conclude that blackmail is generally socially harmful when the act threatened to be exposed is socially harmless.[34]

Consider next blackmail where the information pertains to a *socially harmful activity other than a crime*, for example, the wasteful but not illegal spending of church funds by a minister. The primary difference between this case and the previous one is that here, to the extent that blackmail reduces victims' activities, it is socially

---

[34] This justification for the illegality of blackmail incorporates what others have said. In particular, Ginsburg and Shechtman emphasize the notion that blackmail encourages blackmailers to expend effort on gathering embarrassing information. *See* Ginsburg & Shechtman, *supra* note 5, at 1859-65. Further, the closely related explanation for the illegality of robbery—that it induces wasteful effort on the part of both robbers and victims—is commonplace.

valuable. If ministers are induced to use church funds more responsibly because of fear of blackmail, this is a good thing.[35]

That blackmail in the present case has the beneficial aspect of suppressing undesirable activities, and yet causes wasteful efforts to obtain information and to guard against blackmail, renders the social evaluation of blackmail ambiguous. To amplify, it is not possible to say whether the effort expended to undertake and avoid blackmail is more or less important than its effect in reducing undesirable activities. For example, it could be that potential victims of blackmail can almost entirely avoid detection if they make an expenditure of effort (suppose the minister can avoid detection if he goes to the trouble of making all purchases with cash instead of his credit card). If so, the primary effect of blackmail threats would be to induce expenditure of effort, not to reduce the scale of victims' activities, and blackmail would thus be socially undesirable. Conversely, if there is little potential victims can do to prevent blackmail, and its principal effect would be to reduce their undesirable activities, blackmail would be socially advantageous.

Now consider blackmail where the information that would be revealed is that a person *committed a crime*. Recall from previous discussion[36] that blackmail should generally increase the probability that a criminal is punished in the sense that he will be blackmailed more often, but that the magnitude of punishment in the form of blackmail will frequently be lower than the specified legal sanctions. This means that the effect of blackmail on deterring crime is unclear, and thus we cannot say whether or not the blackmail of crime is socially desirable. If we allow blackmail of thieves, then more thieves would be punished because they would be forced to pay blackmail rather than go scot-free. On the other hand, some thieves who today would be reported and go to prison would instead pay modest amounts to blackmailers.

There is, however, an important factor not yet considered that suggests that blackmail need not be viewed as necessary to increase the likelihood of punishment. Suppose that society offers *rewards* to people for identifying criminals whenever this would be socially beneficial. Rather than inducing individuals to obtain information by allowing them to blackmail someone, like a thief, these individu-

---

[35] Additionally, if information is revealed, such disclosure is perhaps more likely to be socially beneficial here because it may allow desirable actions to be taken as a consequence, such as the church's more careful monitoring of its spending.

[36] *See supra* part I.D.

als could be equivalently induced, were that desired, by offering them a reward equal to the amount they could obtain through blackmail–and by making blackmail illegal at the same time. What, though, is the affirmative argument for making blackmail illegal and having the state impose sanctions? One reason has already been discussed–the state can impose higher penalties, in the form of imprisonment and the stigma accompanying criminal convictions, than blackmailers. Thus state-imposed sanctions achieve a more appropriate level of deterrence. Second, presuming the judicial process has been designed to guard against errors, it is better to have this mechanism determine punishment than blackmailers. Third, in some circumstances, blackmailers would devote socially excessive efforts to finding information about criminals.[37] Hence, my conclusion is that blackmail should be made illegal in the present case.[38]

Two further comments are worth making about blackmail and information about crime. First, the argument just given hardly implies that society does not want to take advantage of the information that people have, or can readily obtain, about criminality. On the contrary, society should seek to harness the information that people have about criminality–this is often far more efficient than having law enforcement officials try to obtain the information. The argument is that society can obtain the information through the use of rewards.

---

[37] Landes & Posner, and recently Posner alone, have asserted that if blackmail were legal, blackmailers would *generally* devote socially excessive efforts to finding information. *See* Landes & Posner, *supra* note 5, at 43; Posner, *supra* note 5, at 1827-33. However, this is only a possibility, not a general tendency. Indeed, an important example for our purposes is that when the criminal sanction includes jail, and criminals have relatively small assets, the prospect of blackmail would hardly result in excessive private efforts to find criminals–private efforts would be inadequate. In addition, private incentives to find wrongdoers may be inadequate even if sanctions are entirely monetary; this point is developed in an intellectually compelling way by A. Mitchell Polinsky. *See* A. Mitchell Polinsky, *Private Versus Public Enforcement of Fines*, 9 J. LEGAL STUD. 105, 107 (1980) (concluding that "[r]egardless of relative enforcement costs, private . . . enforcement leads in a wide range of circumstances to less enforcement than public enforcement, rather than more").

[38] This conclusion differs from that reached by Brown, *see supra* note 29, at 1943, because I, unlike Brown, allow for the state to employ rewards. The conclusion is the same as that of Landes & Posner, *supra* note 5, at 42, and Posner, *supra* note 5, at 1823-27, but my justification for it differs from theirs. They would find the legalization of blackmail of criminals socially undesirable because it would generally stimulate excessive efforts to find criminals, but as I have explained, *see supra* note 37, this is incorrect.

Second, in the case where the parties with information are law enforcement officers, there is an additional set of disadvantages with permitting blackmail, that is, with allowing officers to collect privately arranged bounties from criminals as payment for their work. Strong incentives would be created for law enforcement officers to invent offenses and then profit from blackmail (such incentives are not strong when individual arrests have small impact on the well-being of enforcement officers). In addition, excessive risk would be imposed on enforcement officers, since an officer's pay would depend on whether he happened to make a successful arrest. Also, officers' allocation of efforts toward detecting different types of criminals would be skewed. For instance, a poor murderer would not be sought after since he could not pay much, whereas a wealthy man who got involved in a brawl would be a prime target. Similarly, the allocation of effort among different law enforcement tasks might be distorted; too much energy would be devoted to activities leading to final detection and not enough to background work. Altogether, then, the advantages of making blackmail illegal for law enforcement officers seem eminently clear.

3. Commonly Made Threats in Commercial Life and Other Legally Permissible Threats

The general analysis of the welfare effects of threats suggests that the threats we discussed in Part I.D ought not be discouraged or made illegal. First, it is obvious that threats to withdraw business unless price or some other term is altered are usually good things. Such threats are part of the competitive process and promote efficiency. When a seller is induced by the prospect of threats of withdrawal of business to operate at a lower cost, this is socially desirable; where a threat is actually carried out and a person takes his business elsewhere because he can secure a more favorable arrangement, this is also socially desirable. Second, with regard to threats to bring civil suits, it was suggested before that the settlement process does not seriously compromise deterrence, unlike blackmail arrangements between a victim of a crime and a criminal. Thus, a concern about deterrence is not a reason to bar civil settlements, and their legality can be justified by the savings in litigation costs and reduction of risk that they engender. Third, with respect to the other types of threats mentioned herein, many are not socially undesirable, or at least hard to delineate as such—they are part of the normal bargaining process. A threat to fence off one's property unless a dog is restrained will tend to result in the dog being restrained unless the fence is cheaper to erect. It is true that threats made during bargaining can involve bluffs and result in social waste (such as when a person begins to erect a fence to demonstrate his willingness to carry forward with the threat). But such undesirable outcomes generally emanate from the inability of one of the parties to gauge the other side's position. In such cases, the courts are unlikely to have information superior to the parties and will thus be unable to intervene beneficially.

III. CONCLUDING COMMENTS

I want to conclude with several observations about the so-called paradox of blackmail and about the economic analysis of blackmail, extortion, and robbery.

Some writers have described the illegality of blackmail as paradoxical in that it makes punishable the threat to reveal information even though revealing information itself is not punishable.[39] This does not seem paradoxical, however, when viewed through the lens of economics. We know that permitting blackmail will lead potential victims to curtail innocent behavior and take other steps to avoid blackmail, and also will induce potential blackmailers to invest efforts in obtaining embarrassing information. These effects are undesirable and warrant making blackmail illegal. We also know that people usually have little reason to gather embarrassing information or to reveal it if they are not profiting from blackmail threats. Thus, there is no clear reason to make the revelation of information unaccompanied by threats illegal.

Of course, a resolution of the paradox of blackmail need not be cast in economic terms, that is, in terms of the effects of blackmail, and Lindgren has criticized the economic explanation in his influential article. One of Lindgren's primary criticisms[40] concerns information that is adventitiously acquired, such as when a workman going up a ladder happens to look into a room and sees

[39] *See* Lindgren, *supra* note 1, at 670 (noting that "[i]n blackmail, the heart of the problem is that two separate acts, each of which is a moral and legal right, can combine to make a moral and legal wrong"); Williams, *supra* note 1, at 162-63 (demonstrating that a demand and a threat can both be lawfully made, but taken together, they constitute blackmail).

[40] *See* Lindgren, *supra* note 1, at 695 (noting that "[i]f our principal concern is to discourage people from digging up damaging information, it makes no sense to punish people for selling innocently acquired information").

someone in awkward circumstances. In such a case, the workman is not induced to go up the ladder to gain an opportunity for blackmail; he is going up the ladder anyway. Lindgren thus says, correctly, that the illegality of blackmail in such a case cannot be explained by a need to discourage wasteful efforts to obtain information. Nevertheless, there is still an obvious incentive-based reason for making blackmail illegal: to avoid being blackmailed by workmen or others who might by chance be present, potential *victims* will exercise excessive precautions or reduce their level of innocent, yet embarrassing, activities.

Although it seems to me that economic analysis supplies a sound justification for the illegality of blackmail, I do not think that it offers an explanation that jurists, lawyers, or legislators generally would find congenial. Instead, I suspect that most individuals view blackmail as deserving of punishment because it is an act that is very close to robbery, which they believe to be wicked, and because blackmail involves the calculated imposition of suffering upon its victims.

In any event, independent of any light economic analysis may shed, or fail to shed, on why the law is as we find it, economic analysis has its two usual virtues. First, it helps to describe behavior, which sometimes has complex and interesting aspects (such as the repetition of blackmail and extortion threats). Second, it aids in making recommendations. Thus, for example, the analysis suggests that although blackmail should be illegal even when the information that would be exposed pertains to crimes, we should perhaps consider making greater use of rewards for reporting crimes.

Part II
Doctrinal Issues: The Limits of Responsibility

[6]

ARTICLES

WILFUL IGNORANCE, KNOWLEDGE, AND THE "EQUAL CULPABILITY" THESIS: A STUDY OF THE DEEPER SIGNIFICANCE OF THE PRINCIPLE OF LEGALITY

DOUGLAS N. HUSAK*
&
CRAIG A. CALLENDER**

This Article challenges the traditional understanding of the principle of legality—nulla poena sine lege. Conventional wisdom concerning the principle fails to express the full range of values at stake in preserving the rule of law. In order to appreciate the deeper significance of these values, this Article considers an application of the principle of legality to a dispute about mens rea rather than to a controversy about actus reus. This discussion helps to reveal some of the larger issues that are involved in protecting the principle of legality. In addition, a focus on mens rea indicates the limitations of statutory solutions to some of the problems raised by the principle. Finally, this perspective demonstrates how the rule of law serves to protect law-abiding persons, and not only scoundrels. The most general conclusion drawn is that fidelity to law cannot be construed merely as fidelity to statutory law, but must be understood as fidelity to the principles of justice that underlie statutory law.

The deeper significance of the principle of legality is revealed in the context of a discussion of the problem of wilful ignorance. The discussion begins by clearly characterizing the culpable mental state associated with wilful ignorance. The unsatisfactory treatment of wilful ignorance by both courts and commentators is then reviewed. This Article shows that some (but not all) wilfully ignorant defendants are held liable despite their failure to satisfy the mens rea requirement of the statutes under which they are convicted. After considering whether the culpability of such defendants is equal to that of defendants who actually satisfy the mens rea of these statutes, this Article argues that the problem of wilful ignorance should not be assessed apart from the larger political significance of drug policy. Finally, this Article discusses the limitations of proposed statutory solutions to the problem of wilful ignorance, and defends a preferable alternative.

---

* Professor of Philosophy, Rutgers University. Ph.D. (Philosophy), Ohio State University (1976); J.D., Ohio State University, (1976); B.A., Denison University (1970).

** Ph.D. (Philosophy), Rutgers University (expected 1995); B.A., Providence (1990).

I. The Principle of Legality: Conventional Wisdom

The principle of legality—*nulla poena sine lege*[1]—is fundamental in Anglo-American criminal law. Like other fundamental principles, legality protects the moral rights of persons by limiting the coercive power of the state to create and enforce criminal legislation.[2] Every theorist pays homage to the importance of these rights, and acknowledges the injustice if they are violated. Hitler and Stalin were notorious for achieving terror partly by flouting the principle of legality. The infamous Nazi "principle of analogy" provided that:

> Whoever commits an act which the law declares to be punishable or which is deserving of punishment according to the fundamental idea of a penal law and sound perception of the people, shall be punished. If no determinate penal law is directly applicable to the action, it shall be punished according to the law, the basic ideal of which fits it best.[3]

There is a broad consensus about the injustice of this provision. Analogical reasoning in the enforcement of the criminal law is clearly incompatible with the principle of legality.

Despite the centrality of the principle of legality, most Anglo-American theorists have become complacent about it.[4] The wide spectrum of rights protected by the rule of law has received insufficient attention from contemporary commentators. As Francis Allen has observed, it is much easier to interest students in the rights conferred by the First Amendment than in those protected by the principle of legality.[5] He speculates that the principle has been slighted because its truth seems

---

1. *The principle of legality has no single formulation. Other common formulations include* "*nullum crimin sine lege*" and "*nullum crimen, nulla poena, sine lege.*"

2. *See* DOUGLAS N. HUSAK, PHILOSOPHY OF CRIMINAL LAW 30-49 (1987).

3. *Lawrence Preuss, Punishment By Analogy in National Socialist Penal Law*, 26 J. CRIM. L. & CRIMINOLOGY 847, 847 (1936) (discussing principles of analogy). The comparable provision (Article 16) of the Soviet Code provided that "if any socially dangerous act is not provided for by the present Code, the basis and limits of responsibility for it shall be determined by application of those articles of the Code which provide for crimes most similar to it in nature." HAROLD BERMAN, SOVIET CRIMINAL LAW AND PROCEDURE 22 (2d ed. 1972).

4. *"The very fact of widespread acceptance has worked to inhibit full exploration of the legality concept."* CRIMINAL LAW *34 (Peter Low et al. eds., 1986).*

5. *Francis Allen, The Erosion of Legality in American Criminal Justice: Some Latter-Day Adventures of the* Nulla Poena *Principle*, 29 ARIZ. L. REV. 385 (1987).

so obvious that there appears to be little to say about it.[6] Surely the monstrous violations of the rule of law perpetrated by totalitarian regimes could never occur in our legal system, and more subtle evasions of legality are rarely noticed. Many of the cases included in current textbooks are English, suggesting that the American legal system has a nearly unblemished record in preserving the principle of legality.[7]

Moreover, the cases that find their way into textbooks conform to a familiar pattern. Typically, the state prosecutes a person for an actus reus that appears wrongful, but has not clearly been defined as criminal by the legislature in advance. Paradigm examples are as follows. Does a defendant "unlawfully effect a public mischief" by making false allegations to the police?[8] Does a defendant "conspire to corrupt public morals" by publishing either a directory of prostitutes[9] or classified advertisements by male homosexuals?[10] Does a defendant commit a homicide by killing a human fetus without the mother's consent?[11] Such examples, of course, could be multiplied.[12]

The use of such examples serves to reinforce the following three propositions, which have come to express conventional wisdom about the principle of legality. First, whatever may be true in theory, in practice the principle serves mainly to protect scoundrels bent on mischief.[13] Noting that "it is hard for the legislature in advance to conceive of all possible anti-social behavior that ought to be criminal," Wayne LaFave and Austin Scott contend that "[t]he question in the criminal law field is whether judges can create (or discover) new crimes for which to punish the ingenious fellow who conceives and carries out a new form of anti-social conduct not covered by the criminal code."[14] They conclude with a query, designed to indicate why the judiciary is frequently tempted to

---

6. *Id.* at 387.

7. *But see* Commonwealth v. Mochan, 110 A.2d 788, 790 (Pa. Super. 1955) (holding that the defendant's act of making obscene phone calls is a misdemeanor because "from its nature [it] scandalously affects the morals or health of the community") (internal citation omitted); Commonwealth v. Donoghue, 63 S.W.2d 3, 8 (Ky. Ct. App. 1933) (holding that "a nefarious plan for the habitual exaction of gross usury" was punishable despite the absence of an explicit legislative enactment).

8. *Rex v. Manley, 1 K.B. 529 (1933).*

9. *Shaw v. Director of Pub. Prosecutions, [1961] 2 All E.R. 446.*

10. Knuller v. Director of Pub. Prosecutions, [1972] 2 All E.R. 898.

11. Keeler v. Superior Court, 470 P.2d 617 (Cal. 1970).

12. Additional examples can be found in 1 FRANCIS WHARTON, CRIMINAL LAW §§ 18-24 (12th ed. 1932).

13. "The malicious ingenuity of mankind is constantly producing new inventions in the art of disturbing their neighbors." Commonwealth v. Taylor, 5 Binn. 277, 281 (Pa. 1812).

14. 1 WAYNE R. LAFAVE & AUSTIN W. SCOTT, JR., SUBSTANTIVE CRIMINAL LAW 89 (1986).

infringe the rule of law: "If someone intentionally or by chance finds a loophole, may the courts create a new crime to plug that gap?"[15] According to this account, the principle of legality constitutes a "loophole" through which clever criminals manage to escape. After all, even the Nazi principle of analogy applied only to persons "deserving of punishment."[16] Rarely is legality understood to protect persons whose behavior is not "anti-social."

Second, any problem raised by the principle of legality is amenable to a straightforward statutory solution. Presumably, the foregoing difficulties could be overcome simply by redefining the statutes in question to explicitly prohibit making false allegations to the police, publishing a directory of prostitutes or classified advertisements by male homosexuals, or killing a human fetus. The issue is not whether persons who perform these acts are deserving of punishment, but which branch of government has the proper authority to impose it. No deeper questions are at stake than the division of power between the legislature and the judiciary.

Third, controversy about the principle of legality invariably involves disagreement about the scope and boundaries of the actus reus of an offense. Indeed, some commentators apparently are unable to distinguish the demands of legality from those raised by the principle that criminal liability requires an actus reus. If the defendant's conduct clearly satisfies the actus reus of an existing criminal offense, narrowly defined to avoid vagueness, no further question about legality remains to be resolved.

This Article will challenge the conventional wisdom conveyed by these three propositions. The traditional understanding of legality fails to express the full range of values at stake in preserving the rule of law.[17] In order to appreciate the deeper significance of these values, it will be necessary to consider an application of the principle of legality to a dispute about mens rea rather than to a controversy about actus reus. Apart from enlarging the focus of the rule of law, this discussion will help to reveal some of the larger issues that may be involved in protecting the principle of legality. In addition, a focus on mens rea will indicate the limitations of statutory solutions to some of the problems raised by the principle of legality. Finally, this focus on mens rea will demonstrate how the rule of law serves to protect law-abiding persons, and not only scoundrels. The most general conclusion to be drawn is that fidelity to

---

15. *Id.* at 89-90.

16. Preuss claims that legality had become regarded by the Nazis as "the Magna Carta of the criminal." Preuss, *supra* note 3, at 847.

17. "The generality with which the legality principle is usually stated . . . tends to obscure the variety of concerns comprehended by this label and to ignore its dynamic character." CRIMINAL LAW, *supra* note 4, at 34.

law cannot be construed merely as fidelity to statutory law, but must be understood as fidelity to the principles of justice that underlie statutory law.[18]

The deeper significance of the principle of legality will be revealed in the context of a discussion of the problem of wilful ignorance. Part II of this Article will raise this problem, and clarify the concept of wilful ignorance. Part III will argue that some (but not all) wilfully ignorant defendants are held liable despite their failure to satisfy the mens rea requirement of the statutes under which they are convicted. Part IV will consider but ultimately dismiss the relevance of inquiring whether the culpability of such defendants is equal to that of defendants who do satisfy the mens rea requirement of these statutes. Part V will show why the infringement of legality involved in the conviction of these defendants is politically significant. Part VI will indicate the limitations of proposed statutory solutions to the problem of wilful ignorance and will defend a preferable alternative.

This challenge to the conventional wisdom about the principle of legality should help to rekindle interest in the rule of law. Against the background of conventional wisdom, it is not surprising that contemporary commentators have tended to display little enthusiasm for the principle of legality. No one is especially interested in creating legal loopholes through which clever wrongdoers escape their just deserts. The importance of the principle of legality would become more evident if it sometimes protected persons who are innocent—not innocent in some technical, legal sense, to which scoundrels can appeal—but innocent in a deeper, moral sense that is important to life in a free society.

II. THE CONCEPT OF WILFUL IGNORANCE

Suppose that criminal liability under a particular statute requires that a defendant act with the mens rea of knowledge. For example, consider the offense of knowing possession of a controlled substance with the intent to distribute.[19] Virtually all courts and commentators agree that a mental state they alternatively describe as "wilful ignorance" or "wilful

---

18. This suggestion is developed more fully in LON L. FULLER, THE MORALITY OF LAW (1969). The importance of "fidelity not just to rules but to the theories of fairness and justice that these rules presuppose by way of justification" is also emphasized in RONALD DWORKIN, LAW'S EMPIRE 185 (1986).

19. 21 U.S.C. § 841(a)(1) (1988) ("[I]t shall be unlawful for any person knowingly or intentionally—to manufacture, distribute, or dispense, or possess with intent to manufacture, distribute, or dispense, a controlled substance . . . ."). Possession is a necessary element in the substantive charge of either distribution or sale of narcotics. *See* United States v. Jackson, 526 F.2d 1236, 1237-38 (5th Cir. 1976).

blindness"[20] is sufficient to satisfy the requirement of knowledge.[21] Whether and under what circumstances defendants with this mental state should be held liable for acting knowingly constitutes "the problem of wilful ignorance."[22]

United States v. Jewell[23] is probably the leading case in which the concept of wilful ignorance was invoked to uphold a conviction. The defendant was arrested after driving an automobile in which 110 pounds of marijuana had been concealed in a secret compartment between the trunk and rear seat. The defendant testified that he had been paid $100 by a stranger to drive the car into the country, and that he was not actually aware that it contained contraband. Liability under one count required that the defendant knowingly brought the drugs into the country.[24] The court affirmed the defendant's conviction, and upheld the following instruction:

> The Government can complete their burden of proof by proving, beyond a reasonable doubt, that if the defendant was not actually aware that there was marijuana in the vehicle he was driving when he entered the United States his ignorance in that regard was solely and entirely a result of his having made a conscious purpose to disregard the nature of that which was in the vehicle, with a conscious purpose to avoid learning the truth.[25]

---

20. Other terms include "connivance," "conscious avoidance," "wilful shutting of the eyes," "deliberate ignorance," "studied ignorance," "purposely abstaining from all inquiry as to the facts," "avoidance of any endeavor to know," "a conscious purpose to avoid learning the truth," and "deliberately chose not to learn." *See* ROLLIN M. PERKINS & RONALD N. BOYCE, CRIMINAL LAW 867-68 (3d ed. 1982).

21. "For well-nigh a hundred years, it has been clear from the authorities that a person who deliberately shuts his eyes to an obvious means of knowledge has sufficient *mens rea* for an offence based on such words as . . . 'knowingly.'" J. Edwards, Comment, *The Criminal Degrees of Knowledge*, 17 MOD. L. REV. 294, 298 (1954).

22. Of course, several other "problems of wilful ignorance" could be identified. For example, one might examine whether and under what circumstances wilfully ignorant defendants should be held liable for satisfying culpable states of mind other than those included in the Model Penal Code. *See* Robin Charlow, *Wilful Ignorance and Criminal Culpability*, 70 TEX. L. REV. 1351, 1360-61 (1992).

23. 532 F.2d 697 (9th Cir. 1976).

24. Jewell was charged with a violation of 21 U.S.C. § 841(a)(1) (1988), as well as 21 U.S.C. § 952(a) (1988) ("It shall be unlawful to . . . import . . . into the United States . . . any controlled substance."). Possession is not an element of this latter offense. United States v. Valencia, 492 F.2d 1071, 1074 (9th Cir. 1974).

25. *Jewell*, 532 F.2d at 700.

The Court added that "knowingly" should not be equated with "positive knowledge" because such an interpretation "would make deliberate ignorance a defense."[26]

What exactly is the mental state of wilful ignorance possessed by the defendant in *Jewell*? Commentators[27] and courts[28] differ not only in the names they give to this state, but also in the details of the descriptions they provide—if, indeed, they provide any details at all. An immediate methodological problem is to identify the criteria that should be used to decide between competing conceptions of wilful ignorance. Legal terms with familiar non-legal usages should probably be construed according to their meanings in ordinary language.[29] But unlike other mental states commonly employed in criminal statutes, such as knowledge and belief, the concept of wilful ignorance is more of a technical, stipulative term of legal art with no precise analogue in everyday speech. This concept has not been borrowed from ordinary language; attributions of wilful ignorance are extremely rare outside of legal contexts. Consequently, semantic considerations would seem to have little bearing on how to identify the mental state involved in *Jewell*.

How, then, should an explication of wilful ignorance proceed? A good start is to allow the purpose of the term to guide deliberations about competing conceptions of wilful ignorance.[30] Legal theorists have invented the term to serve a given objective. Once this purpose is identified, a particular conception of wilful ignorance may be defended as superior to its rivals. Simply, the conception of wilful ignorance that serves this objective most effectively is best among its competitors.

The purpose of having the concept of wilful ignorance is relatively clear. This concept has been created by courts to describe the culpable mental state found in cases like *Jewell*. The objective of the courts is to convict a defendant who may lack genuine knowledge (and who otherwise might have been acquitted) for acting knowingly. This purpose can be

---

26. *Id.* at 703.

27. One commentator juxtaposes one three-part distinction upon another to generate nine different "forms" of definitions of wilful ignorance. Charlow, *supra* note 22, at 1366-72.

28. Courts of appeals in each circuit have adopted some form of wilful ignorance instruction. These different formulations are contrasted in Kristen L. Chestnut, United States v. Alvarado*: Reflections on a Jewell*, 19 GOLDEN GATE U. L. REV. 47, 49 (1989). Thus "the cases . . . are at sixes and sevens on what wilful blindness means." GLANVILLE L. WILLIAMS, TEXTBOOK OF CRIMINAL LAW 125 (1983).

29. For a defense of this claim, see ALAN R. WHITE, MISLEADING CASES (1991).

30. Here the analysis follows the recent advice of some philosophers regarding attempts to analyze and to clarify concepts. Many philosophers believe that accounts of concepts should stress the *role* concepts play in the realm of interest. *See* Michael A. Bishop, *The Possibility of Conceptual Clarity in Philosophy*, 29 AM. PHIL. Q. 267 (1992).

accomplished either by describing a mental state that is a kind of knowledge or by describing a mental state that is not a kind of knowledge but can plausibly be construed to be the moral equivalent of knowledge. Of course, it is doubtful that *any* conception of wilful ignorance which adequately describes the culpable mental state found in cases like *Jewell* can accomplish this objective unproblematically.[31] Still, the particular conception of wilful ignorance is best that encounters the fewest difficulties in satisfying this objective. The aim of this section is to develop a conception of wilful ignorance that is less objectionable than its competitors in enabling courts to convict such defendants for acting knowingly.

The draftsmen of the Model Penal Code sought to achieve this purpose in the following way. The Code generally defines "knowledge" of the "nature of [a defendant's] conduct" to require that "he is aware that his conduct is of that nature."[32] But a subsection of the Code provides that "knowledge of the existence of a particular fact" is established "if a person is aware of a high probability of its existence, unless he actually believes that it does not exist."[33] The commentaries explain that this subsection is designed to deal with the phenomenon of "wilful blindness," in which the defendant "is aware of the probable existence of a material fact but does not determine whether it exists or does not exist."[34] The explanatory note describes this subsection as an "elabora[tion] on the definition of 'knowledge.'"[35] Yet this "elaboration" apparently applies only to wilful ignorance; a defendant who only believed a fact to be highly probable would not be said to know it unless his lack of genuine knowledge were due to wilful ignorance.[36]

31. *See infra* part IV.

32. MODEL PENAL CODE § 2.02(2)(b)(i) (Official Draft, review and commmentaries, 1985).

33. *Id.* § 2.02(7).

34. *Id.* commentary at 248.

35. *Id.* explanatory note at 228.

36. If § 2.02(7) were intended as a universal definition of knowledge, the earlier definition in § 2.02(2)(b)(i) would serve no purpose. If both "definitions" had the same scope, the drafters would not have included two distinct versions. When this observation is coupled with the explanation in the commentaries that § 2.02(7) is designed to deal with wilful ignorance, it is natural to suppose that this "elaboration" is intended only for cases of wilful ignorance.

One commentator who maintains that § 2.02(7) is meant as a general definition of knowledge proposes to solve the problem of wilful ignorance by consistently applying this "elaboration." *See* Jonathan L. Marcus, *Model Penal Code Section 2.02(7) and Willful Blindness*, 102 YALE L.J. 2231 (1993). If § 2.02(7) is taken as a general definition of knowledge, anyone who believes a fact to be highly probable would be said to know that fact. This proposal would solve the problem of wilful ignorance, according to the commentator, because all wilfully ignorant defendants presumably believe the fact to be

If intended as a definition of wilful ignorance, the foregoing provision of the Model Penal Code is defective on a number of grounds. First, not all cases in which a defendant would seem to be wilfully ignorant involve "aware[ness] of a high probability" of the "existence of a particular fact."[37] Consider the following example. Suppose that a foreigner approaches two American tourists who are about to return home. He offers to pay either of them one hundred dollars to deliver a suitcase to a contact in America. When the tourists inquire about the contents of the suitcase, the foreigner replies: "You have no need to know." Both tourists are tempted, but decline because they are apprehensive that the act would be illegal. So the foreigner modifies his offer in order to persuade them. He proposes to pay *each* of them one hundred dollars to deliver *two* suitcases, and assures them that one of the suitcases (he will not identify which one) is empty. Both of the tourists accept this modified offer. Suppose that the tourists are stopped by customs officers, who open the suitcases and discover that one contains illegal drugs. Can the tourist whose suitcase contained the drugs be convicted under a statute that forbids knowingly possessing a controlled substance?

If either tourist had accepted the foreigner's original offer, his mental state would be a paradigm case of wilful ignorance. But what is to be said about the state of mind of the arrested tourist who accepts the modified proposal?[38] This question must be answered by inquiring whether categorizing his mental state as wilful ignorance helps to achieve the purpose for which that concept was invented. By this standard, it seems the question should be answered affirmatively. Anyone who proposes that the tourist in the original hypothetical should be convicted for violating a statute that requires that he act knowingly is unlikely to change his opinion when the example is modified. It seems more

---

highly probable. However, the present investigation demonstrates that this proposal is both too strong and too weak to solve the problem of wilful ignorance. This proposal is too strong inasmuch as a defendant who believes a fact to be highly probable may still not be wilfully ignorant. *See infra* notes 162-64 and accompanying text. In addition, this proposal is too weak inasmuch as a defendant who is wilfully ignorant may still not believe a fact to be highly probable. *See infra* text accompanying notes 40-43.

37. This aspect of the Model Penal Code account has been endorsed by many commentators. "The best view is that [wilful blindness] applies only when a person is virtually certain that the fact exists." WILLIAMS, *supra* note 28, at 125.

38. It may be interesting to speculate about whether each tourist in this hypothetical could be convicted of a conspiracy. Liability for conspiracies also requires knowledge. Moreover, such speculation does not resolve the question of whether the arrested tourist is wilfully ignorant. *See* Christine L. Chinni, *Whose Head Is in the Sand? Problems With the Use of the Ostrich Instruction in Conspiracy Cases*, 13 W. NEW ENG. L. REV. 35 (1991).

plausible to conclude that the tourists are wilfully ignorant in both the original and the modified hypotheticals,[39] even though the tourist in the latter example does not believe that it is highly probable that he is carrying a controlled substance.[40] Thus the "highly probable" component of the Model Penal Code account of wilful ignorance must be rejected.

Moreover, it is not even clear that the Model Penal Code account is correct in specifying that a defendant cannot be wilfully ignorant of a material fact that "he actually believes . . . does not exist."[41] As further modifications of the foregoing example indicate, some defendants who seem to be wilfully ignorant would estimate the probability of the truth of a given proposition p (such as "my suitcase contains illegal drugs") as less than fifty percent. Suppose that the example is altered to involve three tourists, two of whose suitcases were known to be empty. Then, each tourist would actually *dis*believe that his suitcase contained illegal drugs.[42] But this fact does not seem to entail that none of these defendants could be wilfully ignorant.[43]

---

39. One commentator claims that "where there is direct evidence of a deliberate plan to avoid knowing the truth, the degree of probability is unimportant." Rollin M. Perkins, *"Knowledge" as a Mens Rea Requirement*, 29 HASTINGS L.J. 953, 964 (1978). But Perkins' claim may be overstated. Presumably there is *some* lower limit to the probability of a proposition about which a defendant can be wilfully ignorant. If the probability is sufficiently low, the defendant's suspicion will not be warranted.

40. One commentator's proposal that § 2.02(7) of the Model Penal Code function as a general definition of knowledge is therefore deficient. *See* Marcus, *supra* note 36. The agent in this hypothetical, though wilfully ignorant, does not believe it is highly probable that he possesses a controlled substance.

41. MODEL PENAL CODE, § 2.02(7) (Official Draft, review and commentaries, 1985).

42. Some epistemologists have thought it preferable to abandon attempts to answer the question whether or not a person believes a proposition p. Instead of constructing an epistemology of belief, these philosophers (sometimes called 'probabilists') have opted to construct an epistemology of degrees of belief. These epistemologists refuse to answer the further question whether this degree of confidence is sufficient to give rise to belief *simpliciter*. In the present example, the wilfully ignorant defendant has a given degree of confidence in proposition p. Whether this low degree of confidence counts as disbelief or not for some epistemologists is irrelevant for present purposes. The reason for the irrelevance is that the Model Penal Code uses the concept of belief, and the example can be modified (by adding more tourists with empty suitcases) to create mental states which would certainly warrant attributions of disbelief to the defendant. Additionally, if belief *simpliciter* is to be entirely shunned, then the belief requirement in the Model Penal Code must be expressed in terms of degrees of belief; and again, the example can be modified so that the wilfully ignorant defendant's degree of belief falls well below that mentioned by the Model Penal Code. *See* RICHARD FOLEY, WORKING WITHOUT A NET § 4 (1993).

43. Of course, this example requires commitment to a position about the connection between probability and belief. How high must an agent estimate the

The agent's estimation of the probability of the truth of a proposition does not seem to be essential to judgments about whether he is wilfully ignorant. Even a belief in the material fact's existence is not an essential component of the phenomenon of wilful ignorance.[44] Reconsider the foregoing hypotheticals. If a defendant need not actually believe p in order to be willfully ignorant of p—and might actually *dis*believe p—what mental state must he have? In the last example, all three defendants would appear to be wilfully ignorant because they are (and have good reason to be) *suspicious* of the illegal contents of the suitcase.[45] This conclusion indicates that the potentially complex relationship between belief and probability is somewhat tangential to the analysis of wilful ignorance.

The requirement of suspicion explains why otherwise troublesome cases qualify as examples of wilful ignorance. Judge (now Justice) Kennedy's example of a child who is "given a gift-wrapped package by his mother while on vacation in Mexico" and has "a conscious purpose to take it home without learning what is inside"[46] is not wilfully ignorant (in the event that the package contains drugs), not because he lacks the relevant belief—since belief is not required—but because he lacks the relevant suspicion. Kennedy, however, draws the wrong conclusion from his example. He mistakenly infers that the "state of mind" of this child "is totally innocent unless he is aware of a high probability that the package contains a controlled substance."[47] However, the state of mind of the defendant who does not believe with a high probability that his conduct is criminal need not be "totally innocent." Instead, the defendant's state of mind is culpable rather than innocent if he is (and has good reason to be) suspicious that his conduct is illegal. His culpability decreases as he becomes less and less suspicious, but does not reach total innocence until he lacks suspicion altogether.

Wilful ignorance cannot be equated with suspicion alone, however. At least three nonmental conditions differentiate the wilfully ignorant defendant from the suspicious defendant. The first, which qualifies the

---

likelihood of a proposition before he can be said to believe it? No general answer seems possible. The foregoing examples, however, assume only that a necessary condition for believing a proposition is that the agent believes that proposition to be true. Clearly this requirement, known as "Moore's paradox," is plausible. G.E. Moore noticed that it would be absurd to believe a proposition p and at the same time believe it to be false. *See* PAUL A. SCHILPP, THE PHILOSOPHY OF G.E. MOORE 386 (2d ed. 1952).

44. For a discussion of the nature of belief, see WILLIAM LYCAN, JUDGEMENT AND JUSTIFICATION (1988) (especially chapters 3 and 4).

45. Suspicion need not be a kind of belief. *See* WHITE, *supra* note 29, at 134.

46. This example is described by Judge Kennedy in his dissent in United States v. Jewell, 532 F.2d 697, 707 (9th Cir. 1976) (Kennedy, J., dissenting).

47. *Id.* (Kennedy, J., dissenting).

suspicion requirement, might be called the *warranted suspicion* condition. Because wilful ignorance should not be extended to those with unfounded suspicions, that is, to persons suffering from paranoia or other delusions, the suspicion must be restricted to those who have good, objective, reasons for their suspicion. Ideally, wilfully ignorant agents are suspicious because the evidence demands it.

The second condition to differentiate the wilfully ignorant defendant from the suspicious defendant might be called the *availability* condition. In many (but not all) potential cases of wilful ignorance, there exists information highly relevant to a defendant's determination of the truth of the proposition about which he is wilfully ignorant. If a defendant has the means to learn the truth (or to gather more evidence) about the significance of his actions, and is aware of these means, his failure to act on these suspicions is a plain sign of wilful ignorance. In most cases, the wilfully ignorant defendant will not have considered (or evaluated) all of the evidence that honest persons in those circumstances would have considered. Typically, these defendants fail to pursue reliable, quick, and ordinary measures to discover the facts. Each of these three factors is important. The wilfully ignorant defendant cannot simply fail to pursue unreliable, time-consuming, or extraordinary means to learn the truth. The facts must be readily available to anyone disposed to discover them.[48]

The third condition to differentiate the wilfully ignorant defendant from the suspicious defendant might be called the *motivational* condition. The wilfully ignorant defendant must have a given motive for remaining unaware of the truth—he must consciously desire to preserve a possible defense from blame or liability in the event that he is apprehended. His failure to gain more information cannot be due to mere laziness, stupidity, or the absence of curiosity.

Alternative conceptions of wilful ignorance that do not include these three conditions appear to be inferior to the present characterization. Each condition eliminates consequences seemingly incompatible with the phenomenon of wilful ignorance. If the warranted suspicion requirement is not posited, then a person with an extremely low degree of confidence in p—or a deluded person—may be held to be wilfully ignorant of p. Additionally, if the availability condition is not posited, a person who

48. In some cases, the means to learn the truth may not exist. Suppose, for example, the defendant has no key to a locked suitcase. Perhaps the availability requirement should be conditional upon the existence of these means. In such cases, however, it should be recognized that the means to learn the truth would have been available to a wilfully ignorant defendant at an earlier time. In the locked suitcase example, the wilfully ignorant defendant would not have made reasonable inquiries to the person who gave him the suitcase.

lacks the means to learn the truth of p may be held to be wilfully ignorant of p. Finally, if the motivational condition is not posited, then a person who does not act on his suspicion about p, merely because of laziness or a lack of curiosity, may be held to be wilfully ignorant of p. Thus each of these three conditions is important to an adequate conception of wilful ignorance.

In summary, a defendant is wilfully ignorant of an incriminating proposition p when he is suspicious that p is true, has good reason to think p true, fails to pursue reliable, quick, and ordinary measures that would enable him to learn the truth of p, and, finally, has a conscious desire to remain ignorant of p in order to avoid blame or liability in the event that he is detected. In a paradigm case of wilful ignorance, the defendant will have a warranted suspicion regarding the illegal contents of the trunk of a car, and have readily available means to learn the truth, but will remain ignorant in order to retain a possible defense if he is arrested. This characterization of wilful ignorance is defensible in light of the purpose for inventing the concept: to identify the culpable mental state found in cases such as *Jewell*. Arguably, this mental state either is a kind of knowledge[49] or is the moral equivalent of knowledge.[50] Thus, it seems plausible to hold such a defendant liable for violating a statute that requires that he act knowingly.

III. Two Views of the Relationship Between Wilful Ignorance and Knowledge

The aim of this section is to refine further the concept of wilful ignorance by comparing and contrasting it with other culpable mental states with which it might be confused. The most difficult part of this task will be to clarify the relationship between wilful ignorance and knowledge. This section will contrast two competing views about this relationship, and will give reasons to conclude that the second provides a better account of the elusive connection between wilful ignorance and knowledge.

Wilful ignorance is easily contrasted with what is sometimes called culpable ignorance.[51] The culpably ignorant defendant is simply negligent or reckless in failing to learn the facts that a reasonable person would have discovered. But unlike the negligent defendant, who is unaware of a proposition that a reasonable person would have known to be true, the wilfully ignorant defendant is not totally oblivious to the truth

---

49. *See infra* part III.
50. *See infra* part IV.
51. *See* Holly Smith, *Culpable Ignorance*, 92 PHIL. REV. 543 (1983).

of a proposition; he must believe or at least be suspicious of it. And unlike the reckless defendant, the wilfully ignorant defendant satisfies the motivational condition; he has a particular incentive to fail to learn the facts. Moreover, many culpably ignorant defendants will not satisfy the availability condition. These differences, however, should not obscure the similarity between the reckless and the wilfully ignorant defendant. Both defendants consciously entertain the risk that an incriminating proposition is true. Thus all wilfully ignorant defendants are reckless, but—largely because not all reckless defendants satisfy the motivational condition—not all reckless defendants are wilfully ignorant.[52]

The relationship between wilful ignorance and knowledge is more complicated and requires a more detailed discussion. Two views about this relationship must be contrasted. Elaboration of both views requires that a name be given to the mental state that is unquestionably knowledge. Call such a state *genuine* knowledge. The first view about the relationship between wilful ignorance and genuine knowledge might be called the "actual knowledge" account. According to this interpretation, wilful ignorance is a species of genuine knowledge; thus the wilfully ignorant defendant *does* possess genuine knowledge after all. The second view might be called the "substitute for knowledge" account. According to this interpretation, wilful ignorance is not a species of genuine knowledge; although the wilfully ignorant defendant does *not* possess genuine knowledge, there is a reason to treat him as though he did. Either of these two views provides a basis to allow the wilfully ignorant defendant to be held liable for violating a statute that requires that he act knowingly, although only those who embrace the "substitute for knowledge" interpretation need provide a further reason to defend the justice of this result.[53] Obviously, there is no difficulty in holding a wilfully ignorant defendant liable for acting knowingly if wilful ignorance is a species of genuine knowledge.

Unfortunately, courts are seldom clear about which of these competing views they endorse.[54] Commentators have not been especially helpful in resolving this dispute. Some conceal the difference between the "actual knowledge" and "substitute for knowledge" views by

52. Contrast this account of the relationship with Ira Robbins' statement that "deliberate ignorance constitutes recklessness, rather than knowledge." Ira P. Robbins, *The Ostrich Instruction: Deliberate Ignorance as a Criminal Mens Rea*, 81 J. CRIM. L. & CRIMINOLOGY 191, 195 (1990).

53. *See infra* part IV.

54. "Those American courts that have accepted the concept of willful blindness are themselves divided on the question whether such blindness constitutes actual knowledge or instead some lesser degree of knowledge." Comment, *Willful Blindness as a Substitute for Criminal Knowledge*, 63 IOWA L. REV. 466, 472 (1977).

expressing their position in terms of what the wilfully ignorant defendant is "deemed" to know.[55] The claim that a wilfully ignorant defendant is "deemed" to know a proposition is ambiguous between saying that wilful ignorance *is* a species of genuine knowledge and saying that wilful ignorance is *not* a species of genuine knowledge, although it can and should be treated as though it were. Other theorists have changed their minds about these competing views over time, without acknowledging their shift in position.[56] Still others seemingly embrace both interpretations simultaneously, even though they are incompatible.[57] Confusion about whether the wilfully ignorant defendant possesses genuine knowledge or a substitute for knowledge infects many of the hypotheticals[58] and real cases commentators use[59] to illustrate the

55. Perkins and Boyce write: "Circumstances sometimes cause a person to realize that what he plans to do may bring about a result which the law seeks to prevent. If he wilfully goes ahead with his plan, while deliberately refusing to find out about this, he is deemed at common law to have knowledge of what he would have known had he not made it a point not to know." PERKINS & BOYCE, *supra* note 20, at 867.

56. In his first treatise, Glanville Williams defended the "substitute for knowledge" view, writing that wilful ignorance should be regarded as an "exception" to the requirement of actual knowledge. GLANVILLE L. WILLIAMS, CRIMINAL LAW: THE GENERAL PART 157 (2d ed. 1961). In his subsequent textbook, however, Williams came to endorse the "actual knowledge" view, holding that wilful ignorance "can reasonably be said to be an explanation of what is meant by knowledge as a matter of common sense, rather than an illegitimate extension of the meaning of the term." WILLIAMS, *supra* note 28, at 125. Williams fails to explain, or even to acknowledge, his shift in position.

57. Andrew Ashworth writes: "Although, strictly speaking, [the wilfully ignorant defendant] does not *know*, since he has refrained from finding out, he has an overwhelmingly strong belief (he believes it is virtually certain) that the prohibited circumstance exists. Thus, wilful blindness may be treated not as reckless knowledge, but as a form of actual knowledge." ANDREW ASHWORTH, PRINCIPLES OF CRIMINAL LAW 167-68 (1991). This passage contains support for both the actual knowledge and the substitute for knowledge conceptions of wilful ignorance. The "thus" in this quotation is especially mysterious. Ashworth appears to infer that the mental state of the wilfully ignorant defendant "may be treated . . . as a form of actual knowledge" from a number of premises, one of which is that he "does not *know*."

58. The example of wilful ignorance provided by Williams seems to involve genuine knowledge. He writes: "An example of wilful blindness in the proper sense is where an employer knew that his business was being run in an illegal way, and absented himself without having altered the arrangements; he was held to 'know' that the law was being broken in his absence even though he had no direct information about what was happening then." WILLIAMS, *supra* note 28, at 125. *Ex hypothesi*, the employer "knew that his business was being run in an illegal way." About what proposition, then, is he alleged to be wilfully ignorant?

59. *See* Robbins, *supra* note 52, at 192 n.5. The first case cited in his comprehensive discussion may not exemplify wilful ignorance at all. In United States v. Batencort, 592 F.2d 916 (5th Cir. 1979), the defendant admitted that he knew there was "something illegal" in the suitcase a stranger had paid him to carry from Colombia to

phenomenon. This confusion is intolerable. An adequate understanding of wilful ignorance requires commitment to one view or the other.[60]

Problems in deciding between these competing views of the relationship between wilful ignorance and knowledge are partly due to the enormous theoretical difficulties in understanding and applying the concept of knowledge. Epistemologists have sought to elucidate the concept of knowledge and have found this project no small task. A brief examination of what recent philosophy has had to say about knowledge is therefore required.[61] This investigation will assist a determination of whether wilful ignorance is a kind of genuine knowledge. The conclusion of this inquiry is that the wilfully ignorant defendant need not have knowledge of the incriminating proposition p. This conclusion is not reached simply by applying an overly stringent, philosophically demanding analysis of knowledge. A less rigorous, more colloquial understanding of knowledge may be more useful for purposes of imposing criminal liability. But the conclusion is not altered even when such an understanding of knowledge is applied. Some wilfully ignorant defendants lack knowledge.

Contemporary epistemology began in 1963 with Edmund Gettier's well-known challenge to the then-received understanding of knowledge.[62] Prior to 1963, the consensus was that knowledge of a proposition p consisted of three distinct components: justified true belief.[63] Exactly how justification was to be defined was (and is) a subject of much dispute. However, the intuitive idea was that an agent's belief be based

---

Texas, although he did not investigate what that illegal something might be. If such a case really involves wilful ignorance, as Robbins alleges, it must be because a defendant can be wilfully ignorant when he does not know what law he is breaking, even though he knows that he is breaking some law or another. But according to the conception of wilful ignorance endorsed here, a defendant need not have genuine knowledge that he is breaking any law at all.

60. "[T]here is tremendous confusion in this area of law and a lurking sense that something is fundamentally awry." Charlow, *supra* note 22, at 1353.

61. Though some philosophers question whether humans can ever really *know* anything, or more than very few things, their concerns do not touch upon the present inquiry. Knowledge skeptics are generally concerned with only a very strict understanding of "knowledge," and not the legal sense of knowledge used here. The positions of skeptics vary widely, but it is safe to say that they would not hesitate in claiming knowledge possible, in the sense needed here. *See* BARRY STROUD, THE SIGNIFICANCE OF PHILOSOPHICAL SCEPTICISM (1984).

62. Edmund L. Gettier, *Is Justified True Belief Knowledge?*, 23 ANALYSIS 121 (1963). The kinds of counterexamples that Gettier proposes to this analysis of knowledge involve what might be called coincidences: cases in which a proposition p happens to be true for reasons other than those that justify the agent's belief that p.

63. *See, e.g.*, RODERICK M. CHISHOLM, *Theory of Knowledge in America*, *in* THE FOUNDATIONS OF KNOWING (1982).

on good evidence for the proposition in question. Roughly, to be justified was to have reasoned in the appropriate fashion from the available data. The mental state of knowledge was hence identified with an agent correctly believing a proposition for which he possessed good evidence. Exactly what form good evidence would take was again controversial, but for present purposes an intuitive understanding of "evidence" is more than sufficient. Gettier challenged this analysis by describing cases in which an agent lacked what would be called knowledge while still having a justified true belief. The subjects in his cases correctly believe a proposition which resulted from scrupulous reasoning from all of the available data, yet they do not have what most would call "knowledge." The result is that even if one's doxastic house is perfectly in order, even if one reasons flawlessly from the available evidence, one still cannot be guaranteed to possess genuine knowledge of any particular proposition. Consequently, subsequent analyses of knowledge have sought to delineate those features external to one's subjective state that are required for knowledge.[64]

Despite the preceding difficulty for understanding knowledge as justified true belief, for ease of exposition let *any* third condition added to the truth and belief conditions be called "justification."[65] Philosophical analyses of this elusive third condition may be divided into two kinds: internalist and externalist. Internal justification for a belief p is a relation that obtains exclusively between p and some of a subject's other noetic states.[66] The relation is usually thought to provide evidence for p; further, the noetic states are thought to be cognitively accessible to the subject. External justification is non-internal justification; that is, (broadly) it maintains that justifiedness is, in part, a function of external

64. This interpretation of contemporary epistemology may be verified by examining any recent textbook. *See, e.g.*, JONATHAN DANCY, INTRODUCTION TO CONTEMPORARY EPISTEMOLOGY (1985); JOHN L. POLLOCK, CONTEMPORARY THEORIES OF KNOWLEDGE (1986).

65. Having noted that Gettier and subsequent philosophers take justified true belief to be insufficient for knowledge, it will be easier simply to call all recent (post-Gettier) accounts of what elevates true belief to knowledge "justification" than to describe each proposal in detail. Many epistemologists object to calling the proposed further conditions "justification," since this description may have the wrong connotations. *See* William P. Alston, *An Internalist Externalism*, 74 SYNTHESE 265 (1988). Despite this worry, it is easier for the sake of presentation to place all further conditions for knowledge under the umbrella of justification. Nothing more is implied by "justification" than "that condition which elevates true belief to genuine knowledge."

66. For a recent example of internalism, see LAURENCE BONJOUR, THE STRUCTURE OF EMPIRICAL KNOWLEDGE (1985). For an example of traditional internalism, the reader can do no better than RODERICK M. CHISHOLM, THEORY OF KNOWLEDGE (3d ed. 1989).

factors to which the agent lacks cognitive access.[67] Gettier is commonly taken to have refuted internalism, and to have demonstrated that genuine knowledge consists of true belief that is to some extent externally justified.[68]

Return now to the issue of whether wilful ignorance is a kind of genuine knowledge. To begin, in any case in which a defendant is prosecuted and convicted for illegal possession, the incriminating proposition p about which he is wilfully ignorant is true.[69] Thus, the wilfully ignorant agent satisfies the first condition of knowledge. Must he believe p? Not necessarily; he may be wilfully ignorant of p merely by suspecting that p is true.[70] Yet genuine knowledge requires belief, not mere suspicion. Hence some cases of wilful ignorance are straightforwardly *not* cases of genuine knowledge. In many cases, however, the wilfully ignorant defendant *does* believe p.[71] If forced to report sincerely about his belief, he would almost certainly admit that he believes p. Moreover, it is likely that the relevant behavior of most wilfully ignorant defendants—their attempts to avoid detection, their lack of surprise when illegal substances are found—would warrant third parties attributing a belief in p to them.

In most cases, the (sincere) wilfully ignorant defendant would admit that he *believes* p, but would deny that he *knows* p. On the assumption

67. Externalists are numerous; a good sample would include: WILLIAM P. ALSTON, EPISTEMIC JUSTIFICATION: ESSAYS IN THE THEORY OF KNOWLEDGE (1989); DAVID M. ARMSTRONG, BELIEF, TRUTH AND KNOWLEDGE (1973); FRED I. DRETSKE, KNOWLEDGE & THE FLOW OF INFORMATION (1982); ALVIN I. GOLDMAN, EPISTEMOLOGY AND COGNITION (1986); ROBERT NOZICK, PHILOSOPHICAL EXPLANATIONS (1981); MARSHALL SWAIN, REASONS AND KNOWLEDGE (1981).

68. *See* DANCY, *supra* note 64; RICHARD FOLEY, THE THEORY OF EPISTEMIC RATIONALITY 174-208 (1987); POLLOCK, *supra* note 64.

69. It may be interesting to speculate about whether a defendant who is wilfully ignorant of the truth of the incriminating proposition p can be held liable in the event that p happens to be false. Perhaps he can be held liable for some offense other than illegal possession. *See infra* text accompanying note 167. Or perhaps he can be held liable for attempted possession. The resolution of this issue depends, inter alia, on what degree of mens rea is required to give rise to liability for an attempt. If (at least) knowledge is required, the problem of wilful ignorance resurfaces. *But see* Glanville L. Williams, *The Problem of Reckless Attempts*, 1983 CRIM. L. REV. 365.

70. *See supra* text accompanying note 42.

71. Some commentators, however, apparently define wilful ignorance to preclude belief. According to one commentator, a wilfully ignorant defendant "suspects that the fact exists (although the strength of his conviction is insufficient to constitute a 'belief') and he purposely avoids learning that his suspicions are accurate." JOSHUA DRESSLER, UNDERSTANDING CRIMINAL LAW 106 (1987). There is a great deal of controversy about exactly what conditions need to be met for a mental state to constitute a belief. *See* LYCAN, *supra* note 44. Nonetheless, it is clear that on any definition not inordinately strict, some wilfully ignorant defendants will meet its conditions and hence believe p.

that knowledge consists of some kind of externally justified true belief, this denial can only be interpreted as an allegation that the quantum of justification possessed by the wilfully ignorant defendant is insufficient to give rise to knowledge. The foremost question in deciding between the two views about the relationship between wilful ignorance and knowledge, and thus in deciding whether the wilfully ignorant defendant possesses genuine knowledge, is whether his belief in the incriminating proposition is justified.[72]

Is the wilfully ignorant defendant justified in his true belief that p? There is no reason to believe that a single answer will suffice for all cases in which the issue of wilful ignorance has been raised and litigated. In many such cases, defendants may well have sufficient justification for p to know p. After all, wilfully ignorant defendants typically possess a wealth of evidence in favor of the proposition that, for example, "my suitcase contains illegal drugs," and frequently occupy situations favorable to the acquisition of external justification. Justification for p is often provided by the very same facts that discourage these defendants from making further inquiries.[73] For instance, the defendant may overhear discussions about the truth of p. This incident at once makes a defendant apprehensive about what he might find if he investigates further, and gives him an incentive not to look. On many theories of external justification, these factors provide *some* justification for his belief in p. In some such cases, this quantum of evidence may well be sufficient to conclude that the defendant is externally justified in believing p, and thus that he knows p.

Of course, these defendants will have failed to conform to a standard of how honest persons in their circumstances would have behaved. They

---

72. If justification is crucial to the question of whether wilful ignorance is a kind of genuine knowledge, then one commentator is seriously mistaken in claiming that "criminal knowledge is correct belief." Robin Charlow contends that true belief is sufficient for knowledge. She mistakenly infers from the philosophical controversy about the nature of justification that justification is not essential for knowledge. By contrast, the present examination notes the controversial status of any particular justificatory condition, but retains the common opinion that *some* such condition is required. Some kind of justificatory condition is necessary for both the legal and philosophical senses of knowledge. Indeed, it is especially crucial to the legal sense. As Charlow is aware, criminal knowledge is a culpable state of mind. For a state of mind to be culpable, one must be to some extent responsible for it. But that an agent has a belief, and that the belief is correct, are not usually thought to be states for which an agent is responsible. By and large, persons have little voluntary control over what they believe, and, of course, no control over what propositions are true. Thus correct belief is inadequate for the legal sense of knowledge. Its adequacy for the philosophical sense of knowledge is discussed below, *infra* note 79.

73. Evidence of wilful ignorance has frequently been used to provide proof of genuine knowledge. *See, e.g.*, People v. Brown, 16 P. 1, 2 (Cal. 1887).

will not, for example, have opened their suitcases to look inside. But this failure does not always entail a lack of sufficient justification for p to know p. Why suppose that they cannot know p in the absence of all the conditions that people in their circumstances would ordinarily satisfy? The additional evidence they would have gained by opening the suitcase may only provide further confirmation for what they know already. To insist that a defendant cannot have sufficient justification to know p without actually *looking* inside the suitcase creates an unwarranted bias in favor of visual means of obtaining knowledge.[74] Hence, the wilfully ignorant defendant may have genuine knowledge of the incriminating proposition; or put differently, a subject displaying all those characteristics of genuine knowledge may still manifest wilful ignorance.

In many, if not most, cases, however, the wilfully ignorant defendant will have *in*sufficient external justification for his belief that p. Many philosophers would conclude that these defendants do *not* possess genuine knowledge, and should not be convicted under statutes that require that they act knowingly. But this conclusion may be too hasty; perhaps the mental state of these defendants can qualify as knowledge in the relevant sense after all. The conception of justification typically employed by philosophers is idealized, and may be unsuitable for purposes of imposing criminal liability.

The futility of using external justification for legal purposes can be illustrated with a troublesome example. Consider a defendant suffering from a hearing loss who uses a generally unreliable hearing aid. If he manages to hear a discussion affirming the truth of the incriminating proposition p, it seems plausible to judge that he gains knowledge of p. His mental state can qualify as knowledge despite the fact that his hearing aid is often unreliable. But many philosophers resist this judgment. Since they claim that knowledge is true belief produced from a reliable process, many philosophers conclude that no belief formed from an unreliable process can qualify as an instance of knowledge.[75] Consequently, even if a defendant overheard that a bag of heroin had been placed in his suitcase, and believed (accurately) that he was carrying heroin, he may still not know p according to many philosophical conceptions of knowledge. He may lack knowledge for the simple reason

74. *See* United States v. Jewell, 532 F.2d 697, 705 (9th Cir. 1976) (Kennedy, J., dissenting).

75. These epistemologists are called "reliabilists." Reliabilism is a kind of externalism with respect to knowledge. While many varieties exist, the core idea is that if a belief is produced from a mechanism, e.g., one's auditory apparatus or an intelligent person, which generally supplies one with beliefs that are true, then a belief so produced is, if true, an instance of knowledge. Many of the externalists cited in *supra* note 67 are reliabilists.

that his belief might not have been produced by a reliable process, e.g. his hearing aid may be unreliable. Clearly many wilfully ignorant defendants will not possess genuine knowledge in this sense.

This kind of example points to an important problem with adopting such an idealized conception of knowledge for present purposes. The state of external justification is seemingly irrelevant to determinations of culpability. As Gettier has shown, one can have justified true belief without having knowledge. A proposition p might accidently be true for reasons other than those that justify (in the internalist sense) the belief of the agent. Thus Gettier is commonly understood to have demonstrated that some factors external to a subject's cognitive access are required in order for him to have knowledge. One can reason and reflect upon all one's available evidence in the most scrupulous possible fashion and still lack knowledge. As a consequence, it is clear that one is to some extent lucky to be knowledgeable. Yet it is perverse to fault someone for being unlucky. Criminal culpability cannot be thought to be in part a function of whether an agent is epistemically fortunate or not. What matters for culpability is how a defendant performs with respect to factors accessible to him; whether his cognizing has been *responsible* is important, for irresponsible cognizing may well count as culpable behavior. The fact that external environmental factors prevent him from gaining knowledge in this idealized sense seems irrelevant to his culpability. Thus, whether or not the wilfully ignorant defendant possesses what a contemporary epistemologist would call knowledge may be unhelpful to the attempt to describe a culpable mental state.[76]

Perhaps a less idealized conception of knowledge would include the state of wilful ignorance in its extension. A more familiar, intuitive understanding of knowledge is found in the pre-Gettier sense of knowledge, and in a few recent formulations of knowledge. Here

---

76. Contrast this result with Robbins, *supra* note 52. Robbins surveys the philosophical literature to see whether the philosophical sense of knowledge conflicts with the Model Penal Code's definition of knowledge in terms of a person's awareness of a high probability of the existence of a particular fact. Since he examines only epistemology prior to 1960, however, he rightly concludes that the two definitions conflict—but for the wrong reasons. Robbins presupposes an extreme form of internalism and concludes that "subjective certainty" is needed for philosophical knowledge. This conflicts with the mere high probability aspect of the Model Penal Code's definition. As noted, however, epistemology in the latter half of this century has been unkind to extreme internalism, and so philosophical knowledge does not conflict with the high probability aspect. However, knowledge that is externally justified does conflict with the requirement that a subject must be *aware* of a high probability of the material fact's existence. On many epistemological theories, all that is required is that a true belief be acquired in the correct manner. Ironically, the philosophical sense of knowledge conflicts with that of the Model Penal Code not by being too strict, as Robbins believes, but by being too loose.

knowledge is justified true belief, where justification is understood as some kind of internal justification. In other words, justification is a function of the evidence cognitively accessible to a subject. On this conception, justification is a result of one's own efforts; it is a matter of being intellectually responsible. Consequently, if a subject is not justified on this view, he has not been an entirely careful cognizer.[77] Contrary to the situation with external justification, a person may indeed be faulted for lacking this notion of justification.[78]

The question now to be answered is whether the wilfully ignorant defendant is justified, in this internalist sense, in his true belief that p. For the same reasons described above, many defendants will have sufficient justification for p to know p. Evidence for p is often provided by the very same facts that discourage these defendants from making further inquiries. Often this evidence will be enough to conclude that the defendant knows p, even if he has not considered all the evidence that honest people would ordinarily consider. Consider the additional evidence that would have been gained if the defendant had looked inside the suitcase. Suppose the defendant would have seen a white powder wrapped in a plastic bag. He still would not have obtained the *best* evidence to justify his suspicion that the suitcase contains an illegal drug, since he would not have ingested the substance or submitted it to a chemical analysis. Perhaps the defendant may not know the incriminating proposition on an idealized conception of knowledge, but on the more ordinary sense of knowledge, no one would insist that he could not know that what he sees is an illegal drug because he failed to collect the best evidence to justify his belief. Sufficient justification to know p does not require considering the *best* evidence for p—it simply requires considering *enough* evidence for p. How much evidence is enough? That is a question about which epistemologists have disagreed. Fortunately, it need not be resolved here. Suffice it to say that many wilfully ignorant

---

77. Epistemologists recognize this as a classical deontological form of internal justification. It is espoused, for example, by John Locke: he who has justification "may have this satisfaction in doing his duty as a rational creature, that, though he should miss truth, he will not miss the reward of it [i.e., of having done his duty, being justified]." 2 JOHN LOCKE, AN ESSAY CONCERNING HUMAN UNDERSTANDING, bk. 4.17.24, at 413 (Alexander C. Fraser ed., Dover Pub. 1959) (1690).

78. "[O]ne's cognitive endeavors are epistemically justified only if and to the extent that they are aimed at this goal [truth], which means very roughly that one accepts all and only those beliefs which one has good reason to think are true. To accept a belief in the absence of such a reason . . . is to neglect the pursuit of truth; such acceptance is, one might say, *epistemically irresponsible*. My contention here is that the idea of avoiding such irresponsibility, of being epistemically responsible in one's believings, is the core of the notion of epistemic justification." BONJOUR, *supra* note 66, at 8.

defendants will have considered enough evidence for p to justify their belief that p, and thus to know p.

Nonetheless, for whatever reason, many wilfully ignorant defendants will lack sufficient justification for p, and thus will not know p. The remainder of this section will present two reasons to conclude that such cases exist. The "substitute for knowledge" rather than the "actual knowledge" view of the relationship between wilful ignorance and knowledge offers a better account of such cases. Thus many (but not all) wilfully ignorant defendants do not possess knowledge of the incriminating proposition p in either the philosophical or the more colloquial senses.[79]

Conceptual analysis provides the first argument in favor of concluding that some wilfully ignorant defendants do not have genuine knowledge. Consider the example of Smith, who is not wilfully ignorant and possesses a true belief about a proposition p, but lacks sufficient justification to know p. He believes, for example, that a gem he found is a real diamond. The gem looks and feels like a real diamond to him, but, despite his efforts, he is unable to gather sufficient evidence to justify his true belief. He asks his friends, most of whom concur that the gem looks and feels like a diamond. But he does not know how to justify his belief without consulting a jeweler, and no jeweler is available. Smith lacks knowledge; it might be said that he is nonwilfully ignorant. Contrast his case with that of Jones, who possesses the exact quantum of evidence about the nature of the diamond as Smith. Jones has the same beliefs about the gem as Jones, and for precisely the same reasons. Unlike Smith, however, Jones knows that real diamonds can be identified by performing a simple and reliable test—only diamonds scratch rubies. As luck would have it, Jones has a ruby readily available. However, Jones fails to perform this test precisely because he does not want to know the truth about the gem. Jones' ignorance, unlike Smith's, is wilful.[80]

---

79. Indeed, the conclusion can be put even stronger. Perhaps the loosest conception of knowledge sanctioned by ordinary language is knowledge as merely true belief. *See* Crispin Sartwell, *Knowledge is Merely True Belief*, 28 AM. PHIL. Q. 157 (1991); Crispin Sartwell, *Why Knowledge is Merely True Belief*, 89 J. PHIL. 167 (1992). Since a wilfully ignorant defendant need not believe an incriminating proposition, but must merely be suspicious of it (*see supra* part II), in some cases he will fail to know p on even this extremely weak sense of knowledge. Consequently, the foregoing considerations show that the wilfully ignorant subject may not have knowledge in *any* remotely plausible understanding of that term.

80. According to the definition in *supra* part II, Jones would not be wilfully ignorant unless he satisfied the motivational condition; his motive for remaining ignorant must be to avoid blame or liability. For the present example to involve wilful ignorance, Jones must have this motive for failing to perform the test to identify the diamond.

Despite this important difference between Smith and Jones, there is no reason to conclude that the latter, unlike the former, has genuine knowledge that the gem is a real diamond. *Ex hypothesi*, both Jones and Smith have a true belief about the gem, as well as the same quantum of evidence in favor of their belief. If knowledge consists in justified true belief, either both Jones and Smith have knowledge, or neither does. Since Smith lacks knowledge, so does Jones. The fact that Jones' ignorance is wilful does not by itself provide him with *more* of a justification for believing a proposition than that possessed by Smith, whose ignorance is nonwilful. Surely the fact that Jones fails to perform the relevant test cannot be used to demonstrate that he *already has* the knowledge that he *would* have gained by performing the test.

The same conclusion can be applied to many cases of wilful ignorance. Wilfully ignorant defendants frequently have no more evidence of p than nonwilfully ignorant defendants. Although the wilfully ignorant defendant would know p if he looked inside the suitcase, for example, it does not follow that he already knows p *without* looking inside the suitcase, just because his failure to look is wilful. Tests would be superfluous if persons already knew the information that would be revealed by performing these tests. Thus, many wilfully ignorant defendants lack even the more intuitive sense of justification defined above. Consequently, many of these defendants do not possess knowledge of the incriminating proposition p in either the philosophical or more colloquial senses of "knowledge."

A second reason can be given to conclude that some wilfully ignorant defendants do not have genuine knowledge. Many of the cases that illustrate the phenomenon of wilful ignorance do not appear to involve knowledge. Consider again the jury instructions in *Jewell*. The court instructed the jury that guilt could be established if the "ignorance" of the defendant "was solely and entirely a result of his having made a conscious purpose . . . to avoid learning the truth."[81] Liability was not predicated on a finding of knowledge, but rather on a particular explanation of *why* the defendant remained ignorant. But it is hard to see how ignorance, from whatever cause, can *be* knowledge.[82] A particular explanation of why a defendant remains ignorant might justify treating him *as though* he had knowledge, but it cannot, through some mysterious alchemy, convert ignorance *into* knowledge.

---

81. United States v. Jewell, 532 F.2d 697, 700 (9th Cir. 1976). Other instructions lead to comparable results. One instruction said that the defendant's "self-imposed ignorance cannot protect him from criminal responsibility." United States v. Murrieta-Bejarano, 552 F.2d 1323, 1324 n.1 (9th Cir. 1977).

82. "It is implicit in the definition of willful blindness that the defendant does not have knowledge." Comment, *supra* note 54, at 476.

Many of these cases contrast the mental state of the defendant with something else he lacks, called "genuine knowledge" here.[83] Some commentators describe wilful ignorance as an "exception" to the requirement of genuine knowledge.[84] Of course, no "exception" to this requirement would be needed if wilful ignorance *were* genuine knowledge. It seems safe to conclude that the mental state of many (but not all) defendants who allege wilful ignorance does not amount to genuine knowledge, even though, in Glanville Williams' words, it is "almost" knowledge.[85]

Again, however, it is important to emphasize that many wilfully ignorant defendants might possess genuine knowledge despite their failure to evaluate all the evidence for p that honest persons in their circumstances would ordinarily consider. A jury might well conclude that, despite his failure to look inside his suitcase, a wilfully ignorant defendant still has enough justification for p to know p. But not all cases are comparable. In some cases, the wilfully ignorant defendant will lack knowledge, and will possess, at best, only a substitute for knowledge.

IV. THE "EQUAL CULPABILITY" THESIS

If some wilfully ignorant defendants do *not* possess genuine knowledge—as the "substitute for knowledge" view entails—what reason can be given for treating them as though they did? The only plausible answer to this question is that wilful ignorance is the "moral equivalent" of knowledge; it involves a degree of culpability that is equal to genuine knowledge.[86] Unless these two distinct mental states were equally culpable, it would be outrageous to hold a defendant with the first mental state liable for violating a statute that required the second mental state.[87] Many commentators apparently regard this supposed equivalence as

83. In *Jewell*, the mental state of wilful ignorance is contrasted with "positive" knowledge (and called "genuine" knowledge here), although the concept of positive knowledge is never analyzed. *Jewell*, 532 F.2d at 700.

84. *See* 1 LAFAVE & SCOTT, *supra* note 14, at 307.

85. "A court can properly find wilful blindness only where it can almost be said that the defendant actually knew." WILLIAMS, *supra* note 56, at 157. Of course, "almost" knowledge is recklessness, it is not genuine knowledge.

86. "The notion that [wilful blindness] is properly classified as knowledge in the hierarchy of mental states is grounded in the conclusion 'that deliberate ignorance and positive knowledge are equally culpable.'" 1 LAFAVE & SCOTT, *supra* note 14, at 302 (quoting *Jewell*, 532 F.2d at 700).

87. "We want to punish wilful ignorance as knowledge only if and when the two are comparably morally reprehensible." Charlow, *supra* note 22, at 1357.

beyond dispute,[88] and most courts concur with this assessment.[89] Yet the judgment that wilful ignorance and knowledge are equivalent in culpability, though frequently asserted, is seldom defended.

Rollin Perkins and Ronald Boyce are perhaps the only theorists to have made an explicit attempt to argue in favor of the "equal culpability" thesis. Their defense refers to what an "honest person" would have done under the circumstances. They write: "No honest person would *deliberately fail* to find out the truth *for fear of learning* that what he was thinking of doing would violate the law."[90] Perkins and Boyce are clearly correct in their generalization about honest people. Their argument shows that the wilfully ignorant defendant is indeed culpable; his behavior hardly conforms to an ideal of honesty.[91] Nonetheless, their argument does not show that the culpability of the wilfully ignorant defendant is *equal* to that of the defendant who possesses genuine knowledge. How can the *degree* of culpability of a particular defendant be ascertained by reference to the objective standard of an honest person? Not all dishonest persons are equally culpable.

The "equal culpability" thesis may or may not be true, depending on the criteria by which two distinct mental states are held to be equally culpable. Controversy about the equal culpability thesis cannot be resolved in the absence of a theory to identify what makes one mental state more or less culpable than another. Unfortunately, no adequate theory to measure degrees of culpability has yet been proposed.[92] In the absence of such a theory, commentators are left with only their unsupported (and frequently conflicting) intuitions about whether one

---

88. "Up to the present day, no real doubt has been cast on the proposition that connivance is as culpable as actual knowledge." Edwards, *supra* note 21, at 302.

89. The *Jewell* court referred to wilful ignorance as a "calculated effort to avoid the sanctions of the statute while violating its substance." 532 F.2d at 704. Another characterized the phenomenon as a "loophole" for "circumventing criminal sanctions." United States v. Sarantos, 455 F.2d 877, 881 (2d Cir. 1972).

90. PERKINS & BOYCE, *supra* note 20, at 873.

91. "Wilful blindness has about it an invitation to punishment. A person who is wilfully blind appears to court criminal liability." David Lanham, *Wilful Blindness and the Criminal Law*, 9 CRIM. L.J. 261, 267 (1985).

92. Some of the available theories are discussed and critiqued in Jeremy Horder, *Criminal Culpability: The Possibility of a General Theory*, 12 LAW & PHIL. 193 (1993).

Perhaps the inability to measure degrees of culpability is partly due to the oversimplified structure of culpability in modern criminal codes such as the Model Penal Code. One recent proposal would measure culpability along two independent dimensions: belief-states and desire-states. A wilfully ignorant defendant may be quite culpable with respect to his desire—he may be callously indifferent to whether a harm occurs—but less culpable with respect to his belief. *See* Kenneth W. Simons, *Rethinking Mental States*, 72 B.U. L. REV. 463 (1992).

mental state is more or less culpable than another.[93] Thus it is prudent to suspend judgment about the equal culpability thesis until arguments supporting its truth or falsity are produced. Still, it may be helpful to speculate about what any such arguments are likely to reveal. The most probable result of these arguments is that the culpability of wilfully ignorant defendants is highly sensitive to the facts of their particular circumstances. Some wilfully ignorant defendants may be just as culpable as defendants who act knowingly, while others may be less culpable.[94] Still others may even be *more* culpable than defendants who act knowingly.[95] No general conclusion about the culpability of wilfully ignorant defendants, relative to defendants who act knowingly, is likely to prove defensible.

At least one reason can be given to suspect that a great many wilfully ignorant defendants are *not* as culpable as defendants who possess genuine knowledge. Notice that only persons who play very limited roles in a criminal scheme involving several participants have the realistic opportunity to remain wilfully ignorant. Consider the role played by the typical wilfully ignorant defendant. He is almost always the carrier or "mule" who transports illegal drugs for the benefit and profit of others. He is neither the drug producer, the ultimate user, nor the "kingpin" who organizes and reaps great profits from a scheme to distribute drugs. Indeed, it is barely possible to imagine how those who produce or organize the distribution of drugs—and thus are more centrally involved in the criminal scheme—*could* be wilfully ignorant. The intermediary role of the "mule," however, is very different. With a little ingenuity, such a person may well succeed in remaining ignorant of what he is doing.

---

93. One commentator's intuition is as follows: "By engaging in conduct while aware of a high probability that such conduct is criminal, the [wilfully blind] actor has manifested his *indifference* to the values underlying the criminal prohibition in much the same way as the actor who is certain his conduct is criminal. Consequently, the criminal law should not differentiate between them." Marcus, *supra* note 36, at 2236 (emphasis added). But why assume that relative culpability is solely a function of the degree to which the defendant manifests indifference to the values underlying the law? A more complete account of the factors that affect culpability is provided in Simons, *supra* note 92, at 463.

94. One commentator describes a number of inculpating factors that are typically present in cases of wilful ignorance. *See* Charlow, *supra* note 22, at 1400. Presumably a wilfully ignorant defendant who lacks one or more of these inculpating factors is less culpable than a defendant who possesses them.

95. One commentator has gone so far as to suggest that "[r]ecklessness/deliberate ignorance may indicate greater culpability [than genuine knowledge] in some situations." *See* Robbins, *supra* note 52, at 234.

Anglo-American law has been reluctant to recognize that persons who play distinct roles in a criminal plan involving several participants may be culpable to different degrees. As a general rule, Anglo-American law treats all parties in a criminal scheme as equally culpable.[96] But there is no reason why the criminal law should disregard ordinary judgments of culpability and recognize that the contribution of the typical wilfully ignorant defendant renders him less culpable than other, more central participants in the scheme.[97] Paul Robinson has proposed the rudiments of a theory to incorporate these ordinary judgments of culpability into the criminal law. He distinguishes between four kinds of involvement in a criminal enterprise: organizers, managers, participants, and supporters.[98] He suggests punishing participants half or two-thirds as severely as organizers and managers.[99] Implementing these suggestions would result in more lenient treatment for most wilfully ignorant defendants.[100]

Suppose, however, that the "equal culpability" thesis is true, and that all wilfully ignorant defendants *are* as culpable as defendants who act knowingly. Even so, it is crucial to realize that invoking the equal culpability thesis to punish a wilfully ignorant defendant for violating a statute requiring knowledge is incompatible with the principle of legality. The rule of law should not be construed to allow liability to be imposed when the particular mens rea required by the statute *or its equivalent in culpability* is present. Instead, the rule of law should be construed to allow liability to be imposed only when the particular mens rea required by the statute is present *simpliciter*. Using the equal culpability thesis to justify punishing the wilfully ignorant defendant under a statute requiring that he act knowingly is to employ the very kind of analogical reasoning condemned by the principle of legality.[101]

---

96. *See* K.J.M. SMITH, A MODERN TREATISE ON THE LAW OF CRIMINAL COMPLICITY 73 (1991). Prosecutors may choose not to prosecute persons whose role in the criminal scheme is relatively minor, and authorities with sentencing discretion may punish such persons less severely. These facts only serve to demonstrate that the substantive law is morally troublesome. *See* DRESSLER, *supra* note 71, at 420.

97. *See* Joshua Dressler, *Reassessing the Theoretical Underpinnings of Accomplice Liability: New Solutions to an Old Problem*, 37 HASTINGS L.J. 91 (1985).

98. Paul H. Robinson, *A Sentencing System for the 21st Century?*, 66 TEX. L. REV. 1, 49 (1987).

99. *Id.*

100. According to Robinson's proposal, wilfully ignorant defendants would typically be classified as mere supporters rather than as participants, since they generally are compensated by a fixed amount rather than by a percentage of the profits of the criminal scheme. *Id.*

101. *See supra* part I.

Appeals to the supposed equal culpability of defendants as a justification for imposing criminal liability would seem outrageous in other contexts; the judgment that two defendants are equally culpable is not accepted as a good reason to violate the principle of legality.[102] Consider contexts in which allegations of equal culpability are frequently expressed. For example, many theorists contend that defendants who fail in their attempts are equally culpable as those who succeed.[103] After all, these theorists reason, it is simply a matter of luck whether the bullet of an attempted assassin happens to be fatal, and luck should play no part in assessments of culpability. Suppose that these theorists are correct,[104] and that the murderer and the attempted murderer are equally culpable. Even so, no one would conclude that the principle of legality allows holding these two defendants liable for the same offense. As long as existing homicide statutes require an actual killing, and not the "moral equivalent" of a killing, the principle of legality allows only a real killer, and not a defendant whose culpability is identical to that of a killer, to be punished for a homicide.[105] And so with wilful ignorance. As long as existing possessory statutes require knowledge, and not the "moral equivalent" of knowledge, the principle of legality allows only a knower, and not a defendant whose culpability is identical to that of a knower, to be punished for possession. All commentators agree that statutory reform would be needed if attempts are to be punished under homicide statutes.[106] On parallel grounds, statutory reform is needed if wilfully

---

102. Perhaps Paul Robinson is correct to maintain that the doctrine of transferred intent relies upon a theory of equivalent culpability: "The best explanation of why the intent to shoot the desired victim should be 'transferred' to the actual victim is that both intentions are equally culpable." *See* Paul H. Robinson, *Imputed Criminal Liability*, 93 YALE L.J. 609, 620 (1984). But it is arguable that the mens rea of intentional homicide is the intention to kill *some* human being. If the precise identity of the victim is irrelevant, no theory of equivalent culpability may be required to explain the doctrine of transferred intent. See the treatment of transferred intent in Michael Moore, *Intentions and Mens Rea*, *in* ISSUES IN CONTEMPORARY LEGAL PHILOSOPHY 245, 267-68 (Ruth Ganison ed., 1987).

103. *See* Andrew Ashworth, *Criminal Attempts and the Role of Resulting Harm Under the Code, and in the Common Law*, 19 RUTGERS L.J. 725 (1988).

104. *But see* R.A. Duff, *Actions, Lotteries, and the Punishment of Attempts*, 9 LAW & PHIL. 1 (1990).

105. Punishing attempted killers under homicide statutes would be a clear violation of the principle of legality because the actus reus of the offense has not been committed. It is the hypothesis of this Article that the principle of legality should be construed to oppose the punishment of persons who lack the mens rea of an offense as well.

106. The reform recommended most frequently is to rewrite existing statutes to delete reference to actual results. *See* Stephen Schulhoffer, *Harm and Punishment: A Critique of Emphasis on the Results of Conduct in the Criminal Law*, 122 U. PA. L. REV. 1497 (1974). But in the absence of such statutory reform, the principle of legality clearly

ignorant defendants (who possess only a substitute for knowledge) are to be punished under possessory statutes.[107] In short, fidelity to the principle of legality requires resistance to analogical reasoning in the enforcement of the criminal law.

V. THE DEEPER SIGNIFICANCE OF THE PRINCIPLE OF LEGALITY

It is highly unlikely that redescriptions of the phenomenon of wilful ignorance can help to resolve the incompatibility between the rule of law and the practice of holding such defendants liable for statutes requiring that they act knowingly. Short of the "actual knowledge" account, *any* conception of wilful ignorance that serves its purpose *must* infringe the principle of legality.[108] The whole point of inventing this concept is to describe a mental state that is alleged to be the moral equivalent of knowledge, thereby providing courts with a basis to convict a defendant (who otherwise might have been acquitted) for acting knowingly.[109] Attempts to reconcile the principle of legality with the punishment of wilfully ignorant defendants are almost certain to be unsuccessful, since the concept has been created for the sole purpose of circumventing the principle of legality.

It is easy to miss the significance of the inconsistency between the principle of legality and the practice of holding all wilfully ignorant defendants liable under a statute requiring that they act knowingly. Theorists who emphasize the importance of fair notice to the exclusion of other values promoted by the rule of law[110] will not be especially impressed by the threat that wilful ignorance poses to the legality principle. The wilfully ignorant defendant who is held to have acted knowingly can hardly complain that he has not received fair notice of the offense charged. After all, wilfully ignorant defendants satisfy the motivational condition; their ignorance is wilful precisely because they are all too aware of the existence of the offense.[111] Fair notice is not the

---

precludes holding defendants whose attempts are unsuccessful liable for the completed offense, regardless of their relative culpability.

107. The limitations of statutory reforms are discussed *infra* part VI.

108. "[A]ny definition of wilful ignorance in which the construct is used for a purpose other than as evidence from which to infer actual knowledge, or as pretended ignorance, implies true ignorance." *See* Charlow, *supra* note 22, at 1388.

109. *See supra* part II.

110. "The basis [of the maxim *nullum crimen sine lege*] is that the criminal law ought to be certain, so that people can know in advance whether the conduct on which they are about to embark is criminal or not." 1 LAFAVE & SCOTT, *supra* note 14, at 101.

111. Thus wilfully ignorant defendants are even more likely to be aware that their conduct is illegal than defendants who act knowingly—since knowledge that conduct is illegal is not part of the mens rea of knowledge. *See* MODEL PENAL CODE, § 2.02(9)

problem here.

But values other than fair notice to defendants are protected by the principle of legality as well. Some commentators have noted that an additional value achieved by adherence to the rule of law is the check on arbitrary and selective law enforcement. According to Herbert Packer, "[t]he real importance of the principle of legality . . . [is] to control the discretion of the police and of prosecutors rather than of judges."[112] Legality helps to promote this objective by ensuring "[t]hat the police and prosecutors confine their attention to the catalogue of what has already been defined as criminal."[113]

This goal is obviously valuable. But the need to ensure that police and prosecutors are concerned only with matters that are in "the catalogue of what has already been defined as criminal" is important only when defendants are punished for what is not clearly the actus reus of an offense.[114] Applications of the principle of legality to issues of mens rea raise a somewhat different set of concerns. Clearly, the state has determined that the arrest and prosecution of a defendant found in possession of a controlled substance is the proper business of police and prosecutors.[115] Packer's account of the importance of legality offers no explanation of why this principle should be preserved in cases in which a defendant unquestionably commits the actus reus of an existing offense, although he lacks the requisite mens rea.

A more compelling reason to uphold the rule of law in the context of mens rea begins by placing the equal culpability thesis in its broader political context. Whether the wilfully ignorant defendant is likely to be found guilty of having acted knowingly may depend on the particular offense charged.[116] Although this hypothesis may be impossible to test directly, conformity to the demands of legality should undermine any suspicion that the meaning of mens rea terms might vary with the offense in question. There is some basis for doubting that these demands of legality have been satisfied. It cannot be accidental that the overwhelming majority of the recent convictions of wilfully ignorant defendants involve drug offenses that include possession as an element.[117] Although wilful

(Official Draft, review and commentaries, 1985).

112. HERBERT PACKER, THE LIMITS OF THE CRIMINAL SANCTION 88 (1968).

113. *Id.* at 90.

114. *See supra* text accompanying notes 8-12.

115. *But see* DOUGLAS N. HUSAK, DRUGS AND RIGHTS (1992).

116. "The courts are greatly influenced in their construction of the statute by the degree of social danger which they believe to be involved in the offence in question." J.C. SMITH & BRIAN HOGAN, CRIMINAL LAW 92 (1983).

117. According to one commentator, the doctrine of wilful blindness originated in England but was given a somewhat cooler reception in the United States until it

ignorance instructions are given for a broad range of statutes that require a mens rea of knowledge,[118] drug offenses are by far the most common crimes for which wilfully ignorant defendants are punished.[119] It seems naive to assess the problem of wilful ignorance apart from the larger political significance of drug policy.

Many commentators have called attention to the fact that precious civil liberties have been sacrificed in the ongoing "war on drugs."[120] In this highly-charged atmosphere, police, prosecutors, and jurors are unlikely to sympathize with persons found with drugs in their possession. Political pressures have distorted the meaning of possession itself in the context of drug offenses,[121] and there is no reason to believe that the criteria for what constitutes knowing possession should be immune from these same pressures.[122] Allowing the conviction of defendants whose culpability is *different* from what is required by the statute—because their *degree* of culpability is alleged to be comparable to what is required by the statute—gives the State an opportunity to bend the law in order to more successfully wage war on drugs.

Ample evidence exists that these very political pressures were operative in *Jewell*. The court did not defend the equal culpability thesis

---

"[r]eemerged during the 1960s, coinciding with a dramatic increase in drug abuse and a resultant increase in prosecutions for the possession, transportation and use of drugs." Comment, *supra* note 54, at 471.

118. *See* Chestnut, *supra* note 28, at 48 n.12.

119. "Federal narcotics violations are the most common source of current deliberate-ignorance case law." Robbins, *supra* note 52, at 192 n.6. "Because the [wilful ignorance] instruction seems to lend itself particularly to those cases involving illegal contraband, the conscious ignorance doctrine and *Jewell* instruction have become increasingly important as the federal government expands the prosecution of cases involving smuggled drugs." Chestnut, *supra* note 28, at 49. "The increased application of willful blindness can be correlated with the rise in federal narcotics prosecutions." Marcus, *supra* note 36, at 2234 n.24. For a discussion of the many drug offenses utilizing a wilful ignorance instruction, see Charlow, *supra* note 22, at 1418 n.276; *see also* Marcus, *supra* note 36, at 2241-53.

120. Commentators have been especially concerned with how the war on drugs has eroded Fourth Amendment rights. *See, e.g.*, Scott E. Sundby, *A Return to Fourth Amendment Basics: Undoing the Mischief of* Camera *and* Terry, 72 MINN. L. REV. 383 (1988); Silas J. Wasserstrom, *The Incredibly Shrinking Fourth Amendment*, 21 AM. CRIM. L. REV. 257 (1984); Steven Wisotsky, *Crackdown: The Emerging 'Drug Exception' to the Bill of Rights*, 38 HASTINGS L.J. 889 (1987).

121. *See* Charles Whitebread & Ronald Stevens, *Constructive Possession in Narcotics Cases: To Have and Have Not*, 58 VA. L. REV. 751 (1972); Seth Davidson, Note, *Criminal Liability for Possession of Nonuseable Amounts of Controlled Substances*, 77 COLUM. L. REV. 596 (1977).

122. In England, Lord Guest alleged that requiring any degree of mens rea for the offense of drug possession was "a drug peddlar's charter." Warner v. Metropolitan Police Comm'r, [1968] 2 All E.R. 356.

directly, but noted that the acquittal of the wilfully ignorant defendant would be "inconsistent with the Drug Control Act's general purpose to deal more effectively 'with the growing menace of drug abuse in the United States.'"[123] The conviction of a wilfully ignorant defendant was explicitly tied to the urgency of the war on drugs. The court offered no reason to convict a wilfully ignorant defendant for acting knowingly except for its allegations that the "menace" of "drug abuse" was "growing," and that "those who traffic in drugs would make the most of" a statutory interpretation that required genuine knowledge.[124]

It is disappointing that commentators apparently approve of this tendency to distort or to stretch the application of mens rea terms in order to wage war on drugs more effectively.[125] Robin Charlow writes:

> Even if the suggested definition of wilful ignorance is not adopted as a wholesale knowledge equivalent, it nevertheless might be advisable to lower the mens rea for the crime of drug importation to a level that would include less culpable forms of wilful ignorance, such as those commonly in use.[126]

Why does Charlow propose singling out drug offenses for special treatment? Her answer does not explore why legislatures included a knowledge requirement in offenses of drug possession. Instead, she writes:

> One possible reason for Congress to distinguish drug importation . . . may be the devastating effect that drugs are currently thought to have on our society . . . . If the gravity of the problem posed by a particular crime, in this case drug importation, is perceived as more serious than in the case of other crimes, it may be advisable to consider a broader level of culpability.[127]

---

123. United States v. Jewell, 532 F.2d 697, 703 (9th Cir. 1976) (quoting H.R. Rep. No. 1444, 91st Cong., 2d Sess. 1 (1970), *reprinted in* 1970 U.S.C.C.A.N. 4566-67)).

124. *Id.*

125. One commentator cites the "severity of the drug problem currently afflicting our society" as a reason to hold defendants outside the country liable for a conspiracy to import drugs into the United States even though they did not know where the drugs would be exported. *See* Jennifer E. Raiola, Comment, *Crossing the Border Line: Interpreting Federal Drug Trafficking Statutes in* United States v. Londono-Villa, 66 ST. JOHN'S L. REV. 487, 503 (1992).

126. Charlow, *supra* note 22, at 1426.

127. *Id.* at 1427 n.306 (citation omitted).

The reasoning in *Jewell*, apparently endorsed by Charlow, should be resisted. *Any* criminal statute is designed to deal effectively with a perceived menace, and whatever mens rea requirement is used in the statute inevitably restricts the authority of the state to punish defendants who commit the actus reus of that offense.[128] Such a restriction is likely to prove especially burdensome to law enforcement officials as the severity or incidence of a particular crime increases. Yet the fact that a given offense is committed frequently hardly provides a compelling reason to erode the meaning of the mens rea requirement of that offense. Would anyone seriously propose that wilfully ignorant defendants should not be convicted once the "menace" of "drug abuse" stops "growing"?[129] The meaning of "knowingly" should not vary with the actus reus of the offense modified by this adverb, and should not be affected by fluctuations in crime rates.[130] Part of the function of the rule of law should be to insulate findings of criminal liability from these very sorts of political pressures. The above reasoning of courts and commentators cannot be reconciled with the demands of the rule of law, when the scope of this rule is expanded beyond the conventional wisdom that surrounds it to encompass mens rea as well as actus reus.

VI. Statutory Reforms and Their Limitations

Many commentators have sought a statutory solution to the problem of wilful ignorance. To be successful, any such reform must enable the state to impose criminal liability on the wilfully ignorant defendant "without manipulating the definition of knowledge to achieve a desired but unwarranted result."[131]

The statutory reform proposed most frequently would encourage legislatures to substitute recklessness for knowledge as the level of culpability required for liability.[132] A radical version of this proposal

128. *See* Morissette v. United States, 342 U.S. 246 (1952).

129. According to most surveys, marijuana use peaked in 1979, and cocaine use peaked in 1985. *See, e.g.*, HUSAK, *supra* note 115, at 11.

130. Allen reports that compromises of the principle of legality have been most frequent during periods of "high anxiety about crime." *See* Allen, *supra* note 5, at 400. This remark surely characterizes contemporary attitudes about the drug menace.

131. Robbins, *supra* note 52, at 233.

132. *See, e.g.*, *id.* A second possible statutory solution to the problem of wilful ignorance would alter the mens rea required for liability under a given statute from "knows p" to "knows p or is wilfully ignorant of p." A few existing offenses already incorporate such language. The Anti-Drug Abuse Act of 1988, Pub. L. No.100-690, 102 Stat. 4181 (1988) (codified as amended at 21 U.S.C. §§ 1501-08 (1988 & Supp. 1991)), provides for forfeiture of vehicles used in drug-related offenses unless the offense is "established by that owner to have been committed or omitted without the knowledge,

would modify *all* existing criminal statutes so that no offense required knowledge. A more moderate version would continue to require knowledge as the mens rea of some offenses, while modifying others so that recklessness would suffice for liability. Statutes proscribing drug possession, of course, are the prime candidates for modification.[133] Most wilfully ignorant defendants would be acquitted under those statutes that continued to require knowledge.

This reform would achieve the objective of convicting wilfully ignorant defendants under the modified statutes, since all such defendants are at least reckless.[134] However, not all reckless defendants are wilfully ignorant.[135] Lowering the degree of culpability required for liability under some or all statutes from knowledge to recklessness would succeed in convicting not only wilfully ignorant defendants, but also a great many nonwilfully ignorant (but reckless) defendants who otherwise would have been acquitted. Nonwilfully ignorant defendants would be punished if they consciously disregarded a substantial and unjustifiable risk about which they lacked knowledge.

Superficially, this reform appears to solve the problem of wilful ignorance,[136] since no defendant would be punished without having the degree of mens rea expressly provided by statute. The legislature would accomplish what the judiciary could not—a change in the level of mens rea required for conviction from knowledge to recklessness. If fidelity to the rule of law means mere conformity to statutory law, as conventional

---

consent, or willful blindness of the owner." *See also* DRESSLER, *supra* note 71, at 106 n.30.

This proposal would be an improvement over the proposed reform that substitutes recklessness for knowledge as the mens rea of possessory offenses. Since the wilfully ignorant defendant is not innocent, this proposal seemingly avoids the punishment of innocent activity. However, it is not without costs of its own. It seemingly accepts the controversial thesis that the wilfully ignorant defendant is equally culpable as the defendant who possesses genuine knowledge, since it results in convicting wilfully ignorant defendants of the same offense as defendants who act knowingly. Thus the recommendation defended in the text accompaning notes 135-36, *infra*, appears to improve on this proposal.

133. Significantly, the examples of statutory reforms proposed by both Robbins and Dressler to solve the problem of wilful ignorance involve drug offenses. *See* Robbins, *supra* note 52, at 233; DRESSLER, *supra* note 71, at 106 n.30.

134. *See supra* note 52.

135. *See supra* text accompanying note 52.

136. This solution, however, would not eliminate all the problems associated with wilful ignorance. If the severity of the punishment for acting knowingly were greater than that for acting recklessly, and a wilfully ignorant defendant were punished more severely, the question of whether the defendant had acted knowingly would still have to be determined.

wisdom would indicate,[137] the problem of wilful ignorance is indeed amenable to this statutory solution. But this Article hypothesizes that the rule of law raises more fundamental concerns, requiring fidelity to the principles that underlie statutory law. The merits of this proposal cannot be evaluated without examining the reasons why legislatures require a mens rea of knowledge for many offenses, including possessory offenses, in the first place.[138] If sound principles explain why possessory offenses should require genuine knowledge, fidelity to law is not achieved by disregarding them and by redefining statutes so that reckless defendants are convicted of illegal possession. Such a proposal "solves" the problem by ignoring the principles that persuaded legislatures to define such offenses as they did.[139] A more defensible approach would ensure that these principles are respected.

Why do legislators require knowledge as the mens rea of possessory offenses? Should it be legally possible to commit a possessory offense recklessly? After all, recklessness suffices for liability for the majority of crimes. Why should possessory offenses be an exception to this general rule? To propose simply that knowledge should not be required for liability for possessory offenses is to advocate a return to an earlier era without inquiring why courts and commentators found that era so dissatisfying.[140] Criminal liability for possession of narcotics was first imposed by the Harrison Act of 1914.[141] In *Balint v. United States*,[142] the Supreme Court held that liability under this Act could be imposed despite the lack of knowledge that the substance possessed was a narcotic. Most state statutes based on the Harrison Act failed to include an explicit knowledge requirement.[143] Soon, however, the situation changed dramatically. The Uniform Controlled Substances Act of 1970, which provides that "a person may not knowingly or intentionally . . . possess

137. *See supra* part I.

138. Robbins proposes "the addition of recklessness or specific deliberate-ignorance provisions as a basis for conviction for particular crimes" without inquiring why the legislature employed a knowledge standard in the first place. *See* Robbins, *supra* note 52, at 233.

139. One commentator admits that "there may be reasons to punish wilfully ignorant behavior in situations in which we would not want to punish reckless behavior,' but declines to mention what these reasons are. *See* Charlow, *supra* note 22, at 1386.

140. For a historical discussion, see Richard G. Singer, *The Resurgence of Mens Rea: III—The Rise and Fall of Strict Criminal Liability*, 30 B.C. L. REV. 337, 387-88 (1989).

141. Harrison Act, ch. 1, 38 Stat. 785 (1914) (repealed 1970).

142. 258 U.S. 250 (1922).

143. *See* Singer, *supra* note 140, at 388.

a controlled substance,"[144] was adopted by almost every state.[145] Knowledge came to be the standard mens rea for drug offenses that include possession as an element. Even Washington, one of the only states not to have enacted the Uniform Act, does not make ignorance irrelevant, since it allows the lack of knowledge to function as an affirmative defense to liability.[146]

What accounts for this trend? The most plausible reason to require knowledge as the mens rea of possessory offenses is to avoid punishing persons whose activity is innocent. A concern that innocent activity might be punished arises with all anticipatory offenses. Possessory offenses are anticipatory;[147] their objective is not to punish possession itself—which is harmless—but to punish the harmful conduct that is facilitated and evidenced by possession.[148] A legal system committed to preserving personal freedom must be cautious in creating anticipatory offenses; such crimes expand state power exponentially. The central difficulty facing the legislature is to define carefully and narrowly the conduct prohibited by an anticipatory offense so that behavior that does not threaten harm is not proscribed.

Consider, for example, a statute prohibiting the possession of burglar's tools. The point of this statute, of course, is to prevent the illegal use of these tools. But even those persons whose purpose in possessing such tools is innocent are guilty of this anticipatory offense.[149] Thus, this statute clearly gives rise to anxiety that innocent activity will be punished.[150] However, the concern that innocent activity will be punished may seem less worrisome in the context of statutes proscribing the possession of various drugs. Schedule I narcotics

---

144. UNIF. CONTROLLED SUBSTANCES ACT § 401(a), 9 U.L.A. 36 (Supp. 1992). For the text of the federal controlled substances prohibition, see *supra* note 19.

145. *But see* State v. Ripley, 319 N.W.2d 129 (N.D. 1982) (noting that North Dakota's adaptation of the Uniform Act contains no culpability requirement).

146. *See* State v. Cleppe, 635 P.2d 435, 439-40 (Wash. 1981).

147. A few possessory offenses might not be anticipatory. Sometimes possession itself, as with the possession of radioactive materials, may be harmful.

148. *See* DRESSLER, *supra* note 71, at 72 ("Crimes of possession are 'inchoate' or incomplete offenses . . . . Their real purpose is to provide law enforcement officials with a legal mechanism by which to stop a person from performing some later, more dangerous, act."); Robinson, *supra* note 102, at 629 ("It is extremely difficult to argue that possession alone is really the harm or evil prohibited and punished by possession offenses."); Whitebread & Stevens, *supra* note 121, at 753 ("Possession of an object in and of itself is not the law's real concern."). *See also* Davidson, *supra* note 121, at 616-17.

149. *See* GEORGE FLETCHER, RETHINKING CRIMINAL LAW 198-99 (1978).

150. *See* Benton v. United States, 232 F.2d 341 (D.C. Cir. 1956).

have no legitimate medical use;[151] how can it be innocent to possess them? The key to answering this question is to understand the connection between possession and the requirement of an actus reus.

A fundamental principle of criminal liability is that all offenses require an actus reus.[152] This requirement is designed to insure that criminal liability is imposed only for what persons *do*. Like other fundamental principles of criminal liability, the requirement of an actus reus protects the moral rights of citizens by limiting the coercive power of the state to create and enforce criminal legislation. This requirement, however, is difficult to reconcile with the existence of anticipatory offenses in general, and of possessory offenses in particular. Possession itself does not seem to be an act.[153] What act(s) could such offenses proscribe? According to the Model Penal Code, possession *is* an act "if the possessor knowingly procured or received the thing possessed or was aware of his control thereof for a sufficient period to have been able to terminate his possession."[154] Otherwise, possession is *not* an act and may not be subjected to criminal liability.

Notice that this description of the actus reus of a possessory offense makes the concept of reckless possession incoherent: it is logically impossible to commit the actus reus of a possessory offense without knowingly procuring or receiving the thing possessed. Surely, however, the story does not end here. The issue of whether a possessory offense should require a mens rea of knowledge cannot be resolved by definitional stipulation. In the law of property, possession does not entail knowledge.[155] Why define crimes of possession so that their actus reus entails knowledge? The concept of reckless possession does not seem to be incoherent; it is easy to imagine that a person might procure or receive something without being aware that he has done so.

The relevant provisions of the Model Penal Code should be construed to express a normative rather than a conceptual point. In other words, the difficulty is not that the idea of reckless possession is logically incoherent, but that proscribing reckless possession would be morally objectionable.[156] Notice that the Model Penal Code does not characterize procurement or receipt (knowingly or otherwise) as the

---

151. *See* 21 U.S.C. § 812(b)(1)(B) (1988).

152. This requirement is critically examined in HUSAK, *supra* note 2, at 78-121.

153. "Possession is not, strictly speaking, an act." 1 LAFAVE & SCOTT, *supra* note 14, at 279.

154. MODEL PENAL CODE § 2.01(4) (Official Draft, review and commentaries, 1985).

155. *See, e.g.*, South Staffordshire Water Co. v. Sharman, 2 Q.B. 44 (1896).

156. Even though legislating an offense of reckless possession might be morally objectionable, it does not follow that such an offense need be unconstitutional.

complete description of the actus reus of a possessory offense. Clearly, a statute proscribing the immediate procurement or receipt of a prohibited item would sweep too broadly, punishing much behavior that is innocent. A person should not be criminally liable if he procures or receives an illegal substance for an innocent purpose. The most obvious (but not the only) such innocent purposes are to dispose of the prohibited item, or to surrender it to the authorities.[157] A well-drafted offense of possession should therefore allow a "grace period" before liability can be imposed.[158] For this reason, the Model Penal Code includes within its description of the actus reus of possession the requirement that a person must "have been able to terminate his possession."[159] Imposing liability on persons who had no opportunity to dispose of a prohibited item, although logically coherent, would be manifestly unfair. States came to appreciate the injustice of punishing unknowing possessors, and modified their statutes accordingly.[160]

The opportunity to terminate unlawful possession would not be especially valuable to those defendants who did not actually know that they possessed something illegal. Suppose the proposed statutory reforms were enacted and recklessness replaced knowledge as the mens rea of possessory offenses. A defendant would be required to take steps to terminate his possession of something he did not know he had, as long as he consciously disregarded a substantial and unjustifiable risk that he had it.[161] Confronted with the prospect of criminal liability for reckless

---

157. *See* People v. Mijares, 491 P.2d 1115 (Cal. 1971).

158. *See* 1 LAFAVE & SCOTT, *supra* note 14, at 280 n.47.

159. MODEL PENAL CODE § 2.01(4) (Official Draft, review and commentaries, 1985).

160. Two representative statements will suffice to indicate that many courts came to appreciate the injustice of punishing unknowing possessors. One court wrote: "Otherwise seeming 'possession' by accident or the design of another . . . would suffice; and it is not within the competency of the lawgiver to render that criminal which in its very nature is innocent and essentially nonculpable." State v. Labato, 80 A.2d 617, 622 (N.J. 1951). Another court, in holding that a statute proscribing "unknowing possession" of a controlled substance is unconstitutional, wrote: "It requires little imagination to visualize a situation in which a third party hands the controlled substance to an unknowing individual who then can be charged with and subsequently convicted for violation of [the statute] without ever having been aware of the substance he was given. A situation such as the above does indeed offend the nature of the conscious [sic]. The 'unknowing' possession of a dangerous drug cannot be made criminal." State v. Brown, 389 So. 2d 48, 51 (La. 1980).

161. Some of the concerns about punishing innocent behavior would be mollified by requiring that persons guilty of reckless possession must consciously disregard a *substantial* and *unjustifiable* risk. See the definition of recklessness in the MODEL PENAL CODE § 2.02(2)(c) (Official Draft, review and commentaries, 1985). It is difficult to anticipate the conditions under which jurors would find that the risk of illegal possession

possession, defendants would be required to invest substantial amounts of time and energy to ascertain whether they possessed something illegal.[162] Legislators should be very cautious before adopting a statutory reform that requires this effort. Many persons are employed in the legitimate business of importing legal goods from drug-producing countries. Surely the (potentially high) risk that drugs might be concealed among their legal imports must have occurred to such persons. The State should be reluctant to impose affirmative duties of inspection on these individuals. Changing the mens rea of possessory offenses from knowledge to recklessness will punish these persons for activities that might best be left beyond the reach of the criminal sanction. Contrary to the conventional wisdom that surrounds the principle of legality, the considerations of justice that oppose this statutory reform serve to protect law-abiding persons, and not only scoundrels.

It does not follow, however, that criminal liability should not be imposed on persons who are wilfully ignorant. Their conduct is not innocent, and they clearly deserve punishment. Liability, however, should not be imposed by changing the mens rea terms that appear in existing statutes[163]—or by redefining these terms.[164] The problem of wilful ignorance has proved intractable because commentators have sought to hold defendants liable for violating possessory offenses. But preferable alternatives are available. The key to a better solution is to identify exactly what a wilfully ignorant defendant did—or failed to do—that is the proper concern of the criminal law. This problem is easily solved. Most wilfully ignorant defendants allow themselves to be used in a criminal scheme by failing to inform themselves of the relevant facts. In many cases, it is relatively clear what such a defendant should have done to learn the truth. He need only have opened his suitcase, for example. In general, a defendant who is wilfully ignorant and thus is suspicious that he is committing the actus reus of a crime should be required to take whatever steps are *reasonable* to learn the facts.[165] If wilfully ignorant

---

is unjustifiable. Of course, the best guarantee that such possession is unjustifiable is the requirement that defendants have knowledge that they possess something illegal. The concern that persons will be punished for innocent behavior becomes more pressing to the extent that defendants are held liable for less than knowing possession.

162. The same result would follow if criminal liability were imposed for knowing possession, but knowledge were redefined pursuant to § 2.02(7) of the Model Penal Code, so that a person knows a fact if he "is aware of a high probability of its existence." *See* Marcus, *supra* note 36.

163. *See* Robbins, *supra* note 52.

164. *See* Marcus, *supra* note 36.

165. In this light, reconsider United States v. Jewell, 532 F.2d 697, 699 n.2 (9th Cir. 1976). Here the defendant, upon suspecting that his vehicle contained drugs, testified that he "looked in the glove box and under the front seat and in the trunk" and "didn't

defendants are to be held liable, the proper course is to draft a new statute that imposes reasonable duties of inspection on them. Presumably, such an offense would be less serious than that of knowing possession.

This recommendation differs in three crucial respects from the proposed statutory reforms critiqued here. First, the rejected reforms would impose duties of inspection and the threat of criminal liability on *all* reckless defendants,[166] not only on those who are wilfully ignorant. As a result, the rejected reform would create anxiety about the punishment of innocent activity. Second, the rejected reforms would impose criminal liability on reckless and wilfully ignorant defendants *for possession*. Thus these defendants would be punished for what they would have discovered had they made further inquiries, and not for their failure to have made such inquiries in the first place. The recommendation endorsed here provides a more accurate description of the guilty conduct that wilfully ignorant defendants actually perform. Finally, the recommendation endorsed here would allow liability to be imposed even on wilfully ignorant defendants whose suspicions were unfounded and who were not in possession of drugs after all. Since the new statute would punish the failure to make reasonable inquiries, and not possession per se, the existence of illegal drugs would be immaterial to liability. Theoretically, wilfully ignorant defendants who actually possessed illegal drugs would be guilty of the same offense as those who did not.[167] For these reasons, the proposed recommendation is preferable to the rejected reforms, and respects the deeper considerations of justice that underlie the principle of legality.

---

find anything." Drugs were eventually discovered in a secret compartment in the trunk. Is it clear that wilfully ignorant defendants should be required to search for secret compartments in which drugs may be concealed? Perhaps. New statutes that impose reasonable duties of inspection on wilfully ignorant defendants will shift the focus of inquiry away from the issue of whether such persons possess the moral equivalent of knowledge toward the question of what duties of inspection are reasonable.

166. A similar reform would achieve the same result by redefining knowledge to resemble recklessness. Duties of inspection and the threat of criminal liability would be imposed on defendants who were "aware of a high probability" that they possessed something illegal. *See* Marcus, *supra* note 36.

167. Of course, it would be very difficult to prove that a defendant was wilfully ignorant of an incriminating proposition p unless p were true. Still, the truth of p would not be required to impose criminal liability.

[7]

ESSAY

IGNORANCE OF LAW *IS* AN EXCUSE — BUT ONLY FOR THE VIRTUOUS

*Dan M. Kahan**

> If you want to know the law and nothing else, you must look at it as a bad man, who cares only for the material consequences which such knowledge enables him to predict, not as a good one, who finds his reasons for conduct, whether inside the law or outside of it, in the vaguer sanctions of conscience.
>
> Oliver Wendell Holmes, Jr.[1]

> It is no doubt true that there are many cases in which the criminal could not have known that he was breaking the law, but to admit [mistake of law as an] excuse at all would be to encourage ignorance where the law-maker has determined to make men know and obey, and justice to the individual is rightly outweighed by the larger interests on the other side of the scales.
>
> Oliver Wendell Holmes, Jr.[2]

It's axiomatic that "ignorance of the law is no excuse." My aim in this essay is to examine what the "mistake of law doctrine"[3] reveals about the relationship between criminal law and morality in general and about the law's understanding of moral responsibility in particular.

The conventional understanding of the mistake of law doctrine rests on two premises, which are encapsulated in the Holmesian epigrams with which I've started this essay. The first is *liberal positivism.* As a descriptive claim, liberal positivism holds that the content of the law can be identified without reference to morality: one needn't be a good man to perceive what's lawful, Holmes tells us;

* Professor of Law, University of Chicago Law School. B.A. 1986, Middlebury; J.D. 1989, Harvard. — Ed. I am grateful to the Russell J. Parsons & Jerome S. Weiss Funds for Faculty Research at the University of Chicago Law School for generous financial support; to Albert Alschuler, Kate Anderson, Darryl Brown, Elizabeth Garrett, Jack Goldsmith, Tracey Meares, Martha Nussbaum, John Parry, and Eric Posner for instructive comments on an earlier draft; and to Jason Fliegel for first-rate research assistance.

1. Oliver Wendell Holmes, Jr., *The Path of the Law*, 10 HARV. L. REV. 457, 459 (1897).

2. OLIVER WENDELL HOLMES, THE COMMON LAW 41 (Belknap Press 1963) (1881).

3. I will use this phrase as a generic shorthand for the proposition that neither ignorance of the existence of penal law nor a mistake as to the meaning of that law is (ordinarily) an excuse. *See generally* JOSHUA DRESSLER, UNDERSTANDING CRIMINAL LAW 147 (2d ed. 1995) (setting forth rule and exceptions).

one need only understand the consequences in store if one should choose to act badly.[4] The normative side of liberal positivism urges us to see the independence of law from morality as a good thing. In a pluralistic society, the law should aspire to be comprehensible to persons of diverse moral views. What's more, it should avoid embodying within itself a standard of culpability or blame that depends on an individual's acceptance of any such view as orthodox; in a liberal society, even the bad man can be a good citizen so long as he lives up to society's rules.[5]

Liberal positivism supports denying a mistake of law defense when combined with a second premise: the *utility of legal knowledge.*[6] Under the liberal positivist view, the law disclaims any reliance on the moral knowledge of citizens, as well as any ambition to make them value morality for its own sake. Accordingly, to promote good (that is, law-abiding) conduct, it becomes imperative that citizens be made aware of the content of the law and the consequences of breaking it. Hence, the law shows no mercy for those who claim to be ignorant of what the criminal law proscribes, a position that maximizes citizens' incentive to learn the rules that "the law-maker has determined to make men know and obey."[7]

I want to challenge the accuracy of this account of why ignorance of law does not excuse. In its place, I'll suggest an alternative understanding, which rests on premises diametrically opposed to the Holmesian aphorisms that undergird the classic account.

The first premise of this anti-Holmesian conception is *legal moralism.*[8] This principle asserts that law is suffused with morality and, as a result, can't ultimately be identified or applied law without the making of moral judgments. It asserts, too, that individuals are appropriately judged by the law not only for the law-abiding quality of

4. On the independence of law from morals, see H.L.A. HART, THE CONCEPT OF LAW 185-212 (2d ed. 1994).

5. On the connection between legal positivism and liberal political theory, see Jeremy Waldron, *Kant's Legal Positivism,* 109 HARV. L. REV. 1535 (1996).

6. Jerome Hall, at least, viewed liberal positivism as more or less sufficient to support the mistake of law doctrine. *See* JEROME HALL, GENERAL PRINCIPLES OF CRIMINAL LAW 383 (2d ed. 1960) ("[T]here is a basic incompatibility between asserting that the law is what certain officials declare it to be . . . and asserting, also . . . that the law is, what defendants or their lawyers believed it to be."). For a compelling rebuttal, see GEORGE P. FLETCHER, RETHINKING CRIMINAL LAW § 9.3, at 733-34 (1978).

7. HOLMES, *supra* note 2, at 41; *see also* GLANVILLE WILLIAMS, CRIMINAL LAW: THE GENERAL PART 289 (2d ed. 1961) (justifying the doctrine on the same grounds).

8. For a general account of this idea and a discussion of the tension between liberalism and a conception of punishment that takes account of an offender's character and values, see Jeffrie G. Murphy, *Legal Moralism and Liberalism,* 37 ARIZ. L. REV. 73 (1995).

their actions but also for the moral quality of their values, motivations, and emotions — in a word, for the quality of their *characters*.[9]

The second premise of the anti-Holmesian view can be called the *prudence of obfuscation*. Moral judgments are too rich and particular to be subdued by any set of abstract rules; as a result, law will always embody morality only imperfectly. That means that from the standpoint of legal moralism, private knowledge of the law *isn't* unambiguously good. The more readily individuals can discover the law's content, the more readily they'll be able to discern, and exploit, the gaps between what's immoral and what's illegal. The law must therefore employ strategies to discourage citizens from gaining knowledge for this purpose. One is to deny an excuse for ignorance of law. Punishing those who mistakenly believe their conduct to be legal promotes good (that is, moral) behavior less through encouraging citizens to learn the law — an objective that could in fact be more completely realized by excusing at least some mistakes — than by creating hazards for those who choose to rely on what *they think* they know about the law. By denying a mistake of law defense, the law is saying, contra Holmes, that if a citizen suspects the law fails to prohibit some species of immoral conduct, the only certain way to avoid criminal punishment is to be a good person rather than a bad one.

This anti-Holmesian account, I'll argue, not only offers a superior explanation of why ignorance of the law is *not* ordinarily regarded as an excuse; it also does a better job in explaining why it sometimes *is*. Sometimes it's a crime to engage in an act — for example, omitting to file a tax return or failing to report certain financial transactions — that wouldn't be viewed as immoral were it not for the existence of a legal duty. Crimes of this sort are often referred to as *malum prohibitum* — wrong because prohibited — and are distinguished from crimes that are *malum in se* — wrong in themselves independent of law. Malum prohibitum crimes are the ones most likely to be interpreted as permitting mistake of law defenses.[10] This aspect of the doctrine defies both premises of the classic position: to distinguish malum prohibitum crimes from ma-

9. For the exploration of this theme in connection with various other doctrines of substantive criminal law, see Kyron Huigens, *Virtue and Inculpation*, 108 HARV. L. REV. 1423 (1995), and Dan M. Kahan & Martha C. Nussbaum, *Two Conceptions of Emotion in Criminal Law*, 96 COLUM. L. REV. 269 (1996).

10. *See, e.g.*, Meir Dan-Cohen, *Decision Rules and Conduct Rules: On Acoustic Separation in Criminal Law*, 97 HARV. L. REV. 625, 646 (1984); Dan M. Kahan, *Is* Chevron *Relevant to Federal Criminal Law?*, 110 HARV. L. REV. 469, 478-79 (1996); Michael L. Travers, Comment, *Mistake of Law in Mala Prohibita Crimes*, 62 U. CHI. L. REV. 1301 (1995).

lum in se ones, courts must employ moral judgments of the sort that liberal positivism forbids; and by allowing a mistake of law defense for malum prohibitum crimes, courts relax citizens' incentives to learn the law. Excusing someone for ignorance of a malum prohibitum crime makes perfect sense, however, under the anti-Holmesian view: since morality abstracted from law has nothing to say about the underlying conduct, a person can't be expected to rely on her perception of morality rather than her understanding of what such laws prohibit; because even a good person could make that kind of mistake in such circumstances, the defendant is excused.

A final advantage associated with the anti-Holmesian understanding of mistake of law is that it more completely defends the doctrine from the standard criticism made of it. Denying a mistake of law defense, it is said, sanctions punishment of the morally blameless.[11] The classic conception demurs: "[J]ustice to the individual is rightly outweighed by the larger interests on the other side of the scales."[12] But the anti-Holmesian conception goes further, showing that the standard criticism rests on a truncated understanding of when punishment is just: a person is rightly condemned as a criminal wrongdoer not only for knowingly choosing to violate the law, but also for exhibiting the kind of character failing associated with insufficient commitment to the moral norms embodied in the community's criminal law.

My argument will unfold in three Parts, each of which tells the story of a citizen who made, or at least claimed to have made, a mistake of law. Part I describes the case of Julio Marrero, a federal prison guard who reasonably but mistakenly concluded that he was authorized to carry a handgun; the failure of his mistake of law defense discredits the claim that the doctrine is geared toward maximizing citizens' incentive to learn the law. Part II takes up the case of Cleora Olive King; her conviction for possession of a controlled substance exposes the jaundiced eye with which the law regards those who do what *they think* is legal rather than what *they know* is moral. Part III examines the case of John Cheek, an offender

11. *See, e.g.*, FLETCHER, *supra* note 6, § 9.3, at 731, 735; Douglas Husak & Andrew von Hirsch, *Culpability and Mistake of Law*, *in* ACTION AND VALUE IN CRIMINAL LAW 157, 159, 174 (Stephen Shute et al. eds., 1993); John T. Parry, *Reasonable Reliance on Official Interpretations of Criminal Law: Entrapment by Estoppel, Mistake of Law, and the Risk Against Estopping the Government*, 25 AM. J. CRIM. L. (forthcoming 1997); *cf.* John Calvin Jeffries, Jr., *Legality, Vagueness, and the Construction of Penal Statutes*, 71 VA. L. REV. 189, 209 (1985) ("If notice of illegality is an essential prerequisite to the fairness of punishment, how can the law be indifferent to claims of honest and reasonable mistake?").

12. HOLMES, *supra* note 2, at 41.

whose right to assert a mistake of law defense for criminal tax evasion proves that ignorance of the law *is* an excuse — but only for the virtuous.

I. *Marrero:* The Impudence of Legal Knowledge

Who exactly is the mistake of law doctrine afraid of? The answer suggested by the classic view is the *strategically heedless.* Were mistake of law a defense, a person bent on violating the rights of others — Holmes's "bad man" — could evade punishment by remaining studiously ignorant of his legal duties.

But the specter of strategic heedlessness is a fairly obvious piece of misdirection. To be sure, strict liability for mistakes of law takes the profit out of deliberate ignorance, but it's such a wildly overinclusive solution to that problem that it's impossible to view the strategically heedless as more than a bit player in the mistake of law drama. The real protagonist is someone else; to see who, consider *People v. Marrero.*[13]

Julio Marrero was charged with unlicensed possession of a handgun. When police arrested him (at 1:00 a.m. at a Manhattan disco), Marrero protested that he was authorized to carry the weapon under New York law because he was a guard at a federal prison in nearby Danbury, Connecticut.[14] Marrero's understanding of the law was mistaken.

But understandably so. New York's gun law expressly exempted "peace officers,"[15] a term defined, under a section of the state's criminal procedure code, to include "correction officers of any state correctional facility or of any penal correctional institution."[16] Marrero concluded that "any penal correctional institution," as distinguished from "any *state* correctional facility," meant any *federal* prison. That was how his instructor in a local criminal justice course explained it to him, and it was also how the statutes were understood by local gun dealers, who routinely sold weapons to federal prison guards without demanding proof that the guards were licensed to carry such weapons.[17]

Indeed, Marrero's reading of the law was so plausible that the courts nearly accepted it as correct. The trial court dismissed the

13. 507 N.E.2d 1068 (N.Y. 1987).

14. *See* 507 N.E.2d at 1068-69; David De Gregorio, Comment, People v. Marrero *and Mistake of Law,* 54 Brook. L. Rev. 229, 231-33 (1988).

15. N.Y. Penal Law § 265.20(a)(1)(a) (McKinney 1987).

16. N.Y. C.P.L. 2.10(26) (McKinney 1987).

17. *See* De Gregorio, *supra* note 14, at 240-41 & n.54.

indictment after ruling that federal corrections officers were indeed "peace officers" for purposes of the gun law;[18] that decision was overturned on appeal, but by a court that divided 3-2.[19] At the end of the day, three of six judges had sided with Marrero's interpretation. It's hard to imagine a more demonstrably reasonable mistake of law.

At trial, however, Marrero was not afforded the opportunity to assert a mistake of law defense to the jury, or even to present evidence about the reasonable basis of that mistake. According to the trial court, and ultimately to the New York Court of Appeals, Marrero's ignorance of the law — however reasonable — was no excuse.[20]

Even this aspect of the case, however, was subject to reasonable disagreement. It's usually accepted that a reasonable mistake of law *is* a defense when the mistake relates to an issue of law "collateral" to the "penal law" and negates the mental element of the crime.[21] For example, a person commits bigamy only if she knows that the person she is marrying is already married to someone else; although she wouldn't have a defense if she professed to be unaware that bigamy is a crime, she might if she made a reasonable mistake about the effectiveness of an out-of-state divorce proceeding — an issue collateral to the penal law — and thus didn't *know* that the man she was marrying was the spouse of another.[22] By the same token, the court could have held that Marrero's reasonable mistake about whether a federal prison counts as "any penal correctional facility" negated the requirement that he *know* he wasn't a "peace officer" for purposes of the gun possession statute.

One could try to distinguish *Marrero* from the bigamy case on the ground that the law defining "peace officer" wasn't genuinely collateral to the criminal offense charged. But this distinction isn't analytically compelled: Why regard the *criminal procedure code's* definition of "peace officer" as any less collateral to the New York gun possession statute than is the law defining who counts as an-

18. *See* People v. Marrero, 404 N.Y.S.2d 832 (Sup. Ct. 1978).

19. *See* People v. Marrero, 422 N.Y.S.2d 384 (App. Div. 1979).

20. *See* People v. Marrero, 507 N.E.2d 1068 (N.Y. 1987).

21. *See, e.g.*, United States v. Anton, 683 F.2d 1011, 1018 (7th Cir. 1982) (holding that the issue of what constitutes "consent of the Attorney General" to re-entry following deportation is a "collateral" issue for mistake of law purposes). *See generally* MODEL PENAL CODE, § 2.02 cmt. 11 (1985); 1 WAYNE R. LAFAVE & AUSTIN W. SCOTT, JR., SUBSTANTIVE CRIMINAL LAW § 5.1(d), at 585-86 (1986).

22. *See, e.g.*, Squire v. State, 46 Ind. 459, 463 (1874). This conclusion is not universal, however. *See generally* WAYNE R. LAFAVE & AUSTIN W. SCOTT, JR., CRIMINAL LAW 408-09 (2d ed. 1986) (noting contrary authority).

other's spouse to the crime of bigamy? Either characterization of the definition of the peace officer statute — collateral or intrinsic to penal law — is conceptually supportable; to choose between them requires a reason.

The New York Court of Appeals's reason for denying a mistake of law defense was the Holmesian *utility of knowledge* principle. The point of punishing the legally mistaken, the court explained, is "to encourage the societal benefit of individuals' knowledge of and respect for the law."[23] Were Marrero to be afforded a defense, "[m]istakes about the law would be encouraged."[24]

There's nothing persuasive in this account. The anxiety of strategic heedlessness obviously rang false in Marrero's individual case. Marrero hadn't deliberately shielded himself from legal knowledge; rather he had tenaciously attempted to ferret it out, displaying exactly the type of dedication to legal learning that the utility of knowledge purports to value.

Nor would an excuse for Marrero have promoted strategic heedlessness in others. Marrero sought to present a *reasonable mistake of law* defense. Had the court sided with Marrero, it would have been establishing, in effect, a negligence standard with respect to the existence or meaning of the law defining who counts as a "peace officer" under the New York gun possession statute. Under such a standard, heedlessness would be a foolish strategy, for a lawbreaker who deliberately failed to take reasonable steps to learn the law would be deemed negligent and hence denied a defense.

In fact, if the goal were truly to maximize private knowledge of law, a negligence standard would be unambiguously superior to a strict liability standard. This is so because the value of learning the law is always higher when the law excuses reasonable mistakes of law than when it doesn't.

A person will take reasonable steps to learn the law when the expected benefit of having legal information exceeds the expected cost of obtaining it.[25] This benefit can take a number of forms. If a person invests in learning the law, she might discover that some course of conduct that she would otherwise have engaged in — for example, carrying an unlicensed handgun — is unlawful and conse-

23. *Marrero,* 507 N.E.2d at 1069.

24. 507 N.E.2d at 1073.

25. *See* Louis Kaplow & Steven Shavell, *Private Versus Socially Optimal Provision of Ex Ante Legal Advice,* 8 J.L. ECON. & ORG. 306, 307 (1992); Steven Shavell, *Legal Advice About Contemplated Acts: The Decision to Obtain Advice, Its Social Desirability, and Protection of Confidentiality,* 17 J. LEGAL STUD. 123, 127 (1988).

quently not worth undertaking given the penalty. Alternatively, she might learn that some course of conduct that she otherwise would have forgone is in fact perfectly legal and hence worth engaging in after all. But unless she believes the possibility of some such benefit is sufficiently high, she won't bother to invest in learning the law and will instead rely on her untutored judgment about what the law happens to be.[26]

The probability of realizing a benefit sufficient to defray the cost of legal research will always be higher when the law excuses reasonable mistakes of law than when it doesn't. As Marrero himself discovered, even after a person takes reasonable steps to learn the law, there always remains some residual risk that a court will disagree with that person's conclusions. In a regime that imposes strict liability, that person will be punished notwithstanding her reasonable effort to learn the law; the prospect that one's legal information will turn out to be incorrect thus diminishes the value of obtaining such information ex ante. Under a negligence standard, however, reasonable mistakes of law *are* a defense; accordingly, once a person takes reasonable steps to learn the law, she is insured against punishment *even if* it turns out that her information is mistaken. Because the expected value of having legal information is thus higher under a negligence standard than under a strict liability standard, more individuals will conclude that investing in legal knowledge is worthwhile if the law in fact excuses reasonable mistakes.[27]

26. *See generally* Richard S. Murphy & Erin A. O'Hara, *Mistake of Federal Criminal Law: A Study of Coalitions and Costly Information,* 5 SUP. CT. ECON. REV. 217, 227-30 (1997) (modeling incentives to acquire legal information).

27. This point can be illustrated mathematically. Imagine a person is contemplating conduct that would confer a benefit of 40. Before she engages in legal research, she believes that the conduct is illegal and that the expected penalty for engaging in it is 100. She won't engage in the conduct at that point because the expected return is 40 - 100, or -60. Now imagine that the cost of doing "reasonable research" into the law is 5; imagine further that the person believes there is a 50% chance that the research will give her a reasonable belief — one she estimates, say, is 80% likely to be correct — that the conduct is actually legal. She will invest in learning the law at that point only if the 50% chance that her prior belief will change in this way is worth more than 5. It will be under a negligence rule: in that case, the expected value of obtaining the information is the benefit from acting on the basis of a changed belief about the legality of the conduct, discounted by the likelihood that her belief will change, minus the cost of obtaining the information, or (40)(0.5) - 5, which equals 15. The 0.2 chance that the changed belief will prove to be wrong — that is, that the conduct engaged in will be deemed illegal, contrary to the actor's expectations — does not diminish the value of obtaining the information, because in that event the actor's mistake will be reasonable and hence furnish a defense to criminal liability. Under a strict liability rule, however, such a mistake would be no defense; as a result, the actor would have to subtract from the expected value of obtaining and acting on favorable information not just the cost of getting that information, but also the expected penalty for acting on what turns out to be a *mistaken* reasonable belief, or (40)(.5) - 5 - (.2)(100), which equals -5. Since the expected value of obtaining and acting on favorable information under a strict liability rule is negative, the individual won't bother to invest in legal research.

The relative effects of strict liability and negligence in promoting legal knowledge expose the first crack in the classic conception of the mistake of law doctrine. Both strict liability and negligence punish the heedless; however, negligence rewards *all,* and strict liability only *some,* of the citizens who take reasonable steps to learn the law's commands. In other words, if the goal is only to protect society from the legally stupid, either strict liability or negligence will suffice; but if society genuinely aspires to make its citizens legally wise, it should pick negligence. The steadfast refusal of the law to excuse reasonable mistakes, then, displays much more ambivalence about private learning of the law than is suggested by the Holmesian utility of knowledge principle.

This ambivalence is laid bare by a second holding in *Marrero.* Marrero grounded his reasonable mistake of law defense in a New York statute that was meant to liberalize the common law position on when such mistakes excuse.[28] That statute — section 15.20(2) of the New York criminal code — provided:

> A person is not relieved of criminal liability for conduct because he engages in such conduct under a mistaken belief that it does not, as a matter of law, constitute an offense, unless such mistaken belief is founded upon an official statement of the law contained in (a) a statute or other enactment . . . or (d) an interpretation of the statute or law relating to the offense, officially made or issued by a public servant, agency, or body legally charged or empowered with the responsibility or privilege of administering, enforcing or interpreting such statute or law.[29]

Read literally, section 15.20(2) seemed to excuse Marrero: his mistake was "founded upon an official statement of the law contained in . . . a statute," namely, the criminal procedure code provision defining who qualifies as a "peace officer."

The New York Court of Appeals, however, rejected this argument.[30] According to the court, section 15.20(2) was modeled on section 2.04(3) of the Model Penal Code, which states:

> A belief that conduct does not legally constitute an offense is a defense to a prosecution for that offense based upon such conduct when . . . [a person] acts in reasonable reliance upon an official statement of the law, afterward determined to be invalid or erroneous, contained in . . . a statute or other enactment . . . .[31]

28. *See Marrero,* 507 N.E.2d at 1070.

29. N.Y. Penal Law § 15.20(2) (McKinney 1987).

30. *See Marrero,* 507 N.E.2d at 1070.

31. Model Penal Code § 2.04(3) (1985).

Marrero's mistake clearly didn't entitle him to a defense under this standard: the "statement of the law . . . contained in" the New York procedural code, and on which Marrero relied, was not "afterward determined to be invalid or erroneous"; only Marrero's private understanding of that statement was. As construed by the court of appeals, section 15.20(2), like section 2.04(3) of the Model Penal Code, excuses reasonable reliance only on the mistakes of courts, legislatures, and other *official interpreters,* and not reasonable reliance on a *private citizen's* own mistakes.

But was it proper for the court of appeals to read the language of section 15.20(2) as if it were identical to section 2.04(3)? That depends on how far one thinks the New York legislature was trying to go in modifying the common law position. The court of appeals concluded that the legislature meant to go as far as the drafters of the Model Penal Code, who decided to permit reasonable mistake as a defense only when a citizen was misled by a *government official;* the court of appeals concluded that the legislature, contrary to the literal meaning of the statutory text, did not intend to take the additional step of excusing even reasonable *private* misreadings of statutes because the idea that the legislature meant to do something that outrageous was, to the court, all but unthinkable:

> [T]he idea was simultaneously to encourage the public to read and rely on *official statements* of the law, not to have individuals *conveniently and personally* question the validity and interpretation of the law and act on that basis. If later the statute was invalidated, one who mistakenly acted in reliance on the authorizing statute would be relieved of criminal liability. That makes sense and is fair. To go further does not make sense and would create a legal chaos based on individual selectivity.[32]
>
> . . . .
>
> . . . If defendant's argument were accepted, the exception would swallow the rule. . . . There would be an infinite number of mistake of law defenses which could be devised from a good-faith, perhaps reasonable but mistaken, interpretation of criminal statutes, many of which are concededly complex. . . . Our holding comports with a statutory scheme which was not designed to allow false and diversionary stratagems to be provided for many more cases than the statutes contemplated. This would not serve the ends of justice but rather would serve game playing and evasion from properly imposed criminal responsibility.[33]

By now it should be clear who the mistake of law doctrine is really afraid of. It's not, or at least not only, the strategically heed-

32. *Marrero,* 507 N.E.2d at 1071 (emphasis added).
33. 507 N.E.2d at 1073.

less, but also the impudently inquisitive — the lay interpreter who isn't content to rely on her untutored judgment, supplemented by what officials tell her the law means, but who insists on inspecting the law for herself and forming her own admittedly reasonable view about what the law is saying. It is not that person's deliberate ignorance of, but rather her exacting attention to, the law's fine points that we must regard as a "false and diversionary stratagem[ ]," a form of "game playing and evasion" that we should construe the law to discourage. But this question remains: What exactly makes this person's diligent efforts to decode the law so unwelcome?

II. *King:* Do What's Right, Not What You *Think* Is Legal

To see why the law might regard a little legal knowledge as dangerous and a lot as even more so, consider the story of Cleora Olive King. King was convicted of possession of a "controlled substance," namely, the stimulant phentermine.[34] On appeal, King argued that phentermine wasn't on the state's controlled substance list at the time she possessed it. The Minnesota Supreme Court rejected that contention, as well as any suggestion that King had a viable mistake of law defense about the controlled status of the drug: "It is a deeply rooted concept of our jurisprudence that ignorance of the law is no excuse."[35]

King wasn't the only one surprised to discover that phentermine was a controlled substance at the time she was arrested; so was the Minnesota legislature. Only the day before King was charged, the legislature had enacted a statute putting phentermine on the list but with an effective date of three months hence.[36] What the legislature didn't know when it passed this statute, however, was that phentermine was already a controlled substance in Minnesota and had been for over a year.[37]

The source of the legislature's mistake was the complexity of the scheme by which drugs become controlled substances. Under the Uniform Controlled Substances Act, there are three ways to add substances to the state's list: by statute, by administrative regulation, and by what amounts to legal osmosis — the automatic inclu-

34. *See* State v. King, 257 N.W.2d 693, 695 (Minn. 1977).

35. 257 N.W.2d at 697.

36. *See* 257 N.W.2d at 698 (Otis, J., dissenting).

37. *See* 257 N.W.2d at 695.

sion of any substance controlled by federal law.[38] When a federally controlled substance is automatically added to a state's list — as was the case for phentermine in Minnesota — no public notice ever needs to appear in any species of state law; rather, notice must appear only if a state agency decides to *exclude* a federally controlled substance from the state's list.[39] Consequently, to determine whether a particular substance is controlled under state law, one must carefully consult not just state but also federal law.[40] It's not that hard to miss something, as the Minnesota legislature's own mistake about phentermine suggests. No one can seriously maintain that the Uniform Controlled Substances Act was designed to make it easy for members of the general public to figure out the law.

On the contrary, the Act reflects an undisguised resentment of such knowledge, and for a very simple reason: it enables loopholing. Substances on a jurisdiction's controlled substance list are defined by their chemical composition. But it's often possible to alter the composition of such a substance slightly without changing its pharmacological effects. This creates the opportunity for a legally adroit chemist to evade punishment by continually reformulating her wares in response to legislative attempts to ban them. In order to deal with this form of strategic behavior, federal and state law delegates the power to designate controlled substances to administrative agencies, which can respond much more quickly than can legislatures to the development of new designer drugs.[41]

The loopholing problem generalizes. Because the means by which bad people can invade the rights of others are infinitely numerous and diverse, any attempt to specify them all by statute is bound to be incomplete. If the law prohibits altering or counterfeiting vehicle titles, for example, offenders will attempt to achieve the same effect by inducing state agencies to issue genuine titles con-

38. *See* Uniform Controlled Substances Act § 201(d), 9 U.L.A. pt. II, at 28-29 (1988); Curry v. State, 649 S.W.2d 833, 836 (Ark. 1983) (noting that a federally controlled substance becomes a state controlled substance "by operation of law" unless a state agency affirmatively blocks designation).

39. *See* Uniform Controlled Substances Act § 201(d), 9 U.L.A. pt. II, at 28-29 (1988).

40. *See, e.g., King,* 257 N.W.2d at 698 ("Had defendant made an effort to ascertain whether her possession was lawful, she, as any other member of the public, would have been directed to the Federal Register and the delegation provisions here considered . . . .").

41. *See, e.g.,* Touby v. United States, 500 U.S. 160, 163 (1991) (discussing federal delegation to administrative agencies).

taining false information;[42] if it prohibits the interstate transportation of forged checks, they'll wait until they cross state lines before signing them;[43] if it bans sawed-off shotguns defined as those with barrels of less than 17.5 inches, they'll meticulously cut them down to 18.[44] Delegating power to an agency to close such gaps as quickly as they are discovered is one device for responding to the law's persistent incompleteness; another, even more common one is *prudent obfuscation* of the law's outer periphery.[45] Statutory terms like "fraud," "thing of value," and criminal "enterprise" are vague enough to "encompass a wide range of criminal activity, taking many different forms and [attracting] a broad array of perpetrators operating in many different ways."[46] They remove offenders' temptation to look for loopholes ex ante by giving courts the flexibility to adapt the law to innovative forms of crime ex post.

The mistake of law doctrine reinforces the prudent obfuscation strategy.[47] Strict liability makes loopholing hazardous; it says, in effect, that the law will punish any misstep should a person attempt to negotiate the deliberate complexities and uncertainties of the law. A negligence standard, in contrast, would actually magnify the loopholing problem — not by encouraging ignorance, but by increasing the returns from investing in legal knowledge. Were the law to excuse reasonable mistakes of law, designer drug manufacturers and other strategically inquisitive wrongdoers would be rewarded not only for discovering actual loopholes, but also for discovering what they *mistakenly but reasonably perceived* to be loopholes.[48] Presumably there would be lots of mistakes like those,

42. *Cf.* Moskal v. United States, 498 U.S. 103, 108 (1990) (construing the statute to avoid such a loophole).

43. *Cf.* McElroy v. United States, 455 U.S. 642, 655 (1982) (refusing to read the statute in a manner that would create such a loophole).

44. *Cf.* Staples v. United States, 511 U.S. 600, 634 (1994) (Stevens, J., dissenting) (criticizing the majority for reading the statute to exacerbate such a loophole).

45. *See generally* Dan M. Kahan, *Lenity and Federal Common Law Crimes*, 1994 Sup. Ct. Rev. 345, 409-12 (discussing the use of statutory vagueness to deter loopholing).

46. H.J. Inc. v. Northwestern Bell Tel. Co., 492 U.S. 229, 248-49 (1989) (discussing "enterprise" as used in RICO); *see also* United States v. Maze, 414 U.S. 395, 405-06 (1974) (Burger, C.J., dissenting) ("When a 'new' fraud develops — as constantly happens — the mail fraud statute becomes a stopgap device to deal on a temporary basis with the new phenomenon, until particularized legislation can be developed and passed to deal directly with the evil."); Kahan, *supra* note 10, at 475-77, 481-82 (discussing the generative character of federal fraud and property offenses).

47. *Cf.* Stephen McG. Bundy & Einer Elhauge, *Knowledge About Legal Sanctions*, 92 Mich. L. Rev. 261, 287-88 (1993) (recognizing the utility of vagueness and restrictions on dissemination of legal information if law is believed to be underinclusive).

48. Again, this point can be illustrated mathematically. Imagine an individual believes that the benefit of some form of unlawful conduct is 40, and the expected penalty 100; she won't engage in that conduct because the expected return is 40 – 100, or –60. But now imag-

given the deliberate complexity of criminal laws such as the Uniform Controlled Substances Act. Indeed, because a negligence standard would give a defense to anyone who could say that she reasonably understood her conduct to be legal, it would almost completely vitiate the benefits of statutory vagueness, which seeks to combat loopholing precisely by making the outer reaches of the law reasonably uncertain.

The use of prudent obfuscation to discourage loopholing might be thought to raise a puzzle from a deterrence point of view. If the law aspires to be deliberately vague and complex, and if it tries to discourage rather than reward inquiry into the fine points of law by punishing even reasonable mistakes, how can it expect individuals who want to be law-abiding to know what their legal duties are?

The answer is supplied by *legal moralism.* Most individuals know how to live law-abiding lives without ever consulting their community's criminal code. This is so because they assume that the criminal law tracks certain basic moral norms, with which the law-abiders and law-breakers alike *are* thoroughly familiar. It seems unlikely, for example, that King, who made her living as a prostitute, not as a designer-drug manufacturer, ever looked up phentermine on Minnesota's controlled substances list; yet her assumption that the drug was illicit is confirmed by her concealment of it in a small foil packet discovered in her underwear upon her arrest for soliciting.[49] Even the loopholer is aware that her conduct conflicts with the moral norms that determine criminal law, or else it would never occur to her that there was a need to search out a means of evading punishment for her behavior. The law's resentment of legal knowledge is consistent with deterrence, then, be-

ine that she believes that the cost of loopholing — that is, searching for an analogous form of apparently unregulated conduct — is 5; imagine further that the individual believes that there is a 50% chance that such searching will disclose conduct that she is 80% sure (that is, reasonably sure) is legal. Whether loopholing will be worthwhile to that person at that point turns on the standard for assessing mistakes of law. Under a negligence standard, loopholing pays: the expected value of loopholing is the benefit from engaging in the analogous but apparently unregulated form of conduct, discounted by the likelihood that the person will discover such conduct, minus the cost of searching for it, or (40)(.5) - 5, which equals 15. There's a .2 chance, of course, that what appears to be a loophole won't be one in fact — that is, that the analogous conduct will also turn out to be illegal, contrary to the individual's expectations. But because that mistake of law will be deemed reasonable and hence a defense, this pseudo-loophole will be worth just as much as a genuine one. Loopholing won't be worthwhile, however, under a strict liability rule. For in that case, the individual must subtract from the expected value of loopholing not just the cost of such activity, but also the expected penalty for acting on what turns out to be a mistaken reasonable belief, or 15 - (.2)(100), which equals -5. Because the expected value of loopholing is negative, strict liability should deter the individual from seeking to evade the law in that manner.

49. *See* State v. King, 257 N.W.2d 693, 698 n.4 (Minn. 1977).

cause the law expects that in the absence of such knowledge individuals will be more reliably guided by their knowledge of what is moral.

This expectation, moreover, inflicts another blow to the classic conception of the mistake of law doctrine. The Holmesian understanding asserts that the doctrine seeks to encourage knowledge of the law *(utility of knowledge)* in order to compensate for the law's own indifference to the moral goodness of citizens' motivations *(liberal positivism)*. The truth, though, is that the doctrine attempts to discourage legal knowledge *(prudent obfuscation)* so that individuals will be more inclined to behave morally *(legal moralism)*. Strict liability warns citizens *not* to be Holmes's bad man. It tells them that if they suspect that some species of immoral conduct may evade the reach of the law, the only sure way to avoid punishment is to do what they *know* is right, not what they *think* is legal.[50]

This account makes it easier to see why *Marrero* came out the way it did. Marrero ignored the law's injunction to do what's right rather than what one thinks is legal. New York's restrictive gun possession law embodies its citizens' strong antipathy toward, and fear of, handguns. But rather than defer to those norms, Marrero decided to be strategic, availing himself of what must have appeared even to him to be a largely fortuitous gap in the law. That's the attitude that made the court see in Marrero's efforts to decode the law not an earnest and laudable attempt to obey but rather a "false and diversionary stratagem[ ]," a form of "game playing and evasion."[51] Other facts, not even mentioned by the court, also likely played a role: that the policy of the federal prison at which Marrero worked forbade guards to carry guns either on or off duty; that Marrero had supplied his girlfriend and another companion with guns, even though they clearly had no grounds for believing their possession to be lawful; and that Marrero menacingly reached for his weapon when the police approached him in the Manhattan club.[52] These facts might not have been formally relevant to the court's disposition, but they no doubt helped the court to see Mar-

50. *Cf.* Boyce Motor Lines, Inc. v. United States, 342 U.S. 337, 340 (1952) ("[M]ost statutes must deal with untold and unforeseen variations in factual situations, and the practical necessities of discharging the business of government inevitably limit the specificity with which legislators can spell out prohibitions. Consequently, no more than a reasonable degree of certainty can be demanded. Nor is it unfair to require that one who deliberately goes perilously close to an area of proscribed conduct shall take the risk that he may cross the line.").

51. People v. Marrero, 507 N.E.2d 1068, 1073 (N.Y. 1987).

52. *See* De Gregorio, *supra* note 14, at 231-32, 233 n.24.

rero as a Holmesian bad man. And in the eyes of the court, a Holmesian bad man is plenty bad enough to be designated a criminal.

Another way to see the doctrine's repudiation of liberal positivism is to consider the relative effects of strict liability and negligence on *marginally legal behavior.* By marginally legal behavior, I mean conduct that is just barely legal because of its exceedingly close proximity to the line between what's lawful and what's not. This is exactly the kind of conduct that Holmes's bad man wants to engage in. A negligence standard makes engaging in such conduct relatively safe: even when the line between what's lawful and what's not is indistinct, individuals may approach it without apprehension so long as they have taken reasonable steps to ascertain where that line is drawn, for in that case inadvertent trespasses into the territory of illegality will be forgiven.

Strict liability, in contrast, is much less accommodating. It punishes persons who inadvertently cross the line notwithstanding their reasonable efforts to stay on the lawful side of it. To avoid this residual risk of penalty, some persons will choose to steer well clear of the line between lawful and unlawful behavior and thus forgo even marginally legal behavior.[53] From the point of view of liberal positivism, this chilling effect on marginally legal behavior is unfortunate, because the law expects no more from individuals than that they behave lawfully. But from the point of view of legal moralism, the chilling effect of strict liability is *good:* because of the persistent incompleteness of the law relative to morality, marginally lawful behavior — whether the distribution of an uncontrolled designer drug or the possession of an unregulated but dangerous firearm — is still likely to be immoral and thus worth deterring.

This preference for moral over purely legal motivation also sharpens the focus of the normative issue surrounding the mistake of law doctrine. The debate is ordinarily framed as one between retributivists, who object to the doctrine's supposed indifference to blameworthiness,[54] and utilitarians, who (like Holmes) defend punishing the blameless for the sake of securing important collective ends.[55] The grounding of the doctrine in legal moralism, however,

53. *See generally* Murphy & O'Hara, *supra* note 26, at 233-36.

54. *See, e.g.,* Husak & von Hirsch, *supra* note 11, at 158-59, 174; Edwin R. Keedy, *Ignorance and Mistake in the Criminal Law,* 22 HARV. L. REV. 75, 84-85 (1908).

55. *See* HOLMES, *supra* note 2, at 41; WILLIAMS, *supra* note 7, at 289; *cf.* 1 JOHN AUSTIN, LECTURES ON JURISPRUDENCE 482 (reprint 1911) (Robert Campbell ed., 5th ed., London, John Murray 1885) (asserting that the rule is justified by the interest in avoiding fraud).

suggests that the debate is really about something else: not whether it's justified to punish the morally blameless, but rather *when* someone should be regarded as morally blameworthy. Critics of the doctrine view only those who knowingly choose to violate the law as deserving of punishment, whereas proponents are unwilling to excuse from blame a person who behaves immorally merely because she happens to believe (mistakenly) that her conduct is legal.

The proponents' stance is more compelling. Consider, first, a person who knows that some species of harmful conduct — whether assaulting a pregnant woman for the purpose of killing her fetus,[56] or writing a series of bad checks as part of a "check kiting" scheme[57] — is immoral, but (mistakenly) believes it to be legal. On any viable theory of morality, the choice to harm another in this way justifies condemnation, *whether or not* the conduct is unlawful. Because the person would deserve moral condemnation *even if* it turned out that such conduct was legal, it's obvious that her mistake about the legality of the conduct doesn't excuse her as a moral matter. Indeed, if the person comes to the (mistaken) conclusion that such conduct is lawful on the basis of legal research, we are likely to condemn her more, not less, severely: for in that case her action reflects not only the culpable choice to harm another, but also the culpable choice to search out means of evading accountability for such action. If there is a reason to afford such a person a legal excuse, that reason can't be that she is morally blameless.

Now consider the only slightly more complicated case of a person who engages in wrongful conduct mistakenly believing it to be both legal and moral. In her case, we couldn't say that she knowingly *chose* to do wrong. But we might well say that she was *culpably inattentive* to her moral obligations. The moral norms that typically inform the criminal law express judgments about the high worth of important goods and values.[58] We expect individuals — at least if they are mentally competent adults — to recognize and assent to these appraisals, and if they don't, we judge them negatively on that account.[59] Imagine a person who assaulted another out of

56. *Cf.* Keeler v. Superior Court, 470 P.2d 617 (Cal. 1970) (holding that such conduct is not within the terms of the state homicide statute).

57. *Cf.* Williams v. United States, 458 U.S. 279 (1982) (holding that a statute prohibiting "false statement" to a bank should be read not to reach check kiting).

58. *See generally* Jeffrie G. Murphy & Jean Hampton, Forgiveness and Mercy 25, 43-44 (1988); Dan M. Kahan, *What Do Alternative Sanctions Mean?*, 63 U. Chi. L. Rev. 591, 597-98 (1996).

59. *See* Leo Katz, Ill-Gotten Gains: Evasion, Blackmail, Fraud and Kindred Puzzles of the Law 128-30 (1996).

racial animus, or who engaged in sexual relations with a ten-year-old, and who professed to be unaware that such conduct was immoral (much less illegal). Rather than being a ground for sympathy, that person's moral ignorance would itself provide grounds for condemning her, for it would reveal that she doesn't care about things — the equal dignity of all persons, the psychological and physical well-being of children — that she ought to care about, and that she does care about other things — racial hatred, sexual domination of vulnerable and dependent persons — that she shouldn't.

This sensibility is grounded in an understanding of morality that's willing to blame people not just for knowingly choosing to do wrong, but also for having bad character. When we condemn someone for being inattentive to moral obligations, we are saying that she lacks the values that would have motivated a good person to perceive the real value of things.[60] This understanding of blame is commonplace in our ordinary moral practices: "But it was an accident!"; "So? If you had *cared* about me, you wouldn't have said that/done that/forgotten that." It's also commonplace in criminal law: the punishment of *negligent* homicides condemns persons for caring so little about others that they fail to perceive the unreasonable danger they are exposing them to;[61] the punishment of persons who kill because of unjustifiable anger or hate — even when those dispositions are unwilled and interfere with the capacity to conform to the law — condemns them for having the bad values that inspire bad emotions.[62] The mistake of law doctrine likewise condemns individuals for a character defect — namely, an insufficient commitment to the moral values that stand behind the criminal law.[63]

60. *Cf.* R.B. Brandt, *A Motivational Theory of Excuses in the Criminal Law, in* CRIMINAL JUSTICE: NOMOS XXVII 165, 176-77 (J. Roland Pennock & John W. Chapman eds., 1985) (suggesting a theory of blame that rests on dispositional commitment to appropriate values).

61. *See* R.A. Duff, *Choice, Character, and Criminal Liability*, 12 LAW & PHIL. 345, 349-50 (1993).

62. *See* Kahan & Nussbaum, *supra* note 9, at 313-14, 353.

63. Whether or not these values are universal, people do not always universally subscribe to them. Indeed, an individual whom we might be inclined to condemn for being inattentive to community norms might well owe her ignorance to her immersion in competing, subcommunity norms. Sometimes the law accommodates moral diversity of this kind. *See, e.g.*, Staples v. United States, 511 U.S. 600, 610-15 (1994) (reading a mistake of fact defense into the National Firearms Act to avoid criminalizing possession of weapons that are not condemned by common experience). More often, however, it does not, as reflected in the refusal of the law to recognize the so-called "cultural defense" — the claim that the defendant's ignorance of the law should be excused because the conduct in question is moral in her native land. *See generally* Note, *The Cultural Defense in the Criminal Law*, 99 HARV. L. REV. 1293 (1986). Obviously, individuals don't always "choose" their formative communities; the willingness of the law to condemn them for having the values that such unchosen attachments engender testifies to the depth of the law's commitment to appraising individuals for their characters. Whether a commitment this deep is warranted is another question.

III. *Cheek:* A Defense for the Virtuous

Not every mistake of law, however, displays bad character. When a person makes the kind of error that even a morally virtuous person could make, then her ignorance of the law *should* be an excuse. That is the moral of *Cheek v. United States.*[64]

Cheek neglected to file tax returns for several years. His defense to charges of criminal tax evasion was that he honestly believed he owed no tax on the salary he earned as a pilot for American Airlines. Cheek claimed to have formed this belief on the basis of lectures by members of a tax protest group, who persuaded him that wages were not taxable income for purposes of the federal tax code and that any form of income tax violated the Constitution. After being instructed that these beliefs were not a defense, the jury convicted.[65]

But the Supreme Court reversed. Reaffirming precedents of over a half century's standing, the Court held that a person can be convicted of criminal tax evasion only if he "intentional[ly] violat[es] . . . a *known* legal duty."[66] Under this standard, Cheek's mistaken beliefs about the unconstitutionality of income taxes would *not* be a defense, the Court reasoned, because a person who declines to comply with the law on that basis is nevertheless aware that he has a duty to pay under the tax code.[67] However, a person who honestly believes — however unreasonably — that wages or any other species of income aren't taxable under the code *would* have a defense, for in that circumstance he couldn't be said to "know" that he had a duty to pay.[68] The Court remanded the case for retrial under this standard.

The Supreme Court, like other courts, tends to give meaning to an ambiguous criminal statute not by mechanically parsing its text but by imputing to the legislature an intent to enact the reading that the Court itself views as best.[69] This was so in *Cheek.* A person is guilty of criminal tax evasion only if her failure to pay is "willful[ ],"[70] a term that can be understood to refer merely to knowl-

64. 498 U.S. 192 (1991).

65. *See* 498 U.S. at 194-96.

66. 498 U.S. at 196 (emphasis added).

67. *See* 498 U.S. at 205-06.

68. *See* 498 U.S. at 202-03.

69. *See* Kahan, *supra* note 45, at 370-89. In other words, the Court does exactly what Hart and Sacks said it should do with respect to statutes generally. *See* Henry M. Hart, Jr. & Albert M. Sacks, The Legal Process: Basic Problems in the Making and Application of Law 1378 (William N. Eskridge, Jr. & Philip P. Frickey eds., 1994).

70. *See* 26 U.S.C. §§ 7201, 7203 (1994).

edge of the factual elements of a crime.[71] The Court in *Cheek* construed "willful" to mean knowledge of legal duty because of the "the complexity of the tax laws."[72] "The proliferation of statutes and regulations has sometimes made it difficult for the average citizen to know and comprehend the extent of the duties and obligations imposed by the tax laws."[73] It was thus implausible to think that Congress "'intend[ed] that a person, by reason of a bona fide misunderstanding as to his liability for the tax, as to his duty to make a return, or as to the adequacy of the records he maintained, should become a criminal.'"[74]

Had the Court accepted the premises of the classic conception of the mistake of law doctrine, it certainly wouldn't have used its interpretive discretion to engraft a mistake of law defense onto the tax code. Denying an excuse for any type of mistake might not be the best way to promote knowledge of the law, but allowing one for all such mistakes is the surest way to discourage it. If a person can be convicted only for intentionally violating *known* tax obligations, then she is better off ignorant. The complexity of the tax code, moreover, only multiplies the opportunities for this form of strategic heedlessness. Thus, far from being a ground for softening the traditional mistake of law doctrine as the Court in *Cheek* suggested, complexity — as the court in *Marrero,* for instance, recognized[75] — is a ground for hardening the law's resolve not to excuse ignorance.

Or at least it is if one accepts the premises of the classic conception of the doctrine. Matters are more complicated under the anti-Holmesian conception.

On the anti-Holmesian view, it's just to punish a person notwithstanding her ignorance of law — even complex laws, like the Uniform Controlled Substances Act — insofar as her conduct reveals that she is insufficiently committed to the moral values that the law reflects. Obviously, such an account presupposes that the

71. *See, e.g.,* United States v. Gunn, 97 F. Supp. 476, 480 (W.D. Ark. 1950) (so construing "willfully"); Model Penal Code § 2.02(8)-(9) (1985) (defining "willfully" as "knowingly" and indicating that the mental element of the statute is presumed to apply only to facts and not to law). *See generally* Ratzlaf v. United States, 510 U.S. 135, 141 (1994) ("'Willful,' this Court has recognized, is a 'word of many meanings,' and 'its construction [is] often . . . influenced by its context.'" (alteration in original) (quoting Spies v. United States, 317 U.S. 492, 497 (1943))).

72. *Cheek,* 498 U.S. at 200.

73. 498 U.S. at 199-200.

74. 498 U.S. at 200 (quoting United States v. Murdock, 290 U.S. 389, 396 (1933)).

75. *See* People v. Marrero, 507 N.E.2d 1068, 1073 (N.Y. 1987) (noting that precisely because criminal law is "complex," dispensing with strict liability could create "an infinite number of mistake of law defenses [based on] good-faith, perhaps reasonable but mistaken, interpretation[s]").

criminal law embodies moral norms that have an existence independent of the law itself. Criminal tax provisions don't. Individuals don't have a moral duty, independent of law, to turn over a portion of their income to the government. Consequently, we can't disregard what a person understood her legal duties to be when we are morally appraising her failure to pay a tax. If she *knew* she owed the tax, then we are almost certain to condemn her — not for engaging in an intrinsically immoral act, but for attempting to exempt herself from obligations to which other members of the community have submitted in the interest of the common good.[76] But if she didn't know, then we must press deeper to see whether such ignorance was itself morally culpable.

It is at this point that the complexity of the tax code becomes relevant. The obligation to pay a tax on one's salary or wages is a simple matter; ignorance of it displays such a gross degree of inattention to civic duty that one can justly be blamed for that very lack of knowledge.[77] But the tax code extends far beyond the obligation to pay tax on one's wages or salaries: it encompasses as well one's duty to pay tax on barter transactions,[78] to recognize taxable gains associated with swapping comparable mortgage portfolios,[79] and to make withholdings from the wages of once-weekly maids.[80] *Good* persons — from the "average citizen"[81] to the prospective Supreme Court Justice[82] — can make mistakes about these duties, which involve no independent moral obligation and which aren't a matter of common civic knowledge. A mistake of law defense protects these excusably inattentive actors from punishment. Of course, it might protect some culpably inattentive ones from punishment, too, insofar as courts are obliged, as a matter of statutory construction, to treat all mistakes of law alike. Excusing the vicious Cheek for his

76. *See* HERBERT MORRIS, ON GUILT AND INNOCENCE 33-34 (1976) (developing a theory of desert along these lines).

77. *Cf. Cheek,* 498 U.S. at 209-10 (Blackmun, J., dissenting) ("[I]t is incomprehensible to me how, in this day, more than 70 years after the institution of our present federal income tax system with the passage of the Revenue Act of 1913, any taxpayer of competent mentality can assert as his defense to charges of statutory willfulness the proposition that the wage he receives for his labor is not income, irrespective of a cult that says otherwise and advises the gullible to resist income tax collections." (citation omitted)).

78. *See* 26 C.F.R. § 1.61-2(d) (1996).

79. *See* Cottage Sav. Assn. v. Commissioner, 499 U.S. 554, 559-67 (1991).

80. *See generally* Rita L. Zeidner, *W&M Panel Hears Pleas for Simplification of Domestic Employee Tax Laws,* 58 TAX NOTES 1282, 1284 (1993) (reporting the IRS position that housekeepers are employees and not independent contractors).

81. *See Cheek,* 498 U.S. at 199.

82. *See* Richard L. Berke, *Favorite for High Court Failed to Pay Maid's Taxes,* N.Y. TIMES, June 13, 1993, at 1.

ignorance was thus necessary to avoid condemning many virtuous ones for theirs.[83]

Another way to see this point is to reflect on the difference in how we typically regard marginally legal behavior in the tax field and how we regard it in other domains of criminal law. When the law implements independent moral norms, members of society are likely to view marginally legal behavior with disapproval. Because of the persistent incompleteness of law relative to morality, persons who deliberately try to skirt the line of what separates, say, legal from illegal drug distribution, or mere sharp dealing from fraud, strike us (usually) as morally *bad* persons. Punishing them if they miscalculate gives them exactly what they deserve and helps to reinforce for the rest of us what being *good* entails. But society feels differently about persons who try to find "loopholes" in the tax code; we don't condemn those persons, but instead compensate them with hundreds of dollars an hour, and honor them with status and respect. Giving them an excuse for ignorance of law implements the widely shared (but by no means uncontentious) judgment that persons *like that* shouldn't be deemed criminals when they make honest mistakes.

The anti-Holmesian conception of the doctrine can also explain why the Court in *Cheek* declined to make mistakes of constitutional law a defense. These beliefs, the Court explained, "do not arise from innocent mistakes caused by the complexity of the [code]"; "[r]ather, they reveal full knowledge of the provisions at issue and a studied conclusion, however wrong, that those provisions are invalid and unenforceable."[84] In other words, it is not morally "innocent" but morally *culpable* to insist on one's own understanding of one's civic obligations when one knows that one's position has been considered and rejected by legislatures, administrative agencies, courts, and other institutions authorized to define what those obligations are. The willingness to abide by the judgments of those in-

83. This tradeoff, however, might not be as stark as it seems. Although ignorance of the obligation to pay a tax on wages stands on the same formal footing as ignorance of the tax status of a complex business transaction, the reality is that juries are much less likely to believe the genuineness of the claimed ignorance in the former case than in the latter. A court that crafts a mistake of law defense to protect excusably inattentive actors can thus bank on the jury's situation sense as a hedge against the appropriation of that defense by culpably inattentive ones. *Cf. Cheek*, 498 U.S. at 203-04 ("Of course, the more unreasonable the asserted beliefs or misunderstandings are, the more likely the jury will consider them to be nothing more than simple disagreement with known legal duties imposed by the tax laws and will find that the Government has carried its burden of proving knowledge."). Cheek was in fact convicted on remand. *See* United States v. Cheek, 3 F.3d 1057, 1059 (7th Cir. 1993).

84. *Cheek*, 498 U.S. at 205-06.

stitutions, while not an uncontested understanding of moral and civic virtue, is nevertheless clearly recognizable as such.

Of course, the tax code isn't the only complex body of criminally enforceable law that doesn't implement independent moral norms; the same can be said for banking law, broadcasting law, and election law, among others. If the point of strict liability is to punish individuals who are culpably inattentive to society's moral norms, then we should expect to see courts fashioning exceptions to the mistake of law doctrine for all manner of malum prohibitum offenses.

Which is exactly what we do see. Structuring banking transactions so as to avoid having to report them is not "obviously 'evil'" or "inevitably nefarious."[85] There's "nothing inherently wrong in making" a campaign contribution without disclosing it to the government.[86] There's nothing about broadcasting on a CB radio without an FCC license that's "likely to create danger" or otherwise make a "reasonable man . . . aware that he [is doing something] forbidden."[87] Exporting and importing "amphibious vehicles, pressure-breathing suits, [and] aerial cameras" can be done "innocently" and thus can't be analogized to distribution of illicit "substances which are known generally to be controlled by government regulation, such as heroin or like drugs."[88] In all of these settings, and in various others,[89] courts have recognized mistake of law as a defense because the underlying conduct violates no moral norms independent of the law that prohibits it.

85. *See* Ratzlaf v. United States, 510 U.S. 135, 144-48 (1994).

86. State v. Azneer, 526 N.W.2d 298, 300 (Iowa 1995); *see also* United States v. Curran, 20 F.3d 560, 569 (3d Cir. 1994) (holding that unreported campaign contributions are not "obviously 'evil' or inherently 'bad'").

87. United States v. Simpson, 561 F.2d 53, 62 (7th Cir. 1977).

88. United States v. Lizarraga-Lizarraga, 541 F.2d 826, 828 (9th Cir. 1976).

89. *See, e.g.,* Liparota v. United States, 471 U.S. 419, 426-27 (1985) (recognizing a mistake of law defense for the misuse of food stamps on the ground that regulations relating to their use cover "a broad range of apparently innocent conduct," from destroying them to using them to buy food from a store charging above-normal prices to food stamp program participants); United States v. Jonas Bros., 368 F. Supp. 783, 784-85 (D. Alaska 1974) (holding that the mistake of law defense is available to the federal offense of transporting wildlife in violation of state law if the state law in question is a malum prohibitum state hunting restriction); Long v. State, 65 A.2d 489, 498 (Del. 1949) (recognizing a reasonable mistake of law defense where the conduct is "neither immoral nor anti-social in our culture"); Commonwealth v. Rudnick, 60 N.E.2d 353, 355 (Mass. 1945) ("The indictment being for conspiracy to commit an offense which is malum prohibitum only [alteration of building without a permit from building commissioner], there must have been an intent to do wrong . . . and . . . knowledge of the existence of the law and knowledge of its actual or intended violation."); *cf.* United States v. Ehrlichman, 376 F. Supp. 29, 35 (D.D.C. 1974) (recognizing the "rule that mistake of law often *is* a defense to *malum prohibitum* crimes" but concluding that "unauthorized entry and search . . . are *malum in se*").

Still, courts don't invariably recognize mistake of law defenses for crimes of this kind. As a statement of black letter law, the rule that ignorance of law excuses malum prohibitum — but not malum in se — crimes is overbroad; indeed, it takes no real detective work to find cases that say just the opposite — that ignorance of law is no excuse "whether the crime charged is *malum prohibitum* or *malum in se*"[90] — although that proposition too is (as I've just shown) wildly overstated. So why do courts permit mistake of law as a defense only selectively across malum prohibitum crimes?

The answer, the anti-Holmesian view suggests, is in part a matter of timing. Well into the first decades of the twentieth century, the law's resistance to excusing legal ignorance was nearly absolute. But it wasn't until about that time that the criminal law was pressed into the service of regulating essentially malum prohibitum conduct. So long as there was an essential unity between criminal law and community moral norms, the uncompromising application of strict liability was the best means for implementing prudent obfuscation and legal moralism. The absolutism of this approach came into tension with the (anti-Holmesian) premises of the doctrine, however, with the advent of malum prohibitum crimes, and it wasn't long after that that courts began to recognize exceptions to the principle that ignorance of the law is no excuse.[91] There was a transition period, though, during which some courts resisted any softening of the doctrine; and their resistance, memorialized in the case reports, continues to furnish a convenient rhetorical foothold when a contemporary court is inclined to deny a mistake of law defense for a crime that looks malum prohibitum.

A court is most likely to feel this inclination in two circumstances. The first, again, is when ignorance of the law — even a malum prohibitum one — connotes bad character. Ignorance doesn't connote bad character when the statutory scheme in question regulates the common place activities of ordinary citizens whose contact with intricate laws — such as the tax code — is understandably irregular and fleeting. But matters are different when, say, the defendant is a sophisticated participant in a "closely regulated" industry;[92] we expect "repeat players" to be attentive to the

90. *E.g.*, Blumenthal v. United States, 88 F.2d 522, 530 (8th Cir. 1937); State v. McDermott, 220 A.2d 38, 43 (Conn. Cir. Ct. 1965).

91. *See, e.g.*, United States v. Murdock, 290 U.S. 389, 396 (1933).

92. *See* United States v. Weitzenhoff, 35 F.3d 1275, 1285 (9th Cir. 1993); *see also* United States v. Gunn, 97 F. Supp. 476, 480 (W.D. Ark. 1950) (justifying the denial of a mistake of law defense for a company ignorant of the licensing requirement for interstate shippers on

rules of the game.[93] Matters are different, too, when someone is engaged in behavior that, while not strictly speaking immoral, nevertheless exposes the public to unusually high risks: it might not occur to someone who is transporting "[p]encils, dental floss, [or] paper clips" that his conduct is subject to stringent safety regulations, but if it doesn't to someone who is transporting "dangerous or deleterious devices . . . or obnoxious waste materials,"[94] then he's missing a critical faculty of moral perception. In these particular settings, ignorance of a malum prohibitum obligation, no less than ignorance of a malum in se one, expresses a culpable failure to attune oneself to basic civic norms.

The second circumstance in which judges might be tempted to deny that malum prohibitum crimes get special treatment is when they want to avoid the burden of explaining why they really view the conduct in question as malum in se. It goes without saying that the line between *prohibitum* and *in se* will often be blurry. It should go without saying as well that drawing the line will often be a controversial and even politically perilous task for a court to undertake. It's inconvenient to declare the transporting of alcohol during and immediately after Prohibition to be intrinsically immoral;[95] it's risky to be seen as jumping into the fray when management ejects a union official from company property.[96] Life is much easier for a court in these and like cases when it can simply invoke a rule — "ignorance of the law is *never* an excuse, for malum prohibitum offenses *or* malum in se ones" — that spares it the burden of justifying the denial of a defense. But against the background of all the malum prohibitum crimes that now *do* get mistake of law defenses, the invoking of such a rule serves only to conceal, and does not

---

the ground that the company engaged in sustained dealings with an interstate shipper and thus "is presumed to have a practical knowledge of the law commensurate with its duties").

93. *Cf.* Murphy & O'Hara, *supra* note 26, at 257. Indeed, courts sometimes draw distinctions between sophisticated, repeat players and unsophisticated, intermittently regulated parties, affording a mistake of law defense to the latter but not the former. *Compare* United States v. Speach, 968 F.2d 795, 796-97 (9th Cir. 1993) (allowing a mistake of law defense for an independent transporter who was unaware of permit requirements for customer's waste) *with* United States v. Weitzenhoff, 35 F.3d 1275, 1284 n.5 (9th Cir. 1993) (denying the defense for managers of a toxic waste facility because they "are clearly in the best position to know their own permit status").

94. United States v. International Minerals & Chem. Corp., 402 U.S. 558, 564-65 (1971) (transportation of hazardous chemicals); *accord* United States v. Weitzenhoff, 35 F.3d 1275, 1284-85 (9th Cir. 1993) (discharge of toxic wastes).

95. *Cf.* Blumenthal v. United States, 88 F.2d 522, 530-31 (8th Cir. 1937) (denying the defense for transporting liquor across state lines without proper labeling).

96. *Cf.* State v. McDermott, 220 A.2d 38, 43 (Conn. Cir. Ct. 1965) (denying the defense to a union official convicted of trespass who believed, allegedly mistakenly, that he had a statutory right to be on plant property).

genuinely eliminate, the need for the court to make contentious, context-specific judgments about which actors have characters good enough to be excused for their mistakes of law.

That such discretion must be exercised, moreover, completes the indictment of the classic conception of the mistake of law doctrine. Had the doctrine embodied the normative side of liberal positivism — that is, had it been accepted by courts that the law ought to judge persons only by the conformity of their actions to the standard laid down by law and not by the conformity of their characters to an extralegal conception of moral virtue — courts would never have perceived the need to reform the doctrine upon the advent of malum prohibitum crimes. Moreover, had courts been intent on conserving the positivistic character of the law as a descriptive matter, they would never have reformed it by making an exception for malum prohibitum crimes, much less only for certain of them. For one can determine whether a particular species of conduct — whether possessing a gun, distributing a drug, or neglecting to pay a tax — is malum in se or malum prohibitum only by appraising that conduct in light of moral norms external to positive law. Once it is acknowledged that an important component of the law depends on this kind of appraisal, a person who "want[s] to know the law," even if she wants to know "nothing else,"[97] has no choice but to view the world through a good person's eyes.

Conclusion

This essay had two aims. One was to identify the true basis of the mistake of law doctrine; the other was to distill from that account some general conclusions about the relationship between criminal law and morality. I'll now take stock.

The classic conception of the mistake of law doctrine, I've argued, is false. That understanding asserts the utility — indeed, the indispensability — of widespread legal knowledge in a political regime that disclaims any reliance on its citizens' commitment to a moral orthodoxy. If maximizing legal knowledge were really the objective, however, the law would apply a negligence standard, rather than a strict liability standard, to legal mistakes. Refusing to excuse even reasonable mistakes *discourages* investments in legal knowledge by making it hazardous for a citizen to rely on her private understanding of the law. This resentment of legal knowledge makes sense because the doctrine assumes, contrary to the classic

97. Holmes, *supra* note 1, at 459.

conception, that individuals are and should be aware of society's morality and that morality furnishes a better guide for action than does law itself. Thus, far from trying to maximize the incentive that presumptively bad men have to know the law, the doctrine seeks to obscure the law so that citizens are more likely to behave like good ones.

What does this conception of the doctrine reveal about the criminal law more generally? One lesson is that the criminal law is intensely moralistic. The mistake of law doctrine is an integral part of a strategy of prudent obfuscation aimed at remedying the persistent imperfection of criminal law relative to morality. The standard of culpability reflected in the doctrine, moreover, judges individuals not just for the conformity of their conduct to law, but also for the conformity of their values to society's moral norms. Indeed, because it generally excuses individuals for mistakes of law that even a virtuous person would make, the doctrine demands that courts interpret society's morality in the course of interpreting its criminal statutes so that they can determine which mistakes of law reflect bad character.

But another lesson that emerges from the anti-Holmesian account is that the law is ambivalent — indeed, almost embarrassed — about exactly this kind of moralizing. The positivistic idiom of the classic account drives the rhetoric of the decisions, even when the decisions defy that account's central premises in substance. Legal moralism, secured by prudent obfuscation, is the truth of the mistake of law doctrine. But it is a truth that one can get at only by prying back the doctrine's antimoralistic, Holmesian veneer.

Stealthy moralizing is in fact endemic to criminal law. The principle of *legality,* for example, proclaims that legislatures alone are responsible for defining crimes and disavows any lawmaking role for courts;[98] the truth, however, is that criminal statutes typically emerge from the legislature only half-formed and must be completed through contentious, norm-laden modes of interpretation that are functionally indistinguishable from common-law making.[99] Public debate about the death penalty is dominated by empirical claims relating to deterrence, when in fact parties on both sides ground their positions in nonempirical but contested moral beliefs.[100] The rhetoric of duress, provocation, and insanity depicts

98. *See* Herbert L. Packer, The Limits of the Criminal Sanction 79-102 (1968).

99. *See* Kahan, *supra* note 45, at 367-89.

100. *See generally* Phoebe C. Ellsworth & Samuel R. Gross, *Hardening of the Attitudes: Americans' Views on the Death Penalty,* J. Soc. Issues, Summer 1994, at 19; Tom R. Tyler &

emotions in pseudo-scientific, mechanistic terms that obscure the judgmental appraisals that decisionmakers make about the values that emotions embody.[101] The false prominence of liberal positivism and the utility of legal knowledge in the mistake of law doctrine is of a piece with the law's general reticence about displaying its moral core.

I have defended the moralizing that animates the mistake of law doctrine, but not the duplicity that surrounds it. As the stories of Julio Marrero, Cleora Olive King, and John Cheek should make clear, the kinds of moral judgments that the mistake of law doctrine reflects are highly contentious. Is possession of a handgun malum in se or malum prohibitum?[102] Are the persons who seek out "tax loopholes" truly virtuous? Are the ones who make mistakes about the status of controlled substances invariably vicious?[103] If not, why do courts see the world this way? The moralizing that occurs with other criminal law doctrines is subject to just as much contestation. Such judgments are on balance a good thing, and are probably inevitable in any event, but they ought at least to be made openly. When contentious moral judgments are camouflaged in seemingly nonjudgmental rhetoric, decisionmakers are freed from the constraints of public accountability, and citizens are denied the opportunity to examine, criticize, and reform the judgments that their law reflects.

It might not be realistic to expect the criminal law always to get it right when it moralizes, particularly in light of the dissensus that characterizes moral issues in contemporary society. But precisely because citizens disagree about what's good, insisting that the law be *honest* when it moralizes is definitely not too much to ask.

Renee Weber, *Support for the Death Penalty: Instrumental Response to Crime, or Symbolic Attitude?*, 17 L. & Socy. Rev. 21 (1982).

101. *See* Kahan & Nussbaum, *supra* note 9, at 372-74.

102. Compare the New York Court of Appeals's decision in *Marrero* with *Staples v. United States*, 511 U.S. 600, 613 (1994), in which the U.S. Supreme Court read a mens rea requirement into a silent statute in order to respect "the common experience that owning a gun is usually licit and blameless conduct."

103. *Cf.* Idaho v. Fox, 866 P.2d 181 (Idaho 1993) (holding that a mistake of law is no defense for the possession of the asthma medication ephedrine, which was a controlled substance in Idaho but an over-the-counter drug in other states).

[8]

ARTICLES

EXEGESIS OF THE LAW OF DURESS: JUSTIFYING THE EXCUSE AND SEARCHING FOR ITS PROPER LIMITS

BY JOSHUA DRESSLER*

INTRODUCTION

Our society has a love-hate relationship with the criminal law defense of duress.[1] Although "of venerable antiquity,"[2] the defense was frequently condemned as illegitimate,[3] narrowly defined at common

---

* Professor of Law, Wayne State University. B.A., J.D., University of California, Los Angeles. More people than I have room to name here read portions of earlier drafts of this Article or patiently listened to my musings on the subject. I thank them *en masse*. I also thank Laura Eisele and Christine Scarnecchia for their research assistance.

1. Although many observations herein have broader significance, this Article purports to deal only with the criminal law defense of duress. As a result, I use the word "duress" in this limited context. For those interested in a broader view of the subject, see Fingarette, *Victimization: A Legalist Analysis of Coercion, Deception, Undue Influence, and Excusable Prison Escape*, 42 WASH. & LEE L. REV. 65 (1985). *See also* Beatson, *Duress as a Vitiating Factor in Contract*, 33 CAMBRIDGE L.J. 97 (1974) (discussing the limits of the duress doctrine).

I also will use the terms "coercion" and "compulsion" synonymously with "duress," although in early common law the word "coercion" generally was used to describe an independent defense pertaining to pressures a husband applied on his wife. R. PERKINS & R. BOYCE, CRIMINAL LAW 1018 (3d ed. 1982). *See infra* note 20.

2. Regina v. Howe, [1987] 2 W.L.R. 568, 575 (Lord Hailsham). Indeed, Blackstone recognized "duress per minas" as one of three forms of compulsion exculpating criminal actors. 4 W. BLACKSTONE, COMMENTARIES ON THE LAWS OF ENGLAND *30. *See also* Fingarette, *supra* note 1, at 67 ("By the 19th and 20th centuries the common law regarding coercion as a defense to a criminal charge was well established.") (footnote omitted).

3. *E.g.*, 2 J. STEPHEN, A HISTORY OF THE CRIMINAL LAW OF ENGLAND 108 (1883) ("Compulsion by threats ought in no case whatever to be admitted as an excuse for crime."); *see* G. FLETCHER, RETHINKING CRIMINAL LAW 829 (1978) (observing that "text writers in the common law have resisted recognition of the excuse," and citing Hale, Stephen, and Glanville Williams in support of this assertion); Hitchler, *Duress as a Defense in Criminal Cases*, 4 VA. L. REV. 519, 520 (1917) ("The impropriety of admitting duress as a defense in any case has been seriously asserted.").

law,[4] comparatively rarely invoked in criminal prosecutions,[5] and not often successfully pleaded.[6]

Nonetheless, our society also seems to love the plea or, at least, to be intrigued by it. Despite criticisms, our society has retained the defense,[7] expanded it over the years,[8] and paid close attention to the calls of those who would apply the defense in novel ways.[9]

Our conflicting reactions to the defense coincide with our emotions toward coerced actors. In a world that often seeks to avoid moral ambiguity by finding victims and villains, it is unclear which appellation more fairly describes a person who accedes to an unlawful threat. Consider a person who, gun pointed at his head, kills an innocent child at the behest of a terrorist. Is he a victim who merely chose life over death? Or, is he the villain because "his aversion to dying was greater than his aversion to killing"?[10] Most people are apt to feel much like Judge Tatting in the

---

This view has not been abandoned by all modern commentators. *See, e.g.*, Waslik, *Duress and Criminal Responsibility*, 1977 CRIM. L. REV. 453 (duress should function only in discretionary sentencing mitigation).

4. O'Regan, *Duress and Criminal Conspiracies*, 1971 CRIM. L. REV. 35, 35 ("The criminal law has admitted the defense . . . only with reluctance and has imposed numerous, if vaguely formulated restrictions on its operation.") (footnote omitted); *see also* J. HALL, GENERAL PRINCIPLES OF CRIMINAL LAW 443-44 (2d ed. 1960) (Hall suggests that the defense is "formally" broad, but that "in the context of actual administration of the law, it all but disappears. It has met a judicial hostility which has drastically reduced its potential effectiveness.") (footnote omitted).

5. Goodhart, *Perjury and Duress—A Rejoinder*, 121 NEW L.J. 909, 910 (1971); Hitchler, *supra* note 3, at 519 ("the law concerning [duress] is . . . meagre").

6. *See* J. HALL, *supra* note 4, at 443-44. George Fletcher is somewhat more upbeat than Hall about the successes of duress claims. *See also* G. FLETCHER, *supra* note 3, at 829 (in which he suggests that courts "have been more compassionate" than text writers regarding duress); Fletcher, *Excuse*, in 2 ENCYCLOPEDIA OF CRIME AND JUSTICE 724 (S. Kadish ed. 1983) (stating that "[a]s compared with insanity, . . . claims of duress receive highly differential treatment").

7. Leo Katz has observed that few people "want to own up" to the fact that the same reasoning that permits the common law to deny the defense in homicide cases, *see infra* notes 82-87 and accompanying text, and has resulted in the hanging of coerced killers, applies to all duress cases. L. KATZ, BAD ACTS AND GUILTY MINDS 69 (1987).

8. *See infra* notes 88-95 and accompanying text.

9. For example, duress serves as the underlying rationale for such proposed new defenses as brainwashing, *see* Alldridge, *Brainwashing as a Criminal Law Defence*, 1984 CRIM. L. REV. 726; Delgado, *Ascription of Criminal States of Mind: Toward a Defense Theory for the Coercively Persuaded ("Brainwashed") Defendant*, 63 MINN. L. REV. 1 (1978) [hereinafter Delgado, *Brainwashing*]; and "rotten social background," *see* Bazelon, *The Morality of the Criminal Law*, 49 S. CAL. L. REV. 385 (1976); Delgado, *"Rotten Social Background": Should the Criminal Law Recognize a Defense of Severe Environmental Deprivation?*, 3 LAW & INEQUALITY 9 (1985) [hereinafter Delgado, *RSB*]. The latter defense is discussed *infra* at notes 238-68 and accompanying text.

10. Brudner, *A Theory of Necessity*, 7 OXFORD J. LEGAL STUD. 339, 353 (1987).

fictional, but hardly fanciful,[11] Speluncean Case,[12] who conceded that "I find myself torn between sympathy for [the coerced actor] . . . and a feeling of abhorrence and disgust at the monstrous act . . . committed."[13]

Even if our emotions were not in conflict, moral questions regarding duress would still abound. When, if ever, is a coerced act justified? Should a person who accedes to a wrongful threat ever be excused? If so, what theory of excuse explains society's willingness to hold the actor unaccountable for his intentional, wrongful actions?

Although legal scholars have considered these questions,[14] albeit not as often as philosophers,[15] neither the law nor the commentators have reached a definitive conclusion. Indeed, the leading legal treatises reach diametrically opposing conclusions about the defense—one identifying duress as a justification,[16] the other as an excuse.[17] If, as I believe, legal doctrine ought to be, whenever possible, consistent with a coherent moral theory, society's moral intuitions, and the emotions that shape society's reactions to dilemmatic circumstances, current duress law may fail these criteria.

This Article rethinks duress as a legal defense.[18] It is my hope that by clarifying the moral issues, and by examining the feelings people express regarding coerced actors and their deeds, the legal system can

11. *E.g.*, Regina v. Dudley and Stephens, 14 Q.B.D. 273 (1884); United States v. Holmes, 26 F. Cas. 360 (C.C.E.D. Pa. 1842) (No. 15,383). For a marvelous account of *Dudley and Stephens*, see A. SIMPSON, CANNIBALISM AND THE COMMON LAW 92-270 (1984).

12. Fuller, *The Case of the Speluncean Explorers*, 62 HARV. L. REV. 616 (1949). In Lon Fuller's account, after they were imprisoned in a cave by a landslide and all reasonable hope of rescue was lost, Roger Whetmore, a member of the Speluncean Society, was killed and eaten by fellow members of the Society. Although the case technically raises the issue of necessity rather than duress, *see infra* notes 111-23 and accompanying text, most of the moral issues are indistinguishable.

13. Fuller, *supra* note 12, at 626.

14. Among the fairly recent literature on duress and/or the excuse counterpart, necessity, are G. FLETCHER, *supra* note 3, at 818-35; Brudner, *supra* note 10, at 339; Fingarette, *supra* note 1; Morgan, *The Defence of Necessity: Justification or Excuse?*, 42 U. TORONTO FAC. L. REV., Fall 1984, at 165; Smith, *Duress*, 1978 CRIM. L. REV. 122.

15. One of the most well-known recent philosophical accounts of duress is Nozick, *Coercion*, in PHILOSOPHY, SCIENCE AND METHOD: ESSAYS IN HONOR OF ERNEST NAGEL 440 (S. Morgenbesser, P. Suppes & M. White eds. 1969).

16. W. LAFAVE & A. SCOTT, CRIMINAL LAW § 5.3 (2d ed. 1986).

17. R. PERKINS & R. BOYCE, *supra* note 1, at 1059.

18. This Article is an outgrowth of a paper this author gave at an American Law Institute and Rutgers-Camden Law School conference commemorating the twenty-fifth anniversary of the Model Penal Code. Dressler, *Reflections on Excusing Wrongdoers: Moral Theory, New Excuses and the Model Penal Code*, 19 RUTGERS L.J. 671 (1988) is the published later version of that paper. In that paper and resulting article, this author expressed concededly "tentative" thoughts about the concept of excuse. *Id.* at 673. Duress received brief focus in the process. *Id.* at 708-15.

move toward developing legal rules regarding the defense that are more just.

A brief road map of the Article will help. Part I describes the law of duress that developed at common law and in modern American criminal codes, especially the Model Penal Code (MPC). In Part II, moral arguments for treating duress as a justification defense are considered. The defense sometimes is defended in lesser-harm justification terms, but this only simplistically, and not entirely accurately, explains the law that has developed. It does not conform to our intuitions about coercion. Although a more sophisticated moral argument, based on permissible, self-interested action, can coherently justify a class of compelled actions, this explanation will prove repellent to many, and probably fails to explain why people are tempted to exculpate compelled actors.

Part III examines and rejects various plausible arguments for excusing coerced wrongdoers. Ultimately, I conclude that, in a system of excuses ordinarily premised on the specialness—indeed, superiority to other creatures—of human beings, duress ironically is a plea based on inherent human weakness. One who pleads duress concedes "I'm *only* human." For duress to make sense as an excuse, however, it must constitute more than an empirical claim that the defendant acted like most other humans would have acted in the same situation. Unlike other excuses, duress is a normative defense: the actor should be excused only if he attained or reflected society's legitimate expectations of moral strength.

Finally, Part IV looks at the possible outer limits of the excuse. In light of the theory of duress posited, this Article considers three controversial questions raised in the law and literature of duress. First, the rule that duress cannot ever excuse coerced killings is considered and rejected. This view, along with the MPC, conflicts with common law.

Second, the rule that the defense should be limited to human threats, thus leaving unfortunate persons such as the Spelunceans without an excuse for their wrongdoing, is considered and rejected.[19] This view opposes both the common law and the MPC.

Finally, this Article considers and rejects the frequent claim that the defense should be more broadly defined to permit an excuse for criminal wrongdoing that is the result of social and economic deprivation. This view affirms the position of both the MPC and the common law.

19. They would have a possible *justification* for their action, however, under MODEL PENAL CODE § 3.02 (1985). *See infra* note 111 and accompanying text.

I. DEFINING DURESS

A. Common Law

1. *In General*

Duress is one of three forms of compulsion to which early commentators and courts accorded exculpatory significance.[20] Nonetheless, it is an "extremely vague and elusive juristic concept,"[21] one for which, surprisingly, "very little learning [is] to be found in any of the books or cases on the subject."[22]

Blackstone described duress as "threats and menaces which induce a fear of death or other bodily harm, and which take away, for that reason, the guilt of many crimes and misdemeanors . . . ."[23] Reduced to a more easily digested analytic form, but subject to the clarification that follows, *D*[24] will be acquitted of an offense other than murder on the basis of duress if he pleads and proves that: (1) *C* unlawfully threatened imminently to kill or grievously injure him or another person; and (2) he was not at fault in exposing himself to the threat.[25]

20. A second concept of compulsion, now antiquated, involved the marital relationship. A wife was not punished for criminal conduct if she acted under the coercion of her husband. Coercion, however, was presumed by the mere presence of the husband at the time of her offense. Even in his absence, proof of a command by him to commit the crime was sufficient to excuse the wife. 4 W. BLACKSTONE, *supra* note 2, at *28-29; 1 MODEL PENAL CODE AND COMMENTARIES § 2.09 commentary at 385 (1985) [hereinafter MPC COMMENTARIES]. This form of compulsion was grounded on the idea that a wife was an obedient servant—even marionette—of her husband. Smith v. Meyers, 54 Neb. 1, 7, 74 N.W. 277, 278 (1898) (The wife is a "marionette, moved at will by the husband."). MPC COMMENTARIES, *supra*, at 385. The ancient rule has virtually disappeared and will not be considered further in this Article.

"Necessity" is a third form of compulsion. Its problematic relationship to duress is discussed *infra* at notes 111-23 and accompanying text.

21. D.P.P. v. Lynch, 1975 App. Cas. 653, 686 (Lord Simon); *see also* Regina v. Hurley & Murray, 1967 V.R. 526, 542 ("This . . . is a branch of the law in which there is much uncertainty . . . ."); O'Regan, *supra* note 4.

22. Rex v. Steane, 1947 K.B. 997, 1005 (Lord Goddard); *but see* G. WILLIAMS, TEXTBOOK OF CRIMINAL LAW 577 (1978) ("Happily, the law of this subject is not shrouded in quite the same doubt as the defence of necessity."). In light of the fact that courts frequently fail to distinguish between the defenses of duress and necessity, see *infra* notes 111-23 and accompanying text, Professor Williams's observation is debatable.

23. 4 W. BLACKSTONE, *supra* note 2, at *29.

24. Throughout this Article I will use "*D*" (Defendant) to denote the person coerced and "*C*" to denote the coercer.

25. *See* Fingarette, *supra* note 1, at 67 n.9 (where the author concluded that a person is excused if: "(a) [t]he otherwise innocent defendant (b) . . . had a well-grounded belief (c) in a threat of imminent (d) death or serious injury (e) from which there was no escape except through compliance with the demands of the threatener; . . . (g) except where the alleged criminal act is murder.") (emphasis in original deleted).

2. *In Particular*

a. *Duress implicates threats,*[26] *not offers:* In matters of the criminal law, a threat is distinguishable from an offer. Threats potentially legally coerce; offers do not. For example, *C* "threatens" *D* if, with the intent of changing *D*'s course of action, she proposes to render him or another person worse off than he would be in the ordinary course of events.[27] An "offer" would improve another's position. Thus, if *C* tells *D* that she will hire him if and only if he performs a specified illegal act, *C* is an offeror, assuming she makes the statement for the purpose of convincing *D* to commit the criminal act. She "threatens" *D*, however, if she informs him that she will fire him unless he performs the illegal act.[28]

---

26. It is not precisely accurate to imply that an *actual* threat is a prerequisite to exculpation. A person may be acquitted of a crime in the absence of an actual threat if he acted as the result of a well-founded, albeit incorrect, belief that a threat of the sort described in the text was issued. D'Aquino v. United States, 192 F.2d 338, 358 (9th Cir. 1951); People v. Pena, 149 Cal. App. 3d Supp. 14, 27, 197 Cal. Rptr. 264, 272 (1983); Regina v. Valderramma-Vega, [1985] CRIM. L.R. 220; Regina v. Graham, [1982] 1 All E.R. 801, 804; Hitchler, *supra* note 3, at 540. This also appears to be the case under the MPC, although it is not evident from the language of the duress provision. MPC COMMENTARIES, *supra* note 20, § 2.09 commentary at 380.

For example, suppose that *C* tells *D* that if the latter does not perform a particular criminal act, she will "do something" to *D*. *D*'s exculpation does not depend upon proof that *C* intended imminently to kill or seriously injure him, as long as a reasonable person in his situation would have interpreted *C*'s words in that way (e.g., if *C* was armed and had a reputation for the use of violence in such circumstances).

C's conduct in such circumstances is a putative threat, and the defense claim is one of putative duress. Alldridge, *Developing the Defence of Duress*, 1986 CRIM. L. REV. 433, 433. Conceptually, *D* is acquitted in such circumstances based on the conjunction of two "defenses," mistake-of-fact and duress. As in other mistake situations, as long as an actor's understanding of the factual circumstances was reasonably based, the common law usually interprets the situation as if the reasonable appearances were reality.

27. A. WERTHEIMER, COERCION 204 (1987); Nozick, *supra* note 15, at 447.

28. Threats ordinarily are also distinguishable from warnings. *See* Greenawalt, *Criminal Coercion and Freedom of Speech*, 78 NW. U.L. REV. 1081, 1096-97 (1983); Nozick, *supra* note 15, at 445, 453-58. Unlike a threat, which is expressed for the purpose of changing another's behavior, a warning merely informs another of the unpleasant consequences (Y) that will befall him if he behaves (or fails to behave) in a particular manner (X). Thus, if I tell my son that "If you do not study hard (X), you will not get into a good college (Y)," I am not threatening him, but am predicting a future event over which I have no control. A warning does not necessarily become a threat merely because X is an illegal act (e.g., "If you do not embezzle money (X), your creditors will take away your property (Y).").

Of course, a warning may also be a disguised threat. If the "warner" has control over whether the unpleasant consequence (Y) occurs, the statement that connects conduct (X) to (Y) may be intended as a warning threat. Thus, if I tell my son that "If you do not do your homework tonight (X), you will not be able to go to the basketball game with me tomorrow (Y)," I may simply be issuing a warning—a reminder, of sorts—about the pleasant consequence that will be lost if he has to forego the game in order to do his work at the last moment. But it may fairly be interpreted as a warning threat, since it is in my power to cause (Y) to occur, and I may have issued the "warning" in order to induce him (not) to do (X).

Some suggest the criminal law distinguishes between threats and offers because the former play on our fears, whereas offers—temptations—merely play on our desires.[29] Intuitively, society believes that conduct is freer when individuals respond to temptations than when they act out of fear. Individuals want what is offered, but not what is threatened. Consequently, when a threatened *D* acts unwillingly, society will impute his wrongful actions to *C*. In distinction, offeree *D* desires the consideration presented, so his will is considered predominant.[30] As such, D must accept the moral consequence of his actions.

To a strict determinist, this distinction is incomprehensible, since no human act can be free in a meaningful sense.[31] Even among those who accept the existence of human freedom, however, the threat-offer dichotomy is unpersuasive. Some parties reason that the distinction between threat and offer is illusory because it is based on the invalid fear-desire dichotomy.[32] Fear, it is argued, is itself a desire, namely, the desire to avoid unpleasant consequences. The typical coercer "tempts" her victim with his life.[33]

It is also counterintuitive to some critics to assume that "offers" inevitably are less coercive than "threats." Is it evident, for example, that when *C* tempts impecunious *D1* with an offer of one million dollars to commit a minor crime, the pressure he feels is meaningfully less than that which wealthy *D2* experiences when *C* threatens him with the loss of one million dollars unless he commits the same crime?

Doubtlessly, the fear-desire and threat-offer distinctions are semantically questionable. The fact remains, however, that it correctly expresses our intuitive sense about the two types of cases. Society believes that the contract killer is freer to reject a million dollar deal to commit a homicide (and, therefore, is more deserving of condemnation), than someone who is ordered to kill on pain of losing an equivalent amount of money or suffering bodily harm.[34]

29. Norrie, *Freewill, Determinism and Criminal Justice*, 3 LEGAL STUD. 60, 71 (1983).

30. L. KATZ, *supra* note 7, at 69-70; Nozick, *supra* note 15, at 459.

31. Norrie, *supra* note 29, at 71; *see infra* note 156 and accompanying text.

32. Pennock, *Coercion: An Overview*, in COERCION: NOMOS XIV 5 (1972) (author observes that two of five contributing scholars believe that a promise of benefit can be as coercive as a threat).

33. L. KATZ, *supra* note 7, at 70 ("When I *threaten* to kill you if you don't do what I tell you, am I not *tempting* you with your life to do what I tell you?"); Norrie, *supra* note 29, at 71 ("[F]ears and desires are no more than different kinds of the same thing, the forces that motivate us to act.").

34. *See* Kruglanski & Yinon, *Evaluating an Immoral Act Under Threat Versus Temptation: An Illustration of the Achievement Principle in Moral Judgment*, 3 J. MORAL EDUC. 167 (1974) (study shows that a person who commits an immoral act in order to gain a benefit is considered more

Typical life experiences confirm this belief in comparative freedom. It is probably harder for persons to give up what they already have (whether it is their bodily safety or decent living conditions) than to reject that to which they have not yet grown accustomed. These differential feelings are no less real or morally relevant because they cannot be empirically verified,[35] or even logically justified.[36]

---

immoral than one who commits the same act to avoid a loss). The study is briefly discussed in L. KATZ, *supra* note 7, at 70.

35. Some validation may exist. Fear (from a threat), like anger, can physiologically incapacitate us, at least to some degree. *See* Dressler, *Rethinking Heat of Passion: A Defense in Search of a Rationale*, 73 J. CRIM. L. & CRIMINOLOGY 421, 462 n.287 (1982). This author knows of no evidence that temptations physiologically affect us in this manner.

36. Professor Andrew Ashworth recently argued, however, that "natural" feelings and intuitions should not be "regarded as benchmarks of criminal responsibility and punishment," since "[i]ntrospection may be revealing, but it cannot be a substitute for rational argument." Ashworth, *Criminal Attempts and the Role of Resulting Harm Under the Code, and in the Common Law*, 19 RUTGERS L.J. 725, 748 (1988).

Perhaps so. Certainly, not all intuitions or feelings deserve our respect, even if they are strongly held. *See* R. DWORKIN, TAKING RIGHTS SERIOUSLY 248-53 (1977). Nonetheless, we should not depreciate the importance and value of feelings and intuitions in moral philosophy. If feelings are not a substitute for rational argument, the converse is also true.

We do not need to validate all of our moral beliefs. For example, there is no need to prove that torture of babies is morally wrong. Are not our intuitive responses of shock or repugnance at the thought of such conduct sufficient? Do we have any doubt that our beliefs on this matter are right? Indeed, do we have any doubt that our feelings are right even if torturing babies might actually prove rational and sensible in certain circumstances?

In straightforward cases, no moral theory ought to be accepted if it is counterintuitive. Intuitions should trump rational arguments. *See* Fischer, *Responsiveness and Moral Responsibility*, in RESPONSIBILITY, CHARACTER, AND THE EMOTIONS 82 (F. Schoeman ed. 1987) ("A theory of moral responsibility should capture our intuitive judgments about clear cases."); Moore, *Causation and the Excuses*, 73 CALIF. L. REV. 1091, 1144 (1985) ("The only moral argument I can imagine that would establish one interpretation over the other is one that appeals to the totality of our moral experience involving praise and blame.").

Furthermore, some moral concepts, such as desert and responsibility, are not susceptible to rational proof, but will persist as long as people are people. *See* Weinreb, *The Complete Idea of Justice*, 51 U. CHI. L. REV. 752, 782 (1984) [hereinafter Weinreb, *Justice*] ("We may acknowledge that we do not and cannot know [desert's] . . . bases . . . . One might have thought that unavoidable ignorance of that kind would defeat the notion altogether. Evidently that is not so."); Weinreb, *Desert, Punishment, and Criminal Responsibility*, 49 LAW & CONTEMP. PROBS., Summer 1986, at 47, 78-79 [hereinafter Weinreb, *Desert*]. *See also infra* note 156 and accompanying text.

As long as this is so, as Ashworth recognizes, *supra*, at 748, any society that allows its rules of criminal responsibility to diverge too far from such deeply held moral feelings runs the unacceptable risk of severing the criminal law from its moral underpinnings and jeopardizing its moral legitimacy and practical efficacy.

Finally, it is worth noting that emotions have independent moral significance. Certain feelings are more morally desirable than others. People are judged by their feelings. The person who empathizes with an injured person is considered a better person than one who is apathetic to another's pain. M. MOORE, LAW AND PSYCHIATRY: RETHINKING THE RELATIONSHIP 107 (1987); Sabini & Silver, *Emotions, Responsibility and Character*, in RESPONSIBILITY, CHARACTER, AND THE EMOTIONS 165-75 (F. Schoeman ed. 1987).

b. *Nature of the threat:* Not all threats exculpate. As a matter of law, a threat only exculpates if it: (i) emanates from a human being, (ii) is unlawful, and only if the threat is to (iii) imminently cause, (iv) death or grievous bodily harm, (v) to *D* or *X*, a third person.

i. *Human threat:* A rabid dog's menacing actions may threaten my safety. Similarly, a threat of rain can cause cancellation of an outdoor event.[37] Nonetheless, duress only applies to threats arising from humans. Nonhuman threats, or "conditions," exculpate actors, if at all, on the grounds of necessity, a separate defense.[38]

ii. *Unlawfulness:* Scholars disagree about whether a person can be coerced by a lawful threat.[39] Solely as an empirical phenomenon, the answer should be yes. When I tell my son that I will not take him to the basketball game unless he finishes his homework, I probably am coercing him to do his homework—i.e., he is doing something unpleasant that he would not have done but for the threat. Similarly, the police officer who orders a drunk to leave private premises where he is trespassing[40] uses a lawful threat of arrest to compel compliance. The degree to which an actor's will is constrained by a threat need not have anything to do with the lawfulness of the command.

Understandably, lawful threats rarely arise in criminal cases in which duress is pleaded. A justifiable demand will not often result in unlawful conduct (i.e., conduct that requires exculpation).[41] Although courts rarely articulate the requirement,[42] it is doubtlessly true that coercion does not exculpate unless the threat was unlawful.

The unlawfulness requirement is consistent with the concept of duress as an excuse.[43] Excuses are recognized when wrongdoers are

---

37. Of course, it could be argued that the threat here does not arise from natural causes but from the prognosticator of the inclement weather. However, if we seek to "blame" someone for the cancellation of the game, Nature, not the weather forecaster, is the likely culprit.

38. *See infra* notes 111-23 and accompanying text.

39. *E.g.*, Cohen, *Robert Nozick and Wilt Chamberlain: How Patterns Preserve Liberty*, in JUSTICE AND ECONOMIC DISTRIBUTION 259 (J. Arthur & W. Shaw eds. 1978) (yes); R. NOZICK, ANARCHY, STATE, AND UTOPIA 262 (1974) (no); Westen, *"Freedom" and "Coercion" - Virtue Words and Vice Words*, 1985 DUKE L.J. 541, 548 (yes).

40. *See* O'Sullivan v. Fisher, [1954] S.A. St. R. 33, *cited in* G. WILLIAMS, CRIMINAL LAW: THE GENERAL PART 759 (1961).

41. For an excellent discussion of the few cases that arise in this context, see Fingarette, *supra* note 1, at 80 n.42.

42. *But see* Regina v. Hurley & Murray, 1967 V.R. 526, 543 (court emphasized the requirement that the threat be an unlawful act).

43. The excusing aspect of duress is developed *infra* at notes 153-95 and accompanying text.

blameless for their conduct.[44] One who commits an *unlawful* act as the result of a *lawful* threat could not be blameless.[45]

iii. *Imminency:* To exculpate, a threat must be imminent or, as courts sometimes require, "present, imminent and impending."[46] These latter terms actually suggest two related but independent concepts.

First, the threat must be present "in the sense that it is effective to neutralise the will of the accused at that time [when the offence was committed]."[47] That is, the fear caused by the threat must be operating on the mind of the actor at the time of the criminal act.[48] This requirement insures the existence of a causal connection between the threat and the wrongful act.

Second, the threat must be "imminent and impending." At a minimum, this means that the actor would not have sufficient time to avoid future violence.[49] Courts rarely clarify the concept further, but successful duress claims typically involve threatened injuries that will follow nearly instantly if the coerced actor fails to obey. The defense may apply even if the threat "may not follow instantly but [only] after an interval,"[50] i.e., if there is no reasonable opportunity for delaying tactics.[51]

iv. *Death or grievous bodily injury:* Although court language varies, death and grievous bodily injury are the only two types of threatened harm that unambiguously exculpate a coerced actor.[52]

---

44. *See infra* notes 154-55 and accompanying text.

45. This assumes, of course, that the actor is not insane or otherwise independently excusable.

46. Hitchler, *supra* note 3, at 537; *see* People v. Sanders, 82 Cal. App. 778, 785, 256 P. 251, 254 (1927); Koontz v. State, 204 So. 2d 224 (Fla. Dist. Ct. App. 1967); Commonwealth v. Robinson, 382 Mass. 189, 199, 415 N.E.2d 805, 812 (1981); State v. Toscano, 74 N.J. 421, 432-33, 378 A.2d 755, 760 (1977) (quoting R. PERKINS, CRIMINAL LAW 916-18 (2d ed. 1969)); State v. Lee, 78 N.M. 421, 423, 432 P.2d 265, 267 (1967); Regina v. Hurley & Murray, 1967 V.R. 526, 543 (C.A.).

The imminency requirement is so entrenched in American legal history that at least one court has grafted it on to a statute even though the American Law Institute's Model Penal Code does not so require it. People v. Maes, 41 Colo. App. 75, 583 P.2d 942 (1978).

47. Regina v. Hudson and Taylor, [1971] 2 Q.B. 202, 206 (C.A.).

48. People v. Luther, 394 Mich. 619, 623, 232 N.W.2d 184, 187 (1975).

49. *Sanders*, 82 Cal. App. at 785, 256 P. at 254; Slater v. State, 185 Ga. App. 889, 890-91, 366 S.E.2d 240, 241-42 (Ga. Ct. App. 1988); Burton v. State, 51 Tex. Crim. 196, 201, 101 S.W. 226, 229 (1907).

50. *Hudson & Taylor*, 2 Q.B. at 207 (citing Subramaniam v. Public Prosecutor, [1956] 1 W.L.R. 965, 972 for the principle).

51. For example, in *Subramaniam*, 1 W.L.R. 965, *D* was charged with unlawful possession of ammunition. He asserted that he was forced to accept the contraband by terrorists because he feared for his safety if they returned. The Privy Council ruled that his plea of duress should go to the jury.

52. *E.g.*, *Sanders*, 82 Cal. App. at 785, 256 P. at 254; Commonwealth v. Robinson, 382 Mass. 189, 199, 415 N.E.2d 805, 812 (1981); *Luther*, 394 Mich. at 623, 232 N.W.2d at 187; People v.

Courts rarely define the phrase "grievous bodily injury" in duress cases, but in other contexts it has come to mean "injury periling life,"[53] "is likely to be attended with dangerous or fatal consequences,"[54] or "seriously interfere[s] with [the victim's] health and comfort."[55] Although these definitions differ in significant ways,[56] force that would cause grievous bodily injury is generally considered force that falls within the broad definition of "deadly force."[57] Thus, it is fair to say that common law duress requires a threat of deadly force.

v. *Harm to D or others:* Most duress cases involve a threat to the well-being of the person compelled to commit the crime. Only occasionally do appellate decisions speak about threats to others. Although the law is not wholly consistent, the plea is generally recognized if the deadly force is directed at a third person, especially if that person is a family member.[58]

c. *Lack of fault of the coerced actor:* Little case law on the subject exists,[59] but duress probably may not be pleaded by one who is at fault for placing himself in the coercive situation.[60] For example, a person who joins a terrorist organization and later is coerced to commit a crime, is denied the defense.[61]

Repke, 103 Mich. 459, 471-72, 61 N.W. 861, 865 (1895); State v. Toscano, 74 N.J. 421, 434, 378 A.2d 755, 760-61 (1977); State v. Lee, 78 N.M. 421, 423, 432 P.2d 265, 267 (1967); State v. Kearns, 27 N.C. App. 354, 357, 219 S.E.2d 228, 230-31 (1975); State v. Knapp, 147 Vt. 56, 59, 509 A.2d 1010, 1011-12 (1986); Pancoast v. Commonwealth, 2 Va. App. 28, 33-34, 340 S.E.2d 833, 836-37 (1986); State v. Tanner, 301 S.E.2d 160, 163 (W. Va. 1982); *Hudson & Taylor*, 2 Q.B. at 206; Regina v. Hurley & Murray, 1967 V.R. 526, 543 (C.A.).

A few cases suggest, at least in dictum, that a threat of imprisonment may suffice. *E.g.*, Regina v. Steane, [1947] 1 K.B. 997, 1005 ("Duress is a matter of defence where a prisoner is forced by fear of violence or imprisonment to do an act which in itself is criminal."). In such circumstances an implied threat of death usually exists if the kidnapper's demands are not met. Yeo, *The Threat Element in Duress*, 11 CRIM. L.J. 165, 167 (1987).

53. Wellar v. People, 30 Mich. 16, 20 (1874).

54. People v. Crenshaw, 298 Ill. 412, 416, 131 N.E. 576, 577 (1921).

55. Commonwealth v. Dorazio, 365 Pa. 291, 301, 74 A.2d 125, 130 (1950).

56. *See* J. DRESSLER, UNDERSTANDING CRIMINAL LAW § 31.05 (1987).

57. State v. Clay, 297 N.C. 555, 562-63, 256 S.E.2d 176, 182 (1979) (defining "deadly force" in context of self-defense as "force likely to cause death or great bodily harm").

58. J. DRESSLER, *supra* note 56, at § 23.01; W. LAFAVE & A. SCOTT, *supra* note 16, at § 5.3(a); R. PERKINS & R. BOYCE, *supra* note 1, at 1061-62; Yeo, *supra* note 52, at 167. *Contra* Herring v. State, 152 Ga. App. 150, 262 S.E.2d 529 (1979).

59. O'Regan, *supra* note 4, at 35.

60. Ross v. State, 169 Ind. 388, 390, 82 N.E. 781, 781 (1907); State v. Clay, 220 Iowa 1191, 1203, 264 N.W. 77, 83 (1935); People v. Merhige, 212 Mich. 601, 611, 180 N.W. 418, 422 (1920); Regina v. Hurley & Murray 1967 V.R. 526, 543 (C.A.); *see* D.P.P. v. Lynch, 1975 App. Cas. 653, 668 (Lord Morris of Borth-y-Gest).

61. Regina v. Fitzpatrick, 1977 N.Ir. 20.

Like the usually implicit rule that a threat be unlawful,[62] the requirement that the coerced actor come to the situation free from fault is consistent with the nature of the defense as an excuse. A person should not be permitted to plead blamelessness, as an excuse implies, if he was culpably responsible for the predicament in which he found himself.[63]

d. *Crimes for which the defense applies:* Duress has been recognized, in holdings or dictum, as a defense to the offenses of armed robbery,[64] attempted robbery,[65] arson,[66] bigamy,[67] burglary,[68] conspiracy to commit larceny,[69] forgery,[70] illegal presence in the country,[71] malicious damage,[72] mutiny,[73] perjury,[74] prison escape,[75] receiving stolen property,[76] riot,[77] sale of illegal drugs,[78] treason,[79] and unlawful possession of ammunition.[80] Case law is divided regarding the applicability of the defense to rape.[81]

---

62. *See supra* notes 39-45 and accompanying text.

63. A different result is appropriate if duress is rationalized as a justification, *see infra* notes 124-52 and accompanying text. As a justification, duress arguably merges with the lesser-harm defense of necessity, *see infra* notes 111-23 and accompanying text. In such a case, if one seeks to defend duress/necessity on utilitarian grounds, the defense should be available to persons who negligently or recklessly created the emergency that justified the necessitous conduct. Robinson, *Causing the Conditions of One's Own Defense: A Study in the Limits of Theory in Criminal Law Doctrine*, 71 VA. L. REV. 1, 27-28 (1985).

64. People v. Adcock, 29 Ill. App. 3d 917, 920, 331 N.E.2d 573, 576 (1975).

65. Koontz v. State, 204 So. 2d 224, 226 (Fla. Dist. Ct. App. 1967).

66. Ross v. State, 169 Ind. 388, 389, 82 N.E. 781, 781 (1907); Regina v. Shiartos, unreported opinion of September 29, 1961, *cited in* Beaumont, *Duress as a Defence to Murder*, 1976 DALHOUSIE L.J. 580, 581.

67. Burton v. State, 51 Tex. Crim. 196, 201, 101 S.W. 226, 229 (1907).

68. Beal v. State, 72 Ga. 200, 200 (1883).

69. Regina v Gill, [1963] 1 W.L.R. 841, 843.

70. United States v. Birch, 470 F.2d 808, 812 (4th Cir. 1972), *cert. denied*, 411 U.S. 931 (1973).

71. United States v. Palmer, 458 F.2d 663, 665 (9th Cir. 1972).

72. People v. Martin, 13 Cal. App. 96, 98, 108 P. 1034, 1034 (1910) (dynamiting a house); Rex v. Crutchley, 172 Eng. Rep. 909 (1831).

73. United States v. Haskell, 26 F. Cas. 207 (C.C.E.D. Pa. 1823) (No. 15,231).

74. United States v. Nickels, 502 F.2d 1173, 1177 (7th Cir. 1974), *cert. denied*, 426 U.S. 911 (1975); McCoy v. State, 78 Ga. 490, 492, 3 S.E. 768, 769 (1887); Bain v. State, 67 Miss. 557, 560, 7 So. 408, 409 (1890); Regina v. Hudson & Taylor [1971] 2 Q.B. 202, 206 (C.A.).

75. United States v. Bailey, 444 U.S. 394 (1980).

76. Robinson v. State, 141 Tex. Crim. 380, 386, 148 S.W.2d 1115, 1118 (1941); Attorney General v. Whelan, 1934 I.R. 518 (C.C.A.).

77. Rex v. Crutchley, 172 Eng. Rep. 909 (1831).

78. United States v. McClain, 531 F.2d 431, 438 (9th Cir.), *cert. denied*, 429 U.S. 835 (1976).

79. Hitchler, *supra* note 3, at 525 (discussing applicable cases).

80. Subramaniam v. Public Prosecutor [1956] 1 W.L.R. 965, 968 (P.C.).

81. People v. Patton, 25 Ill. App. 3d 840, 844, 322 N.E.2d 592, 595 (1975) (permitting the defense); State v. Dowell, 106 N.C. 722, 11 S.E. 525 (1890) (disallowing the defense).

Thankfully, coerced homicides (or, at least, reported prosecutions) have been rare. Nonetheless, there is considerable authority or dictum[82] for the proposition that the defense may not be pleaded in murder prosecutions.[83] Indeed, recent judicial efforts to narrow the no-defense rule have been overruled.[84]

Some courts also state that the defense may not be pleaded in any situation "where innocent life is taken,"[85] thus apparently disallowing the defense in manslaughter prosecutions.[86] Similarly, some courts disallow the defense in any case in which the coerced actor unsuccessfully attempted to take life.[87]

B. Statutory Reform

1. *Model Penal Code*[88]

Thirteen states[89] have adopted in whole or in substantial part the

82. While noting the general rule against the defense in murder prosecutions, courts often place their decisions on alternative grounds, such as a lack of imminency of the deadly threat. J. HALL, *supra* note 4, at 439.

83. Arp v. State, 97 Ala. 5, 12, 12 So. 301, 303 (1892); Brewer v. State, 72 Ark. 145, 153, 78 S.W. 773, 776 (1904); Cawthon v. State, 382 So. 2d 796, 797 (Fla. Dist. Ct. App. 1980); State v. Fisher, 23 Mont. 540, 556-57, 59 P. 919, 924 (1900); State v. Fuller, 203 Neb. 233, 243, 278 N.W.2d 756, 762, *supplemented by* 204 Neb. 196, 281 N.W.2d 741 (1979); State v. Little, 67 N.C. App. 128, 130, 312 S.E.2d 695, 697 (1984); State v. Metcalf, 60 Ohio App. 2d 212, 215, 396 N.E.2d 786, 789 (1977); Leach v. State, 99 Tenn. 584, 595, 42 S.W. 195, 197 (1897); Abbott v. The Queen, 1977 App. Cas. 755, 758; Regina v. Bourne, 36 Crim. App. 125, 128 (1952); Rex. v. Steane, 1947 K.B. 997, 1005; Attorney General v. Whelan, 1934 I.R. 518, 526 (C.C.A.); 4 W. BLACKSTONE, *supra* note 2, at *27; 1 M. HALE, HISTORY OF THE PLEAS OF THE CROWN 50 (1736); 2 J. STEPHEN, *supra* note 3, at 107. This rule even applies to unintentional felony-murders: State v. Ng, 110 Wash. 2d 32, 750 P.2d 632, 636 (1988); State v. Moretti, 66 Wash. 537, 540, 120 P. 102, 104 (1912).

There is scant authority for the proposition that duress may serve as a partial defense by reducing the seriousness of an intentional killing to manslaughter. Wentworth v. State, 29 Md. App. 110, 121, 349 A.2d 421, 428 (1975); Regina v. Hercules, [1954] 3 S. African 826, 832.

84. The most significant inroad was Director of Public Prosecutions for Northern Ireland v. Lynch, 1975 App. Cas. 653, 677, in which the House of Lords ruled that the defense could be pleaded by a principal in the second degree to the murder. *Lynch* was overruled twelve years later. Regina v. Howe, [1987] 2 W.L.R. 568, 583.

85. Corujo v. State, 424 So. 2d 43, 44 (Fla. Dist. Ct. App. 1982).

86. Not all courts agree with this approach. *E.g.*, R. v. Evans & Gardiner (No. 1), [1976] V.R. 517 (although the defense is not available to accomplices to murder, it may be pleaded in manslaughter prosecutions).

87. Cawthon v. State, 382 So. 2d 796, 797 (Fla. Dist. Ct. App. 1980) (attempted murder); Watson v. State, 212 Miss. 788, 793-94, 55 So. 2d 441, 443 (1951) (assault with intent to kill).

88. *See generally* J. DRESSLER, *supra* note 56, § 23.07 (summary of the Model Penal Code's approach to the defense of duress).

89. ALASKA STAT. § 11.81.440 (1983); ARK. STAT. ANN. § 5-2-208 (1987); COLO. REV. STAT. § 18-1-708 (1986); CONN. GEN. STAT. ANN. § 53a-14 (West 1985); DEL. CODE ANN. tit. 11, § 431 (1987); HAW. REV. STAT. § 702-231 (1985); KY. REV. STAT. ANN. § 501.090 (Michie/Bobbs-Merrill 1985); MO. ANN. STAT. § 562.071 (Vernon 1979); N.J. STAT. ANN. § 2C:2-9 (West 1982); N.Y.

definition of duress framed by the American Law Institute (ALI) in the MPC:

> (1) It is an affirmative defense that the actor engaged in the conduct charged to constitute an offense because he was coerced to do so by the use of, or threat to use, unlawful force against his person or the person of another, which a person of reasonable firmness in his situation would have been unable to resist.
> (2) The defense . . . is unavailable if the actor recklessly placed himself in a situation in which it was probable that he would be subjected to duress. The defense is also unavailable if he was negligent in placing himself in such a situation, whenever negligence suffices to establish culpability for the offense charged.[90]

This version of the defense differs from the common law in five significant ways. First, it dispenses with the requirements of deadly force and imminency. A defendant is excused as long as the unlawful force was of the type such that a "person of reasonable firmness" in the actor's situation "would have been unable to resist," or, more accurately, would not have resisted.[91] Thus, it is not necessarily fatal to a duress claim that *D* committed a crime in reaction to a threat by *C* that she would kill or grievously injure him or *X* at a *future* date, or even that she would cause some other, more moderate, physical injury to *D* or *X*.[92]

Second, the defense may be pleaded as an excuse for any crime, including murder. Third, the defense applies if *D* was coerced by *C*'s *prior* use of physical force, even if *D* no longer is threatened. Thus, under appropriate circumstances, a victim of coercive persuasion (commonly called "brainwashing") could be excused for criminal activity.[93]

Fourth, the defense applies in the following atypical situation: *C* threatens harm unless *D* commits a particular act; *D* seeks to avoid the threatened physical injury by performing a different, albeit criminal, act that was not desired by *C*. For example, suppose that *C*, a prison inmate,

---

PENAL LAW § 40.00 (McKinney 1987); 18 PA. CONS. STAT. ANN. § 309 (Purdon 1983); S.D. CODIFIED LAWS ANN. § 22-5-1 (1988); UTAH CODE ANN. § 76-2-302 (1978).

90. MODEL PENAL CODE § 2.09(1)-(2) (1985).

91. Dressler, *supra* note 18, at 708-09.

92. For example, if *C* threatened minor physical harm to *D*'s three young children unless *D* committed a larceny, a jury would not be precluded from excusing *D* for acceding to the threat.

In such circumstances, *D*'s conduct might also be justifiable as a choice of lesser evils, under MODEL PENAL CODE § 3.02 (1985). MODEL PENAL CODE § 2.09(4) (1985) provides: "When the conduct of the actor would otherwise be justifiable under Section 3.02, this Section does not preclude such defense." The advantage in pleading duress is that *D* would not have to show that the harm that would have befallen the children was a greater evil than the theft.

93. MPC COMMENTARIES, *supra* note 20, § 2.09 commentary at 376-77.

threatens serious physical harm to *D*, another inmate, unless the latter accedes to *C*'s sexual demands. Rather than do so, *D* flees confinement and seeks later to be excused for his escape. At common law, this excuse claim might fail for various reasons, including the fact that *C* never ordered *D* to escape. Under the MPC, the conduct of the escapee could be excused.[94]

Finally, as the previous differences suggest, the MPC involves the jury (assuming it is not waived) more deeply in the determination of the excuse than is the case at common law. The jury determines whether the hypothetical "person of reasonable firmness" would have resisted the threat. On its face, this appears to be a factual determination, but in reality the jury must also make a moral judgment about the degree of moral firmness that can be expected of persons in the actor's circumstances.[95] In contrast, at common law, the jury's role was limited to straightforward factfinding to determine whether there was a threat and, if so, was it deadly, unlawful, and imminent.

2. *Non-MPC Reform*

In contradistinction to the MPC, eighteen states by statute,[96] and twelve by common law,[97] retain the common law rule that duress applies

94. *Id.* at 377. The inmate might also successfully claim that his flight was justified under MODEL PENAL CODE § 3.02 (1985). *See supra* note 92 and accompanying text.

MODEL PENAL CODE § 2.09 (1985) may also excuse deadly self-defense against innocent aggressors. Thus, if *V*, a child too young to know what he is doing, threatens to kill *D*, *D* would be excused in killing the youth if a person of ordinary firmness would have been unable to resist. Alexander, *Justification and Innocent Aggressors*, 33 WAYNE L. REV. 1177, 1187 (1987). Normally, such cases are treated as justifiable self-defense since *V* was a deadly aggressor. Indeed, the MPC would also seem to justify such conduct. MODEL PENAL CODE § 3.04(1) (1985).

95. *See infra* notes 192-95 and accompanying text.

96. ALA. CODE § 13A-3-30 (1975); ARIZ. REV. STAT. ANN. § 13-412 (1978); CAL. PENAL CODE § 26(6) (West Supp. 1988); GA. CODE ANN. § 16-3-26 (1988); IDAHO CODE § 18-201(4) (1987); ILL. ANN. STAT. ch. 38, para. 7-11 (Smith-Hurd 1972); IND. CODE ANN. § 35-41-3-8 (Burns 1988); IOWA CODE ANN. § 704.10 (West 1979); KAN. STAT. ANN. § 21-3209 (1988); LA. REV. STAT. ANN. § 14:18(6) (West 1986); ME. REV. STAT. ANN. tit. 17-A, § 103-A (1983); MINN. STAT. ANN. § 609.08 (West 1987); MONT. CODE ANN. § 45-2-212 (1987); NEV. REV. STAT. ANN. § 194.010(8) (Michie 1986); N.D. CENT. CODE § 12.1-05-10 (1985); TEX. PENAL CODE ANN. § 8.05 (Vernon 1974); WASH. REV. CODE ANN. § 9A.16.060 (1988); WIS. STAT. ANN. § 939.46 (West 1988).

97. Koontz v. State, 204 So. 2d 224, 226 (Fla. Dist. Ct. App. 1967); Wentworth v. State, 29 Md. App. 110, 118, 349 A.2d 421, 426 (1975); Commonwealth v. Robinson, 382 Mass. 189, 199-200, 415 N.E.2d 805, 812 (1981) (including MPC-like language that the actor "be put in a condition of mind where neither he nor a person of reasonable firmness could have acted otherwise in the circumstances"); People v. Merhige, 212 Mich. 601, 610-11, 180 N.W. 418, 422 (1920); State v. Fuller, 203 Neb. 233, 243, *supplemented by* 204 Neb. 196, 278 N.W.2d 756, 762 (1979); State v. Lee, 78 N.M. 421, 423, 432 P.2d 265, 267 (1967); State v. Kearns, 27 N.C. App. 354, 357, 219 S.E.2d 228, 230-31

only if the coercer threatens use of deadly force. In addition, five states, which have no duress statute or relevant case law,[98] presumably would apply the common law rule in the absence of legislative direction.[99]

The ALI recommendation that the defense apply to all offenses also has failed to be generally accepted. In addition to the seventeen jurisdictions that have not codified the defense at all[100] (and, therefore, would not allow the defense to be pleaded in murder cases), twenty-one other states (including four MPC states[101]) statutorily disallow the defense in the prosecution of one or more crimes.

All twenty-one codification states prohibit the defense in some or all murder cases.[102] Three of these states go further and disallow a duress plea in the prosection of all intentional homicides (thereby precluding use of the plea in voluntary manslaughter prosecutions).[103] Two jurisdictions prevent its use in all criminal homicide prosecutions.[104] Three states further disallow the defense in various nonhomicide circumstances,

(1975); State v. Procter, 51 Ohio App. 2d 151, 158, 367 N.E.2d 908, 913 (1977); State v. Robinson, 622 S.W.2d 62, 73, (Tenn. Crim. App. 1980) *appeal dismissed, cert. denied sub nom.* LeMay v. Tennessee, 454 U.S. 1096 (1984); State v. Knapp, 147 Vt. 56, 59, 509 A.2d 1010, 1011 (1986); Pancoast v. Commonwealth, 2 Va. App. 28, 33, 340 S.E.2d 833, 836 (1986); State v. Tanner, 301 S.E.2d 160, 163 (W. Va. 1982).

98. These states are Mississippi, New Hampshire, Rhode Island, South Carolina, and Wyoming.

99. Two states have ambiguous statutes. OKLA. STAT. ANN. tit. 21 §§ 152(7), 155, 156 (West 1983) (excuses persons who act "while under involuntary subjection to the power of superiors," or in "actual compulsion by use of force or fear"); OR. REV. STAT. § 161.270 (1985) (excuses conduct coerced by "use of or threatened use of unlawful physical force upon the actor of a third person, which force or threatened force was of such nature as to overcome earnest resistance").

100. *See supra* notes 97-99 and accompanying text.

101. These states are Colorado, Kentucky, Missouri, and New Jersey.

102. ALA. CODE § 13A-3-30 (1975) (murder); ARIZ. REV. STAT. ANN. § 13-412 (1978) (homicide or serious physical injury); CAL. PENAL CODE § 26(6) (West Supp. 1988) (crime punishable with death); COLO. REV. STAT. § 18-1-708 (1986) (class 1 felony); GA. CODE ANN. § 16-3-26 (1988) (murder); IDAHO CODE § 18-201(4) (1987) (crime punishable with death); ILL. ANN. STAT. ch. 38, para. 7-11 (Smith-Hurd 1972) (offense punishable with death); IND. CODE ANN. § 35-41-3-8 (Burns 1985) (offense against the person); IOWA CODE ANN. § 704.10 (West 1979) ("intentionally or recklessly causes physical injury to another"); KAN. STAT. ANN. § 21-3209 (1988) (murder or voluntary manslaughter); KY. REV. STAT. ANN. § 501.090 (Michie/Bobbs-Merrill 1985) (intentional homicide); LA. REV. STAT. ANN. § 14:18(6) (West 1986) (murder); ME. REV. STAT. ANN. tit. 17-A, § 103-A (1983) ("intentionally or knowingly committed the homicide"); MINN. STAT. ANN. § 609.08 (West 1987) (murder reduced to first degree manslaughter); MO. ANN. STAT. § 562-071 (Vernon 1979) (murder); MONT. CODE ANN. § 45-2-212 (1987) (offense punishable with death); NEV. REV. STAT. ANN. § 194.010(8) (Michie 1986) (crime punishable with death); N.J. STAT. ANN. § 2C:2-9 (West 1982) (murder reduced to manslaughter); OR. REV. STAT. § 161-270 (1985) (murder); WASH. REV. CODE ANN. § 9A.16.060 (1988) (murder or manslaughter); WIS. STAT. ANN. § 939.46 (West 1988) (murder reduced to manslaughter.

103. *See supra* note 102, regarding Kansas, Kentucky, and Maine.

104. *See supra* note 102, regarding Arizona and Washington.

including offenses involving serious physical injury.[105] One state rejects the defense for all crimes in which intent-to-kill is an element.[106]

Like the twelve common law jurisdictions[107] and thirteen MPC jurisdictions, eight additional states explicitly preclude use of the defense by those who culpably placed themselves in the situation in which it was probable that they would be subjected to duress.[108] Finally, in light of later discussion in this Article,[109] it is noteworthy that four criminal codes explicitly treat duress as a justification rather than as an excuse.[110]

C. Duress Versus Necessity

For purposes of clarity, duress should be distinguished from necessity, an independent defense recognized in most modern penal codes, including the MPC,[111] as well as in the common law of the United States[112] and, probably, England.[113] In general, necessity exculpates when, as the result of a naturally-caused condition, "a man has his choice of two evils before him, and, being under a necessity of choosing one, he chooses the least pernicious of the two."[114]

---

105. *See supra* note 102, regarding Arizona and Iowa.

106. N.M. Stat. Ann. § 14-5131 (1986) (jury instruction).

107. *See supra* note 97 and accompanying text.

108. Seven non-MPC states preclude the defense if the defendant was intentionally or recklessly (or, sometimes more precisely, intentionally, knowingly, or recklessly) at fault: Ala. Code § 13A-3-30(b) (1988); Ariz. Rev. Stat. Ann. § 13-412 (1978); Ind. Code Ann. § 35-41-3-8(b)(1) (West 1986); Kan. Stat. Ann. § 21-3209(2) (1981) ("willfully or wantonly"); Or. Rev. Stat. § 161.270(2) (1985); Tex. Penal Code Ann. § 8.05(d) (Vernon 1974); Wash. Rev. Code Ann. § 9A.16.060(3) (1988).

An eighth state, Maine, provides that the defense is inapplicable in cases of recklessness. Me. Rev. Stat. Ann. tit. 17-A, § 103-A (1983). Presumably, however, the defense is also unavailable to one whose *mens rea* is more culpable.

Two of the above statutes provide that the defense is unavailable in prosecutions of crimes if the actor was negligently at fault. Ala. Code § 13A-3-30(b) (1988); Me. Rev. Stat. Ann. tit. 17-A, § 103-A (1983).

109. *See infra* notes 124-52 and accompanying text.

110. Ariz. Rev. Stat. Ann. § 13-412 (1978); Iowa Code Ann. § 704.10 (West 1979); La. Rev. Stat. Ann. § 14.18(6) (West 1986); Me. Rev. Stat. Ann. tit. 17-A, § 103-A (1983).

111. Model Penal Code § 3.02(1)(a) (1985)

> Conduct that the actor believes to be necessary to avoid a harm or evil to himself or to another is justifiable, provided that: (a) the harm or evil sought to be avoided by such conduct is greater than that sought to be prevented by the law defining the offense charged.

112. MPC Commentaries, *supra* note 20, § 3.02 commentary at 10.

113. Glanville Williams "somewhat confidently" reports that it was a defense in England. G. Williams, *supra* note 40, at 724. Some commentators disagree; *see* The Law Commission, No. 83, Criminal Law Report on Defenses of General Application 20 (1977). The Law Commission recommended that the defense "as may exist" be abolished. *See generally* Williams, *Necessity*, 1978 Crim. L. Rev. 128.

114. 4 W. Blackstone, *supra* note 2, at *30-31.

Unfortunately, modern courts frequently blur the distinction between duress and necessity[115] or treat the dichotomy as "narrow and unreal."[116] Some American treatise authors promote the latter view. For example, Professors Perkins and Boyce treat necessity as if it were a type of duress,[117] while Professors LaFave and Scott consider duress a subspecies of necessity.[118]

In one sense, such judicial and scholarly treatment of the defenses is understandable. Often, the only difference between the defenses is the nature of the threat. At common law, necessity involves the situation in which the greater evil—the one properly avoided by the actor—was naturally caused. An example of this is when a lightning storm forces *D* to trespass on *V*'s land in order to seek safety. When the threat is human in origin—e.g., an armed terrorist threatens to kill *D* unless he drives on *V*'s land—only a plea of duress potentially may be invoked.[119]

Nonetheless, as the law has developed, necessity and duress are distinguishable. As Blackstone and most modern statutes (including the MPC) define necessity, the plea is properly understood to be a justification defense since it is based on the premise that the actor "chooses the least pernicious" of two evils.[120] On the other hand, duress is more commonly an excuse.[121] Since important differences exist between

115. *E.g.*, United States v. Bailey, 444 U.S. 394, 410 (1980) ("Modern cases have tended to blur the distinction between duress and necessity."); Commonwealth v. Thurber, 383 Mass. 328, 330, 418 N.E.2d 1253, 1256 (1981) ("Necessity is similar to duress, and differences have sometimes been blurred.").

A prime example of the merger of the defenses is the judicial reaction to prison escapes by inmates who fled confinement due to allegedly intolerable, imminent prison conditions, usually threats of physical or sexual assaults by fellow inmates. Increasingly, courts have permitted escapees to raise such claims. *See generally* Comment, *Intolerable Conditions as a Defense to Prison Escapes*, 26 UCLA L. REV. 1126 (1979). Some courts identify the defense as one of necessity; others call precisely the same claim duress. *E.g.*, State v. Reese, 272 N.W.2d 863 (Iowa 1978) (necessity); People v. Haromon, 53 Mich. App. 482, 220 N.W.2d 212 (1974), *aff'd*, 394 Mich. 625, 232 N.W.2d 187 (1975) (duress).

116. D.P.P. v. Lynch, 1975 App. Cas. 653, 701 (Lord Kilbrandon) ("The difference between the defence of duress, which comes from coercion by the act of man, and that of necessity, which comes from coercion by the forces of nature, is narrow and unreal.").

117. R. PERKINS & R. BOYCE, *supra* note 1, at 1065.

118. W. LAFAVE & A. SCOTT, *supra* note 16, § 5.4, at 443.

119. *Id.* § 5.4, at 441.

120. If the actor chooses to save one life by taking another life, the ordinary view is that "the doctrine of necessity must generally be silent, because the two lives must be accounted equal in the eye of the law and there is nothing to choose between them." G. WILLIAMS, *supra* note 22, at 562. This view is not universally accepted. *Id.* at 562 n.1. For example, Jerome Hall would recognize the defense in "the preservation of at least an equal value." J. HALL, *supra* note 4, at 426.

121. *See infra* notes 182-95 and accompanying text.

justifications and excuses,[122] lawyers should understand the difference between the two defenses.[123] Consequently, unless otherwise indicated, the term "necessity" is used in this Article only in the Blackstone/MPC sense of a concept of justification.

II. DURESS AS A JUSTIFICATION

A. IN GENERAL

Why does coercion exculpate? More precisely, does society acquit persons who act under duress because their actions were *justifiable*, or is it that we *excuse* them—render them personally blameless—for their unjustifiable conduct?[124]

Neither the law nor legal literature answers these questions consistently. Some statutes identify duress as a justification,[125] while most

122. *See infra* notes 124-29 and accompanying text.

123. This does not mean necessity could not serve as an excuse. Fletcher, *The Individualization of Excusing Conditions*, 47 S. CAL. L. REV. 1269, 1273, 1274 (1974) (describing necessity as "the protypical ambiguity" which has the "capacity to function now as a justification and now as an excuse."). *See infra* notes 228-37 and accompanying text.

124. Many scholars and some courts now appreciate the difference between justifications and excuses. Although much more can be said on the matter, *see* J. DRESSLER, *supra* note 56, at 179-90; Dressler, *Justifications and Excuses: A Brief Review of the Concepts and the Literature*, 33 WAYNE L. REV. 1155 (1987), the difference between the two classes of defenses is straightforward.

When the law tolerates, permits, or actively encourages otherwise wrongful, socially harmful conduct, we say that the law *justifies* the act. Self-defense, defense of third persons, and crime prevention are among the recognized modern justification defenses.

On the other hand, we recognize *excuse* defenses when we do not blame the actor for his unjustified conduct. By excusing a person for his wrongdoing, society does not hold him accountable for the harm caused. In other words, "an excuse shows that *one* was not to blame, whereas a justification shows that one was not to *blame*." Watson, *Responsibility and the Limits of Evil*, in RESPONSIBILITY, CHARACTER, AND THE EMOTIONS 260 (F. Schoeman ed. 1987). Or, as Joel Feinberg has explained it, "to plead excuse is in effect to admit that one's action 'wasn't a good thing to have done, but to argue that it is not quite fair or correct to say *baldly*,' or without qualification, that one did the thing at all, that it was one's *action*." J. FEINBERG, HARM TO OTHERS 108 (1984) (quoting J. L. Austin, *A Plea for Excuses*, in PROCEEDINGS OF THE ARISTOTELIAN SOCIETY 57 (1956-57)) (footnote omitted). Insanity, mistake, and involuntary intoxication are excuse defenses.

Practical, not merely academic, reasons merit concern by lawyers about the justification-excuse distinction. Dressler, *supra*, at 1167-74; *but see* L. KATZ, *supra* note 7, at 65 ("With only a little verbal legerdemain, you can turn any justification into an excuse (and vice versa)."); Greenawalt, *Distinguishing Justifications from Excuses*, 49 LAW & CONTEMP. PROBS., Summer 1986, at 89 [hereinafter Greenawalt, *Distinguishing*] (arguing that because of the law's need for rigid labels, the law should not strive for clear distinctions); Greenawalt, *The Perplexing Borders of Justification and Excuse*, 84 COLUM. L. REV. 1897 (1984) [hereinafter Greenawalt, *Justification and Excuse*] (agreeing that differences exist and that legal theorists should attend to the distinctions, but arguing that Anglo-American law should not attempt to distinguish between the concepts in a systematic way).

125. *See supra* notes 109-10 and accompanying text.

consider it an excuse.[126] Legal scholars also disagree. For George Fletcher, duress is "a paradigmatic example of an excuse,"[127] while an influential criminal law treatise treats it as a subspecies of the lesser-harm justification defense of necessity.[128]

In part, such disagreement may be the result of confusion about, or insensitivity to, the differences between the concepts of justification and excuse generally.[129] Nonetheless, some of the disagreement is principled. Unlike insanity, which can only be characterized as an excuse, or the defense of crime prevention, which doubtlessly is a justification, duress is not easily explained.

As a purely descriptive matter, the defense *can* function either as a justification or as an excuse. Normatively, as well, an intellectually coherent case for duress as a justification can be mounted. Nonetheless, as I discuss more fully in Part III, duress is more satisfactorily viewed in excuse terms.

B. Lesser-Harm Justification Theory

Professors LaFave and Scott consider duress a justification.[130] Their statement seems intended merely as a description of the common law. In the paradigmatic case, *D* commits a crime short of homicide

126. *E.g.*, statutes that model the defense upon the MPC treat it as an excuse. *See supra* notes 89-95 and accompanying text.

127. G. Fletcher, *supra* note 3, at 830; *but see id.* at 798-99 (describing insanity and involuntary intoxication as paradigmatic excuses, and observing that duress is regarded as an excuse in some, but not all, legal systems).

128. W. LaFave & A. Scott, *supra* note 16, at 433 ("The rationale of the defense of duress is that, for reasons of social policy, it is better that the defendant, faced with a choice of evils, choose to do the lesser evil . . . in order to avoid the greater evil threatened by the other person."); *see also id.* at 433, 434, 436, 443 (in which they explicitly treat the conduct of the coerced actor as "justified").

129. As an example of such apparent justification/excuse confusion, see Borins, *The Defence of Duress*, 24 Crim. L.Q. 191, 191-93 (1981-82) (in which the author, a York County Court judge, described duress as an excuse, cited the Canadian Criminal Code as support, but then rationalized the defense by quoting both from Glanville Williams's justification-based explanation of the defense, G. Williams, *supra* note 40, at 755-56, and from Attorney General v. Whelan, 1934 I.R. 518, 526, (C.C.A.), an Irish case which explicitly described duress as a justification). *See also* Feliciano v. Delaware, 332 A.2d 148, 149 (Del. 1975) (applying the MPC's excuse-oriented definition of duress to explain that duress and self-defense "are different species of justification defense . . . [and] are kindred defenses in that each involves compulsion in a 'choice of evils' setting."); Crawford v. State, 61 Md. App. 620, 622, 630-31, 487 A.2d 1214, 1215, 1219-20 (1985) (discussing "duress of circumstances" in terms of "excuse," yet equating it to self-defense, a justification).

130. *See supra* notes 118, 128 and accompanying text. I do not mean to suggest that these legal scholars stand alone in this view. Indeed, Professor Glanville Williams, in his extremely influential English treatise, rationalized duress in lesser-harm justification terms. G. Williams, *supra* note 40, § 246, at 755 ("Most persuasively, it is allowed where the evil of breaking the letter of the law is less than the evil that was illegally threatened against the accused.").

because of an imminent deadly threat by *C*. Under these circumstances, commission of the crime is a lesser evil or social harm than that threatened. *D*'s conduct is, therefore, justifiable.

By this view, duress lacks any independent force as a defense. It is simply a special version of the justification defense of necessity,[131] special only because the circumstances were produced by a human rather than a natural force. The moral reasoning (whether utilitarian[132] or nonconsequentialist[133]) that justifies performing a lesser evil in the latter case would similarly justify the coerced actor to accede to the threat.

This explanation of duress is unsatisfactory. First, even if we are satisfied with a merely descriptive account of duress, it only explains the traditional version of the defense. The lesser-harm concept does not explain the law in those jurisdictions, such as MPC-based states, that reject the common law no-homicide rule or that treat the defense as an excuse.[134]

---

131. *See supra* notes 111-23 and accompanying text.

132. The defense of necessity is often justified on utilitarian grounds. At the time of a threatening tornado, from a utilitarian perspective, it is preferable that *D* trespass on *V*'s property rather than that he die as the result of the tornado. One can similarly argue that duress is justified when *D* avoids his or another's death at the hands of a coercer by committing a property offense.

133. The defense of necessity can be defended on nonconsequentialist grounds. For example, a rights-oriented view of justification theory would suggest that *D*'s act of injuring *V*'s property to save his own life is justifiable because *D* was defending his human right of autonomy which overrides *V*'s defeasible property right. Brudner, *supra* note 10, at 370.

134. Unfortunately, although the MPC treats justification as a discrete concept, it nowhere defines "excuse" or identifies obvious excuse defenses in such terms. Nonetheless, the commentary to § 2.09 explicitly treats duress as an excuse. MPC COMMENTARIES, *supra* note 20, at 368-84. While conceding this, Professor Hyman Gross has argued that the defense "appear[s] more like a justification than an excuse." H. GROSS, A THEORY OF CRIMINAL JUSTICE 288 (1979).

Gross offers two unpersuasive reasons for his observation. First, the Code makes no allowance for pecuniary and reputational threats; only physical threats suffice. Gross reasons that this limitation "makes sense in the design of a justification, though not of an excuse, for interests in remaining free of physical harm may be deemed sufficiently important to justify acts undertaken for their protection, though interests in income or reputation may be thought not to be important enough." *Id.* at 288-89.

This reasoning cannot be correct, however, since the Code's "choice of evils" defense would potentially justify an actor in precisely these circumstances. For example, if *D* were ordered by *C* to slap *V* in the face or else suffer immense reputational or economic loss, a jury could reasonably conclude that *D* was justified in committing the minor physical harm demanded. MODEL PENAL CODE § 3.02 (1985).

The duress defense is limited to physical threats because, according to the commentary, "threats to property or even reputation cannot exercise sufficient power over persons of 'reasonable firmness' to warrant consideration in these terms." MPC COMMENTARIES, *supra* note 20, § 2.09 commentary at 375. The drafters' reasoning on this matter is also unpersuasive, *see* Dressler, *supra* note 18, at 712, but their decision on this matter hardly converts duress to a justification.

Gross's second argument supporting the MPC duress defense as a justification is its limitation to *unlawful* threats. He reasons that this rule makes sense in a justification context: quite obviously,

Second, as the latter point suggests, it is the disallowance of the defense in murder cases that renders the lesser-harm justification analysis facially plausible. Yet, it is unlikely that this rule is the consequence of a prior determination that duress is a justification. Rather, the no-homicide rule is likely based on the deontological claim that it is morally wrong to kill innocent persons, even if the coerced homicidal act might constitute a lesser social evil.[135] Thus, the irony is that a nonconsequentialist moral imperative assists a consequentialist explanation of duress as a justification.

Third, as a descriptive assertion, it is not entirely accurate to conclude that all common law duress cases involve the commission of the lesser evil. Duress exculpates not only when the actor is threatened with death, but also when the actor accedes to a threat of serious bodily injury. The actor can be acquitted although the actor has caused equal or slightly greater harm than was threatened. For example, suppose that *C* threatens to cut off *D*'s arm unless *D* rapes *V*. Presumably,[136] *D* will be acquitted of rape; yet it is unlikely that the exculpatory force of the case depends on an analysis of whether the loss of an arm or rape is the greater evil.

Or, suppose the harm threatened is precisely the same as the harm commanded: *D* must cut off *V*'s right arm or else lose his own right

---

one is not justified in committing an unlawful act in response to a lawful threat; but, Gross states, with duress as an excuse "the matter is quite different. Force or its threatened use, whether lawful or unlawful, will equally deprive the actor of his ability to do otherwise, for opportunities are equally foreclosed regardless of the legitimacy of the acts foreclosing them." H. GROSS, *supra*, at 289.

Again, Gross misapprehends the nature of duress as an excuse. Duress does not exculpate an actor for lacking the capacity to choose to act lawfully or, even as Gross's statement suggests, because he lacks the opportunity to conform his conduct to the law. Rather, duress is an excuse because the actor lacked a *fair* opportunity to behave lawfully. This is a normative judgment. As such, it is reasonable to conclude that a person has a fair opportunity to behave lawfully if the coercive threat was a lawful one.

Gross apparently values this point. After making his case for analyzing the defense as a justification, Gross concedes that "a case of sorts" can be made for duress as an excuse by arguing that "coercion deprives the one coerced of *fair* opportunity to do otherwise." *Id*. at 289 (emphasis added). Thus, when coercion is lawful, obedience to the law is a reasonable course to be taken; likewise, when only pecuniary or reputational harm is threatened, "there are available to him (in theory, at least) satisfactory remedies that he may later pursue to repair the harm that is done." *Id*. Nonetheless, inexplicably, Gross states that "conceived in this way as an excuse, the defense of duress seems forced and unnatural, while as a justification its special requirements come naturally into play." *Id*. at 290.

135. Fletcher, *supra* note 123, at 1279. For further discussion of the no-homicide rule, *see infra* notes 205-27 and accompanying text.

136. Some jurisdictions do not excuse coerced rapes. *See supra* note 81 and accompanying text.

appendage. The harm is equal,[137] and the defense applies. Yet, the usual view is that conduct is not justified (although excusable) unless it prevents a greater, not simply an equal, harm.[138]

Fourth, as previously observed,[139] the common rule that the coerced actor must enter the situation free of fault is defensible if duress is an excuse, but not if the defense is a lesser-harm justification. Finally, a lingering question remains: If duress is a subspecies of necessity, why do courts and legislatures persist in recognizing a separate claim of duress? Courts and legislatures have not failed to see the obvious. The lesser-harm analysis only explains the easy cases of duress.

The theory does not adequately capture our moral intuitions in morally troubling circumstances. My intuitions may not be the reader's nor can I empirically prove that my intuitions are more commonly held than another's, but I submit that people do not intuitively equate the decision by *D1* to avoid a storm by trespassing on *V1*'s land (a typical case of necessity) with *D2*'s act of raping *V2* because *C* threatens *D2*'s young child with death, although both cases involve lesser-harm events.

Indeed, society's moral intuitions regarding *D2*—whether to justify, excuse, or punish—do not fundamentally change whether he attacks *V2* because his child was threatened with death or because his child would suffer an equal or somewhat lesser bodily injury, such as a severe beating. More is going on here than simply weighing comparative harms.[140] The feeling in the pit of our stomachs tells us so.[141] Society must go beyond the lesser-harm theory to find out why duress persists as a separate defense from necessity, as well as to provide a normative justification for its retention.

C. Self-Interest as a Justification

If the lesser-harm theory does not adequately explain our reaction to cases of duress (or, at least, not to all cases), is there another, more satisfying, explanation to justify committing an otherwise criminal act as the result of coercion, *even when the harm caused by the coerced actor is*

137. Of course, an act-utilitarian might argue that the harms are not necessarily equal. The loss of a hand by an artist or surgeon, for example, would be greater than a law professor's loss of a hand.

138. *See supra* note 120 and accompanying text.

139. *See supra* notes 59-63 and accompanying text.

140. Balancing the threat against the crime *is* involved, but in the context of determining whether to excuse the coerced actor, rather than to justify him. *See infra* note 195 and accompanying text.

141. L. Katz, *supra* note 7, at 64.

equal to, or greater than, that threatened by the coercer? The answer depends in part on one's understanding of the concept of justification. If one believes that a justified act "typically reflects well on the actor's courage or devotion to the public interest,"[142] duress hardly qualifies as a justification defense. But, this view of justification is surely too narrow; it could not even justify most cases of self-defense.[143]

It is also difficult to justify compelled conduct if, as many scholars assert,[144] justifications are truly universal principles (i.e., if *A* is objectively the right thing to do, anyone should be justified in doing *A*, or assisting another to do *A*), and, further, incompatible justifications are necessarily impossible (i.e., no one can be justified in resisting the commission of justified act *A*). Therefore, notice the implications of the universalization-incompatibility view of justification. If coerced actor *D* is justified in raping *V* to protect his child from serious harm or death, it necessarily would be justifiable for *X*, a stranger, to rape *V*, in order to protect *D*'s child, or for *X* to assist *D* in raping *V* by holding a knife at *V*'s throat. Consequently, it would also be unjustifiable for *V* forcibly to resist the attack. It is unlikely that such conclusions satisfy ordinary moral intuitions. If so, then the initial premise justifying coerced conduct should be questioned.

The conclusion that duress is not based on justification analysis may be correct, but the universalizability-incompatibility premise, which is thought to support the conclusion, is incorrect.[145] Justifications can be agent-relative.[146] In another context, it is not morally incoherent for society to permit an on-duty police officer to use deadly force in self-defense without retreating to a place of known safety because he acts in our behest, while society often denies the same justification to a non-retreating private person who acts solely in self-defense. Indeed, many criminal codes take precisely this position.[147]

Similarly, a limited, intellectually coherent argument for a non-universizable version of duress as a justification is possible, and has been

142. G. FLETCHER, *supra* note 3, at 799.

143. *See generally* Dressler, *New Thoughts About the Concept of Justification in the Criminal Law: A Critique of Fletcher's Thinking and Rethinking*, 32 UCLA L. REV. 61, 78-81 (1984) (arguing that justified actors are not necessarily "good characters").

144. *E.g.*, G. FLETCHER, *supra* note 3, at 761-69; Robinson, *A Theory of Justification: Societal Harm as a Prerequisite for Criminal Liability*, 23 UCLA L. REV. 266, 277-79 (1975).

145. Dressler, *supra* note 143, at 87-91, 95-98; Greenawalt, *Justification and Excuse*, *supra* note 124, at 1915-27; Greenawalt, *Distinguishing*, *supra* note 124, at 91.

146. The term is from Nagel, *The Limits of Objectivity*, in 1 TANNER LECTURES ON HUMAN VALUES 102 (1980).

147. MODEL PENAL CODE § 3.04(2)(b)(ii)(B) (1985).

suggested.[148] The duress-as-justification argument is based on the general principle that, at least within certain limits, self-interested conduct, even when it results in equal or greater social harm, is morally permissible.

On this theory, it would be morally justifiable for a person to value his own interests, or perhaps that of a family member, over the equivalent interests of a stranger, although a noninterested person and society would value the interests equally.[149] For example, under this theory *D* could justifiably kill *V* to avoid his own death because *D* may value his own life over *V*'s, although society would treat the losses as equal. Or, *D* could justifiably kidnap *V*, rather than allow *C* to kidnap *D*'s child, although the harms again are equal. Yet, in each of these cases, *X*, a third person unrelated to *D*, would not be justified in committing or assisting in the intended crime.[150]

It cannot be gainsaid that such a moral position is plausible. Even if it is accepted, it would have rather limited applicability. First, and most obviously, it does not apply to the case where a coerced person causes harm to an innocent person in order to protect a stranger from less harm. Such conduct ordinarily exculpates, so one must look elsewhere to explain such a rule.

Second, it is likely that few who would justify self-interested conduct are willing to take the theory to its logical conclusion. Some people might only permit an actor to cause rather minor harm to another to protect himself from similar or lesser harm. For example, *D* is arguably justified in pushing *V* in order to avoid a similar battery threatened by *C*,

148. A. WERTHEIMER, *supra* note 27, at 165-69.

149. It is beyond the scope of this Article to develop fully the moral arguments that might support this claim. A rule-utilitarian might conclude that criminal laws that require a person to value interests in a non-self-interested manner might create societal dissatisfaction (and consequent disregard for the law) that outweigh the benefits of the principle. Indeed, even Bentham considered it "right and proper" within limits to aim to promote one's own personal happiness. H. SIDGWICK, THE METHODS OF ETHICS 119 (7th ed. 1962).

Similarly, egoism, a nonutilitarian consequentialist theory that philosophers Hobbes and Spinoza, and classical capitalist theorist Adam Smith espouse, posits that "[e]ach person ought to do that which will most benefit himself." Bayles, *Introduction*, in CONTEMPORARY UTILITARIANISM 4 (M. Bayles ed. 1978). Finally, a nonteleological theory, based on the right of personal autonomy, can be propounded in favor of self-interested conduct. *See* Nagel, *supra* note 146, at 120.

150. This moral theory of justification would also apply outside the realm of duress. Thus, it would be justifiable for an adult to kill an innocent aggressor, such as a child, in necessary self-defense, although a stranger would be unjustified in killing the youth in defense of the adult. *See* Alexander, *supra* note 94, at 1189.

It must be emphasized that the point here is not whether a legislature or court ought to draw the distinctions laid out here, only that such a position is morally coherent.

but *D* is not similarly justified in kidnapping or killing *V*, even to avoid a similar fate. In this case, duress as a justification would have little practical significance because it is unlikely that minor batteries would be prosecuted. One would presumably have to look to excuse theory to defend exculpation in most criminal cases, in particular, to defend abandonment of the no-homicide rule of the MPC.

Similarly, other advocates of this moral theory might not agree that self-interest justifies causing substantially greater harm. *D* might be justified in raping *V* in order to deter *C* from raping his wife, but he would not be justified in doing so to avoid a minor battery of his wife. *D* might be justified in killing one person to save his own life, but would not be justified in killing ten to save one.[151] Indeed, given the qualitative difference between death and other nondeadly forms of harm, it is not at all clear that *D* can ever be justified in killing another, even to save himself or a loved one from very serious personal injury.[152]

Ultimately, most people probably reject self-interest as a justification of coerced action, even in limited circumstances. It is much easier to excuse than to justify the person who places his own well-being above that of another. If *D1* kills or robs *V1* in order to avoid rape by *C*, or if *D2* rapes *V2* in order to protect his wife from the same fate, we may conclude that the actor has committed an equal or only slightly greater harm than was threatened, but it matters little to our reaction. *D1* and *D2* may escape punishment for their actions not because society condones these actions, but rather because they, like the persons whom they have wronged, are victims who deserve to be excused. It is excuse theory, therefore, that justifies the duress defense.

III. DURESS AS AN EXCUSE

A. The Problems with Excusing Coerced Actions

Although cases of justifiable coerced action potentially exist, most states treat duress as an excuse. But, it must be recognized at the outset that it is an atypical excuse.[153] In general, a person is excused for his wrongdoing when it is unjust to punish him.[154] It is unjust to punish a person for his wrongdoing when he does not deserve to be blamed for

151. Wertheimer agrees. A. Wertheimer, *supra* note 27, at 167 n.91.

152. *Cf.* Coker v. Georgia, 433 U.S. 584 (1977) (given the irrevocability of death, capital punishment is per se disproportionate punishment for the crime of rape).

153. *See* Brudner, *supra* note 10, at 351 (discussing the concept of necessity as an excuse).

154. *See infra* note 155.

it.[155] In most excusing situations—e.g., in cases of insanity, infancy, or involuntary intoxication—the wrongdoer is blameless because he substantially lacked the capacity for free choice.[156] That is, due to the excusing condition at the time of the crime, he substantially lacked the

155. Obviously, I am presenting a retributive rather than utilitarian explanation of excuses. As is now commonly accepted by nearly all but the most die-hard utilitarians, deterrence theory does not adequately explain the existence of excuses in the criminal law. H.L.A. HART, PUNISHMENT AND RESPONSIBILITY 40-53 (1968), powerfully rebuts Jeremy Bentham's original analysis of excuses, based on the nondeterrability of excused actors in J. BENTHAM, AN INTRODUCTION TO THE PRINCIPLES OF MORALS AND LEGISLATION § 3 (1789). *See also* H. PACKER, THE LIMITS OF THE CRIMINAL SANCTION 117-18 (1968) (further rebutting the utilitarian analysis).

In turn, Hart has offered a more sophisticated utilitarian explanation for excuses, centering on the premise that excuses enable individuals to plan their lives with reasonable confidence that the coercive forces of the law will not intervene unless they freely choose to break the law. In this way, excuses maximize societal satisfaction. H.L.A. HART, *supra*, at 45. However, as Professor Kadish has observed, "[s]omething is missing in this account." Kadish, *Excusing Crime*, 75 CALIF. L. REV. 257, 264 (1987). That "something" is this:

> To blame a person is to express a moral criticism, and if the person's action does not deserve criticism, blaming him is a kind of falsehood and is, to the extent the person is injured by being blamed, unjust to him. It is this feature of our everyday moral practices that lies behind the law's excuses. Excuses, then, . . . represent no sentimental compromise with the demands of a moral code; they are, on the contrary, of the essence of a moral code.

Id.

It is for this reason that utilitarian reasoning receives very little attention in this Article. *But see infra* notes 212-15 and accompanying text.

156. Any thoughtful discussion of excuses runs up against the claim of determinists that, in simplest terms, "things must be as they are." Goodman, *Determinism and Freedom in Spinoza, Maimonides, and Aristotle: A Retrospective Study*, in RESPONSIBILITY, CHARACTER, AND THE EMOTIONS 107 (F. Schoeman ed. 1987). To the modern, psychoanalytically inclined determinist, free will is an illusion since our will "is only an instrument, a slave, in the hands of a deep unconscious motivation which determines his action." Hospers, *Free Will and Psychoanalysis*, in REASON AND RESPONSIBILITY 357 (J. Feinberg 5th ed. 1981). We cannot control our past and, therefore, are not responsible for it, yet it shapes our character, and consequent motives and actions. The past, therefore, in conjunction with the laws of nature, makes us who we are and do what we do. Eagle, *Responsibility, Unconscious Motivation, and Social Order*, 6 INT'L J.L. & PSYCHIATRY 263, 264 (1983); Fischer, *supra* note 36, at 100.

The trouble that determinism creates for criminal law theory is obvious enough: "*[J]ust* punishment and *moral* condemnation imply moral guilt and guilt implies moral responsibility and moral responsibility implies freedom and freedom implies the falsity of determinism." Strawson, *Freedom and Resentment*, in FREEDOM AND RESENTMENT AND OTHER ESSAYS 2 (1974). Freedom and cause are mutually exclusive concepts; "[a]s soon as one is eliminated, the other occupies the field." Weinreb, *Justice*, *supra* note 36, at 781. If one accepts as true both determinism and the necessity of moral guilt and desert as preconditions of punishment, duress not only is the only true excuse in the law, but it is a universal one. (Of course, one can favor punishment in the absence of moral desert. We can punish people for the same reason that "men strive to extirpate poisonous snakes," namely because they are dangerous, and even though they "offend only by their own nature and cannot do otherwise." Spinoza, COGITATA METAPHYSICA II cap. 8, Gebhardt, vol. 1, 265, *as cited in* Goodman, *supra*, at 123 n.42.)

Some philosophers have sought to prove that moral responsibility is compatible with determinism. Termed "compatibilists" or "soft determinists," they have reasoned that a person possesses freedom (at least, sufficient to blame and punish) in the sense that "he was free to do otherwise," as

capacity to understand the relevant facts regarding his conduct, to appreciate its wrongfulness, or to conform his conduct to the law.[157]

In such circumstances, the excused actor lacks the unique and, for purposes of punishment, critical attribute of personhood:[158] the ability to apply what Professor Michael Moore has termed "practical reasoning" skills.[159] With this disability, he cannot be a responsible moral agent. At least at the time of the wrongdoing, he is not a member of the moral community.[160] Although he may communicate, he cannot reason morally with society.[161] He is "no more the proper subject[ ] of moral evaluation than . . . [an] animal[ ], or even [a] stone[ ]."[162]

---

long as the latter phrase means simply, "he could have done otherwise if he had had the desire or will to do otherwise."

The problem with soft determinism is also obvious enough: "the desire or will to do otherwise" is itself determined, assuming the truth of determinism. Thus, freedom to the compatibilist means "determined choice," an apparent oxymoron. Norrie, *supra* note 29, at 67.

Despite the logical problems of soft determinism, and the incompatibility of the hard variety with the premise of moral responsibility, the issue of determinism's truth or falsity is commonly relegated to a footnote like this—often with an intellectual shrug of the shoulders—because nearly all of us, including determinists, live our lives as if we have freedom. As Jerome Hall put it, determinist theory "falls like snowflakes on a mountain." J. HALL, *supra* note 4, at 415.

Science increasingly demonstrates that freedom is a myth—that the "autonomous capacity [of humans] that remains is squeezed into a corner," Weinreb, *Desert*, *supra* note 36, at 57—yet we—including the scientists—persist in believing that we are free.

Einstein has written, for example, that he did "not at all believe in human freedom . . . . Everybody acts not only under external compulsion but also in accordance with inner necessity." A. EINSTEIN, IDEAS AND OPINIONS 8 (1982). Yet, he also observed that "[e]xternal compulsion can . . . reduce but never cancel the responsibility of the individual." *Id.* at 27. Likewise, Freud, a determinist, stated that one aim of his psychoanalytic theory was "to give the patient's ego *freedom* to decide one way or another." P. GAY, FREUD: A LIFE FOR OUR TIME 119 (1988) (quoting Freud).

If Einstein and Freud persisted in believing in freedom and responsibility and acting upon it, it is unlikely any of us can live as if determinism is true. Blame, praise, the sense that we have freedom of choice, and similar "irrational feelings" are simply too much a part of human life to ignore.

157. Dressler, *supra* note 18, at 701.

158. Dressler, *supra* note 124, at 1166.

159. *See* M. MOORE, *supra* note 36, at 9-43 (1984); Moore, *supra* note 36, at 1148

> At a bare minimum, the ability to reason practically involves: (1) the ability to form an object we desire to achieve through action, (2) the ability to form a belief about how certain actions will or will not achieve the objects of our desires, and (3) the ability to act on our desires and our beliefs . . . .

160. Strawson, *supra* note 156, at 17

> [H]e is not seen as one on whom demands and expectations lie in that particular way in which we think of them as lying when we speak of moral obligation; he is not . . . seen as a morally responsible agent, as a term of moral relationships, as a member of the moral community.

161. *Id.* at 9.

162. Moore, *supra* note 36, at 1137. As a result, Moore describes insanity, involuntary intoxication, and infancy as status excuses. *Id.* at 1099, 1109-11. Kadish describes them as nonresponsibility excuses. *See* Kadish, *supra* note 155, at 278. In distinction to these defenses, Moore considers duress a "true" excuse. Moore, *supra* note 36, at 1097.

Thus, just as we do not blame the pit bull who kills, or the stone that breaks our window, but rather blame the person who lets the dog free or throws the stone, the insane person or similarly excused actor is immune[163] from moral blame for his wrongdoing. In the language of P.F. Strawson, such excuses "invite us to suspend our ordinary reactive attitudes towards the agent, either at the time of his action or all the time."[164] We may feel many emotions regarding the excused actor: fear, repulsion, compassion; but we do not feel the type of anger that results in blame.

A coerced wrongdoer is unlike the insane person. The coerced actor is a whole person, free of sickness. As such, he possesses the capacity for free choice; he has practical reasoning skills. Unlike the insane actor, he is a morally responsible agent. Even while coerced, he is a member of the moral community, a person who by status is entitled to blame or praise. When he commits a crime, he is not intrinsically free from blame.

Furthermore, the coerced actor not only possesses the capacity to understand the attendant factual and legal circumstances, but he does *in fact* realize what it is he is doing. When *D* steals a watch under duress, he knows that he is taking a watch; when he commits perjury, he realizes that he is uttering a falsehood under oath; and when he succumbs to a kill-or-be-killed command, he knows perfectly well that he is taking a human life.[165] In none of these cases could *D* reasonably deny that he knew that his actions were unlawful.

Indeed, what most weakens the case for excuse is that the coerced

---

163. The excusing condition may only partially impair the actor. In such circumstances, we can and do blame the actor, but we may consider him less responsible than if the disability were more extreme. Partial excuses are appropriate in such circumstances.

164. Strawson, *supra* note 156, at 8.

165. Courts have frequently and erroneously made a contrary claim. *E.g.*, People v. Anderson, 409 Mich. 474, 491, 295 N.W.2d 482, 490, *cert. denied*, 449 U.S. 1101 (1981) (duress "goes to the central issue of criminal intent"); People v. Luther, 394 Mich. 619, 622, 232 N.W.2d 184, 186-87 (1975) (duress excuses *D* because "the compulsion . . . overcomes the defendant's free will and his acts lack the required mens rea"); State v. Tanner, 301 S.E.2d 160, 163 (W. Va. 1982) (the actor is excused because "the necessary ingredient of intent . . . is then lacking"); Regina v. Bourne 36 Crim. App. 125, 129 (1952) (Lord Goddard, C.J.) ("she could have set up the plea of duress, not as showing that no offense had been committed, but as showing that she had no *mens rea*").

Occasionally, coercion may negate a *mens rea*, particularly a specific intent required in a criminal offense. For example, in Regina v. Steane, [1947] 1 K.B. 997, the defendant was charged with "doing acts likely to assist the enemy *with intent to assist the enemy*." *Id.* Lord Goddard believed that the coerced defendant might have lacked the latter specific intent. *Id.* at 1003-04. Similarly, it could happen that *D*, while stealing property under duress, may have reason to believe that police officers will arrive imminently. If so, *D* may lack the specific intent to permanently deprive the owner of his property, the required *mens rea* of common law larceny.

actor *chooses* to violate the law.[166] He chooses to commit the criminal offense rather than to accept the threatened consequences. He would not have chosen to commit the crime but for the threat, but it *is* still his choice, albeit a hard and excruciatingly difficult choice. His act may be unwilling, but it is not unwilled.[167]

In no other circumstance does the law excuse a person for his rational and intentionally chosen harmful acts. Only duress cases excuse one who "self-consciously subordinates [the law] to the primacy of the person who is the subject of the desire."[168] If law is paramount, so the argument might proceed, a person who knowingly places his own interests above that of the community, as represented by the law, should not be excused.

B. Potential Excusing Explanations

1. *Expressing Compassion*

Perhaps the coerced actor is excused because society empathizes with him. Again, compare insanity to duress. The insane actor is a sick human being, not an animal or stone.[169] We should, and perhaps sometimes do, feel compassion for him because of his illness. However, in fact, the dominant emotion we probably experience is fear. Insane people do not seem like the rest of us; they are different. Literally, we may segregate them from us; figuratively, they are pushed away. In a more fundamental sense, they are already apart from the rest of society because of a lack of moral agency.

Societal feelings toward the duress defendant, however, are much warmer. The tragic circumstances often create unmitigated compassion for the defendant.[170] We can identify with him and imagine ourselves in the same predicament.[171] We recognize that his acts, although wrongful,

---

166. J. Smith & B. Hogan, Criminal Law 200 (4th ed. 1978); Brudner, *supra* note 10, at 348-49. *See infra* note 194 and accompanying text.

167. Fingarette, *supra* note 1, at 73; Waslik, *supra* note 3, at 455; A. Wertheimer, *supra* note 27, at 9-10 (describing duress as "constrained volition"). Thus, a coerced act is a voluntary act, in the sense that it involves use of the mind, rather than simply of the brain. Takacs v. Engle, 768 F.2d 122, 126-27 (6th Cir. 1985) (duress does not negate the voluntary act requirement); Dressler, *supra* note 143, at 68; Fingarette, *supra* note 1, at 73. Coerced acts involve, at most, "metaphorical involuntarism." Kadish, *supra* note 155, at 266.

168. Brudner, *supra* note 10, at 349.

169. *See supra* note 162 and accompanying text.

170. D.P.P. v. Lynch, 1975 App. Cas. 653, 670 (Morris of Borth-y-Gest) ("[I]s the law to pay no heed to the miserable, agonizing plight of such a person?").

171. Dressler, *supra* note 18, at 683 ("We feel a close connection to the coerced wrongdoer. He is perceived as a normal person in an abnormal situation. His weakness is our weakness.").

were performed to avoid personal loss rather than to secure some personal gain. The duress defendant is seen as a victim rather than as a victimizer. Unlike the insane person, who is excused but excluded, the coerced is symbolically embraced even as he is condemned for the harm he caused.

Compassion alone, however, cannot entirely explain the force of the duress excuse. Just as the insane actor is excused without passion, there can be, and often is, compassion toward people and their personal struggles in life despite the fact that they must be punished for their wrongdoing. Compassion and blame are not mutually exclusive emotions.[172]

It is too simplistic to treat coerced actors as victims rather than as victimizers, for they are both. They are victims of a coercive threat; but they are also victimizers because they have chosen to protect themselves at another innocent person's expense. Indeed, most victimizers are also victims. Even the worst criminals are victims of a poor genetic pool, of an unhealthy environment, or of both. No one acts free of inherited and environmental constraints.[173] Yet, people are *not* excused for their wrongdoing simply because their criminal activities are causally related to some factor beyond their control.[174] In the final analysis, if a person is blamed or excused on the basis of the presence or absence of empathetic feelings, society will run the risk of reaching false positive or negative conclusions. Ultimately, excusing is a matter of justice, not of compassion.[175]

---

172. *Id.*

173. *See supra* note 156 and accompanying text.

174. Moore, *supra* note 36, at 1129-39.

175. In a previous Article on the subject of excuses, Dressler, *supra* note 18, I stated that "[a]n intimate relationship exists between showing compassion and excusing." *Id.* at 682 (footnote omitted). While not going so far as to say that it was a necessary condition for excusing, I reflected that it "is closely linked to the excusing process." *Id.* at 683. Although I conceded that we do not always feel compassion for some excused actors, in particular the insane, "[e]ven here, in our best moments, we believe that we *should* feel compassion." *Id.* at 682 n.71; *cf.* G. FLETCHER, *supra* note 3, at 808 ("Excuses are motivated by compassion for persons caught in a maelstrom of circumstance."); Fletcher, *supra* note 123, at 1283 n.49 ("excusing . . . is an expression of compassion").

Upon further reflection, I do not now believe that the link between compassion and excusing is as strong as suggested. Indeed, just as I sought to show in the prior Article that feeling compassion can result in false positives—i.e., excusing persons who deserve punishment—it is doubtlessly the case that the linkage suggested can, even more often, result in false negatives—i.e., denial of excuses to persons who do not deserve punishment. Quite simply, emotions such as fear too often prevent us from feeling compassion or, at least, so overwhelm us that the compassion we do feel is hidden. Ultimately, it is a sense of justice, not a feeling of compassion, that causes us to excuse certain wrongdoers.

2. *The "I'm Just Like You" Character Claim*

Another argument closely tied to the compassion claim may seem to explain duress as an excuse: persons who act under duress are excused because they do not possess bad characters. They are not bad persons, even as they commit a bad act. In the language of Robert Nozick, they are not "anti-linked" to correct moral values.[176]

Some scholars consider evaluation of an actor's character central to the blaming-excusing process. The thesis is that a person only deserves punishment if and to the extent that his wrongdoing manifests his bad character. A wrongdoer is excused when society is satisfied that he possesses a good character or, at least, when we cannot infer badness from the wrongful conduct.[177]

The role of character in the blaming process is most plausible in duress cases. We often see ourselves when looking at the coerced defendant. We imagine ourselves in his position, doing as he did. We assume that his compelled actions do not represent his true self, that in normal circumstances he would reject his own behavior.[178] Considering ourselves decent individuals, we assume the same about the defendant. Therefore, as the coerced wrongdoer does not flout correct values, he does not deserve punishment.

The difficulties with the character theory of excuses have been noted elsewhere, so I will not reiterate them here except briefly by footnote.[179]

---

176. R. Nozick, Philosophical Explanations 382 (1981).

177. *E.g.*, G. Fletcher, *supra* note 3, at 800.

178. *See* Lynch v. D.P.P., 1975 App. Cas. 653, 678 (Lord Morris of Borth-y-Gest) (observing that *L*, a coerced actor, assisted in the crime "even though he regretted the plan or indeed was horrified by it"); Watson, *supra* note 124, at 266 (the actions of a person who acts under stress do not reflect his true moral self).

179. Dressler, *supra* note 18, at 692-701; *see also* Brudner, *supra* note 10, at 353 (unjust to punish these actors because he acts as others in his situation would act). Among the difficulties with the character theory is that character-based desert assumes that people deserve their character. Since a person's initial character is determined by heredity and early environment, and thus cannot be deserved at this early stage, a critical question for character-desert theorists is: When does a person deserve his bad character? One's character may be immutable, at least at its core. If so, desert can only be justified on a noncharacter basis. *See* Kadish, *supra* note 155, at 276 n.56.

Others, like Maimonides, believe that "[w]e can reject and overcome our inner urges and tendencies, combat and conquer our own nature, regardless of the depth, intensity, or direction of its thrust." Goodman, *supra* note 156, at 150-51. But, even if character is malleable, various questions remain. Does desert of character exist as soon as a person becomes (or should become) aware of his antisocial character and omits any effort to change? *See* A. Wertheimer, *supra* note 27, at 270 n.6. Or, does desert exist when he not only possesses a bad value system but affirmatively identifies with it, i.e., when he not only desires to be bad, but desires such a desire? It is doubtful that any human, and certainly no court, is able to answer these questions.

It is sufficient to note that a person's alleged good character, although relevant to the believability of an excuse claim[180] and critical in the forgiveness process,[181] does not render him free from responsibility for his wrongdoing.

3. *The "I Am Only Human" Claim*

a. *The empirical version:* The previous arguments move to another reason why duress is recognized as an excuse: Duress excuses because the coerced wrongdoer behaved in a statistically normal manner in particularly compelling circumstances. In a sense, the conduct should be excused because the wrongdoer is "only human."[182] The problem with this argument is that empirical normality does not by itself equate to moral excusability.

The empirical claim runs as follows.[183] Human conduct, including criminal behavior, is a function of personal characteristics and external, "environmental" factors. The issue in any case is whether primary responsibility for human conduct should be attributed to personal or to environmental factors.

According to empirical attribution theory, whether responsibility for conduct is affixed to the individual or to the environment depends on whether the individual's behavior conforms to the statistical norm for that given situation. Responsibility for conduct is attributable to the individual only when the individual acts in a statistically uncommon manner. Thus, since most people do not commit crimes in the usual state of affairs, society attributes responsibility for criminal conduct by the statistically uncommon wrongdoer to the latter's personality. Either the individual is victim of some statistically rare, excusing disability or of a nonexcusing criminal disposition.

In the usual case of duress, the statistical norm *is* criminal conduct. Most people *do* intentionally violate the law in specified coercive circumstances. Therefore, since such criminal conduct is the norm, and since

180. It is doubtlessly true that in interpersonal relations we are more apt to look for an excuse, and to believe an excuse claim, if we believe the wrongdoer possesses a good character.

181. We are more willing to forgive the good person his rare transgressions than we are willing to overlook of the bad person his usual wrongdoing. But to forgive is not to excuse or render a person blameless. Forgiveness presupposes existing blameworthiness. Dressler, *supra* note 18, at 698-701.

182. Kadish, *supra* note 155, at 266 ("[H]is action does not merit blame because it fails to distinguish him from the common run of humankind.").

183. *See generally* Schoeman, *Statistical Norms and Moral Attribution*, in RESPONSIBILITY, CHARACTER, AND THE EMOTIONS 287-315 (F. Schoeman ed. 1987) (discussing the appropriateness of attributing fault to an agent for behavior caused by something external to the agent).

such wrongdoing runs counter to the norm in noncoercive circumstances, we attribute responsibility for the intentional wrongdoing to the environment[184]—to the threat—rather than to the actor.[185]

Although the argument is appealing, duress cannot be defended simply on empirical grounds.[186] The fact that the coerced wrongdoer acts typically (and, presumably, as the juror would in the same situation) does not prove by itself that leniency toward the wrongdoer is appropriate. It only proves that most people share a tendency—more accurately, share a weakness—with the actor. Something more is required to turn an empirical norm into a moral claim for excuse.[187]

The implausibility of the empirical argument as a moral position becomes obvious as empirical examples are sought. A majority of all citizens (let us assume) cheat on their taxes, drive above the speed limit, and steal trifles from their employers. It also may be provable that a majority of defense contractors overcharge the Department of Defense or cut corners in the production of military equipment. However, it is hardly self-evident that such wrongdoers are not responsible for their actions, or that the claim "I'm only [a typical] human" should excuse.

Similarly, and more to the point of duress, even if Milgram[188] and others[189] have demonstrated that people all too readily accept commands

---

184. Conversely, we attribute responsibility to the *person* who withstands the coercion and refuses to act unlawfully. We assume that such an individual possesses an unusual personality, i.e., greater than normal courage.

185. Goodman, *supra* note 156, at 609 (quoting Professor Rupert Cross: "Duress is an excuse, because the law recognizes that the average man can only endure a limited amount of pressure from others.").

> Why, then, is it unjust to blame a person in this situation? The answer is . . . in yielding to a threat to which most of us would yield the person has not shown herself to be more blameable than the rest of us. All that distinguishes her is the accident that produced her predicament.

Kadish, *supra* note 155, at 273.

These arguments slide easily into the claim that it is hypocritical to punish a coerced actor. *See infra* notes 197-200 and accompanying text.

186. Brudner, *supra* note 10, at 353 ("A moment's reflection will reveal . . . that the empirical equality of behaviours [of the coerced actor and the average person] produces a semblance of innocence rather than innocence itself.").

187. The "something," as described *infra* at notes 192-95 and accompanying text, is evidence that the actor shares with others an incapacity or lack of fair opportunity to behave lawfully.

188. S. MILGRAM, OBEDIENCE TO AUTHORITY: AN EXPERIMENTAL VIEW (1974). The subjects of Milgram's test were told by the experimenter to give increasingly painful electrical shocks to another person (in fact, a fellow experimenter) if the latter made a mistake in answering the experimenter's questions. Milgram found that the subjects were generally willing to do as ordered, even when the shocks ostensibly caused great pain or apparent unconsciousness.

189. Various studies purport to demonstrate that persons can easily be seduced, not so much coerced, into doing things they would otherwise disapprove. *See* L. KATZ, *supra* note 7, at 74-76.

from persons in apparent authority, this need not mean that we must attribute sole or primary *moral* responsibility for all actions to authority figures. To admit that the majority would have done X in a specified circumstance—that the coerced actor has "not shown herself to be more blameable than the rest of us"[190]—may less properly acquit the actor than convict the majority.

We expect people to avoid acting unlawfully in a broad range of difficult factual circumstances. People should handle emotional and moral conflicts in a correct manner. If many or most fail this test, it demonstrates that some of life's conflicts are more difficult to resolve than originally thought.[191] But, by itself, this does not undermine the established moral rules or our culpability for violating them.

In short, duress is not like other excuses. The excusing basis is not merely empirical but primarily normative. Unlike insanity, infancy, and intoxication, the issue is not simply whether, as an empirically-verifiable matter, the actor lacked volitional or cognitive capacity; nor does duress merely involve a Gallup poll-like factual determination that a majority of persons would have acted as the defendant did in similar circumstances. This does not mean that the "I'm only human" thesis is irrelevant. Rather, something more—the normative component—must be included.

b. *The normative component:* The empirical component of the "I'm only human" claim demonstrates that sometimes life's choices are very difficult to effect. Duress excuses when the available choices are not only hard but also unfair. A person acting under duress is excused, although he possessed the capacity to make the right choice, if he lacked a fair opportunity to act lawfully or, slightly more accurately, if he lacked a fair opportunity to avoid acting unlawfully.[192]

Some studies tend to show that "once a person has been induced to comply with a small request he is more likely to comply with a larger demand." Freedman & Fraser, *Compliance Without Pressure: The Foot-in-the-Door Technique*, 4 J. PERSONALITY & SOC. PSYCHOLOGY 195, 195 (1966). Studies of small group interaction also demonstrate that the perceptions of others can substantially influence individual judgment (or, at least, expressed individual judgment). *E.g.*, Deutsch & Gerard, *A Study of Normative and Informational Social Influences Upon Individual Judgment*, 51 J. ABN. & SOC. PSYCHOLOGY 629 (1955).

190. *See* Kadish, *supra* note 155, at 273.

191. As a result, we may want to be more generous—i.e., more merciful—to transgressors than we otherwise would be.

192. One should distinguish between a "fair opportunity to act lawfully" and "fair opportunity to *avoid* acting *un*lawfully." In some cases of duress, *D* will have no opportunity, fair or otherwise, to act lawfully. *D*'s options are either to act unlawfully (do as ordered) or do nothing at all and accept the consequences of refusing to do as he was ordered. *D* does not have the chance (fairly or otherwise) to turn on *C* and resist the threatened attack (i.e., to act lawfully). Thus, where resistance

Even this statement must be carefully clarified. By definition, a coerced person never has a "fair opportunity" if we focus on the wrongfulness of *C*'s threat. That is, in cases of compulsion, *D* must choose between harm to himself or harm to another innocent person.[193] Since that choice was forced upon him unlawfully by *C*, we can always conclude that *D* has an unfair choice. Nonetheless, people are not exculpated in law or in our personal judgments simply because they were confronted with unfair, hard choices. For example, if *D* commits an aggravated battery upon *V* to avoid suffering an economic injury, neither the law nor most of society would excuse him. Nevertheless, *D*'s options may properly be described as unfair.

At its core, the defense of duress requires us to determine what conduct we, a society of individual members of the human race, may legitimately expect of our fellow threatened humans. Can society fairly expect the coerced actor to risk suffering the loss in question (or allow the loss to occur if the threat is to *X*)? Ultimately, society does not and should not expect the *impossible*; indeed, it should not always expect even the *possible*.[194]

---

is impossible, it is more accurate to describe *D*'s dilemmatic choice in terms of whether *D* lacked a fair opportunity to avoid acting unlawfully.

193. Even if *D* can attempt to resist *C*, *D* is unfairly forced to risk the possibility that his resistance will fail, and that *C* will inflict serious injuries on him.

194. Sometimes we say of one acting under duress that "the actor had no choice." In fact, we really mean "the actor had no meaningful choice," or "the actor had no fair choice." Similarly, when we say that "the actor could not have acted otherwise," we really mean "the actor could not fairly be expected to have acted otherwise." *See generally* A. ROSS, ON GUILT, RESPONSIBILITY AND PUNISHMENT 159-79 (1975) (it is futile to assign responsibility to a person once it is admitted that the person could not have acted differently). It is the latter statement that I assert here as the appropriate test.

A common refrain in duress analysis is that threats excuse when the actor's only "viable and reasonable choice" was to do as ordered. Fingarette, *supra* note 1, at 106 n.160. Or, put most starkly, one's choice process is excused if the coerced actor had "only one non-idiotic, non-'suicidal' move." D. DENNETT, ELBOW ROOM 72 (1984), *quoted in* A. WERTHEIMER, *supra* note 27, at 193. The point apparently is that the coerced actor has made the "obviously correct" choice. It is "*as if* . . . the 'world' had chosen for us." A. WERTHEIMER, *supra* note 27, at 196.

Such a test is wrong. First, focusing on the "suicidal" nature of the situation, the test seems to require us to excuse all coerced homicides. It assumes that we never can expect a sensible person to choose death over life. It is as if, as George Bernard Shaw once suggested, persons of great common sense are nothing more than people lacking moral courage.

Yet, putting aside for now the questionable wisdom of the common law no-homicide rule, it is not self-evident that we want to (or do) excuse all "nonsuicidal" actions, as, for example, when *D* kills 100 innocent persons to save his own life. In such a case, we may have a right to expect sacrifice rather than single-minded, self-interested action. We may conclude that common sense sometimes does suggest that courage is appropriate, and that we can fairly expect a person to take some suicidal routes.

More basically, many cases of excusable duress do not seem to meet the test of being the *only* reasonable or the "obviously correct" choice. After all, duress is not a justification. At most this test

To determine when coercion should excuse, we must conduct a balancing process somewhat similar to that which occurs in choice-of-evils justification analysis. The distinction at issue, however, is not whether the actor made the right or a permissible decision, nor even whether the choice was expected as a predictive matter, but rather whether, in light of the nature of the demand and the expected repercussions from noncompliance, *we could fairly expect a person of nonsaintly moral strength*[195] *to resist the threat.*

This test provides no simple or noncontroversial answers. Duress always is a matter of line drawing about which reasonable minds can differ. All that can be said with certainty is that, assuming the threat remains constant, our willingness to excuse an actor doubtlessly recedes as the offense becomes more heinous. Some, but not all, persons who are forced into a corner and wrongfully choose to harm innocent persons rather than accept the threatened consequences will be excused.

IV. DURESS: DRAWING LINES

A. General Considerations

As demonstrated in Part III, duress is a normative excuse that ought to exculpate anyone who is a victim of a threat that a person of reasonable moral strength could not fairly be expected to resist. This view of duress coincides imperfectly[196] with the MPC's approach. The MPC dramatically expands upon the common law, especially when applied in homicide cases. At the same time, the MPC does not excuse

means that the person has made the "obviously correct *wrong* choice." If the difference between the coercer's threat and the action he demands strongly supports acceding to the demand, then it is because the threat to the coerced actor is great, and the demand is minor, in which case *D* acts justifiably in acceding. On the other hand, if the threat is minor and the demand is great, we will not excuse.

Most often, duress will involve fairly close cases where the demand is worse than the threat, but the difference is small. In those cases we may excuse, but the reason is not that the actor's choice was obviously correct. Indeed, we may wish to conclude that we excuse precisely because there is *no* obviously correct choice. We come closer to the point of duress if we say, as does Kadish, that *D* is excused when "guilty" of a "deficient, but reasonable action." Kadish, *supra* note 155, at 259, 262. The action is both wrongful (deficient) and reasonable (in the sense that it is one that we could expect of a person of reasonable moral firmness), but it is surely not the *only* reasonable alternative.

195. Obviously, this approximates the MPC "person of reasonable firmness" language. Presumably, the MPC intends to measure *moral* firmness. This author has no idea whether a jury would reach a different result in a particular case if my "nonsaintly person" test were applied instead of the "reasonable person" inquiry.

The key difference between my test and the MPC language is that the Code seems to treat duress as an incapacity-oriented excuse: Was the person of reasonable firmness *unable* to resist? As I have shown, the real issue is one of opportunities, so the test ought to be drafted this way.

196. *See supra* note 195 and accompanying text.

wrongdoing that results from coercive nonhuman threats or from poor socioeconomic conditions. These three situations—kill-or-be-killed threats, coercive natural conditions, and environmentally induced crime—raise a more general question: In light of the underlying rationale of the excuse, what are the proper outer limits of the defense?

At the outset, certain overarching considerations that ought to go into the line drawing process deserve brief attention. First, and most simply, it must be remembered that since duress is a normative excuse reasonable minds can and will differ regarding its proper boundaries. Hence, this author cannot suggest that the lines drawn below are beyond fair controversy. Second, line drawing in duress cases is a highly sensitive matter. The rules of duress say something very important about the actor (i.e., that the actor is (or is not) a person of reasonable moral strength) as well as the characteristics of the hypothetical objective person to whom the actor is compared (i.e., the degree of moral strength that human beings may fairly be expected to manifest). In setting standards, therefore, we need to be honest about our weaknesses and optimistic about our strengths. We must avoid unfairly stigmatizing persons who find themselves in compelling circumstances by setting standards too high, yet we must not demean ourselves by setting standards that are too low. We need to avoid the conflicting evils of hypocrisy and overzealousness, on the one hand, and moral abstention, on the other.

First, we must refrain from acting hypocritically. In the realm of duress, hypocrisy is the result of holding others to a standard of moral strength to which we would not hold ourselves if we were similarly situated. The MPC Commentary makes this point, albeit inartfully,[197] when it warns that:

> [T]he law is ineffective in the deepest sense, indeed . . . it is hypocritical, if it imposes on the actor who has the misfortune to confront a dilemmatic choice, a standard that his judges are not prepared to affirm that they should and could comply with if their turn to face the problem should arise. Condemnation in such a case . . . is unjust.[198]

But, as wrong as hypocrisy is, the MPC drafters have overstated the problem with regard to duress cases. It is not inevitably hypocritical for a juror to concede that most people in the same situation, including the juror, would[199] have acted as the defendant did, yet still believe that the

197. *See infra* note 199 and accompanying text.

198. MPC COMMENTARIES, *supra* note 20, § 2.09 commentary at 374-75.

199. Contrary to the quoted language, the question is not whether the defendant or the jurors "should" or even "could" comply with the law's demands in the same circumstances. "Should"

coerced actor deserves to be punished. As long as the juror believes that the juror also would be deserving of punishment[200] (and, presumably, would accept it) in the same situation, there is no hypocrisy. We avoid duplicity by only blaming others when we are prepared to blame ourselves.

But, *should* we blame others whenever we would blame ourselves? If we do, we run a second risk: overzealous or even self-righteous use of the criminal law. The criminal law is not intended to correlate perfectly with our personal moral values. More specifically, the introspective form of guilt persons are apt to feel when they do something wrong should not be treated as a perfect measure of the criminal law's denunciatory version of guilt. Most of us are harder on ourselves than we are on those around us. We attempt to live virtuous lives. We are apt to reproach ourselves when we fail to live up to our highest moral standards. Although we cannot be perfect, we try to be, and feel guilty when we fail. We do not excuse our shortcomings.

However, the criminal law is not perfectionistic. It sets only minimum standards of conduct. It does not, nor should it, function as the moral police, requiring us, upon threat of death or loss of liberty and resulting stigma, to act virtuously. Thus, although in the general run of cases we should expect excuse law to conform roughly with our feelings about blame and guilt, a perfect relationship should not be expected. In some cases, it is proper for the law to excuse me, although I do not excuse myself.[201] We should set criminal law standards of conduct somewhat *below* the level to which we tend to hold ourselves in our private lives.[202]

Nevertheless, we also should avoid the conflicting danger of setting standards too low or, even worse, abstaining entirely from expressing moral judgments of others. Our compassion for the coerced actor should not cause us to treat human beings as if they cannot be expected to demonstrate a reasonable degree of moral courage. Nor should we fall prey to the idea that because we share a moral fault with the actor

implies a justificatory analysis; "could" is an incapacity-oriented claim. Neither point is relevant to duress.

200. Punishment need not imply imprisonment. *See* Dressler, *supra* note 18, at 683-84, especially at 684 n.80.

201. *E.g.*, consider the statement of a defense lawyer in a recent case in which a wife and mother, herself physically abused, allowed her child to be beaten to death by the child's father, and was exonerated: "The law had to excuse her, but she hasn't excused herself and she never will." Sullivan, *Judge Dismisses Murder Charge for Nussbaum*, N.Y. Times, Oct. 27, 1988, at B3, col. 1.

202. Dressler, *supra* note 18, at 691 n.100, 713 n.197.

(namely, our mutual lack of absolute moral strength), and because the difference between us and the wrongdoer may simply be a matter of moral luck, that it is not "our business" to blame the actor, or that we should be "cleaning our own house first."[203]

Notice the significance of the latter argument. It is *not* a claim that the coerced wrongdoer is not blameworthy. It is not an argument to excuse. Rather, it is an argument against imperfect people throwing stones at other imperfect wrongdoers. It suggests that those who would judge the wrongdoer lack the moral standing to do so or, at least, should voluntarily abstain from invoking their standing.[204] If accepted in the context of the criminal law, its effect is not to have us draw liberal lines of excuse, but to draw no lines at all.

Society will not do that, nor should it. As long as we remain mindful of our connection to the wrongdoer, including our shared fallibilities, it is not unseemly for us to set reasonable, minimal standards of personal responsibility (standards to which, lest we forget, we are willing to be held ourselves), codify them in our criminal codes, and punish those who fail to live up to them.

B. Coerced Homicides

Stemming from antiquity,[205] the nearly "unbroken tradition"[206] of Anglo-American common law is that duress never excuses murder, that the person threatened with his own demise "ought rather to die himself, than escape by the murder of an innocent."[207] Indeed, one recent English judicial venture from this traditional path[208] in which the House of Lords permitted the defense to be pled by an accomplice to a murder was recently overruled.[209] And, although the MPC would abrogate the common law rule, most statutory authority in this country runs contrary to reform.

We ought to be respectful of such common law tradition and not assume that centuries of nearly consistent rejection of the duress defense

203. Watson, *supra* note 124, at 283.

204. A version of this argument is frequently raised in the specific context of the rotten social background (RSB) defense: society has caused, or allowed to fester, the horrible conditions that create the criminal environment. Therefore, society is not entitled to sit in condemnation of the urban criminal. *See infra* note 246 and accompanying text.

205. Waslik, *supra* note 3, at 461.

206. Regina v. Howe, [1987] 2 W.L.R. 568, 575 (Lord Hailsham).

207. 4 W. Blackstone, *supra* note 2, at *30.

208. D.P.P. v. Lynch, 1975 App. Cas. 653.

209. *Howe*, 2 W.L.R. at 568.

in murder cases is self-evidently wrong, "obsolescent or inhumane or unjust."[210] The burden is placed correctly on those who would allow the defense to murder. Nonetheless, and despite my earlier published reservations on the subject,[211] I am now satisfied that the American Law Institute was correct in rejecting the common law no-homicide rule.

Utilitarian reasoning, although not without dissenters, probably supports the excuse.[212] But, in this context, as with excuses in general, the argument of utility "smells of the lamp."[213] The question is more properly framed as an issue of just deserts:[214] Does a person always deserve to be punished as a murderer if he kills another innocent individual as the result of coercion? While the common law punishes in these instances, the underlying basis for this position almost certainly is the Kantian moral principle that "a human being can never be manipulated merely as a means to the purposes of someone else . . . . His innate

---

210. *Id.* at 581. Lord Hailsham made the point even more forcefully: "[I]t ill becomes those of us who have participated in the cruel events of the 20th century [such as genocides and international terrorism] to condemn as out of date those who wrote in defence of innocent lives in the 18th century." *Id.* at 582.

211. Dressler, *supra* note 18, at 712, 716.

212. Bentham justified what lawyers today would call an excuse in those cases in which punishment is inefficacious, i.e., when threat of punishment will not deter misconduct. *See supra* note 155 and accompanying text. Nonetheless, some courts and commentators believe that coerced individuals can be deterred from killing others. Lord Hailsham has observed, for example, that "[d]oubtless in actual practice many will succumb to temptation . . . . But many will not . . . . I have known in my own lifetime of too many acts of heroism by ordinary human beings of no more than ordinary fortitude to [reject the common law position]." *Howe*, 2 W.L.R. at 579. Jerome Hall has also reasoned that the proposition that people inevitably act in self-preservation is debatable; therefore, the wise course "is to proceed on the hypothesis that a substantial percentage of persons in such situations will act against their instinctual desires . . . ." J. HALL, *supra* note 4, at 446-47.

In essence, these advocates of the common law rule believe that if a person finds himself standing between the devil and the deep blue sea, it is unwise to concede the person's soul to the Devil. He ought to be taught how to swim or, at least, convinced that jumping in the water is preferable to conspiring with the Devil. The threat of moral stigma and punishment may cause a person to resist evil. *Cf.* A. KENNY, *Duress per Minas as a Defence to Crime*, in THE IVORY TOWER 37-38 (1985), *quoted in* L. KATZ, *supra* note 7, at 69 ("[A]ny man must pray never to be thus placed between the devil and the deep blue sea. But if the law takes away the deep blue sea, a man will go wherever the devil drives.").

The difficulty with this argument is that although some people *do* act heroically in coercive circumstances, no one has demonstrated that duress law encourages such heroism. Neither is there any evidence that heroism is more often exhibited in common law jurisdictions than in states that excuse such homicides. Heroes may just be heroes, regardless of legal doctrine. (Indeed, if moral messages affect human conduct in such circumstances, it would seem that the more potent message is one that announces that killing innocent humans is not *justified*.) Utilitarians should (and do) loathe the infliction of punishment in the absence of such evidence or, at least, some common sense reason to believe that it is so.

213. H. PACKER, *supra* note 155, at 118.

214. *See supra* note 155 and accompanying text.

personality [that is, his right as a person] protects him against such treatment . . . ."[215]

The moral imperative against killing innocent persons was evident in the recent House of Lords opinion reaffirming the common law rule. In the most significant opinion, Lord Hailsham described the common law rule as "good morals" and categorically rejected the conclusion "that the law must 'move with the times' in order to keep pace with the immense political and social changes since what are alleged to have been the bad old days of Blackstone and Hale."[216] At least for this Lord, the question of excusing a coerced killer should not be determined by juries deciding moral deserts on a case-by-case basis. As he put it, "[t]he question is not one of the reliability of juries. *It is one of principle*."[217]

The difficulty with Hailsham's reasoning is not with the moral principle he reveres, but with its relevance to the question at hand. His essential point is that Kant's imperative against killing innocents is (or should be) as powerful today as it was in the past. But this position only demonstrates that such homicides are as wrong, as *unjustifiable*, today as in earlier times. By this he has only "proven" that those who accept the categorical imperative should reject modern departures from the imperative, such as the MPC's version of the necessity justification defense,[218] as well as its apparent justification of self-defense against morally innocent aggressors.[219]

But, since duress is an excuse rather than a justification, the real issue (it bears repeating with some additional emphasis) is whether a coerced person who unjustifiably violates the moral principle *necessarily, unalterably, and unfailingly* deserves to be punished as a murderer, as the common law insists.[220] If a murderer were insane, involuntarily intoxicated, or especially young, society would not necessarily, unalterably,

215. I. KANT, THE METAPHYSICAL ELEMENTS OF JUSTICE 100 (J. Ladd trans. 1965).

216. *Howe*, 2 W.L.R. at 579, 581.

217. *Id.* at 581 (emphasis added).

218. MODEL PENAL CODE § 3.02 (1985). The underlying theory of § 3.02 may be, as the Lord puts it, the "morally disreputable principle that the end *justifies* the means." *Howe*, 2 W.L.R. at 580 (emphasis added).

219. *See* MODEL PENAL CODE §§ 3.04(1) (general self-defense provision, justifying the use of force as is immediately necessary to repel unlawful force), 3.11(1) (defining "unlawful force" to include force which would constitute a tort of criminal offense except for a defense, such as insanity or infancy) (1985); Greenawalt, *A Vice of its Virtues: The Perils of Precision in Criminal Codification, as Illustrated by Retreat, General Justification, and Dangerous Utterances*, 19 RUTGERS L.J. 929, 932-37 (1988). *See also supra* note 94 and accompanying text.

220. There is some support for reducing murder to manslaughter. *See supra* note 83 and accompanying text. Indeed, as a conceptual matter, whatever else may be the judgment of the law, duress ought to serve at least as a partial excuse to murder. Fear can affect volitional *capacity* as effectively

and unfailingly demand punishment. These excuses affirm the moral imperative, but render the actor blameless who violates it. Why treat duress differently?

Admittedly, duress is unlike these other excuses because it is a normative defense. A reasoned advocate of the common law rule can, therefore, assert that as a matter of principle there *always* is a fair opportunity to avoid killing another person, regardless of the coercive circumstances. Although there is no way to disclaim the plausibility of this position, I reject it. I am afraid that such a rule, like Lord Hailsham's opinion, has the imprint of self-righteousness, which the law should avoid.[221] The rule asks us to be virtuous; more accurately, it *demands* our virtual saintliness, which the law has no right to require. It is precisely in the case of kill-or-be-killed threats that the criminal law ought to be prepared in some cases to attempt to assuage the guilt feelings of the homicidal wrongdoer by excusing him—by reminding him that he acted no less valiantly than any person of reasonable moral strength would have done.

I am *not* suggesting that all coerced homicides should be excused. The desirability of the MPC approach is that the excusing decision is made by the jury on a contextual basis. It is realistic to believe that juries will not excuse all coerced killers.[222] It is not inherently implausible to contend that persons of reasonable moral strength will accede to some, but not all, homicides.

For example, juries would probably excuse many coerced accomplices to murders, especially those whose participation in the crime was relatively minor, while usually punishing triggermen.[223] Society also has

---

as anger does. If we reduce murder to manslaughter, largely on the ground that a person, when adequately provoked, excusably has less self-control, the same rule ought to apply in cases of duress. Dressler, *supra* note 35, at 461-63.

221. Lord Hailsham's analysis is quite unrestrained. According to him, the law is neither " 'just [n]or humane' which withdraws the protection of the criminal law from the innocent victim and casts the cloak of its protection upon the coward and the poltroon in the name of a 'concession to human frailty' " *Howe*, 2 W.L.R. at 579.

222. *See* D.P.P. v. Lynch, 1975 App. Cas. 653, 681 (Lord Wilberforce)

> [N]o convincing reason, on principle [exists], why . . . [the defence] should be absolutely excluded in murder charges whatever the nature of the charge; hard to establish, yes, in the case of direct killing so hard that perhaps it will never be proved: but in other cases to be judged, strictly indeed, on the totality of facts.

223. *See* Dressler, Thompson, & Wasserman, *Effect of Legal Education Upon Perceptions of Crime Seriousness: A Response to Rummel v. Estelle*, 28 WAYNE L. REV. 1247, 1269-70 (1982) (among accomplices to crime, law students consider those who solicit murder most deserving of punishment, major participants at the scene of the crime less deserving, and minor participants least culpable); Dressler, *The Jurisprudence of Death by Another: Accessories and Capital Punishment*, 51 U. COLO. L. REV. 17, 64-72 (1979) (empirical study showing that execution of accessories was comparatively uncommon from 1935-1979).

a right to expect a person to demonstrate a higher level of moral strength when ordered to kill a hundred innocent children than when commanded to kill one. A jury might also rightly expect people to manifest the utmost moral strength—even, at some point, to choose death—when they have reason to know that they are playing a part, even a minor role, in an especially barbaric scenario, such as the Holocaust.[224] But there is a far more compelling reason to support the MPC. Once one realizes, as Lord Hailsham may not, that the issue with duress is desert of punishment and not justification of the act, the jury is an especially suitable institution to determine whether and when coercion excuses.

Justification defenses amend the law; excuses provide justice to the individual who violated it.[225] In general, it is proper for legislatures to define justifications, but juries are better suited to determine desert of punishment in particular cases,[226] especially when the issue is whether an actor has lived up to society's legitimate expectations of moral courage. If criminal trials are morality plays,[227] they are especially so when excuses are pleaded, and perhaps most of all when a claim of duress is raised. Juries should write the final act of such plays. When a unanimous jury, despite modern heterogeneity of thought on the subject, convicts a coerced actor, its judgment of guilt—its conclusion to the play—is all the more dramatic and powerful.

C. Coercive Conditions

Dudley and Stephens cannibalized a seriously ill, unoffending youth in their lifeboat in order to preserve three lives, including their own, from impending death by starvation.[228] Neither the common law nor the MPC excuses[229] such actions. Even if coercion excuses a homicide, the defense of duress is inapplicable in this case for the simple reason that no human being coerced the conduct. A natural condition, rather than a human threat, caused Dudley and Stephens to kill the victim.

---

224. "[T]is true that we are in great danger; The greater therefore should our courage be." W. Shakespeare, *Henry V*, act 4, scene 1, lines 1-2.

225. G. Fletcher, *supra* note 3, at 810-13.

226. *See* A. De Tocqueville, Democracy in America 302 (H. Reeve trans. 1899)

> Trial by jury, as applied to the repression of crime, appears to me to introduce an eminently republican element . . . . [I]t places the real direction of society in the hands of the governed, or of a portion of the governed, instead of leaving it under the authority of the Government.

227. N. Morris & G. Hawkins, The Honest Politician's Guide To Crime Control 182 (1970).

228. Regina v. Dudley & Stephens, 14 Q.B.D. 273 (1884).

229. Although it is debatable whether the common law *justifies* killing in such circumstances, the MPC does so. Model Penal Code § 3.02 (1985).

The refusal of common law jurists to excuse Dudley and Stephens is not surprising in light of their already extremely narrow conception of duress. The ALI's refusal, however, is more surprising. Why permit a jury to excuse Dudley and Stephens if another had ordered the men to kill the youth, but prevent a jury from considering the actors' excusability when the coercion stems from a natural condition or a natural threat?[230]

The ALI's explanation for the distinction is pragmatic: the "significant difference" between excusing the two classes of cases is that in the case of human threats "the basic interests of the law may be satisfied by prosecution of the agent of unlawful force," whereas with natural threats, "if the actor is excused, no one is subject to the law's application."[231]

Others have also drawn a similar, albeit nonconsequentialist, justification for the distinction. Robert Nozick, for example,[232] questions the difference between being confined in one's house by a lightning storm and being similarly imprisoned by a person threatening to electrocute him if he leaves. His answer is that in the former case, one attributes the dweller's decision to his own will. In the latter case, however, "another's intentions are so closely linked with the action as to make it not fully one's own, less so than an act done in the face of equal costs due solely to inanimate nature."[233] Thus, in the sentence, "I, the coerced actor, am not to blame for the wrongdoing," the critical word becomes "I," and the

---

230. Unlike the MPC, Jerome Hall would recognize a defense in the case of a homicide committed due to necessitous circumstances but deny the defense in duress cases. He reasons that whereas in cases of human threat "the situation may be completely transformed in a split second by the malefactor's change of mind," J. HALL, *supra* note 4, at 447, this possibility is absent in cases of natural threats. Also, in cases of duress, there may be ways to remove the threat by positive action or by flight; in cases of necessity, however, "man bows to the inevitable." *Id.*

Even if these distinctions are empirically accurate, they do not adequately answer the question at hand. Hall inadequately focuses on the distinction between justifiable and excusing forms of the two defenses. *See generally id.* at 415-48 (Hall treats both defenses as justifications, although the issue is actually whether necessity should excuse an actor in the same way as does duress.).

231. MPC COMMENTARIES, *supra* note 20, § 2.09 commentary at 379. In the case of excusable duress, *C* is treated as the principal in the first degree of the wrongdoing where she uses *D* as an innocent instrumentality of the crime. *See generally* J. DRESSLER, *supra* note 56, at § 30.03[A][2][b] (using same example).

The Commentary seeks to play down the harshness of its rule by making the following prediction:

> [i]t will be an extraordinarily rare case in which a person will not be able to claim successfully that a response to natural causes was a choice of a lesser evil [and, thus, be justified under the MPC § 3.02] but could successfully claim that the choice was one a person of reasonable firmness would make.

MPC COMMENTARIES, *supra* note 20, § 209 commentary at 379.

232. *See* R. NOZICK, *supra* note 176, at 49, 520.

233. *Id.* at 520.

assumption is that to excuse me there must be another person whose wrongful will is preempting mine.[234]

Nozick's understanding of duress approximates that of Herbert Fingarette, who views duress as part of a broader conception of victimization. "Victimization" implies the existence of a victim (the coerced actor) who is wronged by a victimizer, namely, "one who intends to elicit certain conduct from another person."[235] This concept fits the duress paradigm nicely, but since necessity involves no victimizer, there is no victim remaining to excuse.

But why should it be the case that before the criminal law excuses a person there must exist another actor with a wrongful will who potentially can be punished for the wrongdoing? Certainly, as a descriptive matter, this claim is inconsistent with other excuses. The pleas of insanity, infancy, involuntary intoxication, and mistake of law do not require the existence of a culpable party to whom legal responsibility may be shifted. In these contexts, the issue is whether the particular defendant deserves punishment, not whether someone else can be deservedly punished for the crime.[236]

It should be kept in mind that the question at hand is whether the actor—the immediate law violator—had a fair chance to avoid acting unlawfully, i.e., whether a person of reasonable moral firmness would have resisted the human or natural threat. Assuming that natural and human threats are equal in coerciveness, the immediate actors' blameworthiness are also equal, as their opportunities to act lawfully were equally constrained. The MPC and the common law, therefore, wrongly limit duress to human threats.[237]

234. Actually, taken literally, Nozick's explanation, which is not limited to homicide cases, cannot explain either the MPC or the common law rule of duress. He suggests only that *D*'s conduct is "not fully" his own. This implies that *D*'s conduct *is* partially his own; yet, this is hardly a reason not to excuse *D*. In many cases of group attribution, one person possesses the stronger will, yet society is also prepared to punish the weaker one. At most, Nozick's arguments suggest that duress should function as a partial excuse.

235. Fingarette, *supra* note 1, at 106; *see also id*. at 84 nn.54, 109 (emphasizing the significance of the requirement that the coercive threat be wrongful).

236. *See* Dressler, *supra* note 18, at 713 (footnote omitted) ("We do not need a culprit to convict. Letting *A* off the hook need not always require putting *B* on the hook.").

237. Others agree with this conclusion. *E.g.*, K. GREENAWALT, CONFLICTS OF LAW AND MORALITY 289 (1987); Kadish, *supra* note 155, at 273-74.

A state that has adopted the MPC duress provision, but which wishes to include coercive conditions within the excuse, might redraft the defense as follows:

> It is an affirmative defense that the actor engaged in the conduct charged to constitute an offense because he was coerced to do so by the use of, or a threat to use, unlawful force against his person or the person of another, *or as the result of a non-human threat to his or*

D. Poor Socioeconomic Conditions as an Excuse

Dudley and Stephens were faced with a horrible, but extremely rare, moral dilemma. Although they intentionally committed a crime, their actions presented for them a moral dilemma. Their actions did not reflect their true selves.[238]

Some people who commit crimes, however, perceive no dilemma in their actions. Their wrongdoing represents their true or present selves. Often, these actors not only possess antisocial values but also identify with them; they repudiate the surrounding dominant culture. Many people who fall into this general category are criminals who live in economically-deprived circumstances, i.e., the urban youths and adults of society's underclass.

These people are who they are—and commit the crimes they do—because they were born into, brought up in, and influenced by a subculture whose values conflict in significant part with those of the majority in their community. As a result, it is sometimes suggested that these actors were not "given the opportunities that promote responsible attitudes."[239] Nonetheless, neither the common law nor the MPC excuses the wrongdoing of these people because of their socioeconomic adversity.

Various commentators have urged for the acquittal of such criminal defendants from urban ghettoes because of their social deprivation.[240] The claim of these commentators, sometimes coined the "rotten social background" (RSB) defense,[241] merits attention, especially by those who favor the broader MPC "person of reasonable firmness" version of the duress defense, and even more particularly by those who believe, as I, that the MPC defense should be expanded to excuse persons who commit crimes as the result of coercive conditions.

In a recent article advocating the RSB defense,[242] Professor Richard Delgado provided the most complete justification of this defense. Some

another person's bodily well-being, that a person of reasonable firmness in his situation would have been unable to resist.

The requirement in the italicized language that the threat be to a person's *bodily* well-being is based on the general MPC position that the defense is inapplicable in the case of threatened non-physical harm. I reject this limitation. Dressler, *supra* note 18, at 712.

238. Watson, *supra* note 124, at 266.

239. Schoeman, *supra* note 183, at 311.

240. *See supra* note 9 and accompanying text.

241. According to Professor Richard Delgado, the RSB appellation was coined by the trial judge in United States v. Alexander and later used by Judge Bazelon at the appellate level, 471 F.2d 923, 961 (D.C. Cir. 1973) (Bazelon, J., dissenting). Delgado, *RSB, supra* note 9, at 11 n.11.

242. Delgado, *RSB, supra* note 9, at 9.

of the potential arguments sound in justification theory.[243] Delgado also provides possible excuse[244] claims based on the theory that the RSB defendant is incapacitated.[245] Additionally, Delgado posits the claim that society may lack standing to punish the RSB defendant, even if the

243. Delgado reasons that "[a]n individual may justifiably use force to protect his or her interests in freedom from violence itself." *Id.* at 57. He points out that "justification will often depend on what 'violence' means." *Id.* Although he does not provide a definition, he does quote Greenawalt, *Violence - Legal Justification and Moral Appraisal*, 32 EMORY L.J. 437, 439 (1983), who asked whether violence may include "psychological persecution or a social and economic order that produces impoverishment of body or spirit?" Delgado, *RSB*, *supra* note 9, at 57. He also cites Professor John Harris, who concluded that "harm which others could have prevented may sometimes be regarded as a form of violence." *Id.* (citing Harris, *The Marxist Conception of Violence*, 3 PHIL. & PUB. AFF. 192, 212-20 (1974)). Further, Delgado suggests that an RSB defendant may justifiably protect—presumably by violence—other interests, such as "the right to have the community treat him with full and equal respect and concern" and "the right to full and equal participation in society." Delgado, *RSB*, *supra* note 9, at 58-59.

Delgado concedes that there are "difficulties" with this justification reasoning. *Id.* at 61. He acknowledges that justification defenses require that an actor's conduct both be necessary to prevent the injury to the right and proportional to the threatened harm. Also, in a remarkable understatement, Delgado observes that "[t]he effect of justification is to condone and encourage the RSB defendant's conduct, *a result that may seem morally and prudentially wrong*." *Id.* at 63 (footnotes omitted) (emphasis added).

Ultimately, Delgado concludes "[w]ith some ambivalence, . . . that justification is not an acceptable model for a new defense based on rotten social background." He cites "moral, practical, and political hurdles" for his conclusion. *Id.* at 78.

244. It is not always clear that Professor Delgado's understanding of "justification" and "excuse" theory are consistent with the general understanding of those terms. In some portions of his article, Delgado seems to accept the traditional understanding. *See, e.g.*, *id.* at 56 ("Generally, justification asserts that conduct is not wrongful, while excuse asserts that although the conduct is wrongful, the actor cannot be blamed for it.") (footnote omitted).

This is not always his understanding of the concepts. For example, he states that most justification and excuse defenses are "non-accountability" pleas, or defenses which "focus on the circumstances of the actor at the time of the offense to determine whether the *wrongful* act can properly be attributed to the actor." *Id.* at 15 (emphasis added) (citing G. FLETCHER, *supra* note 3, at 496-97). In fact, as the quoted language should suggest, the concept of nonaccountability, based as it is on wrongful conduct, involves excuses only.

Professor Delgado augments the confusion with another assertion that "[j]ustification defenses hold the defendant unaccountable because by acting *unlawfully*, he or she furthered an important social interest." Delgado, *RSB*, *supra* note 9, at 15 (emphasis added). In fact, of course, a person who asserts a justification defense claims thereby that he acted lawfully. As such, he takes full responsibility for his actions.

245. Delgado makes various incapacity-oriented excuse arguments for the RSB claim. First, he claims that some RSB defendants may suffer from environmentally produced rage, which he equates to seizures and automatic reflexes. Delgado, *RSB*, *supra* note 9, at 64, 75-76. According to Delgado, "long-term exposure to environmental insult can make an individual a virtual 'time-bomb.'" *Id.* at 75. In such cases, he asserts, the rage becomes so powerful as to block the sufferer's consciousness.

If this claim is empirically provable, it would suggest that the RSB defendant is entitled not so much to an excusing defense for which the burden of proof may properly be placed on the defendant, but rather to acquittal on the basis that the prosecutor did not prove a prima facie element of the crime, a voluntary act. To make such a claim, an RSB advocate would have to show that the enraged conduct of the actor was not the result of a willed contraction of a muscle. *See* O. HOLMES,

latter's conduct is unjustified and inexcusable.[246] In view of the focus of this Article, however, this author will only consider Delgado's claims

THE COMMON LAW 54 (1881), or, as the authors of the MPC state, "a product of the effort or determination of the actor." MODEL PENAL CODE § 2.01(2)(d) (1985).

The empirical evidence supporting this claim is unclear. Many of the studies reported by Delgado only reach the rather unsurprising conclusion that "[h]umans subjected to stress and danger become irritable and aggressive." Delgado, *RSB*, *supra* note 9, at 35 (footnote omitted). Delgado does cite sources that claim that abnormal or prolonged stimulation of brain circuits, which environmental irritations presumably cause, can result in hyperdevelopment of brain circuits responsible for aggression. *Id.* at 34. It is not clear whether these studies are meant to suggest that persons with such brain circuits act unthinkingly, unconsciously, or reflexively as proof of genuine involuntarism requires.

The rage thesis is probably better analyzed like provocation claims. Such pleas *are* based on a claim of partial incapacity. *See* Dressler, *supra* note 35, at 463-65; Dressler, *Provocation: Partial Justification or Partial Excuse?*, 51 MOD. L. REV. 467, 471-72 (1988); *but see* Delgado, *RSB*, *supra* note 9, at 49-50 (who interprets the defense as a "limited range of choice" defense based on external forces rather than incapacity). Even here, however, the claim is not based on a claim of strict involuntarism.

Second, Delgado argues that RSB may undermine the actor's ability to control his conduct or "alter perception and interpretation, causing the person to perceive incorrectly the nature or consequences of his or her actions." *Id.* at 65 (footnote omitted). Assuming that such disability is medically provable, an RSB claim might constitute a form of insanity.

Third, Delgado also suggests that the RSB "defendant's existence might lead him or her to a conclusion that his or her conduct is not wrongful, or less wrongful than any other available alternative." *Id.* Unless the claim is that the RSB actor's misapprehension is based on a mental disability, which Delgado does not suggest, he is no more entitled to be excused than a devout Nazi who believes that killing non-Aryans is morally right. Indeed, even in the context of the *McNaghten* right-from-wrong insanity prong, *see* McNaghten's Case, 10 CLARK & FIN. 200 (1843), the defense is not proven unless it is demonstrated that, as a result of mental disease, the actor did not realize that his views were inconsistent with those of the dominant culture. *See generally* A. GOLDSTEIN, THE INSANITY DEFENSE 51-53 (1967). The usual RSB defendant, however, is fully aware that the society, including the general subcommunity in which he lives, considers killing, robbing, and raping to be morally and legally wrong.

246. The basis of the defense is that "[t]o say that a person deserves a certain punishment is not to say that someone is justified in inflicting it." Delgado, *RSB*, *supra* note 9, at 68 (quoting Hospers, *Punishment, Protection and Retaliation*, in JUSTICE AND PUNISHMENT 24 (1977)). Similarly, Judge Bazelon has observed that, to be morally valid, a decision for conviction requires not only a condemnable act, and an actor deserving of condemnation but also a society whose "conduct in relation to the actor entitles it to sit in condemnation of him with respect to the condemnable act." Bazelon, *supra* note 9, at 388 (footnote omitted).

Just as with the more general claim discussed in the text, *see supra* notes 203-04 and accompanying text, this argument does not support a recognizable excuse for wrongdoing; rather, it leaves society without moral jurisdiction over the wrongdoer.

Society allegedly lacks moral standing in the RSB case because it "brings about crime by ignoring or permitting intolerable living conditions that make crime inevitable." Delgado, *RSB*, *supra* note 9, at 77. Indeed, we have a "responsibility to generate a society in which the powerful, humanly distorting conditions [present in the RSB actor's subsociety] are not present." Schoeman, *supra* note 183, at 311 (footnote omitted). The urban criminal is effectively " 'entrapped' in a ghettoized existence." Delgado, *RSB*, *supra* note 9, at 77.

This claim has significant moral power. However, the issue is partially clouded by the fact that the RSB defendant is often judged by a jury, which, at least potentially, includes his peers from the same unwholesome environment. *These* people, certainly, have standing to condemn the violator.

that the RSB defendant ought to be excused on the ground that he lacked a fair opportunity to act lawfully.

Unfortunately, the overarching moral principle that animates Delgado's position is misleading. His argument comes down to this: (1) blame is inappropriate when an actor's criminal behavior is caused by factors beyond his control; (2) the social adversity causes an RSB actor's conduct, a factor which cannot be controlled; and, therefore, (3) the RSB actor is not to be blamed for his criminal conduct.[247]

This is a straightforward causal theory of excusing.[248] Causation alone, however, cannot be the basis for excusing, for if a person were to be excused whenever his criminal conduct was caused by some factor over which he had no control, all crime would be excusable. All crime, like all other behavior, is an effect of earlier causes.[249] The proper issue in excusing is whether the actor had the capacity and fair opportunity to apply practical reasoning skills or to act freely.[250]

Delgado's two specific excusing arguments, based on the proposition that the ghetto actor lacks a fair opportunity to act lawfully, are also troubling. First, he effectively raises a cultural defense claim,[251] stating that "[a] person who has lived since birth in . . . [the ghetto] environment may be so strongly socialized by it that he or she has little sense of the values of the larger society or opportunity to acquire the norms necessary to function responsibly in that society."[252] In essence, ghetto defendants lack a "fair opportunity to acquaint themselves with right

Interestingly, Delgado would only treat this as a partial defense or, perhaps, as a matter for sentencing mitigation. *Id.* at 99.

247. Delgado, *RSB*, *supra* note 9, at 55.

248. For a carefully explained rejection of this theory, see Moore, *supra* note 36.

249. For discussion of determinism, see *supra* note 156 and accompanying text. Acceptance of its antithesis, indeterminism, does not resolve the moral problem: If a criminal intent can exist free from any prior causes, then it is a capricious event, for which it would appear equally morally unfair to punish the actor.

250. *See* Kadish, *supra* note 155, at 284.

> Social deprivation may well establish a credible explanation of how the defendant has come to have the character he has. But it does not establish a[n] . . . excuse . . . for there is a difference between explaining a person's wrongful behavior and explaining it away . . . . The . . . argument fails to make out a moral excuse . . . [because] it fails to establish the breakdown of rationality and judgment that is incompatible with moral agency.

251. *See generally* Note, *The Cultural Defense in the Criminal Law*, 99 HARV. L. REV. 1293 (1986) (arguing that recognition of a cultural defense is justified and setting forth factors to define its scope); Note, *Cultural Defense: One Person's Culture is Another's Crime*, 9 LOY. L.A. INT'L & COMP. L.J. 751 (1987) (authored by Malek-Mithra Sheybani) (discussing whether a cultural defense should be recognized in the criminal justice system).

252. Delgado, *RSB*, *supra* note 9, at 76.

moral norms . . . ."[253] As a result, they lack a "fair opportunity to see problems as problems."[254]

Even according to Delgado, this excuse model would only be available to persons raised in "extreme cultural isolation, in which knowledge of laws and norms simply never filters through, or does so only in the most attenuated form."[255] It is hard to imagine in the modern world that an RSB defendant could factually demonstrate such extreme isolation. If an RSB defendant claims that he does not know that murder, robbery, and rape violate the dominant society's moral and legal norms, then it is likely that "his ears are not deaf, but [only that] his heart is frozen."[256]

Second, Delgado would also excuse RSB defendants who were victims of "pressured adoption of deviant subcultural values."[257] What does he mean by "pressured adoption" of such values? RSB defendants do not ordinarily incorporate such attitudes at the point of a gun. Values are not adopted as the result of any single incident.[258] Moreover, if the actor's criminal conduct were the result of such pressure, traditional duress would apply.

Delgado asserts that the RSB defense would be appropriate in the case of a young defendant "for whom acquiescence to ghetto norms was required to survive."[259] Again, what does he mean by "required to survive"? Delgado has helpfully provided a hypothetical example:

> A youth moves into a ghetto neighborhood dominated by vicious street gangs. To survive, he must join one or the other of the gangs. Membership is achieved through intensive indoctrination in gang values, including instant obedience to the gang leaders. The members are required to spend most of their time with the group, returning to the home only for meals and sleep. Violation of gang rules is punished by beatings or expulsion. Gang members are taught a code of conduct that includes robbery, arson, and hatred of adults.[260]

253. Schoeman, *supra* note 183, at 308.

254. *Id.* at 309.

255. Delgado, *RSB*, *supra* note 9, at 87-88 (footnote omitted).

256. Watson, *supra* note 124, at 271.

257. Delgado, *RSB*, *supra* note 9, at 88 (footnote omitted).

258. Even in cases of alleged brainwashing, value changes are not implemented on a single occasion, but are the result of "multiple forces, both physical and psychological, intensively applied over a short period of time." Delgado, *Brainwashing*, *supra* note 9, at 3; *see also* Dressler, *Professor Delgado's "Brainwashing" Defense: Courting a Determinist Legal System*, 63 MINN. L. REV. 335, 347 n.79 (1979) (summarizing the various theories of the cause of brainwashing).

259. Delgado, *RSB*, *supra* note 9, at 76 (footnote omitted).

260. Delgado, *A Response to Professor Dressler*, 63 MINN. L. REV. 361, 365 (1979) [hereinafter Delgado, *Reply*]. Delgado cites this example in his RSB article. Delgado, *RSB*, *supra* note 9, at 76 n.429.

What is one to make of this example? First, it is worth noting that when he originally formulated the hypothetical as part of his advocacy of a new defense of coercive persuasion ("brainwashing"), Delgado doubted that this gang-member-turned-criminal was entitled to that defense.[261] He offers no explanation now why he would excuse the actor under the different title of "rotten social background," although both defenses are based at their core on a conception of coercion.

Second, Delgado does not explain what he means in the quoted hypothetical above that "[t]o survive, he must join one or the other of the gangs." Does he mean, literally, that the youth would be killed if he refused to join one of the gangs? Apparently not, since he concedes that "[t]he moral case for exculpating such a defendant is weakened by the youth's ability to make the initial decision to join the gang."[262]

Since Delgado concedes that the youth can be held responsible for the initial entry into the gang, what else could constitute the "necessary to survive" form of coercion? It must be in the fact that "[v]iolation of gang rules is punished by beatings or expulsion."

Should this be sufficient? In the case of severe beatings, it could be adequate under the MPC.[263] On the other hand, how can it possibly be said that the RSB actor lacked a fair opportunity to behave lawfully because failure to conform his conduct to the antisocial values of the gang would result in expulsion from—and, presumably, freedom from the coercion of—the antisocial group? Is the desire for peer validation a sufficient excuse for violent crimes?

The error in equating the pressures of joining or staying within the gang subculture with traditional duress (or even with the nontraditional form of duress or necessity) is the same as that which equates temptations with threats.[264] Gangs tempt potential members by offering them the prospect of power, wealth, and esteem that society wrongfully denies them. Such temptations are not threats. Gang temptations create *motivational* conflicts for the RSB actor (e.g., "I want to be rich/liked/respected by my peers, but I would like to have a chance to succeed in the larger society"). Threats, however, create *moral* conflicts (e.g., "I

261. Delgado, *Reply*, *supra* note 260, at 365.

262. *Id.* at 365 n.32.

263. *E.g.*, if gang leaders severely beat the member in the past, any subsequent "suggestion" that he commit a crime might excuse his criminal conduct. In such circumstances, he was arguably " 'coerced' to do so by the use of . . . unlawful force against his person . . . that a person of reasonable firmness in his situation would have been unable to resist." MODEL PENAL CODE § 2.09(1) (1985); *see* MPC COMMENTARIES, *supra* note 20, § 2.09 commentary at 376-77.

264. *See supra* notes 26-36, and accompanying text.

know what I am about to do is morally wrong, but I fear I will be hurt if I do not cooperate"). It is the latter which, if severe enough, excuses.[265]

The real question to be answered is not whether the ghetto criminal had a fair chance to learn proper values or to live a decent life, but rather whether he lacked a fair chance to avoid robbing the particular store, raping the particular neighbor, selling the particular "crack" cocaine, or killing the specific homeowner who surprised him during a certain burglary.

The answer to this question ought to be yes. The RSB defendant's case is plainly distinguishable from Dudley and Stephens's. The typical ghetto defendant does not commit his crime in response to a bodily threat, immediate or otherwise. Rather, he acts as the result of devotion to (or, at least, current acceptance of) the skewed values of the gang or subculture in which he is enmeshed. The ghetto defendant's life is awful, and the temptations to commit crime are great, but society can legitimately expect him to resist the temptation to improve his life by committing violent acts against an innocent person.

It may be argued that my normative conclusion is just that—the debatable moral views of one person, or even of many persons, but not the inevitable position of all. If I am prepared to allow juries to determine whether and when a homicide is excusable or what natural conditions a person of reasonable firmness may legitimately be expected to overcome, perhaps I must leave the issue of the RSB defendant's accountability to the same institution.

Two reasons convince me that the issue should not be left to the jury. First, there is a moral consensus about RSB defendants that is lacking in the cases of coerced homicides and compelled conditions. Even morally sensitive and compassionate people who believe that society has a responsibility to improve the lives of poor persons, as well as[266] the RSB actor's neighbors, *do* believe that RSB defendants are accountable for their actions. They *do* blame the ghetto murderer, robber, rapist, and

265. None of this means that excusing the RSB defendant is not emotionally tempting. When many of us think about the impoverished ghetto defendant, we are apt to experience various powerful emotions favorable to him. We understand him: his gang membership, even his criminal conduct, makes sense to us in an awful way. We also feel compassion for his current plight. We may feel guilty about not having improved his living conditions.

But, understanding is not excusing, *see supra* note 250, feeling compassion is not reason enough to excuse, *see* Dressler, *supra* note 18, at 682-89; Kadish, *supra* note 155, at 284-85, and being partially responsible for the RSB actor's poverty does not render him blameless for his own wrongful actions. *See supra* notes 203-04 and accompanying text.

266. Perhaps, especially.

drug peddler for his actions. Therefore, it is not inappropriate for the legislature to preempt the jury on this matter.

But there is another, more basic, reason for disallowing the excuse. The powerful emotions felt in response to our own and others' actions—feelings such as guilt, blame, praise, anger, remorse, disgust, compassion, and antipathy—are inextricably tied to the belief that humans, as a species, possess free choice, and that people who possess normal, adult human reasoning skills are morally accountable for their intentional acts. The duress defense represents a very limited, and slightly disquieting, exception to that rule.

Whether our reactive attitudes—our moral feelings—are the cause or the effect of our moral premises may be debated. The immutable reality is, however, that we possess these feelings and believe in accountability. It would be wrong, and ultimately self-defeating, to develop and enforce rules of criminal responsibility alien to these reactions.

Under this assumption, the difference between the person who acts with a gun at his head, sharks in the sea, or starvation on the immediate horizon, on the one hand, and the RSB actor, on the other, is too basic to ignore. The law must distinguish, as in our personal relations, between those who act as the result of specific, articulable threats, however caused, and those who choose *in the absence of threats* to behave in conformity with admittedly strongly inculcated countervalues.

To blur this distinction is to ignore our belief in the uniqueness of humans, to create emotionally unacceptable moral ambiguity,[267] and to run afoul of our natural reactions to wrongdoing.[268] In short, to excuse

267. One commentator has put it this way:

> Often we are able to say "he's to blame," or the law to pronounce "he is guilty," only by eliminating complexities that might serve as excuses. A fuller . . . account might acknowledge that perhaps others might have stopped a criminal or might have removed temptation from him, or that perhaps his character structure made it extraordinarily difficult for him to act differently. As a last resort, we can even say "society made him what he is." But the law cannot retain ambiguities to that degree and cannot present such a balanced account. It must hold individuals responsible for what may indeed be the product of broader social circumstances . . . .

Y. ROGAT, THE EICHMANN TRIAL AND THE RULE OF LAW 10 (1961).

268. As anomalous as it may sound to some, when RSB defendants are held accountable for their actions, they are respected, not pitied. To acquit them because of their environment smacks of condescension. Kadish, *supra* note 155, at 284-85; Moore, *supra* note 36, at 1147. Even Delgado concedes that the defense potentially "undermine[s] the dignity and courage of those who choose to abide by the law despite their hardships." Delgado, *RSB, supra* note 9, at 65.

When society punishes the RSB actor by incarcerating him in our prisons the actor may feel like saying, "Thanks, but if this is how you show me your respect, I think I'd prefer your pity." But, as I have argued before, Dressler, *supra* note 18, at 684, punishment need not (and, in my view, should not) inevitably imply imprisonment, particularly in the awful institutions that we have constructed.

the RSB defendant would not cause us to slip on a slope, but rather to fall off a moral cliff.

CONCLUSION

Neither the law nor the theory of duress runs smoothly or satisfactorily. The courts and commentators are not certain whether duress justifies or excuses, if they are even concerned about the question. As a result, the law that has developed lacks consistent theoretical foundation and often does not conform to our moral intuitions.

As a purely descriptive matter, at least at first glance, the common law version of the plea looks like a subspecies of the justification defense of necessity. Upon closer inspection, it is evident that the defense cannot fully be explained in this manner and should not be. Although other moral theories can justify coerced actions in a limited number of cases, our intuitions and better theory suggest that duress, if anything, excuses wrongdoing.

As an excuse, duress is atypical. In no other situation are people who knowingly choose to violate the law excused. When we examine our temptation to excuse coerced wrongdoers, we find that various common explanations for the excuse are not acceptable. Specifically, we ought not to excuse a person who accedes to threats on the grounds of compassion, evaluation of the actor's character, or simply because the wrongdoer has behaved in a manner that statistically is normal or predictable. Rather, the defense must be based on the normative claim that the actor lacked a fair opportunity to avoid acting unlawfully. Such an opportunity is lacking if a person of reasonable moral strength cannot fairly be expected to resist the threat.

So understood, duress is at once a fascinating and very troubling excuse, for it requires us to ask ourselves what level of moral courage we have a right to demand of others through the criminal justice system. In seeking to draw the proper outer limits of the defense, we must avoid acting hypocritically or overzealously, yet we should be prepared to make moral judgments about those who were unluckily confronted with dilemmatic choices we have only faced in our nightmares. In this context, I would draw the lines so as to allow juries to excuse persons who kill under duress, and I would equate natural coercive conditions with

Moreover, it is unwise to reshape our concepts of moral responsibility simply as a strategy to frustrate the prison system. (Candor suggests that I disclose, however, that this argument may be the most vigorously criticized point in my previous article, at least based on letters from readers.)

human threats. But, I would not recognize a duress-based defense of social adversity.

I am not sure at all that my line drawing is correct. The primary purpose of this Article, however, is not to advocate a particular result, but rather to suggest that legal scholars and lawmakers need to confront the moral questions that arise in this realm more carefully. If they do, the law may ultimately make more sense and more closely correlate with our moral intuitions.

There is another, more compelling reason to think about duress. An honest view of coercion teaches or reminds us that countless ordinary people, like ourselves, have weaknesses and susceptibilities that allow us to contribute to the world's injustices and cruelty. That we are human really means, at times, that we are all too human. It is not as easy as we sometimes think to "plac[e] the greatest distance between us and responsibility for evil."[269] Perhaps there are fewer moral monsters in this world than "ordinary men [who] . . . do monstrous things."[270]

This realization is disquieting but critical. Only when we realize how prone we are to acceding to immorality can we combat it. Only when we are aware of our own weaknesses and assail them can we fairly condemn them in others.

269. Y. ROGAT, *supra* note 267, at 8.
270. *Id.* at 10.

[9]

A THEORY OF NECESSITY†

ALAN BRUDNER*

'The several modes of feeling, perception, desire, and will, so far as we are aware of them, are in general called ideas (mental representations) and it may be roughly said that philosophy puts thoughts, categories, or, in more precise language, adequate notions, in the place of generalized images we ordinarily call ideas. Mental impressions such as these may be regarded as the metaphors of thoughts and notions. But to have these figurate conceptions does not imply that we appreciate their intellectual significance, the thoughts and rational notions to which they correspond. Conversely, it is one thing to have thoughts and intelligent notions, and another to know what impressions, perceptions, and feelings correspond to them'.[1]

INTRODUCTION

Commentary on the law of necessity has for centuries been marked by a sharp discordance between the views of philosophic writers on the one hand and those of judges and text-writers on the other. Whereas philosophers have generally conceded a legal defence to someone who breaks the law under compulsion of circumstances, common-law judges have reacted far more sternly and more discriminatingly to pleas of this kind. Two illustrations will suffice to exhibit the contrast. Both Bacon and Kant argue that someone who wrests from another a life-preserving plank in order to save himself from drowning is entitled to an acquittal.[2] He is not simply a worthy candidate for the mercy of the court; he has a right to go unpunished. Yet in *Dudley and Stephens*,[3] the shipwrecked seamen who cannibalized the cabin-boy in order to keep from starving were denied a defence of necessity. They were denied it, moreover, not only because their circumstances of peril were insufficient to call forth the application of the defence, but because there was, in Lord Coleridge's view, no right to an acquittal based on the strength of temptation, not even if the standard of

†Research for this article was funded by a grant from the Connaught Program in Legal Theory and Public Policy.
*Faculty of Law, University of Toronto.

1 *The Logic of Hegel*, trans Wallace (1892), p 7.

2 Bacon, *Maxims* (1630) Reg 25; Kant, *The Metaphysical Elements of Justice*, trans Ladd (1965), p 41. See also Hobbes, *Leviathan*, ed Oakeshott (1957), p 197: 'If a man, by the terror of present death, be compelled to do a fact against the law, he is totally excused; because no law can oblige a man to abandon his own preservation. And supposing such a law were obligatory; yet a man would reason thus, if I do it not, I die presently; if I do it, I die afterwards; therefore by doing it, there is time of life gained; nature therefore compels him to the fact'. Blackstone's views on the plank case accord with those of Bacon; see *Commentaries*, IV, 186.

3 (1884), 14 QBD 273.

firmness demanded of the accused was one which the judge himself could not have satisfied.[4] A similar disagreement exists on the availability of a defence where the competing interests are of unequal value. Aquinas says that 'if the need be so manifest and urgent . . . then it is lawful for a man to succour his own needs by means of another's property'.[5] Yet in *London Borough of Southwark* v *Williams*,[6] the English Court of Appeal denied that extreme hunger could excuse a theft or that homelessness could excuse a trespass. The reason, said Lord Denning, was that 'if hunger were once allowed to be an excuse for stealing, it would open a door through which all kinds of disorder and lawlessness would pass'.[7]

It is tempting to view this tension between the law and philosophy of necessity as a fixed and essential one, rooted in a deeper cleavage between the standpoints of moral and legal thought. One might think, in other words, that a defence of necessity can be justified only by appeal to a moral end that relativizes individual rights to life, physical integrity, and property, and from the perspective of which the invariance of legal obligation has significance only as a salutary illusion.[8] Were this the case, a defence of necessity would be understandably anathema to legal thought, which characteristically priorizes personal rights rather than a conception of the good, and which strives to secure these rights against the solvent of teleological reasoning. In fact, the most common arguments for a defence of necessity appeal to a moral good. The right of someone to break the law to avoid a greater evil is typically viewed as instrumental to the goal of welfare maximization.[8a] The supposed right to an acquittal of someone who has taken innocent life as a necessary means of saving his own is usually explained as mirroring a moral duty of compassion owed to one whose loss of self-control manifested ordinary human frailty rather than a criminal disdain for the rights of others.[8b] There is, however, a notable exception to this pattern of argument. In *Perka* v *The Queen*,[9] the Supreme

4 Ibid, at 288.

5 *Summa Theologica*, II-II, Q 66, A 7. Cf Bacon, *Maxims*, 25.

6 [1971] 2 All ER 175.

7 Ibid, at 179. Lord Denning relied on the authority of Hale, who reasoned that if necessity could justify theft, 'men's properties would be under a strange insecurity, being laid open to other men's necessities, whereof no man can possibly judge, but the party himself'.

8 See Finnis, *Natural Law and Natural Rights* (1980), pp 308–320.

8a See, for example, Williams, *Criminal Law: The General Part* (1961), pp 728–31.

8b See Fletcher, *Rethinking Criminal Law* (1978), pp 807–10.

9 (1985), 13 DLR (4th) 1. The accused in this case were drug smugglers charged with importing cannabis into Canada. They were en route from Colombia to Alaska in international waters when bad weather and mechanical difficulties induced the captain to seek refuge in a cove on the west coast of Vancouver Island. There the cargo of marijuana was off-loaded in order to prevent the ship from capsizing. At trial, the accused pleaded, inter alia, the defence of necessity and were acquitted. The Supreme Court of Canada, however, ordered a new trial, holding that the trial judge had erred in failing to direct the jury properly on the question of the availability of a legal means of avoiding the danger to the crew.

Court of Canada affirmed the existence of a defence of necessity and, in doing so, explicitly sought to conceive it in a way that permits its accommodation to a rights-based view of the common law. The majority saw this reconciliation as possible only if necessity is conceived as an excuse based on 'a realistic assessment of human weakness . . . in emergency situations where normal human instincts . . . overwhelmingly impel disobedience'.[10] For Madame Justice Wilson, on the other hand, a defence of necessity is compatible with the logic of rights only if it is conceived as a justification rather than an excuse, and only if its availability is restricted to those caught in a conflict between legal duties.

This essay takes up the problematic of *Perka*. In it I argue that neither the majority judgment of Chief Justice Dickson nor the concurring judgment of Madame Justice Wilson succeeds in reconciling a common-law defence of necessity with the idea of a right. Against the former I argue that such a reconciliation is possible only if common-law necessity operates solely as a justification, and if necessitous circumstances falling short of justification are relevant only to the mitigation or remission of sentence. Against the latter, I contend that law-breaking is justified not only in the service of other legal duties, but whenever necessary to affirm a hierarchy of values itself necessitated by the idea of a right. In arguing, however, against the common-law recognition of necessity as an excuse, I shall also attempt to explain the origin in the imagination of the idea for such an excuse, and therewith to provide reasons for its recognition by statute. The argument will be that necessity as mitigation is a sensuous analogue of the conceptual truth about excuses, and that this close resemblance makes it undesirable as a matter of policy to leave mitigation or pardon to the vagaries of discretion.

THE UTILITARIAN THEORY OF NECESSITY AS JUSTIFICATION

The Anglo-American theory of necessity as justification has traditionally been formulated in utilitarian terms.[11] Thus, on the so-called choice-of-evils branch

10 Ibid, at 14.

11 See Williams, *Criminal Law: The General Part* (1961), pp 728–31; Williams, 'The Defence of Necessity', [1953] *Current Legal Problems*, 216; Fletcher, *Rethinking Criminal Law* (1978), pp 788–98; Robinson, 'A Theory of Justification: Social Harm as a Prerequisite for Criminal Liability', (1975), 23 *UCLA L Rev* 266; Conde, 'Necessity Defined: A New Role in the Criminal Defence System', (1981), 29 *UCLA L Rev* 409. According to section 3.02 of the American Law Institute's Model Penal Code, 'conduct which the actor believes to be necessary to avoid an evil to himself or to another is justifiable, provided that: (a) the evil sought to be avoided by such conduct is greater than that sought to be prevented by the law defining the offence charged; and (b) neither the Code nor the law defining the offence provides exceptions or defenses dealing with the specific situation involved; and (c) a legislative purpose to exclude the justification claimed does not otherwise plainly appear'. Note that this provision would justify taking innocent life to achieve a net saving of lives.

of necessity, law-breaking is said to be justified whenever necessary to avoid a harm greater than the one inflicted. The requirements that an emergency exist and that there be no legal exit from the accused's dilemma ensure that the benefit gained by the unlawful conduct is purchased by the least costly means. Indeed, since necessity as justification seems to imply the subordination of rights to the greater good of others, it is difficult to see how the justificatory theory of necessity can be anything other than utilitarian. Certainly the majority in *Perka* takes this connection for granted, as does George Fletcher, on whose writings the *Perka* majority chiefly relies.[12] Once the justificatory theory of necessity is identified with utilitarianism, moreover, it becomes a relatively simple matter to discard it. For in situations where overall welfare is served by infringing rights, utilitarianism proves more than its foundations will bear. Not only does it justify the sacrifice of the few by the many in its own self-interest; it also imposes on the few a moral obligation to sacrifice themselves. Thus the moral theory whose premise is that pleasure is the good must, in order to be a theory of moral (as distinct from prudential) obligation, embrace a conclusion that contradicts that premise. Nor does the obligation of altruism rest any more comfortably on the foundations of the common law. The latter, it seems, cannot accept a utilitarian theory of necessity without committing itself in principle to a legal duty of beneficence destructive of the distinction between acts and omissions.[13]

There are other, more obvious, difficulties with a utilitarian interpretation of necessity. If law-breaking is justified on act-utilitarian grounds, then the objectivity of law dissolves in an individualistic calculus of net social benefit. Right action becomes indistinguishable in principle from criminality, the essence of which is the self-elevation of the individual above the objective order of reciprocal rights. It is no answer to say that private judgments about social welfare will be reviewable by courts. For if courts may dispense with law for the greater good, then they may also substitute their judgment about social welfare for that of the legislature. Law then consists of nothing but the *ad hoc* decrees of judges applied retroactively. If in order to preclude these possibilities, necessity is conceived in rule-utilitarian terms, then the legal order is doubtless preserved, but at the expense of a defence of necessity. For since the universalization of any breach of law will produce counter-utilitarian results, no breach will ever be permissible.[14] In any case, there is no reason for a utilitarian to be concerned

12 See Fletcher, 'The Individualization of Excusing Conditions', 47 *S Cal L Rev* 1269, 1280–88. In *Rethinking Criminal Law,* however, Professor Fletcher sees the possibility (reflected in German law) of a non-utilitarian theory of necessity as justification, one based on the concept of a transcendent right; see *supra* note 11, pp 779–88.

13 In fact, Bentham could make no sense of this distinction; see *An Introduction to the Principles of Morals and Legislation* (Hafner, 1970), p 323.

14 The rule-utilitarian position is embodied in the recommendation of the English Law Commission to exclude a defence of necessity from a criminal code and to abolish it insofar as it exists at common law; see Law Com No 83, Part IV.

about the universalizability of an unlawful act as distinct from its actual consequences on law-abidingness in general. It would be perverse from a utilitarian standpoint to forego an act approved by the greatest happiness principle simply because that act would fail the utilitarian test in a counterfactual world. Accordingly, the only self-consistent utilitarian is an act-utilitarian, one who considers the likely repercussions of a decision to acquit a law-breaker on the ground that his conduct was necessary to promote a greater good.

There are a number of reasons to reject even so modified a utilitarian theory of necessity. In the first place, this theory implies the notional if not the actual dissolution of the legal order, for it replaces the sovereignty of law with the moral virtuosity of judges. The fact that in practice judges will almost always confirm the political decisions of legislatures cannot affect the principle of judicial supremacy entailed by their power continually to re-evaluate those decisions. Secondly, a theory of necessity that makes justification dependent on the social effects of an acquittal will be incapable of formulating a law which actors can apply to themselves. Indeed, it will be incapable of supporting a *law* of necessity. Since the net benefit of the unlawful act is but a minor component of the total analysis, the utilitarian will eschew any articulation in advance of defensible types of conduct, preferring to decide each case as it arises.[15] There will thus be no law of necessity by which an agent could determine at the time of acting whether his act was lawful. The more broad-gauged and sophisticated the calculus, therefore, the more will a law of necessity degenerate into a series of retroactive decrees.

Furthermore, a theory of necessity that balances the utility of an acquittal against that of the accused's activity will determine guilt or innocence by reference to factors having no connection with the conduct of the accused. Lord Denning's judgment in *Southwark* illustrates what must inevitably occur if a judge, in determining whether necessity is available in the circumstances, may consider the probable social impact of a successful plea. In *Southwark* there was little doubt that, taken in isolation, the squatting of the homeless defendants was welfare enhancing. Their circumstances were evidently dismal and the house they occupied had been boarded up by the municipality for future renovation. Since the dwelling had thus been withdrawn from the pool of low-rent housing, the defendants' trespass cannot be said to have subverted the rationality of the public scheme of distribution. In effect, the boarding-up had created an

15 See Stephen, *A History of the Criminal Law of England* (1883), II, 108: 'It is just possible to imagine cases in which the expediency of breaking the law is so overwhelmingly great that people may be justified in breaking it, but these cases cannot be decided beforehand, and must be adjudicated upon by a jury afterwards'. Cf Kenny, *Outlines of Criminal Law*, 19th ed, 73. The authors of the English Draft Code of 1879 omitted inclusion of a defence of necessity because of the problems of stipulating in advance the conditions under which it would apply. They preferred to leave the defence to the common law and recommended that each case be decided as it arises; see *Report of the Criminal Code Bill Commission*, Parl Pap (1878–79), XX, pp 10, 43–44.

alternative pool of housing available to the first person willing to make the necessary repairs and whose need for housing was so urgent as to making living in such conditions preferable to any alternative. Independently considered, therefore, the defendants' conduct very likely yielded benefits in excess of the costs both to themselves and to the municipality. Yet the net benefit of the defendants' trespass naturally paled when set alongside the putative costs of a judgment in their favour, for would not that outcome encourage risk-taking by persons ever inclined to pity their circumstances and hence open the door to widespread breaches of the peace? As a result of this reasoning, the defence was denied not to persons who exaggerated their need but to persons common sense tells us were entitled to the premises until otherwise accommodated by the community.[16]

Finally, an act-utilitarian theory of necessity distorts the significance which the defence of necessity has for legal discourse. By legal discourse I mean not the actual speech of judges and lawyers, but the speech that preserves the legal order as an autonomous and objective sphere of right insulated from subjective moral judgment. In legal thought, the right of necessity comes forward as an extraordinary right, one that defines the outer perimeter or conceptual limit of the sphere of legal justice. It is understood, in other words, as an overriding of rights that are determined independently of the necessitous circumstances, something notionally as well as practically peripheral. By contrast, the act-utilitarian theory of necessity views the latter as constitutive of the sphere of legal rights itself. Empirically, no doubt, law-breakers will only exceptionally be acquitted owing to the perceived social consequences of a successful plea. However, for the act-utilitarian, the defence of necessity simply embodies a particular conclusion of a teleological reasoning that standardly determines rights. All utilitarian rights, therefore, are rights of necessity.[17] But if rights are determined rather than overridden by necessity, then on the one hand necessity loses its peculiar meaning, and on the other legal rights, understood as rights against subjection to the pleasure of others, are relativized to the point of non-existence.

NECESSITY AND THE RATIONALE FOR EXCUSES

It is the position of Professor Fletcher and of the majority in *Perka* that since the utilitarian theory of necessity as justification is subversive either of the legal order

16 The prison escape cases are notorious examples of the application of a consequentialist reasoning to convict persons whose conduct would be justified if considered independently of the effects of an acquittal. See *State* v *Green*, 470 SW 2d 565 (1971); *People* v *Richards*, 269 Cal App 2d 768 (1969); *People* v *Noble*, 18 Mich App 300 (1969). On the other hand, a necessity defence to prison escapes has been recognized in *People* v *Lovercamp*, 118 Cal Rptr 110 (1974); *People* v *Luther*, 232 NW 2d 184 (1975); *State* v *Baker*, 598 SW 2d 540 (1980).

17 Williams, 'The Defence of Necessity', *supra* n 11, at 217: 'In a manner of speaking the whole law is based upon social necessity; it is a body of rules devised by the judges and the legislature to provide for what are felt to be reasonable needs'.

or of the defence of necessity, the latter must be conceptualized as an excuse.[18] Necessity is to be understood as negating not the wrongfulness of the act but the culpability of the actor. Once necessity is assimilated to the category of excuses, however, the problem arises of formulating a theory of excuses that will rationally integrate defences like mistake, insanity, and involuntary intoxication on the one hand, and necessity and duress on the other.[19] Necessity, after all, fits awkwardly with the other excuses. Whereas mistake, insanity, and intoxication negate the intentionality of the wrongful act, necessity presupposes an act that is intentional both as to its consequences and its wrongfulness. In the usual circumstances under which necessity is invoked as an excuse, the accused consciously and wilfully infringes a right to further particularistic ends. His act thus seems quintessentially criminal. What theory of excuses can unify such seemingly disparate defences?

Fletcher offers two possibilities. One conceivable rationale for excuses, he argues, is that they preclude an inference from the wrongful act to the character of the actor:

> Typically, if a driver knowingly runs over someone lying in the roadway, we might infer something about the driver's indifference to human life. But we cannot make that inference if the choice open to the driver was going over a cliff or continuing down the incline and running over someone lying in the roadway. Similarly, if someone violates a legal prohibition under an unavoidable mistake about the legality of his conduct, we cannot infer anything about his respect for law and the rights of others. The same breakdown in the reasoning from conduct to character occurs in cases on insanity, for it is implicit in the medical conception of insanity that the actor's true character is distorted by his mental illness.[20]

We can agree that the presence of excusing conditions precludes an inference from conduct to character. Something more is needed, however, to explain why the illicitness of such an inference should excuse the wrongdoer. Fletcher sets out the reasoning in the following steps. First, punishment is just only if its distribution is just; second, the just distribution of sanctions presupposes an allocation of burdens according to the desert of the offender; third, the desert of the offender is a function of his character as manifested in the commission of a legally prohibited act; fourth, in a case of excused conduct, one cannot determine the character of the offender; fifth, it is therefore unjust to punish excused offenders.[21]

18 *Perka, supra* n 9, at 13–14; Fletcher, 'The Individualization of Excusing Conditions', *supra* n 12, at 1299–1309.

19 This article will not deal separately with the defence of duress. For the purposes of our discussion, duress may be regarded as a special case of necessity, one where the threat to the accused emanates from a human rather than from an impersonal source. Accordingly, the analysis presented here is intended to apply indifferently to both necessity and duress.

20 *Rethinking Criminal Law, supra* n 11, at 800.

21 Fletcher, 'The Individualization of Excusing Conditions', *supra* n 12, at 1271 n 8.

The crucial link in this chain of reasoning is the third. It is that a vicious character is the criterion of criminal desert. One need not subscribe to a thesis of environmental determinism to regard this premise with scepticism. Inasmuch as a wicked character may be manifest in ways other than through the perpetration of criminal acts, this theory renders problematic the act requirement of criminal law. There is no difference in point of character between the person who commits adultery in a jurisdiction where adultery is an offence and one who commits adultery mistakenly believing it to be an offence. The character theory would convict the latter as well as the former. Fletcher, to be sure, has a response to this objection. He argues that the limitation of the inquiry to the criminal act is dictated by a requirement of respect for the suspect's privacy. 'Disciplining the inquiry in this way', he says, 'restricts the range of relevant information, but it secures the individual against a free-ranging inquiry of the state into his moral worth'.[22] Yet once it is conceded that all evidence of character is relevant, there is no principled ground for making the *criminal* act the curtain for the suspect's privacy. From the standpoint of privacy, the criminal act is fair game only because it is a public manifestation of the character of the accused. But then the way seems open to attaching criminal liability to any pattern of public acts which, criminal or not, manifests a wicked character.

Not only does the character theory of excuses threaten the act requirement; it also renders unintelligible the limitation of excusing conditions to a finite set of nominate factors. If the only significance of mistake, drunkenness, insanity and necessity is that they preclude the inference from conduct to character, there is no reason to exclude evidence of happenings extrinsic to the act that might do so as well. Indeed, since it is manifestly unfair to judge a person's character by a single act, the accused ought on Fletcher's theory to be permitted to adduce character evidence, not simply to support a denial of commission but as exculpatory in itself. Thus, if it could be shown that the criminal act was a momentary aberration from, rather than an expression of, the accused's enduring moral character, he should be entitled to an acquittal. Nor is this all. Could one exclude from the scope of relevant evidence attestations of the sincerity and generosity of the accused's motives in committing the crime? The person who, out of an abundance of love for mankind, privately redistributes wealth to the poor is certainly not deserving of punishment on account of the inward disposition of his character. On the contrary, that disposition taken by itself merits only reward and praise. Yet to allow the purity of the accused's motives objectively to excuse his crime is to dissolve the objectivity of right in an absolutism of conscience.[23] Indeed, the problem in general with Fletcher's 'individualization of excusing conditions' is that, by relating these conditions to moral states of being rather than to the elements of wrong*doing*, it submerges

22 *Rethinking Criminal Law, supra* n 11, at 801.

23 See Hegel, *Philosophy of Right*, trans Knox (1967), para 126.

the notion of a legal wrong, and correlatively, of a human right. Punishment then ceases to be an enforcement of rights, becoming instead an external incentive to virtue, one which must fail to the extent that it succeeds.

Accordingly, the defence of necessity cannot be integrated with the other excuses on the basis of the character theory of excusing conditions, for the latter is unable to preserve the notion of wrongdoing as both condition and determinant of criminal desert. The other possibility suggested by Fletcher and adopted by the majority in *Perka* is this: excusing conditions render wrongful acts involuntary in the sense that those acts cannot be regarded as expressions of the actor's free choice. The act is no doubt voluntary in the sense that the physical movements of the actor are consciously willed. If, however, any of the excusing conditions are present, the act is 'normatively involuntary'; that is, its consequences are not freely chosen by the accused and so are not justly attributable to him.[24]

It is easy to see that mistake, involuntary intoxication, and insanity accord with this theory of excuses. It is less obvious that necessity does so. Consider the case in which someone kills an innocent victim as the only alternative to dying himself. Here the involuntariness theory gains plausibility from the fact that the accused is in one sense free and in another sense unfree.[25] He is free in the thin or purely formal sense that his act is the intended one of a self-conscious agent and so unquestionably the embodiment of a choice. No doubt the pressure of the impulse to survive was, given the immediacy of the peril, such as would have overpowered even a will of reasonable fortitude. However, we must reject as a product of cloudy thinking any suggestion that inordinately pressing instincts can negate freedom in the formal sense, for inasmuch as this freedom consists precisely in a transcendence of determination by instinct, quantitative considerations are irrelevant to it.[26] The will cannot be compelled by powerful desire unless it is compelled by desire as such, in which case we are committed to a determinism destructive of the entire edifice of criminal responsibility, blame and punishment. On the other hand, the accused was doubtless unfree relative to a more robust and concrete sense of freedom, which requires not only

24 *Rethinking Criminal Law, supra* n 11, at 802–7; *Perka, supra* n 9, at 14–15. 'The lost Alpinist who on the point of freezing to death breaks open an isolated mountain cabin is not literally behaving in an involuntary fashion. He has control over his actions to the extent of being physically capable of abstaining from the act. Realistically, however, his act is not a "voluntary" one. His "choice" to break the law is no true choice at all; it is remorselessly compelled by normal human instincts. This sort of involuntariness is often described as "moral or normative involuntariness".'

25 See Gombay, 'Necessitate Without Inclining', (1985), XXIV *Dialogue* 579–87; McCall, 'Incline Without Necessitating', (1985), XXIV *Dialogue* 489–96; Brodeur, 'Compelled to Choose', (1985), XXIV *Dialogue* 597–603; Baker, 'Duress, Responsibility, and Deterrence', (1985), XXIV *Dialogue* 605–612.

26 The *Perka* majority slips into this error when it says that in necessity situations, the accused's act is 'remorselessly compelled by normal human instincts'. See *supra* n 9, at 15.

that the agent choose the consequence begotten by him, but also that the content of his choice be itself something which he can affirm as his own.[27] In situations of necessity, the accused can affirm none of the options available to him. Those options are externally imposed and pre-emptive of any he might voluntarily embrace. His freedom of choice prior to action is thus contradicted by his being compelled to accept a content for action that he would never have chosen for himself.

Few would deny that the concrete sense of freedom is the one most adequate to the notion of freedom. Whether it is the sense relevant to criminal responsibility is, however, another matter. Certainly the excuses of mistake, involuntary intoxication, and insanity are wholly explicable as conditions which vitiate formal freedom.[28] When any of these conditions are present, the accused is exonerated not because he had no choices of which he could approve, but because he did not choose the consequence he caused. Indeed, it can be shown that the formal sense of freedom, however inadequate as a full account of freedom, is the only sense relevant to criminal desert. Suppose that, owing to the combined circumstances of my birth, upbringing, natural endowments, and a depressed economy, I am now faced with a choice of receiving social assistance or embarking on a criminal career. I regard neither of these options as desirable in itself but despise a life of crime less than the humiliation I would feel in accepting welfare. I therefore choose crime. Having regard solely to the issue of voluntariness, this situation seems structurally identical to that in which someone must either take innocent life or die. Neither option is choiceworthy in itself; neither would be chosen if the agent were free to choose an object of desire. Accordingly, if the person who kills rather than die is excused, but the person who steals rather than accept welfare is not, it cannot be because the former's act is involuntary while the latter's is free. The actions of both are, as Aristotle says, partly voluntary and partly involuntary.[29] If one is excused and the other is not, it can only be because we expect the down-and-outer to overcome his aversion to accepting welfare, whereas we regard with understanding and sympathy the killer's failure to overcome his aversion to death. The free choice he exercised was one that a person of reasonable fortitude would likewise have made. But this places the theory of necessity on a footing entirely different from that of voluntariness and from that on which the other excuses rest. The other excuses deny the attributability of the act to the actor; necessity concedes attributability but denies that the man of ordinary firmness would have acted differently.

That the formal sense of freedom is the only one relevant to criminal responsibility can be shown conceptually as well. The difference between formal and concrete freedom corresponds to a difference between two dimensions of the

27 See Hegel, *Philosophy of Right*, paras 10–21.

28 See H. L. A. Hart, *Punishment and Responsibility* (1968), ch 2.

29 Aristotle, *Nicomachean Ethics*, 1110a–1110b.

person. The formal capacity of uncaused choice is a capacity of personality considered as a universal subjectivity or ego abstracted from the manifold qualities and preferences that differentiate one individual from another.[30] It is a capacity of the person *qua* person. Concrete freedom, on the other hand, is this formal capacity objectively realized by a particular individual acting from determinate purposes in particular circumstances.[31] Whether a person is concretely free depends not on the universal nature of self-consciousness but on a harmony of inner powers and outward circumstances on the one hand with the peculiar desires of the individual on the other. Now if wrongdoing is to be understood as a contradiction of law, then it must lay claim to the same universality as the law itself. It must lay claim, in other words, to the validity of a principle. This it can do, however, only if it is the act of a purposive self, for the latter is the only universal whose dominion can oppose the universality claimed by the law. The concept of wrong is thus completed by an unlawful act intended by a self-conscious agent. It does not require in addition that the content of choice be itself willed as the agent's own, because whether the unlawful consequence is desired or unwillingly accepted as a necessary means of satisfying another desire, the implication is the same: the law is self-consciously subordinated to the primacy of the person who is the subject of desire. The reason that motive is regarded by the law as irrelevant to culpability is that, from the standpoint of the authority of law, all motives are on a par; they are the motives of an individual ego. Accordingly, the concept of law cannot rationally admit as a ground of exculpation the fact that a choice was coerced, for if the law is contradicted by an unlawful consequence that is desired by the agent, it must also be contradicted by an unlawful consequence that is intended by the agent because necessary for the satisfaction of another desire. Rather, the only excusing conditions consistent with the notion of law are those under which the law, though breached, is undisturbed in its supremacy. However, such conditions are precisely those which negate the implicit claim to validity of the wrongful act because they signify that the consequence was not chosen.

If the formal sense of freedom is the only sense relevant to criminal wrongdoing, it follows that necessity, which does not negate this kind of freedom, cannot be integrated with the other excuses on the basis of the voluntariness theory. It is indeed doubtful whether any theory of excuses that saves the notion of wrongdoing can integrate necessity with mistake, involuntary intoxication, and insanity.[32] On a retributivist account of criminal desert, the basis for the true excuses is that they negate the claim of validity implicit in

30 Hegel, *Philosophy of Right*, para 5.

31 Ibid, para 6.

32 Bentham's theory of inefficacious punishment will not do either, for it illogically confines the deterrent force of punishment to its power to deter those with the same characteristics as the accused. This criticism has been elaborated by Hart, *Punishment and Responsibility*, *supra* n 28, at 40–44, and by Fletcher, *Rethinking Criminal Law*, *supra* n 11, at 813–17.

intentional infringements of rights, and therewith also the rationale and legitimating grounds of punishment. Where intent is present, the wrongful act signifies not simply a challenge of the victim's right to a particular thing or to a particular scope of activity; rather it signifies a denial that the victim is a bearer of rights equal in moral worth to the aggressor.[33] The act thus implicitly claims a right of the arbitrary freedom of the will against freedom actualized in the mutual recognition of persons as equals. The loss, then, of the criminal's actual liberty is the inner consequence of his own claim, a claim thereby shown to be self-contradictory and null. Accordingly, the presence of intent reconciles punishment with the right of the criminal in a dual sense: first, as the universalization of the criminal's own principle, punishment is immanent in his actual will; second, as the vindication of concrete human rights, punishment is immanent in his rational will, something to which he would, if he saw clearly, assent. Where, on the other hand, intent is absent, there is no ontological challenge to the validity of rights that could awaken the inner retribution of the law, or that could confer a right of coercion on the order of freedom. Any force inflicted on the individual would violate his rights, for it could only be applied for ends external to his own.

Now this rationale for excuses has no application to necessity. In the circumstances under which necessity is invoked as an excuse for homicide, all the objective elements of criminality are present. This is most clearly the case in situations like that in *Dudley and Stephens* or in the example of the sailor on the plank, where the homicide is committed from an interest in self-preservation. As between the life of the victim and the life of the accused, the latter's self-preference is wholly arbitrary from an objective point of view. He has thus implicitly asserted a right to an arbitrary freedom, the content of which is pleasure, against the order of concrete rights. Suppose, however, the accused was a detached observer, not himself at risk, who diverted an inevitable catastrophe away from the many and onto the few. Consider, in particular, Judith Thomson's example of the bystander at the switch who redirects a trolley running out of control so as to kill one instead of five.[34] At first sight, no doubt, it seems absurd to say that someone acting to minimize the cost of an inevitable catastrophe is in the same position with respect to criminal desert as the person who, to save himself, takes innocent life. Yet this is indeed the case. The killing of one to save many cannot be legally justified except on a utilitarian calculus that would deny the victim his right not to be subordinated to the self-interest of others, and that incoherently obliges the one to a self-sacrifice from which nothing is received in return. If the bystander is innocent of wrongdoing, therefore, it can only be on the basis of an excuse. An excuse presupposes, however, that the victim had a right against his one-sided subjection to the

33 See Hegel, *Philosophy of Right*, para 95.

34 Thomson, 'The Trolley Problem', (1985), 94 *Yale LJ* 1395.

advantage of the five, a right that was violated. What is the bystander's excuse? It can only be that he acted out of a purely moral duty to save as many lives as possible. However, this moral duty (supposing it exists),[35] inasmuch as it stands opposed to the public, legal order of rights, obligates the bystander, if at all, as a private individual. And it was as a private legislator, as it were, that he determined that the saving in suffering was worth the violation of the victim's rights. To raise, however, the value preferences of the private conscience above the victim's rights is to assert a right of the particular will against the order of reciprocal freedom secured by law. The principle of a private, duty-based ethic turns, when absolutized, into the principle of crime, because the content of such an ethic can have no other origin than subjective inclination, which then claims priority over law.[36] Since, however, the moral necessity to which the bystander appeals shades into the principle of crime, it can hardly count as an objective excuse for crime.

All this is to show that if circumstances of necessity excuse a wrongdoer, it cannot be because the act is objectively blameless in a criminal sense. It is impossible for necessity objectively to excuse a crime because the very invocation of necessity, asserting the priority of a particularistic freedom over law, is crime itself. If necessity is an excuse, therefore, it must be one that is *sui generis*. And it must be one that signifies not that the accused is objectively blameless, but that *we* withhold blame from him out of compassion for his predicament, or as a concession to the human-all-too-human in his behaviour. Yet even this is insufficient as a theoretical basis for necessity as excuse. For one must go on to explain why compassion for the accused is not in this context justly remitted to the benevolence and good sense of the judge or executive, but is rather something to which the accused has a right. The focus now shifts, therefore, from the culpability of the accused to his punishability by us. The argument might be stated thus: objectively speaking the accused did wrong; we, however, have no right to punish him, because it is unlikely that we would have done otherwise.

This is in fact the theory on which Fletcher and the Model Penal Code ultimately rest the excuse of necessity.[37] It is also the theory that implicitly underlies the majority judgment in *Perka,* for (as we have seen) what ultimately distinguishes coerced choices that are excusable from coerced choices that are culpable is a judgment as to whether the unlawful act was resistible by a person

35 That there is no such moral duty to sacrifice the one to the five has been convincingly argued by Taurek, 'Should the Numbers Count', (1977), 6 *Philosophy and Public Affairs* 293.

36 See Hegel, *Philosophy of Right,* paras 137–40.

37 See Fletcher, *Rethinking Criminal Law, supra* n 11, at 807–10; Fletcher, 'The Individualization of Excusing Conditions', *supra* n 12, at 1308–9. Under section 2.09(1) of the Model Penal Code (Proposed Official Draft, 1962), a person has a defence if he was coerced into criminal conduct by force or a threat of force that 'a person of reasonable firmness in his situation would have been unable to resist'.

of ordinary firmness.[38] I want to show, however, that neither this nor cognate theories succeed in revealing necessity as a genuine excuse, that is, as conferring on the accused a right to an acquittal. However, I also want to show why it is reasonable to create such a right understood as a statutory entrenchment of compassion.

THE STRANGE CONFUSION OF JURISTS

It is clear, to begin with, that the compassion theory will not work as a comprehensive theory of necessity. It will not work because it fails to account for the situations in which breaking the law seems positively justified, and in which even an acquittal from compassion is unjust to the accused. If someone drives through a red light to save the life of his child, he does nothing for which he requires an excuse. We would not think anyone had a right to stop him; on the contrary, we would applaud the conduct of someone who manually stopped traffic and so assisted him in breaking the law. Since this stranger to the calamity cannot be the object of our compassion, his blamelessness must be an objective one, rooted in the rightness in these circumstances of breaking the law.[39]

Furthermore, it is the characteristic feature of the compassion theory that it raises subjective considerations normally relevant only to sentence into considerations that objectively negate liability to conviction. The argument is that in necessity scenarios, the circumstances that make compassion for the accused appropriate also render punishment unjust. Now there are a number of ways in which this curious mixture of objective and subjective considerations can be made to appear intellectually coherent. We shall see, however, that they rest either on a confusion between a metaphorical innocence and the conceptual one it images, or on untenable assumptions concerning the nature of the legal order.

Let us for convenience assume the facts in the classic scenario painted by Kant.[40] Two shipwrecked sailors are in the water. A has hold of a plank that will

38 That the compassion theory underlies the majority reasoning in *Perka* is revealed by the following passage: '[The defence of necessity] rests on a realistic assessment of human weakness, recognizing that a liberal and humane criminal law cannot hold people to the strict obedience of laws in emergency situations where normal human instincts, whether of self-preservation or of altruism, overwhelmingly impel disobedience. . . . Praise is indeed not bestowed, but pardon is, when one does a wrongful act under pressure which, in the words of Aristotle . . . "overstrains human nature and which no one could withstand" '. (*Supra* n 9, at 14).

39 In *Perka,* the identification of necessity as excuse with the whole defence of necessity produces an incoherence in the limitations attached to the defence. The restrictions laid down by Dickson C. J. – that the harm avoided be objectively greater than the harm done and that the peril be objectively imminent leaving no legal alternative – are more consistent with necessity as justification than with necessity based on a 'realistic assessment of human weakness'. See Wells, 'Necessity and the Common Law', 5 *Oxford J Legal Stud* 471.

40 *Metaphysical Elements of Justice, supra* n 2, at 41.

support only one; B, to save himself, wrests the plank from A, who drowns. Fletcher's (and Dickson C J's) argument for B's acquittal is that his act was normatively involuntary. B killed A only because his aversion to dying was greater than his aversion to killing, and in giving effect to the former preference, he exhibited a weakness of will to which a man of reasonable fortitude would likewise have succumbed. For the reasons I have already elaborated, the cogency of this argument has nothing to do with our inability to draw inferences from the sailor's conduct to his character. Its real force lies, rather, in its having borrowed a truth from the retributivist rationale for excuses and in having recast it in empirical terms.[41] If it seems unjust to punish the sailor, it is because, in exhibiting no less firmness than the man of ordinary character, he has done nothing that sets him apart from the human community. It is, however, precisely the *notional* separation from the human community that is the objective ground of criminal liability. Through his intentional violation of his victim's rights, the criminal asserts a right of unlimited freedom against the framework of reciprocal rights secured by law. And it is only this implicit self-separation that justifies the punishment which casts him out explicitly. Necessity scenarios thus present a remarkable paradox in which is no doubt rooted the long history of controversy as to whether and under what circumstances the defence exists. The paradox consists in this: in circumstances in which necessity is invoked as an excuse, the accused satisfies the notional criterion of criminal isolation without, however, empirically differentiating himself from ordinary humanity.

A moment's reflection will reveal, however, that the empirical equality of behaviours produces a semblance of innocence rather than innocence itself. If someone were charged with the offence of jay-walking, no one would think he had a right to an acquittal based solely on the fact that everyone (including the judge) is frequently guilty of the same offence. Similarly, if I assault someone in the heat of anger, I cannot claim a right to an acquittal simply because a man of reasonable self-control would have been similarly moved to violence. These examples appeal, no doubt, only to intuitions. The reason, however, that parity of behaviour cannot be the criterion of immunity from punishment is that such a criterion is incompatible with law. No standard of right conduct can have its enforcement tied to acceptable standards of non-compliance and still be a standard of right conduct. If the drowning sailor has a right to an acquittal based on parity of conduct, then the law has been displaced by the standard of acceptable weakness as the criterion of right. But then the sailor's homicide is justified; he has no need of an excuse; and the right of personality is subject to the variable weaknesses of human beings.

There is, however, another way of defending a right to an acquittal in the case of the drowning sailor. One might argue that the defendant's duty to forbear

41 This is also seen by Bruce Chapman, 'Criminal Law Liability and Fundamental Justice: Toward a Theory of Substantive Judicial Review', (1986) 44 UT Fac L Rev 153, at 170–171.

from killing is imperfect, that is, purely moral in the circumstances.[42] In fact much of the language typically used to defend the excuse of necessity resembles the language of imperfect duties. Breach of the duty is considered not vice but moral weakness of a kind to which human beings as such are susceptible. Observance of the duty is viewed as meritorious rather than as morally neutral; and the claimed right to an acquittal suggests that non-observance is neutral rather than morally blameworthy. Is there any basis for the extraordinary claim that a duty to forbear from violence is imperfect in necessitous circumstances?

Of one thing we may be certain. It cannot be the peculiar strength of the inclination toward breach of the duty that renders the latter imperfect. My duty not to steal the crown jewels is a legal rather than a purely moral one, and remains so even if I come across them one day in a deserted street. The basis of imperfect duties is not that they confront intersubjectively strong temptations, but that they are duties which cannot be externally compelled without contradiction.[43] Private beneficence is a purely ethical duty, because its moral worth inheres in the good will that animates it. Compelling it would thus destroy it as beneficence. Moreover, since the duty of private beneficence is grounded in the demands of moral perfection on the donor, it cannot generate rights to specific acts on the part of others.[44] The duty is an indeterminate one, inasmuch as the manner of its concrete fulfillment is remitted to the moral prudence of the individual. Negative duties, on the other hand, are normally compellable because they relate to external actions rather than to inner virtue, and because their basis is not the good of the person obliged but the rights of him to whom the duty is owed. Accordingly, we can now perhaps see the subtle appeal of a claim that the sailor's quiet submission to fate would be meritorious in the circumstances. If duties of forbearance seem imperfect in cases of necessity, it is because the accused is, *as a matter of fact,* non-compellable in the circumstances. No threat of future punishment could induce him to submit to the present certainty of death. If he forbears from violence, therefore, he necessarily does so not from fear of punishment but from virtue, and his forbearance is thus praiseworthy. If he resorts to violence, his act is morally neutral, a failure to exercise praiseworthy self-control.

The sense that the duty of forbearance is imperfect in situations of necessity thus rests on a further confusion between a phenomenal reality and the conceptual one it imperfectly images. That *de facto* non-compellability produces only the appearance of an imperfect duty can be seen from the following example. Suppose two brothers each sentenced to life imprisonment kill a fellow inmate in response to an insult to both that would have similarly provoked a man of ordinary self-control. One brother has no hope of parole whereas the

42 See Bickenbach, 'The Defence of Necessity', (1983), 13 *Canadian Journal of Philosophy* 79, at 86.

43 Kant, *Ethical Philosophy,* trans Ellington (1983), pp 38–9.

44 Ibid, p 40.

other does, and capital punishment has been outlawed in the jurisdiction. If the combination of strong temptation and immunity from fear renders the duty of self-restraint imperfect, then the brothers deserve different outcomes solely by virtue of the difference in their prospects for early release. The brother with no hope of parole will be entitled to an acquittal, whereas the other will not. If this result seems absurd, it is because the rationale for imperfect duties has no application in these circumstances. Punishment would not here contradict the duty of forbearance, nor would it enforce conduct undetermined by that duty. On the contrary, it would vindicate in the usual way the right by which the duty was generated. Furthermore, the moral praiseworthiness of forbearance is nothing intrinsic to it (as it is with positive acts of beneficence) but is entirely relative to the non-deterrability of the accused in the circumstances. Accordingly, to allow the high moral worth of forbearance to nullify the enforceability of the law is to make the rights of personality hostage to the contingent deterrability of assailants.

A third way of rendering coherent the elevation of sentencing considerations to factors pertinent to conviction is the way suggested by Kant. In his discussion of the right of necessity, Kant sees that the theory of necessity as excuse involves a 'strange confusion among jurists' of subjective considerations relevant to punishment and objective considerations of culpability.[45] He himself has no doubt that the sailor who appropriates the plank is objectively culpable and bereft of excuse. Nevertheless, he presents an argument purporting to show why, in that situation, the guilty accused is entitled to an acquittal.

The argument rests on a particular conception of the relationship between law and ethics, or between the right and the good. As Kant conceives them, the legal order and the realm of ethics are each constituted by the exclusion of the other.[46] While there are, to be sure, duties common to both spheres, the ground of the obligation to conform to duty is fundamentally different in each. In the sphere of ethics, the individual obeys the law purely for the sake of the freedom inherent in making the dictates of reason the exclusive object of the will.[47] The basis of obligation is thus the inward, ontological priority of freedom. In the legal order, by contrast, the ground of the obligation to obey the law is that of external compulsion.[48] The incentive relied upon by the law is not that of virtue but the desire for self-preservation. The point, however, is not simply that the legal order is externally coercive for the egoistic man; nor is it simply that legal norms, applying as they do only to external actions, need not rely on virtue as an incentive for obedience. Kant's more controversial point is that the legal order is in essence coercive, so that autonomy is necessarily a matter of private rather than of public ethics.

45 *Metaphysical Elements of Justice*, *supra* n 2, at 41–2.
46 Ibid, pp 18–21.
47 Ibid, pp 13–14, 19–21.
48 Ibid, p 19.

Now if the purely legal obligation to obey the law arises from compulsion, then in the situation of the drowning sailor, there is no legal obligation to forbear from violence. For, as we have seen, the law is without deterrent force in those circumstances. Hence, although there has doubtless been a violation of right for which punishment is deserved, no *court* can pass sentence on the accused.[49] As the institution through which law in the inward sense becomes law in the external or positive sense, the court finds its jurisdiction circumscribed by the brute efficacy of punishment. In the legal order, if the law cannot operate coercively, then it cannot operate at all.[50]

Since Kant's moral philosophy (of which the legal philosophy is a part) purports to be true to our moral experience, it cannot be irrelevant to point out that no common-law court has been persuaded by this reasoning. In situations akin to the one he adduces, the courts have never thought it beyond their competence to give effect to the moral law whether or not it could effectively deter. However, we need not rely on such extrinsic evidence. Kant's argument for the right of necessity rests on the residual positivism of his legal theory, a positivism that stands in irreconcilable tension with that theory's rationalist core. The fundamental principle of Kantian ethics is the ontological priority of the laws of freedom, their capacity spontaneously and without admixture of anything foreign to move the will.[51] When Kant comes to justify the coercion of the legal order, he does so solely by reference to this principle. Coercion is authorized only when rationally necessitated by the general freedom, or only when applied against acts that are inconsistent with the freedom of all under universal laws.[52] There is thus for Kant no purely legal right to coerce that is separate from the right derived from justice. The authority to coerce is unitary and it is moral. If this is so, it is difficult to see how there can be a legal obligation that is conceptually divorced from moral obligation and that rests exclusively on compulsion. The obligation to obey the law is, after all, merely the logical correlate of the right to coerce. If the right to coerce is derived solely from freedom, can the obligation to obey rest on anything else? But if the obligation to obey is indeed an undifferentiated one resting on the justice of the law, then that obligation is independent of the deterrability of the accused and

49 Ibid, p 39.

50 I am indebted to Peter Benson for this interpretation of a difficult passage in Kant. It is important to distinguish Kant's position from that of Bentham, to which it bears a superficial resemblance. For Bentham, the fact that punishment is powerless to deter the accused renders it objectively unjust (see *Introduction to the Principles of Morals and Legislation, supra* n 13, at 170 ff). For Kant, punishment in the plank case would be just if only one could find someone who could justly execute it; this, however, is impossible, because the execution of the moral law is a function of the legal order, the authority of which is co-extensive with its power.

51 See Kant, *Metaphysical Elements of Justice, supra* n 2, at 22; cf Kant, *Foundations of the Metaphysics of Morals,* trans Beck (1959), pp 59 ff; Kant, *Critique of Practical Reason,* trans Beck (1956), pp 26–51.

52 Kant, *Metaphysical Elements of Justice, supra* n 2, at 36.

may be enforced by external courts no less than by the court of conscience. Furthermore, the implication of Kant's position is that courts are powerless to exact the retribution of the moral law not only in cases of necessity, but whenever the sanction of the law is insufficient to daunt a powerful aggressor. But if this is so, what becomes of the practical reality of pure reason, the demonstration of which is precisely the burden of Kant's moral theory?

We can also attack Kant's argument for the right of necessity by showing that the positivist premises on which it rests are unnecessary for the purpose for which Kant thinks they are necessary and indeed are antithetical to that purpose. Kant insists on the separation of the right and the good because he thinks that united they will destroy each other. Freedom for Kant consists in willing the form of universality in law, a form abstracted from the material content that originates in contingent preferences.[53] Accordingly, the multiplicity of positive laws can have no significance for the good of freedom, which is why the obligation to obey them cannot be moral. Were human beings inwardly obligated to obey positive law, they would be obligated to obey that which could not be the object of a universal legislation; hence they would not be essentially free. Conversely, if respect for the rights of personality depended on the obligatory force of the good, these rights would evaporate. For the good that obligates is an abstract freedom that renders particular duties contingent and imperfect.

It is evident, however, that this antagonism between the right and the good arises only because Kant has taken as his starting-point the action of the atomistic individual, from whose arbitrary preferences the philosopher must abstract in order to arrive at a universal good. It is this initial repulsion of particularity from the idea of freedom that determines the character of positive law as something essentially external to the self. If, however, we begin from the idea of freedom itself, and if particular laws are seen as inwardly necessitated by the idea of freedom actualized, then neither would the inner obligation to obey them contradict freedom, nor would the priority of the good (now concretized in laws embodying rights of personhood) destroy the integrity of rights.[54] Surely it is this synthesis of the right and the good rather than their separation that is the authentic realization of each. Kant's antithesis really accomplishes the opposite of what it intends. Intending to vindicate freedom as the good, it consigns freedom to the inner life, leaving the individual unfree in his public existence; intending to vindicate freedom as a right, it leaves the right subject to the hazards of deterrence.

It is doubtful, then, that there exists any theory of necessity that can reveal it as conferring a right to an acquittal in circumstances where the act is admittedly wrongful. All the attempts to do so succeed only in subverting the idea of a

53 Ibid, p 13; *Critique of Practical Reason, supra* n 51, at 26 ff.

54 This is the synthesis of Hegel's *Sittlichkeit*; see *Philosophy of Right*, paras 142–155.

right. However, in examining the possible ways of defending necessity as excuse, we have perhaps come to understand why it has exerted such a powerful hold on the human imagination. In circumstances where necessity makes compassion for the accused appropriate, the conceptual conditions both for true excuses and for imperfect duties are present in a phenomenal shape. Necessity, we can say, simulates the conditions that excuse an offence and that render duties moral rather than legal. Now this analogical relationship of necessity to the true grounds for acquittal provides a powerful reason for legislatively privileging compassion above the considerations of policy that might otherwise overwhelm it. Normally the compassion expressed in mitigation or remission of sentence is evoked by factors that transcend the act toward the actor – factors such as his moral character, signs of repentance, the circumstances of his background and environment and so on. Such considerations are, of course, quite alien to the issue of culpability for an isolated wrongful act, and as such are relevant only to a discretion that itself begins where the demands of right leave off. Here, however, what evokes compassion is precisely the sense that the act itself in all its isolation is strangely equivocal – culpable and not culpable at once.[55] While the drowning sailor has no objective excuse, the fact remains that he has not *by his act* empirically differentiated himself from the human community, and forbearance really would have been praiseworthy in the circumstances. The close resemblance between these reasons and the reasons that genuinely exculpate qualitatively differentiates the compassion that is appropriate in necessity cases from that which normally goes to sentencing discretion. Since the latter invokes considerations extrinsic to the act, it is logically defenceless against countervailing considerations equally extrinsic; since, however, the former appeals to nothing beyond the act other than our identification with the accused, it is inherently more resistant to arguments from expediency. If, therefore, mercy in the usual sense is a mere benefaction, and if true excuses confer rights, then the compassion evoked by wrongful acts committed from necessity is something in between a benefaction and a right. I can think of no other way of adequately reflecting this objectively unique status than through the creation of a statutory excuse.[56]

TOWARD A NON-CONSEQUENTIALIST THEORY OF NECESSITY AS JUSTIFICATION

Thus far we have argued that a utilitarian theory of necessity as justification

55 See Fletcher, *Rethinking Criminal Law, supra* n 11, at 808–9.

56 Such an excuse is recognized in section 35 of the German Penal Code of 1975. The latter provides: 'Whoever commits an unlawful act in order to prevent a present danger to the life, limb or liberty of himself, a relative or a close person, acts without guilt. However, this does not apply if under the circumstances, and in particular if he has brought about the danger or has a special legal obligation, the perpetrator should be expected to cope with the danger'.

cannot reconcile a defence of necessity with the idea of a legal order, and that no theory of necessity as excuse can reveal it as generating a right to an acquittal. Nevertheless, it is indisputable that there are situations in which a breach of the law should go unpunished as a matter of right and hence too as a matter of common law. The driver who breaks the speed limit to rush an accident victim to hospital, or the lost mountaineer who trespasses on property to seek shelter from the cold – these persons deserve not simply our understanding but an acquittal. The challenge, then, is to develop a non-consequentialist theory of necessity as justification to account for this intuition.

A. *The Conflict of Duties Approach*

In *Perka,* Madame Justice Wilson attempted to sketch such a theory. The only cicumstance that can justify the violation of a legal duty, she argues, is the need to discharge another duty. The duty that justifies law-breaking cannot, however, be a purely ethical duty unrecognized by law. This would entail the priority of the good over the right and therewith the subjection of rights to the moral prudence of the private individual. Furthermore, she argues, to justify an infringement of rights by a moral duty owed another would be tantamount to imposing on the victim a legal duty to rescue. Since, however, duties of assistance cannot be generated from the idea of reciprocal liberty under law, any attempt to coerce their observance in the sphere of private transactions violates rights. For Wilson J, therefore, the only kind of duty that can justify the breach of a legal duty is another legal duty.[57]

There are several problems with this solution. For one thing, it produces the odd result that I am justified in trespassing to save the life of my wife or child but not to save my own life or that of a stranger. It seems anomalous that my guilt or innocence, or that of someone who resists the trespass, should depend on the relationship to me of the person benefited. Since, moreover, the scope of legal duties can always be expanded by legislation, Wilson J's solution makes the inherent rightness of conduct subject to the vicissitudes of legislative policy. However, the most serious problem with the conflict-of-duties standard of justification is its emptiness. By itself, this criterion cannot tell us which legal duty we are justified in breaching, and it is thus indifferent to our choice. This indeterminacy leads Wilson J to a further elaboration of her principle. 'The crucial question for the justification defence', she says, 'is whether the accused's act can be said to represent a furtherance of, or a detraction from the principle of the universality of rights'.[58] Accordingly, the choice between legal duties will be constrained by the requirement to respect the 'notion of right'. Presumably this means that it will be determined by a hierarchy of values objectively necessitated by this notion. But if this is the case, why bother with the requirement that the

57 *Perka, supra* n 9, at 35–6. See also Morgan, 'The Defence of Necessity: Justification or Excuse', (1984), 42 *UT Fac L Rev* 165, at 174-5.

58 *Perka, supra* n 9, at 36.

conflicting duties be legal ones? Inasmuch as this requirement was introduced merely to preserve the integrity of rights against a teleology of the good, it becomes redundant if the idea of a right can itself generate a ranking of interests.

But what of Wilson J's concern that a right of necessity in favour of non-legal duties amounts to the imposition of a broad legal duty to rescue? This argument depends for its force on the equation of a duty to tolerate an invasion with a duty to assist the person in need. As a physical matter, of course, there is no difficulty in distinguishing tolerances from rescues. In the one case I passively allow my resources to be appropriated; in the other I actively donate them to the person in need. Yet to impose a legal duty to do either is to effect a compulsive transfer of resources, and it is indeed difficult to conceive of a principle that would justify a duty to tolerate without also justifying a duty to rescue. This, however, is precisely the desideratum of a theory that would reconcile a defence of necessity with the idea of a right. For recall that the decisive objection to a legal duty to rescue was that such a duty implied a degree of coercion in excess of that demanded by the idea of the equal liberty of persons under universal laws. It is therefore a duty irreconcilable with the right of the person not to be used for ends external to his will.[59] Persons may have positive rights to life and health, but these rights are generated by the idea of community rather than of civil liberty, and so are rights against persons considered as citizens rather than as private individuals.[60] Accordingly, Wilson J is correct in thinking that a theory of necessity as justification must avoid the implication of justifying a general duty to rescue in emergencies. It must therefore avoid any appeal either to private moral duties or to the demands of social justice implicit in the idea of community. Yet once again the notion of a right will accomplish this purpose without the aid of a conflict-of-legal duties constraint. If the theory that justifies the infringement of a right reveals this infringement as itself necessitated by the idea of a right, then it will have defended a duty to tolerate the infringement without spilling over into a defence of a legal duty to rescue.

B. Rights, Limits, and Overridings

To say that a right can be justifiably infringed is to say, of course, that the right is not absolute. If an absolute right is one that is indefeasible simply, then a non-absolute right is one that is defeasible only by certain kinds of considerations. The considerations that are admissible as bounding rights are those that are necessary to the intelligibility of the right. When circumscribed by such factors, the right is, as it were, stopping of its own accord. The limit is rationally required by the concept of the right, so that the right-holder would, if he saw clearly, assent to it. Now there are two ways in which a right may be said to be defeasible.[61] An abstract right, say to liberty, is internally limited by the

59 See Weinrib, 'The Case for a Duty to Rescue', (1980), 90 *Yale LJ* 247, at 266–7.

60 See Rawls, *A Theory of Justice* (1971), pp 100–8.

61 See Morris, 'The Status of Rights', (1981), 92 *Ethics* 40.

conditions necessary to assure equality of freedom to all those who share the right-bearing characteristic. The aggregate of these conditions defines the nature and scope of the final or true right. Considerations of equality limit rights internally because they are the conditions for the self-identity of the right. A claim of right invokes a principle which, because implicitly universal, must be capable of remaining what it is when explicitly enforced as a rule. Since a right to an unlimited liberty becomes the opposite of itself when universalized, respect for the equal liberty of all rational agents is an intrinsic limit to the right of liberty. Alternatively, a final right may itself be defeasible by a certain type of consideration, in which case we say not that the right has been more concretely defined but that it has been overridden. What constitutes a restriction an overriding rather than an internal limit is the end for the sake of which it is imposed. Overriding ends are ends which, if invoked to curtail rights in ordinary circumstances, would render conduct a violation of rights, indeed would amount to the reassertion of an abstract right. For example, the detention without process of suspected enemy sympathizers may be a legitimate restriction of their rights if done during a wartime emergency; if done, however, in normal circumstances and merely for the greater peace of mind of the majority of citizens, it would most certainly constitute a violation of their rights.

Accordingly, we can distinguish between internal limits of abstract rights and overridings of final rights as ways of bounding rights. This distinction is, however, not one that *we* make; it is one that is necessitated by the idea of a right. If all boundaries to rights were overridings of final rights, then conflicts between rights of the same order (e.g. property rights) would be arbitrable only by reference to a metric of welfare capable of assigning relative weights to each. But such a metric would subordinate rights to the greater happiness of others and so would effectively undermine rights. On the other hand, if all boundaries to rights were internal limits, then rights would cease to exist in situations calling for their subordination to a superior value. Hence there would be no right to compensation for the abridgement of the right, just as there is none for the restriction of a nuisance. But rights would then be hostage to fortune, a limit hardly consistent with the notion of a right. If, however, rights are overridden rather than determined in extraordinary situations, then these rights logically endure throughout the period of their *de facto* suspension, and may thus claim compensation for their infringement.[62] Paradoxically, then, it is for the sake of rights that some boundaries must be conceived as overridings of final rights rather than as internal limits of *prima facie* rights. Specifically, those boundaries which entail the sacrifice of one individual's interests for the sake of another's, and which thus seem to violate the constraint of equality as between right-bearing persons, must be conceived, if at all, as overridings. Since the

62 See Melden, *Rights and Persons* (1977), pp 18–20. Feinberg, 'Voluntary Euthanasia and the Inalienable Right to Life', (1978), 7 *Philosophy and Public Affairs* 93, at 102.

situations in which necessity is invoked as a justification call for precisely these kinds of sacrifices, necessity must be defended, if at all, as an overriding of rights. The problem then becomes to determine the peculiar kind of consideration conceptually admissible as defeating a final right.

Whereas the sole considerations admissible for limiting rights internally are those assuring the equality of rights, the sole consideration admissible for overriding final rights relates to the preservation of their logical ground. By the logical ground of a right I mean the basis upon which a right is claimed and acknowledged. The logical ground of private rights is moral personality, understood as a capacity for purposiveness of which the specific aims of a human being are expressions, and hence as an objective end necessarily presupposed in all action. The attribution of rights to this capacity for agency signifies a claim that the inherent purposive structure of personality is the structure of reality itself, or that personality is an end not simply for itself but in itself as well. This claim is specified in particular rights whose significance is that they give practical confirmation to the person's self-certainty of its final worth. Thus freedom from physical constraint is a human right, because the person's self-ownership is the condition for executing any of its purposes, and so for objectively expressing its purposiveness in general. The acquisition and exclusive ownership of objects is a right of the person, because property objectively manifests the instability and merely instrumental value of things relative to persons, who are in turn confirmed as bearers of intrinsic value.[63] It follows that personality is logically prior to property as that by which the right of property is originally constituted. It is also, therefore, the conceptual limit of the right of property in the sense that the latter must yield to the former as to the basis of its own existence. Hence in any conflict between the right of property in a particular thing and values (such as life) indispensable to moral agency, the more essential value must be preferred both for its own sake and for the sake of property.[64] Were a property-owner to prefer (by resisting a taking) his property to another's life, he would be committing a legal wrong, for such a choice would, no less than theft, undermine the conceptual basis of property. Conversely, the taking of property to save life is rightful as an affirmation of the ground upon which alone property rests.

What limitations on a right of necessity are generated by this analysis? In the first place, this theory justifies only the minimum intrusion on property necessary to protect the value more essential to agency. Since property rights are affirmed rather than destroyed by the right of necessity, they endure even as they are justifiably infringed. Hence the victim, while he has no right to enjoin a taking, has a right to restitution.[65] Secondly, the right of necessity arises only in

63 See Hegel, *Philosophy of Right*, para 44.

64 See Gewirth, *Human Rights* (1982), p 59.

65 The right to compensation for justified rights-infringements is embodied in section 904 of the German Civil Code of 1871. See Fletcher, *Rethinking Criminal Law, supra* n 11, at 776–7.

situations of genuine conflict, when the threat to agency is imminent and no other legal alternative is available. This is so because it is only in these circumstances that subordinate rights reach their logical limit. Short of such extremities, the right infringed is yielding not to the higher value but to the self-preference of the accused. It follows that the inquiry into whether the circumstances were sufficiently perilous must be a rigidly objective one. Mistake, whether reasonable or not, cannot justify an infringement, for otherwise rights are self-contradictorily determined by the subjectivity of the aggressor.[66] On the other hand, the prior fault of the accused in bringing about the necessitous situation should not preclude a defence. Once the conflict materializes, the solution sanctioned by the order of rights is the one that prefers the objectively more essential value. How the conflict came about is irrelevant to the question of the accused's guilt for the intentional action taken in response to the necessity. It is, however, directly relevant to a lesser charge of criminal negligence causing the unlawful consequence.[67]

The foregoing account of necessity yields in addition the following conclusion with respect to the rights of victims and third parties: if the infringement of rights is justified, then the victim cannot rightfully resist and third parties are justified in assisting the person in need.[68] Some commentators have recently disputed the existence of a necessary connection between these propositions.[69] No doubt the connection does not exist if the right of necessity is justified by utility. For while overall welfare might be furthered by a right to effect the lesser evil, it would be a further question whether, in any particular case, the benefit of a restriction on the victim's liberty to resist is worth the cost. And it would be a further question still whether the social good is advanced by encouraging the intervention of third parties who might misapprehend the balance of utilities.[70] We have seen, however, that a right of necessity cannot be coherently founded on utilitarianism, both because the latter dictates a duty of self-sacrifice inconsistent with its own hedonistic premises; and because its internal logic leads to a rejection of a law of necessity in favour of a case-by-case calculus impossibly weighted against the accused. By contrast, the agency theory of necessity says nothing about a duty to rescue and supports a true law

66 Of course, none of these limitations apply if necessity is conceived as an excuse based on compassion for the accused. Here we simply ask whether, in the circumstances as perceived by the accused, he acted differently than a person of reasonable firmness would have acted.

67 See Gur-Arye, 'Should the Criminal Law Distinguish Between Necessity as a Justification and Necessity as an Excuse', 102 *LQ Rev* 71, at 78–9.

68 The opposite is the case in circumstances where necessity only excuses, for in such cases the act is concededly wrongful; see Robinson 'A Theory of Justification . . .', *supra* n 11, at 277–79.

69 See Gur-Arye, 'Should the Criminal Law . . .', *supra* n 66; Greenawalt, 'The Perplexing Borders of Justification and Excuse', (1984), 84 *Col L Rev* 1897; Conde, 'Necessity Defined . . .', *supra* n 11, at 442–45; Stuart *Canadian Criminal Law* (1982), p 380.

70 See Gur Arye, Should the Criminal Law . . .', *supra* n 66, at 80–1, 84–5; Conde, 'Necessity Defined . . .', *supra* n 11, at 442–45.

of necessity applicable in advance to the conduct of the agent. On this theory, moreover, the duty not to resist is logically entailed by the right to appropriate, since that right is generated not by the demands of welfare but by the concept of property itself. To resist the taking is thus to violate property. Similarly, third parties may assist, for they commit no wrong in transferring to the person in need what is his by right.

The connection between justified rights-infringements and the duty not to resist has, however, been disputed from another perspective. Kent Greenawalt believes that the following example severs the link:

> Young came upon two middle-aged men beating and struggling with a youth. Reasonably believing the youth was being unlawfully assaulted, Young went to his rescue, pulling on or punching the seeming assailants. They turned out to be plain clothes detectives trying to make an arrest for disorderly conduct.[71]

Greenawalt contends that Young's reasonable mistake operates as a justification rather than an excuse because 'Young is to be praised, not blamed, for what he did, and members of society would wish that others faced with similar situations requiring instant judgment would act as Young did'.[72] And yet it is clear that the detectives had a right to fend off Young's 'assault'. It cannot be true, therefore, that justifications imply a duty not to resist.

The argument depends, of course, on the claim that a reasonable but mistaken belief in the existence of justificatory circumstances itself justifies an infringement of rights. This claim not only makes rights self-contradictorily subject to determination by the opinion of others; it also destroys the basis for rational adjudication. It is, of course, part of the logic of rights that they imply correlative duties to respect the interests they protect. Yet according to Greenawalt, Young has a right to intervene in the scuffle and the detectives have a right to stop him. Assuming the detectives could apply to a judge for an injunction restraining Young, what result?

Greenawalt's root error lies in having confused moral with legal justification. Young is justified in assaulting the detectives, Greenawalt thinks, because we praise his altruistic conduct and would encourage others to emulate it. However, what we find praiseworthy in Young is not his external actions but the principle that animated them. It is characteristic of moral praise and blame that they apply to the principles of acts rather than to acts themselves, since on the one hand, acts are morally good or evil only according as the will is good or evil, and on the other, purely moral duties do not imply rights in others to specific acts.[73] By contrast, it is characteristic of legal right and wrong that they apply to

71 Greenawalt, 'The Perplexing Borders . . .', *supra* n 68, at 1919. See also *R* v *Mark,* [1961] *Crim L Rev* 173; *Kenlin* v *Gardiner,* [1967] 2 QB 510; Howard, 'Assaulting Policemen in the Execution of Their Duty', (1963) 79 *LQ Rev* 247–265.

72 Greenawalt, *supra* n 68, at 1919.

73 See Kant, *Ethical Philosophy, supra* n 42, at 47–50.

external acts, and the criterion for the legal justification of acts is not the moral praiseworthiness of the actor but their consistency with the rights of those acted upon. Accordingly, it is no contradiction to say that Young deserves moral approbation for his conduct and yet that his conduct is legally wrong though excused.

CONCLUSION: THE RELEVANCE OF CONTRACT

The account of necessity presented thus far explains the clear cases of justified law-breaking. It explains, for example, why it is not unlawful to jettison cargo for the safety of passengers,[74] to break out of a burning prison,[75] or illegally to put into port in order to avoid danger of death.[76] It also explains why it is not inherently unlawful to take food to avoid starvation or to take shelter on private property to avoid death by exposure. However, the agency theory of necessity would also justify rights-infringements in more controversial cases where the conflicting interests are closer in value as measured by their worth to agency. Thus, taking blood from an unwilling donor would be justified if the battery were objectively necessary to the saving of life and if it imposed no real risk to the capacity for action of the victim. Killing a foetus would be justified when necessary to save the life of the mother, because the basis of rights in personality privileges actual over potential personality.[77] On the other hand, necessity as justification cannot avail anyone who imposes grave risks on the life or health of persons regardless of the magnitude of the net saving of lives. The justification afforded by necessity is based on a hierarchy of qualitative values whose order is governed by agency, not on a balancing of quantitative harms in pursuit of an indeterminate welfare.

There is, however, one famous American case for which the foregoing analysis cannot account. In *Vincent* v *Lake Erie Trans Co*,[78] a ship's captain kept his vessel moored to a dock after its cargo had been offloaded rather than risk losing the ship in a storm. The ship repeatedly struck against the dock, causing damage assessed at $500. The Minnesota Supreme Court held the shipowner liable for the damage even though it conceded that the plaintiff had a

74 *Mouse's Case* (1608), 12 Co Rep 63.

75 *Reniger* v *Fogossa* (1551), 1 Plowden 1, per Brook, Recorder of London, f 13.

76 *The William Gray* 29 Fed Cas 1300 (1810). But see *R* v *Kitson* (1955), 39 Cr App R 66, where the court unaccountably upheld the conviction for drunk driving of someone who, having fallen asleep alone and drunk in an automobile, awoke to find it moving and steered it to safety.

77 See *R* v *Bourne*, [1939] 1 KB 687.

78 109 Minn 456 124 NW 221 (1910). Cf *Munn* v *M/V Sir John Crosbie*, [1967] 1 Ex Ct R 94.

duty to tolerate the invasion.[79] Commentators on the case have typically viewed as unproblematic the court's assumption that the defendant's action was justified, having sought instead to explain the court's finding of liability.[80] From our point of view, the liability rule presents no difficulty once one understands the right of necessity as affirming rather than as extinguishing property. What is perplexing, however, is that the defendant was held justified in appropriating the plaintiff's property simply in order to preserve his own more valuable property. Can this aspect of the case be explained again without recourse to moral principles that would commit us to a legal duty to rescue?

My argument will parallel in its structure the one presented earlier as an explanation for the sentiment in favour of a legal excuse of necessity. The circumstances in which property is pitted against property do not, I shall argue, give rise to a true justification for a private taking. Nevertheless they reproduce in a sensuous form the conceptual conditions under which true justifications do arise; and it is this resemblance which, through a confusion of metaphor and concept, creates the appearance of a valid defence.

Professor Ernest Weinrib has argued that private necessity cases as well as cases imposing a duty of an easy rescue can be explained in terms of a suspension of contract values in situations where bargaining would likely prove grossly exploitative.[81] Applied to a case like *Vincent* v *Lake Erie,* this analysis would suggest that the shipowner can unilaterally appropriate the dock provided he pay for its damage because any refusal by the dock owner would amount in the circumstances to a coercive exploitation of monopoly power inconsistent with the equality of moral agents. Now a theory of unconscionable contracts is indeed an essential adjunct of the foregoing account of necessity as justification, because such a theory is needed to explain why contract is not

79 The court followed *Ploof* v *Putnam* 81 Vt 471, 71 A 188 (1908), in which a Vermont court had held the owner of a dock liable in damages to a shipowner for refusing to allow the latter access to the dock during a storm. There is, however, a difference between this case and *Vincent*. In *Ploof* lives were in danger, whereas in *Vincent* the captain could have set the vessel adrift without risking life.

80 The case is discussed by Epstein, 'A Theory of Strict Liability', (1973), 2 *Journal of Legal Studies* 151, by Fletcher, 'Fairness and Utility in Tort Theory', (1972), 85 *Harvard Law Review* 537 and 'The Search for Synthesis in Tort Theory', (1983), 2 *Law and Philosophy* 63, and by Coleman, 'Moral Theories of Torts: Part II', (1983), 2 *Law and Philosophy* 5. Epstein sees *Vincent* as illustrative of strict liability, inasmuch as the defendant is made to compensate the plaintiff even though his conduct is deemed justifiable. Fletcher sees *Vincent* as illustrating the principle of non-reciprocal risk-taking as the basis of tort liability. Since, however, both writers view the rightness of the taking in utilitarian terms, they cannot adduce *Vincent* to support their non-utilitarian liability rules without rendering the case incoherent. Coleman sees *Vincent* as a challenge to a corrective justice theory of tort law, since the defendant has a duty to compensate the plaintiff even though his gains are not wrongful. From our point of view, however, it is not the duty to compensate that brings *Vincent* into conflict with corrective justice, but the fact that the gains are not considered wrongful.

81 Weinrib, 'The Case for a Duty to Rescue', *supra* n 58, at 268–79.

always a legal alternative to the defendant's dilemma. Where contract is feasible, its legal possibility would remove the defendant's justification for taking and entitle the victim to resist. Where it is not feasible, its legal possibility would be alone sufficient to entitle the victim to damages reflecting the expropriation of his power to bargain. As Weinrib notes, however, it is difficult to formulate a principle that would delegitimate contract in situations of necessity without sweeping along with it the everyday exploitation of market advantage. The crane cases, in which property-owners hold construction companies up to ransom for permission to trespass on their airspace, have long been deemed by the courts to illustrate a legitimate form of market coercion.[82] How are they to be distinguished from *Vincent* v *Lake Erie*?

Let us begin with the easier task of distinguishing the crane cases from one in which a man on the point of starvation must either steal bread, exchange his labour for bread, or die. It is possible to explain why contract is acceptable in the former situation, but not in the latter, or why coercion is compatible with freedom in the one but not in the other. The difference has to do with the nature of a market. The latter would seem to imply a liberation of human beings from natural necessities (which are satiable in isolation) and a relation to each other through wants originating not in nature but in the will.[83] As an interrelation of individuals through wants, moreover, the market is a system of external dependence and hence also the possibility of mutual coercion. Nevertheless, this coercion is consistent with freedom, because (or when) it is only the want or free will of one individual that confers on another the power to coerce. When this is the case, the person in thrall need only renounce his preference in order to set himself free. Since in the crane cases the parties are related through wants, their relations are essentially market relations and the coercion exercised is legitimate market coercion. There is, however, no market relation between one who stands in peril of death and one who holds the means of his salvation. Here it is not caprice that gives the property-owner the power to coerce, but a need—an objective requirement of moral agency, something the individual cannot rightfully renounce. Here, therefore, the withholding of the property is an act of pure or extra-market coercion inconsistent with rights.[84]

Now *Vincent* v *Lake Erie* is both like and unlike the case of the starving person. It is like that case because it appears that nature rather than the will of the shipowner has suddenly conferred on the dock owner a power to coerce. The

82 See, for example, *Woollerton and Wilson Ltd* v *Richard Costain Ltd*, [1970] 1 WLR 411.

83 See Rousseau, *Discourse on the Origin and Foundations of Inequality*, ed Masters (1964), pp 151–56; Hegel, *Philosophy of Right*, para 194.

84 See *Post* v *Jones* 60 US (19 How) 150 (1856), in which the Supreme Court of the United States refused to enforce a contract made between whalers marooned in the Arctic and their rescuers. The transaction, said the Court (at 159), 'where one party has absolute power, and the other no choice but submission – where the vendor must take what is offered or get nothing – is a transaction which has no characteristic of valid contract'. Note that the suspension of contract values thesis does not establish a duty to rescue; it merely establishes a duty to tolerate a taking.

sudden incursion of the elements creates the impression of a 'necessity' that is extra-social. Indeed, the only circumstance that distinguishes *Vincent* from the crane cases is that in the latter the project of the builders creates the opportunity for exploitation by the property-owner, whereas in *Vincent* it is the sudden onset of the storm. Yet clearly this distinction is illusory. The naturalness of the storm is but an image of the inward naturalness of the needs of moral agency. And the image is obviously an imperfect one, for at bottom it is only the shipowner's contingent desire for his boat that binds him to the owner of the dock. Theirs is indisputably a market relation, in which any bargain struck is consistent with rights. Should the shipowner exclaim that his action was justified by necessity, therefore, the appropriate response is the one Richelieu inappropriately gave to the prisoner who, charged with a minor offence, pleaded the necessity to preserve his life. Richelieu replied: 'Je n'en vois pas la necessite'.

Part III
Punishment

[10]

Torture and Plea Bargaining*

John H. Langbein†

In this essay I shall address the modern American system of plea bargaining from a perspective that must appear bizarre, although I hope to persuade you that it is illuminating. I am going to contrast plea bargaining with the medieval European law of torture. My thesis is that there are remarkable parallels in origin, in function, and even in specific points of doctrine, between the law of torture and the law of plea bargaining. I shall suggest that these parallels expose some important truths about how criminal justice systems respond when their trial procedures fall into deep disorder.

I. The Law of Torture[1]

For about half a millennium, from the middle of the thirteenth century to the middle of the eighteenth, a system of judicial torture lay at the heart of Continental criminal procedure. In our own day the very word "torture" is, gladly enough, a debased term. It has come to mean anything unpleasant, and we hear people speak of a tortured interpretation of a poem, or the torture of a dull dinner party. In discussions of contemporary criminal procedure we hear the word applied to describe illegal police practices or crowded prison conditions. But torture as the medieval European lawyers understood it had nothing to do with official misconduct or with criminal sanctions. Rather, the application of torture was a routine and judicially supervised feature of European criminal procedure. Under certain circumstances the law permitted the criminal courts to employ physical coercion against suspected criminals in order to induce them to confess. The law went to great lengths to limit this technique of extorting confessions to cases in which it was thought that the accused was highly likely to be guilty, and to surround the use of torture with other safeguards that I shall discuss shortly.

This astonishing body of law grew up on the Continent as an adjunct to the law of proof—what we would call the system of

---

* The William Crosskey Lecture in Legal History, The University of Chicago Law School, October 19, 1978. Suggestions and criticisms from Albert Alschuler, Paul Bator, Richard Epstein, Thomas Green, Emile Karafiol, Richard Lempert, Norval Morris, Richard Posner, Geoffrey Stone and Peter Westen are gratefully acknowledged.

† Professor of Law, The University of Chicago.

[1] This section of this article is based upon and reproduces some language from J. Langbein, Torture and the Law of Proof: Europe and England in the Ancien Régime 1-16 (1977).

trial—in cases of serious crime (for which the sanction was either death or severe physical maiming[2]). The medieval law of proof was designed in the thirteenth century to replace an earlier system of proof, the ordeals, which the Roman Church effectively destroyed in the year 1215.[3] The ordeals purported to achieve absolute certainty in criminal adjudication through the happy expedient of having the judgments rendered by God, who could not err. The replacement system of the thirteenth century aspired to achieve the same level of safeguard—absolute certainty—for human adjudication.

Although human judges were to replace God in the judgment seat, they would be governed by a law of proof so objective that it would make that dramatic substitution unobjectionable—a law of proof that would *eliminate human discretion* from the determination of guilt or innocence. Accordingly, the Italian Glossators who designed the system developed and entrenched the rule that conviction had to be based upon the testimony of two unimpeachable eyewitnesses to the gravamen of the crime—evidence that was, in the famous phrase, "clear as the noonday sun." Without these two eyewitnesses, a criminal court could not convict an accused who contested the charges against him. Only if the accused *voluntarily* confessed the offense could the court convict him without the eyewitness testimony.

Another way to appreciate the purpose of these rules is to understand their corollary: conviction could not be based upon circumstantial evidence, because circumstantial evidence depends for its efficacy upon the subjective persuasion of the trier who decides whether to draw the inference of guilt from the evidence of circumstance. Thus, for example, it would not have mattered in this system that the suspect was seen running away from the murdered man's house and that the bloody dagger and the stolen loot were found in his possession. Since no eyewitness saw him actually plunge the weapon into the victim, the court could not convict him of the crime.

In the history of Western culture no legal system has ever made a more valiant effort to perfect its safeguards and thereby to exclude completely the possibility of mistaken conviction. But the Europeans learned in due course the inevitable lesson. They had set the level of safeguard too high. They had constructed a system of proof

[2] The use of imprisonment as a sanction for serious crime was a development of the Renaissance and later times. Langbein, *The Historical Origins of the Sanction of Imprisonment for Serious Crime*, 5 J. LEGAL STUD. 35 (1976), substantially reproduced in J. LANGBEIN, *supra* note 1, at 27-44, 151-64.

[3] J. LANGBEIN, *supra* note 1, at 5-7.

that could as a practical matter be effective only in cases involving overt crime or repentant criminals. Because society cannot long tolerate a legal system that lacks the capacity to convict unrepentant persons who commit clandestine crimes, something had to be done to extend the system to those cases. The two-eyewitness rule was hard to compromise or evade, but the confession rule seemed to invite the "subterfuge"[4] that in fact resulted. To go from accepting a voluntary confession to coercing a confession from someone against whom there was already strong suspicion was a step that began increasingly to be taken. The law of torture grew up to regulate this process of generating confessions.

The spirit of safeguard that had inspired the unworkable formal law of proof also permeated the subterfuge. The largest chapter of the European law of torture concerned the prerequisites for examination under torture. The European jurists devised what Anglo-American lawyers would today call a rule of probable cause, designed to assure that only persons highly likely to be guilty would be examined under torture. Thus, torture was permitted only when a so-called "half proof" had been established against the suspect. That meant either one eyewitness, or circumstantial evidence of sufficient gravity, according to a fairly elaborate tariff.[5] In the example where a suspect was caught with the dagger and the loot, each of those indicia would be a quarter proof. Together they cumulated to a half proof, which was sufficient to permit the authorities to dispatch the suspect for a session in the local torture chamber.

In this way the prohibition against using circumstantial evidence was overcome. The law of torture found a place for circumstantial evidence, but a nominally subsidiary place. Circumstantial evidence was not consulted directly on the ultimate question, guilt or innocence, but on a question of interlocutory procedure—whether or not to examine the accused under torture. Even there the law attempted to limit judicial discretion by promulgating predetermined, ostensibly objective criteria for evaluating the indicia and assigning them numerical values (quarter proofs, half proofs, and the like). Vast legal treatises were compiled on this jurisprudence of torture to guide the examining magistrate in determining whether there was probable cause for torture.[6]

[4] Maitland's famous term, 2 F. Pollock & F.W. Maitland, The History of English Law 660 (2d ed. 1898).

[5] J. Langbein, *supra* note 1, at 14.

[6] These works are canvassed in 1 & 2 P. Fiorelli, La tortura giudiziaria nel diritto comune (1953-54).

CAPVT XXXVIII.

De repetitione quæſtionis, ſiue tor-
turæ.

This woodcut from a leading sixteenth-century European criminal procedure manual shows the accused being examined under torture in the presence of the court, clerk, and court functionaries. The illustration, from Joost Damhouder's *Praxis Rerum Criminalium* 91 (Antwerp ed. 1562), appears in chapter 38, which discusses the rules for repeating the infliction of torture on an accused who has previously resisted confession despite examination under torture. (Reproduced with permission from the rare book collection of The University of Chicago Law Library.)

In order to achieve a verbal or technical reconciliation with the requirement of the formal law of proof that the confession be voluntary, the medieval lawyers treated a confession extracted under torture as involuntary, hence ineffective, unless the accused repeated it free from torture at a hearing that was held a day or so later. Often enough the accused who had confessed under torture did recant when asked to confirm his confession. But seldom to avail: the examination under torture could thereupon be repeated. An accused who confessed under torture, recanted, and then found himself tortured anew, learned quickly enough that only a "voluntary" confession at the ratification hearing would save him from further agony in the torture chamber.[7]

Fortunately, more substantial safeguards were devised to govern the actual application of torture. These were rules designed to enhance the reliability of the resulting confession. Torture was not supposed to be used to elicit an abject, unsubstantiated confession of guilt. Rather, torture was supposed to be employed in such a way that the accused would disclose the factual detail of the crime—information which, in the words of a celebrated German statute, "no innocent person can know."[8] The examining magistrate was forbidden to engage in so-called suggestive questioning, in which the examiner supplied the accused with the detail he wanted to hear from him. Moreover, the information admitted under torture was supposed to be investigated and verified to the extent feasible. If the accused confessed to the slaying, he was supposed to be asked where he put the dagger. If he said he buried it under the old oak tree, the magistrate was supposed to send someone to dig it up.

Alas, these safeguards never proved adequate to overcome the basic flaw in the system. Because torture tests the capacity of the accused to endure pain rather than his veracity, the innocent might (as one sixteenth-century commentator put it) yield to "the pain and torment and confess things that they never did."[9] If the examining magistrate engaged in suggestive questioning, even accidentally, his lapse could not always be detected or prevented. If the accused knew something about the crime, but was still innocent of it, what he did know might be enough to give his confession verisimilitude.

---

[7] J. Langbein, *supra* note 1, at 15-16. An accused who resisted any confession under torture was supposed to be set free (subject to rules permitting further torture if new evidence was thereafter discovered); it was said that the accused had "purged" the incriminating evidence when he endured the torture without confession. *Id.* at 16.

[8] Constitutio Criminalis Carolina art. 54 (1532), *translated in* J. Langbein, Prosecuting Crime in the Renaissance: England, Germany, France 282 (1974).

[9] J. Damhouder, Practique judiciaire es causes criminelles ch. 39, at 44 (Antwerp ed. 1564) (first edition published as Praxis rerum criminalium (Louvain 1554)).

In some jurisdictions the requirement of verification was not enforced, or was enforced indifferently.

These shortcomings in the law of torture were identified even in the Middle Ages and were the subject of emphatic complaint in Renaissance and early modern times. In the eighteenth century, as the law of torture was finally about to be abolished along with the system of proof that had required it, Beccaria and Voltaire became famous as critics of judicial torture, but they were latecomers to a critical legal literature nearly as old as the law of torture itself. Judicial torture survived the centuries not because its defects had been concealed, but in spite of their having been long revealed. The two-eyewitness rule had left European criminal procedure without a tolerable alternative. Having entrenched this unattainable level of safeguard in their formal trial procedure, the Europeans found themselves obliged to evade it through a subterfuge that they knew was defective. The coerced confession had to replace proof of guilt.

II. The Law of Plea Bargaining

I am now going to cross the centuries and cross the Atlantic in order to speak of the rise of plea bargaining in twentieth-century America.

The description of the European law of torture that I have just presented has been meant to stir among American readers an unpleasant sensation of the familiar. The parallels between the modern American plea bargaining system and the ancient system of judicial torture are many and chilling. I have lived with them for some years now, and the least that I hope to achieve in this essay is to unburden myself somewhat by sharing the disturbing vision that I think would come to any American who had spent time studying the European law of torture.

By way of preface, let me set forth briefly some of the rudiments of our plea bargaining system. Plea bargaining occurs when the prosecutor induces a criminal accused to confess guilt and to waive his right to trial in exchange for a more lenient criminal sanction than would be imposed if the accused were adjudicated guilty following trial. The prosecutor offers leniency either directly, in the form of a charge reduction, or indirectly, through the connivance of the judge, in the form of a recommendation for reduced sentence that the judge will follow. In exchange for procuring this leniency for the accused, the prosecutor is relieved of the need to prove the accused's guilt, and the court is spared having to adjudicate it. The court condemns the accused on the basis of his confession, without independent adjudication.

Plea bargaining is, therefore, a nontrial procedure for convicting and condemning people accused of serious crime. If you turn to the American Constitution in search of authority for plea bargaining, you will look in vain. Instead, you will find—in no less hallowed a place than the Bill of Rights—an opposite guarantee, a guarantee of trial. The Sixth Amendment provides: "In *all* criminal prosecutions, the accused shall enjoy the right to . . . trial . . . by an impartial jury . . . ."[10]

In our day, jury trial continues to occupy its central place both in the formal law and in the mythology of the law. The constitutions have not changed, the courts pretend to enforce the defendant's right to jury trial, and the television transmits a steady flow of dramas in which a courtroom contest for the verdict of the jury leads inexorably to the disclosure of the true culprit. In truth, criminal jury trial has largely disappeared in America. The criminal justice system now disposes of virtually all cases of serious crime through plea bargaining. Depending on the jurisdiction, as many as 99 percent of all felony convictions are by plea.[11] This nontrial procedure has become the ordinary dispositive procedure of American law.

Why? Why has our formal system of proof and trial been set out of force? What has happened in the interval of less than two centuries between the constitutionalization of jury trial in 1791 and the present day to substitute this nontrial system for the trial procedure envisaged by the Framers? Scholars are only beginning to investigate the history of plea bargaining,[12] but enough is known to permit us to speak with some confidence about the broad outline. In the two centuries from the mid-eighteenth to the mid-twentieth, a vast transformation overcame the Anglo-American[13] institution of criminal jury trial, rendering it absolutely unworkable as an ordinary dispositive procedure and requiring the development of an alterna-

[10] U.S. CONST. amend. VI (emphasis added).

[11] The figure of 99 percent is given for Detroit in J. BOND, PLEA BARGAINING AND GUILTY PLEAS 13 (1975). Professor Alschuler reports 95 percent for Houston in 1975. Alschuler, *The Trial Judge's Role in Plea Bargaining* (pt. I), 76 COLUM. L. REV. 1059, 1063 n.20 (1976). In New York in 1971, 97 percent of felony convictions were by plea. *See* VERA INSTITUTE OF JUSTICE, FELONY ARRESTS: THEIR PROSECUTION AND DISPOSITION IN NEW YORK CITY'S COURTS 7 (1977). In a large statistical study of New York City felony data about to be published, Hans Zeisel computes that 98 percent of convictions were obtained by plea. H. ZEISEL, THE ANATOMY OF LAW ENFORCEMENT chs. 4, 12, 28 (1979) (forthcoming).

[12] *See* Alschuler, *Plea Bargaining and its History*, 13 LAW & SOC'Y REV. (1979) (forthcoming); Friedman, *Plea Bargaining in Historical Perspective, id.* (forthcoming); Langbein, *Understanding the Short History of Plea Bargaining, id.* (forthcoming).

[13] On the extent of plea bargaining in England, see Baldwin & McConville, *Sentencing Problems Raised by Guilty Pleas: An Analysis of Negotiated Pleas in the Birmingham Crown Court*, 41 MOD. L. REV. 544, 545 n.3 (1978).

tive procedure, which we now recognize to be the plea bargaining system.

In eighteenth-century England jury trial was still a *summary proceeding.*[14] In the Old Bailey in the 1730s we know that the court routinely processed between twelve and twenty jury trials for felony in a single day. A single jury would be impaneled and would hear evidence in numerous unrelated cases before retiring to formulate verdicts in all. Lawyers were not employed in the conduct of ordinary criminal trials, either for the prosecution or the defense. The trial judge called the witnesses (whom the local justice of the peace had bound over to appear), and the proceeding transpired as a relatively unstructured "altercation" between the witnesses and the accused.[15] In the 1790s, when the Americans were constitutionalizing English jury trial, it was still rapid and efficient. "The trial of Hardy for high treason in 1794 was the first that ever lasted more than one day, and the court seriously considered whether it had any power to adjourn . . . ."[16] By contrast, we may note that the trial of Patricia Hearst for bank robbery in 1976 lasted forty days[17] and that the average felony jury trial in Los Angeles in 1968 required 7.2 days of trial time.[18] In the eighteenth century the most characteristic (and time-consuming) features of modern jury trial, namely adversary procedure and the exclusionary rules of the law of criminal evidence, were still primitive and uncharacteristic. The accused's right to representation by retained counsel was not generalized to all felonies until the end of the eighteenth century in America and the nineteenth century in England.[19] Appellate review was very re-

[14] *See generally* Langbein, *The Criminal Trial before the Lawyers,* 45 U. Chi. L. Rev. 263 (1978).

[15] *See id.* at 272-84. The word "altercation" is the famous term of Sir Thomas Smith. T. Smith, De Republica Anglorum 80 (London 1583).

[16] MacKinnon, *The Law and the Lawyers,* in 2 Johnson's England 287, 307 (A.S. Turberville ed. 1933) (referring to Rex v. Hardy, 24 St. Tr. 199 (1794)).

[17] [1976] Administrative Office of the United States Courts Ann. Rep. 335.

[18] The figure for Los Angeles appears in San Francisco Committee on Crime, A Report on the Criminal Courts of San Francisco, Part I: The Superior Court Backlog—Consequences and Remedies 1 (1970). (I am grateful to Professor Albert W. Alschuler for the reference.) Of course, this figure must reflect the diversion of most easy cases into non-jury-trial channels such as plea bargaining, bench trial, and conditional nonprosecution. Reliable figures for New Jersey criminal trials conducted in 1976-77 (bench and jury) are less spectacular, although they hardly detract from the contrast with eighteenth-century trial duration figures. Only five percent of the trials lasted more than five days, whereas 49 percent lasted from one to three days, 35 percent less than a day, and 11 percent from three to five days. Administrative Director of the Courts, State of New Jersey, Ann. Rep. 1976-1977, at F-2 (1978). (I owe this reference to Professor Jerome Israel.)

[19] U.S. Const. amend. VI (1791); 6 & 7 Will. IV, ch. 114 (1836). For the American colonies, see the valuable compilation in the appendix to Note, *An Historical Argument for*

stricted into the twentieth century; counsel for indigent accused was not required until the middle of this century. The practices that so protract modern American jury trial—extended voir dire, exclusionary rules and other evidentiary barriers, motions designed to provoke and preserve issues for appeal, maneuvers and speeches of counsel—all are late growths in the long history of common law criminal procedure.[20]

Nobody should be surprised that jury trial has undergone great changes over the last two centuries. It desperately needed reform. The level of safeguard against mistaken conviction was in several respects below what civilized peoples now require. What we will not understand until there has been research directed to the question is why the pressure for greater safeguard led in the Anglo-American procedure to the law of evidence and the lawyerization of the trial, reforms that ultimately destroyed the system in the sense that they made jury trial so complicated and time-consuming that they rendered it unworkable as the routine dispositive procedure.[21] Similar pressures for safeguard were being felt on the Continent in the same period, but they led to reforms in nonadversarial procedure that preserved the institution of trial.[22]

the Right to Counsel During Police Interrogation, 73 YALE L.J. 1000, 1055-57 (1964).

[20] The latter portion of this paragraph is derived from Langbein, *Controlling Prosecutorial Discretion in Germany*, 41 U. CHI. L. REV. 439, 445-46 (1974).

[21] In isolating the transformation of jury trial as the root cause of plea bargaining, we do not mean to imply that this procedural development is the sole cause of a practice so complex. When the history of plea bargaining is ultimately written, there will certainly be other chapters. In particular, it will be necessary to investigate the influence of the rise of professional policing and prosecution and the accompanying changes in the levels of crime reporting and detection; changes in the social composition of victim and offender groups; changes in the rates and types of crime; and the intellectual influence of the marketplace model in an age when laissez faire was not an epithet. However, these other phenomena were largely experienced in Continental countries that did not turn to plea bargaining. Anyone looking beyond the uniquely Anglo-American procedural development that we have emphasized needs to explain why plea bargaining has characterized lands with such disparate social composition as the United States and England, but not Germany, France, or the other major European states.

In the middle of the 19th century, when German criminal procedure was being given its modern shape, German scholars routinely studied English procedure as a reform model. They found much to admire and to borrow (including the principle of lay participation in adjudication and the requirement that trials be conducted orally and in public), but they were unanimous in rejecting the guilty plea. It was wrong for a court to sentence on "mere confession" without satisfying itself of the guilt of the accused. *See, e.g.*, von Arnold, *Geständniss statt des Verdicts*, 7 GERICHTSSAAL pt. 1, 265, 275 (1855); Walther, *Ueber die processualische Wirkung des Geständnisses im Schwurgerichtsverfahren*, 1851 ARCHIV DES CRIMINALRECHTS (Neue Folge) 225; *Das Schwurgericht: Geständniss und Verdikt und Kollision zwischen beiden*, 18 GOLTDAMMERS ARCHIV 530 (1870).

[22] This paragraph (with note 21) is derived from Langbein, *supra* note 12.

III. The Parallels

Let me now turn to my main theme—the parallels in function and doctrine between the medieval European system of judicial torture and our plea bargaining system. The starting point, which will be obvious from what I have thus far said, is that each of these substitute procedural systems arose in response to the breakdown of the formal system of trial that it subverted. Both the medieval European law of proof and the modern Anglo-American law of jury trial set out to safeguard the accused by circumscribing the discretion of the trier in criminal adjudication. The medieval Europeans were trying to eliminate the discretion of the professional judge by requiring him to adhere to objective criteria of proof. The Anglo-American trial system has been caught up over the last two centuries in an effort to protect the accused against the dangers of the jury system, in which laymen ignorant of the law return a one- or two-word verdict that they do not explain or justify. Each system found itself unable to recant directly on the unrealistic level of safeguard to which it had committed itself, and each then concentrated on inducing the accused to tender a confession that would waive his right to the safeguards.

The European law of torture preserved the medieval law of proof undisturbed for those easy cases in which there were two eyewitnesses or voluntary confession. But in the more difficult cases (where, I might add, safeguard was more important), the law of torture worked an absolutely fundamental change within the system of proof: it largely *eliminated the adjudicative function.* Once probable cause had been determined, the accused was made to concede his guilt rather than his accusers to prove it.

In twentieth-century America we have duplicated the central experience of medieval European criminal procedure: we have moved from an adjudicatory to a concessionary system. We coerce the accused against whom we find probable cause to confess his guilt. To be sure, our means are much politer; we use no rack, no thumbscrew, no Spanish boot to mash his legs. But like the Europeans of distant centuries who did employ those machines, we make it terribly costly for an accused to claim his right to the constitutional safeguard of trial. We threaten him with a materially increased sanction if he avails himself of his right and is thereafter convicted. This sentencing differential is what makes plea bargaining coercive. There is, of course, a difference[23] between having your

[23] This difference is related to differences in the sanctions that characterize the medieval and the modern worlds. The law of torture served legal systems whose only sanctions for

limbs crushed if you refuse to confess, or suffering some extra years of imprisonment if you refuse to confess, but the difference is of degree, not kind. Plea bargaining, like torture, is coercive.[24] Like the

serious crime were severe physical maiming and death. The torture victim was coerced into a confession that condemned him to the most severe of punishments, whereas the plea bargain rewards the accused with a lesser sanction, typically some form of imprisonment, in exchange for his confession. Obviously, the greater the severity of the sanction that the accused's confession will bring down upon himself, the greater the coercion that must be brought to bear upon him to wring out the confession. Plea bargaining is as coercive as it has to be for the modern system of sanctions.

[24] Defenders of plea bargaining sometimes try to minimize the force of this point with a reductio-ad-absurdum argument: granted that plea bargaining is coercive, so is virtually every exercise of criminal jurisdiction, since few criminal defendants are genuine volunteers. I think that the answer to this argument is straightforward. The accused is made a criminal defendant against his wishes, but not contrary to his rights. The Constitution does not grant citizens any immunity from criminal prosecution, but it does grant them the safeguard of trial. Coercion authorized by law is different from coercion meant to overcome the guarantees of law. Coercing people to stand trial is different from coercing them to waive trial and to bring upon themselves sanctions that should only be imposed after impartial adjudication.

Sometimes, as I have mentioned in the text, a rather opposite argument is made in behalf of plea bargaining—not that everything is coercive, but that a mere sentencing differential is not serious enough to be reckoned as coercion. One can test this point simply by imagining a differential so great (*e.g.*, death versus a fifty-cent fine) that any reasonable defendant would waive even the strongest defenses. Like torture, the sentencing differential in plea bargaining elicits confessions of guilt that would not be freely tendered. It is, therefore, coercive in the same sense as torture, although not in the same degree.

The question whether significant numbers of innocent people do plead guilty is not, of course, susceptible to empirical testing. It is known that many of those who plead guilty claim that they are innocent. *See* A. Blumberg, Criminal Justice 89-92 (1970). *See also* text at note 29 *infra* (discussing *North Carolina v. Alford*). Alschuler thinks that "the greatest pressures to plead are brought to bear on defendants who may be innocent." Alschuler, *The Prosecutor's Role in Plea Bargaining*, 36 U. Chi. L. Rev. 50, 60 (1968). See *id.* at 59-62 for evidence that the threatened "sentence differential between guilty-plea and trial defendants increases in direct proportion to the likelihood of acquittal." *Id.* at 60. Alschuler reports one case that resembles the hypothetical choice between death penalty and fifty-cent fine:

> San Francisco defense attorney Benjamin M. Davis recently represented a man charged with kidnapping and forcible rape. The defendant was innocent, Davis says, and after investigating the case Davis was confident of an acquittal. The prosecutor, who seems to have shared the defense attorney's opinion on this point, offered to permit a guilty plea to simple battery. Conviction on this charge would not have led to a greater sentence than thirty days' imprisonment, and there was every likelihood that the defendant would be granted probation. When Davis informed his client of this offer, he emphasized that conviction at trial seemed highly improbable. The defendant's reply was simple: "I can't take the chance."

Id. at 61.

I do not think that great numbers of American defendants plead guilty to offenses committed by strangers. (The law of torture was also not supposed to apply in circumstances where the accused could explain away the evidence that might otherwise have given cause to examine him under torture. *See* J. Langbein, *supra* note 8, at 183.) I do believe that plea bargaining is used to coerce the waiver of tenable defenses, as in Attorney Davis's example, *supra*, or when the offense has a complicated conceptual basis, as in tax and other white collar crimes.

The objection is sometimes voiced that if an accused is innocent, it stands to reason that

medieval Europeans, the Americans are now operating a procedural system that engages in condemnation without adjudication.[25] The maxim of the medieval Glossators, no longer applicable to European[26] law, now aptly describes American law: *confessio est regina probationum*, confession is the queen of proof.

I have said that European law attempted to devise safeguards for the use of torture that proved illusory; these measures bear an eerie resemblance to the supposed safeguards of the American law of plea bargaining. Foremost among the illusory safeguards of both systems is the doctrinal preoccupation with characterizing the induced waivers as voluntary. The Europeans made the torture victim repeat his confession "voluntarily," but under the threat of being tortured anew if he recanted. The American counterpart is Rule 11(d) of the Federal Rules of Criminal Procedure, which forbids the court from accepting a guilty plea without first "addressing the defendant personally in open court, determining that the plea is voluntary and not the result of force or threats or of promises *apart from a plea agreement*."[27] Of course, the plea agreement is the *source* of the coercion and already embodies the involuntariness.

The architects of the European law of torture sought to enhance the reliability of a torture-induced confession with other safeguards designed to substantiate its factual basis. We have said that they required a probable cause determination for investigation under torture and that they directed the court to take steps to verify the accuracy of the confession by investigating some of its detail. We have explained why these measures were inadequate to protect many innocent suspects from torture, confession, and condemnation. Probable cause is not the same as guilt, and verification, even

he will press his defense at trial; if an innocent accused does plead guilty, he must necessarily be calculating that there is a significant probability that the trier will fail to recognize his innocence despite the great safeguards of trial designed to prevent such error. If trials were perfectly accurate, plea bargaining would be perfectly accurate, since no innocent person would have an incentive to accuse himself. Ironically, therefore, anyone who would denigrate plea bargaining because it infringes the right to trial must also assume that the trial itself is to some extent recognized to be mistake-prone. The response, of course, is that paradox is not contradiction. So long as human judgment is fallible, no workable trial procedure can do more than minimize error. The social cost of a rule of absolute certainty—massive release of the culpable—would be intolerable. This was the lesson of the medieval European law, and it explains why the standard of our law is not "beyond doubt" but "beyond reasonable doubt."

[25] "A plea of guilty . . . is itself a conviction . . . . More is not required; the court has nothing to do but give judgment and sentence." Kercheval v. United States, 274 U.S. 220, 223 (1927).

[26] *See* Casper & Zeisel, *Lay Judges in the German Criminal Courts*, 1 J. LEGAL STUD. 135, 146-47 (1972).

[27] FED. R. CRIM. P. 11(d) (emphasis added).

if undertaken in good faith, could easily fail as a safeguard, either because the matters confessed were not susceptible of physical or testimonial corroboration, or because the accused might know enough about the crime to lend verisimilitude to his confession even though he was not in fact the culprit.

The American law of plea bargaining has pursued a similar chimera: the requirement of "adequate factual basis for the plea." Federal Rule 11(f) provides that "the court should not enter judgment upon [a guilty] plea without making such inquiry as shall satisfy it that there is a factual basis for the plea."[28] As with the tortured confession, so with the negotiated plea: any case that has resisted dismissal for want of probable cause at the preliminary hearing will rest upon enough inculpating evidence to cast suspicion upon the accused. The function of trial, which plea bargaining eliminates, is to require the court to adjudicate whether the facts proven support an inference of guilt beyond a reasonable doubt. Consider, however, the case of *North Carolina v. Alford,*[29] decided in this decade, in which the U.S. Supreme Court found it permissible to condemn without trial a defendant who had told the sentencing court: "I pleaded guilty on second degree murder because they said there is too much evidence, but I ain't shot no man . . . . I just pleaded guilty because they said if I didn't they would gas me for it . . . . I'm not guilty but I plead guilty."[30] I invite you to compare Alford's statement with the explanation of one Johannes Julius, seventeenth-century burgomaster of Bamberg, who wrote from his dungeon cell where he was awaiting execution, in order to tell his daughter why he had confessed to witchcraft "for which I must die. It is all falsehood and invention, so help me God . . . . They never cease to torture until one says something."[31]

The tortured confession is, of course, markedly less reliable than the negotiated plea, because the degree of coercion is greater. An accused is more likely to bear false witness against himself in order to escape further hours on the rack than to avoid risking a longer prison term. But the resulting moral quandary is the same.[32]

[28] *Id.* 11(f).

[29] 400 U.S. 25 (1970).

[30] *Id.* at 28 n.2.

[31] *Quoted in* H.R. TREVOR-ROPER, THE EUROPEAN WITCH-CRAZE OF THE 16TH AND 17TH CENTURIES 84 (1969) (Pelican ed.).

[32] Some of those who have favored me with prepublication critiques of this paper have resisted this point—largely, I think, because they do not give adequate weight to the seriousness with which the law of torture undertook to separate the guilty from the innocent. My critics suggest that plea bargaining is in theory meant to have a differential impact upon the guilty and the innocent, whereas torture was not. They contend that the plea bargaining

Judge Levin of Michigan was speaking of the negotiated guilty plea, but he could as well have been describing the tortured confession when he said, "there is no way of knowing whether a particular guilty plea was given because the accused believed he was guilty, or because of the promised concession."[33] Beccaria might as well have been speaking of the coercion of plea bargaining when he said of the violence of torture that it "confounds and obliterates those minute differences between things which enable us at times to know truth from falsehood."[34] The doctrine of adequate factual basis for the plea is no better substitute for proof beyond reasonable doubt than was the analogous doctrine in the law of torture.

The factual unreliability of the negotiated plea has further consequences, quite apart from the increased danger of condemning an innocent man. In the plea bargaining that takes the form of charge bargaining (as opposed to sentence bargaining), the culprit is convicted not for what he did, but for something less opprobrious. When people who have murdered are said to be convicted of wounding, or when those caught stealing are nominally convicted of attempt or possession, cynicism about the processes of criminal justice is inevitably reinforced.[35] This wilful mislabelling plays havoc with

system means to tell the accused, "Don't put us to the trouble of a trial unless you are really innocent," whereas the law of torture gave the same message to both the innocent and the guilty, "Confess or the pain will continue."

I think that both branches of the argument are mistaken. I have already pointed out, *supra* note 24, that plea bargaining can and does induce innocent defendants to convict themselves. As for the law of torture, I should reiterate that the safeguards discussed above, *see* text at notes 6-9 *supra*, were designed for the sole purpose of separating the innocent from the guilty, and the law of torture made express provision for releasing those who did not confess under torture. *See* J. LANGBEIN, *supra* note 1, at 16, 151 n.55. I am very willing to concede that the safeguards of the law of torture were even less effective than those of plea bargaining, but as I have said in the text, the difference is one of degree and not kind.

[33] People v. Byrd, 12 Mich. App. 186, 206-07, 162 N.W.2d 777, 787 (1968) (Levin, J., concurring) (italics deleted).

[34] Beccaria, *Of Crimes and Punishment* (1st ed. 1764) (J. Grigson trans.), *reprinted in preface to* A. MANZONI, THE COLUMN OF INFAMY 33 (1964).

[35] *See, e.g.*, Sudnow, *Normal Crimes: Sociological Features of the Penal Code in a Public Defender Office*, 12 SOC. PROB. 155, 158-59 (1964) (child molestation cases resulting in no serious harm to the victim regularly reduced to the charge of loitering around a schoolyard, even if the offense was committed nowhere near a schoolyard). (I owe this reference to Profesor Richard Lempert.)

The sentences prescribed by statute in the United States are markedly more severe than for comparable offenses in European states. In the words of Judge Frankel, ours is "a nation where prison sentences of extravagant length are more common than they are almost anywhere else." United States v. Bergman, 416 F. Supp. 496, 502 (S.D.N.Y. 1976). I know of no study of the point, but I would be surprised if Hans Zeisel were far wrong in his suggestion that each month of imprisonment in Continental sentences corresponds to a year in the United States. Zeisel, *Die Rolle der Geschworenen in den USA*, 21 ÖSTERREICHISCHE JURISTENZEITUNG 121, 123 (1966). The severity of our prescribed sentences contributes to the

our crime statistics, which explains in part why Americans—uniquely among Western peoples—attach so much importance to arrest records rather than to records of conviction. I think that the unreliability of the plea, the mislabelling of the offense, and the underlying want of adjudication all combine to weaken the moral force of the criminal law, and to increase the public's unease about the administration of criminal justice. The case of James Earl Ray is perhaps the best example of public dissatisfaction over the intrinsic failure of the plea bargaining system to establish the facts about crime and guilt in the forum of a public trial.[36] It is interesting to remember that in Europe in the age of Beccaria and Voltaire, the want of adjudication and the unreliability of the law of torture had bred a strangely similar cynicism towards that criminal justice system.

Our law of plea bargaining has not only recapitulated much of the doctrinal folly of the law of torture, complete with the pathetic

---

plea bargaining system by expanding the potential differential between sentence following trial and sentence pursuant to plea bargain.

In the nineteenth and twentieth centuries, when the Europeans were ameliorating their sentences, we were not. It is tempting to wonder whether the requirements of the plea bargaining system have been somewhat responsible.

Of course, plea bargaining is not responsible for all of the downcharging and resultant mislabelling in which modern American prosecutors engage. If the prosecutor views the statutorily prescribed minimum sentence for an offense as too severe, he can downcharge without exacting a concessionary quid pro quo from the accused.

[36] Of course, not every trial resolves the question of guilt of innocence to public satisfaction. The Sacco-Vanzetti and the Rosenberg cases continue to be relitigated in the forum of popular opinion. However, plea bargaining leaves the public with what I believe to be a more pronounced sense of unease about the justness of results, by avoiding the open ventilation of evidence that characterizes public trial. Just this concern appears to have motivated the government in the plea-bargained bribery case of Vice-President Agnew to take such extraordinary steps to assure the disclosure of the substance of the prosecution case. *See* N.Y. Times, Oct. 11, 1973, § 1, at 35-38.

The public's hostility to plea bargaining should suggest why some of my colleagues in the law-and-economics fraternity are mistaken in their complacent assimilation of plea bargaining to the model of the negotiated settlement of civil disputes. However great the operational similarity, there is a profound difference in purpose between civil and criminal sanctions. Henry Hart was surely correct that "[t]he core of the difference" between a confined mental patient and an imprisoned convict is "that the patient has not incurred the moral condemnation of his community, whereas the convict has." Hart, *The Aims of the Criminal Law*, 23 LAW & CONTEMP. PROB. 401, 406 (1958). The moral force of the criminal sanction depends for part of its efficacy on the sanction having been imposed after rational inquiry into the facts, culminating in an adjudication of guilt. To assert the equivalency of waiver and adjudication is to overlook the distinctive characteristic of the criminal law.

It is for the same reason that the sentence differentials required by plea bargaining are so repugnant to any tenable theory of sentencing. Nothing in the theory of deterrence, reformation, or retribution justifies the enormous differentials needed to sustain plea bargaining. Those differentials exist without a moral basis. On their extent, *see, e.g.*, H. ZEISEL, *supra* note 11; Alschuler, *supra* note 11, at 1082-87.

safeguards of voluntariness and factual basis that I have just discussed, but it has also repeated the main institutional blunder of the law of torture. Plea bargaining concentrates effective control of criminal procedure in the hands of a single officer. Our formal law of trial envisages a division of responsibility. We expect the prosecutor to make the charging decision, the judge and especially the jury to adjudicate, and the judge to set the sentence. Plea bargaining merges these accusatory, determinative, and sanctional phases of the procedure in the hands of the prosecutor. Students of the history of the law of torture are reminded that the great psychological fallacy of the European inquisitorial procedure of that time was that it concentrated in the investigating magistrate the powers of accusation, investigation, torture, and condemnation. The single inquisitor who wielded those powers needed to have what one recent historian has called "superhuman capabilities [in order to] . . . keep himself in his decisional function free from the predisposing influences of his own instigating and investigating activity."[37]

The dominant version of American plea bargaining makes similar demands: it requires the prosecutor to usurp the determinative and sentencing functions, hence to make himself judge in his own cause. I cannot emphasize too strongly how dangerous this concentration of prosecutorial power can be. The modern public prosecutor commands the vast resources of the state for gathering and generating accusing evidence. We allowed him this power in large part because the criminal trial interposed the safeguard of adjudication against the danger that he might bring those resources to bear against an innocent citizen—whether on account of honest error, arbitrariness, or worse.[38] But the plea bargaining system has largely dissolved that safeguard.

While on the subject of institutional factors, I have one last comparison to advance. The point has been made, most recently by the Attorney-General of Alaska,[39] that preparing and taking cases to trial is much harder work than plea bargaining—for police, prosecutors, judges, and defense counsel. In short, convenience—or

[37] 1 E. Schmidt, Lehrkommentar zur Strafprozessordnung und zum Gerichtsverfassungsgesetz 197 (2d ed. 1964).

[38] One need not necessarily accept Jimmy Hoffa's view that Robert Kennedy was conducting a personal and political vendetta against him in order to appreciate the danger that he might have been. The power to prosecute as we know it contains within itself the power to persecute. Hoffa contended "that special investigators from the Justice Dept. and hundreds of agents from the Federal Bureau of Investigation were used to satisfy 'a personal hate' of Robert Kennedy." Bus. Week, Feb. 13, 1965, at 48.

[39] Gross, *Plea Bargaining: The Alaska Experience*, 13 Law & Soc'y Rev. (1979) (forthcoming).

worse, sloth—is a factor that sustains plea bargaining. We suppose that this factor had a little to do with torture as well. As someone in India remarked to Sir James Fitzjames Stephen in 1872 about the proclivity of the native policemen for torturing suspects, "It is far pleasanter to sit comfortably in the shade rubbing red pepper into a poor devil's eyes than to go about in the sun hunting up evidence."[40] If we were to generalize about this point, we might say that concessionary criminal procedural systems like the plea bargaining system and the system of judicial torture may develop their own bureaucracies and constituencies. Here as elsewhere the old adage may apply that if necessity is the mother of invention, laziness is the father.

IV. The Jurisprudence of Concessionary Criminal Procedure

Having developed these parallels between torture and plea bargaining, I want to draw some conclusions about what I regard as the lessons of the exercise. The most important is this: a legal system will do almost anything, tolerate almost anything, before it will admit the need for reform in its system of proof and trial. The law of torture endured for half a millennium although its dangers and defects had been understood virtually from the outset; and plea bargaining lives on although its evils are quite familiar to us all. What makes such shoddy subterfuges so tenacious is that they shield their legal systems from having to face up to the fact of breakdown in the formal law of proof and trial.

Why is it so hard for a legal system to reform a decadent system of proof? I think that there are two main reasons. One is in a sense practical: nothing is quite so imbedded in a legal system as the procedures for proof and trial, because most of what a legal system does is to decide matters of proof—what we call fact-finding. (Was the traffic light green or red, was this accused the man who fired the shot or robbed the bank?) Blackstone emphasized this point in speaking of civil litigation, and it is even more true of criminal litigation. He said: "experience will abundantly shew, that above a hundred of our lawsuits arise from disputed facts, for one where the law is doubted of."[41] Every institution of the legal system is geared to the system of proof; forthright reconstruction would disturb, at one level or another, virtually every vested interest.

The inertia, the resistance to change that is associated with

[40] 1 J.F. Stephen, A History of the Criminal Law of England 442 n.1 (1883). Stephen's forceful quotation has been cited for this point elsewhere; McNabb v. United States, 318 U.S. 332, 344 n.8 (1943); J. Langbein, *supra* note 1, at 147 n.14; Alschuler, *supra* note 11, at 1103 n.137.

[41] 3 W. Blackstone, Commentaries on the Laws of England *330 (1768).

such deep-seated interests, is inevitably reinforced by the powerful ideological component that underlies a system of proof and trial. Adjudication, especially criminal adjudication, involves a profound intrusion into the lives of affected citizens. Consequently, in any society the adjudicative power must be rested on a theoretical basis that makes it palatable to the populace. Because the theory of proof purports to govern and explain the application of the adjudicative power, it plays a central role in legitimating the entire legal system. The medieval European law of proof assured people that the legal system would achieve certainty. The Anglo-American jury system invoked the inscrutable wisdom of the folk to justify its results.[42] Each of these theories was ultimately untenable—the European theory virtually from its inception, the Anglo-American theory after a centuries-long transformation of jury procedure. Yet the ideological importance of these theories prevented either legal system from recanting upon them. For example, I have elsewhere pointed out how in the nineteenth century the ideological attachment to the jury retarded experimentation with juryless trial—that is, what we now call bench trial—while the plea bargaining system of juryless nontrial procedure was taking shape out of public sight.[43] Like the medieval European lawyers before us, we have been unable to admit that our theory of proof has resulted in a level of procedural complexity and safeguard that renders our trial procedure unworkable in all but exceptional cases. We have responded to the breakdown of our formal system of proof by taking steps to perpetuate the ideology of the failed system, steps that closely resemble those taken by the architects of the law of torture. Like the medieval Europeans, we have preserved an unworkable trial procedure in form, we have devised a substitute nontrial procedure to subvert the formal procedure, and we have arranged to place defendants under fierce pressure to "choose" the substitute.

That this script could have been played out in a pair of legal cultures so remote from each other in time and place invites some suggestions about the adaptive processes of criminal procedural systems. First, there are intrinsic limits to the level of complexity and safeguard that even a civilized people can tolerate. If those limits are exceeded and the repressive capacity of the criminal justice system is thereby endangered, the system will respond by developing subterfuges that overcome the formal law. But subterfuges are intrinsically overbroad, precisely because they are not framed in a

[42] *See* T.F.T. PLUCKNETT, EDWARD I AND CRIMINAL LAW 74-75 (1960).
[43] Langbein, *supra* note 12.

careful, explicit, and principled manner directed to achieving a proper balance between repression and safeguard. The upshot is that the criminal justice system is saddled with a lower level of safeguard than it could and would have achieved if it had not pretended to retain the unworkable formal system.

The medieval Europeans insisted on two eyewitnesses and wound up with a law of torture that allowed condemnation with no witnesses at all. American plea bargaining, in like fashion, sacrifices just those values that the unworkable system of adversary jury trial is meant to serve: lay participation in criminal adjudication, the presumption of innocence, the prosecutorial burden of proof beyond reasonable doubt, the right to confront and cross-examine accusers, the privilege against self-incrimination. Especially in its handling of the privilege against self-incrimination does American criminal procedure reach the outer bounds of incoherence. In cases like *Griffin v. California*[44] we have exaggerated the privilege to senseless lengths in formal doctrine, while in the plea bargaining system—which is our routine procedure for processing cases of serious crime—we have eliminated practically every trace of the privilege.

Furthermore, the sacrifice of our fundamental values through plea bargaining is needless. In its sad plea bargaining opinions of the 1970s, the Supreme Court has effectively admitted that for reasons of expediency American criminal justice cannot honor its promise of routine adversary criminal trial,[45] but the Court has simply assumed that the present nontrial plea bargaining procedure is the inevitable alternative. There is, however, a middle path between the impossible system of routine adversary jury trial and the disgraceful nontrial system of plea bargaining. That path is a streamlined nonadversarial trial procedure.

The contemporary nonadversarial criminal justice systems of countries like West Germany have long demonstrated that advanced industrial societies can institute efficient criminal procedures that nevertheless provide for lay participation and for full adjudication in every case of serious crime. I have described the German system in detail elsewhere,[46] and I have made no secret of my admiration for the brilliant balance that it strikes between safeguard and procedural effectiveness. Not the least of its achieve-

[44] 380 U.S. 609 (1965).

[45] In Santobello v. New York, 404 U.S. 257 (1971), Chief Justice Burger explained that plea bargaining "is to be encouraged" because "[i]f every criminal charge were subjected to a full-scale trial, the States and the Federal Government would need to multiply by many times the number of judges and court facilities." *Id.* at 260.

[46] *See generally* J. LANGBEIN, COMPARATIVE CRIMINAL PROCEDURE: GERMANY (1977).

ments is that in cases of serious crime it functions with no plea bargaining whatsoever.[47] Confessions are still tendered in many cases (41 percent in one sample[48]), but they are not and cannot be bargained for; nor does a confession excuse the trial court from hearing sufficient evidence for conviction on what amounts to a beyond-reasonable-doubt standard of proof.[49] In a trial procedure shorn of all the excesses of adversary procedure and the law of evidence, the time difference between trial without confession and trial with confession is not all that great.[50] Because an accused will be put to trial whether he confesses or not, he cannot inflict significant costs upon the prosecution by contesting an overwhelming case. Confessions are tendered at trial not because they are rewarded, but because there is no advantage to be wrung from the procedural system by withholding them.

I hope that over the coming decades we who still live under criminal justice systems that engage in condemnation without adjudication will face up to the failure of adversary criminal procedure. I believe that we will find in modern Continental criminal procedure an irresistible model for reform. That, however, is a theme about which I can say no more if I am to remain within the proper sphere of the Crosskey Lecture in Legal History.

Thus, I am brought to conclude with a paradox. Today in lands where the law of torture once governed, peoples who live in contentment with their criminal justice systems look out across the sea in disbelief[51] to the spectacle of plea bargaining in America, while American tourists come by the thousands each year to gawk in disbelief at the decaying torture chambers of medieval castles.

---

[47] For recent discussion see Langbein & Weinreb, *Continental Criminal Procedure: "Myth" and Reality*, 87 YALE L.J. 1549, 1561-65 (1978). For the observation that modern Continental nonadversarial procedure confers more safeguards upon the accused than does American plea bargaining, see Damaska, *Evidentiary Barriers to Conviction and Two Models of Criminal Procedure: A Comparative Study*, 121 U. PA. L. REV. 506, 552 (1973).

[48] Casper & Zeisel, *supra* note 26, at 146-47, 150-51.

[49] *See* J. LANGBEIN, *supra* note 46, at 66-67, 73-74.

[50] *See id.* at 77; Casper & Zeisel, *supra* note 26, at 150.

[51] *See* Langbein, *supra* note 20, at 457 n.44 (1974):

Plea bargaining is all but incomprehensible to the Germans, whose ordinary dispositive procedure is workable without such evasions. In the German press the judicial procedure surrounding the resignation of Vice President Agnew was viewed with the sort of wonder normally inspired by reports of the customs of primitive tribes. "The resignation occurred as part of a 'cow-trade,' as it can only in the United States be imagined." Badische Zeitung, Oct. 12, 1973, at 3, col. 2.

[11]

Northwestern University Law Review

Printed in U.S.A.
Vol. 91, No. 2

ARTICLES

THE UTILITY OF DESERT

*Paul H. Robinson and John M. Darley**

---

* Paul H. Robinson is Professor of Law, Northwestern University School of Law. John M. Darley is Dorman T. Warren Professor of Psychology, Princeton University. The authors wish to acknowledge the contributions of Dan Kahan, George Fletcher, Dick Craswell, Tom Tyler, Robert Boeckmann, and the participants of a faculty workshop at Northwestern University School of Law, and of the Justice, Authority, and Legitimacy Seminar at the University of California, Berkeley.

Criminal punishment can be justified on two broad grounds. The first is utilitarian (sometimes called "consequentialist"): Punishment for a past offense is justified by the future benefits it provides. Characteristically, the future benefit is to avoid, or at least to reduce, future crimes. The other ground of justification is anchored in the past: Punishment that gives an offender what he or she deserves for a past crime is a valuable end in itself and needs no further justification (such as a showing of a future benefit). This is typically referred to as the "retributivist" or "just deserts" view. The arguments of these two positions are generally considered irreconcilable: Consequentialist grounds are justified on the basis of utility, desert grounds on the basis of fulfilling a deontological moral mandate. In this Article, we argue that, while the underlying rationales of the two views may be irreconcilable, their practical applications, properly done, suggest similar distributions of liability and punishment. More specifically, while we argue that society ought to assign criminal punishments on essentially just desert grounds, our arguments are based on purely utilitarian considerations. We argue that, because it promotes forces that lead to a law-abiding society, a criminal law based on the community's perceptions of just desert is, from a utilitarian perspective, the more effective strategy for reducing crime. While much empirical work remains before we fully understand the dynamics of the forces that we cite as suggesting this conclusion, we can say, at very least, that utilitarians must include in their policy calculations the likelihood of a significant cost to crime control in any deviations from a desert distribution.

The debate over the justification for punishing criminals has been deeply confused, and the confusion has a long and honorable history. In the late eighteenth century, Jeremy Bentham argued that "general prevention ought to be the chief end of punishment, as it is its real justification."[1] From this, Bentham went on to develop the classic formulation of the deterrence rationale for punishment. Thus, tautologically to him (but not tautologically to utilitarians who think rehabilitation could minimize crime, for example) an offender's punishment ought to be set not according to the amount deserved, but rather according to the amount needed to deter future instances of the offense. "If the apparent magnitude, or rather value of [the] pain be greater than the apparent magnitude or value of the pleasure or good he expects to be the consequence of the act, he will be absolutely prevented from performing it."[2] Immanuel Kant, a contemporary of Bentham, summarized an opposing "just deserts" rationale. "[P]unishment can never be administered merely as a means for promoting another good . . . ."[3] Punishment ought to be "pronounced over all criminals proportionate to their internal wickedness . . . ."[4] Of course, the history of justifications goes back further; Kant was giving a particular formulation of the Aristotelian view that criminals should be given punishments and penalties, not rehabilitation.[5] Plato weighed in with a justification for punishment that foreshadows the modern rehabilitation justification, arguing that punishment ought not be inflicted for vengeance, but rather to make the offender a better person.[6] The debate between the desert justification and the various utilitarian justifications such as deterrence, incapacitation, and rehabilitation has continued to divide criminal law thinkers to this day.[7] Perhaps more importantly, it has divided practitioners. In the history of incarceration in this country we have seen repeated confusions in what we might call the "public philosophy of punishment," the reasons claimed for the justification of criminal sanctions by policy-makers and legislators.

---

1 JEREMY BENTHAM, *Principles of Penal Law*, *in* 1 THE WORKS OF JEREMY BENTHAM 396 (John Bowring ed., 1962).

2 *Id.*

3 IMMANUEL KANT, THE SCIENCE OF RIGHT (W. Hastie trans.), *reprinted in* GREAT BOOKS OF THE WESTERN WORLD: KANT 397, 446 (Robert M. Hutchins ed., 1952).

4 *Id.* at 447.

5 ARISTOTLE, NICOMACHEAN ETHICS (W.D. Ross trans.), *reprinted in* GREAT BOOKS OF THE WESTERN WORLD: ARISTOTLE II 335, 359, 383 (Robert M. Hutchins ed., 1952).

6 PLATO, THE LAWS 241 (A.E. Taylor trans., 1960). Rothman reminds of us of an historical fact that it is extraordinarily hard to remember given our modern perceptions of penitentiaries as grim, grey places of brutal convict violence: a rehabilitationist philosophy motivated the development of the modern penitentiary, a place in which the convict would be incarcerated until private contemplation showed him the error of his ways, until, in other words, he became "penitent" for his wrongs and could be discharged a better man. DAVID J. ROTHMAN, THE DISCOVERY OF THE ASYLUM: SOCIAL ORDER AND DISORDER IN THE NEW REPUBLIC 79-108 (1971).

7 For a discussion of the rationales-of-punishment debate and its historical roots, see Matthew A. Pauley, *The Jurisprudence of Crime and Punishment from Plato to Hegel*, 39 AM. J. JURIS. 97 (1994); *see also* JAMES Q. WILSON & RICHARD J. HERRNSTEIN, CRIME AND HUMAN NATURE (1985).

Recently, the confusion has seemed to accelerate; the last decades have seen a rapid oscillation among these rationales for the distribution of criminal liability. The rehabilitationist approach, popular in the 1960s, has lost credibility. Deterrence, grounded in a theory of rational conduct, has ceased to command much confidence among thoughtful criminologists, for a number of reasons that we shall show. Incapacitation, currently popular in the form of "three strikes and you're out" laws, can also be expected to run into difficulties for reasons we shall explain. Part I of this article details the limitations of the standard utilitarian theories. Those limitations mean that policy-makers and legislators, not just academics, should be interested in examining our claim that the greatest utility in controlling crime is found in doing justice.

As we signalled, we argue for a just desert allocation of liability, although a particular and unusual form of desert-based liability: one based upon the community's shared principles of justice rather than on those developed by moral philosophers. Our arguments for this system are, as far as we know, unique: The major claim for our desert-based liability assignment system lies in its advantages in promoting future law-abiding behavior. We give, in other words, a utilitarian justification for the only non-utilitarian system for allocating punishment.

The desert-based liability system that we advocate is one that normally assigns liability and punishment according to the principles of justice that the community intuitively uses to assign liability and blame. We ought to mark here that this is a sufficiently heretical variation on desert theory that it is likely that those who argue for a more standard desert theory, Kantians and others working from philosophical perspectives, will find it repugnant, first because it derives liability assignments from community sentiments rather than a reasoned logical system, and second because our arguments for a desert-based system are blatantly utilitarian.

Our goal then is to persuade those who determine rules of criminal liability and punishment—criminal law theorists, code drafters, legislators, and judges—that a criminal law that assigns punishment in ways that closely reflects the community's intuitions about appropriate condemnation and punishment has a number of hitherto unrecognized advantages over alternative systems. Specifically, a distributive theory that tracks the community's perceived principles of justice has a greater power to gain compliance with society's rules of lawful conduct. Therefore, we suggest, those who base criminal liability on the traditional utilitarian considerations—whether deterrence-based, rehabilitationist, or incapacitationist—run the considerable risk of causing a net drop in the law's effectiveness in controlling crime.

Here is a brief summary of our argument as detailed in Part II of this Article: The real power to gain compliance with society's rules of prescribed conduct lies not in the threat or reality of official criminal sanction, but in the power of the intertwined forces of social and individual moral control. The networks of interpersonal relationships in which people find themselves, the social norms and prohibitions shared among those relationships and transmitted through those social networks, and the internalized representations of those norms and moral precepts cause people to obey the law.

Next, the core of our argument, set out in Part III: The law is not irrelevant to these social and personal forces. Criminal law, in particular, plays a central role in creating and maintaining the social consensus necessary for sustaining moral norms. In fact, in a society as diverse as ours, the criminal law may be the only society-wide mechanism that transcends cultural and ethnic differences. Thus, the criminal law's most important real-world effect may be its ability to assist in the building, shaping, and maintaining of these norms and moral principles. It can contribute to and harness the compliance-producing power of interpersonal relationships and personal morality.

The criminal law can have a second effect in gaining compliance with its commands. If it earns a reputation as a reliable statement of what the community, given sufficient information and time to reflect, would perceive as condemnable, people are more likely to defer to its commands as morally authoritative and as appropriate to follow in those borderline cases in which the propriety of certain conduct is unsettled or ambiguous in the mind of the actor. The importance of this role should not be underestimated; in a society with the complex interdependencies characteristic of ours, an apparently harmless action can have destructive consequences. When the action is criminalized by the legal system, one would want the citizen to "respect the law" in such an instance even though he or she does not immediately intuit why that action is banned. Such deference will be facilitated if citizens are disposed to believe that the law is an accurate guide to appropriate prudential and moral behavior.

The extent of the criminal law's effectiveness in both these respects—in facilitating and communicating societal consensus on what is and is not condemnable, and in gaining compliance in borderline cases through deference to its moral authority—we argue is to a great extent dependent on the degree of moral credibility that the criminal law has achieved in the minds of the citizens governed by it. Thus, we assert, the criminal law's moral credibility is essential to effective crime control, and is enhanced if the distribution of criminal liability is perceived as "doing justice," that is, if it assigns liability and punishment in ways that the community perceives as consistent with the community's principles of appropriate liability and punishment.

Conversely, the system's moral credibility, and therefore its crime control effectiveness, is undermined by a distribution of liability that deviates from community perceptions of just desert. In Parts IV, V, and VI, we discuss how past reforms have hurt the criminal law's moral credibility, and we propose reforms by which its moral credibility might be enhanced.

We begin the argument for our position by criticizing all of the alternatives. That is, before we detail the case for enhancing the criminal law's moral credibility, we comment on the other utilitarian theories for distributing criminal liability and the difficulties that each face. Our conclusion is not that these standard utilitarian mechanisms for controlling crime have no effect in reducing crime, but rather that they have only a limited benefit that is outweighed by their cost in undercutting the law's crime control power by reducing its moral credibility. Remember that sentences based upon desert do provide the opportunity for rehabilitation, incapacitation, and deterrence. In arguing for a desert distribution, then, we need show only that the *additional crime control benefit* that the standard utilitarian analysis claims by *deviating from a desert distribution* is outweighed by the additional cost that such deviation incurs as it inevitably undercuts the criminal law's moral credibility. The optimum distributive principle, we argue, is one that rehabilitates, incapacitates, and deters, but only through the use of liability and punishment that tracks the community's principles of perceived desert.

I. Limitations of the Standard Utilitarian Theories for Distributing Criminal Liability

A. Deterrence

Social scientists have increasingly suspected that the threat of official punishment by the criminal justice system is of modest effect in limiting crime. One reason for its limited effect is the low risk of punishment an offender faces for the contemplated offense. Consider the many ways that an offender can routinely escape punishment for an offense.

An astounding number of serious offenses are never reported to police (*e.g.*, 21% of rapes, 40% of burglaries), either out of embarrassment or fear of reprisal or from a belief that the police are impotent or unwilling to do anything.[8] Of the offenses reported, clearance rates (the rate at which police identify and arrest a suspect for reported

8 Phillip J. Cook, *Punishment and Crime: A Critique of Current Findings Concerning the Preventative Effects of Punishment*, 41 Law & Contemp. Probs. 164, 172 (1977). *Compare* Table 1, Personal and household crimes, 1990, 1990 Criminal Victimization in the United States 16 (1992), *with* Table 3.122, Estimated number and rate of offenses known to police, 1990, 1992 Sourcebook of Criminal Justice Statistics 357 (1993).

offenses) have been steadily dropping for decades. The homicide clearance rate nationwide, which was 93% in 1955, has steadily declined to a current 67%. Rape has declined from 79% to 52%. Burglary went from a not very high 32% to a sad 13%.[10] And, of course, getting arrested is a far cry from punishment. The overall conviction rate of those arrested for the most serious offenses—homicide, rape, robbery, burglary, aggravated assault—is 30%.[11] Further, less than half of those convicted of a felony are sentenced to prison.[12]

The cumulative effect of the many escape hatches leaves a deterrent threat that looks like this: Homicide offers a 44.7% chance of being caught, convicted, and imprisoned for that offense. A person contemplating a rape faces a 12% chance of going to prison for that offense. Robbery presents a 3.8% chance. Assault, burglary, larceny, and motor vehicle theft are each a 100-to-1 shot.[13] To put it mildly,

9 The chart statistics are drawn from the following sources:

Column (a): Table 1, Personal and household crimes, 1990, 1990 CRIMINAL VICTIMIZATION IN THE UNITED STATES 16 (1992).

Column (b): Table 3.122, Estimated number and rate of offenses known to police, 1990, 1992 SOURCEBOOK OF CRIMINAL JUSTICE STATISTICS 357 (1993).

Column (c): Table 4.2, Number and rate of arrests, 1990, 1991 SOURCEBOOK OF CRIMINAL JUSTICE STATISTICS 424 (1992).

Column (d): Federal figures from Table 5.15, Defendants convicted in U.S. District Courts, 1990, 1992 SOURCEBOOK OF CRIMINAL JUSTICE STATISTICS 486 (1993); State figures from Table 5.49, Felony convictions in state courts, 1990, *id.* at 528.

Column (e): Federal figures from Table 5.19, Offenders sentenced to prison in U.S. District Courts, 1990, *id.* at 490; State figures from Table 5.52, Felony sentences imposed by state courts, 1990 (figures determined by converting percentage incarcerated back to totals through Table 5.49), *id.* at 529.

10 *Compare* 1955 statistics from: Table 15, Offenses known, cleared by arrest, and persons charged - 1955, 27 UNIFORM CRIME REPORTS FOR THE UNITED STATES 48 (1956) with 1991 statistics from: Table 4.19, Offenses known to police and percent cleared by arrest, 1991, 1992 SOURCEBOOK OF CRIMINAL JUSTICE STATISTICS 450 (1993); *see also infra* note 13.

11 *See supra* note 9 and accompanying text; Table 4.5, Arrests, by offense charged, 1992 SOURCEBOOK OF CRIMINAL JUSTICE STATISTICS 429 (1993); Table 5.15, Defendants convicted in U.S. District Courts, *id.* at 486; Table 5.50, Most serious offense of felony offenders convicted in State courts, *id.* at 528.

12 *See supra* note 9 and accompanying text; Table 5.52, Felony sentences imposed by State courts, 1992 SOURCEBOOK OF CRIMINAL JUSTICE STATISTICS 529 (1993) (this figure does not include the many offenders who, before or after conviction, may spend several months in local jails). Of those actually sentenced to prison, the median time served ranges from 5.5 years for murder to 2.2 years for kidnapping to 1.4 years for arson. Table 6.125, First releases from prisons in 35 states, 1988, 1991 SOURCEBOOK OF CRIMINAL JUSTICE STATISTICS 693 (1992). Even these short terms of imprisonment seriously overestimate the typical length of time served because these figures include only those offenders who are sentenced to prison. In reality more violent offenders are sentenced to jail than to prison, and for property offenses twice as many criminals are sentenced to jail. *See* Table 5.57, Sentences received in 14 States, 1988, 1991 SOURCEBOOK OF CRIMINAL JUSTICE STATISTICS 549 (1992).

13 *See supra* text accompanying note 9, col. (d). Note that the calculation gives the chance of being caught and convicted for that offense. No doubt many offenders will be caught and con-

our potential offender may not be entirely cowed by these threats. Table 1 summarizes the relevant statistics.

Even these risks of punishment, however, may tend to overstate the effectiveness of the deterrent threat. As one review remarked,

> From an empirical perspective, the existing literature seeking to estimate the expected utility model of criminal choice calls the model into question. . . . A number of laboratory and survey studies . . . of criminal choice provide possible explanations of the poor predictive performance of expected utility models . . . . These studies have found that probabilities used in decision making tend to be subjective rather than objective.[14]

As this suggests, if the task of the criminal justice system is the Bentham-Beccaria notion of deterrence,[15] then it is not the abstract "objective" probabilities that we want to examine, but the representations of these probabilities contained in the heads of potential offenders, and the disutilities that these persons place on the possible prison sentence. We want, in other words, to consider psychological theories of deterrence. A psychological theory of deterrence is a specific case of a "subjective expected utility theory," in which both the estimates of the probabilities of events and the utilities of those events are estimated for the individual about whom the predictions of actions are being made.

The result is worse from the point of view of those who wish to rely on deterrence to prevent crime. Many, if not most, offenders may be unrealistically optimistic about the precautions they take to avoid being caught, or the simple likelihood of being caught, and thus may underestimate that probability.[16] At the same time, just as people notoriously place high discounts on rewards that exist far in the future, so also do they on punishments.[17] The punishment of the prison term

---

victed of a lesser offense. But of course this effect exaggerates the success of the system in capturing and convicting for lesser offenses.

14 Pamela Lattimore & Ann Witte, *Models of Decision Making Under Uncertainty: The Criminal Choice*, *in* THE REASONING CRIMINAL: RATIONAL CHOICE PERSPECTIVES ON OFFENDING 129, 131 (Derek Cornish & Ronald Clarke eds., 1986) [hereinafter THE REASONING CRIMINAL].

15 *See supra* note 7.

16 Floyd Feeney's interviews with robbers suggest that first-time robbers feel a good deal of fear and apprehension, while more experienced robbers were much less tentative and fearful while committing robberies. Floyd Feeney, *Robbers as Decision-Makers*, *in* THE REASONING CRIMINAL, *supra* note 14, at 53, 65-66.

17 In general, people discount future events a great deal. The research method to determine this involves offering a person a choice of, say, $100 now or $200 after some delay and asking them to set the delay length so that they would be indifferent between the two choices. The typical delay time was around 31 days. One way of putting this result is that people were demanding a very high annual interest rate, far higher than available at banks, for keeping their money invested for that 31 days. George Anslie & Nick Haslam, *Hyperbolic Discounting*, *in* CHOICE OVER TIME 69 (G. Loewenstein & J. Elster eds., 1992). For pain, the case is less clear. If a future pain, such as an unavoidable electric shock, is certain, people often choose to get it

TABLE 1[9]

Type of offense	(a) Number Committed	(b) Number Reported (% of col. a)	(c) Number Arrests (% of col. a)	(d) Number Convictions (% of col. a)	(e) Prison Sentence (% of col. a)	(f) (Months) Sentence Imposed	(g) 1989 Time Served
Total	26,122,820	14,475,630 **55.4%**	2,313,247 **8.9%**	379,292 **1.5%**	279,909 **1.1%**	Fed=61.4 State=91.0	Fed=36.23 State=35.9
Murder and Non-Negligent Manslaughter	NA	23,440 ——	18,298 **78.1%**	Fed=133 State=10,895 **47%**	Fed=124 State=10,350 **44.7%**	Fed=134.7 State=233.0	Fed=53.3 State=83.0 6.9 years
Rape	130,260	102,560 **78.7%**	30,966 **23.8%**	Fed=149 State=18,024 **14.0%**	Fed=120 State=15,500 **12.0%**	Fed=78.9 State=128.0	Fed=NA State=55.0 4.6 years
Robbery	1,149,710	639,270 **55.6%**	136,300 **11.9%**	Fed=1,337 State=47,446 **4.2%**	Fed=1,313 State=42,701 **3.8%**	Fed=100.7 State=97.0	Fed=58.6 State=41.0 3.4 years
Assault	4,728,810	1,054,860 **22.3%**	376,917 **8.0%**	Fed=455 State=53,861 **1.1%**	Fed=282 State=38,780 **0.8%**	Fed=34.8 State=52.0	Fed=41.9 State=23.0 1.9 years
Burglary	5,147,740	3,073,900 **59.7%**	341,192 **6.6%**	Fed=99 St.=109,250 **2.1%**	Fed=83 State=82,313 **1.6%**	Fed=34.4 State=61.0	Fed=26.0 State=22.0 1.8 years
Larceny-Theft	12,975,320	7,945,700 **61.2%**	1,241,236 **9.6%**	Fed=2,709 St.=113,094 **0.9%**	Fed=940 State=73,511 **0.6%**	Fed=18.8 State=33.0	Fed=16.3 State=14.0 1.2 years
Motor-Vehicle Theft	1,967,540	1,635,900 **83.1%**	168,338 **8.6%**	Fed=275 State=21,065 **1.1%**	Fed=200 State=13,692 **0.7%**	Fed=27.6 State=33.0	Fed=21.3 State=13.0 1.1 years

in our criminal justice system is well understood to exist far in the future, if it exists at all. Further, newspaper articles frequently report on prisons as "revolving doors"; thus, possibilities of early discharge may be exaggerated in the potential offender's mind. Still further, time in prison may not be as hateful for a person living poorly in the present, thus diminishing its deterrent value.[18]

Finally, recent work tends to suggest that the threat of prison is less than one might expect in other ways. For instance, research on the recollection of painful experiences suggests that the duration of the experience is less important than the peak of the pain felt during it, and that the level of discomfort felt at the *end* of the experience is overweighed in recollection. Kahneman points out what that might mean for recidivism:

> [T]he well being of prison inmates is likely to improve in the course of their sentence, as they gain seniority and survival skills. . . . Suppose . . . that prisoners apply a Peak and End rule in retrospective evaluations of their prison experience. The result would be a global evaluation that becomes steadily less aversive with time in prison, implying a negative correlation between sentence length and the deterrence of individual recidivism. This is surely not a socially desirable outcome.[19]

It surely also suggests that lengthy prison terms are not a particularly useful method of increasing deterrence effects on those who experience them.

All of these effects, factored into a perceptual deterrence theory, make the effects of prison term as deterrent less potent than they are in the objective calculations described above.[20] Consider the implica-

---

over with quickly, probably to avoid anticipatory dread and anxiety. *See* George Loewenstein, *Anticipation and the Valuation of Delayed Consumption*, 97 ECON. J. 667 (1987). But, of course, as we have shown, prison terms are by no means certain, or even likely. Elster and Loewenstein suggest a relationship between probability and dread that probably fits the present case. "At very low probability levels, below a threshold of conceivability, . . . dread will be nil. Beyond this threshold, we would expect a sudden jump and then low marginal sensitivity over a wide range of probabilities beyond that point . . . ." Jon Elster & George Loewenstein, *Utility from Memory and Anticipation*, *in* CHOICE OVER TIME, *supra*, at 213-34.

18 Feeney quotes one robber as saying,"I don't really have any fear of prisons or things like that. I always sort of felt like I was going back someday . . . ." Feeney, *supra* note 16, at 59.

19 Daniel Kahneman, *New Challenges to the Rationality Assumption*, 150 J. INST. & THEORETICAL ECON. 18, 33-34 (1994).

20 A review of the empirical evidence on perceptual deterrence theories confirms what this suggests. The theories predict an inverse relationship between perceived severity and certainty of punishment and crime. But the earlier empirical studies of the theory, which were done using cross-sectional survey study methods, generally found that perceived certainty of punishment deterred crime but the perceived severity did not. In a cross-sectional design, a respondent is asked, for example, about his or her perceptions of the severity and certainty of punishment and arrest record at the same time. These perceptions, reported after experiencing arrest, are assumed to be identical with those held before the arrests, obviously a questionable assumption. Longitudinal, or panel study methods, measure respondent perceptions at time one, and determine respondent arrest records at time two, a better design from the point of view of establishing

tions of this for designing a deterrence-based system that might actually have a significant effect. The logic of a deterrence-based system drives toward the adoption of a fixed "quantum" of punishment for an offense, set according to the stake that society has in lowering the rate of that offense. Inexorably, then, as the probability of arrest or conviction is reduced, and the time of the onset of the already problematic prison term is pushed into the distant and discountable future, one can achieve the fixed quantum of punishment only by increasing the magnitude of the prison sentence or the severity of the conditions under which it is served.

Refer to our earlier figures to see why longer prison terms can have only a limited effect in deterring crime: If a robber faces a 3.8% chance of going to prison, why should it matter to him whether the likely sentence is 2 years or 10 years? The impact of this difference in prison terms on the total disutility score is trivial.[21] If we wished to make it non-trivial, look what we would have to do. If, for instance, we thought that a real threat of a four year sentence was needed to deter burglary, and noticed that only 1.6% of those committing burglary eventually went to prison for their offense, would we wish to impose a 250 year sentence, to keep the quantum of anticipated punishment around that of the 4 year sentence? No. As a practical matter, the community is likely to be morally offended by the suggestion. As one reviewer has remarked, observing the current high levels of crime that are not being deterred by threat of punishment:

> If we cannot live with this, we must lower our ethical standard as the amount of pain we are willing to inflict on others if necessary, and we must considerably tighten police control. . . . If we want to change this,

causality. Later studies, using more sophisticated panel study methods, generally found no evidence of a deterrence effect for either perceived severity or certainty of punishment. Daniel Nagin & Raymond Paternoster, *The Preventive Effects of the Perceived Risk of Arrest: Testing an Expanded Conception of Deterrence*, 29 CRIMINOLOGY 561, 570-72 (1991). None of this is encouraging for those arguing for a deterrence-based system of crime prevention.

The analysis can be made to get worse from the perspective of one wishing to rely on deterrence. Lately in social science there has been increasing skepticism about the validity of the subjective expected utility model that forms the core of perceptual deterrence models. Decision models are being substituted that more closely follow empirical evidence about people's actual representations of events, outcomes, and probabilities. Prospect theory is one contender to replace subjective expected utility theory, and Lattimore and Witte develop a version of Kahneman and Tversky's prospect theory for application to the prediction of criminal behavior. Lattimore & Witte, *supra* note 14, at 137-44. In summary, it does not lead to any more optimistic views on criminal sanction as a successful deterrent of criminal acts. It does not, in other words, rescue a deterrence theory of crime prevention.

21 Assume that we think that 10 years is a reasonable deterrent sentence for a robbery, as long as it is certain and swift and served in full. In other words, we wanted a deterrence value of 10 for robbery. The simple deterrence value of a 10 year sentence with a 3.8% chance of going to jail, then, is 0.38, of a 2 year sentence, 0.076. Neither deters. *See supra* note 9 and accompanying text.

> there is a terrible price to pay: a police state operating a brutal criminal justice system.[22]

Realistically and happily, we are not going to pay this price; as a concomitant of that, the deterrence approach to preventing criminality is gravely weakened.

B. *Rehabilitation*

The rehabilitationist approach to sentencing has lost credibility, based on the findings of numerous studies indicating that criminal rehabilitation programs, as practiced, do not produce impressive, or often even detectable reductions in recidivism of those who have participated in the programs. As Cook comments, a number of true experiments on rehabilitation were conducted, and "[t]he failure of these studies to demonstrate efficacy in reducing recidivism rates has been a major impetus in the current trend away from indeterminant sentencing and the 'rehabilitative ideal.'"[23] Further, "[i]t is safe to conclude that correctional rehabilitation programs, taken collectively, have had a small effect on crime rates in the past, and that a number of notable programs failed completely."[24]

C. *Incapacitation*

Incapacitation, particularly of repeat offenders, is currently attracting a good deal of popular and legislative attention. Part of the reason for its popularity, we suspect, lies in its apparent realism. An incapacitation-based sentencing system implicitly gives up on rehabilitative possibilities and on the possibilities of deterring the specific criminals to which it is applied. It prevents crime in only one way: by preventing the specific criminal from committing crimes during the duration of his sentence. (Actually, it does not even do that; it prevents the commission of crimes outside, but not inside, the prison.)

The attractiveness of incapacitation stems from the belief that an enormous number of crimes are committed by a relatively small group of repeat offenders.[25] If one locks these offenders away, then crime rates will be greatly decreased. However, several assumptions intervene between the fact of repeat criminality and the postulated success of incapacitation, and these assumptions need to be examined. The possibility exists that we are entering a period of unexamined enthusi-

---

22 Hans F. M. Crombag, *When Law and Psychology Meet*, *in* CRIMINAL BEHAVIOR AND THE JUSTICE SYSTEM: PSYCHOLOGICAL PERSPECTIVES 1, 11 (Hermann Wegener et al. eds., 1989).

23 Cook, *supra* note 8, at 166.

24 *Id.* Cook goes on to point out that if one or more specific rehabilitation programs can be shown to work, then rehabilitation deserves consideration in that specific instance.

25 A Rand Corporation study was highly influential in establishing this fact and making the case for an incapacitation-based system. For this study, see PETER W. GREENWOOD, SELECTIVE INCAPACITATION (1982).

asm for incapacitation that will lead to an uncritical adoption of sentencing programs based on it, followed by its rejection, if it produces less than its proponents claim for it.

The central task of an incapacitationist system is to identify those offenders who are likely to commit repeated offenses in the future. By assigning long sentences to those offenders, an incapacitation-based system will have its differential success rate over other sentencing systems. In other words, the system depends on predicting "dangerousness," with dangerousness defined as a high likelihood of committing future crimes, defined, in other words, as recidivism.

Those who have reviewed the empirical status of the prediction of dangerousness do not claim the accuracy rates that would provide confidence in an incapacitation-based system. Schmidt and Witte report a careful and statistically sophisticated study, the conclusions of which are not encouraging for an incapacitation strategy. First, they demonstrate that the accuracy of the prediction of recidivism is highly dependent on the statistical system that one uses to model it.[26] Second, their best model predicts recidivism in a way that is too inaccurate, in their view, to be used in assigning people to such important fates as prison or freedom.[27] That is, the predictions are not entirely inaccurate, but they are too inaccurate for the purposes to which we wish to put them.[28] Specifically, the system falsely identified 47% of those predicted to recidivate; that is, 47% of those predicted to recidivate did not in fact do so in their study.[29] As they remark:

> Our predictions for individuals were reasonable. However, they suffered from a high false positive rate. We were not able to accurately identify a group of career criminals that might be selectively incapacitated. Our false negative rate was lower (28%) and in that sense we were able to identify a group that usefully might be considered for fewer restrictions on their freedom. . . .
>
> A policy of selective incapacitation would be far easier to market if there were some "objective" scientific evidence of one's power to identify a particularly crime-prone group of individuals. We have been able

26 PETER SCHMIDT & ANN WITTE, PREDICTING RECIDIVISM USING SURVIVAL MODELS 158 (1988).

27 The model does meet one set of criteria for success, suggested by David Farrington, *Predicting Individual Crime Rates*, 9 CRIME AND JUSTICE: AN ANNUAL REVIEW OF RESEARCH 53 (1987). He suggests that a successful predictive system should have less than a 50% false positive rate and less than a 50% false negative rate. What this means is that, of each 100 people predicted to recidivate, at least 50 should do so, and of each 100 people predicted to not commit further crimes, at least 50 should not do so. The reader will notice that this set of criteria do not seem highly rigorous, and yet it has proved in practice quite hard for recidivism prediction systems to reach it.

28 SCHMIDT & WITTE, *supra* note 26, at 160.

29 A false positive rate of 47% and a false negative rate of 28% are better than those obtained in other studies of a similar sort. Schmidt & Witte review the rates from other studies. *See* SCHMIDT & WITTE, *supra* note 26, at 142.

> to identify such a group only with a level of error that we feel is unacceptable. . . .
>
> We find the false positive rates too high to use current methods as models for selecting individuals for harsher treatment than they would receive otherwise.[30]

Other studies have suggested that available models are less successful, showing false positive rates of nearly 80%.[31]

It is reasonable to suppose that predictor systems could improve by reducing their error rates, but there are real limits to any prediction of a particular person's future behavior. This means that, in an incapacitation-based system, some people will receive long sentences because they are falsely predicted to be repeat offenders, and others will receive short sentences because they are not predicted to be dangerous but will prove to be repeat offenders on release. With the first sort of error, we will confine for lengthy sentences many people who do not in fact require such treatment, crowding the prison system and increasing its already substantial cost. However, the fact that many of those incarcerated would have committed no crimes were they out of prison cannot become visible because they are in prison. With the second sort of error, we will fail to confine some who will offend again on discharge, and that fact will become highly, publicly visible. Among those who look to incapacitation as a panacea for what they see as crime out of control, this is likely to lead to a dynamic in which, seeking to avoid letting out of prison those who offend again, we increasingly move to assign incapacitative sentences to those for whom the prediction of dangerousness is weaker and weaker, a fact that arouses concerns for justice in many who think about the issue.

Consider also the ethical issues in an incapacitation strategy. Taking a position similar in some respects to our own, Morris and Miller suggest that an increase in penalties based on predictions of future recidivism is moral only if it does not increase the punishment beyond what would be assigned from a just desert perspective.[32] Gottfredson and Gottfredson are willing to use predictive equations to select those for deinstitutional treatments, but not for selecting those who should receive longer sentences.[33] Consider also what variables are likely to appear in the prediction of dangerousness equations. Certainly race will appear there; certainly also gender, as crimes are disproportionately committed by men, not women. Age also is a remarkably strong predictor of crimes. All of these predictors

---

30 *Id.* at 149.

31 John Monahan, *Violence Prediction: The Last 20 and the Next 20 Years*, *in* 23 CRIM. JUST. & BEHAV. 107 (1996).

32 Norval Morris & Marc Miller, *Predictions of Dangerousness*, 6 CRIME AND JUSTICE: AN ANNUAL REVIEW OF RESEARCH 1, 35 (1985).

33 Stephen D. Gottfredson & Don M. Gottfredson, *Accuracy of Predictive Models*, *in* 2 CRIMINAL CAREERS AND "CAREER CRIMINALS" 212, 280 (A. Blumstein et al. eds., 1986).

emerge as significant.[34] What these predictors will lead to, if they are used, is a remarkably strong tendency to incarcerate, for a long sentence, a young, African-American male who commits one crime.

There is an obvious ethical dilemma here; these are attributes that the individual was born with, and many would object to using them as indicators that a person should be sentenced to a longer prison term. The report of the National Panel on Research on Criminal Careers comments that "[c]haracteristics such as race, ethnicity and religion are especially unacceptable as candidate predictors because they have no relationship to blameworthiness . . . and their use affronts basic social values . . . ."[35]

A different sort of objection is found in the failure of the terms of incarceration to match their rationale. The conditions of prison life can be quite harsh; to go to prison in the United States in 1996 can mean exposure to a debased, mind-numbing environment, including significant possibilities of forcible rape, contracting AIDS, and contracting a virulent strain of tuberculosis. The conditions of confinement upon commitment under the criminal justice system are conditions of punishment. Yet, the justification for confinement under an incapacitation strategy is not punishment but prevention, akin to the system of preventive detention that we use for those with infectious diseases or mental illness that is likely to lead to violent behavior. Systems of preventative detention are morally ambiguous, but certainly we are most comfortable with them when they involve detention conditions that are not punitive in nature, involve "treatment" efforts that attempt to remove the elements in the individual that cause the presumed dangerousness, and continually reassess the dangerousness of the individual who is incarcerated. This is not a good description of the workings of the prison system in the United States. Indeed, the current trend toward increased use of a dangerousness rationale is accompanied by a trend to increase the harshness of prison life and to abolish periodic review.

To us, the most severe criticism of an incapacitation-based sentencing system is that it requires a distribution of liability very different from what the community regards as just punishment for the

---

34 Schmidt & Witte, *supra* note 26, ch. 8.

35 Joseph G. Weis, *Issues in the Measurement of Criminal Careers*, *in* 2 Criminal Careers and "Career Criminals", *supra* note 33, at 8-12. There is certainly a desire on the part of the community to protect itself from crime, and a willingness to consider incapacitation as one of the least objectionable options for preventing crime. This has led one of us to suggest that an incapacitation system should exist, but that such a system should be located within the civil rather than the criminal commitment system. The system there will be more familiar with the assessment of the continuing dangerousness of the individual and more able to provide detention conditions that are non-punitive in nature. *See* Paul H. Robinson, *Foreword: The Criminal-Civil Distinction and Dangerous Blameless Offenders*, 83 J. Crim. L. & Criminology 693, 706-14 (1993).

offense committed. First, it assigns sentences of very different lengths to two individuals who have committed exactly the same crime, where one is predicted to be a repeat offender and the other is not. Further, the predicted repeat offender is being punished for an action that he has not yet done, or perhaps even thought of: the future offense. If he is one of the 47% of those predicted from the current best predictor system to commit another offense who would not, the "false positives," he is being punished for an offense that he never would have committed. Finally, an incapacitation strategy assigns liabilities based on considerations that do not figure into the community's perceptions of the appropriate sentences for the crime committed, such as the strong predictors of race, gender, and age. This brings us to what will become our familiar argument: an incapacitation-based sentencing system undercuts the moral credibility of the criminal law and thus the system's ability to produce voluntary compliance with its mandates.

D. *Summary*

To summarize our arguments about the standard utilitarian-based punishment systems: Rehabilitation-based systems, formerly popular, rarely worked and are now rarely under active consideration as a sentencing strategy. Incapacitation-based systems, currently generating a great deal of interest, have a number of difficulties that are likely, at best, to make them less attractive than they seem and, at worst, to cause intolerable injustice on a broad scale. A system centered on deterrence also has a number of difficulties, most prominently the remarkably low detection and conviction rates on many crimes and conflict with the upper limits on sentences that people consider just. This suggests that a system that would truly deter would be regarded as excessively draconian by the community. The evidence suggests that the fear of arrest and incarceration in prison is not effective in causing people to obey the law. This confronts us with the question: Why, then, do people obey the law? Perhaps if we understood better the dynamics of these forces, we might discover ways in which law-abiding behavior could be enhanced.

II. Why Do People Obey the Law?

Given the weak deterrent threat facing people, why do the vast majority of those free in society still act in a way consistent with the law? Social scientists have a preliminary answer: More than because of the threat of legal punishment, people obey the law (1) because they fear the disapproval of their social group if they violate the law, and (2) because they generally see themselves as moral beings who want to do the right thing as they perceive it. In social science, these two factors are referred to as (1) compliance produced by normative social influence, and (2) behavior produced by internalized moral standards and rules.

These informal sources of behavioral control function in a variety of ways. The normative pressures from other people, generally experienced as an external force by the actor, function like the more formal deterrence mechanisms were thought to function. People obey the social norms of their groups because those groups have rewards to give for doing so and sanctions for failing to do so. Three classes of "informal sanctions" are usually identified and can be incurred when one's group judges that one has transgressed: "commitment costs," in which past accomplishments are in jeopardy; "attachment costs," involving the loss of valued relationships with others; and "stigma," discreditation in the eyes of others.[36] These sanctions may follow arrest for a crime, but if the harm-doing act becomes known or suspected within one's community, even if one is not arrested, informal sanctioning processes may occur.[37] The social costs to the offender may extend beyond the offender's friends and family. If one is thought to have committed a crime, one may lose one's job, ability to borrow money, ability to command trust from others, and possible business partners.[38]

People's own moral rules and action proscriptions are generally experienced as internal forces; people recognize that they come from the moral rules that they have adopted. Phenomenologically, we all have experienced this sense of obligation to act in a certain way, to avoid harm to another, or to fulfill some commitment we have made.

These two barriers to deviant behavior—social sanctions and internal moral sanctions—are analytically and often experientially separable, but in the longer term they converge. Children are trained by a powerful socialization process into internalizing the beliefs represented in the social norms of the culture to which they belong. People come to hold the moral standards of the cultures in which they are

36 Exactly what loss counts in what category is not perfectly resolvable; loss of marriage prospects is often listed as a commitment cost, while loss of an existing relationship with a significant other is an attachment cost. Stigma may be feared because it causes others to be unwilling to enter attachments with the stigmatized individual, hire that individual, and so on. The point is that a good many informal sanctions may be risked when one transgresses, and the initial application of some sanctions may lead to further ones.

37 Anonymity, often thought to be a cause of crime in cities, works by severing the informal social sanctions from the individual.

38 Nagin & Paternoster, *supra* note 20, at 562; Kirk R. Williams & Richard Hawkins, *Perceptual Research on General Deterrence: A Critical Review*, 20 LAW & SOC'Y REV. 545, 565-66 (1986). For an examination of the effect of criminal conviction on an offender's future earning potential, see John Lott, Jr., *An Attempt at Measuring the Total Monetary Penalty from Drug Convictions: The Importance of an Individual's Reputation*, 21 J. LEGAL STUD. 159 (1992); John Lott, Jr., *Do We Punish High Income Criminals Too Heavily?*, 30 ECON. INQUIRY 583 (1992).

raised; internal moral standards and external norms generally label the same actions right or wrong.

What is the evidence concerning crime prevention due to fear of social sanction or fulfillment of moral obligation? It is scattered but supportive. Since many of the studies that provide evidence for the operation of social sanctions also report evidence about the role of internalized moral control in inhibiting criminal acts, we review evidence for both forces simultaneously.[39]

Harold Grasmick and his associates have done the most sustained work documenting the role of the informal determinants of law-abidingness. Their research consistently finds that fear of social disapproval and moral commitment to the law both inhibit the commission of illegal activity.[40] They comment that their "findings highlight the importance of internal control in producing conformity to the law."[41] Other researchers reach similar conclusions. Paternoster and Iovanni conclude that "the greatest effects on delinquent involvement are those from informal forces of social control."[42] Meir and Johnson conclude: "despite contemporary predisposition toward the importance of legal sanction, our findings are . . . consistent with the accumulated literature concerning the primacy of interpersonal influence" over legal sanction.[43] Tom Tyler's review of existing studies con-

39 In a study measuring the frequency of property and drug offenses committed by juveniles, it was found that offense frequency was predicted by whether the actor perceived that his friends would approve of the delinquent actions, and negatively predicted by possession of a set of conventional moral beliefs that delinquent acts are wrong. Nagin & Paternoster, *supra* note 20, at 574. (Some evidence was also found for an effect of certainty of arrest on delinquent acts.) Commitment but not attachment or stigma costs were measured in this study.

40 Harold Grasmick & Donald Green, *Legal Punishment, Social Disapproval and Internalization as Inhibitors of Illegal Behavior*, 71 J. CRIM. L. & CRIMINOLOGY 325 (1980).

41 Harold Grasmick & Robert Bursik, *Conscience, Significant Others, and Rational Choice*, 24 LAW & SOC'Y REV. 837, 854 (1990). They came to this conclusion based on the repeated discovery that those who reported that certain actions were immoral, wrong, bad, or seen by others about whom they cared as wrong, were less likely to engage in those actions.

42 Raymond Paternoster & Lee Ann Iovanni, *The Deterrent Effect of Perceived Severity: A Reexamination*, 64 SOCIAL FORCES 751, 769 (1986). They came to this conclusion based on the correlation between an individual reporting that certain actions would be disapproved of by others who were significant to that individual, for instance friends or peers, and the individual's comparatively low rate of committing those actions. One is less likely to commit actions of which those around him will disapprove.

43 Robert Meir & Weldon Johnson, *Deterrence as Social Control: The Legal and Extralegal Production of Conformity*, 42 AM. SOC. REV. 292, 302 (1977). Here the authors are commenting both on their review of the related literature and their own findings. Characteristically, these studies have some assessment of a person's judgment that certain actions are right or wrong, moral or immoral, of concerns about what sanctions that people in his social networks would inflict on him if he did those actions, and of concerns about what sanctions such as arrest, conviction, and jail term the legal system would inflict on him if he did those actions. The power of each of these classes of variables to predict whether he actually commits the actions is tested. The first two sets of variables to predict criminal actions are characteristically demonstrated in this research, and their predictive power is often higher than that of the fear of legal sanctions.

cludes, "Testing the ability of each of the attitudinal factors . . . to predict variance in compliance . . . the most important incremental contribution is made by personal morality . . . ."[44]

III. Criminal Law's Influence on the Social Forces of Compliance

The evidence reviewed suggests that the influences of social group sanctions and internalized norms are the most powerful determinants of conduct, more significant than the threat of deterrent legal sanctions. But, we argue, the law is not irrelevant to the operation of these powerful forces. Criminal law in particular can influence the norms that are held by the social group and that are internalized by the individual. Criminal law's influence comes from being a societal mechanism by which the force of social norms is realized and by which the force of internal moral principles is strengthened. That is, the law has no independent force, the way social group norms and internalized norms do. It has power to the extent that it can amplify and sustain these two power sources; it has power to the extent that it influences what the social group thinks and what its members internalize.

A. *The Criminal Law's Ability to Facilitate the Creation of Shared Norms*

Our first claim is that the criminal law influences the powerful social forces of normative behavior control through its central role in the creation of shared norms. The norms at issue here are of a limited sort, of course. Criminal law ought to and does have little interest in norms that influence everyday matters of style, dress, speech, manners, etc. Cutting in line, being rude, or wearing revealing clothing may be annoying to some people, but it generally is not and ought not be criminal. Even if such violations of norms were frowned upon by most people, the conduct ought not be criminal because it fails to reach the level of seriousness that deserves the condemnation of criminal liability, which is typically and properly limited to the violation of

This is not inconsistent with finding that the fear of criminal sanctions has some deterrent effect in some of the studies.

[44] Tom R. Tyler, Why People Obey the Law 60 (1990). In a subset of studies that Tyler reviews, respondents reported on whether they considered certain actions moral or immoral, on other reasons for committing or not committing those actions, and on the frequency with which they committed those actions. Consistently, "personal morality," the degree to which the individual regarded those actions as right or wrong, predicted the frequency with which those actions were engaged in, and predicted this frequency more strongly than did the other possible predictors.

norms against violence and dishonesty.[45] As Gottfriedson and Hirshi have remarked, the criminal law is about force and fraud.[46]

1. The Educative Function of Criminal Law Adjudication and Legislative Debate.—As to norms against force and fraud, social science suggests that the criminal law builds and maintains societal norms in several related ways. First, criminal law enforcement and adjudication activities send daily messages to all who read or hear about them. Every time criminal liability is imposed, it reminds us of the norm prohibiting the offender's conduct and confirms its condemnable nature.[47] The public condemnation expressed in reaction to the offense supports and encourages the efforts of those who have resisted temptation and continued to remain law-abiding. Having avoided breaking that law, people can regard themselves favorably, which in turn reinforces their moral commitment to the norm expressed in the offense.

Further, every adjudication offers an opportunity to confirm the exact nature of the norm or to signal a shift or refinement of it. Thus, an endangerment or manslaughter prosecution of a polluter points out that some instances of polluting can violate the norm against endangering others. The publicity surrounding an adjudication can teach all people about the consequences of certain kinds of polluting and, therefore, that it ought to be avoided. Kai Erikson's studies point out the role of criminal law in marking the limits between allowable, although perhaps regrettable, conduct and criminal conduct: The prosecution of a deviant brands the deviant as a criminal and casts a bright light on the exact location of a boundary that previously might have been obscure to the community.[48]

Further, people are likely to attend to the comparative liabilities that are assigned by sentencing provisions of legal systems; people intuit that more morally serious offenses should command greater penalties. As Cook remarks, "The legislated (and actual) severity of penalty for a particular offense may influence the public's feeling for the seriousness or moral repugnance of this offense."[49] In the long run, for those crimes in which "moral inhibition" plays an important

---

45 There are some exceptions, however. Eating human flesh and bestiality, for example, remain criminal because the norms against such conduct remain strongly and widely felt.

46 MICHAEL R. GOTTFRIEDSON & TRAVIS HIRSCHI, A GENERAL THEORY OF CRIME 4 (1990).

47 At the same time, regular non-enforcement or a declination to prosecute or to convict tends to undermine the norm prohibiting the conduct. Thus, adultery may remain on the books but a policy of not prosecuting it takes away the criminal law's support of any norm against such conduct that may have existed.

48 KAI ERIKSON, THE WAYWARD PURITANS: A STUDY IN THE SOCIOLOGY OF DEVIANCE (1966).

49 COOK, *supra* note 8, at 177.

role, announcing high severity of punishment may be an important communication; more important than ensuring high probability of punishment, which we have argued is generally not possible.

The criminal adjudication process is not the only forum for public discussion and announcement. Legislative proposals for criminalization or decriminalization, or increased or decreased punishment, also provide an occasion for public debate that can help build norms, with the conclusion of the debate announced by legislative action or inaction. The public discussion about the problem of hate speech and proposals to criminalize it, for example, help strengthen the shared public understanding that such conduct is condemnable. When one seeks to criminalize an act, the debate should say why that act endangers others, or otherwise fits the case of those things we are willing to criminalize. In our complex, interdependent society, this can be usefully instructive. If lawmakers argue that an act should not be criminalized, or should be decriminalized, then they should be able to say why it does not resemble the sorts of things that are now criminalized.

2. The Relationship Between Criminal Law and Community Norms.—Notice that we said that laws can *contribute* to the formation and change of community norms and individuals' moral reasoning; laws cannot themselves compel community acceptance. Passing a law cannot itself create a norm, and not passing a law against certain conduct cannot make that conduct morally acceptable to the community. The passage and subsequent failure of National Prohibition shows the law's limited ability to change norms even when the change is supported by a significant portion of the public.[50] Some would argue that the continuing controversy over our "war on drugs" raises a similar issue.[51] The law is, rather, a vehicle by which the community debates, tests, and ultimately settles upon and expresses its norms. The passage of criminal legislation more often reflects a critical level of support for an incipient norm. The act of criminalization sometimes nurtures the norm, as does faithful enforcement and prosecution, and over time the community view may mature into a strong consensus. The criminal law is not an independent player in that process, but it is a contributing mechanism by which the norm-nurturing process moves forward.

We have seen the process at work recently in enhancing prohibitory norms against sexual harassment, hate speech, drunk driving, and domestic violence. It has also been at work in diluting existing norms

50 In December of 1933, the repeal of the Eighteenth Amendment was completed by the adoption of the Twenty-First Amendment. It was, "[i]n hindsight . . . the legal outcome of a foolish, unpopular reform." DAVID E. KYVIG, REPEALING NATIONAL PROHIBITION 3 (1979).

51 *See, e.g.*, Anthony Lewis, *Prohibition Folly*, N.Y. TIMES, Feb. 12, 1996, at A13.

against homosexual conduct, fornication, and adultery. While it is difficult to untangle how much the criminal law reform followed and how much it led these shifts, it seems difficult to imagine that these changes could have occurred without the recognition and confirmation that comes through changes in criminal law legislation, enforcement, and adjudication.

Perhaps more than any other society, ours relies on the criminal law for norm-nurturing. Our greater cultural diversity means that we cannot expect a stable pre-existing consensus on the contours of condemnable conduct that is found in more homogeneous societies. We require more public debate and discussion to reconcile conflicting views and more public education on the refinements and consensuses that result. Unlike many other societies, we share no religion or other arbiter of morality that might perform this role. Our criminal law is, for us, the place we express our shared beliefs of what is truly condemnable.

B. The Criminal Law's Compliance Power as a Moral Authority in Unanalyzed Cases

The discussion above describes the criminal law's role as a forum and communicator in the process by which moral norms are reinforced, established, or diluted. The criminal law also has a second effect in shaping conduct, specifically in gaining compliance with its demands. If it has developed a reputation as a reliable statement of existing norms, people will be willing to defer to its moral authority in cases where there exists some ambiguity as to the wrongfulness of the contemplated conduct.

1. Evidence of the Criminal Law's Power as a Moral Authority.—There is evidence, largely collected and analyzed by Tyler, that people are inclined to accept the law as a source of moral authority that they themselves should take seriously. This is referred to in social science as informational influence—influence produced by the information transmitted by a specific institution, in which one accepts the validity of the definition of right and wrong behavior conveyed by that institution, internalizes that definition, and expects other people to have internalized it as well. Tyler reviews the literature that relates a person's belief that a law reflects a valid moral rule to obedience to that law, and finds them to be quite strongly related.[52] He notes: "This high level of normative commitment to obeying the law offers an important basis for the effective exercise of authority by legal officials. People clearly have a strong predisposition toward following the

52 TYLER, *supra* note 44, at 37.

law. If authorities can tap into such feelings, their decisions will be more widely followed."[53]

Tyler reviews a number of studies that suggest that the level of commitment to obey the law is proportional to what Tyler calls the law's perceived "legitimacy," by which he means a community's perceptions that, first, the law instantiates their moral beliefs, and, second, that the law came into being via fair procedures conducted by the appropriate authorities.[54] Tyler reasons that, if one regards the law as a legitimate source of rules, if it has what we have called "moral credibility," then one should be more likely to regard the law's judgments about right and wrong actions as an appropriate input to one's own moral thinking; in turn, one should be more likely to obey the law. Further, one should be more likely to support the authorities that promulgated the law. To test this contention he reviews a number of studies that examine individual differences in perceptions of the law's legitimacy and relate those differences to differences in support for legal authorities and felt obligations to obey the law.

> Six studies . . . address the question of whether feelings of [the law's] legitimacy lead to behavioral compliance with the law and legal authorities, regardless of whether those feelings are expressed as support for the authorities or as an obligation to obey . . . . These studies suggest that those who view authority as legitimate are more likely to comply with legal authority, whether the legitimacy is expressed as obligation or as support . . . .[55]

Also as one would expect, those who perceive the political authority that governs them to be less legitimate are more likely to engage in acts of social or political protest, some of which are illegal. More research on this issue is obviously needed, but we conclude that the current research supports our claim of a connection between perceptions of the law's moral credibility and obedience to the law.

2. *Actions That Are Not Obviously Harmful.*—Notice that, as a matter of common sense, the law's moral credibility is not needed to tell a person that murder, rape, or robbery is wrong. The criminal law's influence as a moral authority has effect primarily at the border-

53 *Id.* at 60. In another study, Grasmick and Green conclude: "[E]ach of the three independent variables [of deterrence by threat of legal punishment, social disapproval, and personal moral commitment] makes a significant independent contribution to the explained variance [i.e., the rate of criminal behavior]." Grasmick & Green, *supra* note 40, at 326.

54 *See* Tyler, *supra* note 44, at 64-68; studies listed in Tables 3.1, 3.2, and 3.3, *id.* at 32-37.

55 *Id.* at 31. Tyler suggests that the law gains legitimacy in two ways, only one of which we emphasize in our argument. First, and the element we emphasize, the law gains legitimacy because it is seen as being in accord with the moral rules of the community. Second, it gains legitimacy because it is the product of processes such as legislation and judicial debate, which are the processes that society has agreed are the appropriate ones to enact such laws. In other words, the laws are the products of legitimate authority. We agree that procedural fairness is an important additional element producing moral credibility for the law.

line of criminal activity, where there may be some ambiguity as to whether the conduct really is wrong.

How does this ambiguity arise? Historically, scholars have distinguished between two kinds of "crimes": crimes that are *mala in se* and those that are *malum prohibitum*; crimes that are wrong in themselves and actions that are crimes because they are prohibited by law. This distinction gained use because of the possibilities of remote consequences that arise in modern, complexly interdependent societies. We all may take actions that are harmful in ways that may not be immediately obvious. The harm may be to specific others or to society as a whole or to society's institutions. If these harms are reasonably predictable from certain kinds of conduct, and of sufficient magnitude, then it is appropriate to criminalize the conduct. Driving faster than the speed limit, driving while intoxicated, or insider trading are all examples of this class of conduct.

To be maximally effective, the legal system must publicize why these kinds of conduct lead to outcomes that are sufficiently damaging to be criminalized. But realistically, the legal system cannot constantly generate public understanding of why each specific prohibited act is wrong, and its ability to discourage the conduct shifts to its general reputation for being a reliable judge of what is sufficiently objectionable to merit the condemnation of criminal conviction. If the law has a good reputation, people are more likely to defer to its judgement. If it has a bad reputation, people are more likely to discount its prohibition as one more example of a criminal law focused on something other than imposing liability for wrongs that deserve condemnation.

C. Summary

Internalized moral rules and social norms that are enforced by community sanctions are important sources of compliance with the moral prohibitions of the community. Criminal law rules can contribute to normative forces; they can shape, alter, and guide those forces, but only if the community accepts the law as a legitimate source of moral authority. If the law has this acceptance, debates over legislative proposals or publicity about criminal prosecutions can educate the public about what actions are sufficiently serious to deserve criminal condemnation. If the law has moral authority, it can be a reliable guide in shaping conduct for those cases in which the moral justifications for its prohibitions are not immediately obvious. In an increasingly complex and interdependent society, there may be many cases of this sort, conduct that on analysis proves to be harmful, but is not immediately apparently so. Public conviction and condemnation of an inside trader, for example, can help spread the word that the conduct really is condemnable. Public conviction and condemnation of one who kills another while driving drunk can and probably has helped to spread the word that driving while drunk is morally reprehensible because of its potential to kill.

But the criminal law can only hope to shape moral thinking or to have people follow its rules in ambiguous cases if it has earned a reputation as an institution whose focus is morally condemnable conduct and is seen as giving reliable statements of what is and is not truly condemnable. A criminal law that is seen as having a different criterion for criminalization—such as criminalization whenever the greater penalties of criminal law can provide useful deterrents—is not likely to gain such a reputation. How the law gains—and loses—its reputation as a reliable moral guide is the topic with which we deal next.

IV. The Determinants of Criminal Law's Moral Credibility

Our central point is this: The criminal law's power in nurturing and communicating societal norms and its power to have people defer to it in unanalyzed cases is directly proportional to criminal law's moral credibility. If criminalization or conviction (or decriminalization or refusal to convict) is to have an effect in the norm-nurturing process, it will be because the criminal law has a reputation for criminalizing and punishing only that which deserves moral condemnation, and for decriminalizing and not punishing that which does not. If, instead, the criminal law's reputation is one simply of a collection of rules, which do not necessarily reflect the community's perceptions of moral blameworthiness, then there would be little reason to expect the criminal law to be relevant to the societal debate over what is and is not condemnable and little reason to defer to it as a moral authority. What then are the requirements for a criminal law system to gain this credibility? How can this credibility be lost?

A. *A Central Concern for Doing Justice*

Enhancing the criminal law's moral credibility requires, more than anything, that the criminal law make clear to the public that its overriding concern is doing justice. Therefore, the most important reforms for establishing the criminal law's moral credibility may be those that concern the rules by which criminal liability and punishment are distributed. The criminal law must earn a reputation for (1) punishing those who deserve it under rules perceived as just, (2) protecting from punishment those who do not deserve it, and (3) where punishment is deserved, imposing the amount of punishment deserved, no more, no less. Thus, for example, the criminal law ought to maintain a viable insanity defense that excuses those who are perceived as not responsible for their offense, ought to avoid the use of strict liability (imposing liability in the absence of a culpable state of mind), and ought to limit the use of non-exculpatory defenses.[56] In other words, it ought to adopt rules that distribute liability and punishment according to desert, even if a non-desert distribution appears in the short-run to offer the possibility of reducing crime.

The point is that every deviation from a desert distribution can incrementally undercut the criminal law's moral credibility, which in turn can undercut its ability to help in the creation and internalization of norms and its power to gain compliance by its moral authority. Thus, contrary to the apparent assumptions of past utilitarian debates,[57] such deviations from desert are not cost free, and their cost must be included in the calculation when determining which distribution of liability will most effectively reduce crime.

The law's moral credibility also may depend upon procedural and institutional reforms, as one of us has suggested elsewhere.[58] Some of these include less use of the exclusionary rule to exclude reliable evidence, less plea bargaining for reasons unrelated to genuine factual disputes, less restriction on police power where affected citizens want more, and insistence that non-incarcerative sanctions have sufficient punitive bite to inflict the amount of punishment deserved. Such reforms also would include increased protection of inmates against prison violence, decreased use of dangerousness as a criterion in setting prison terms, and more vigorous police training, discipline, and leadership to bring greater respect and restraint by police in dealing with citizens.

---

[56] It is not feasible to eliminate some non-exculpatory defenses, such as diplomatic immunity, but others can be narrowed if not eliminated. The length of statutes of limitation can be increased to avoid barriers that frustrate prosecutions that the society remains interested in. *See* PAUL H. ROBINSON, 2 CRIMINAL LAW DEFENSES 465-66 (1984). The entrapment defense can be eliminated or, at least, limited to cases of overwhelming coercion. *See* Christopher D. Moore, Comment, *The Elusive Foundation of the Entrapment Defense*, 89 NW. U. L. REV. 1151, 1187-88 (1995).

[57] Consider Shavell's assertion: "Whether or not a party will actually commit an act . . . depends on his perception of the possibility that he will suffer a sanction, either monetary or nonmonetary. A party will commit an act if, and only if, the expected sanction would be less than the expected private benefits. If he decides not to commit an act, he will be said to be deterred." Steven Shavell, *Criminal Law and the Optimal Use of Nonmonetary Sanctions as a Deterrent*, 85 COLUM. L. REV. 1232, 1235 (1985). Certainly if one believes, as Shavell does, that only the threatened sanction affects a person's decision whether to commit an offense, then the extent to which the distribution of sanctions deviates from that perceived as deserved is irrelevant to the calculations. But one may also discount the importance of a distribution of perceived desert if one thinks that the effects of deviation are minor. For the discussion of the danger of any deviation, see *infra* Part VI.

[58] Paul H. Robinson, *Moral Credibility and Crime*, THE ATLANTIC MONTHLY, Mar. 1995, at 72.

B. The Detrimental Effect of Blurring the Criminal-Civil Distinction

The single most important structural reform may be a resharpening of the criminal-civil distinction, which has grown increasingly muddled over the past two decades. Civil law has been "criminalized" with the increased use of punitive damages.[59] But, of greater concern to us, is the "civilization" of the criminal law; the tendency to criminalize actions that are not those that the community would conceive of as condemnable conduct. As Jack Coffee has noted, there is a strong trend toward the criminalization of regulatory offenses, leading to the astounding number of some 300,000 federal "crimes."[60] The problem with this, from our point of view, is that current law has extended criminalization beyond even the domain of traditional *malum prohibitum* offenses, to criminalize conduct that is "harmful" only in the sense that it causes inconvenience for bureaucrats. Thus, most federal regulations are now routinely converted to federal crimes to give the regulators greater leverage in enforcement. Of similar effect is the increased use of strict liability and vicarious liability,[61] common features of civil law but out of place in a criminal system.

Examples of concrete cases will make our point clear. As is well known, individuals and organizations are required to provide large amounts of information to federal, state, and local governments. Providing false information is sometimes a criminalized regulatory offense. If false information knowingly is supplied to evade pollution regulations, taxes, or safety precautions, then the community will agree that this is conduct worthy of criminalization. However, if erroneous information is provided unwittingly or if such information has little bearing on matters of importance, then the community is not likely to see the action as criminal. Or consider a case in which an employer inadvertently fails to put all required information in a federally-required report (as opposed to knowingly putting false information in the report). This may arguably hurt society in some sense, but it is hard to see how; and even if it does, the degree of the injury is so infinitesimal that no one—even those who have full information about the need for the reporting requirement—would think that the failure

59 Punitive damages at civil law may well have been created for a different reason than to mimic criminal liability, and might properly be maintained for this different reason, even in a system that returned to a sharp criminal-civil distinction. Specifically, one might speculate that in cases of intentional wrongdoing, which is where punitive damages typically are imposed, the harm of the violation to the victim is actually greater than where the harm is caused negligently. Note, for example, that the sting of discrimination often lies in its intentionality. The victim of the discrimination suffers more when the motive is clear than where the actions might be accidental. The introduction of punitive damages in cases of intentional torts may well have been out of recognition of this great harm.

60 John C. Coffee, Jr., *Does "Unlawful" Mean "Criminal"?: Reflections on the Disappearing Tort/Crime Distinction in American Law*, 71 B.U. L. REV. 193, 216 (1991).

61 *See id.* at 210-15.

rises to the level of harm that deserves the moral condemnation traditionally associated with criminal conviction. If an adult-appearing twenty-year-old, with high-quality forged ID papers, buys an alcoholic beverage from a harassed bartender, the community has trouble seeing the action as criminal, although a strict liability statute holds the bartender liable and a vicarious liability statute holds the absent bar owner criminally liable.

The law, we suggest, cannot have moral credibility outside of a system with a clear criminal-civil distinction for several reasons. Much of civil law is governed by principles unrelated to desert. While there is some disagreement on the issue, one might well justify, for example, a tort system that uses forms of strict liability or vicarious liability. Even if fairness were adopted as the primary distributive principle for tort liability, no one would claim that tort liability ought to be limited to cases where moral condemnation is appropriate. A mixed criminal-civil system, then, will inevitably have some cases where the result is driven by moral desert and others where it is not. It would be difficult, if not impossible, for such a system to build a reputation with the public as a system devoted exclusively to judging moral blameworthiness. Every instance of liability based upon non-desert criteria would undercut the system's moral credibility, and the "criminal" label could not be used as a clear signal that moral condemnation is deserved. In the cases where the criminal system wishes to wave the red flag of moral condemnation, it would have only an ambiguous pink flag at its disposal. The separation of the two systems, into criminal and civil, enables for the criminal law to focus exclusively on desert and, perhaps more importantly, to make clear to the public that it is so focused. It allows the "criminal" label to be a red flag.[62]

To our minds, the current trend toward blurring the distinction is particularly foolish because it can provide little or no long term gain, even with respect to the very cases brought within the expansion. First, cases of regulatory offenses, strict liability, and vicarious liability are just the cases where the likelihood of a prison sentence is remote;[63] the sentences typically are fines and restitution, the sanctions that are available at civil law. Thus, by criminalizing these offenses, we do not effectively access more severe sanctions.

62 *See* Paul H. Robinson, *The Criminal Civil Distinction and Dangerous Blameless Offenders*, 83 J. CRIM. L. & CRIMINOLOGY 693 (1993); Paul H. Robinson, *The Criminal-Civil Distribution and the Utility of Desert (Symposium on the Intersection of Crime and Tort)*, 76 B.U. L. REV. 201 (1996).

63 The majority of regulatory offenses are misdemeanors, for which a serious prison term is not authorized. Even for the most egregious forms of these offenses, where danger to life or property is created, the likelihood of an incarcerative sentence is not high. In 1989, the number of convicted federal regulatory violators sentenced to prison was: 37 agricultural, 22 antitrust, 2 labor, 24 food and drug. Table 5.17, Sentences imposed in cases terminated in U.S. District Courts, 1992 SOURCEBOOK OF CRIMINAL JUSTICE STATISTICS 488 (1993).

But, of course, access to more severe sanctions is not the reason that many have argued for the extension of the criminal sanction to these cases. More severe sanctions could be provided within the civil system. The arguments for such criminal expansion often focus upon the possibility for the moral stigmatization that criminal liability brings that civil liability does not.[64] Obviously, given our previous discussion, we agree that stigmatization can have a substantial effect in shaping the conduct of potential offenders. But this attempted use of stigmatization is likely to be ineffective because it offends rather than educates the moral code of the community. Passing a statute that criminalizes new conduct does not itself cause that conduct to be perceived as immoral. As the previous discussion suggests, law does not create norms but only acts as a participant in the process by which consensuses are built. Making a regulatory violation a "crime" is not in itself likely to do much to cause people to attach stigma to liability for the violation. Making 300,000 regulatory violations "crimes" makes it even less likely that people will take the resulting liability as evidence that moral condemnation is deserved.[65] Similarly, criminalizing actions that are offenses only from a strict or vicarious liability perspective fails to bring the stigmatization of criminality to bear on those violations. Far from being an independent and respected source of moral authority, a collection of laws of this sort becomes a pettifogging caricature.

More important to us, the expansion of criminal law to punish these various violations is not only ineffective but destructive. The more criminal law's stigmatizing effect is sought to be applied to non-condemnable conduct, the less stigmatizing effect there exists to apply. With each additional non-blameworthy use, the meaning of "criminal liability" becomes incrementally less tied to blameworthiness and incrementally less able to evoke condemnation. As each strict liability case, or vicarious liability case, or case of innocent or trivial conduct is criminalized—such as the woman charged with a criminal offense for picking an eagle feather from the floor of a cage

[64] *See* John C. Coffee, Jr., *"No Soul to Damn: No Body to Kick": An Unscandalized Inquiry Into the Problem of Corporate Punishment*, 79 MICH. L. REV. 386, 424-34 (1981); Brent Fisse, *The Use of Publicity as a Criminal Sanction Against Business Corporations*, 8 MELB. U. L. REV. 107 (1971); Ernest Gellhorn, *Adverse Publicity by Administrative Agencies*, 86 HARV. L. REV. 1380, (1973). *But see* Michael K. Block, *Optimal Penalties, Criminal Law and the Control of Corporate Behavior*, 71 B.U. L. REV. 395 (1991).

[65] We understand that it is sometimes appropriate to apply greater sanctions to regulatory violations. Serious deterrent sanctions can and ought to be imposed but they can as easily and effectively be imposed under an administrative system that is distinct from criminal law and that carries a non-criminal label, perhaps "violation," as many European countries do. Note the similarity to the situation regarding preventive detention—it may be that dangerous people need to be detained, but it is best that the criminal system not be the device for doing it, for to do so carries with it a false claim that these people deserve punishment, which they do not, and this false claim in turn hurts the criminal law's moral credibility.

and using it in a piece of art work that she then sold[66]—more and more people will conclude that the criminal law is being used not to reflect community notions of desert but rather as a tool of a powerful government to intervene destructively in the lives of ordinary people. Expanding the criminal law beyond the bounds of perceived desert initially weakens the stigmatizing effect that that expansion seeks to enlist. Finally, it destroys the stigmatizing effect; criminal penalties for non-condemnable conduct cause the public to sympathize with the person charged, and to despise the legal system that brings the charge. And it is the credibility of the criminal law in general that may be destroyed. Criminal conviction for a violation that the community sees as non-condemnable conduct affects not just the meaning of liability imposed for those offenses but the condemnatory message for all criminal convictions. More on this in Section D, "The Generalization of Disrespect."

C. The Problem of Moral Divisions Within the Community

Our thinking predicts a set of circumstances in which the law's moral credibility will be at risk regardless of the criminalization policy that it chooses. When a society contains groups with a strong and deeply felt moral disagreement, as ours does at this time on the morality of abortion, for example, the situation is destructive of the law's moral credibility and thus its power to gain compliance. More critically, one side will feel that the law is immoral, either because it criminalizes an innocent act, or because it fails to criminalize a morally abhorrent act—in this case fails to criminalize what is seen as a particular kind of murder. Our thinking predicts the destructive consequences that this conflict has. Specifically, it suggests that the "losing" side, at this moment those who wish abortion to be criminal, will lose respect for the legislative process, for the courts that enforce the laws, and eventually, for the legitimacy of the entire criminal law system.[67]

When one thinks that the law does not prohibit murder, one is inclined to "take the law into one's own hands," and we have seen anti-abortion people do this. Note the sequence of steps in what we might call the radicalization of the "pro-life" individual. Perhaps it begins with picketing the abortion clinic and then moves toward more coercive forms of picketing that are arguably legal violations of the rights of others. For some, it moves toward spraying noxious sub-

66 *They Swooped*, THE ECONOMIST, Aug. 19, 1995, at 27.

67 Perspective also predicts that a more diverse society, with its less total agreement on norms, will have more crime, all other things being equal. If this is true, the dramatic difference in crime rates between the United States and Japan, for example, has little to do with criminal justice policies and more to do with the extent of community consensus on norms for condemnable conduct.

stances into the clinics at night—a line has been crossed to committing an undeniable and more substantial legal offense. The next step is setting fire to the abortion clinic, perhaps at night so "no one will get hurt," but certainly this is an act of arson and possibly life-risking. Then death threats and finally the murder of a doctor or nurse who does abortions.

A similar destructive tension exists in Britain at this time. Those who are convinced that animals deserve more humane treatment are outraged at what one is allowed to do to animals under Common Market laws. They protest, seeking to block animal-transporting lorries before they cross the channel. As a recent article comments, for the activists, "[t]he issue is radicalizing . . . . It begins as a protest against abuse of animals. But if the law permits outrages, can it claim moral legitimacy? And if the police protect atrocities, are they not complicit?"[68] Again notice the radicalizing dynamic at work here. The people in question begin as classically law-abiding citizens, typically middle class, middle aged, conservative individuals, but some become willing to commit illegal acts because they regard those acts as morally required. What we have called the process of radicalization occurs most easily and dramatically when there is a group of individuals who are morally opposed to the content of some aspect of the criminal law, but also can occur for a single individual who opposes a law.

D. *The Generalization of Disrespect*

One might discount the danger of such moral disagreements on the ground that people who disapprove of a particular law—be it Prohibition or giving a right to an abortion—can distinguish this "bad" law from the remainder of the system. But we think the possibility for such compartmentalization of disrespect is limited; more likely is what we might call "the generalization of disrespect." Consider the psychological processes that are begun when, for instance, a constitutional amendment prohibiting the use of alcohol is put in place. Examine the situation from the perspective of a person whose cultural traditions have a place for alcohol consumption on certain occasions, and whose individual opinion supports such use.

A law that criminalizes an activity, such as drinking, that I consider not immoral, may initially seem to me to be an isolated and aberrant one, and only the moral validity of that specific law will be denied by me. However, I cannot deny that it was a criminalization action taken by the same authorities that produced the entire criminal code, and I must now be willing to entertain doubts about the moral correctness of the criminalizing of the other activities that those authorities have chosen to sanction. By a process that is easily under-

68 *Also a part of Creation*, THE ECONOMIST, Aug. 19, 1995, at 21.

stood psychologically, if not logically, when the police apprehend me for violation of the drinking laws, I have a revelatory experience canceling the equation of all police actions with the apprehension of wrong-doers, and if the court system convicts, the hypocrisy that I feel that this court manifests is a candidate for generalization to other courts. If I become aware of another instance of the code violating my moral sensibilities, then all these generalizations, and others, are likely to occur. There is a natural process of spreading generalization of disrespect that the reader can intuit here.

The potential for the generalization of disrespect is even greater where the disapproval does not concern a particular controversial law. Where the system generates objectionable case results because of a highly publicized and controversial position, as with Prohibition or the right to an abortion, there is at least the potential to limit the system's discredit to the controversial law. But it is much more frequently the case that the cause of an objectionable result is not so apparent, and in these cases the compartmentalization of disrespect is essentially impossible. The criminal law may conflict with community views in an endless number of ways in its definition of offenses or general principles of liability. An objectionable definition of rape or a counterintuitive rule governing offense culpability requirements, accomplice liability, or causal accountability for a harmful result, or any of a wide range of the general rules relied upon in most cases, can generate an objectionable result. Yet, the specific source of the perceived error will not be apparent to the observer, just the improper result. Without a segregable and visible "bad" law to blame, the observer can do little other than be suspicious of the entire enterprise.[69]

What are the consequences of a generalized discontent with the criminal law and the criminal justice system? Johannes Andenaes remarks that "a certain degree of respect for the formal law is probably essential for the smooth functioning of society. Where it is lacking, law enforcement agencies play a role similar to that of an occupying

69 We would suggest that the dimensions along which generalizations of disrespect occur for legal codes and criminal justice institutions is an urgent topic for psychological research to address. One available example is Jeffrey Kaplan, *Absolute Rescue: Absolutism, Defensive Action and the Resort to Force*, J. TERROR. & POLIT. VIOL. 128 (1993). He uses interview and archival techniques to trace the evolution among the pro-life constituency of a deviant subgroup that has come to accept the use of illegal violent tactics, including killing of abortion workers, to further their aims. To give an example from his work that connects with our argument, it is often the encounter of the pro-lifer with some specific evidence that convinces him of the immorality of abortion—perhaps the sight of an aborted fetus. When that evidence is presented by the pro-lifer to the public, and the legal authorities, and they do not react by outlawing abortion, the moral judgment of the legal authorities is destroyed. Further, encountering the police as the demonstrators were arrested in clinic demonstrations produced more radicalization. "If indifference was the first step in the disillusionment of rescuers with American society, the experience of violence at the hands of those that the civics texts of the 1950's and 1960's held to be the guardians of order was the next great shock." *Id.* at 132.

army in foreign territory . . . ."[70] World War II helped create a popular view that violently opposing the rules imposed by an occupying army is not only not immoral; it is highly moral. A set of laws that is not seen as just is likely to be seen as unjust. When a criminal law offends the moral intuitions of the governed community, the power of the entire criminal code to gain compliance from the community is risked. That there exists such unavoidable sources of injury to the criminal law's moral credibility means that it is that much more important that the criminal law be formulated to maximize its moral credibility in all those respects that are within the control of law makers.

E. Persuasion v. Contempt

The previous discussion in Parts III and IV enable us to clarify a potential ambiguity in our claims. We claim that sometimes the law can convince persons that they should respect and obey the provisions of the criminal code, and internalize those prohibitions as part of their own moral code. But at other times, a conflict between the legal code and individual moral intuitions can lead people to persevere in their own judgements and move toward contempt for the legal code. In this subpart, we specify the conditions under which one or the other outcome will occur, when the code will be persuasive, and when it well be rejected. The psychological literature on persuasion and attitude change provides a basis for doing so.

Social science research suggests that two factors are particularly relevant: the credibility of the source that is attempting to persuade the individual who is the target of the message and the certainty or strength with which the target holds his or her own opinion. Intuition, as well as research, makes clear that the two factors interact as follows: the higher the credibility of the source, the more likely the source's message is to persuade the target;[71] the more strongly or cer-

---

70 JOHANNES ANDENAES, PUNISHMENT AND DETERRENCE 34 (1974).

71 The credibility of a source of communication is generally thought to be a joint function of the source's expertise on the communication topic and the source's trustworthiness as a communicator. One reviewer concludes, "Few areas of research in social psychology have produced results as consistent as the findings that sources high in expertise and/or trustworthiness are more persuasive than those low in these qualities." Glen Hass, *Effects of Source Characteristics on Cognitive Responses and Persuasion*, *in* COGNITIVE RESPONSES IN PERSUASION 141 (Richard Petty et al., eds. 1981). In a major recent review of the attitude literature, the review authors reach the same conclusion: "[S]ubjects typically exhibited greater agreement with the beliefs and attitudes recommended in persuasive messages when the source of these messages were portrayed as higher in expertise [and] trustworthiness." ALICE EAGLY & SHELLY CHAIKEN, THE PSYCHOLOGY OF ATTITUDES 429-30 (1993). McGuire, another leading figure in attitude research, suggests that both expertise and trustworthiness must be jointly present for persuasion to take place. William McGuire, *Attitudes and Attitude Change*, *in* HANDBOOK OF SOCIAL PSYCHOLOGY 233 (Gardiner Lindzey & Elliot Aronson, eds., 3d ed. 1985).

tainly held the original opinion, the less likely the target is to be persuaded to change his or her opinion.[72]

The application of these factors to the present case is fairly direct. The source of the message is the legal code and the intentions and motivations of the drafters who stand behind it.[73] The message is, in essence, that this or that action ought to be criminalized, is wrong, and deserves the specified level of punishment. When will the legal code, as source, be regarded as credible? Much of our argument up to now has been directed to answering this question. We conclude that the legal code is credible to the extent that it has what we have called moral credibility. For the present discussion, we note two components of this credibility. First, the law's credibility is a function of the trustworthiness of its judgement. The code gains trustworthiness by assigning punishment in accord with the principles of justice of the person it is attempting to convince. Second, the law's credibility is a function of its perceived expertise, relevant in this instance when the code asserts that some conduct that is not obviously harmful should be treated as such because the conduct has less apparent but real harmful consequences. The law is saying, in essence, "Trust those of us who drafted the code. We have thought this through. This action is sufficiently harmful or evil that it deserves to be criminalized."

The other factor that influences whether the law will persuade or will draw contempt is the strength of the original opinion on the issue. When are individuals relatively certain of their opinions in the domain of criminal law? People are likely to be certain about the criminality of actions such as killing, arson, and theft—those offenses that historically have been referred to as *malum in se*, "actions that are wrong in and of themselves." Different people may have somewhat different mappings here; as we noted in our section on cultural descensus—abortion and animal cruelty are held to be wrong with great certainty

[72] Eagly & Chaiken, *supra* note 71, reviews the theories that link attitude strength with resistance to change, and the evidence that supports those theories. Theoretically, people are motivationally linked to their strongly held attitudes. They have strong convictions about their rightness and often have publicly committed themselves to this view. Further, strongly held attitudes are generally connected to the values and beliefs that people hold, as well as other attitudes. To change that attitude would require the change in linked values, beliefs, and other attitudes. For both of these theoretical reasons, then, strongly held attitudes can be expected to be resistant to change. Eagly & Chaiken concludes, "we believe that few researchers would disagree with the idea that [the strength of] people's prior attitudes represent an important source of the resistance to attitude change." *Id.* at 589.

[73] McGuire's analysis indirectly supports our extension of the concept of trustworthiness from individuals to institutions and gives a sense of where, among institutions, the trustworthiness of the judicial system might be found: "[I]nstitutional as well as individual sources differ in trustworthiness: Science, medicine, and academic groups tend to elicit a high degree of confidence; the military, police and judiciary somewhat less; followed by business and media leaders, with political officeholders and labor union officials trusted still less." McGuire, *supra* note 71, at 63.

by some. People in general can be expected to be less certain on the actions historically referred to as *malum prohibitum* and may have quite differential certainties produced by past personal histories. A parent whose child has been killed by a drunk driver is likely to hold, with a high degree of certainty, that drunk driving is a serious wrong.

Thus, the social science literature suggests five generalizations, most of which reaffirm conclusions developed in earlier sections. First, the credibility of the legal code depends on it being perceived as a trustworthy guide to assigning liabilities according to the community's perception of which actions are moral, which are immoral, and how severely the immoral actions should be punished. Second, the higher the credibility of the code (that is, the greater its reputation for assigning liabilities according to perceived desert), the more persuasive it will be in convincing people of the correctness of its judgement, and thus, the more they will be inclined to behave in compliance with the code and internalize its judgements as morally appropriate. Third, since people are likely to be relatively less certain about *malum prohibitum* offenses, the code will be more likely to convince people with regard to those offenses. Fourth, when a legal code condemns an action that a person is certain is not morally condemnable, or fails to condemn an action that a person is certain is morally condemnable, its credibility is, at minimum, put at risk, normally lowered, perhaps eventually destroyed, by the spreading processes of radicalization that we have suggested. Fifth, when the criminal law, asserting its expertise, criminalizes an act that is not obviously harmful, if people later discover that the act does not lead to the consequences that they generally regard as properly criminal, the law loses credibility, although not as decisively as in the fourth conclusion above.

Suppose that code drafters wish to adopt a specific proposal that is known to be in conflict with the moral intuitions of the community or a section of the community. They face a difficult but not impossible task; they must convince the community that the community's intuitions are wrong and that justice would be better served by distributing liabilities according to the new principle. From our point of view, they must engage in this persuasive task directly and forcibly and assess the success of their efforts. If they do not succeed in convincing the community, they then risk lowered credibility if they nonetheless adopt the proposal. When, as sometimes happens, the code provisions are adopted without this sort of educational debate, the potential for community contempt for the code has been established, and that potentiality is likely to become an actuality when the first publicized prosecution for violation of the new provision takes place.

F. Summary

We have every reason to think that, more than any other body of law, criminal law plays a central role in the creation of new norms, and that the criminal law can have a direct effect in gaining compliance when it is seen as a moral authority. And both of these sources of influence by the criminal law—in building and maintaining norms and in gaining compliance through moral authority—depend upon the criminal law's moral credibility with the community. The criminal law's moral credibility with the community, we argue, requires a distribution of liability that follows the community's perceptions of principles of deserved punishment and requires a separate and distinct criminal justice system, a system which can demonstrate its exclusive focus on blameworthiness and can effectively convey the special condemnation of criminal conviction. This credibility is risked when the legal system criminalizes actions that the community regards as not criminal or does not criminalize actions that the community regards as serious moral violations that deserve criminal condemnation. A society that contains groups in deep disagreement about what should count as a criminal offense is a society in which the moral authority of the criminal law is in tension and at risk.

V. Determining Community Perceptions of Desert

A. Code Drafting to Community Standards

We have argued for a criminal law based upon principles of desert, specifically, principles of desert as shared by the community. We need to say more about how such a distribution of liability would be determined. We need to distinguish our view of such a law-drafting system from some of the caricatures of it that could be advanced. Basing the criminal law on community standards does not mean resolving individual cases as the public or press see them in the heat of the moment. We know that the public and the press can lose perspective when buffeted by the biases and prejudices inspired by the facts of any particular case. The tendency of people to be more sympathetic to defendants more like themselves is well documented.[74] Nor does our position support legislators' hastily passing laws driven by public reactions to some recent court case that outrages public opinion.

We envision code-drafting being done by commissions of lawyers, criminal law experts, and social scientists. They would seek community input by means of research studies in which respondents make judgments of cases that elicit their principles for the just distribution of liability. Community judgments on the minimal requirements for

[74] *See, e.g.*, Jeffrey T. Frederick, The Psychology of the American Jury 166-67 (1987).

criminalization of conduct, on the justification of conduct that otherwise would be criminal, on the conditions under which wrongful conduct should be excused, and on the grading of offenses would, at a minimum, have claims on the code drafters' attentions. The code drafters would incorporate such shared community intuitions into the code, unless they had well-worked-out reasons not to do so. If they had such reasons, they would make clear what they were, and attempt to educate the community on their validity. The commission's deliberations would be public, and the maximum attention of the community would be sought.

The output of the commission, of course, would be submitted to the legislature, which is the institution to which our constitutional system grants standing to make laws. Many if not most of the commission's recommendations would be non-controversial, especially because they will generally track community views. But where there is disagreement among the community, the commission will have no consensus to report, and it will be in these instances of disagreements that it will be left primarily to the legislature itself to sort out the position that the law will take. Given our general account, we cannot deny the problems inherent in such cases, although we suspect that their existence is rare. Some benefits may arise when the general public sees genuine moral disagreement on one or two of these issues, but these are the truly difficult cases, in which the potential for the radicalization of some segment of the community is present.

We stress the importance of the moral intuitions of the community as a valued beginning for code drafting, followed by a process of code drafting done in public with an eye to educating and involving the community. The establishment of public understanding of the criminal law provides the best chance of a code gaining the respect of the community, and surviving the occasional case of deep community disagreement.

We do not underestimate how complex a task it is to determine liability rules that will capture such shared community intuitions of justice. But, as we show in our recent book, *Justice, Liability, and Blame: Community Views and the Criminal Law*, it is a feasible undertaking given the state of current social science methodology,[75] and it is also an important undertaking. Over the long term, it is by this means that the system will earn its moral credibility with the community.

---

[75] Paul H. Robinson & John M. Darley, Justice, Liability, and Blame: Community Views and the Criminal Law 217-28 (1995).

B. *The Content of a Community-Based Code*

Based on our preliminary research, a community-based criminal code would retain most of the foundational principles on which current criminal law doctrine is based: a focus on a person's level of culpability, the extent of the harm attempted or risked, the degree to which that harm actually came about, and the presence of any justifying or excusing conditions.

There seems a strong consensus, for example, that the degree of an offender's liability should follow to a considerable degree the person's level of culpability toward the conduct constituting the offense. However, for most offenses other than homicide, current codes set a minimum level of culpability, frequently recklessness, and assign a constant degree of liability once that minimum level is reached. The respondents in our research studies generally imposed higher degrees of liability as the culpability level of the offender increased above the minimum required for liability. A person who commits a crime purposefully, rather than recklessly, receives a stiffer prison sentence from our respondents, and this seems reasonable to us.[76]

Our respondents also recognized and granted validity to many of the excusing conditions that are recognized in criminal law. Specifically, they judged that the effects of mental dysfunction could exculpate a person, and they based their judgments of whether to grant an insanity defense on the degree of cognitive and control dysfunction, as do most legal codes.[77] Our respondents similarly recognized and gave validity to the broad notion of justification defenses—defenses that approve of and therefore exculpate a person for normally unlawful conduct in certain circumstances, such as self-defense or citizen's arrest to prevent commission of a crime.[78]

But our research suggests that a community-based code would differ from current codes in some important respects. Systematic disagreements between the criminal law and our community of respondents were not uncommon. Our respondents disagreed with the Model Penal Code's treatment of various kinds of rape. For instance, where forcible rape has occurred, the Code gives a mitigation to the rapist if the victim had been "a voluntary social companion" of the rapist who had "previously permitted him sexual liberties" or if the victim is the rapist's spouse.[79] Our respondents do not.[80]

Similarly, our respondents do not agree with the Model Penal Code's assertion that a substantial step toward committing a crime

[76] *Id.* at 169-70.

[77] *Id.* ch. 5.

[78] *Id.* ch. 3.

[79] MODEL PENAL CODE § 213.1(1), .1(1)(d)(ii).

[80] ROBINSON & DARLEY, *supra* note 75, at 160-69.

alone ought to be sufficient grounds for punishment. And, even for very advanced attempts, they disagree with the Code's grading attempts the same as the completed offense.[81]

Our book gives a more complete characterization of the code that would emerge if one took community intuitions as a basis for criminal sentencing practices. Here we have only described enough to give the reader some sense of what the law would look like and to dispel any notions that it would be excessively savage, excessively lenient, or in marked deviation from the general outlines of existing criminal laws.

C. Apparent Deviations from Deserved Punishment: Amount, Method, and Forgiveness

Would the liability and sentencing practices we recommend ever deviate from strict reliance on just desert? Our preferred answer is "no," but this need not mean that considerations of rehabilitation or incapacitation need never enter into decisions about the fate of specific criminals. While the amount of punishment to be imposed must match the amount required by community perceptions of desert, the method of inflicting that punishment is generally irrelevant to the goal of desert.[82] Thus, once judges ensure that the total amount of punishment is the amount deserved, they are free to select a sanctioning method that will maximize rehabilitation or incapacitation (or deterrence or any other worthwhile crime reduction strategy) without fear that their selection of method may endanger the criminal law's moral credibility. To do this, the judge need only take account of the "punishment bite" of each sanctioning method used and ensure that the total "bite" of all sanctions add up to the amount deserved, not noticeably more or less.[83] We have recently published research on public perceptions of the punitive bite of alternative sanctioning methods that can serve as a guide to judges in constructing sentences.[84] It shows that non-incarcerative sentences frequently can be used to inflict the punishment deserved, even for many non-minor offenses.

A second possibility exists, which we do not favor. In some cases, in which the possibility of rehabilitation of the criminal is thought to be high (preferably documentably high), the sentencing system may decide to assign a rehabilitative course of treatment to the criminal

---

81 *Id.* Study 1.

82 *See* Paul H. Robinson, *Desert, Crime Control, Disparity, and Units of Punishment*, *in* PENAL THEORY AND PRACTICE: TRADITION AND INNOVATION IN CRIMINAL JUSTICE 93 (Antony Duff et al. eds., 1994). *But see* Dan Kahan, *What Do Alternative Sanctions Mean?*, 63 U. CHI. L. REV. 591 (1996).

83 *Id.* at 593.

84 Robert Harlow et al., *The Severity of Intermediate Penal Sanctions: A Psychophysical Scaling Approach for Obtaining Community Perceptions*, 11 J. QUANTITATIVE CRIMINOLOGY 71 (1995).

that does not meet the just desert criterion. What the system is doing here is essentially deciding to forgive the individual (by forgoing the deserved punishment for the crime) because it is thought that this increases the possibility of making that person less likely to commit crimes in the future.

Because it deviates from a desert-based system, we do not favor this option. However, it at least begins with recognizing the desert-based considerations and deviates from them openly, giving reasons for doing so. That is, it acknowledges that there is something to be *forgiven*; it acknowledges the offender's blameworthiness. This might well be a tenable system if it were limited to cases in which research suggested that shared community notions might support such a show of forgiveness while nonetheless agreeing that the offender was blameworthy. For example, research might show that a genuine feeling of great remorse, evidenced by acts of restitution performed before arrest, was one of several preconditions to forgiveness. If that were so, one could limit the damaging effect on such a forgiveness program by limiting it to such cases.

D. Desert and Dangerousness

A desert-based system such as we advocate would not disguise lengthy incarceration based on predictions of dangerousness as legitimate punishment. However, it could include more severe sentences for second-time offenders. Andrew von Hirsch has developed an account of why repeat offenses may justify higher sentences under a desert theory.[85] Community intuitions may mirror his reasoning. Thus, the system might give a "first offense discount" in many, even most cases, on the theory that the absence of any prior offense suggests that this conduct may be an aberration and may not truly reflect the offender's free choice, but rather a response to the pressures of the peculiar situation—a kind of mini-mitigation for coercion, extreme emotional disturbance, or the like. Alternatively one could conceive of the harsher sentence for a second-time offender as giving an extra slap on the wrist to an offender who has previously been reprimanded and nonetheless committed another violation, thumbing his nose at the society's law, as it were. We will be more inclined to support an increase in sentence for a second-time offender only after research suggests that the public has these intuitions.

Obviously, a reliance upon these theories might seem to generate a distribution of liability that keeps more dangerous offenders (that is, repeat offenders) in jail longer. It might well have that effect, but the likelihood of future criminality would be only a useful coincidence; it

85 *See* Andrew von Hirsch, *Desert and Previous Convictions in Sentencing*, 65 MINN. L. REV. 591 (1981).

would play no role in the distribution of liability. Note also that these two desert-based theories would not operate for all dangerous offenders but only for some; each would apply only to a specific set of cases that logically followed from the rationale. Finally, note that the amount of adjustment in sentence, even for cases where both theories are relied upon, would be rather modest; neither the first-offense discount nor the nose-thumbing penalty concerns factors that are of central concern in determining desert. They certainly would not support the kinds of dramatic increases for apparent dangerousness that we see in current practice.[86]

We should note that we do not think that a society must stand defenseless in the face of dangerous offenders. Our point is simply that it is bad policy to pretend that incarceration based upon a prediction of future criminality can be justified as "punishment," because to do so undercuts the law's moral credibility in assigning deserved punishment for past offenses. Society does and should detain people who are shown to be dangerous. Sometimes that showing, that prediction, is based on an assessment of mental state, sometimes it is based on criminal records. However, we ought to be open about what we are doing, and we ought to structure that incarceration to match the rationale. Specifically, incarceration based upon a claim of dangerousness ought to be under conditions consistent with its non-punitive purpose, much like the conditions of confinement of a person with a contagious disease that we confine for our protection. This does not describe current prisons. Even more importantly, such confinement ought to be subject to regular reviews to confirm the confinee's continuing dangerousness, a practice abandoned under the current "three strikes and you're out" legislation that provides for life imprisonment without possibility of parole.[87]

A recent program in the State of Washington, which civilly commits sexual predators if they are judged to remain dangerous after the expiration of their prison term, follows the course we suggest, and we

86 It has been argued that people, often in their function as jurors, use the prison system as a means of locking up dangerous people, and that this suggests that people may conceive of dangerousness as contributing to an actor's blameworthiness and as grounds for deserved punishment. We agree that people under the current system often imprison (or impose the death penalty) on defendants who they think are dangerous. It does not follow, however, that people are ignorant of or indifferent to the difference between imprisonment as punishment for a past crime and incarceration to prevent a future crime. That the distinction is widely recognized is shown by the nearly universal practice of having a separate civil commitment system, distinct from criminal commitment. People are willing to use criminal commitment to protect society against defendants perceived as dangerous because the current system—with its limitations on the use of civil commitment—gives them no alternative means of protection. If they were given the choice, we think lay persons would elect civil commitment rather than criminal if they thought a defendant was dangerous but did not deserve punishment. The issue can be resolved by empirical research.

87 *See* Robinson, *supra* note 35, at 714-16.

note that it is much maligned. Obviously, it is difficult to generate a method of holding sexual predators in custody that does not have punitive elements, and those making the predictions of dangerousness may be swayed by considerations of what would happen if they predicted non-dangerousness for a predator who then offended again. Still, the proposal almost certainly makes the situation better for those incapacitated for "dangerousness" than when they are instead sentenced to long terms or life terms of punitive confinement in prisons, with no right of review for dangerousness. We suspect that some of the criticism of this admittedly imperfect system of preventive detention comes from people who do not realize how rampant is the use of dangerousness in current practice as the primary justification for lengthy prison sentences.[88]

VI. Attempts at Justifying Deviations from Desert

In the previous section we considered some possible deviations from a liability and punishment system based on just desert, and showed how those deviations are more apparent than real: Greater use of non-incarcerative sanctions is not necessarily inconsistent with a distribution of punishment according to perceived desert; and forgiveness of some offenders is not necessarily detrimental to the criminal law's moral credibility. In this section we consider some deviations from just desert that may seem attractive but that we regard as undesirable.

Some utilitarians apparently believe that only the threat of sanction or lack thereof determines whether a person will commit an offense.[89] But other utilitarians might agree with our claim that personal morality and interpersonal relations have effect and that the operation of these forces can be influenced by altering community perceptions of the criminal law's moral credibility. They nonetheless may be tempted by a system that intentionally and regularly deviates from a distribution of criminal liability according to perceived desert.[90] They might argue that the crime-control value of one or another deviation from desert outweighs the incremental loss in the criminal law's moral credibility.[91]

88 Notice how a consistent focus on just desert and blameworthiness clarifies issues. If one does not focus on the proper proportionality between blameworthiness and punishment, then it is not apparent that the current sentencing practices are as disproportionate as they are, and that they create sentences that the community would perceive as unjust.

89 *See, e.g.*, Shavell, *supra* note 57.

90 To do this, they would have to overcome the objections to the utilitarian approaches that we describe in Part I of this article.

91 For a discussion of how such a hybrid distributive principle might operate, see Paul H. Robinson, *Hybrid Principles for the Distribution of Criminal Sanctions*, 82 Nw. U. L. Rev. 19 (1987).

Such a system of selective deviations would be an improvement over our current state in which little regard is paid to the effect of deviations from desert. Nonetheless, we suggest that the utilitarian be cautious here. If we had perfect data on the dynamics of the forces at work and their relative effects, the cost-benefit analysis would be clear. We do not, of course, and are not likely to have even a crude understanding of the dynamics in our lifetimes. We can only speculate about the relative effects. Let us explain why we think we should err on the side of caution in deviating from the principles of perceived desert.

A. *The Problem of Attributions to the Criminal Justice System: Reputation and Motive*

How will deviations from desert affect the criminal justice system's reputation for doing justice? The general principle that we shall appeal to here is referred to psychologically as an attributional principle. Those studying persons perception have realized that the task that perceivers take on, when they are examining the actions of others, is to determine the dispositions of the other, the abilities the other possesses, the personality, and the immediate or long-term intentions. Dispositional perception of this sort is referred to as "attributional perception."[92] One not only makes attributions to individuals, but to institutions set up by persons; we all can make sense of the question of whether a legal system is "fair." The specific attributional problem here is one of making sense of the cumulative meaning of actions that seem to deviate from the announced purposes of that institution. What conclusions are drawn, what attributions are made, if the system seems to operate by a set of rules (punishment according to just desert) or claims to operate by the set of rules but occasionally deviates from those rules? What conditions determine when those who observe the system conclude that the system does not, in fact, live by the set of rules that it professes? When, in other words, does it lose its "reputation"?

One attributional rule involves whether the deviations are repeated. All of us are aware that there are many reasons that a system could occasionally come to a wrong outcome; rare deviations do not signify. However, repeated ones do signify, especially when the deviations seem to point to the same underlying cause; regular deviations that fall in a regular explanatory pattern, even if they are minor, could

92 The seminal publications on attribution theory are: Edward Jones & Keith Davis, *From Acts to Dispositions*, *in* 2 ADVANCES IN EXPERIMENTAL SOCIAL PSYCHOLOGY 219-66 (L. Berkowitz ed., 1965) and Harold Kelley, *Attribution Theory in Social Psychology*, *in* 15 NEBRASKA SYMPOSIUM ON MOTIVATION 192-238 (D. Levine ed., 1967).

do much to hurt the system's reputation.[93] This would be true even if the number and extent of the deviations were small in comparison to the system's overall output of decisions.[94]

This reflects the fact that a large part of preserving the reputation of a person or an organization is to cause others to see that the person or organization is genuinely motivated to "play by the rules" that it espouses. An error can be forgiven if it is seen as "out of character." This is true of personal reputations; we suggest that it is also true of the reputations of larger entities.[95] People know that they cannot know what all aspects of the criminal justice system are doing at all times. Their view of the system is likely to be governed by what they think the system is trying to do, by what they see as its motivation to do justice. The criminal law's reputation may depend on its public commitment to never intentionally deviating from the principles of perceived desert, while conceding that inadvertent deviations are unavoidable. To admit a policy that intentionally authorizes failures in administering liability and punishment according to desert is to render the system suspect in all its workings.

B. The Advantages of a Morally Credible System

Not only is it easy to underestimate the detriment of intentional deviation from desert, it also is easy to underestimate the benefit of maintaining the system's moral credibility. Unlike the threat of legal punishment, the sources of compliance discussed here are not dependent on the effectiveness of the system in arresting, convicting, and punishing offenders. The real sources of compliance power—a person's family or friends and the person's own conscience—can know of an offender's violation even if the authorities do not or cannot prove it. Thus, harnessing the compliance powers of social group and personal morality can reduce current crime levels even if policing and prosecuting functions cannot be made more effective.

Note as well that these sources of compliance power do not have the staggering costs of increased enforcement, adjudication, and imprisonment that would be required if reduced crime were to be achieved through deterrence (or incapacitation or rehabilitation). Again, their power comes not from catching and punishing every

---

93 Harold Kelley, *Causal Schemata and the Attribution Process*, *in* ATTRIBUTION: PERCEIVING THE CAUSES OF BEHAVIOR 151-74 (Edward E. Jones et al. eds., 1971).

94 In the case of sentences handed out by the criminal justice system, this process is exacerbated by mass media reports that focus on what they see as system failures. Lay persons tend not to see the larger picture and rarely are able to put mass media reports in perspective. (The more cynical observation is that news is more "newsworthy" when it exaggerates the significance and extent of a failure of justice.).

95 *See* BERNARD WEINER, JUDGMENTS OF RESPONSIBILITY: A FOUNDATION FOR THE THEORY OF SOCIAL CONDUCT 212-14 (1995).

criminal but rather from the system's moral power in obviously trying to do justice. That educational and symbolic function can be served in the adjudication of whatever cases are brought to the system, even if many are not. Nor does crime reduction through these mechanisms require the increased intrusions of privacy that more effective crime investigation would require or the increased errors in adjudication that easier prosecution rules would require. In other words, harnessing the social and personal forces of compliance offers the possibility of better compliance at lower cost.

We have argued that a criminal law based on community principles of perceived desert can enhance the law's compliance power and that a criminal law that is seen systematically to deviate from those principles reduces that power. Here we should point out that our account of the role of criminal law assigns it a less powerful role in producing law-abiding behavior than do the traditional theories. One reason for the attractiveness of deterrence theory, for instance, lies in its claims of having great power to autonomously produce compliance. (We have shown the moral and empirical fallaciousness of that possibility earlier in Part II.) We make no such claim for the legal code; its role is secondary and contributive rather than primary and determinative of law-abiding behavior. This seems to us to be an accurate representation of the true state of affairs, and if adopted, might have the useful function of removing from public debate some of the unrealistically high expectations about what can be accomplished by the manipulation of criminal liability and punishment.

VII. Summary and Conclusion

The evidence is reasonably clear that the power of interpersonal relationships and internalized norms to prevent crime is dramatically greater than that of official sanctions. The ability of the law to harness these forces is less clear. Studies suggest that increasing the law's moral credibility can enhance its compliance power, but the studies are preliminary and many important questions remain unanswered. Will research confirm our speculations about the mechanisms by which a morally credible criminal law can increase compliance? Will research confirm our speculations about the practices that most undercut the system's moral credibility and those that would most enhance it?

It will take some time for social scientists to answer these questions, but we need not wait for those answers before we make some changes in what we do. Most importantly, it is clear that a utilitarian calculus in determining the rules for the distribution of criminal liability and punishment must take account of real-world costs that come from deviating from the community's principles of deserved punishment. The costs and benefits of moral credibility may be more difficult to measure than those of the factors typically taken into account by utilitarian calculations in the past, but if they are more powerful in their effect than the other factors, to ignore them risks rendering the calculation meaningless.

While we do not know with any certainty the degree of importance of the criminal law's moral credibility, we can be reasonably sure that it has some. Thus, a corollary to the above is that we ought not tolerate any deviation from desert, or any other measure that may undercut moral credibility, without a clear and significant benefit. And even then, we counsel a close examination of long-term as well as short-term effects. This suggests a number of reforms, which we have mentioned.

Where have we left the long-running debate between desert and utilitarian justifications for punishment? We have used essentially utilitarian reasoning to argue for a desert-based system of criminal law. More specifically, we have argued that people obey the law not so much because they are fearful of being apprehended by the criminal justice system, but because they care about what their social group thinks of them and because they regard obedience as morally appropriate. Criminal laws based on community standards of deserved punishment enhance this obedience. We conclude that desert distribution of liability happens to be the distribution that has the greatest utility, in the sense of avoiding crime. Thus, utility theorists ought to support liabilities assigned according to such a desert-based system.

If our arguments are accepted, we have, in some sense, united two groups of criminal justice philosophers that have characteristically been thought to be at hopeless odds. Desert-based punishment proponents assert that what matters in liability and sentencing is doing justice; utilitarians require an analysis of the consequences of a liability assignment system to justify it, characteristically a showing of how the system is maximally effective in avoiding crimes in the future. We suggest that while these two sides do not agree on the reasons for imposing punishment, if they agree with our analysis, they can, incredibly enough, agree on how punishment should be distributed.

We have, perhaps, united utilitarians and just desert thinkers, but we may have united them in opposition to our recommendations. Liability and punishment should be distributed according to a desert-based distribution system, but the advocate for desert-based punishment systems may not be greatly pleased by this. Our desert-based system is importantly different from the standard one. In the standard desert-based system, what a criminal actually deserves is derived from some underlying systematization of moral principles; in our analysis, desert is not derived from any philosophically-based, coherently-reasoned systematization, but rather is patterned on the principles the community uses in assessing blameworthiness.

Has the utilitarian won the battle if our recommendations are accepted? In one sense, yes; we have used utilitarian arguments to justify our desert-based liability and sentencing scheme. However, the results of that analysis install the kind of liability distribution system that the utilitarians have argued against for decades. Worse, from their point of view, they cannot reject our arguments on principle, as they have rejected desert arguments in the past. If future investigations support the power we claim for the law's moral credibility, there is a powerful utilitarian argument for the adoption of a desert-based criminal law.

If our recommendations are adopted, the utilitarian criminal justice system is in some ways constrained in its distribution of liability, but it is freed from another constraint. During the past decades of the standard utilitarian approach, some criminal justice systems and institutions have had their charters set to a strictly utilitarian purpose, which seemed to exclude considerations of desert.[96] Our thesis suggests that a charge to prevent crime is, as a practical matter, a charge primarily to do justice—to consider just desert—for that will reduce crime more than distributive criteria that ignore desert. Thus, our thesis not only allows these systems and institutions to take account of desert but in fact demands it.

The central point that we seek to make is this—there is practical value, not just "philosophical" value, in maintaining the criminal law's focus on moral blameworthiness. What we have in the past taken to be instances of injustice imposed by the criminal justice system on some individual, when the just desert principle is violated, we ought to understand now as instances of injustice imposed on us all, since each such instance erodes the criminal law's moral credibility and, thus, its power to protect us all.

96 *See, e.g.*, Alaska Const. art. I, § 12; State v. Chaney, 477 P.2d 441 (Alaska 1970); G.A. Res 152, U.N. GAOR, 46th Sess. Supp. No. 49, at 12, U.N. Doc. A/152 (1992) (establishing UN Commission on Crime Prevention).

[12]

SOCIAL INFLUENCE, SOCIAL MEANING, AND DETERRENCE

Dan M. Kahan[*]

INTRODUCTION

WHY do individuals commit crimes? What policies should a community adopt to discourage criminality?

The economic conception of deterrence bases its answers on the assumption that individuals behave rationally to maximize their utility. Individuals commit crimes, this account predicts, when the expected utility of law-breaking exceeds the expected disutility of punishment. To promote obedience, the community should adopt the most cost-effective policies for raising the price of crime. This model yields prescriptions on a diverse range of subjects—from the optimal tradeoff between probability of conviction and severity of punishment,[2] to the relative advantages of public and private investments in discouraging crime,[3] to the most efficient form of punishment.[4]

---

[*] Assistant Professor, University of Chicago Law School. I am grateful to the Russell J. Parsons Fund for Faculty Research at the University of Chicago Law School for its generous financial support; to Richard Craswell, Randal Picker, Richard Ross, Stephen Schulhofer, and the students in my Winter 1997 Criminal Law Seminar for helpful discussions; to Albert Alschuler, Richard Epstein, Elizabeth Garrett, Lawrence Lessig, John Lott, Tracey Meares, Martha Nussbaum, Richard Pildes, Eric Posner, Richard Posner, and Cass Sunstein for instructive written comments; to participants in the workshops at the University of Pennsylvania Law School and at the University of Virginia Law School for probing questions; and to Kenworthey Bilz for phenomenal research assistance.

[1] The classic exposition is Jeremy Bentham, An Introduction to the Principles of Morals and Legislation (J.H. Burns & H.L.A. Hart eds., The Athlone Press 1970) (1780). For contemporary accounts, see Gary S. Becker, Crime and Punishment: An Economic Approach, 76 J. Pol. Econ. 169 (1968); Richard A. Posner, An Economic Theory of the Criminal Law, 85 Colum. L. Rev. 1193 (1985); Steven Shavell, Criminal Law and the Optimal Use of Nonmonetary Sanctions as a Deterrent, 85 Colum. L. Rev. 1232 (1985).

[2] See Becker, supra note 1, at 191-93; George J. Stigler, The Optimum Enforcement of Laws, 78 J. Pol. Econ. 526, 530-31 (1970).

[3] See, e.g., Omri Ben-Shahar & Alon Harel, Blaming the Victim: Optimal Incentives for Private Precautions Against Crime, 11 J.L. Econ. & Org. 434 (1995) [hereinafter

My goal in this Article is to draw attention to two phenomena that the standard economic conception of deterrence overlooks. The first is the contribution that *social influence* makes to individuals' decisions to commit crimes. The second is the role that regulation of *social meaning* can play in determining the direction of social influence.

Individuals don't decide to commit crimes in isolation; rather, their decisions interact with and reinforce each other in various ways. In particular, individuals are much more likely to commit crimes when they perceive that criminal activity is widespread. In that circumstance, they are likely to infer that the risk of being caught for a crime is low. They might also conclude that relatively little stigma or reputational cost attaches to being a criminal; indeed, if criminal behavior is common among their peers, they may even view such activity as status enhancing. Finally, in a community in which crime is perceived to be rampant, individuals are less likely to form moral aversions to criminality. By *social influence*, I refer generically to how individuals' perceptions of each others' values, beliefs, and behavior affect their conduct, including their decisions to engage in crime.[5]

The law can shape these perceptions. The public expects criminal law to protect it from harm, but it also understands the

Ben-Shahar & Harel, Blaming the Victim]; Alon Harel, Efficiency and Fairness in Criminal Law: The Case for a Criminal Law Principle of Comparative Fault, 82 Cal. L. Rev. 1181 (1994); Omri Ben-Shahar & Alon Harel, The Economics of the Law of Criminal Attempts: A Victim-Centered Perspective (Sept. 1995) (unpublished manuscript, on file with the Virginia Law Review Association); Keith N. Hylton, Optimal Law Enforcement and Victim Precaution, 27 Rand J. Econ. 197 (1996); Jan J.M. van Dijk, Understanding Crime Rates: On the Interactions between the Rational Choices of Victims and Offenders, 34 Brit. J. Criminology 105, 114 (1994).

[4] See, e.g., John R. Lott, Jr., Do We Punish High Income Criminals Too Heavily?, 30 Econ. Inquiry 583 (1992); Richard A. Posner, Optimal Sentences for White-Collar Criminals, 17 Am. Crim. L. Rev. 409 (1980); Joel Waldfogel, Are Fines and Prison Terms Used Efficiently? Evidence on Federal Fraud Offenders, 38 J.L. & Econ. 107 (1995).

[5] I take the term from the work of Elliot Aronson and other social psychologists. See Elliot Aronson, The Social Animal 6 (7th ed. 1995) (defining the concept of "social influence" as used in social psychology); David J. Schneider, Introduction to Social Psychology 306 (1988) ("social influence" refers to the "obvious but important fact that much of our behavior is affected by what others say and do"); see also Robert B. Cialdini, Influence: Science and Practice (3d ed. 1993) (describing as principle of "social proof" the tendency of individuals to "*view a behavior as correct in a given situation to the degree that [they] see others performing it.*").

kinds of things the law punishes, and how much, to express shared valuations.[6] Individuals also draw such inferences from the behavior of other individuals; when the law regulates such behavior, it can either accentuate or mute these signals. By the regulation of *social meaning*, I refer to all of the ways in which the law creates and shapes information about the kinds of behavior that members of the public hope for and value, as well as the kinds they expect and fear.[7]

The phenomena of social influence and social meaning matter for deterrence. The decisions of individuals to commit crimes are influenced by their perception of others' beliefs and intentions; the law shapes information about what those beliefs and intentions are. It follows that a community that wants to deter crime should concern itself not just with the effect of particular policies on the price of crime but with the statements that those policies make (and enable others to make) about the public's attitudes toward criminal behavior.

This strategy—which I will call the "social influence conception of deterrence"—will sometimes generate policy insights that elude the standard economic conception. Given the power of social influence, laws that shape individuals' perceptions of each others' beliefs and intentions, for example, may often turn out to be the most cost-effective means of deterring crime. Cracking down on aggressive panhandling, prostitution, open gang activity and other visible signs of disorder may be justifiable on this ground, since disorderly behavior and the law's response to it are cues about the community's attitude toward more serious forms of criminal wrongdoing.

In addition, the social influence conception of deterrence will sometimes subvert the prescriptions of the standard economic conception. Under the standard view, for example, it may sometimes seem efficient to rely more heavily on a severe pen-

---

[6] See, e.g., Dan M. Kahan & Martha C. Nussbaum, Two Conceptions of Emotion in Criminal Law, 96 Colum. L. Rev. 269, 351-52 (1996).

[7] I am following the lead of Lawrence Lessig here. See Lawrence Lessig, The Regulation of Social Meaning, 62 U. Chi. L. Rev. 943 (1995); see also Dan M. Kahan, What Do Alternative Sanctions Mean?, 63 U. Chi. L. Rev. 591 (1996) (discussing social meanings of different types of punishment); Cass R. Sunstein, Social Norms and Social Roles, 96 Colum. L. Rev. 903 (1996) (discussing role of government in the management of social norms).

alty than on a high probability of conviction (which requires large investments in law enforcement). But if individuals infer widespread criminality from a low probability of apprehension, the power of social influence could more than offset any efficiency gains from this tradeoff. Likewise, visible efforts by private citizens to protect themselves from crime may convey the message that criminality is rampant. If so, then it might make sense for the government to assume a greater share of the burden in preventing crime than the standard view suggests is optimal. Or if the expressive significance of one form of punishment (say, imprisonment) more effectively expresses community disapprobation than does another one (say, fines or community service), the effect of the former in directing social influence may justify selecting it even if the latter imposes the same price on crime at a lesser social cost.

I will present my argument in three Parts. In the first, I examine the phenomenon of social influence. In the second, I discuss the phenomenon of social meaning. And in the third, I put the two together, identifying their policy implications for a range of issues in criminal law.

I. SOCIAL INFLUENCE AND CRIME

The concept of social influence refers to a pervasive and familiar phenomenon in our economic and social life: namely, that individuals tend to conform their conduct to that of other individuals.[8] When we say that a particular style of clothing or model of car is in fashion, for example, we are recognizing that consumers attach value to it precisely because other consumers do.[9] Comparable dynamics inform entertainment markets, where the popularity of a particular television show or film can feed on itself because of the value that viewers assign to seeing what oth-

[8] See Aronson, supra note 5, at 13-55 (discussing factors that influence conformity); Cialdini, supra note 5, at 94-133 (arguing that individuals rely on the actions of others as cues indicating appropriate behavior).

[9] See, e.g., Sushil Bikhchandani, David Hirshleifer & Ivo Welch, A Theory of Fads, Fashion, Custom, and Cultural Change as Informational Cascades, 100 J. Pol. Econ. 992 (1992); H. Leibenstein, Bandwagon, Snob, and Veblen Effects in the Theory of Consumers' Demand, 64 Q.J. Econ. 183 (1950).

ers have seen.[10] Social influence often drives political behavior: the value that citizens attach to backing a winner can produce a bandwagon of support for a political candidate;[11] the aversion that citizens feel toward bucking popular opinion can induce them to adopt popular views as their own[12] or to voice support for policies that they actually believe to be misguided.[13] Decisions to commit suicide exhibit similar patterns of interdependence,[14] as do decisions to make charitable donations.[15]

In light of the pervasiveness of social influence, it would be odd if it *didn't* affect decisions to engage in crime. Evidence that it does abounds.

The contribution of social influence is most obvious in "mob" offenses such as looting and lynching. Individuals who would not steal or assault by themselves are often willing to do so as part of a crowd.[16] The severity and atrocity of the harm that

[10] See generally Gary S. Becker, A Note on Restaurant Pricing and Other Examples of Social Influences on Price, 99 J. Pol. Econ. 1109 (1991) (including social interactions in economic modeling of consumer demand).

[11] See, e.g., Larry M. Bartels, Expectations and Preferences in Presidential Nominating Campaigns, 79 Am. Pol. Sci. Rev. 804 (1985).

[12] See Theodore M. Newcomb, Personality and Social Change: Attitude Formation in a Student Community (1943) (documenting adaptation of initially conservative college freshmen to liberal views of upperclassmen and faculty).

[13] See Timur Kuran, Private Truths, Public Lies 3 (1995); see also Dale T. Miller & Deborah A. Prentice, Collective Errors and Errors About the Collective, 20 Personality & Soc. Psychol. Bull. 541, 542-43 (1994) (analyzing phenomenon of "pluralistic ignorance" to describe how and why individuals behave publicly in ways misrepresentative of their personal views).

[14] See, e.g., David P. Phillips, The Influence of Suggestion on Suicide: Substantive and Theoretical Implications of the Werther Effect, 39 Am. Soc. Rev. 340 (1974).

[15] See Peter H. Reingen, Test of a List Procedure for Inducing Compliance With a Request to Donate Money, 67 J. Applied Psychol. 110 (1982).

[16] See, e.g., Robert Curvin & Bruce Porter, Blackout Looting! 6-7 (1979) (documenting that looting draws in individuals without prior criminal records); Kurt Lang & Gladys Engel Lang, Racial Disturbances as Collective Protest, Am. Behav. Sci., March-April 1968, at 11, 12 (same, riots); E.L. Quarantelli & Russell R. Dynes, Looting: A Social Index, 12 New Soc'y 190, 191-92 (1968) (persons arrested for looting do not differ in criminal history or socio-economic background from general population in affected area). The "group" nature of criminality is especially pronounced among juveniles. See Maynard L. Erickson & Gary F. Jensen, "Delinquency Is Still Group Behavior!": Toward Revitalizing the Group Premise in the Sociology of Deviance, 68 J. Crim. L. & Criminology 262, 264-66 (1977) (documenting that juveniles are much more likely to commit wide range of offenses in groups than individually); see also Fox Butterfield, A Team's Shoplifting Spree Shocks

violent mobs are likely to inflict on their victims, moreover, increases with the size of the crowd, suggesting that individuals' propensities to engage in violence interact with and reinforce each other.[17]

Empirical studies of why people obey the law suggest that these effects generalize. Such studies reveal a strong correlation between a person's obedience and her perception of others' behavior and attitudes toward the law.[18] Thus, a person's beliefs about whether other persons in her situation are paying their taxes plays a much more significant role in her decision to comply than does the burden of the tax or her perception of the expected punishment for evasion.[19] Likewise, the perception that one's peers will or will not disapprove exerts a much stronger influence than does the threat of a formal sanction on whether a person decides to engage in a range of common offenses—from larceny, to burglary, to drug use.[20] These findings confirm that

---

Quiet Boston Suburb, N.Y. Times, May 5, 1996, at 14 ("[The principal] added that after carefully questioning all of the students, he had come to believe they really did not understand why they had taken part in the [shoplifting spree], except that they were in a group.").

[17] See Brian Mullen, Atrocity as a Function of Lynch Mob Composition: A Self-Attention Perspective, 12 Personality & Soc. Psychol. Bull. 187 (1986).

[18] See Harold G. Grasmick & Donald E. Green, Legal Punishment, Social Disapproval and Internalization as Inhibitors of Illegal Behavior, 71 J. Crim. L. & Criminology 325 (1980) (finding positive correlation between disposition to follow the law and belief that respected peers obey it); see also Jack P. Gibbs, Preventive Effects of Capital Punishment Other Than Deterrence, 14 Crim. L. Bull. 34, 41 (1978) ("Indeed, an individual is not likely to persist in the condemnation of some type of act if he or she observes that the act is committed openly and frequently with impunity.").

[19] See, e.g., Steven M. Sheffrin & Robert K. Triest, Can Brute Deterrence Backfire? Perceptions and Attitudes in Taxpayer Compliance, *in* Why People Pay Taxes: Tax Compliance and Enforcement 193, 212-13 (Joel Slemrod ed., 1992) (finding that "tax gap" stories can spark greater evasion even when information about noncompliance is combined with publicity of stepped up enforcement efforts); Marco R. Steenbergen, Kathleen M. McGraw & John T. Scholz, Taxpayer Adaptation to the 1986 Tax Reform Act: Do New Tax Laws Affect the Way Taxpayers Think About Taxes?, *in* Why People Pay Taxes, supra at 29-30, 32 (opinions toward tax of those with whom taxpayer interacts exert greater influence on compliance rate than does economic consequence of tax on taxpayer).

[20] See, e.g., John Braithwaite, Crime, Shame, and Reintegration 69-70 (1989); Charles R. Tittle, Sanctions and Social Deviance: The Question of Deterrence 196-99, 320-21 (1980); Grasmick & Green, supra note 18, at 334. For a strikingly powerful demonstration that reputational penalties dominate formal ones from a deterrence point of view, see John R. Lott, Jr. & David B. Mustard, Crime, Deterrence, and Right-to-Carry Concealed Handguns, 26 J. Legal Stud. 1, 58 (1997),

individuals' decisions to engage in crime are interlinked in various ways.

Statistical analyses point in the same direction. In one such study, sociologists Albert Reiss, Jr. and Albert Rhodes examined delinquency rates in a Tennessee county over an eight-year period. They discovered that neighborhood crime rates were in fact a much better predictor of individual delinquency than was social class.[21] In another study, economists Edward Glaeser, Bruce Sacerdote, and José Scheinkman developed a formal model to predict the influence of interdependent decisionmaking among potential criminals.[22] Applying this model to different neighborhoods in New York City, they discovered that it succeeded in explaining substantially more of the variance in crime rates than did demographic and law-enforcement variables. In other words, individuals' decisions to commit crimes are responsive to the decisions of other individuals and not just to the price of crime.[23] Other researchers have found similar patterns of interdependence in the commissions of sensational violent offenses, including assassinations, serial killings, hijackings, and kidnappings.[24]

The role of social influence on law-breaking has even been confirmed experimentally.[25] In one famous—if somewhat im-

which finds that the arrest rates exert an effect on crime rates that is up to ten times greater than that exerted by conviction rates.

[21] See Albert J. Reiss, Jr. & Albert Lewis Rhodes, The Distribution of Juvenile Delinquency in the Social Class Structure, 26 Am. Soc. Rev. 720, 728-29 (1961).

[22] See Edward L. Glaeser, Bruce Sacerdote & José A. Scheinkman, Crime and Social Interactions, 111 Q.J. Econ. 507 (1996).

[23] Id. at 542.

[24] See Albert Bandura, Aggression: A Social Learning Analysis 104-07 (1973) (surveying data and literature suggesting "contagion" effect for such crimes); Leonard Berkowitz, Studies of the Contagion of Violence, *in* Violence as Politics: A Series of Original Essays 41, 41-45 (Herbert Hirsch & David C. Perry eds., 1973). William Landes's data are consistent with a finding of interdependence in the decision to engage in hijacking between 1961 and 1973, although he finds that conventional deterrence variables—including the probability of apprehension and the severity of punishment—exerted a greater influence, particularly in reducing the level of that offense by the end of the period. See William M. Landes, An Economic Study of U.S. Aircraft Hijacking, 1961-1976, 21 J.L. & Econ. 1, 17-18 (1978).

[25] See Robert B. Cialdini, Raymond R. Reno & Carl A. Kallgren, A Focus Theory of Normative Conduct: Recycling the Concept of Norms to Reduce Littering in Public Places, 58 J. Personality & Soc. Psychol. 1015 (1990) (finding that test subjects were more likely to engage in or refrain from littering depending on the observed

pressionistic—study, psychologist Philip Zimbardo uncovered evidence suggesting the interdependence of decisions to pillage an abandoned automobile.[26] Zimbardo placed the car, hood up, on the campus of Stanford University, where it remained in pristine condition for over a week. Zimbardo then smashed the windshield with a sledgehammer. At that point, passersby spontaneously joined in the carnage, gleefully visiting further destruction upon the car and (over time) stripping it of valuable parts. The sight of others openly pillaging the car, Zimbardo concluded, had released passersby from their inhibitions against vandalism and theft.[27]

Social scientists have posited a number of explanations for the phenomenon of social influence generally. Some stress the individual rationality of conforming to behavior of other individuals,[28] some the reputational benefits of conforming to social norms,[29] and still others a deep-seated affinity between individuals that causes them to value conformity for its own sake.[30]

Similar mechanisms can explain the role of social influence in criminal decisionmaking in particular. The most obvious is the signaling effect of criminal behavior. If individuals perceive that their neighbors are freely dealing drugs or routinely evading their taxes, they are likely to infer that the risks of such behavior are small and the potential rewards high.[31] If enough people

behavior of other individuals); Brian Mullen, Carolyn Copper & James E. Driskell, Jaywalking as a Function of Model Behavior, 16 Personality & Soc. Psychol. Bull. 320, 324, 327 (1990) (finding that test subjects were more likely to engage in jaywalking or to refrain from doing so depending on behavior of models, particular when the models were of evidently high social status). Understandably, experiments test for the effect of social influence on the decision to engage in nonviolent rather than violent law-breaking.

[26] Philip G. Zimbardo, The Human Choice: Individuation, Reason, and Order Versus Deindividuation, Impulse, and Chaos, *in* Nebraska Symposium on Motivation, 1969, at 237, 287-93 (William J. Arnold & David Levie eds., 1969).

[27] See id. at 290-93. In another experiment, Zimbardo placed an automobile in the Bronx in New York City. Within hours and without any prompting from the experimenters, the car had been picked clean by clean-cut passersby, many of whom gratuitously inflicted damage upon it. Id. at 287-88.

[28] See, e.g., James S. Coleman, Foundations of Social Theory 197-240 (1990).

[29] See, e.g., Kuran, supra note 13, at 24-37; Sunstein, supra note 7, at 916-17.

[30] See, e.g., Stephen R. G. Jones, The Economics of Conformism (1984).

[31] They may also see that some of these law-breakers are punished. That may counteract the inference that crime is a worthwhile option; or, in contrast, it may

draw this inference and act on it, moreover, it will become self-fulfilling. For the greater the number of individuals engaged in a particular crime, the less effective will be any given investment of resources aimed at detecting and punishing it.[32] The (self-confirming) perception that there is little risk of punishment when large numbers are breaking the law also plays an important role in the dynamics of looting, lynching, and other forms of mob criminality.[33]

Individuals' decisions to commit crimes also reinforce each other because of their cumulative effect on stigma. Most people refrain from engaging in crime not because they fear formal penalties but because they fear damage to their reputation and loss of status.[34] But individuals fear stigma less when they perceive that criminality is rampant. The more prevalent criminal activity is in a particular community the less likely someone is to be condemned for it by either those with criminal records or those without.[35] The enervation of the stigma associated with rampant criminality is particularly acute in inner-city neighborhoods, in which criminal convictions are commonplace and, far from being a mark of disgrace, are for some "a badge of honor."[36]

Indeed, inversion of the ordinary reputational effect of law-breaking can be both a consequence and a self-sustaining cause of rampant criminal behavior. When juveniles see others committing crimes, they infer that their peers value law-breaking; they are then more likely to break the law themselves, which

---

reinforce that inference, if experience with punished offenders suggests to individuals that punishment is less unpleasant than they would otherwise have imagined.

[32] See, e.g., Raaj K. Sah, Social Osmosis and Patterns of Crime, 99 J. Pol. Econ. 1272 (1991).

[33] See Curvin & Porter, supra note 16, at 8-9; Leonard Berkowitz, The Study of Urban Violence: Some Implications of Laboratory Studies of Frustration and Aggression, Am. Behav. Sci., Mar.-Apr. 1968, at 14, 16.

[34] See supra note 20 and accompanying text.

[35] See Eric Rasmusen, Stigma and Self-Fulfilling Expectations of Criminality, 39 J.L. & Econ. 519 (1996) (formally modeling this effect); Curvin & Porter, supra note 16, at 17-18 (using this mechanism to explain decision to engage in looting); James P.F. Gordon, Individual Morality and Reputation Costs as Deterrents to Tax Evasion, 33 Eur. Econ. Rev. 797, 808 (1989) (same, tax evasion).

[36] James Q. Wilson & Richard J. Herrnstein, Crime and Human Nature 304 (1985). See also Franklin E. Zimring & Gordon J. Hawkins, Deterrence: The Legal Threat in Crime Control 215-16 (1973) (describing studies finding that imprisonment is status-enhancing within gang culture).

leads other juveniles to draw the same inference and engage in the same behavior.[37] Violence and destruction can become status-enhancing for the leaders of political protest movements in exactly the same way.[38]

Still another mechanism of social influence is the interaction of perceived criminality with emotional dispositions such as pride and resentment. Most individuals regard compliance with law to be morally appropriate. But most also loathe being taken advantage of. The latter sensibility can easily subvert the former if individuals perceive that those around them are routinely violating a particular law: When others refuse to reciprocate, submission to a burdensome legal duty is likely to feel more servile than moral.[39] This effect can explain the divergence between the relatively high tax-compliance rate in the United States, where paying one's tax is viewed as an important civic duty, and the relatively low ones in Europe, where evasion is viewed as a fairly trivial infraction.[40]

Finally, social influence shapes values. Whether to satisfy a general appetite for conformity[41] or to avoid cognitive dissonance,[42] individuals tend to adapt their moral convictions to those

---

[37] See David Matza, Delinquency and Drift 52-59 (Transaction Publishers 1990) (1964); infra text accompanying notes 88-92.

[38] See Bandura, supra note 24, at 234-35.

[39] See Albert Alschuler, The Descending Trail: Holmes' Path of the Law 100 Years Later, Fla. L. Rev. (forthcoming); Peter H. Huang & Ho-Mou Wu, More Order Without More Law: A Theory of Social Norms and Organizational Cultures, 10 J.L. Econ. & Org. 390, 402-03 (1994).

[40] See generally Frank A. Cowell, Cheating the Government: The Economics of Evasion 102-03 (1990) (noting that differential levels of tax compliance among countries are in part a function of the tax compliance "climate" within those countries); Huang & Wu, supra note 39, at 401-02 (reviewing works arguing for a model of tax evasion which includes social influence); cf. Richard D. Schwartz & Sonya Orleans, On Legal Sanctions, 34 U. Chi. L. Rev. 274, 296-99 (1966-67) (finding that individuals exposed to information emphasizing reciprocity and moral duty declared higher income and claimed fewer deductions in tax than like-situated individuals exposed to information emphasizing possible penalties for evasion). The same effect has also been linked to juvenile criminality. See James F. Short, Jr. & Fred L. Strodtbeck, Group Process and Gang Delinquency 76 (1965).

[41] See Jones, supra note 30, at 2.

of their peers.[43] Experimental and empirical data, moreover, suggest that such adaptation can occur very rapidly once individuals are exposed to information about their peers' attitudes.[44] Accordingly, if a person is surrounded by persons who are (or appear to be) morally opposed to crime, she is likely to share their aversion; if they find (or appear to find) criminal behavior innocuous or even desirable, she is likely to feel the same way. Propensities to engage in crime thus reinforce each other because they determine (at least in part) how much value individuals are likely to attach to such behavior.

Whatever the mechanism, the power of social influence diminishes the explanatory power of the standard economic conception of deterrence. The standard conception assumes that the level of criminal activity is a function of the "price" of crime as determined by the community's law-enforcement policies.[45] The phenomenon of social influence, however, reveals that individuals' assessments of both the value and the price of criminal activity are endogenously related to their beliefs about the attitudes and intentions of others. As a result, at any particular level of expected punishment there can be multiple crime-rate

---

42 See, e.g., Leon Festinger, A Theory of Cognitive Dissonance (1957); Elliot Aronson & J. Merrill Carlsmith, Effect of the Severity of Threat on the Devaluation of Forbidden Behavior, 66 J. Abnormal & Soc. Psychol. 584 (1963).

43 See, e.g., Robert B. Cialdini, Social Motivations to Comply: Norms, Values, and Principles, *in* 2 Taxpayer Compliance 200, 213-14 (Jeffrey A. Roth & John T. Scholz eds., 1989).

44 See, e.g., Leonard Berkowitz & Nigel Walker, Laws and Moral Judgments, 30 Sociometry 410, 415-22 (1967) (finding that information suggesting that peers approved of various forms of conduct induced test subjects to express similar valuation); Nigel Walker & Catherine Marsh, Do Sentences Affect Public Disapproval?, 24 Brit. J. Criminology 27, 37-39 (1984) (same with seat-belt use). Rioting and looting, for example, appear to involve the rapid (and transient) adaptation of individual values to emergent norms. See Quarantelli & Dynes, supra note 16, at 191 (connecting looting to "*temporary and localised redefinitions of property rights*" that makes "plundering . . . the socially supported thing to do"); see also David M. Neal, A Further Examination of Anonymity, Contagion, and Deindividuation in Crowd and Collective Behavior, 26 Soc. Focus 93, 103-04 (1993) (same phenomenon in post-sporting-event rioting).

45 See supra note 1.

equilibria depending on what individuals believe other members of their community believe about crime.[46]

---

[46] This point can be represented graphically:

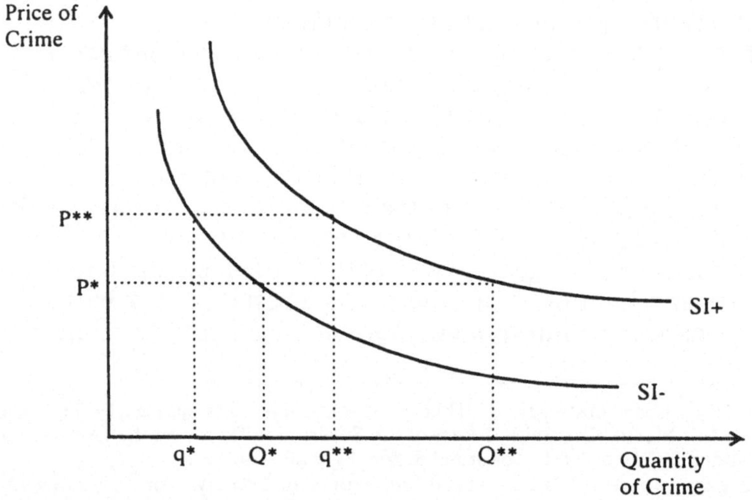

Figure 1

According to the standard economic view, the relationship between the quantity of crime and its price is represented by a downward sloping curve. That is, as the price of crime decreases (from, say, P** to P*), the quantity of it increases (from q** to Q**). But this is an incomplete picture according to the social influence conception. That theory tells us that individuals commit crimes not just because they think that crime is a bargain at its current price, but also because they perceive that others are breaking the law. Accordingly, the price of crime *doesn't* uniquely determine the level of criminality. Rather, at any given price (say, P*), there will be more (Q**) or less (Q*) crime depending on what individuals perceive about the intentions and values of others. As a result, there is not one but at least two crime-rate curves: a high one when social influence points toward crime (SI+), and a low one when it points away from it (SI–). For a formal model of how decisionmaking interdependencies can generate multiple equilibria, and a discussion of the significance of this phenomenon for law, see Randal C. Picker, Simple Games in a Complex World, 64 U. Chi. L. Rev. (forthcoming Fall 1997).

This power of social influence suggests an explanation for disparate crime rates across time. It is well documented that the national crime rate increased significantly in the 1960s and persisted at this level through the early 1990s. The initial jump can be explained consistently with the standard conception of deterrence insofar as a reduction in expected prison time per offense reduced the price of crime in the 1960s. Reliance on imprisonment, however, increased steadily and dramatically through the 1980s; what the standard conception of deterrence can't explain is why this increase in expected punishment did not succeed in reducing crime rates to their earlier levels.[47]

But a theory that takes account of social influence can. It's quite plausible to believe that the jump in the crime rate triggered the various mechanisms by which individual decisions to engage in crime reinforce each other: As they observed their peers turning to crime, individuals concluded that crime isn't particularly risky, that being a criminal doesn't necessarily threaten and might indeed enhance one's status in the community, that obeying the law is servile, and that engaging in crime isn't morally repugnant. These beliefs caused potential offenders to revise upward their assessment of the value of crime and downward their assessment of the cost of it. And these altered evaluations outlived the initial reduction in the price of crime, so that even once expected punishment was restored to its previous level, the higher crime rate persisted.[48]

The phenomenon of social influence reduces not only the explanatory power of the standard economic conception of deterrence, but also its prescriptive power. The standard conception counsels adoption of policies that raise the price of criminal wrongdoing.[49] But because social influence can generate multiple crime-rate equilibria at any given level of expected punishment, it should be obvious that a policy that attends only to price and not to social influence may be ineffective in reducing crime.

---

[47] See, e.g., James Q. Wilson, Culture, Incentives, and the Underclass, *in* Values and Public Policy 54, 59-61 (Henry J. Aaron, Thomas E. Mann & Timothy Taylor eds., 1994) (reviewing crime rates and expected punishments from 1960s to 1980s).

[48] See Rasmusen, supra note 35.

[49] See supra notes 1-4 and accompanying text.

II. SOCIAL MEANING AND CRIMINAL LAW

Social meaning is as pervasive a phenomenon as social influence. Many of the roles we occupy (spouse, parent, teacher) and goods we value (love, dignity, status) are constructed by social norms.[50] Against the background of these norms, actions become invested with meaning; they signify to others what a person (or community) believes and cares about.[51] From our friends, for example, we expect shared time and experience; thus, a person's failure to share time and experiences with others—because, say, she is preoccupied with her professional life—conveys that she either doesn't value them as friends or doesn't really know how to.

Social meaning plays a critical role in criminal law. Economists speak of criminal law as a mechanism for pricing misconduct, but ordinary citizens think of it as a convention for morally condemning it.[52] Against the background of that expectation, the positions that the law takes become suffused with meaning. *What* it punishes (drug possession, sodomy) can tell us what kind of life the community views as virtuous; *how* it punishes (imprisonment, corporal punishment, fines) can tell us what forms of affliction it views as appropriate to mark wrongdoers' disgrace;[53] how *severely* it punishes (the death penalty for the killers of whites, life imprisonment for the killers of blacks) can tell us whose interests it values and how much.[54] Social-meaning effects often explain the tremendous political salience

[50] See Sunstein, supra note 7.

[51] See Lawrence Lessig, Social Meaning and Social Norms, 144 U. Pa. L. Rev. 2181 (1996).

[52] See Joel Feinberg, The Expressive Function of Punishment, *in* Doing and Deserving: Essays in the Theory of Responsibility 95 (1970) (distinguishing between "penalties" designed merely to inflict disutility and "punishments" intended to express additional moral disapproval); Jean Hampton, The Retributive Idea, *in* Jeffrie G. Murphy & Jean Hampton, Forgiveness and Mercy 111 (1988); Kahan, supra note 7.

[53] See generally Kahan, supra note 7 (discussing expressive significations of corporal punishment, imprisonment, fines, community service, and shaming penalties).

[54] See Randall L. Kennedy, *McCleskey v. Kemp:* Race, Capital Punishment, and the Supreme Court, 101 Harv. L. Rev. 1388, 1441 (1988) ("*[I]n Georgia's marketplace of emotion the lives of blacks simply count for less than the lives of whites.*"); see also George Fletcher, With Justice For Some (1995) (examining political stake that those who identify with victim have in severity of punishment).

of many criminal law issues (like capital punishment) that have only trivial or ambiguous regulatory significance.[55]

Generalizing, criminal law can produce social meaning in two ways.[56] First, it can *express* meanings directly by taking positions that, in the context of extant social norms, signify particular valuations. Indeed, it's possible to identify criminal laws that produce little more than this expressive consequence. Few really believed, for example, that the Flag Protection Act of 1989[57] would deter flag burnings—an extremely uncommon form of protest in any case—yet this law provoked tremendous controversy because of what it signified about the virtue of patriotism and the relative status of veterans and dissidents in our society.[58]

Second, criminal law can produce social meaning through the *regulation of social norms*. Because norms construct the context within which action becomes meaningful, regulating norms can reinforce or suppress particular meanings.[59] Consider possession of guns in inner-city public schools. This behavior is infused with social meaning. Possessing a gun confers status because it expresses confidence and a willingness to defy authority. By the same token, not possessing one signals fear, and thus invites aggression.[60] Policies that aim at suppressing possession usually

---

[55] See generally Phoebe C. Ellsworth & Samuel R. Gross, Hardening of the Attitudes: Americans' Views on the Death Penalty, J. Soc. Issues, Summer 1994, at 19 (surveying research that confirms support for death penalty based on "emotion" and not "rational argument"); Tom R. Tyler & Renee Weber, Support for the Death Penalty: Instrumental Response to Crime, or Symbolic Attitude?, 17 L. & Soc'y Rev. 21 (1982) (concluding from survey results that death penalty support results from "political-social" attitudes and not "instrumental" concerns).

[56] See generally Lessig, supra note 7 (discussing how law forms orthodoxy and how this affects social meaning).

[57] Pub. L. No. 101-131, 103 Stat. 777 (1989).

[58] See Frank I. Michelman, Saving Old Glory: On Constitutional Iconography, 42 Stan. L. Rev. 1337 (1990) (describing political controversy surrounding issue of flag burning); Cass R. Sunstein, On the Expressive Function of Law, 144 U. Pa. L. Rev. 2021, 2023 (1996) (same).

[59] See generally Sunstein, supra note 7 (discussing importance of norm management for accomplishment of the objectives of the law).

[60] See generally Louis Harris & Assoc., The Metropolitan Life Survey of the American Teacher 1993: Violence in America's Public Schools 60, tbl.4.7 (1993) (when students were asked the purpose of carrying a gun, 66% listed "to impress friends/be accepted by peers," 56% "for self esteem/to feel powerful/important," and 49% "for

fail; indeed, when authorities aggressively seek out and punish students who possess weapons, their behavior reinforces the message of defiance associated with guns, thereby increasing their expressive value.[61]

One policy that *is* believed to be effective is to pay rewards to students who turn in gun possessors.[62] This tactic appears to work, moreover, not just because it facilitates seizure of the weapons, but because it interferes with norms that give guns their meaning. When students fear that their peers will report them, they are less likely to display their guns; when students are reluctant to display them, guns become less valuable for conveying information about one's attitude and intentions.[63] Students then

protection/self-defense/fear going to and from school"); Daniel W. Webster, Patricia S. Gainer & Howard R. Champion, Weapon Carrying Among Inner-City Junior High School Students: Defensive Behavior vs. Aggressive Delinquency, 83 Am. J. Pub. Health 1604, 1607 (1993) (finding that influence of peers is more significant than fear in motivating gun possession by juveniles); Mary E. Pattillo & Reuben A.B. May, Gun Talk: Culture & Social Control in an African-American Community 13-23 (1996) (unpublished manuscript, on file with the Virginia Law Review Association) (discussing attitudes of inner-city youths toward guns).

[61] See, e.g., David B. Kopel, Children and Guns, *in* Guns: Who Should Have Them? 330-31, 375, 377-79 (David B. Kopel ed., 1995) (critiquing "zero tolerance" and "buyback" policies); Charles M. Callahan, Frederick P. Rivara & Thomas D. Koepsell, Money for Guns: Evaluation of the Seattle Gun Buy-Back Program, 109 Pub. Health Rep. 472, 476-77 (1994) (reviewing ineffectiveness of buyback program in inducing minors to turn in guns under current funding levels); Stephan Hudak, Gun Buybacks: Curb to Violence or Exercise in Futility?, Plain Dealer (Cleveland, Ohio), May 15, 1994, at 1A (reporting perception that buybacks fail to produce significant results); Jeffrey A. Roberts, Firearm Buyback Debated, Some Say Swaps Don't Cut Crime, Denver Post, Jan. 30, 1994, at B1 (reporting perceived ineffectiveness of buyback, particularly among juveniles).

[62] See Fox Butterfield, Police Chief's Success in Charleston, S.C., Is What's Raising Eyebrows Now, N.Y. Times, Apr. 28, 1996, at 16 (reporting success of such a policy in Charleston, South Carolina); see also Donna Harrington-Lueker, Metal Detectors: Schools Turn to Devices Once Aimed Only at Airport Terrorists, Am. School Board J., May 1992, at 26-27 (reviewing perceived ineffectiveness of metal detectors and recommending as alternative use of student informants).

[63] See Butterfield, supra note 62, at 16. According to the city's police chief, the informant program has "reversed the psychology of having a gun[:] . . . 'Before, the more people who knew you had a gun, the greater your prestige. . . . [Now] [t]he more people who know, the more likely you are to get turned in.'" Id.

have less incentive to carry them. Paying students to inform probably doesn't change the meaning of guns, but it does disrupt behavioral norms—including the ready display of guns—that are essential to their expressive value.

What is the significance of social meaning for criminal law? Understanding this phenomenon clearly enriches descriptive accounts of criminal law as a political institution. But I want to show that a vocabulary of social meaning is essential to making sensible prescriptions in criminal law as well; a deterrence program that thinks of criminal law solely as a mechanism for pricing misconduct and that ignores its effects in creating social meaning will often be ineffective. This is so because such an account will consistently overlook the effect of social meaning in determining the direction of social influence.

III. The Social Influence Conception of Deterrence

The argument so far generates a straightforward but abstract policy prescription. Individuals decide to commit crimes, I've suggested, based in part on their perception of the values, beliefs, and behavior of other individuals; the law plays a role in shaping these perceptions through its expressive and norm-regulatory effects. Accordingly, by adopting laws that generate appropriate social meanings, a community should be able to point social influence in a direction that discourages criminality.

My goal in this Part is to make this prescription more concrete. The deterrence strategy that I've identified has theoretical implications for a wide range of issues. It reveals, for example, the potential utility of policies aimed at suppressing public disorder and visible gang activity, forms of behavior that can generate social-influence pressure to engage in crime. It calls into question the utility of substituting severity of punishment for certainty of conviction, and private precautions for public law enforcement, since these tradeoffs can produce negative social meanings that offset their apparent efficiencies. It supplies a reason to select particular forms of punishment that more clearly express public condemnation of crime. And it highlights the costs of certain conceptions of individual rights, which either express undesirable social meanings or inhibit norm regulations that could produce desirable ones.[64]

[64] The arguments in this section can also be illustrated graphically:

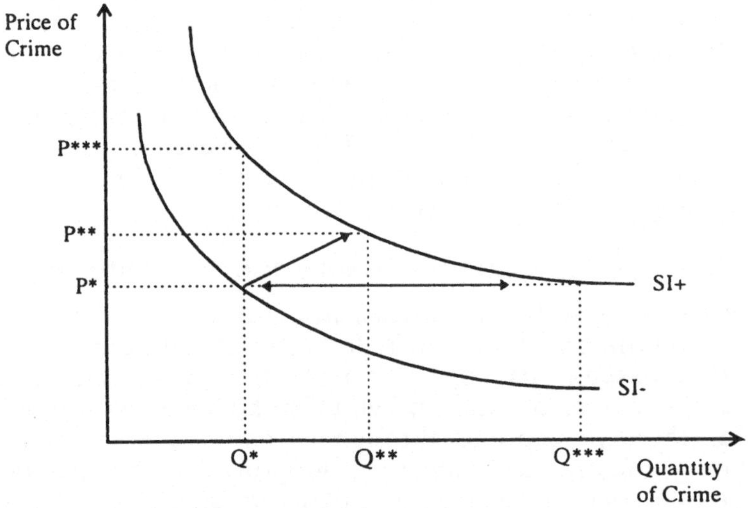

Figure 2

According to the standard economic view, as the price of crime goes up, the quantity of crime goes down, as is true for either curve represented in Figure 2. From a policy point of view, then, a community should aim at policies that either raise the price (from, say, P* to P**) and thus lower the quantity of crime (from Q*** to Q**on the SI+ curve); or maintain the current price (and hence the current quantity of crime) at a lower social cost. The social influence view, in contrast, suggests that there can be multiple crime-rate equilibria at any given price of crime depending on whether social influence is pointing toward (SI+) or away from (SI-) crime. See supra note 46. It follows that we can't rate the deterrent effects of law enforcement policies based solely on their price effects. A policy that maintains the current price of crime (say, P*) but that adversely affects social influence can shift the quantity of crime from a low crime-rate equilibrium (Q* on SI-) at that price to a high one (Q*** on SI+). A policy that raises the price of crime (from, say, P* to P**) but that also adversely affects social influence can also shift the crime-rate curve upward and thereby *increase* law-breaking (from Q* on SI- to Q** on SI+). These are the kinds of arguments I present against the prescriptions associated with the standard view, including the substitution of severe penalties for certainty of conviction, fines for

Of course, identifying these implications as a matter of theory is not the same as proving that these policies will work as a matter of fact. I will, where I can, adduce empirical support for my claims. But for the most part, I will confine myself to informed speculation about the likely interactions between social influence and social meaning.

This pragmatic form of theorizing is commonplace in arguments about deterrence. Working from parsimonious and plausible assumptions about individual behavior, proponents of the standard economic conception—from Bentham to Becker—have produced a rich array of policy prescriptions. By drawing attention to the importance of social influence and social meaning, I hope to uncover additional prescriptions that are every bit as plausible and every bit as worthy of experimentation and study as those suggested by this standard conception. In addition, I hope to unsettle at least some of the standard conception's own prescriptions, which turn out to be much less plausible than they initially appear once the phenomena of social influence and social meaning are brought into view.

A. Law Enforcement Strategies

1. Order Maintenance

New York City has much less crime today than it did just three years ago. Since 1993, the murder rate there has come down nearly 40 percent, the robbery rate more than 30 percent, and the burglary rate more than 25 percent.[65] These drops are

imprisonment, and private for public deterrence. See infra Part III.B-D. In addition, under the social influence view, raising the price of crime isn't the only way to deter it; we can also regulate perceptions of criminality in a way that moves the quantity of crime from a high crime-rate equilibrium to a low one. We should choose moving from one curve to the other (from, say, Q*** on SI+ to Q* on SI-) over moving along one an equivalent amount (from Q*** to Q* on SI+) whenever it's cheaper to change perceptions of crime in the requisite way than it is to increase the price by the requisite amount (from P* to P***). Considerations of this sort, I argue below, support policies like order-maintenance policing, gang-loitering laws, and curfews. See infra Part III.A.

[65] See Composite Crime Statistics (compiled by author from: FBI Uniform Crime Reports, 1980-1995; U.S. Bureau of the Census, City Government and Finances, series GF-89-4 (1981-1995)) (unpublished manuscript, on file with the Virginia Law Review Association).

more than double the national average.[66] Overall, crime in New York is at its lowest level in more than a quarter century.[67] What explains this rapid and dramatic turnaround?

The forces conventionally assumed to drive crime rates don't explain much. New York City has increased its investment in law enforcement over the course of a decade, but no more so than other cities around the country, none of which has seen reductions in crime as dramatic as New York's.[68] Similarly, demographic shifts—including changes in the size of the teenage male population—are far too small to account for New York's drop in crime and are no different from those in other cities.[69]

What has changed significantly is New York's law-enforcement strategy. Beginning in 1993, the New York City Police Department began to focus intensively on so-called "public order" offenses, including vandalism, aggressive panhandling, public drunkenness, unlicensed vending, public urination, and prostitution. City officials and at least some criminologists

---

[66] See id. Indeed, while crime has in fact decreased nationwide since 1990, New York is responsible for much of this drop. If one were to ignore New York, the national homicide rate, instead of decreasing 8% between 1990 and 1995, would have decreased only 4%; the robbery rate, instead of decreasing 9%, would have decreased only 3%; and the car theft rate, instead of dropping 10%, would have dropped only 6%. See id.

[67] See Clifford Krauss, Mystery of New York, the Suddenly Safer City, N.Y. Times, July 23, 1995, § 4, at 1.

[68] Between 1989 and 1993, for example, the state of New York increased its prison population (over half of which comes from New York City) by 24%; the increase nationwide during that same period was 29%. See 1994 Sourcebook of Criminal Justice Statistics 541, tbl.6.20. In the decade ending in 1994, New York increased its spending on police by 74%; the nation's nine largest cities excluding New York increased police spending by 70% on average. See Composite Crime Statistics, supra note 65. In the nation's nine largest cities excluding New York, homicides declined on average 14% from 1993 to 1995 as compared to 40% in New York; robberies declined 15% as compared to 31% in New York; and burglaries declined 13% as compared to 26% in New York. See id. Overall crime dropped on average 6% in these cities (excluding Chicago and Detroit, which failed to supply conforming data to the FBI), as compared to 26% in New York. See id.; see also infra note 85 (comparing crime drop in New York crime to drops in San Diego and San Antonio).

[69] See Craig Horowitz, The Suddenly Safer City, New York Magazine, Aug. 14, 1995, at 20, 24; Krauss, supra note 67, at 1, 4.

credit the larger reduction in crime rates to this recent emphasis on "order maintenance."[70]

But this claim seems to make little sense under the conventional economic conception of deterrence. The legal prices of murder, robbery, and burglary don't depend on how the police respond to vandalism, public drunkenness, prostitution and the like. So why should we think that New York's order-maintenance strategy is in any way responsible for the reduction in the rate of these more serious crimes? The social influence conception of deterrence supplies an answer.

Visible disorder is a self-reinforcing cue about the community's attitude toward crime. James Wilson and George Kelling describe this dynamic as the "broken window" effect.[71] A broken window invites more window-breaking because it is "a signal that no one cares, and so breaking more windows costs nothing."[72] Likewise, prostitution, petty drug dealing, public drunkenness, and the like "lead[] to the breakdown of community controls" because they convey that people in the community either don't value or don't expect order.[73]

The work of criminologist Wesley Skogan supplies empirical support for the "broken window" hypothesis.[74] Skogan collected data on forty urban neighborhoods that varied significantly in their crime rates. The data revealed a strong positive correlation between disorder (both physical and social) and robbery rates. This effect, moreover, persisted when Skogan controlled for demographic variables commonly associated with crime, such as race and poverty; indeed, Skogan's research indicated that these variables explained relatively little of the vari-

---

[70] See, e.g., William J. Bratton, The New York City Police Department's Civil Enforcement of Quality-of-Life Crimes, 3 J.L. & Pol'y 447 (1995); George Kelling & Catherine M. Coles, Fixing Broken Windows: Restoring Order and Reducing Crime in Our Communities 151-56 (1996).

[71] James Q. Wilson & George L. Kelling, Broken Windows, Atlantic Monthly, Mar. 1982, at 29.

[72] Id. at 31.

[73] Id. See also Robert C. Ellickson, Controlling Chronic Misconduct in City Spaces: Of Panhandlers, Skid Rows, and Public-Space Zoning, 105 Yale L.J. 1165, 1177-78, 1182 (1996) (linking "broken window" effect to aggressive panhandling).

[74] See Wesley G. Skogan, Disorder and Decline: Crime and the Spiral of Decay in American Neighborhoods (1990).

ance in the crime rates across the neighborhoods once he controlled for the effects of disorder.[75] Skogan's research also indicated a significant positive correlation between disorder and perceptions of crime.[76]

The effect of disorder on crime can be understood in terms of the effect that social meaning has on the mechanisms of social influence. The meaning of behavior is highly contextual and often complex. A person might infer that others expect aggressive behavior, for example, not only from words or actions to that effect, but from more general signs that they value aggression—such as the presence of a weapon.[77] Disorder is also pregnant with meaning: Public drunkenness, prostitution, aggressive panhandling and similar behavior signal not only that members of the community are inclined to engage in disorderly conduct, but also that the community is unable or unwilling to enforce basic norms. In that circumstance, individuals understandably infer that the odds of being punished for more serious crimes are also low. The very openness of such behavior, moreover, suggests

[75] Id. at 73-75.

[76] Id. at 76-77.

[77] Social psychologists refer to the power of one concept or norm to trigger associations with another concept or norm as "cognitive priming." See Cialdini, Reno & Kallgren, supra note 25, at 1023. The phenomenon has been the subject of experimental study. In one, researchers found that test subjects who were exposed to a gun that they were told had been left behind after another experiment behaved more aggressively (by administering what they believed were more intense electric shocks to a confederate of the experimenter) than those who were not exposed to the gun. See Leonard Berkowitz & Anthony LePage, Weapons as Aggression-Eliciting Stimuli, 7 J. Personality & Soc. Psychol. 202, 205-06 (1967); see also Ladd Wheeler, Toward a Theory of Behavioral Contagion, 73 Psychol. Rev. 179, 185 (1966) (noting one form of aggressive behavior can trigger related but distinct forms of aggressive behavior). In another, researchers first asked subjects to rank on a 9-point scale the "likeness" of various norms to the norm against littering. They then placed fliers on the windshields of parked cars. Some of the fliers contained a message identical to the norm against littering ("April is Keep Arizona Beautiful Month. Please Do Not Litter"); others messages deemed to be related but not identical to the anti-littering norm (including one reminding drivers to recycle and one reminding them to vote); and others a message that was deemed to bear no relation to the anti-littering norm ("April is Arizona's Fine Arts' Month. Please Visit Your Local Art Museum"). Drivers were more likely to throw to the ground a flier bearing a message unrelated to the anti-littering norm than they were to throw to the ground a flier bearing a messaged related but not identical to that norm; fliers bearing an anti-littering message were least likely to be thrown to the ground. See Cialdini, Reno & Kallgren, supra note 25, at 1023-24.

that violating basic norms carries little social sanction. Visible disorder also tells individuals that their own forbearance is unlikely to be reciprocated. In this environment, individuals who are otherwise inclined to engage in crime are much more likely to do so.

The meaning of disorder can also influence the behavior of committed *law-abiders* in a way that is likely to increase crime. If they can, law-abiding citizens are likely to leave a neighborhood that is pervaded by disorder. Their departure increases the concentration of law breakers, thereby multiplying their interactions with each other and accentuating their mutually reinforcing propensities to engage in crime.[78] Law-abiders who stick it out, moreover, are more likely to avoid the streets, where their simple presence would otherwise be a deterrent to crime.[79] They are also more likely to distrust their neighbors, and thus less likely to join leagues with them in monitoring their community for signs of trouble.[80] The law-abiders' fear of crime thus facilitates even more crime.

An order-maintenance strategy should reverse these effects. When citizens obey norms of orderliness—and when authorities visibly respond to those who don't—onlookers see that the community is intolerant of criminality. This message counteracts the inferences that point social influence in the direction of crime. It also reassures law-abiders, inducing them to engage in patterns of behavior that themselves discourage crime.[81] In this way, the perception of obedience to law becomes reality.

---

[78] See Elijah Anderson, Streetwise: Race, Class, and Change in an Urban Community 2-5, 58-59, 69-76 (1990) (describing mutually reinforcing trends of urban decay, middle-class flight, and crime).

[79] See Jane Jacobs, The Death and Life of Great American Cities 29-35 (1961) (describing role of legitimate street life in counteracting crime and deleterious effect of crime in suppressing legitimate street life).

[80] See Skogan, supra note 74, at 68-69 ("[I]n neighborhoods in decline, mutual distrust and hostility are rampant, and antipathy between newcomers and long-term residents prevails.").

[81] See, e.g., Malcolm Gladwell, The Tipping Point, New Yorker, June 3, 1996, at 32 ("On the streets of [Brooklyn] today, it is possible to see signs of everyday life that would have been unthinkable in the early nineties. There are now ordinary people on the streets at dusk—small children riding their bicycles, old people on benches and stoops, people coming out of the subways alone.").

Empirical studies again furnish support. In one, sociologists Robert Sampson and Jacqueline Cohen discovered a significant negative correlation between police activity aimed at disorderly conduct and robbery rates.[82] The data suggested, moreover, that order-maintenance policing reduces robbery directly rather than indirectly through any effect on the arrest rate for that offense.[83] Another study found significant reductions in both recorded crimes and fear of crime after the Newark Police Department implemented a community policing program that focused on order maintenance.[84]

The social-influence account thus makes it plausible to believe that order maintenance has in fact reduced crime in New York.[85] Because social meaning directs social influence independently of the legal price of crime, this dynamic can explain why New York's crime rate has dropped so dramatically without any increase in

[82] See Robert J. Sampson & Jacqueline Cohen, Deterrent Effects of the Police on Crime: A Replication and Theoretical Extension, 22 L. & Soc'y Rev. 163, 169, 176 (1988). Sampson and Cohen's sample consisted of all American cities with populations over 100,000 in 1980. Id. at 169. They treated the number of "disorderly conduct" and DUI arrests per police officer as a proxy for police involvement in order maintenance. Id. at 169-70.

[83] See id. at 176, 185. Sampson and Cohen also found a much weaker but still significant negative correlation between order maintenance and burglary rates. Id. at 176.

[84] See Lawrence W. Sherman, Policing Communities: What Works?, *in* 8 Crime and Justice: Communities and Crime 343, 366, 368-69 (Albert J. Reiss, Jr. & Michael Tonry eds., 1986).

[85] There is also reason to believe that order maintenance is at least partially responsible for crime drops in other large cities. See, e.g., Kelling & Coles, supra note 70, at 198 (describing successful use of order maintenance in Baltimore). Aside from New York, the two cities with the most dramatic recent reductions in crime are San Diego, where crime has fallen 24% since 1993, and San Antonio, where it has fallen 18%. See Composite Crime Statistics, supra note 65. Significantly, like New York, both cities have instituted law-enforcement programs that include order maintenance. In San Diego, these policies include the closing down of liquor stores and the use of volunteer citizen patrols that alert police when they encounter disorderly behavior. See Crackdown On Crime: Recent Trends Focus on Deterrence (editorial), San Diego Union-Tribune, Feb. 9, 1995, at B-12; see also Targeting Nuisance Crimes: City's New Policy Will Upgrade Neighborhoods (editorial), San Diego Union-Tribune, June 30, 1996, at G-2 (describing extension of San Diego order maintenance policies). San Antonio has attacked disorder through strict curfew laws and other policies aimed at suppressing open gang activity. See Anne Belli Gesalman, San Antonio Officials Cite Curfew Benefits, Predict Dallas Success, Dallas Morning News, May 2, 1994, at 1A. See infra text accompanying notes 86-105 (discussing gang-loitering laws and curfews as forms of order maintenance).

the expected punishment for murder, robbery, burglary, and other serious crimes. This account can also explain the rapidity of New York's crime drop. Because decisions to engage in crime are interdependent, policies that alter information about the values and behavior of other individuals can quickly move a community from a high crime-rate equilibrium to a low one.

New York's success in reducing crime also illustrates the potential efficiency of policies aimed at directing social influence. Order maintenance was apparently more effective than simply "raising the price" of serious crimes through either increased investments in law enforcement or longer terms of imprisonment; it was certainly much cheaper than either of those policies. Of course, the proposition that order maintenance is responsible for New York's precipitous drop in crime remains open to empirical challenge. But given the plausibility of this claim under the social influence conception of deterrence, New York's strategy definitely merits further study and emulation.

2. Gang Criminality

The strategy also merits extension. Two other law-enforcement policies that should produce similar effects are "gang loitering" laws and youth curfews.

Criminal youth gangs present a number of puzzles for the standard economic conception of deterrence. Why are some communities plagued by gangs and others not? The kinds of demographic and law-enforcement variables that the standard theory suggests should be relevant turn out not to be.[86] What should be done to suppress gangs? The standard view suggests "raising the price" of gang-related activity—either by shifting law-enforcement resources to crimes committed by gangs, increasing the penalties for gang-related crimes, or both. Yet such policies have proven notoriously ineffective.[87]

---

[86] See Walter B. Miller, Why the United States Has Failed to Solve Its Youth Gang Problem, *in* Gangs in America 263, 280-81 (C. Ronald Huff ed., 1990) (presenting evidence that demographic factors, including income levels and racial composition, do not adequately explain variance in incidence of gang activity across communities).

[87] See C. Ronald Huff, Denial, Overreaction, and Misidentification: A Postscript on Public Policy, *in* Gangs in America, supra note 86, at 310, 313; Miller, supra note 86,

The social influence conception of deterrence again explains much of what the standard view can't. There can be multiple levels of gang activity, it suggests, depending on whether individual juveniles form the impression that others value and expect gang membership. To reduce gang activity, the law should regulate the sources of social meaning that construct that impression.

Juveniles in high-crime neighborhoods do not necessarily value gang membership for its own sake. Indeed, they are just as likely as those in low-crime neighborhoods to see gangs as violent and destructive.[88] Nevertheless, those in high-crime neighborhoods are much more likely than those in low-crime neighborhoods to believe that a *majority of their peers* admire gang members: whereas only 19% of teens in low-crime communities believe that, 66% of those in high-crime communities do.[89]

These perceptions can reinforce themselves and ultimately determine the level of gang criminality in a particular community. In low-crime neighborhoods, the belief that others disvalue gang membership augments the aversion that individual juveniles have toward joining them. In high-crime neighborhoods, in contrast, the belief that others value criminality can make membership seem worthwhile even to those juveniles who are otherwise only weakly committed or even opposed to gangs.[90] Notwithstanding their private reservations, moreover, the decision of such individuals to join gangs conveys *publicly* that they, too, value gang membership, a signal that reinforces the pressure on other teens to do the same.[91] This "system of shared misunderstanding"[92] is one mechanism by which social influence fuels criminal gang activity.

Another is the effect of visible gang activity on emotional dispositions. In a community pervaded by gang activity, individu-

at 263, 267; Office of Juvenile Justice and Delinquency Prevention, Gang Suppression and Intervention: Problem and Response 12, 15-16 (Oct. 1994).

[88] See Louis Harris & Assoc., Inc., Between Hope and Fear: Teens Speak Out on Crime and the Community 104 tbl.5.2 (1995).

[89] Id.

[90] See Matza, supra note 37, at 54-56; Short & Strodtbeck, supra note 40, at 75-76; Gary F. Jensen, Parents, Peers, and Delinquent Action: A Test of the Differential Association Perspective, 78 Am. J. Soc. 562, 565 (1972).

[91] See Matza, supra note 37, at 52-59.

[92] Id. at 59.

als are likely to form the aggressive disposition that gang members themselves prize. The apparent authority and status of gang members imbues their mannerisms with connotations of strength. Indeed, the failure to imitate their demeanor can make one appear weak and vulnerable.[93] These considerations make it rational for individuals to cultivate the aggressive bearing associated with gang membership.[94] When numerous individuals cultivate that bearing simultaneously, however, more of them are likely to turn to crime, both because of the (mis)information those mannerisms impart about public attitudes toward gang membership, and because of the obstacles they create to interactions with law-abiders, who strongly disvalue aggression.[95]

The social influence account not only helps to explain why gangs exist, but also identifies which policies for fighting them are likely to work. The conventional suppression strategy doesn't, in part because policies that "raise the price" of gang activity can actually reinforce the meanings that point social influence in the direction of gang membership. Delinquency is status-enhancing because juveniles view willingness to break the law as a sign of strength and courage.[96] The more severe the penalty, the more strength and courage law-breaking projects. Thus, the crackdown strategy is at war with itself.

A more effective approach is to attack the public signs and cues that inform juveniles' (mis)perception that their peers

---

[93] See Anderson, supra note 78, at 177-179, 181.

[94] See, e.g., id. at 181 (stating that young African-Americans must adopt "an aggressive presentation" to avoid "being ridiculed or even victimized by their own peers"); see also Martin Sanchez Jankowski, Islands in the Street: Gangs and American Urban Society 28 (1991) (noting that gang norms emphasize cultivation of appropriate emotions "because emotions can be either a resource or a sign of vulnerability depending on the situation").

[95] See Anderson, supra note 78, at 177-78, 189. A similar phenomenon exists in the American South: because of the reputational benefits of conforming to local honor norms, it's *individually rational* for men to react with anger to perceived affronts; this shared disposition is *collectively irrational*, however, insofar as it produces a higher incidence of homicide. See Richard E. Nisbett & Dov Cohen, Culture of Honor: The Psychology of Violence in the South 13-22, 92-93 (1996).

[96] See, e.g., Walter B. Miller, Lower Class Culture as a Generating Milieu of Gang Delinquency, 14 J. Soc. Issues, No.3 1958, at 5, 8-9 (discussing how delinquency may signal "toughness" and is overtly prestige-conferring in some communities).

value gang criminality. That's what gang-loitering laws attempt to do. Some versions of these laws authorize the police to disperse known gang members when they congregate in public places;[97] others directly prohibit individuals from displaying gang allegiance through distinctive gestures or clothing.[98] By preventing gangs from openly displaying their authority, such laws counteract the perception that gang members enjoy a high status in the community. As that perception recedes, so does the perceived reputational pressure to join them.

Juvenile curfews operate on the same theory. Participating in nighttime street life appears to be another form of behavior that juveniles engage in not because they find it intrinsically valuable but because they think it's what others expect them to do.[99] Once on the street, moreover, they are exposed to further social-influence pressure to participate in gang criminality, not to mention risks of criminal victimization. Curfews help to extricate juveniles from these pressures. Against the background of such laws, being out at night becomes less a potent means of displaying toughness for the simple reason that fewer of one's peers are around to witness such behavior. Likewise, staying off the street loses much of its reputational sting once the street loses its vitality as a center of nighttime social life.[100]

The suppression of open gang activity also positively influences the attitude and behavior of law-abiding adults. Like public disorder, gang activity drives some law-abiding citizens out of the community and others off the streets. In addition, it drives a wedge between the community and the police. When individuals understand gangs to be in control, they infer that cooperating with law-enforcement officials is likely to be both futile and dangerous.[101] The reluctance of the community to turn on the gangs not only shields the gangs from punishment but

---

[97] See, e.g., Chicago, Ill., Municipal Code § 8-4-015 (1992). Such laws have been challenged on constitutional grounds. See infra note 154 and accompanying text.

[98] See, e.g., Harvard, Ill. Municipal Code § 26.04 (1993).

[99] Teens in high-crime neighborhoods, for example, usually support curfews by an overwhelming margin. See Poll Says 77% of Youths Support District's Curfew, Wash. Post, Nov. 7 , 1995, at B1.

[100] See Dan M. Kahan, Curfews Free Juveniles, Wash. Post, Nov. 14, 1996, at A21.

[101] See George Akerlof & Janet L. Yellen, Gang Behavior, Law Enforcement, and Community Values *in* Values and Public Policy, supra note 47, at 173, 174-184.

also legitimizes gang membership in the eyes of potential recruits.[102] Because they counteract the perception that gangs control the community, gang-loitering laws and curfews give law-abiders the confidence they need to oppose gangs. Once the community withdraws its support for them, the perception of waning gang influence quickly becomes a reality.[103]

There is already a respectable body of evidence documenting the effectiveness of the social-influence strategy for fighting gangs. Law-enforcement officials in Chicago, for example, report dramatic reductions in violent offenses in the neighborhoods where the city's gang-loitering ordinance is most vigorously enforced.[104] Numerous other municipalities report the effectiveness of curfews in reducing the incidence of juvenile victimization and juvenile crime.[105] The evidence that the reductions are a consequence of these laws is obviously far from conclusive. But combined with the merits of such policy as a matter of theory—not to mention the substantial cost savings that it offers relative to the conventional strategy of severe penalties—these results certainly justify continued experimentation with suppression of open gang activity.

B. Certainty v. Severity

The standard economic conception of deterrence treats severity of punishment and certainty of conviction as interchangeable components of the price of crime.[106] Maintaining a high cer-

---

[102] See Jankowski, supra note 94, at 193-202 (discussing dependence of gang on community cooperation).

[103] See id. at 201-02.

[104] See Tracey L. Meares, Social Organization and Drug Law Enforcement 40-41 (Jan. 10, 1997) (unpublished manuscript, on file with the Virginia Law Review Association).

[105] See Office of Juvenile Justice and Delinquency Prevention, U.S. Dept. of Justice, Curfew: An Answer to Juvenile Delinquency and Victimization? Juvenile Justice Bulletin, April 1996, at 1, 3-9 (discussing data on effectiveness of curfews in Chicago, Dallas, Denver, New Orleans, North Little Rock, and Phoenix); James Q. Wilson, What To Do About Crime, Commentary, Sept. 1994, at 25 (discussing success of Charleston, South Carolina curfew law); Gesalman, supra note 85, at 1A (reporting 77% drop in victimization of juveniles in period during which curfew was adopted as part of anti-gang policy in San Antonio).

[106] See Posner, supra note 1, at 1206; Becker, supra note 1, at 183-84.

tainty of conviction, however, requires investment of substantial resources in law enforcement. Of course, punishment, particularly in the form of imprisonment, is not costless; moreover, limiting the severity of punishment for less serious offenses preserves marginal deterrence across offenses that impose different levels of harm.[107] But subject to these qualifications, the efficiency of substituting severity for certainty is generally regarded as a foundational insight of the standard economic conception.[108]

The social influence conception challenges this prescription. The level of crime, this account suggests, turns not just on the price of crime but also on the direction of social influence. A strategy of low-certainty/high-severity can create social meanings that point social influence toward criminality. This is so because of what a low probability of conviction does to the norms of law-breakers and what severe punishments express to law-abiders.

The norms of potential law-breakers matter to deterrence insofar as their propensities to engage in crime are determined in part by their perception of the attitudes and behavior of their peers. The problem for a policy of low-certainty/high-severity is that it is more likely to signal to potential law-breakers that like-situated persons are engaged in crime.

This risk is implicit in how information about the price of crime is transmitted. Again, it is plausible to assume that individuals learn about the expected returns of criminality primarily from observing their peers.[109] In a low-certainty/high-severity regime, potential law-breakers observe two things: that persons who choose to commit crimes usually get away with them; and that some small percentage don't and are punished severely. The social influence conception of deterrence suggests that the behavioral effects of the former observation can counteract the

[107] See generally David Friedman & William Sjostrom, Hanged For A Sheep—The Economics of Marginal Deterrence, 22 J. Legal Stud. 345 (1993) (discussing risk that a high punishment for one crime may influence offender to commit a different and worse crime).

[108] See generally A. Mitchell Polinsky & Steven Shavell, The Optimal Tradeoff between the Probability and Magnitude of Fines, 69 Am. Econ. Rev. 880 (1979) (contending that even the concept of risk aversion does not modify the fundamental tradeoff between severity and probability of punishment).

[109] See Sah, supra note 32, at 1273-74.

effects of the latter. Based on the perception that criminals are unlikely to be caught, some potential law-breakers will infer that crime pays and act accordingly. Their decisions will likely inspire others to do the same by driving down the likelihood of conviction even more, reducing or inverting the reputational costs of criminality, and tainting obedience with connotations of servility.[110] Severe penalties will have some effect in this norm environment, but much less than they would have had if social influence had been pointing away from rather than toward crime. In sum, the low-certainty/high-severity strategy is likely to yield a high crime-rate equilibrium at a given price of crime.

A high-certainty/low-severity strategy, in contrast, is more likely to generate a low crime-rate equilibrium. In that regime, individuals learn about the price of crime primarily from observing that a high percentage of those who choose to break the law are caught. Thus, fewer are likely to draw the initial inference that crime pays. Their compliance with the law sustains a high certainty of conviction, conserves the stigma of criminality, and prevents resentment from eroding the disposition to obey. Because this norm environment points social influence toward obedience, deterrence can be sustained even with relatively low penalties. These considerations suggest a greater investment in certainty of conviction than seems optimal under the standard economic conception of deterrence.

Empirical evidence is consistent with this analysis. Researchers report, for example, that when individuals learn that the IRS is beefing up enforcement policies to close the "tax gap"—the difference between the amount due the government and what taxpayers actually pay—they become less rather than more likely to comply with the tax laws. The inference that evasion is widespread dominates any inference relating to the likely punishment for such behavior.[111]

---

[110] See supra text accompanying notes 31-40.

[111] See Steven M. Sheffrin & Robert K. Triest, Can Brute Deterrence Backfire? Perceptions and Attitudes in Taxpayer Compliance, *in* Why People Pay Taxes, supra note 19, at 193, 212-13; see also Schwartz & Orleans, supra note 40, at 296-99 (individuals exposed to information on penalties declared less income and claimed more deductions than individuals exposed to no information and those exposed to information emphasizing reciprocity and moral duty).

Other empirical studies likewise conclude that certainty of conviction plays a much bigger role in discouraging all manner of crime than does severity of punishment.[112] One interpretation of this finding is that potential offenders are risk-preferring relative to other members of the community,[113] but that conclusion is more a redescription of the underlying phenomenon than an explanation of it. The effect that a low probability of conviction has on the direction of social influence can plausibly explain why potential law-breakers are more deterred by certainty than by severity.

A low-certainty/high-severity strategy can also adversely affect the behavior of law-abiders, particularly in inner-city communities with high crime rates. These citizens face a dilemma. As potential crime victims, they have an obvious interest in disclosing information about the identity and activities of wrongdoers when they believe that cooperating with law-enforcement authorities will make their communities safer. But at the same time, they face powerful incentives not to cooperate. Such behavior can subject them to violent reprisals from law-breakers. In addition, in communities in which crime is widespread, law-abiders are likely to be connected to law-breakers by family and social ties; as a result, when criminals are punished, law-abiders are likely to suffer too, both emotionally and financially.[114] Be-

---

[112] See, e.g., Wilson & Herrnstein, supra note 36, at 398 (drunk driving); Isaac Ehrlich, Participation in Illegitimate Activities: A Theoretical and Empirical Investigation, 81 J. Pol. Econ. 521 (1973) (robbery); Daniel Nagin & Alfred Blumstein, The Deterrent Effect of Legal Sanctions on Draft Evasion, 29 Stan. L. Rev. 241, 269 (1977) (draft evasion).

[113] See generally Michael K. Block & Vernon E. Gerety, Some Experimental Evidence on Differences between Student and Prisoner Reactions to Monetary Penalties and Risk, 24 J. Legal Stud. 123 (1995) (finding that criminals are less risk-averse than students).

[114] See Glenn C. Loury, Black Crime: Answering Conservatives, *in* One by One from the Inside Out: Essays and Reviews on Race and Responsibility in America 298, 300 (1995):

> This ambivalence is rooted in the obvious fact that the young black men wreaking havoc in the ghetto are still "our youngsters" in the eyes of many of the decent poor and working-class black people who are occasionally their victims. For many of these people the hard edge of judgment and retribution is tempered by sympathy for and empathy with the perpetrators.

cause the police depend heavily on information from private citizens, how law-abiders respond to these competing loyalties can have a significant impact on crime rates.[115]

A low-certainty/high-severity policy makes it more likely that law-abiders will side with the law-breakers. For one thing, such a policy adversely affects the returns of cooperation with law-enforcement: by lowering the probability of conviction, it reduces the expected benefit of individual acts of cooperation; and by raising the severity of punishment, it increases the incentive of offenders to retaliate against cooperators and magnifies the financial and emotional costs of implicating members of the community in wrongdoing.

Even more importantly, severe punishments have *expressive* consequences that can change law-abiders' moral assessment of cooperating. Members of poor minority communities often interpret high penalties for crack cocaine distribution, gang-related crimes, and other offenses committed disproportionately by minorities as expressing the larger community's contempt for members of their race and class.[116] For this reason, these punishments become highly potent symbols of the tension between these groups and lawful authority. Against this background, cooperating with the police can become imbued with connotations of collaboration and betrayal.[117]

These dynamics feed on themselves. Low-certainty/high-severity reduces the willingness of law-abiders to cooperate with authorities in fighting crime. Their unwillingness further reduces the probability of conviction, requiring even stiffer penalties to maintain deterrence. This makes members of the community even more reluctant to cooperate. The resentment that even law-abiders feel toward law-enforcement officials, moreover, is a form of social influence that predictably emboldens law-breakers. The result is a high crime-rate equilibrium, fueled by

---

Id. See also Anderson, supra note 78, at 190, 195-96, 201-05 (discussing conflicting loyalties of law-abiders in inner-city neighborhood); Jankowski, supra note 94, at 180-93 (ambivalence of law-abiders toward gang members).

[115] See Jankowski, supra note 94, at 193, 202; Akerlof & Yellen, supra note 101, at 174-75.

[116] See Meares, supra note 104, at 26-32.

[117] See generally Randall Kennedy, Race, Law, and Crime 49-54 (forthcoming Pantheon Press 1997).

the effect that a low-certainty/high-severity policy has on the behavior and attitudes of all members of the community.

A policy of high-certainty/low-severity counteracts these dynamics. It raises the expected benefit of individual acts of cooperation with police, reduces the disruptive collateral effects of punishment, and erases the expressive import of draconian penalties. More cooperation raises the probability of conviction, further easing the need for severe punishments to maintain deterrence. And the improved spirit of cooperation between the community and law-enforcement officials helps to prevent forces of social influence from pushing potential law-breakers toward criminality. These effects are more likely to produce a low crime-rate equilibrium.

In sum, before we can identify the optimal balance of certainty of conviction and severity of punishment, we must know more than how much each costs. We must understand, in addition, how particular combinations of certainty and severity create and shape social meaning. The beneficial effects of high-certainty/low-severity on the direction of social influence might well compensate for what appears to be a greater-than-optimal investment in certainty of conviction.

C. Alternative Sanctions

The standard economic conception also generates a prescription on the optimal form of criminal punishment. The function of punishment, on this view, is to impose disutility on offenders in order to raise the price of criminal wrongdoing. There are many ways to make criminals suffer—from restricting their liberty, to confiscating their property, to requisitioning their labor, to tormenting their bodies. If two afflictions impose comparable levels of disutility, the law, according to the standard economic conception, should prefer the one that costs the least to impose. On this basis, proponents of the standard conception generally advocate substitution of fines and community service for imprisonment, particularly for white collar offenders, who are likely to have assets large enough and skills valuable enough to make these sanctions feasible, and who are likely to be sufficiently nonviolent to make incapacitation unnecessary.[118]

But the phenomena of social influence and social meaning again complicate the analysis. Punishment does more than impose disutility on the offender; it also expresses the community's moral condemnation. This expressive function of punishment matters for deterrence, because the information that punishment conveys about the attitudes of a society's members helps to determine the direction of social influence. If we assume—as seems reasonable—that different sanctions vary in their expressive power, then a community that cares about deterrence ought to concern itself not just with how much pain different punishments impose and how many dollars they cost, but also with how forcefully they communicate society's condemnation.

Although modern Benthamites overlook this point, Bentham himself did not. Bentham stressed the desirability not only of making punishments severe enough to outweigh the expected gain of the offense, but also of making them meaningful enough "to answer the purpose of a moral lesson":

> A punishment may be said to be calculated to answer the purpose of a moral lesson, when, by reason of the ignomy it stamps upon the offence, it is calculated to inspire the public with sentiments of aversion towards those pernicious habits and dispositions with which the offence appears to be connected; and thereby to inculcate the opposite beneficial habits and dispositions.[119]

In effect, the power of an expressively superior punishment to shape the dispositions of potential offenders is a positive externality that ought to be taken into account in considering that punishment's relative deterrent value. The meaning a punishment expresses counts as much as the disutility it imposes, for the more effectively a punishment signals condemnation, Ben-

[118] See, e.g., Douglas Corry McDonald, Punishment without Walls: Community Service Sentences in New York City 27-28 (1986); Norval Morris & Michael Tonry, Between Prison and Probation: Intermediate Punishments in a Rational Sentencing System 114-15 (1990); Posner, supra note 4, at 409-11. Corporal punishment can be defended on the same grounds. See, e.g., Steven S. Kan, Corporal Punishments and Optimal Incapacitation, 25 J. Legal Stud. 121, 122 (1996).

[119] Bentham, supra note 1, at 171 n.o.

tham predicts, the fewer persons there will be who value wrongdoing enough to make engaging in crime worthwhile.

On this account, imprisonment is likely to compare more favorably to conventional alternative sanctions than the standard economic conception of deterrence suggests. Imprisonment is an extraordinarily potent gesture of moral disapproval; because of the symbolic importance of individual liberty in American culture, there is never a doubt that society means to condemn someone when it takes that person's freedom away. Fines, in contrast, condemn much more ambiguously. When combined with imprisonment, no one doubts that fines express moral disapproval, but when used as a substitute for it they are often understood as merely attaching a "price" to misconduct—a connotation that is inconsistent with moral condemnation. Community service, too, frequently fails to express adequate condemnation, in part because of the positive connotations associated with serving the public. Because of the connection between the social meaning of law and the direction of social influence, imprisonment's expressive superiority to fines and community service might make imprisonment preferable even if these alternative sanctions impose comparable disutility at less cost.[120]

Other, less conventional alternatives, however, appear to rival imprisonment in expressive power. Bentham identified corporal punishment as the affliction best suited to place a "stamp" of "ignomy . . . upon the offence."[121] Another highly expressive alternative sanction—one that is much less problematic on moral grounds—is shame.[122] Shaming penalties—from bumper stickers for drunk drivers, to publicity for toxic waste dumpers, to signs or distinctive clothing for sex offenders—are on the rise in American law.[123] Like imprisonment, these punishments convey condemnation in dramatic and unequivocal terms. They can thus be expected to "inspire the public with sentiments of aversion"[124] toward criminality through their effect on the forces of

---

[120] See Kahan, supra note 7, at 615-16, 619-32.

[121] Bentham, supra note 1, at 171 n.o.

[122] Cf. Kahan, supra note 7, at 613-14, 638-52 (reviewing moral objections to corporal punishment and defending shaming penalties).

[123] See id. at 633-36.

[124] Bentham, supra note 1, at 171 n.o.

social influence. Yet like conventional alternative sanctions, shaming punishments cost much less than incarceration. Accordingly, shame might be a worthwhile alternative sanction even if it imposes substantially less disutility on the offender than does incarceration.

D. Public v. Private Deterrence

Both public enforcement of law and private precautions can deter crime. A potential thief is less likely to steal a car in a neighborhood that is heavily patrolled by the police. She's also less likely to commit such a crime when she perceives that the car is equipped with an alarm or that residents of that neighborhood are keeping close tabs on the behavior of suspicious people on their streets.

The standard economic conception of deterrence treats public and private deterrence as interchangeable according to their effect on the price of crime. That is, it predicts that if a precaution by victims reduces the expected return of crime by the same amount as a particular law-enforcement policy, the two should be equivalent in their deterrent effects.[125]

This interchangeability thesis has counterintuitive and potentially important implications. One is that public and private deterrence are at war with each other. Increased investments in public deterrence reduce the need for (and hence the value of) precautions by potential victims, thereby discouraging investments in private deterrence.[126] Philipson and Posner deduce from this dynamic a "natural rate of crime" that is largely impervious to increased public expenditures on law enforcement.[127]

Another implication of the interchangeability thesis is that the law should deliberately underdeter crime. Full deterrence cre-

[125] See Ben-Shahar & Harel, Blaming the Victim, supra note 3, at 434-35; Harel, supra note 3, at 1195; Hylton, supra note 3, at 197-98; Tomas J. Philipson & Richard A. Posner, The Economic Epidemiology of Crime, 39 J.L. & Econ. 405, 408 (1997); van Dijk, supra note 3, at 114.

[126] See Philipson & Posner, supra note 125, at 407-08; van Dijk, supra note 3, at 114.

[127] See Philipson & Posner, supra note 125, at 408; see also Richard A. Posner, The Most Punitive Nation, Times Literary Supp., Sept. 1, 1995, at 3, 4 (characterizing hypothesized off-setting effects of increased public and decreased private deterrence as the "futility thesis").

ates a moral hazard: Since private citizens largely externalize the costs of protecting themselves from crime through law enforcement, they have inadequate incentive to invest in private precautions.[128] One solution is to set the expected penalty for crime below the expected gain for the offenders so that potential victims are forced to purchase a certain measure of private deterrence.[129] Another is a principle of contributory fault that punishes crimes against careless victims less severely than crimes against careful victims, effectively lowering protection for those who free ride on public deterrence.[130] Still another means of shifting the deterrence load away from law is to lower the cost of private deterrence through legal rules that authorize potential victims to resort to physical violence to protect themselves from criminality.[131]

The social influence conception of deterrence suggests reason to be skeptical of the interchangeability thesis. Decisions to commit crimes, according to the social influence account, are influenced not just by the price of crime, but also by individuals' perceptions of others' behavior and attitudes; these perceptions are shaped by the social meaning of law and private conduct. There is no reason to assume that law enforcement and private precautions are equivalent in social meaning. In particular, one might convey public aversion to crime more effectively than the other, and hence exert a considerably greater deterrent effect through the mechanisms of social influence. If so, there would be multiple crime-rate equilibria—not a natural rate of crime—depending on the relative contributions of public and private deterrence. Moreover, it would make sense in that circumstance to structure the law to induce the mix of private and public deterrence most likely to produce a low rather than a high crime-rate equilibrium.

---

[128] See Harel, supra note 3, at 1193; Hylton, supra note 3, at 201-02.

[129] See Hylton, supra note 3, at 198; see also van Dijk, supra note 3, at 117 (suggesting that "radical non-intervention" might result in efficient transfer of deterrence responsibility to victims but noting potential distributional objections).

[130] See Ben-Shahar & Harel, Blaming the Victim, supra note 3, at 435-36; Harel, supra note 3, at 1183.

[131] See Philipson & Posner, supra note 125, at 415.

Which (if either) is more likely to move the forces of social influence in a positive direction—law enforcement or private precautions? Plausible hypotheses can be advanced either way. The punishment of wrongdoers molds public sensibilities by expressing moral condemnation of crime; it's hard to believe that locked doors and barred windows have this effect. Indeed, these and like precautions convey that members of the community believe crime to be rampant and the law impotent.[132] Like other signs of public disorder,[133] then, highly visible private precautions might in fact erode deterrence by emboldening lawbreakers and demoralizing law-abiders.[134] If that's so, then social-meaning effects clearly favor public over private deterrence.

But it's also possible to imagine that the opposite is true. Perhaps some forms of private deterrence—such as neighborhood-watch programs and other forms of organized community self-policing[135]—effectively express the community's opposition to crime and its resolve to fight it. In that environment, individuals are more likely to see crime as both risky and status-diminishing. In poor inner-city neighborhoods, in particular, community self-help might be thought to express condemnation of crime more potently than does law enforcement, which is often viewed by the residents of such neighborhoods as alien and illegitimate.

The conflict between these two hypotheses can't be settled by *a priori* theorizing. The respective effects of private and public deterrence on the mechanisms of social influence must be sorted out empirically.

The empirical evidence that exists, moreover, calls into serious doubt the suggestion that private deterrence rivals or surpasses public deterrence along the dimension of social meaning. As public deterrence diminishes, both crime and the fear of

---

[132] Cf. Skogan, supra note 74, at 50 (noting that barred windows convey disorder and fear).

[133] See supra text accompanying notes 71-80.

[134] Cf. Ellickson, supra note 73, at 1177-78 (suggesting that private efforts to combat disorder reinforce perception of disorder).

[135] See Kevin Merida & Barbara Vobejda, Promoting a Return to "Civil Society," Wash. Post, Dec. 15, 1996, at A1 (discussing program to fund church-organized community self-policing).

crime increase.[136] In response, individuals might increase investments in private precautions, although the evidence that they do is conflicting.[137] What is clear, however, is that increased private deterrence does not counteract, and may even magnify, the perception of rampant criminality associated with the breakdown of public deterrence.[138]

A study conducted by Skogan documents this phenomenon. Skogan assessed the effects of a Chicago program aimed at promoting neighborhood-watch groups and other forms of private crime-avoidance. He found that perceptions of disorder and crime actually *increased* in the neighborhoods selected for the program; efforts to stimulate precautions against being victimized apparently made the existence of wrongdoing more salient to potential victims.[139] What's more, the residents of these communities grew more distrustful of their neighbors and showed less, not more, willingness to intervene in suspicious circumstances.[140] Skogan linked these changes in attitude to increased fear of crime.[141] Such findings suggest that efforts to shift the burden of deterrence to private citizens can backfire by reinforcing norms of behavior that fuel crime.

These effects, moreover, seem to depend on the level of public deterrence. In relatively crime-free communities, individuals are much more inclined to join leagues with their neighbors in policing their communities.[142] They are also much less likely to

---

136 Cf. Wesley G. Skogan, On Attitudes and Behaviors, *in* Reactions to Crime 19, 28 (Dan A. Lewis ed., 1981) (noting that fear of crime and crime have risen in parallel).

137 Compare Philipson & Posner, supra note 125, at 423-27 (presenting evidence that increased crime produces greater investment in private precautions) with Paul J. Lavrakas, On Households, *in* Reactions to Crime, supra note 136, at 67 (finding that use of anti-crime devices *decreases* as crime rate for burglary and robbery go up) and Fran H. Norris & Krzysztof Kaniasty, A Longitudinal Study of the Effects of Various Crime Prevention Strategies on Criminal Victimization, Fear of Crime, and Psychological Distress, 20 Am. J. Comm. Psychol. 625, 638-39 (1992) (increased fear of crime does not correlate with subsequent investment in precautions).

138 See Norris & Kaniasty, supra note 137, at 638-39 (finding that use of private precautions does not reduce fear of crime).

139 Skogan, supra note 74, at 144-45.

140 Id. at 143-44.

141 Id. at 151-52.

142 See Skogan, supra note 74, at 148; Skogan, supra note 136, at 37; Norris & Kaniasty, supra note 137, at 643.

view neighborhood watch programs and other conspicuous forms of private deterrence as cause for alarm.[143] In other words, what private deterrence means is determined in part by the size of a community's investment in public deterrence.

If this is the right conclusion, then the social influence conception supports a much greater investment in public deterrence than seems optimal under the interchangeability thesis. Even when they reduce the expected return of crime equally, law enforcement and private precautions remain inequivalent in social meaning and thus inequivalent in their effects on the direction of social influence. When public deterrence predominates, individuals are much less likely to perceive that criminality is widespread. Moreover, when they feel reassured that law enforcement is adequate, law-abiders are *more* likely to view private precautions as worthwhile, and less likely to see such precautions as signs that those around them lack confidence in the efficacy of law. These attitudes are likely to sustain norms of private behavior that reduce the need for expenditures on public deterrence. In short, a mix tilted toward public law enforcement rather than private precautions would be more likely to generate a low crime-rate equilibrium at any given price of crime.

This is an admittedly speculative—not to mention abstract—conjecture. It's sufficiently plausible, however, to require that proponents of the interchangeability thesis come forward with convincing empirical evidence before their counterintuitive prescriptions are made the basis of public policy.

E. The Cost of Rights

The standard economic conception of deterrence supplies a framework for assessing the social cost of individual rights. Deterrence, on this view, is a function of the probability of conviction and the severity of punishment, which combine to determine the "price" of crime.[144] The "exclusionary rule," the *Miranda* doctrine, and like constraints reduce the price of crime by lowering the probability that offenders will be convicted. The cost of such rights, then, consists of the resulting increase in

143 Skogan, supra note 74, at 130-31; Norris & Kaniasty, supra note 137, at 643.

144 See supra note 106.

crime[145] or the resources that must be invested—primarily in increased severity of punishment—to offset the rights discount on the price of crime.[146]

The social influence conception suggests that rights undermine deterrence in a different and potentially even more costly way. Certain types of rights—including those that constrain the authority of law enforcement officials to obtain evidence[147] or to control the behavior of potential criminals[148]—can move social influence in a negative direction, both because of what they express and because of what they do to the power of the community to regulate expressive norms. These social-meaning effects magnify the consequences of any reduced probability of conviction, and can't necessarily be offset through increased severity of punishment.

Start with the expressive effect of rights. Although it's difficult to demonstrate that the "exclusionary rule," *Miranda* warnings, and like doctrines impede law enforcement,[149] it isn't hard to show that they are *perceived* as having this effect. The majority of the public see such rules as procedural "technicalities" that require courts to let admittedly guilty defendants go free.[150]

---

[145] See, e.g., Raymond Atkins & Paul H. Rubin, The Impact of Changing Criminal Procedure on Crime Rates 19 (Oct. 28, 1995) (unpublished manuscript, on file with the Virginia Law Review Association) (finding that in aftermath of Supreme Court decision requiring exclusion of unlawfully obtained evidence, burglary rate increased 4.4%, larceny rate 3.9%, and auto theft rate 6.1% in states that did not previously exclude such evidence).

[146] See Richard A. Posner, The Costs of Enforcing Legal Rights, East Euro. Const. Rev., Summer 1995, at 71, 75, 82 n.8; Posner, supra note 127, at 3, 4.

[147] See, e.g., Miranda v. Arizona, 384 U.S. 436, 444 (1966) (excluding evidence of custodial confession unless police advise offender of rights); Mapp v. Ohio, 367 U.S. 643, 655 (1961) (requiring state as well as federal courts to exclude evidence obtained in violation of Fourth Amendment).

[148] See, e.g., Papachristou v. City of Jacksonville, 405 U.S. 156 (1972) (invalidating anti-loitering law on due process vagueness grounds).

[149] See generally Stephen J. Schulhofer, *Miranda*'s Practical Effect: Substantial Benefits and Vanishingly Small Social Costs, 90 Nw. U. L. Rev. 500 (1996) (critiquing studies purporting to show negative effect of *Miranda* on conviction rates).

[150] See, e.g., Roper Poll No. 154151 (Mar. 26, 1991) (61% of Americans believe that "balance between victims' rights and defendants' rights favors . . . defendants too much"); Roper Poll No. 48979 (Sept. 1987) (56% believe that Supreme Court "has gone too far" in "[p]rotecting the rights of defendants in criminal cases"); Roper Poll No. 1029692 (Jan. 1987) (74% of Americans believe that a voluntary confession should not be excluded from evidence merely because the police failed to give a

This message—whether or not accurate—can easily push the forces of social influence in a negative direction. When the public learns of rulings that exclude evidence of guilt from trial or overturn convictions based on procedural violations, some individuals will adjust downward their estimation of the odds of being punished for crime. The perception that such decisions rest on grounds unrelated to justice, moreover, will cause others to become resentful and diminish the pride they might otherwise experience in being law abiding.[151] In this environment, more individuals will commit crimes. And their behavior will in turn reinforce the criminal propensities of others by lowering the (actual and perceived) likelihood of conviction, reducing or inverting the stigma attached to criminality, imbuing obedience with connotations of servility, and so forth.[152]

Now consider rights and norms. Norms of order are critical to keeping social influence pointed away from, rather than toward, criminality; the spectacle of open gang activity, vandalism, aggressive panhandling, and other forms of disorder transmit signals that cause both law-breakers and law-abiders to behave in ways conducive to crime.[153] Policies aimed at suppressing these signals, however, are often attacked on civil liberties grounds. Thus, courts have invalidated gang-loitering ordinances,[154] teen curfews,[155] laws against aggressive panhandling,[156] and laws pro-

---

defendant a *Miranda* warning). See generally Herbert McClosky & Alida Brill, Dimensions of Tolerance: What Americans Believe about Civil Liberties 147-64 (1983) (documenting popular resentment of criminal procedural rights).

[151] As one measure of how such resentment can diminish commitment to obey the law, consider a recent poll that showed that Americans were *four times* more likely to agree that individuals are "justif[ied] [in] taking the law into their own hands" when a "criminal goes free . . . on a technicality [or] gets a lenient sentence" than to believe that such behavior is justified in response to the abuse of a child or murder of a family member. Roper Poll No. 154176 (Mar. 26, 1991) (17% agree that vigilantism appropriate response technicality, 4% to abuse or murder of family member).

[152] See supra text accompanying notes 31-44.

[153] See supra text accompanying notes 77-80.

[154] See, e.g., City of Chicago v. Youkhana, 660 N.E.2d 34 (Ill. App. Ct. 1995), appeal granted, 664 N.E.2d 639 (Ill. 1996); City of Harvard v. Gaut, 660 N.E.2d 259 (Ill. App. Ct. 1996) (invalidating on First Amendment overbreadth grounds ordinance prohibiting display of gang clothing and other signs of gang membership).

[155] See, e.g., City of Maquoketa v. Russell, 484 N.W.2d 179, 186 (Iowa 1992). But see Qutb v. Strauss, 11 F.3d 488, 495 (5th Cir. 1993) (upholding constitutionality of Dallas's teen curfew law attacked in part on First Amendment free association and equal protection grounds), cert. denied 511 U.S. 1127 (1994).

hibiting sleeping in public spaces.[157] By inhibiting the power of communities to enforce norms of order through law, such rulings oblige communities to deal instead with the criminal behavior that disorder can trigger.[158]

This analysis predicts a bigger negative impact from rights than does the standard economic conception of deterrence. The social influence conception suggests that there can be multiple crime-rate equilibria at any given price of crime depending on what individuals believe about the behavior and attitudes of other individuals. Certain rights, when enforced in a certain way, are likely to convey that criminality is rampant. Accordingly, the negative impact of such rights on deterrence is not confined to whatever effect they have in reducing the price of crime; by virtue of their social meaning effects, these rights also make it likely that the community will experience a high rather than a low crime-rate equilibrium.

For similar reasons, the social influence conception of deterrence suggests that the effect of rights cannot necessarily be offset by policies that raise the price of crime. The mechanisms of social influence promote crime independently of probability of conviction and severity of punishment. Severe penalties, for example, might compensate for the effect of rights in reducing the

---

[156] See, e.g., Loper v. New York City Police Dep't, 999 F.2d 699, 706 (2d Cir. 1993) (holding unconstitutional a New York law prohibiting loitering "for the purpose of begging").

[157] See, e.g., Pottinger v. City of Miami, 810 F. Supp. 1551, 1583 (S.D. Fla. 1992) (enjoining the arrest of homeless persons for sleeping in public areas and holding the practice cruel and unusual under the Eighth Amendment and violative of the "fundamental right to travel").

[158] Policies that increase the public's perception of the legitimacy of law increase the willingness of citizens to obey. See Tom R. Tyler, Why People Obey the Law 57-68, 161-69 (1990). Accordingly, if it could be shown that the aggressive enforcement of the exclusionary rule, *Miranda*, and the like increased legitimacy, the social influence effects of rights might in fact point toward obedience. But there is little evidence that these doctrines increase the law's legitimacy in the communities in which public confidence in it is most likely to be wanting. Indeed, one consequence of rights that constrain police discretion is *greater distrust* of the police by law-abiding members of the community. Because they perceive that the police are inhibited by constitutional norms from effectively monitoring suspicious individuals from outside the community, law-abiding members of the community become more tolerant of gangs, which are willing to perform that service (free, of course, from constitutional constraint) in exchange for the community's protection of the gang from the police. See Jankowski, supra note 94, at 184.

probability of conviction, but they don't counteract the inferences that citizens draw when they learn that convictions are being reversed because of "technicalities," or when they see disorder in their streets. Accordingly, even if severe penalties restore the price of crime to its pre-rights level, they won't completely offset the negative effect of rights on deterrence.

If anything, the social influence conception of deterrence shows how raising the severity of penalties to compensate for the effect of rights can easily backfire. Because law-abiders in high-crime communities are likely to identify to some extent with law-breakers, high penalties make law-abiding citizens less willing to cooperate with law-enforcement officials. The reluctance of the law-abiders to cooperate, moreover, fortifies the resolve of potential law-breakers; the increased resolve of law-breakers reinforces itself through the mechanisms of social influence, thereby driving up the level of crime even more, and possibly forcing adoption of even stiffer—and even less popular—penalties.[159] Members of high-crime communities are much more likely, in contrast, to support gang-loitering ordinances, curfews, and other order-maintenance policies, which they perceive to be appropriately moderate yet effective devices for reducing crime.[160]

Indeed, the dialectic that yields longer terms of imprisonment from the opposition between rights and order-maintenance policies suggests the short-sightedness of civil libertarian opposition to order maintenance. Increasingly severe prison sentences are not only more expensive and less effective than order-maintenance policies; they are also much more destructive of

[159] See supra text accompanying notes 113-117.

[160] See, e.g., Andrew Fegelman, Gang Loitering Law Is Ruled Illegal, Chi. Trib., Dec. 19, 1995, § 2 at 1, 2 (reporting community support for Chicago gang-loitering ordinance); All Things Considered: Miami Curfew Gaining Support among Many Black Groups (National Public Radio broadcast, Feb. 24, 1994) (reporting that curfew ordinance sponsored by African-American county commissioner is supported by 70% of African-Americans in Dade County and by Greater Miami Urban League); Quinnipiac College Polling Institute, Quinnipiac College Poll (July 24, 1996) (reporting that 81% of Hispanics and 72% of African-Americans in New York City, as compared to 63% of whites, support youth curfew). See generally Tracey L. Meares & Dan M. Kahan, When Rights Are Wrong (unpublished manuscript, on file with the Virginia Law Review Association) (discussing support among inner-city African-Americans for gang-loitering laws, curfews, and public-housing sweeps).

individual liberty. Yet increasingly severe punishments are the predictable—if imperfect—response to rights that block the effective management of social influence and thereby produce more crime. The ironic consequence of resisting the regulation of norms in the name of rights is a society that can protect its citizens' liberty only by extinguishing ever greater amounts of it.

CONCLUSION

Why do individuals commit crimes? Obviously, for many reasons—including necessity, greed, and depravity. In this Article, I have tried to suggest one more: the perception that other individuals are either committing crimes or expecting crimes to be committed. As is so with many other types of behavior, the decisions of individuals to commit crimes are highly interdependent. When they perceive that many of their peers are committing crimes, individuals infer that the odds of escaping punishment are high and the stigma of criminality is low. To the extent that many persons simultaneously draw these inferences and act on them, moreover, their perceptions become a self-fulfilling reality. In addition, the belief that criminality is rampant alters individuals' evaluation of criminality, eroding their moral aversions to it and undercutting their pride in being law-abiders; more individuals will commit crimes in this climate, and their decisions will reinforce the criminal propensities of others. These dynamics can be thought of as the contribution that social influence makes to crime.

What policies should a community adopt to discourage criminality? Obviously, a variety of them, including ones that make unlawful activities less feasible and attractive, and ones that make lawful activities more so. I have tried to identify an additional set: those aimed at regulating social meaning. Laws shape individuals' perceptions of each other's beliefs and intentions in a variety of ways. The types of conduct that a community criminally punishes, as well as the manner and severity of the punishment it imposes, express shared valuations. Laws that regulate social norms determine the background against which private behavior conveys information about citizens' beliefs and intentions. These social meaning effects help to determine whether social influence points toward or away from criminality.

The phenomena of social influence and social meaning generate prescriptions that are materially different from those suggested by the standard economic conception of deterrence. The standard conception counsels the adoption of cost-effective policies that raise the price of crime. The social influence conception, however, reveals the utility of certain law-enforcement strategies—including order-maintenance policies and gang-loitering laws—that have little effect on the price of crime but that nonetheless discourage it through suppressing signals of criminality. The social influence conception also suggests the disutility of some policies that *do* raise the price of crime in a cost-effective manner but that create undesirable social meaning effects. Substituting severity of punishment for certainty of conviction, fines for imprisonment, or private for public deterrence, for example, can create signals that push social influence toward criminality, thereby undermining any efficiency gains associated with such a policy.

The fundamental principle of the social influence conception of deterrence is that a community is more likely to *be* law-abiding when its members *perceive* that it is. Fostering this perception should be regarded as one of the central aims of criminal law.

Name Index